Blackstone's

# Police Investigators' Manual

# Blackstone's
# Police Investigators' Manual
## 2014

Paul Connor
Glenn Hutton
David Johnston
Gavin McKinnon

OXFORD
UNIVERSITY PRESS

# OXFORD
**UNIVERSITY PRESS**

Great Clarendon Street, Oxford, OX2 6DP,
United Kingdom

Oxford University Press is a department of the University of Oxford.
It furthers the University's objective of excellence in research, scholarship,
and education by publishing worldwide. Oxford is a registered trade mark of
Oxford University Press in the UK and in certain other countries

© Oxford University Press 2013

The moral rights of the authors have been asserted

First Edition published in 1998
Sixteenth Edition published in 2013

Impression: 1

Published in the United States of America by Oxford University Press
198 Madison Avenue, New York, NY 10016, United States of America

British Library Cataloguing in Publication Data

Data available

ISBN 978–0–19–968466–3

Printed in Italy by
L.E.G.O. S.p.A.—Lavis TN

# Contents

# How to Use *Blackstone's Police Investigators' Manual 2014*

The National Investigators' Examination (NIE) contains questions based solely on the material within Parts One to Four of the *Blackstone's Police Investigators' Manual*. Part Five contains material for Immigration Enforcement Investigators and National Crime Agency (NCA) Investigators, whilst Part Six is for National Crime Agency (NCA) Investigators only. Please see below for further information on the different candidate groups.

Any feedback regarding content or editorial matters in this Manual can be emailed to police.uk@oup.com.

## Police Investigators

All police candidates taking the NIE exam in 2014 are required to study the material contained in Parts One, Two, Three and Four of the Manual **only**. This includes all the PACE and Disclosure Codes of Practice extracts contained in Part One—see further information on grey lined material below.

Police NIE examinations taking place in 2014 will be based solely on the material contained in Parts One to Four.

## National Crime Agency (NCA) Investigators

All NCA Investigators are required to pass the NIE based on Parts One to Four of this Manual. NCA Investigators will also need to pass an **additional exam** based solely on the material contained within Parts Five and Six. These Parts cover immigration, customs and cross-border offences. NCA Investigators will also be tested on the new provisions of the Crime and Courts Act 2013. This information will be provided separately by the NCA at a later date.

## Immigration Enforcement (IE) Investigators

All IE Investigators are required to pass the NIE based on Parts One to Four of this Manual. IE Investigators will also need to study the material on Immigration Enforcement criminal investigations (reflecting the operational environment of those dealing with immigration-related crime) found in Part Five. The Immigration Enforcement Investigators' Exam (IEIE) tests professional competence and the benchmark for successful completion of the IEIE will mirror the College of Policing's own agreed standards in terms of the National Investigators' Exam (NIE).

## Use of a Grey Line to Denote Legislation

Codes of Practice, specifically PACE and the Disclosure Code of Practice issued under the Criminal Procedure and Investigations Act 1996, are now incorporated within chapters in the main body of the Manual. A thick grey line down the margin is used to denote text that is an extract of the Code itself (i.e. the actual wording of the legislation) and does not form part of the general commentary of the chapter.

# Table of Cases

# Table of Legislation

# Table of Statutory Instruments

# Table of European Legislation

# Table of International Treaties and Conventions

# Table of Circulars

# Table of Codes of Practice

# Table of Practice Directions

# PART ONE

# Evidence

<table>
<tr><td>1.1</td><td></td></tr>
</table>

# 1.1 State of Mind

### 1.1.1 Introduction

The starting point of any analysis of the law begins with an examination of *mens rea* (state of mind) and *actus reus* (criminal conduct). This is because these concepts are fundamental to an understanding of all offences and the idea of criminal liability generally.

To begin with, *mens rea* alone will not amount to an offence; thinking about committing a crime and how it would be accomplished is nothing more than an exercise of the imagination. But while the notion of 'thought crime' is perhaps better left to science fiction, the application of the mind is essential for liability to exist as acts (or omissions) alone cannot amount to a crime unless they are accompanied by '*mens rea*' at the time of the act (or omission).

It is therefore vital to consider, among others, what is meant by terms such as 'intent' and 'recklessness'.

### 1.1.2 Offences of 'Specific' and 'Basic' Intent

Crimes of 'specific' intent are only committed where the defendant is shown to have had a particular intention to bring about a specific consequence at the time of the criminal act. Murder is such a crime, requiring proof of an intention to kill or cause grievous bodily harm. Other examples would be offences such as wounding or inflicting grievous bodily harm with intent (Offences Against the Person Act 1861, s. 18) and burglary with intent to steal, commit grievous bodily harm or criminal damage (Theft Act 1968, s. 9(1)(a)). The common feature with these offences is that the *intention of the offender* is critical—without that intent, the offence does not exist.

Other criminal offences require no further proof of anything other than the 'basic' intention to bring about the given circumstances. For example, burglary under s. 9(1)(b) simply requires proof that the person entered the building/part of a building as a trespasser and that he/she went on to commit one of the prohibited acts (steal/attempt to steal; inflicting/attempting to inflict grievous bodily harm). Other examples would be offences such as maliciously wounding or inflicting grievous bodily harm (Offences Against the Person Act 1861, s. 20) and assault occasioning actual bodily harm (Offences Against the Person Act 1861, s. 47).

The important difference between offences of specific and basic intent is that, in the case of the latter type of offence, *recklessness* will often be enough to satisfy the mental element.

### 1.1.3 Intent

'Intent' is a word often used in relation to consequences. If a defendant intends something to happen, he/she wishes to bring about a certain consequence. In some offences, say burglary under s. 9(1)(a) of the Theft Act 1968, the defendant's *intention* may be very clear; he/she may enter a house as a trespasser *intending* to steal property inside. Provided there is enough admissible evidence (e.g. the possession of articles for use in the theft or perhaps an admission by the defendant), this element of the defendant's intention is relatively straightforward to prove.

However, there will often be consequences following from a defendant's actions that he/she did not *intend* to happen. An example might be where, in the above burglary, it was late at night and the householder came across the burglar and suffered a heart attack as a result of the shock. In such an event it might be reasonable to suggest that it was the defendant's behaviour or actions that had brought about the victim's heart attack. The defendant, however, may well argue that, although he/she intended to break in and steal, there had never been any *intention* of harming or frightening the occupant. At this point you might well say that the defendant should have thought about that before breaking into someone else's house in the middle of the night. This then brings in the concept of *foresight*, a concept that has caused the courts considerable difficulty over the years—for a number of reasons.

First, there is the Criminal Justice Act 1967 which says (under s. 8) that a court/jury, in determining whether a person has committed an offence:

(a) shall not be bound in law to infer that he intended or foresaw a result of his actions by reason only of its being a natural and probable consequence of those actions; but

(b) shall decide whether he did intend or foresee that result by reference to all the evidence, drawing such inferences from the evidence as appear proper in the circumstances.

Secondly, there is the body of case law which has developed around the area of 'probability', culminating in two cases in the House of Lords (*R* v *Moloney* [1985] AC 905 and *R* v *Hancock* [1986] AC 455). Following those cases it is now settled that foresight of the probability of a consequence *does not amount to an intention to bring that consequence about, but may be evidence of it*.

In other words, you cannot claim that a defendant *intended* a consequence of his/her behaviour simply because it was virtually certain to occur. What you can do is to put evidence of the defendant's foresight of that probability before a court, which may infer an intention from it. In proving such a point the argument would go like this:

• at the time of the criminal act there was a *probability* of a consequence;
• the greater the probability, the more likely it is that the defendant *foresaw* that consequence;
• if the defendant foresaw that consequence, the more likely it is that the defendant *intended* it to happen.

Whether or not a defendant intended a particular consequence will be a question of fact left to the jury (or magistrate(s) where appropriate). Most of the problematic cases in this area have arisen in relation to murder. In such circumstances, where death or serious bodily harm was a *virtual certainty* from the defendant's actions and he/she had appreciated that to be the case, the jury *may* infer that the defendant intended to bring about such consequences (*R* v *Nedrick* [1986] 1 WLR 1025). Therefore, where the defendant threw a three-month-old baby down onto a hard surface in a fit of rage, the jury *might* have inferred both that death/ serious bodily harm was a virtual certainty from the defendant's actions and that he must have appreciated that to be the case; they should therefore have been directed by the trial judge accordingly (*R* v *Woollin* [1999] 1 AC 82).

Finally, the relevant intent may have been formed, not of the defendant's own volition, but influenced in some way by other external factors. An example is where the defendant's thinking is affected by duress.

## 1.1.4 Recklessness

This concept has become more important in proving criminal offences than the concept of 'intent' above as proof of recklessness is often enough to fulfil the requirement of *mens rea*.

An advantage of recklessness over intention is that the former is easier to prove by the attendant circumstances; a disadvantage is the different elements attributed to the word 'reckless' by different courts considering different offences.

Take the example of assault occasioning actual bodily harm. In such an offence reckless-ness can suffice in proving the mental element (*R* v *Venna* [1976] QB 421). But recklessness as to what? The defendant may have been reckless as to the assault itself and/or to the harm that was actually caused by the assault. The courts have held that assault occasioning actual bodily harm only requires proof of recklessness as to the assault and there is no need to show that the defendant was reckless as to the extent of the harm caused by his/her assault (see *R* v *Savage* [1992] 1 AC 699).

For many years the application of the concept of 'objective' recklessness caused problems for the courts in cases of criminal damage. 'Objective' recklessness (also called 'Caldwell' recklessness from the House of Lords decision in *Metropolitan Police Commissioner* v *Caldwell* [1982] AC 341) gave rise to difficulties of proof where the defendant failed to consider an *obvious* risk and then went on to damage property. In those cases a defendant was not allowed to claim to have had no *mens rea* simply because he/she had not thought the matter through, and if the prosecution showed that the relevant risk would have been apparent to a reasonable person, it was not necessary to show that the defendant realised that risk. But this notion of obvious risk presented some real problems in practice, e.g. where the defend-ant, because of a mental condition or personal attributes, would not have been able to appreciate the risk even if he/she had stopped to consider the consequences. This meant that defendants could be held criminally liable for the consequences of their actions even where they could not have foreseen those consequences, and the strict application of the rule resulted in some harsh decisions (*Elliott* v *C* [1983] 1 WLR 939; *R* v *R* (*Stephen Malcolm*) (1984) 79 Cr App R 334). The abolition of the *doli incapax* rule meant that, where objective recklessness was the appropriate test—e.g. criminal damage—children who were incapable of appreciating the risks arising from their actions could still be found guilty. Similarly, adults whose mental characteristics prevent them from appreciating the risks created by their behaviour were not able to raise those characteristics as a defence to charges requiring objective recklessness.

Although this type of recklessness was generally confined to offences under the Criminal Damage Act 1971, it still caused concern among practitioners and academics alike. It was a criminal damage case involving children, who did not think that their actions would lead to the ultimately disastrous consequences, that changed the law. In *R* v *G and R and another* [2003] UKHL 50, the House of Lords decided that the objective recklessness approach should be departed from and that recklessness in criminal damage matters should be viewed sub-jectively (**see para. 2.9.2.7**).

---

**KEYNOTE**

The clarification of the law means that the standard approach to dealing with the term 'recklessness' will be that 'subjective recklessness' is the order of the day.

---

The requirements of subjective recklessness can be found in the case of *R* v *Cunningham* [1957] 2 QB 396 and are satisfied in situations where the defendant foresees the consequences of his/her actions as being probable or even possible. In cases requiring subjective recklessness, the fact that the consequences *ought to have been foreseen* by the defendant will not be enough.

A good example of the 'subjective recklessness' issues in action can be seen in *D* v *DPP* [2005] EWHC 967. In that case a police officer attending a domestic incident arrested a man in order to prevent a breach of the peace. During a subsequent struggle the defendant bit the officer on the hand. The magistrates' court convicted the defendant of assaulting the officer in the execution of his duty (**see para. 3.2.14.2**) on the basis that the biting of the officer had been 'reckless'. The defendant appealed, arguing that a bite could not be reckless; either it was deliberate or it was accidental. The Divisional Court dismissed the appeal and held that the test of recklessness involved the defendant having *foreseen the risk* that the victim would be subjected to unlawful force and *having gone on to take the risk*.

### 1.1.5 Malice

The term 'malice' is particularly relevant to ss. 18, 20, 23 and 24 of the Offences Against the Person Act 1861 (offences relating to grievous bodily harm/wounding and poisoning). It *should not* be considered as one relating to ill will, spite or wickedness. 'Malice' requires either the actual intention to cause the relevant harm or at least foresight of the risk of causing *some harm* (though not the extent of the harm) to a person.

---

EXAMPLE

D throws a coin at V thinking that when the coin strikes V, it will result in a small cut to V's forehead (this illustrates that D has the foresight that *some harm*, albeit relatively minor, will befall V as a result of D's actions). The coin actually strikes V in the eye, causing V serious injury resulting in the loss of sight in the eye.

It does not matter that the harm that D foresaw was relatively minor compared to the resultant harm caused to V. D has committed a s. 20 grievous bodily harm offence because D has behaved 'maliciously'—D saw the risk of some harm befalling V but went on to take the risk anyway.

---

### 1.1.6 Wilfully

'Wilfully' is mentioned in offences such as child cruelty (s. 1 of the Children and Young Persons Act 1933) and obstructing a police officer (s. 89(2) of the Police Act 1996). Like the term 'maliciously' (**see para. 1.1.5**) the term 'wilfully' should not be understood in a literal sense as meaning 'deliberate' or 'voluntary'. It is taken to mean intentionally or recklessly (subjective) (*Attorney-General's Reference (No. 3 of 2003)* [2005] QB 73).

### 1.1.7 Dishonestly

The concept of 'dishonesty' is of great importance to a number of offences, including theft and fraud. This expression is defined for certain purposes in s. 2 of the Theft Act 1968. However, it has also been extended by common law decisions of the courts (*R v Ghosh* [1982] QB 1053) and it is critical, in dealing with offences requiring proof of dishonesty, that you identify the nature of the state of mind required and the ways in which it can be proved/disproved.

### 1.1.8 Knowing

The term 'knowing' is relevant to offences such as s. 22 of the Theft Act 1968 (handling stolen goods) and s. 12(1) of the Theft Act 1968 (taking a conveyance without consent). One *knows* something if one is absolutely sure that it is so. Since it is difficult to be absolutely sure of anything, it has to be accepted that a person who feels 'virtually certain' about something can equally be regarded as 'knowing' it (see *R v Dunne* (1998) 162 JP 399).

### 1.1.9 Belief

The degree of certainty required to be experienced by an accused to create a 'belief' would appear to be the same for 'knowing'—the difference is that knowing something implies correctness of belief whereas a 'belief' could turn out to be mistaken. This is how 'belief' has been interpreted by the courts for the purposes of handling stolen goods (s. 22 of the Theft

Act 1968) where it has been stressed that there is a need to distinguish belief from reckless-ness or suspicion and that it is not sufficient that an accused believed it to be more probable than not that the goods were stolen.

## 1.1.10  Negligence

Negligence is generally concerned with the defendant's compliance with the standards of reasonableness of ordinary people. The concept of negligence focuses on the consequences of the defendant's conduct rather than demanding proof of a particular state of mind at the time and ascribes some notion of 'fault' or 'blame' to the defendant who must be shown to have acted in a way that runs contrary to the expectations of the reasonable person.

The most important criminal offence that can be committed by negligence is manslaughter (manslaughter by gross negligence), which is also one of the only offences to include specific reference—at common law—to the word 'negligence'. Other offences that can be committed by negligence do not usually contain the word itself but attract that test in relation to the mental element. Good examples are offences involving the standard of driving.

## 1.1.11  Strict Liability

Some offences are said to be offences of 'strict liability'. This expression generally means that there is little to prove beyond the act itself, however in most cases it is more accurate to say that there is no need to prove *mens rea* in relation to one particular aspect of the criminal activity or behaviour. There have been isolated instances in which the courts have held that an offence does not require any *mens rea* to be proved. An example relates to the offence of driving with excess alcohol, contrary to the Road Traffic Act 1988, s. 5, which was stated in *DPP* v *H* [1997] 1 WLR 1406 not to require proof of any *mens rea*.

In some other, albeit rare, cases absolute liability is imposed, reducing even further the burden on the prosecution.

Situations where strict or absolute liability is imposed are usually to enforce statutory regulation (e.g. road traffic offences), particularly where there is some social danger or con-cern presented by the proscribed behaviour.

Some other offences such as public nuisance at common law require only strict liability in relation to some elements of the criminal conduct.

As a general rule, however, there is a presumption that *mens rea* is required for a criminal offence unless parliament clearly indicates otherwise (see *B (A Minor)* v *DPP* [2000] 2 AC 428). This rule should be borne in mind, not only when approaching the rest of the material in this Manual, but also when considering criminal law in general.

## 1.1.12  Transferred *Mens Rea*

Transferred *mens rea* (an expression now acknowledged as a 'better description' by the Supreme Court in *R* v *Gnango* [2012] 2 WLR 17), was traditionally referred to as 'transferred malice' because it originates from a case involving malicious wounding. The doctrine states that the state of mind required for one offence can, on occasions, be 'transferred' from the original target or victim to another. *The doctrine only operates if the crime remains the same.* In other words, a defendant cannot be convicted if he/she acted with the *mens rea* for one offence but commits the *actus reus* of another offence. For example, in the original case (*R* v *Latimer* (1886) 17 QBD 359) the defendant lashed out with his belt at one person but missed, striking a third party instead. As it was proved that the defendant had the required *mens rea* when he swung the belt, the court held that the same *mens rea* could support a charge of wounding against any other victim injured by the same act. If the *nature of the offence* changes, then the doctrine will not operate. Therefore if a defendant is shown to have thrown a rock at a crowd of people intending to injure one of them, the *mens rea* required for that offence cannot be 'transferred' to an offence of criminal damage if the rock misses that person and breaks a window instead (*R v Pembliton* (1874) LR 2 CCR 119). The House of Lords acknowledged that this doctrine is somewhat arbitrary and is an exception to the general principles of law (*Attorney-General's Reference (No. 3 of 1994)* [1998] AC 245).

The issue of transferred *mens rea* can be important in relation to the liability of accessories (as to which, **see chapter 1.2**). If the principal's intentions are to be extended to an accessory, it must be shown that those intentions were either contemplated and accepted by that person at the time of the offence, or that they were 'transferred' by this doctrine.

......................................................................................................

EXAMPLE

A person (X) encourages another (Y) to assault Z. Y decides to attack a different person instead. X will not be liable for that assault because it was not contemplated or agreed by X. If, however, in trying to assault Z, Y happens to injure a third person inadvertently, the doctrine of 'transferred malice' may result in X being liable for those injuries even though X had no wish for that person to be so injured.

......................................................................................................

<table>
<tr><td>**1.2**</td><td></td></tr>
</table>

# 1.2 Criminal Conduct

## 1.2.1 Introduction

Having considered the concepts relating to state of mind, the next key element is that of the criminal conduct. Many statutory offences spell out exactly the sort of behaviour that will attract liability, but there are some important general rules that also need to be considered.

For a person to be found guilty of a criminal offence you must show that he/she:

- acted in a particular way
- failed to act in a particular way (omissions) or
- brought about a state of affairs.

Known as the *actus reus*, this essential characteristic of any offence is the behavioural element.

## 1.2.2 *Actus Reus*

*Mens rea* is what a defendant must have had; *actus reus* is what a defendant must have done—or failed to do.

When proving the required *actus reus* you must show:

- that the defendant's conduct was voluntary and
- that it occurred while the defendant still had the requisite *mens rea*.

### 1.2.2.1 Voluntary Act

You must show that a defendant acted or omitted to act 'voluntarily', that is, by the operation of free will.

If a person is shoved into a shop window, he/she cannot be said to have damaged it for the purposes of criminal liability, even though he/she was the immediate physical cause of the damage. Similarly, if a person was standing in front of a window waiting to break it and someone came up and pushed that person into the window, the presence of the requisite *mens rea* would still not be enough to attract criminal liability for the resultant damage. In each case, the person being pushed could not be said to be acting of his/her own volition in breaking the window and therefore could not perform the required *actus reus*.

This aspect of voluntariness becomes important, not just when considering offences committed under physical compulsion, but also where defendants have lost control of their own physical actions. Reflexive actions are generally not classed as being willed or voluntary, hence the (limited) availability of the 'defence' of automatism.

Likewise, the *unexpected* onset of a sudden physical impairment (such as severe cramp when driving; actions when sleepwalking) can also render any linked actions 'involuntary'. If the onset of the impairment could reasonably have been foreseen or anticipated (e.g. where someone is prone to blackouts) the defendant's actions may be said to have been willed in the respect that he/she could have prevented the loss of control or at least avoided the situation (e.g. driving) which allowed the consequences to come about.

**Coincidence with *Mens Rea***

It must be shown that the defendant had the requisite *mens rea* at the time of carrying out the *actus reus*. However, there is no need for that 'state of mind' to remain unchanged throughout the entire commission of the offence. If a person (X) poisons another (Y) intending to kill Y at the time, it will not alter X's criminal liability if X changes his mind immediately after giving the poison or even if X does everything he can to halt its effects (see *R v Jakeman* (1983) 76 Cr App R 223).

Conversely, if the *actus reus* is a continuing act, as 'appropriation' is, it may begin without any particular *mens rea* at the start but the required 'state of mind' may come later while the *actus reus* is still continuing. If this happens, whereby the *mens rea* 'catches up' with the *actus reus*, the offence is complete at the first moment that the two elements (*actus reus* and *mens rea*) unite.

This principle can be seen in the offence of rape. The sexual intercourse may be consensual at the time it starts but, if that consent is later withdrawn, any continued intercourse will amount to an offence (*Kaitamaki v The Queen* [1985] AC 147).

A further illustration can be found in a case where a motorist was being directed to pull his car over to the kerb by a police officer. In doing so, the motorist inadvertently drove onto the officer's foot. Having no *mens rea* at the time of driving onto the officer's foot, the defendant was not at that point guilty of battery. However, once the situation was pointed out to him, the fact that he left the car where it was (the *actus reus*) was then joined by the appropriate *mens rea* and he was convicted of assault (*Fagan v Metropolitan Police Commissioner* [1969] 1 QB 439).

## 1.2.3 Omissions

Criminal conduct is most often associated with *actions* but occasionally liability is brought about by a failure to act.

Most of the occasions where failure or omission will attract liability are where a **DUTY** *to act* has been created. Such a **DUTY** can arise from a number of circumstances, the main ones being:

**D** Dangerous situation created by the defendant. See, for example, *R v Miller* [1983] 2 AC 161 where the defendant accidentally started a fire in a house (a fact that he became aware of), but instead of putting the fire out, he moved to another room taking no action to counteract the danger he had created, resulting in the house being damaged by fire.

**U** Under statute, contract or a person's public 'office'. Examples would include:
  • Statute—a driver who is involved in a damage or injury accident fails to stop at the scene of the accident (s. 170 of the Road Traffic Act 1988).
  • Contract—a crossing keeper omitted to close the gates (a job that was part of his contractual obligations) at a level crossing and a person was subsequently killed by a passing train (*R v Pittwood* (1902) 19 TLR 37).
  • Public office—a police officer failed to intervene to prevent an assault (*R v Dytham* [1979] QB 722).

**T** Taken it upon him/herself—the defendant decides to carry out a duty and then fails to do so. Such a duty was taken up by the defendant in *R v Stone* [1977] QB 354 when she accepted a duty to care for her partner's mentally ill sister who subsequently died from neglect.

**Y** Young person—in circumstances where the defendant is in a parental relationship with a child or a young person, i.e. an obligation exists for the parent to look after the health and welfare of the child and he/she does not do so.

Whether or not there is a sufficient proximity between the defendant and the victim brought about by a duty to act will be a question of law (see generally *R v Singh* [1999] Crim LR 582 and *R v Khan* [1998] Crim LR 830).

Having established such a duty, you must also show that the defendant has *voluntarily* omitted to act as required or that he/she has not done enough to discharge that duty. If a defendant is unable to act (e.g. because someone else has stopped him/her) or is incapable of doing more because of his/her own personal limitations, the *actus reus* will *not* have been made out (see *R* v *Reid* [1992] 1 WLR 793).

Some statutory offences are specifically worded to remove any doubt as to whether they can be committed by omission as well as by a positive act (e.g. torture under the Criminal Justice Act 1988, s. 134). Other offences have been held by the courts to be capable of commission by both positive acts and by omission (e.g. false accounting under the Theft Act 1968, s. 17).

The distinction between acts and omissions was considered by the High Court in a case concerning withholding medical treatment from chronically ill patients (*NHS Trust A* v *M* [2001] Fam 348).

## 1.2.4 Causal Link or Chain of Causation

Once the *actus reus* has been proved, you must then show a *causal link* between it and the relevant consequences. That is, you must prove that the consequences would not have happened 'but for' the defendant's act or omission.

In a case of simple criminal damage it may be relatively straightforward to prove this causal link: a defendant throws a brick at a window; the window would not have broken 'but for' the defendant's conduct. Where the link becomes more difficult to prove is when the defendant's behaviour triggers other events or aggravates existing circumstances. For example, in *R* v *McKechnie* [1992] Crim LR 194 the defendant attacked the victim, who was already suffering from a serious ulcer, causing him brain damage. The brain damage (caused by the assault) prevented doctors from operating on the ulcer which eventually ruptured, killing the victim. The Court of Appeal, upholding the conviction for manslaughter, held that the defendant's criminal conduct (the assault) had made a significant contribution to the victim's death even though the untreated ulcer was the actual cause of death.

In some cases a significant delay can occur between the acts which put in train the criminal consequences. An example is where a defendant transported an accomplice to a place near to the victim's house some 13 hours before the accomplice shot and killed the victim. Despite the delay and despite the fact the accomplice had not fully made up his mind about the proposed shooting at the time he was dropped off by the defendant, there was no intervening event that diverted or hindered the planned murder—*R* v *Bryce* [2004] EWCA Crim 1231.

In a case which had similar facts to our 'simple damage' example above, the defendant entered a house after throwing a brick through a window. Although the defendant did not attack the occupant, an 87-year-old who died of a heart attack some hours later, the Court of Appeal accepted that there could have been a causal link between the defendant's behaviour and the death of the victim. If so, a charge of manslaughter would be appropriate (*R* v *Watson* [1989] 1 WLR 684).

## 1.2.5 Intervening Act

The causal link can be broken by a new intervening act provided that the 'new' act is 'free, deliberate and informed' (*R* v *Latif* [1996] 1 WLR 104).

If a drug dealer supplies drugs to another person who then kills him/herself by taking an overdose, the dealer cannot, without more, be said to have *caused* the death. Death would have been brought about by the deliberate exercise of free will by the user. This approach was reaffirmed in *R* v *Kennedy* [2007] UKHL 38 (**see para. 3.1.4.1**). The supplier is unlikely to be held liable for *causing* death in such a case unless he/she actually takes a more active part in the administering of the drug (see *R* v *Dias* [2001] EWCA Crim 2986).

If the medical treatment which a victim is given results in their ultimate death, the treatment itself will not normally be regarded as a 'new' intervening act (*R* v *Smith* [1959] 2 QB 35). However, in *R* v *Jordan* (1956) 40 Cr App R 152, where the defendant had stabbed the deceased, it was held that death could not be attributed to the defendant. In this case the actual cause of death had been the administration of a drug (terramycin) after the deceased had shown he was intolerant to it (treatment described as 'palpably wrong' by the court) and when his original wound had nearly healed. *R* v *Jordan* has been described as a very particular case, depending on its exact facts. The basic rule is that an intervening act will not generally break the causal link/chain of causation.

There is also a rule which says defendants must 'take their victims as they find them'. This means that if victims have a particular characteristic—such as a very thin skull or a very nervous disposition—which makes the consequences of an act against them much more acute, that is the defendant's bad luck. Such characteristics (e.g., where an assault victim died after refusing a blood transfusion on religious grounds (*R* v *Blaue* [1975] 1 WLR 1411)) will not break the causal link.

Actions by the victim will sometimes be significant in the chain of causation such as where a victim of a sexual assault was injured when jumping from her assailant's car (*R* v *Roberts* (1971) 56 Cr App R 95). Where such actions take place, the victim's behaviour will not necessarily be regarded as introducing a new intervening act. If the victim's actions are those which might reasonably be anticipated from any victim in such a situation, there will be no new and intervening act and the defendant will be responsible for the consequences flowing from them. If, however, the victim's actions are done entirely of his/her own volition or where those actions are, in the words of Stuart-Smith LJ 'daft' (see *R* v *Williams* [1992] 1 WLR 380), they *will* amount to a new intervening act and the defendant cannot be held responsible for them.

### 1.2.6    Principals and Accessories

Once you have established the criminal conduct and the required state of mind, you must identify what degree of involvement the defendant had.

There are two ways of attracting criminal liability for an offence: either as a *principal* or an *accessory* (accessories can also be referred to as *secondary parties*).

A principal offender is one whose conduct has met all the requirements of the particular offence. An accessory is someone who helped in or brought about the commission of the offence. If an accessory 'aids, abets, counsels or procures' the commission of an offence, he/she will be treated by a court in the same way as a principal offender for an indictable offence (Accessories and Abettors Act 1861, s. 8) or for a summary offence (Magistrates' Courts Act 1980, s. 44). The expression 'aid, abet, counsel and procure' is generally used in its entirety when charging a defendant, without separating out the particular element that applies. Generally speaking, the expressions mean as follows:

- aiding = giving help, support or assistance
- abetting = inciting, instigating or encouraging.

Each of these would usually involve the presence of the secondary party at the scene (unless, for example, part of some pre-arranged plan):

- counselling = advising or instructing
- procuring = bringing about.

These last two activities would generally be expected to take place before the commission of the offence. These are purely guides by which to separate the elements of this concept and will not necessarily apply in all cases. However, if you are trying to show that a defendant *procured* an offence you must show a causal link between his/her conduct and the offence (*Attorney-General's Reference (No. 1 of 1975)* [1975] QB 773). 'Counselling' an offence requires no causal link (*R v Calhaem* [1985] QB 808). As long as the principal offender is aware of the 'counsellor's' advice or encouragement, the latter will be guilty as an accessory, even if the principal would have committed the offence anyway (*Attorney-General v Able* [1984] QB 795). If an accessory is present at the scene of a crime when it is committed, his/her presence may amount to encouragement which would support a charge of aiding or abetting if he/she was there as part of an agreement in respect of the principal offence. This would not be the case if a person was simply passing by and watched the offence. It is not an offence to do so as the ordinary citizen is not under a duty to prevent an offence occurring and failing to do so will not create liability as an accomplice (see *R v Coney* (1882) 8 QBD 534).

### 1.2.6.1 State of Mind for Accessories

Generally, the state of mind (*mens rea*) which is needed to convict an accessory is: 'proof of intention to aid as well as of knowledge of the circumstances' (*National Coal Board v Gamble* [1959] 1 QB 11 at p. 20). Whether there was such an intention to aid the principal is a question of fact to be decided in the particular circumstances of each case. An example of such a case can be seen in *Gillick v West Norfolk & Wisbech Area Health Authority* [1986] AC 112. The case concerned the question as to whether a doctor who prescribed a contraceptive pill for a girl under the age of 16 could be charged with being an accessory to an offence by the girl's partner of having unlawful sexual intercourse. The requirement for proof of intention to aid means that the wider notions of recklessness and negligence are not enough to convict an accessory.

The *minimum* state of mind required of an accessory to an offence is set out in *Johnson v Youden* [1950] 1 KB 544. In that case the court held that, before anyone can be convicted of aiding and abetting an offence, he/she must at least know the essential matters that constitute that offence. Therefore the accessory to an offence of drink/driving must at least have been aware that the 'principal' (the driver) had been drinking (see *Smith v Mellors and Soar* (1987) 84 Cr App R 279).

Occasionally statutes will make specific provision for the state of mind and/or the conduct of accessories and principals. An example can be found in s. 7 of the Protection from Harassment Act 1997.

### 1.2.6.2 Joint Enterprise

A joint criminal enterprise exists where two (or more) people embark on the commission of an offence by one or both (or all) of them. It is a joint enterprise because all the parties have a common goal—that an offence will be committed.

---

**KEYNOTE**

As the parties to a joint enterprise share a combined purpose, each would be liable for the consequences of the actions of the other in the pursuit of their joint enterprise (but see below for such liability when the nature of the offence changes). This is the case even if the consequences of the joint enterprise are a result of a mistake. For example, two offenders (A and B) agree to carry out a burglary on a particular house. Offender A leads the way but makes an error in trying to identify the house and mistakenly breaks into the wrong house. The fact that the mistake has been made by offender A will not prevent offender B being guilty as an accomplice to the burglary offence.

---

What happens when one party to the joint enterprise goes beyond that which was agreed or contemplated by the other?

Two men (A and B) agree to carry out an offence of theft. During the course of the offence, the owner of the property subject of the offence appears and tries to prevent the offence taking place. Offender A produces a flick-knife and stabs the victim, causing grievous bodily harm. Offender B had no idea whatsoever that offender A had a flick-knife and had never even contemplated the use of violence during the theft offence.

The actions of offender A are a clear departure from the nature and type of crime that was envisaged by offender B who did not know that A possessed a flick-knife; it is an act so fundamentally different from that originally contemplated by B that B is most unlikely to be liable for the injuries caused to the victim (see *R* v *Anderson* [1966] 2 QB 110).

The situation would alter if offender B knew that offender A possessed the flick-knife. Here, offender B could be convicted of a wounding offence if he had contemplated as a real possibility that offender A might commit the wounding offence but nevertheless still took part in the theft.

This line of thinking is also relevant when considering the liability of a joint enterprise offender when a death has taken place. In *R* v *Powell* [1999] 1 AC 1, two defendants accompanied a third defendant to a drug dealer's house to buy drugs. When the drug dealer came to the door he was shot. It was unclear who had fired the fatal shot but the prosecution argued that, if the third defendant had done so, then the first two defendants were guilty of murder because they knew that the third defendant was armed with a gun. The first two defendants were convicted of murder. They appealed but the House of Lords dismissed the appeal holding that where one party (D) to a joint enterprise to commit an offence foresees as a real possibility that another party (E) may, in the course of it do an act, with the requisite *mens rea*, constituting another offence (and E does so), D is liable for that offence. This is the case even if D has not expressly or tacitly agreed to that offence, and even though he expressly forbids it. This approach was re-affirmed in the case of *R* v *Rahman* [2008] UKHL 45 where the House of Lords considered an appeal by a group of men who chased and attacked their victim with weapons including baseball bats, iron bars and knives. The victim died from two stab wounds to his back. There was no evidence that the appellants inflicted the fatal injuries; the participant who did probably escaped arrest but this did not prevent the defendants being convicted for their part in the joint enterprise. The House of Lords ruled that where a defendant was involved in a joint enterprise which resulted in murder, that defendant only had to foresee what his associate might do, not what he specifically intended to do, to be guilty of murder as an accessory. The defendants knew they were taking part in a joint attack with the purpose of causing serious injury, in which one or more of the participants was armed with a knife. Obviously, those participants would not have had a knife unless they were prepared to use it in the attack, a fact the defendants must have realised when they joined the attack. Killing due to the use of the knife could not be regarded as a complete departure from what the defendants contemplated as being involved in the common design.

What of the situation where the accessory or secondary party is not present during the substantive offence? In such circumstances involved in the example above, the position can be summarised as follows:

Where the principal (P) relies on acts of the accessory (D) which assist in the preliminary stages of a crime later committed in D's absence, it is necessary to prove *intentional assistance by D* in acts which D knew were steps taken by P towards the commission of the crime. Therefore the prosecution must prove:

- an act done by D;
- which *in fact* assisted the later commission of the offence;
- that D did the act deliberately realising that it was capable of assisting the offence;

- that D, at the time of doing the act, contemplated the commission of the offence by P, (e.g. D foresaw it as a real or substantial risk or real possibility); and
- that when doing the act D intended to assist P.

(see *R* v *Bryce* [2004] EWCA Crim 1231)

Another practical consideration arises, not from the absence of the accessory, but the failure to trace the *principal*.

If the principal cannot be traced or identified, the accessory may still be liable (see *Hui Chi-ming* v *The Queen* [1992] 1 AC 34). Similarly, an accessory may be convicted of procuring an offence even though the principal is acquitted or has a valid defence for his/her actions. The reasoning for this would seem to be that the principal often supplies the *actus reus* for the accessory's offence. If the accessory also has the required *mens rea*, the offence will be complete and should not be affected by the fact that there is some circumstance or characteristic preventing the principal from being prosecuted.

Additionally, if the accessory had some responsibility and the actual ability to control the actions of the principal, his/her failure to do so may attract liability (e.g. a driving instructor who fails to prevent a learner driver from driving without due care and attention (*Rubie* v *Faulkner* [1940] 1 KB 571)).

It is possible for an accomplice to change his/her mind before the criminal act is carried out. However, the exact requirements of making an effective 'withdrawal' before any liability is incurred is unclear. Evidence such as how far the proposed plan had already proceeded before the withdrawal and the amount and nature of any help or encouragement already given by the accessory will be very relevant. Simply fleeing at the last moment because someone was approaching would generally not be enough. In the absence of some overwhelming supervening event, an accessory can only avoid liability for assistance rendered to the principal offender towards the commission of the crime by acting in a way that amounts to the *countermanding* of any earlier assistance such as a withdrawal from the common purpose. Repentance alone, unsupported by any action taken to demonstrate withdrawal, will not be enough (see e.g. *R* v *Becerra* (1976) 62 Cr App R 212 and *R* v *Mitchell* (1999) 163 JP 75).

A person whom the law is intended to protect from certain types of offence cannot be an accessory to such offences committed against them. For example, a girl under 16 years of age is protected (by the Sexual Offences Act 2003) from people having sexual intercourse with her. If a 15-year-old girl allows someone to have sexual intercourse with her she cannot be charged as an accessory to the offence (*R* v *Tyrrell* [1894] 1 QB 710).

## 1.2.7 Corporate Liability

Companies which are 'legally incorporated' have a legal personality of their own, that is they can own property, employ people and bring law suits: they can therefore commit offences. There are many difficulties associated with proving and punishing criminal conduct by companies. However, companies have been prosecuted for offences of strict liability (*Alphacell Ltd* v *Woodward* [1972] AC 824); offences requiring *mens rea* (*Tesco Supermarkets Ltd* v *Nattrass* [1972] AC 153); and offences of being an 'accessory' (*R* v *Robert Millar (Contractors) Ltd* [1970] 2 QB 54—aiding and abetting the causing of death by reckless (now dangerous) driving). There are occasions where the courts will accept that the knowledge of certain employees will be extended to the company (see e.g. *Tesco Stores Ltd* v *Brent London Borough Council* [1993] 1 WLR 1037).

Clearly there are some offences that would be conceptually impossible for a legal corporation to commit (e.g. some sexual offences) but, given that companies can be guilty as accessories (see *Robert Millar* above), they may well be capable of aiding and abetting such offences even though they could not commit the offence as a principal.

A company (OLL Ltd) has also been convicted, along with its Managing Director, of manslaughter (following the school canoeing tragedy at Lyme Bay in 1994) (*R* v *Kite* [1996] 2 Cr App R (s) 295). Companies can be prosecuted for such offences under the terms of the Corporate Manslaughter and Corporate Homicide Act 2007.

# 1.3 Incomplete Offences

## 1.3.1 Introduction

There are circumstances where defendants are interrupted or frustrated in their efforts to commit an offence. Such circumstances might come about as a result of police intervention (e.g. where intelligence suggests that a serious offence is to take place on a given date) or as a result of things not going as the defendants had hoped (e.g. the property which they intended to steal not being where they thought it was). In these and other cases several general offences, often called inchoate or incomplete offences, may be used to ensure that the defendant's conduct does not go unpunished.

It should be noted that most incomplete offences *cannot* be mixed, and that most *cannot* be attempted. For instance, you *cannot* conspire to aid and abet, neither can you attempt to conspire. There are, as ever, limited exceptions to this rule.

## 1.3.2 Encouraging or Assisting Crime

The common law offence of inciting an offence was abolished by the Serious Crime Act 2007. Incitement was replaced by the offences under ss. 44, 45 and 46 of the Act.

> **KEYNOTE**
>
> Readers should note that any references in existing legislation to the common law offence of incitement are to be read as references to the offences in ss. 44, 45 and 46, i.e. to be read as 'encouraging or assisting an offence'.

OFFENCE: **Intentionally Encouraging or Assisting an Offence—*Serious Crime Act 2007, s. 44***
- Triable in the same way as the anticipated offence • Where the anticipated offence is murder the offence is punishable by life imprisonment • In any other case a person is liable to any penalty for which he/she would be liable on conviction of the anticipated offence

The Serious Crime Act 2007, s. 44 states:

  (1) A person commits an offence if—
    (a) he does an act capable of encouraging or assisting in the commission of an offence; and
    (b) he intends to encourage or assist its commission
  (2) But he is not to be taken to have intended to encourage or assist the commission of an offence merely because such encouragement or assistance was a foreseeable consequence of his act.

> **KEYNOTE**
>
> This offence requires the defendant to *intentionally* encourage or assist an offence. As such, s. 44(2) makes it clear that foresight of a consequence is not sufficient to establish intention.

OFFENCE: **Encouraging or Assisting an Offence Believing it will be Committed—**
***Serious Crime Act 2007, s. 45***

> • Triable in the same way as the anticipated offence • Where the anticipated offence is murder the offence is punishable by life imprisonment • In any other case a person is liable to any penalty for which he/she would be liable on conviction of the anticipated offence

The Serious Crime Act 2007, s. 45 states:

> A person commits an offence if—
> (a) he does an act capable of encouraging or assisting in the commission of an offence; and
> (b) he believes—
>   (i) that the offence will be committed; and
>   (ii) that his act will encourage or assist its commission.

---

**KEYNOTE**

This section creates an offence of encouraging or assisting an offence *believing* it will be committed. The person commits the offence if he/she does an act capable of encouraging or assisting an offence and believes *both* that the offence will be committed and that this act will encourage or assist its commission.

---

OFFENCE: **Encouraging or Assisting Offences Believing One or More will be Committed—***Serious Crime Act 2007, s. 46*

> • Triable on Indictment • Where the reference offence is murder the offence is punishable with life imprisonment • In any other case a person is liable to any penalty for which he he/she would be liable on conviction of the reference offence

The Serious Crime Act 2007, s. 46 states:

> (1) A person commits an offence if—
>   (a) he does an act capable of encouraging or assisting the commission of one or more of a number of offences: and
>   (b) he believes—
>     (i) that one or more of those offences will be committed (but has no belief as to which); and
>     (ii) that his act will encourage or assist the commission of one or more of them.
> (2) It is immaterial for the purposes of subsection (1)(b)(ii) whether a person has any belief as to which offence will be encouraged or assisted.

---

**KEYNOTE**

Under s. 46, the defendant must do an act capable of encouraging or assisting *one or more offences* believing that one or more offences will be committed and that his act will encourage or assist one or more of them.

---

### General Points

Section 47 of the Serious Crime Act 2007 sets out what needs to be proved in order to establish guilt for each of the above offences.

Section 49(1) of the Act states that offences can be committed regardless of whether or not the encouragement or assistance has the effect which the defendant intended or believed it would have.

..............................................................................................

EXAMPLE

D, a surgeon, wishes to sexually assault his patients whilst they are unconscious under anaesthetic. To do so D will need the co-operation of his assistant, V. D puts his idea to V while they are having a drink in a pub, intending to encourage V to take part in the offences. V is outraged and wants nothing to do with D's plan. In this situation, the fact that V is not remotely interested in D's plan and is not encouraged to take part in it will not alter the fact that D has committed an offence under s. 44 of the Act.

......................................................................................................................

A person can be convicted of more than one of these offences (ss. 44, 45 or 46) in relation to the same act (s. 49(3)).

Section 50 of the Act sets out that it will be a defence to the offences under ss. 44, 45 and 46 if the person charged with those offences acted reasonably, that is in the circumstances he/she was aware of, or in the circumstances he/she reasonably believed existed, it was reasonable to act as he/she did.

Section 51 limits the liability of the offence by setting out in statute the common law exception established in the case of *R* v *Tyrrell* [1894] 1 QB 710. A person cannot be guilty of the offences in ss. 44, 45 and 46 if, in relation to an offence that is a 'protective' offence, the person who does the act capable of encouraging or assisting that offence falls within the category of persons that offence was designed to protect and would be considered as the victim.

......................................................................................................................

EXAMPLE

D is a 12-year-old girl and encourages P, a 40-year-old man, to have sex with her. P is not remotely interested and does not attempt to have sex with D. D cannot be liable of encouraging or assisting child rape despite the fact that it is her intent that P has sexual intercourse with a child under 13 (child rape) because she would be considered the 'victim' of that offence had it taken place, and the offence of child rape was enacted to protect children under the age of 13.

......................................................................................................................

The offences under ss. 44, 45 and 46 do not apply to the offence of corporate manslaughter. This means an individual cannot be guilty of an offence of encouraging or assisting the offence of corporate manslaughter (s. 62 of the Serious Crime Act 2007).

## 1.3.3 Conspiracy

Conspiracies can be divided into statutory and common law conspiracies.

### 1.3.3.1 Statutory Conspiracy

OFFENCE: **Statutory Conspiracy—*Criminal Law Act 1977*, s. 1**
  • Triable on indictment • Where conspiracy is to commit murder, an offence punishable by life imprisonment or any indictable offence punishable with imprisonment where no maximum term is specified—life imprisonment • In other cases, sentence is the same as for completed offence

The Criminal Law Act 1977, s. 1 states:

(1) Subject to the following provisions of this Part of this Act, if a person agrees with any other person or persons that a course of conduct will be pursued which, if the agreement is carried out in accordance with their intentions, either—
  (a) will necessarily amount to or involve the commission of any offence or offences by one or more of the parties to the agreement; or
  (b) would do so but for the existence of facts which render the commission of the offence or any of the offences impossible,
he is guilty of conspiracy to commit the offence or offences in question.

### Agreeing with Another

For there to be a conspiracy there must be an agreement. Therefore there must be at least two people involved. Each conspirator must be aware of the overall common purpose to which they all attach themselves. If one conspirator enters into *separate* agreements with different people, each agreement is a separate conspiracy (*R v Griffiths* [1966] 1 QB 589).

A person can be convicted of conspiracy even if the actual identity of the other conspirators is unknown (as to the affect of the acquittal of one party to a conspiracy on the other parties, see the Criminal Law Act 1977, s. 5(8)).

A defendant cannot be convicted of a statutory conspiracy if the only other party to the agreement is:

- his/her spouse or civil partner
- a person under 10 years of age
- the intended victim (Criminal Law Act 1977, s. 2(2)).

A husband and wife can both be convicted of a statutory conspiracy if they conspire with a third party (not falling into the above categories) (*R v Chrastny* [1991] 1 WLR 1381). A person is not guilty of statutory conspiracy if the only other person with whom he agrees is his civil partner. A civil partnership is a same-sex partnership registered under the Civil Partnership Act 2004.

The 'end product' of the agreement must be the commission of an offence by *one or more of the parties to the agreement*. Once agreed upon, any failure to bring about the end result or an abandoning of the agreement altogether will not prevent the statutory conspiracy being committed. An agreement to aid and abet an offence of conspiracy is not, in law, capable of constituting a statutory conspiracy under s. 1(1) of the Criminal Law Act 1977 (*R v Kenning* [2008] EWCA Crim 1534).

Note that if an agreement to commit a *summary offence which is not punishable by imprisonment* is made in contemplation or furtherance of a trade dispute, it must be disregarded (Trade Union and Labour Relations (Consolidation) Act 1992, s. 242).

### 1.3.3.2   Common Law Conspiracies

OFFENCE:   **Conspiracy to Defraud—*Common Law***
  - Triable on indictment  - Ten years' imprisonment and/or a fine

Conspiracy to defraud involves:

...an agreement by two or more [persons] by dishonesty to deprive a person of something which is his or to which he is or would or might be entitled [or] an agreement by two or more by dishonesty to injure some proprietary right [of the victim]...

*(Scott v Metropolitan Police Commissioner* [1975] AC 819).

(See also *Blackstone's Criminal Practice 2013*, para. A5.61.)

This offence has been endorsed by senior judges as representing an effective—if not *the* most effective—means of dealing with multiple defendants engaged in a fraudulent course of conduct.

The common law offence of conspiracy to defraud can be divided into two main types. The first is contained in the case of *Scott* above, the second involves a dishonest agreement to *deceive* another into acting in a way that is contrary to his/her duty (see *Wai Yu-Tsang* v *The Queen* [1992] 1 AC 269).

Although the requirement for an agreement between at least two people is the same, this offence is broader than statutory conspiracy. There is no requirement to prove that the end result would amount to the commission of *an offence*, simply that it would result in depriving a person of something under the specified conditions or in injuring his/her proprietary right.

You must show *intent* to defraud a victim (*R* v *Hollinshead* [1985] AC 975).

You must also show that a defendant was dishonest as set out in *R* v *Ghosh* [1982] QB 1053 (**see para. 2.1.1.2**).

Clearly there will be circumstances where the defendant's behaviour will amount to both a statutory conspiracy and a conspiracy to defraud. The Criminal Justice Act 1987, s. 12 makes provision for such circumstances and allows the prosecution to choose which charge to prefer.

Examples of common law conspiracies to defraud include:

- Buffet car staff selling their own home-made sandwiches on British Rail trains thereby depriving the company of the opportunity to sell their own products (*R* v *Cooke* [1986] AC 909).
- Directors agreeing to conceal details of a bank's trading losses from its shareholders (*Wai Yu-Tsang* above).
- Making unauthorised copies of commercial films for sale (*Scott* above).

A further example can be found in *R* v *Hussain* [2005] EWCA Crim 1866 where the defendant pleaded guilty to conspiracy to defraud after a widespread abuse of the postal voting system. In that case the defendant, an official Labour party candidate, collected uncompleted postal votes from households and completed them in his own favour.

## 1.3.4 Attempts

The Criminal Attempts Act 1981, s. 1 states:

(1) If, with intent to commit an offence to which this section applies, a person does an act which is more than merely preparatory to the commission of the offence, he is guilty of attempting to commit the offence.

…

(2) A person may be guilty of attempting to commit an offence to which this section applies even though the facts are such that the commission of the offence is impossible.

(3) In any case where—

(a) apart from this subsection a person's intention would not be regarded as having amounted to an intent to commit an offence; but

(b) if the facts of the case had been as he believed them to be, his intention would be so regarded,

then, for the purposes of subsection (1) above, he shall be regarded as having had an intent to commit that offence.

(4) This section applies to any offence which, if it were completed, would be triable in England and Wales as an indictable offence, other than—

(a) conspiracy (at common law or under section 1 of the Criminal Law Act 1977 or any other enactment);

(b) aiding, abetting, counselling, procuring or suborning the commission of an offence;

(ba) an offence under section 2(1) of the Suicide Act (c 60) (encouraging or assisting suicide);

(c) offences under section 4(1) (assisting offenders) or 5(1) (accepting or agreeing to accept consideration for not disclosing information about a relevant offence) of the Criminal Law Act 1967.

### More than Merely Preparatory

A defendant's actions must be shown to have gone beyond mere preparation towards the commission of the substantive offence. Whether the defendant did or did not go beyond that point will be a question of fact for the jury/magistrate(s). There is no specific formula used by the courts in interpreting this requirement. An example of where the defendant was held to have done no more than merely preparatory acts was *R* v *Bowles* [2004] EWCA Crim 1608. In that case the defendant had been convicted of several offences involving dishonesty against an elderly neighbour. The neighbour's long-standing will left her estate to charity but, following his arrest, police officers searched the defendant's premises and found a new will, fully complete except for the signature. The defendant and his wife were named as the main beneficiaries and were to inherit the neighbour's house. Although the defendant's son was said to have been heard making reference to the fact that he was going to inherit the house, the 'new' will had been drafted over six months earlier and there was no evidence of any steps to have it executed, nor was there any evidence of it being used. On this basis the Court of Appeal held that the making of the will was no more than merely preparatory and the defendant's conviction for attempting to make a false instrument (as to which **see para. 2.6.11.4**) was quashed.

Courts have accepted an approach of questioning whether the defendant had 'embarked on the crime proper' (*R* v *Gullefer* [1990] 1 WLR 1063) but there is no requirement to have passed a point of no return leading to the commission of the substantive offence. However, to prove an 'attempt' you must show an *intention* on the part of the defendant to commit the substantive offence.

This requirement means that a higher level or degree of *mens rea* may be required to prove an attempt than for the substantive offence. For instance, nothing less than an *intent* to kill can support a charge of attempted murder (*R* v *Whybrow* (1951) 35 Cr App R 141), while in proving the substantive offence, an intention to cause grievous bodily harm will suffice. A defendant's intention may be *conditional*, that is, he/she may only intend to steal from a house if something worth stealing is later found inside. The conditional nature of this intention will not generally prevent the charge of attempt being brought and the defendant's intentions will, in accordance with s. 1(3) above, be judged *on the facts as he/she believed them to be.*

Although 'intent to commit' the offence is required under s. 1(1), there are occasions where a state of mind that falls short of such a precise intention may suffice. For instance, in cases of attempted rape the courts have accepted that recklessness as to whether the victim is consenting was (under the earlier sexual offences legislation) sufficient *mens rea* for attempted rape because it is sufficient for the substantive offence (*R v Khan* [1990] 1 WLR 813).

In proving an 'attempt' it is enough to show that defendants were in one of the states of mind required for the substantive offence and that they did their best, so far as they were able, to do what was necessary for the commission of the full offence (*Attorney-General's Reference (No. 3 of 1992)* [1994] 1 WLR 409).

### 1.3.4.1 Interfering with Vehicles

OFFENCE: **Interfering with Vehicles—*Criminal Attempts Act 1981, s. 9***
 • Triable summarily  • Three months' imprisonment and/or a fine

The Criminal Attempts Act 1981, s. 9 states:

(1) A person is guilty of the offence of vehicle interference if he interferes with a motor vehicle or trailer or with anything carried in or on a motor vehicle or trailer with the intention that an offence specified in subsection (2) below shall be committed by himself or some other person.
(2) The offences mentioned in subsection (1) above are—
    (a) theft of the motor vehicle or trailer or part of it;
    (b) theft of anything carried in or on the motor vehicle or trailer; and
    (c) an offence under section 12(1) of the Theft Act 1968 (taking and driving away without consent);
and, if it is shown that a person accused of an offence under this section intended that one of those offences should be committed, it is immaterial that it cannot be shown which it was.
(3)–(4) …
(5) In this section 'motor vehicle' and 'trailer' have the meanings assigned to them by section 185(1) of the Road Traffic Act 1988.

---

**KEYNOTE**

The term 'interference' is not defined by the Criminal Attempts Act 1981. This offence is one of specific intent and you must prove that the defendant interfered with the vehicle, etc. with one of the intentions listed— (note, however, that it is not necessary to show which *particular* intention).

The above offence is a specified offence for the purposes of the Vehicles (Crime) Act 2001, s. 3(4)(b).

---

## 1.3.5 Impossibility

Practical difficulties have arisen where, despite the best (or worst) efforts of the defendant, his/her ultimate intention has been impossible (such as trying to extract cocaine from a powder which is, unknown to the defendant, only talc). Impossibility is now far clearer following the Criminal Attempts Act 1981 and its interpretation through the courts. It differs however in some incomplete offences.

...........................................................................................................

EXAMPLE

Taking an example of someone who tries to handle goods which are not in fact stolen, the following rules would apply:

• A defendant could *not* be guilty of encouraging another, nor of common law conspiracy to defraud in these circumstances. The *physical* impossibility of what the defendant sought to do would preclude such a charge.

- A defendant *could* be guilty of a statutory conspiracy with another to handle 'stolen' goods and also of attempting to handle 'stolen' goods under these circumstances. The physical impossibility would not preclude such charges as a result of the Criminal Attempts Act 1981 and the House of Lords' decision in *R* v *Shivpuri* [1987] AC 1. The only form of impossibility which would preclude liability under the Criminal Attempts Act 1981 or for a statutory conspiracy would be the *legal* impossibility.

# 1.4 The Regulation of Investigatory Powers Act 2000

## 1.4.1 Introduction

The Regulation of Investigatory Powers Act 2000 provides the law governing the covert acquisition of information about people and the interception of communication. It requires that when public authorities, such as the police or government departments, need to use covert techniques to obtain private information about someone, they do it in a way that is necessary, proportionate and compatible with human rights. Surveillance measures necessarily involve some interference with private life, but have the legitimate aim of protecting national security and economic well-being (*Kennedy* v *United Kingdom* (2011) 52 EHRR 4).

Breach of the Act's provisions in a policing context can have three main consequences: any evidence obtained may be excluded by a court or tribunal as being unfair; proceedings may be taken under the relevant police conduct regulations; or a person may make a claim before the Investigatory Powers Tribunal.

The Secretary of State is required to issue Codes of Practice relating to the exercise and performance of the powers and duties mentioned in the Act (s. 71). A failure to comply with any provision of a Code of Practice is not of itself an offence but the Codes are admissible in evidence (s. 72).

## 1.4.2 Surveillance and Covert Human Intelligence Sources

Part II of the 2000 Act sets up a system for the authorisation and monitoring of various methods of surveillance and the use of 'covert human intelligence sources'. Failure to follow the statutory requirements will render the relevant public authority liable to an action for breaching the 1998 Act and will also risk any evidence that has been obtained as a result being excluded by the courts.

Part II deals with three main types of activity by the police (and other investigators), namely:

- covert human intelligence sources
- directed surveillance and
- intrusive surveillance.

(s. 26(1))

Although only the first of these expressly uses the word 'covert' for the nature of the activity, it is relevant to *all three* of these areas. Part II is concerned with *covert* activity and so, as a general rule, if it is not covert, it is not covered.

Some law enforcement activities fall outside the scope of the Act—an example is 'property interference' which is a very intrusive form of intelligence gathering such as attaching listening devices within people's homes. This type of activity is covered by part III of the Police Act 1997 and is beyond the scope of this Manual.

### 1.4.3 Covert Human Intelligence Sources

The 2000 Act introduces the concept of a 'covert human intelligence source' (CHIS). As with the legislation regulating surveillance (see **para 1.4.4**), it is the *covert* nature of this type of activity that the Act is concerned with. This is because of the effect of such activity on an individual's rights under the European Convention *when carried out by public authorities* (e.g. the police). It is worth noting that, apart from the many other considerations of using CHIS, the police owe a duty to take reasonable care to avoid unnecessary disclosure to the general public of information which an informant has given to them—*Swinney* v *Chief Constable of Northumbria Police (No. 2)* (1999) 11 Admin LR 811.

In accordance with s. 71 of the 2000 Act, the Secretary of State is required to prepare and publish a Code of Practice relating to the powers and duties concerning the use of covert human intelligence sources. The Code of Practice is available from the Home Office website at http://www.homeoffice.gov.uk.

#### 1.4.3.1 What is a CHIS?

Broadly, a covert human intelligence source is someone who establishes or maintains a relationship with another person for the *covert* purpose of:

- obtaining information
- providing access to information

or who *covertly* discloses information obtained by the use of such a relationship.

The full definition is set out in s. 26(8) of the 2000 Act. A purpose is 'covert' here only if the relationship (and the subsequent disclosure of information) is conducted in a manner that is calculated to ensure that one of the parties is unaware of that purpose (see s. 26(9)). Therefore the definition would not usually apply to members of the public generally supplying information to the police. Similarly, people who have come across information in the ordinary course of their jobs who suspect criminal activity (such as bank staff, local authority employees etc.) do not have a covert relationship with the police simply by passing on information. Great care will be needed, however, if the person supplying the information is asked by the police to do something further in order to develop or enhance it. Any form of direction or tasking by the police in this way could make the person a CHIS and thereby attract all the statutory provisions and safeguards.

Practically there are two broad areas to be considered when considering covert human intelligence sources: 'use' of a CHIS and acting as a CHIS. Both areas are strictly controlled by the legislation and require the relevant authorisation if they are to be lawful. 'Using' a CHIS includes inducing, asking or assisting someone to act as such and obtaining information by means of such a source (s. 26(7)(b)).

Generally, covertly recording conversations and other personal information about a particular person will amount to some form of 'surveillance' (and therefore will be governed by the strict rules regulating such operations: see below). However, such use of a CHIS will not amount to 'surveillance' (s. 48(3)).

#### 1.4.3.2 Who Can Authorise a CHIS?

Section 27 of the 2000 Act provides that activity involving a CHIS will be lawful for all purposes if it is carried out in accordance with a properly granted authorisation. Such authorisation can cover activity in the United Kingdom or elsewhere.

The people who can grant authorisations for a CHIS are prescribed by s. 30 and the relevant order(s) made by the Secretary of State. The power to authorise the use of a CHIS extends to public authorities far beyond the police (see sch. 1 to the Act). The Regulation of Investigatory Powers (Directed Surveillance and Covert Human Intelligence Sources) Order

2010 (SI 2010/521), as amended by the Regulation of Investigatory Powers (Directed Surveillance and Covert Human Intelligence Sources) (Amendment) Order 2012 (SI 2012/1500), sets out the relevant people who can authorise the activities of a CHIS. In the case of police services in England and Wales, the relevant rank is superintendent and above. However, where

- it is not reasonably practicable
- to have the application considered
- by someone of that rank in the same organisation
- having regard to the urgency of the case

then an inspector may generally give the relevant authorisation (see r. 6 of the Order). As with other parts of the Act, however, the Code of Practice places further restrictions on this area and must be consulted. For example, in the case of a juvenile CHIS or a situation where the CHIS may obtain confidential material, the Code requires that the relevant authority be given by an assistant chief constable and chief constable respectively.

The Regulation of Investigatory Powers (Covert Human Intelligence Sources: Matters Subject to Legal Privilege) Order 2010 (SI 2010/123) relates to activities involving conduct of a source, or the use of a source, to (a) obtain matters subject to legal privilege, (b) provide access to any matters subject to legal privilege to another person or (c) disclose matters subject to legal privilege. The Order imposes further requirements in these cases that must be satisfied before an authorisation is given or renewed, together with an enhanced regime of prior approval.

### 1.4.3.3    How Long will an Authorisation Last?

Unless it is renewed, the authorisation given by a superintendent will ordinarily cease to have effect after 12 months beginning on the day that it was granted (s. 43(3)(b)). If that authorisation was given orally by the superintendent in an urgent case, it will only last for 72 hours unless renewed (s. 43(3)(a)(i)).

Where the case was urgent and the authority was given by an inspector, it will cease to have effect 72 hours later unless renewed (s. 43(3)(a)).

Special provisions exist where the CHIS is under 18 (see below).

A single authorisation can cover more than one regulated activity (e.g. the use of surveillance—see below—and the use of a CHIS) but they operate independently of each other. This means that when one authorisation lapses, any other authorisation made at the same time does not necessarily end as well.

### 1.4.3.4    When and How Can a CHIS be Used?

A designated person must not authorise any activity by a CHIS unless he/she believes it is necessary:

- for the purpose of preventing or detecting crime or of preventing disorder
- in the interests of national security, public safety or the economic well-being of the United Kingdom
- for the purposes of protecting health or collecting or assessing any tax, duty, etc.
- for any other purpose specified by an order made by the Secretary of State and that to do so is proportionate to what is sought to be achieved (s. 29(3)).

Section 29(2)(c) provides that arrangements must exist for a covert human intelligence source's case which satisfy the requirements of subsection (5). Under s. 29(5) and (9), these arrangements cannot be divided between different public authorities unless the activities of the covert human intelligence source are for the benefit of each of those public authorities. The new provisions require arrangements equivalent to those in s. 29(5) to be in force in relation to sources of police collaborative units comprising two or more police forces. Under the new provisions, these equivalent arrangements could be divided between the police forces in a collaborative unit provided the chief officers of the forces in question had made a collaboration agreement permitting this to happen. The new provisions apply to police forces in England and Wales which have made a collaboration agreement to this effect under s. 23(1) of the Police Act 1996. It will not be enough for a designated person to show that he/she thought the use of a CHIS would be very useful or productive in achieving one of the above purposes; he/she must *believe* that is both *necessary* and *proportionate* to the legitimate objective of the operation.

Generally, the authorisation must be given in writing but, in urgent cases involving superintendents' authority, it may be given orally (s. 43(1)).

In addition to the requirements surrounding authorisation, the 2000 Act makes provisions for the independent management and supervision of a CHIS. A Code of Practice, together with a number of statutory instruments set out clear guidelines for the control and monitoring of CHIS activities and the keeping of records. This regulatory framework sets out specific conditions in relation to the deployment of different types of CHIS, from undercover operatives who change their entire identity in order to infiltrate criminal organisations, to 'decoys' who have no direct communication with suspects.

The Code of Practice sets out the requirements of key personnel in the recruitment and management of CHIS such as *handlers* (broadly the person dealing with, directing, monitoring and recording the activities of the CHIS) and *controllers* (the person with the relevant experience who oversees the use of the CHIS); it also defines some core activity that will be caught by the legislation such as the 'tasking' and 'cultivation' of a CHIS.

In addition, the Code sets out the form and content of the records that must be kept when applying for, authorising, using and maintaining a relationship with a CHIS. Among other things, these records will contain the confidential details of the CHIS's true identity, his/her given name or reference and a risk assessment of his/her deployment. Details of payments or rewards made along with all information provided by the CHIS must also be recorded.

Very strict controls have been put in place where a CHIS is under 18 years of age (see the Regulation of Investigatory Powers Act (Juveniles) Order 2000 (SI 2000/2793)). One such control is the time for which a written authorisation will last; in the case of a juvenile it is reduced from 12 months to one month. Further restrictions are imposed by the Code of Practice.

This discussion is merely a summary of the key aspects of this legislation. To find the full extent of the powers and duties under part II, the statutory text should be used, along with the relevant Code of Practice in force at the time.

### 1.4.4 Covert Surveillance

Along with the deployment of CHIS, covert surveillance has become a vital method of obtaining evidence and intelligence in the reduction of crime and the investigation of offences. Surveillance will only be covert for the purposes of part II of the 2000 Act if it is carried out in a manner that is calculated to ensure that people subject to it are unaware that it is (or might be) taking place (see s. 26(9)). Surveillance includes monitoring, observing, listening to and recording people and their conversations, activities and communications (see s. 48(2)). So, if the police are monitoring a person's movements and are trying to do it without that person knowing, the activities will usually amount to 'covert' surveillance. General monitoring of a particular area such as a shopping precinct by CCTV will not usually be covert and therefore will not be caught by the provisions of part II. There are, however, exceptions (see below). The proper use of covert TV detector equipment is neither directed nor intrusive surveillance (s. 26(6)).

Guidance on the carrying out of directed and intrusive surveillance is contained in the Regulation of Investigatory Powers (Covert Surveillance and Property Interference: Code of Practice) Order 2010 (SI 2010/463).

### 1.4.4.1 Directed Surveillance

It can be seen from s. 26(1) that there are two particular types of surveillance for the purposes of part II—'directed' and 'intrusive'. It is clear from the wording of s. 26 that surveillance must be one or the other; it cannot be both. Why does it matter? Because the controls surrounding *intrusive* surveillance are far tighter than those imposed on *directed* surveillance. If surveillance is:

- covert (but not 'intrusive'—see below)
- for the purposes of a specific investigation or specific operation
- likely to result in the obtaining of private information about a person (including information about his/her family life)
- whether or not that person has been specifically identified for the purposes of the investigation/operation, and
- not carried out in immediate response to events/circumstances where it would not be reasonably practicable to seek prior authorisation

it will generally be 'directed' surveillance (s. 26(2)).

Therefore, if in the example cited above, the police *specifically* use the CCTV camera in connection with a planned operation or they are covertly filming an area in a way that is likely to result in the obtaining of private information about someone, these may amount to directed surveillance. On the other hand, if a police officer in immediate pursuit of a suspect conceals himself/herself behind an obstacle in order to watch that person briefly, this would not amount to directed surveillance—because the activity was carried out in immediate response to events/circumstances where it would not have been reasonably practicable to seek prior authorisation.

The interception of a communication in the course of its transmission by a postal or telecommunication system will be 'directed' surveillance if the communication is sent or intended to be received by someone who has consented to its interception and there is no interception warrant (s. 48(4)). However, the use of a CHIS (see **para 1.4.3**) to record or obtain information will not usually amount to 'surveillance' (s. 48(3)).

### 1.4.4.2 Authorising Directed Surveillance

Directed surveillance must be authorised by a designated person (see below) and the authorisation can cover activity in the United Kingdom or elsewhere. The person must not grant the authorisation unless he/she believes that it is *proportionate* to what is sought to be achieved and *necessary* on the specified grounds (s. 28). These specified grounds are the same as those for 'communications data' (see s. 22) with the exception that there is no provision for emergency actions.

The people who can grant authorisations for directed surveillance are prescribed by s. 30 and the relevant order(s) made by the Secretary of State. The power to authorise directed surveillance extends to other public authorities (see sch. 1 to the 2000 Act). The Regulation of Investigatory Powers (Directed Surveillance and Covert Human Intelligence Sources) Order 2003 (SI 2003/3171) as amended, sets out the relevant roles and ranks of the people in those public authorities who can authorise directed surveillance. In the case of police services, the relevant rank will generally be superintendent and above. However, where it is not reasonably practicable:

- to have the application considered
- by someone of that rank in the same organisation
- having regard to the urgency of the case

then an inspector may give the relevant authorisation (see r. 6 of the Order).

Authorisations must generally be made in writing but, in urgent cases, a superintendent may give an oral authorisation (s. 43(1)(a)).

Authorisations may also be given on an application made by a member of another police force where such police forces are party to a collaborative agreement that provides for them (s. 33(3ZA) to (3ZF)).

Additional procedural safeguards are made by the Codes of Practice. For instance, if the material sought by the surveillance is subject to legal privilege, is confidential personal information or some journalistic material, the authority of the relevant chief officer will be needed. In relation to 'legal privilege' the House of Lords held that the Regulation of Investigatory Powers Act 2000 permits covert surveillance of communications between lawyers and their clients even though these may be covered by legal professional privilege (*Re McE (Northern Ireland)* [2009] UKHL 15).

### 1.4.4.3 How Long will an Authorisation Last?

Unless it is renewed, the authorisation given by a superintendent will ordinarily cease to have effect after three months beginning on the day that it was granted (s. 43(3)(c)). If that authorisation was given orally by the superintendent in an urgent case, it will only last for 72 hours unless renewed (s. 43(3)(a)(i)).

Where the case was urgent and the authority was given by an inspector, it will cease to have effect 72 hours later unless renewed (s. 43(3)(a)).

### 1.4.4.4 Intrusive Surveillance

Intrusive surveillance is broadly what it says—surveillance activity that immediately intrudes on someone's private life. The statutory regulation of this activity is concerned as much with the intrusive *effects* of such surveillance as the means by which they are carried out and is designed to keep such intrusions by public authorities to an absolute minimum. If surveillance is:

- covert,
- carried out in relation to anything taking place on any *residential premises* or in any *private vehicle*, and
- involves the presence of an individual on the premises or in the vehicle, or is carried out by means of a surveillance device

it will generally be 'intrusive' surveillance (s. 26(3)).

The definition of residential premises extends much wider than a conventional home. Covert rural surveillance operations and the use of specialist devices in houses or hotel rooms will generally fall into the category of intrusive surveillance. In addition to the activities authorised under part II of the 2000 Act, the Police Act 1997 makes further provision governing the interference with property for the purposes of evidence/intelligence. These highly specialised areas of property interference are beyond the scope of this Manual.

In *R v Plunkett* [2013] EWCA Crim 261, in admitting evidence of statements and admissions made by the accused in a police van which were covertly recorded on three occasions, the court held that a police van was not a 'private vehicle' for the purposes of s. 26(3) and the authorisation obtained from a superintendent under s. 28 of the Act for directed surveillance was appropriate.

The elements of intrusive surveillance listed above require the presence of people or devices on the relevant premises/vehicle. However, if the surveillance:

- involves a surveillance device and
- relates to activities taking place on residential premises or in private vehicles
- but without the device being present on the premises or in, on or under the vehicle

it will still be 'intrusive' if that device *consistently* provides information of the same quality and detail as might be expected from a device that was actually present on the premises or in the vehicle (s. 26(5)). An example would be long-range audio equipment monitoring conversations or powerful lenses used to watch people inside a house and giving the same quality and detail of image as if a camera had been placed in the premises. This is in keeping with the aims of part II of the Act in this area, namely, to minimise the intrusive effects of such surveillance on people's legitimate right to conduct their private and family life without interference from the State.

Surveillance carried out by means of a device for the purpose of providing information about the location of a vehicle (e.g. a tracking device) is not 'intrusive' (s. 26(4)(a)).

The Regulation of Investigatory Powers (Extension of Authorisation Provisions: Legal Consultations) Order 2010 (SI 2010/461) provides that directed surveillance carried out in relation to anything taking place on any premises that are being used for the purpose of legal consultations shall be treated as 'intrusive surveillance'. The consultation may be between a professional legal adviser and his/her client or person representing the client, or with a medical practitioner, where legal proceedings are contemplated and for the purposes of such proceedings. 'Any premises' include prisons, police stations, legal advisers' business premises, courts, etc.

### 1.4.4.5 Authorising Intrusive Surveillance

Given the type of activity that is covered by this category, the restrictions on its authorisation are very tight. In addition, many types of activity under this heading will involve applications for 'multiple' authorisations and specialist advice must be sought.

Generally, the person who will authorise intrusive surveillance by the intelligence services, the armed forces and other specified bodies is the Secretary of State. In relation to the police (including the armed services police) the authority will be sought from senior authorising officers. Broadly these will be chief officers, the commissioners/assistant commissioners of the Metropolitan and City of London Police and the Director-General of the Serious Organised Crime Agency (to be replaced by the National Crime Agency) (s. 32). Provision is also made for authorisations by designated deputies in some cases. A senior authorising officer is permitted to grant an authorisation for the carrying out of intrusive surveillance on an application made by a member of another police force where such forces are parties to a police force collaboration agreement. This can also apply to authorisations for the carrying out of intrusive surveillance in respect of residential premises (s. 33(3ZA) to (3ZF)).

In keeping with the tenor of the Act, these officers must not grant the relevant authorisation unless they believe that it is necessary and proportionate to do so:

- in the interests of national security;
- for the purpose of preventing or detecting serious crime ('serious crime' means an offence(s) for which a person who has attained the age of 21 and has no previous convictions could reasonably be expected to be sentenced to imprisonment for a term of three years or more, or that the conduct involves the use of violence, results in substantial financial gain, or is conduct by a large number of persons in pursuit of a common purpose—s. 81(3));
- for the purpose of safeguarding the economic well-being of the United Kingdom.

These are very similar to the grounds on which an interception warrant may be authorised. The 2000 Act makes detailed provision for the recording and notification of authorisations. Anyone granting a police, SOCA or Revenue and Customs authorisation for intrusive surveillance must notify a Surveillance Commissioner (as to which, see above) in writing as soon as reasonably practicable (s. 35). This is because, except in urgent cases, the authorisation will not take effect until the Surveillance Commissioner has approved it and given written notification to that effect to the authorising officer (s. 36). The purpose behind this process is to make the system open to independent scrutiny and monitoring, largely in satisfaction of the requirements of the Human Rights Act 1998. Surveillance Commissioners can quash or revoke authorisations and order the destruction of certain records and materials obtained by intrusive surveillance. Senior authorising officers may appeal against decisions of Surveillance Commissioners to the Chief Surveillance Commissioner.

As in the case of directed surveillance, authorisations last for three months and urgent authorisations granted, for example, by an assistant chief constable last for 72 hours. Authorisations can be renewed before they cease to have effect provided that the criteria for authorisation are still satisfied.

# Entry, Search and Seizure

## PACE Code of Practice for Searches of Premises by Police Officers and the Seizure of Property found by Police Officers on Persons or Premises (Code B)

A thick grey line down the margin denotes text that is an extract of the PACE Code itself (i.e. the actual wording of the legislation).

## 1.5.1 Introduction

The main police powers dealing with entry to premises, searching them and seizing evidence from them, are contained within the Police and Criminal Evidence Act 1984; Code B of the Codes of Practice provides detailed guidance in relation to these features.

Whilst PACE and Code B are predominant when considering entry with or without a warrant, there are many other statutes that allow such processes to take place. However, only one common law power of entry without warrant exists—to deal with a breach of the peace. This power is preserved by s. 17(6) of the Police and Criminal Evidence Act 1984 and only applies where officers have a genuine and reasonable belief that a breach of the peace is happening or is about to happen in the immediate future (*McLeod* v *Commissioner of Police for the Metropolis* [1994] 4 All ER 553).

On a general point, it is worth remembering that where police officers enter premises *lawfully* (including where they are there by invitation), they are on the premises for *all lawful purposes* (see *Foster* v *Attard* [1986] Crim LR 627). This means that they can carry out any lawful functions while on the premises, even if that was not the original purpose for entry. For instance, if officers entered under a lawful power provided by the Misuse of Drugs Act 1971, they may carry out other lawful functions such as enforcing the provisions of the Gaming Act 1968. If officers are invited onto premises by someone entitled to do so, they are lawfully there unless and until that invitation is withdrawn. Once the invitation is withdrawn, the officers will become trespassers unless they have a power to be there, and the person may remove them by force (*Robson* v *Hallett* [1967] 2 QB 939). If that invitation is terminated, the person needs to communicate that clearly to the officer; it has been held that merely telling officers to 'fuck off' is not necessarily sufficient (*Snook* v *Mannion* [1982] RTR 321).

The above issues are of broad significance to police officer but the principal features of the Police and Criminal Evidence Act 1984 and Code B remain the most important for the purposes of operational policing and that is the central focus of this chapter.

## PACE Code of Practice for Searches of Premises by Police Officers and the Seizure of Property found by Police Officers on Persons or Premises (Code B)

This Code applies to applications for warrants made after midnight 6 March 2011 and to searches and seizures taking place after midnight on 6 March 2011.

**1.5.2**

## 1 Introduction

1.1 This Code of Practice deals with police powers to:
- search premises
- seize and retain property found on premises and persons

1.1A These powers may be used to find:
- property and material relating to a crime
- wanted persons
- children who abscond from local authority accommodation where they have been remanded or committed by a court

1.2 A justice of the peace may issue a search warrant granting powers of entry, search and seizure, e.g. warrants to search for stolen property, drugs, firearms and evidence of serious offences. Police also have powers without a search warrant. The main ones provided by the Police and Criminal Evidence Act 1984 (PACE) include powers to search premises:
- to make an arrest
- after an arrest

1.3 The right to privacy and respect for personal property are key principles of the Human Rights Act 1998. Powers of entry, search and seizure should be fully and clearly justified before use because they may significantly interfere with the occupier's privacy. Officers should consider if the necessary objectives can be met by less intrusive means.

1.3A Powers to search and seize must be used fairly, responsibly, with respect for people who occupy premises being searched or are in charge of property being seized and without unlawful discrimination. The Equality Act 2010 makes it unlawful for police officers to discriminate against, harass or victimise any person on the grounds of the 'protected characteristics' of age, disability, gender reassignment, race, religion or belief, sex and sexual orientation, marriage and civil partnership, pregnancy and maternity when using their powers. When police forces are carrying out their functions they also have a duty to have regard to the need to eliminate unlawful discrimination, harassment and victimisation and to take steps to foster good relations.

1.4 In all cases, police should:
- exercise their powers courteously and with respect for persons and property
- only use reasonable force when this is considered necessary and proportionate to the circumstances.

1.5 If the provisions of PACE and this Code are not observed, evidence obtained from a search may be open to question.

**1.5.3**

## 2 General

2.1 This Code must be readily available at all police stations for consultation by:
- police officers
- police staff
- detained persons
- members of the public

2.2 The *Notes for Guidance* (incorporated within Keynotes of this Manual) are not provisions of this Code.

2.3 This Code applies to searches of premises:

    (a) by police for the purposes of an investigation into an alleged offence, with the occupier's consent, other than:

- routine scene of crime searches;
- calls to a fire or burglary made by or on behalf of an occupier or searches following the activation of fire or burglar alarms or discovery of insecure premises;
- searches when *paragraph 5.4* applies;
- bomb threat calls;

    (b) under powers conferred on police officers by PACE, sections 17, 18 and 32;

    (c) undertaken in pursuance of search warrants issued to and executed by constables in accordance with PACE, sections 15 and 16;

    (d) subject to *paragraph 2.6*, under any other power given to police to enter premises with or without a search warrant for any purpose connected with the investigation into an alleged or suspected offence.

For the purposes of this Code, 'premises' as defined in PACE, section 23, includes any place, vehicle, vessel, aircraft, hovercraft, tent or movable structure and any offshore installation as defined in the Mineral Workings (Offshore Installations) Act 1971, section 1.

2.4 A person who has not been arrested but is searched during a search of premises should be searched in accordance with Code A.

2.5 This Code does not apply to the exercise of a statutory power to enter premises or to inspect goods, equipment or procedures if the exercise of that power is not dependent on the exist-ence of grounds for suspecting that an offence may have been committed and the person exercising the power has no reasonable grounds for such suspicion.

2.6 This Code does not affect any directions or requirements of a search warrant, order or other power to search and seize lawfully exercised in England or Wales that any item or evidence seized under that warrant, order or power be handed over to a police force, court, tribunal, or other authority outside England or Wales. For example, warrants and orders issued in Scotland or Northern Ireland, and search warrants and powers provided for in sections 14 to 17 of the Crime (International Co-operation) Act 2003.

2.7 When this Code requires the prior authority or agreement of an officer of at least inspector or superintendent rank, that authority may be given by a sergeant or chief inspector authorised to perform the functions of the higher rank under PACE, section 107.

2.8 Written records required under this Code not made in the search record shall, unless other-wise specified, be made:

- in the recording officer's pocket book ('pocket book' includes any official report book issued to police officers) or
- on forms provided for the purpose.

2.9 Nothing in this Code requires the identity of officers, or anyone accompanying them during a search of premises, to be recorded or disclosed:

    (a) in the case of enquiries linked to the investigation of terrorism; or

    (b) if officers reasonably believe recording or disclosing their names might put them in danger.

In these cases officers should use warrant or other identification numbers and the name of their police station. Police staff should use any identification number provided to them by the police force.

2.10 The 'officer in charge of the search' means the officer assigned specific duties and responsi-bilities under this Code. Whenever there is a search of premises to which this Code applies one officer must act as the officer in charge of the search.

2.11 In this Code:

    (a) 'designated person' means a person other than a police officer, designated under the Police Reform Act 2002, Part 4 who has specified powers and duties of police officers conferred or imposed on them;

    (b) any reference to a police officer includes a designated person acting in the exercise or per-formance of the powers and duties conferred or imposed on them by their designation;

(c) a person authorised to accompany police officers or designated persons in the execution of a warrant has the same powers as a constable in the execution of the warrant and the search and seizure of anything related to the warrant. These powers must be exercised in the company and under the supervision of a police officer. See *Note 3C*.

2.12 If a power conferred on a designated person:

    (a) allows reasonable force to be used when exercised by a police officer, a designated person exercising that power has the same entitlement to use force;

    (b) includes power to use force to enter any premises, that power is not exercisable by that designated person except:

      (i) in the company and under the supervision of a police officer; or

      (ii) for the purpose of:

        • saving life or limb; or

        • preventing serious damage to property.

2.13 Designated persons must have regard to any relevant provisions of the Codes of Practice.

---

**1.5.3.1**

**KEYNOTE**

**Application for Warrant—s. 15 PACE**

The Police and Criminal Evidence Act 1984, s. 15 states:

(1) This section and section 16 below have effect in relation to the issue to constables under any enactment, including an enactment contained in an Act passed after this Act, of warrants to enter and search premises; and an entry on or search of premises under a warrant is unlawful unless it complies with this section and section 16 below.

(2) Where a constable applies for any such warrant, it shall be his duty—

    (a) to state—

      (i) the ground on which he makes the application;

      (ii) the enactment under which the warrant would be issued; and

      (iii) if the application is for a warrant authorising entry and search on more than one occasion, the ground on which he applies for such a warrant, and whether he seeks a warrant authorising an unlimited number of entries, or (if not) the maximum number of entries desired;

    (b) to specify the matters set out in subsection (2A) below; and

    (c) to identify, so far as is practicable, the articles or persons to be sought.

(2A) The matters which must be specified pursuant to subsection (2)(b) above are—

    (a) if the application relates to one or more sets of premises specified in the application each set of premises which it is desired to enter and search; and

    (b) if the application relates to any premises occupied or controlled by a person specified in the application—

      (i) as many sets of premises which it is desired to enter and search as it is reasonably practicable to specify;

      (ii) the person who is in occupation or control of those premises and any others which it is desired to enter and search;

      (iii) why it is necessary to search more premises than those specified under sub-paragraph (i); and

      (iv) why it is not reasonably practicable to specify all the premises which it is desired to enter and search.

(3) An application for such a warrant shall be made ex parte and supported by information in writing.

(4) The constable shall answer on oath any question that the justice of the peace or judge hearing the application asks him.

(5) A warrant shall authorise an entry on one occasion only unless it specifies that it authorises multiple entries.

(5A) If it specifies that it authorises multiple entries, it must also specify whether the number of entries authorised is unlimited, or limited to a specified maximum.

(6) A warrant—

    (a) shall specify—

      (i) the name of the person who applies for it;

      (ii) the date on which it is issued;

      (iii) the enactment under which it is issued;

      (iv) each set of premises to be searched, or (in the case of an all premises warrant) the person who is in occupation or control of premises to be searched, together with any premises under his occupation or control which can be specified and which are to be searched; and

    (b) shall identify, so far as is practicable, the articles or persons to be sought.

(7) Two copies shall be made of a warrant (see section 8(1A)(a) above) which specifies only one set of premises and does not authorise multiple entries; and as many copies as are reasonably required may be made of any other kind of warrant.

(8) The copies shall be clearly certified as copies.

**KEYNOTE**

**Execution of a Warrant—s. 16 PACE**

The Police and Criminal Evidence Act 1984, s. 16 states:

(1) A warrant to enter and search premises may be executed by any constable.

(2) Such a warrant may authorise persons to accompany any constable who is executing it.

(2A) A person so authorised has the same powers as the constable whom he accompanies in respect of—

(a) the execution of the warrant, and

(b) the seizure of anything to which the warrant relates.

(2B) But he may exercise those powers only in the company, and under the supervision, of a constable.

(3) Entry and search under a warrant must be within three months from the date of its issue.

(3A) If the warrant is an all premises warrant, no premises which are not specified in it may be entered or searched unless a police officer of at least the rank of inspector has in writing authorised them to be entered.

(3B) No premises may be entered or searched for the second or any subsequent time under a warrant which authorises multiple entries unless a police officer of at least the rank of inspector has in writing authorised that entry to those premises.

(4) Entry and search under a warrant must be at a reasonable hour unless it appears to the constable executing it that the purpose of a search may be frustrated on an entry at a reasonable hour.

(5) Where the occupier of premises which are to be entered and searched is present at the time when a constable seeks to execute a warrant to enter and search them, the constable—

(a) shall identify himself to the occupier and, if not in uniform, shall produce to him documentary evidence that he is a constable;

(b) shall produce the warrant to him; and

(c) shall supply him with a copy of it.

(6) Where—

(a) the occupier of such premises is not present at the time when a constable seeks to execute such a warrant; but

(b) some other person who appears to the constable to be in charge of the premises is present, Subsection (5) above shall have effect as if any reference to the occupier were a reference to that other person.

(7) If there is no person present who appears to the constable to be in charge of the premises, he shall leave a copy of the warrant in a prominent place on the premises.

(8) A search under a warrant may only be a search to the extent required for the purpose for which the warrant was issued.

(9) A constable executing the warrant shall make an endorsement on it stating—

(a) whether the articles or persons sought were found; and

(b) whether any articles were seized, other than articles which were sought; and

unless the warrant is a warrant specifying one set of premises only, he shall do so separately in respect of each set of premises entered and searched, which he shall in each case state in the endorsement.

(10) A warrant shall be returned to the appropriate person mentioned in subsection (10A) below—

(a) when it has been executed; or

(b) in the case of a specific premises warrant which has not been executed, or an all premises warrant, or any warrant authorising multiple entries, upon the expiry of the period of three months referred to in subsection (3) above or sooner.

(10A) The appropriate person is—

(a) if the warrant was issued by a justice of the peace, the designated officer for the local justice area in which the justice was acting when he issued the warrant;

(b) if it was issued by a judge, the appropriate officer of the court from which he issued it.

(11) A warrant which is returned under subsection (10) above shall be retained for 12 months from its return—

(a) by the designated officer for the local justice area, if it was returned under paragraph (i) of that subsection; and

(b) by the appropriate officer, if it was returned under paragraph (ii).

(12) If during the period for which a warrant is to be retained the occupier of premises to which it relates asks to inspect it, he shall be allowed to do so.

**1.5.3.3**

**General Points**

If an application for a warrant is refused, no further application can be made unless it is supported by additional grounds.

'Premises' include any place, and in particular, (a) any vehicle, vessel, aircraft or hovercraft; (b) any offshore installation; (c) any renewable energy installation; (d) any tent or moveable structure (s. 23 of the 1984 Act).

The details of the extent of the proposed search should be made clear in the application and the officer swearing the warrant out must be prepared to answer *any* questions put to him/her on oath under s. 15(4). Many courts will go into background detail about the particular premises, or part of the premises, and who is likely to be present on the premises at the time the warrant is executed (e.g. children).

**1.5.3.4**

KEYNOTE

**Examples**

Sections 15 and 16 of the 1984 Act apply to all search warrants issued to and executed by constables under any enactment, e.g. search warrants issued by:

(a) a justice of the peace under:
  - Theft Act 1968, s. 26—stolen property;
  - Misuse of Drugs Act 1971, s. 23—controlled drugs;
  - PACE, s. 8—evidence of an indictable offence;
  - Terrorism Act 2000, Sch. 5, para. 1;
(b) a Circuit judge under:
  - PACE, Sch. 1;
  - Terrorism Act 2000, Sch. 5, para. 11.

Examples of the other powers in para. 2.3(d) include:

(a) Road Traffic Act 1988, s. 6E(1) giving police power to enter premises under s. 6E(1) to:
  - require a person to provide a specimen of breath; or
  - arrest a person following
    — a positive breath test;
    — failure to provide a specimen of breath;
(b) Transport and Works Act 1992, s. 30(4) giving police powers to enter premises mirroring the powers in (a) in relation to specified persons working on transport systems to which the Act applies;
(c) Criminal Justice Act 1988, s. 139B giving police power to enter and search school premises for offensive weapons, bladed or pointed articles;
(d) Terrorism Act 2000, sch. 5, paras 3 and 15 empowering a superintendent in urgent cases to give written authority for police to enter and search premises for the purposes of a terrorist investigation;
(e) Explosives Act 1875, s. 73(b) empowering a superintendent to give written authority for police to enter premises, examine and search them for explosives;
(f) search warrants and production orders or the equivalent issued in Scotland or Northern Ireland endorsed under the Summary Jurisdiction (Process) Act 1881 or the Petty Sessions (Ireland) Act 1851 respectively for execution in England and Wales.

The Criminal Justice Act 1988, s. 139B provides that a constable who has reasonable grounds for suspecting that an offence under the Criminal Justice Act 1988, s. 139A or 139AA has been or is being committed may enter school premises and search the premises and any persons on the premises for any bladed or pointed article or offensive weapon. Persons may be searched under a warrant issued under the Misuse of Drugs Act 1971, s. 23(3) to search premises for drugs or documents only if the warrant specifically authorises the search of persons on the premises.

The Immigration Act 1971, part III and sch. 2 gives immigration officers powers to enter and search premises, seize and retain property, with and without a search warrant. These are similar to the powers available to police under search warrants issued by a justice of the peace and without a warrant under ss. 17, 18, 19 and 32 of the 1984 Act except they only apply to specified offences under the Immigration Act 1971 and immigration control powers. For certain types of investigations and enquiries these powers avoid the need for the Immigration Service to rely on police officers becoming directly involved. When exercising these powers, immigration officers are required by the Immigration and Asylum Act 1999, s. 145 to have regard to this Code's corresponding provisions. When immigration officers are dealing with persons or property at police stations, police officers should give appropriate assistance to help them discharge their specific duties and responsibilities.

The purpose of para. 2.9(b) of Code B is to protect those involved in serious organised crime investigations or arrests of particularly violent suspects when there is reliable information that those arrested or their associates may threaten or cause harm to the officers or anyone accompanying them during a search of premises. In cases of doubt, an officer of inspector rank or above should be consulted.

**1.5.3.5**

## KEYNOTE

### Officer in Charge of the Search

For the purposes of para. 2.10, the officer in charge of the search should normally be the most senior officer present. Some exceptions are:

(a) a supervising officer who attends or assists at the scene of a premises search may appoint an officer of lower rank as officer in charge of the search if that officer is:
- more conversant with the facts;
- a more appropriate officer to be in charge of the search;

(b) when all officers in a premises search are the same rank. The supervising officer if available must make sure one of them is appointed officer in charge of the search, otherwise the officers themselves must nominate one of their number as the officer in charge;

(c) a senior officer assisting in a specialist role. This officer need not be regarded as having a general supervisory role over the conduct of the search or be appointed or expected to act as the officer in charge of the search.

Except in (c), nothing in this keynote diminishes the role and responsibilities of a supervisory officer who is present at the search or knows of a search taking place.

An officer of the rank of inspector or above may direct a designated investigating officer not to wear a uniform for the purposes of a specific operation.

**1.5.3.6**

## KEYNOTE

### Exclusion of Evidence

If the provisions of these sections are not fully complied with, any entry and search made under a warrant will be unlawful. Although the officers executing the warrant may have some protection from personal liability where there has been a defect in the *procedure* by which the warrant was issued, failure to follow the requirements of ss. 15 and 16 may result in the exclusion of any evidence obtained under the warrant. Therefore, where officers failed to provide the occupier of the searched premises with a copy of the warrant (under s. 16(5)(c)), they were obliged to return the property seized during the search (*R* v *Chief Constable of Lancashire, ex parte Parker* [1993] QB 577).

If a warrant itself is invalid for some reason, any entry and subsequent seizure made under it are unlawful (*R* v *Central Criminal Court and British Railways Board, ex parte AJD Holdings Ltd* [1992] Crim LR 669). After a warrant has been executed, or if it has not been used within three months (or sooner) from its date of issue, it must be returned to the designated officer for the local justice area in which the justice of the peace issued the warrant, or where it was issued by a judge to the appropriate officer of the court from which it was issued (s. 16(10) and (10A)).

Very minor departures from the letter of the warrant, however, will not render any search unlawful (see *Attorney-General of Jamaica* v *Williams* [1998] AC 351).

## 1.5.3.7    KEYNOTE

### Search Warrants for Indictable Offences—s. 8 PACE

The Police and Criminal Evidence Act 1984, s. 8 states:

(1) If on an application made by a constable a justice of the peace is satisfied that there are reasonable grounds for believing—

    (a) that an indictable offence has been committed; and

    (b) that there is material on premises mentioned in subsection (1A) below which is likely to be of substantial value (whether by itself or together with other material) to the investigation of the offence; and

    (c) that the material is likely to be relevant evidence; and

    (d) that it does not consist of or include items subject to legal privilege, excluded material or special procedure material; and

    (e) that any of the conditions specified in subsection (3) below applies in relation to each set of premises specified in the application

he may issue a warrant authorising a constable to enter and search the premises.

(1A) The premises referred to in subsection (1)(b) above are—

    (a) one or more sets of premises specified in the application (in which case the application is for a 'specific premises warrant'); or

    (b) any premises occupied or controlled by a person specified in the application, including such sets of premises as are so specified (in which case the application is for an 'all premises warrant').

(1B) If the application is for an all premises warrant, the justice of the peace must also be satisfied—

    (a) that because of the particulars of the offence referred to in paragraph (a) of subsection (1) above, there are reasonable grounds for believing that it is necessary to search premises occupied or controlled by the person in question which are not specified in the application in order to find the material referred to in paragraph (b) of that subsection; and

    (b) that it is not reasonably practicable to specify in the application all the premises which he occupies or controls and which might need to be searched.

(1C) The warrant may authorise entry to and search of premises on more than one occasion if, on the application, the justice of the peace is satisfied that it is necessary to authorise multiple entries in order to achieve the purpose for which he issues the warrant.

(1D) If it authorises multiple entries, the number of entries authorised may be unlimited, or limited to a maximum.

(2) A constable may seize and retain anything for which a search has been authorised under subsection (1) above.

(3) The conditions mentioned in subsection (1)(e) above are—

    (a) that it is not practicable to communicate with any person entitled to grant entry to the premises;

    (b) that it is practicable to communicate with a person entitled to grant entry to the premises but it is not practicable to communicate with any person entitled to grant access to the evidence;

    (c) that entry to the premises will not be granted unless a warrant is produced;

    (d) that the purpose of a search may be frustrated or seriously prejudiced unless a constable arriving at the premises can secure immediate entry to them.

(4) In this Act 'relevant evidence', in relation to an offence, means anything that would be admissible in evidence at a trial for the offence.

(5) The power to issue a warrant conferred by this section is in addition to any such power otherwise conferred.

This section provides that a constable can apply for two different types of search warrant: a 'specific premises warrant' for the search of one set of premises; and an 'all premises warrant' when it is necessary to search all premises occupied or controlled by an individual, but where it is not reasonably practicable to specify all such premises at the time of applying for the warrant. The warrant allows access to all premises occupied or controlled by that person, both those which are specified on the application, and those which are not. Note that s. 8(1C) and (1D) provide that a warrant (either an 'all premises warrant' or a 'specific premises warrant') may authorise access on more than one occasion, and if multiple entries are authorised these may be unlimited or limited to a maximum.

The officer applying for a warrant under s. 8 must have reasonable grounds for believing that material which is *likely to be of substantial value to the investigation of the offence* is on the premises specified. Therefore, when executing such a warrant, the officer must be able to show that any material seized thereunder fell within that description (*R* v *Chief Constable of the Warwickshire Constabulary, ex parte Fitzpatrick* [1999] 1 WLR 564). Possession of a warrant under s. 8 does not authorise police officers to seize all material found on the relevant premises to be taken away and 'sifted' somewhere else (*R* v *Chesterfield Justices, ex parte Bramley* [2000] QB 576) (see s. 50 of the Criminal Justice and Police Act 2001 for the power to 'seize and sift').

This means that material which is solely of value for *intelligence* purposes may not be seized under a s. 8 warrant.

The power to apply for and execute a warrant under s. 8 and to carry out the actions under s. 8(2) are among those powers that can be conferred on a person designated as an Investigating Officer under sch. 4 to the Police Reform Act 2002.

The conditions set out under s. 8(1)(e) are part of the *application* process, not part of the general execution process (which is set out at s. 16 above). Therefore the officer swearing out a s. 8 warrant will have to satisfy the court that any of those conditions apply.

---

**1.5.3.8**   **KEYNOTE**

**Legally Privileged Material**

Material which falls within the definition in s. 10 of the 1984 Act is subject to legal privilege which means that it cannot be searched for or seized.

The Police and Criminal Evidence Act 1984, s. 10 states:

(1) Subject to subsection (2) below, in this Act 'items subject to legal privilege' means—
   (a) communications between a professional legal adviser and his client or any person representing his client made in connection with the giving of legal advice to the client;
   (b) communications between a professional legal adviser and his client or any person representing his client or between such an adviser or his client or any such representative and any other person made in connection with or in contemplation of legal proceedings and for the purposes of such proceedings; and
   (c) items enclosed with or referred to in such communications and made—
      (i) in connection with the giving of legal advice; or
      (ii) in connection with or in contemplation of legal proceedings and for the purposes of such proceedings,

when they are in the possession of a person who is entitled to possession of them.

Items held with the intention of furthering a criminal purpose are not subject to this privilege (s. 10(2)). When making an application for a warrant to search for and seize such material the procedure under sch. 1 should be used. Occasions where this will happen are very rare and would include instances where a solicitor's firm is the subject of a criminal investigation (see *R v Leeds Crown Court, ex parte Switalski* [1991] Crim LR 559). However, it may be possible during a search to ascertain which material is subject to legal privilege and which might be lawfully seized under the warrant being executed. Therefore, although a warrant cannot authorise a search for legally privileged material, the fact that such material is inadvertently seized in the course of a search authorised by a proper warrant does not render the search unlawful (*R v HM Customs & Excise, ex parte Popely* [2000] Crim LR 388).

---

**1.5.3.9**   **KEYNOTE**

**Excluded Material**

Access to 'excluded material' can generally only be gained by applying to a judge for a production order under the procedure set out in s. 9 of, and sch. 1 to, the 1984 Act and PACE Code B. That strict statutory procedure also applies to the application for and execution of warrants by Investigating Officers designated under sch. 4 to the Police Reform Act 2002.

The Police and Criminal Evidence Act 1984, s. 11 states:

(1) Subject to the following provisions of this section, in this Act 'excluded material' means—
   (a) personal records which a person has acquired or created in the course of any trade, business, profession or other occupation or for the purposes of any paid or unpaid office and which he holds in confidence;
   (b) human tissue or tissue fluid which has been taken for the purposes of diagnosis or medical treatment and which a person holds in confidence;
   (c) journalistic material which a person holds in confidence and which consists—
      (i) of documents; or
      (ii) of records other than documents.

(2) A person holds material other than journalistic material in confidence for the purposes of this section if he holds it subject—
    (a) to an express or implied undertaking to hold it in confidence; or
    (b) to a restriction on disclosure or an obligation of secrecy contained in any enactment, including an enactment contained in an Act passed after this Act.
(3) A person holds journalistic material in confidence for the purposes of this section if—
    (a) he holds it subject to such an undertaking, restriction or obligation; and
    (b) it has been continuously held (by one or more persons) subject to such an undertaking, restriction or obligation since it was first acquired or created for the purposes of journalism.

Medical records and dental records would fall into this category, as might records made by priests or religious advisers.

'Personal records' are defined under s. 12 of the 1984 Act and include records relating to the physical or mental health, counselling or assistance given to an individual who can be identified by those records.

'Journalistic material' is defined under s. 13 as material acquired or created for the purposes of journalism.

## 1.5.3.10    KEYNOTE

### Special Procedure Material

Special procedure material can be gained by applying for a search warrant or a production order under sch. 1 to the 1984 Act.

The Police and Criminal Evidence Act 1984, s. 14 states:

(1) In this Act 'special procedure material' means—
    (a) material to which subsection (2) below applies; and
    (b) journalistic material, other than excluded material.
(2) Subject to the following provisions of this section, this subsection applies to material, other than items subject to legal privilege and excluded material, in the possession of a person who—
    (a) acquired or created it in the course of any trade, business, profession or other occupation or for the purpose of any paid or unpaid office; and
    (b) holds it subject—
      (i) to an express or implied undertaking to hold it in confidence; or
      (ii) to a restriction or obligation such as is mentioned in section 11(2)(b) above.

For items subject to 'legal privilege' and 'excluded material', **see para. 1.5.3.8**

The person believed to be in possession of the material must have come by it under the circumstances set out at s. 14(2)(a) *and* must hold it under the undertakings or obligations set out at s. 14(2)(b).

## 1.5.4    3 Search warrants and production orders

### (a) Before Making an Application

3.1 When information appears to justify an application, the officer must take reasonable steps to check the information is accurate, recent and not provided maliciously or irresponsibly. An application may not be made on the basis of information from an anonymous source if corroboration has not been sought.

3.2 The officer shall ascertain as specifically as possible the nature of the articles concerned and their location.

3.3 The officer shall make reasonable enquiries to:
  (i) establish if:
    • anything is known about the likely occupier of the premises and the nature of the premises themselves;
    • the premises have been searched previously and how recently;
  (ii) obtain any other relevant information.

3.4 An application:

(a) to a justice of the peace for a search warrant or to a Circuit judge for a search warrant or production order under PACE, Schedule 1 must be supported by a signed written authority from an officer of inspector rank or above:

Note: If the case is an urgent application to a justice of the peace and an inspector or above is not readily available, the next most senior officer on duty can give the written authority.

(b) to a circuit judge under the Terrorism Act 2000, Schedule 5 for
- a production order;
- search warrant; or
- an order requiring an explanation of material seized or produced under such a warrant or production order

must be supported by a signed written authority from an officer of superintendent rank or above.

3.5 Except in a case of urgency, if there is reason to believe a search might have an adverse effect on relations between the police and the community, the officer in charge shall consult the local police/community liaison officer:
- before the search; or
- in urgent cases, as soon as practicable after the search.

## (b) Making an application

3.6 A search warrant application must be supported in writing, specifying:

(a) the enactment under which the application is made;

(b)
    (i) whether the warrant is to authorise entry and search of:
- one set of premises; or
- if the application is under PACE section 8, or Schedule 1, paragraph 12, more than one set of specified premises or all premises occupied or controlled by a specified person; and

    (ii) the premises to be searched;

(c) the object of the search;

(d) the grounds for the application, including, when the purpose of the proposed search is to find evidence of an alleged offence, an indication of how the evidence relates to the investigation;

(da) where the application is under PACE section 8, or Schedule 1, paragraph 12 for a single warrant to enter and search:

    (i) more than one set of specified premises, the officer must specify each set of premises which it is desired to enter and search

    (ii) all premises occupied or controlled by a specified person, the officer must specify:
- as many sets of premises which it is desired to enter and search as it is reasonably practicable to specify;
- the person who is in occupation or control of those premises and any others which it is desired to search;
- why it is necessary to search more premises than those which can be specified;
- why it is not reasonably practicable to specify all the premises which it is desired to enter and search;

(db) whether an application under PACE section 8 is for a warrant authorising entry and search on more than one occasion, and if so, the officer must state the grounds for this and whether the desired number of entries authorised is unlimited or a specified maximum;

(e) there are no reasonable grounds to believe the material to be sought, when making application to a:

(i) justice of the peace or a Circuit judge consists of or includes items subject to legal privilege;

(ii) justice of the peace, consists of or includes excluded material or special procedure material;

Note: this does not affect the additional powers of seizure in the Criminal Justice and Police Act 2001, Part 2 covered in paragraph 7.7;

(f) if applicable, a request for the warrant to authorise a person or persons to accompany the officer who executes the warrant.

3.7 A search warrant application under PACE, Schedule 1, paragraph 12(a), shall if appropriate indicate why it is believed service of notice of an application for a production order may seriously prejudice the investigation. Applications for search warrants under the Terrorism Act 2000, Schedule 5, paragraph 11 must indicate why a production order would not be appropriate.

3.8 If a search warrant application is refused, a further application may not be made for those premises unless supported by additional grounds.

## 1.5.4.1 KEYNOTE

The identity of an informant need not be disclosed when making an application, but the officer should be prepared to answer any questions the magistrate or judge may have about:

- the accuracy of previous information from that source
- any other related matters.

Under s. 16(2) of the 1984 Act, a search warrant may authorise persons other than police officers to accompany the constable who executes the warrant. This includes, for example, any suitably qualified or skilled person or an expert in a particular field whose presence is needed to help accurately identify the material sought or to advise where certain evidence is most likely to be found and how it should be dealt with. It does not give them any right to force entry, but it gives them the right to be on the premises during the search and to search for or seize property without the occupier's permission.

The information supporting a search warrant application should be as specific as possible, particularly in relation to the articles or persons being sought and where in the premises it is suspected they may be found. The meaning of 'items subject to legal privilege', 'excluded material' and 'special procedure material' are defined by ss. 10, 11 and 14 of the 1984 Act respectively.

## 1.5.5    4 Entry without warrant—particular powers

## (a) Making an arrest etc

4.1 The conditions under which an officer may enter and search premises without a warrant are set out in PACE, section 17. It should be noted that this section does not create or confer any powers of arrest.

## 1.5.5.1 KEYNOTE

### Power of Entry—s.17 PACE

The Police and Criminal Evidence Act 1984, s. 17 states:

(1) Subject to the following provisions of this section, and without prejudice to any other enactment, a constable may enter and search any premises for the purpose—

(a) of executing—

(i) a warrant of arrest issued in connection with or arising out of criminal proceedings; or

(ii) a warrant of commitment issued under section 76 of the Magistrates' Courts Act 1980;

(b) of arresting a person for an indictable offence;

(c) of arresting a person for an offence under—

(i) section 1 (prohibition of uniforms in connection with political objectives) of the Public Order Act 1936;

      (ii)  any enactment contained in sections 6 to 8 or 10 of the Criminal Law Act 1977 (offences relating to entering and remaining on property);

      (iii)  section 4 of the Public Order Act 1986 (fear or provocation of violence);

      (iiia)  section 4 (driving etc when under influence of drink or drugs) or 163 (failure to stop when required to do so by constable in uniform) of the Road Traffic Act 1988;

      (iiib)  section 27 of the Transport and Works Act 1992 (which relates to offences involving drink or drugs);

      (iv)  section 76 of the Criminal Justice and Public Order Act 1994 (failure to comply with interim possession order);

      (v)  any of sections 4, 5, 6(1) and (2), 7 and 8(1) and (2) of the Animal Welfare Act 2006 (offences relating to the prevention of harm to animals);

  (ca)  of arresting, in pursuance of section 32(1A) of the Children and Young Persons Act 1969, any child or young person who has been remanded or committed to local authority accommodation under section 23(1) of that Act;

  (caa)  of arresting a person for an offence to which section 61 of the Animal Health Act 1981 applies;

  (cb)  of recapturing any person who is, or is deemed for any purpose to be, unlawfully at large while liable to be detained—

      (i)  in a prison, remand centre, young offender institution or secure training centre, or

      (ii)  in pursuance of section 92 of the Powers of Criminal Courts (Sentencing) Act 2000 (dealing with children and young persons guilty of grave crimes), in any other place;

  (d)  of recapturing any person whatever who is unlawfully at large and whom he is pursuing; or

  (e)  of saving life or limb or preventing serious damage to property.

(2)  Except for the purpose specified in paragraph (e) of subsection (1) above, the powers of entry and search conferred by this section—

  (a)  are only exercisable if the constable has reasonable grounds for believing that the person whom he is seeking is on the premises; and

  (b)  are limited, in relation to premises consisting of two or more separate dwellings, to powers to enter and search—

      (i)  any parts of the premises which the occupiers of any dwelling comprised in the premises use in common with the occupiers of any other such dwelling; and

      (ii)  any such dwelling in which the constable has reasonable grounds for believing that the person whom he is seeking may be.

(3)  The powers of entry and search conferred by this section are only exercisable for the purposes specified in subsection (1)(c)(ii) or (iv) above by a constable in uniform.

(4)  The power of search conferred by this section is only a power to search to the extent that is reasonably required for the purpose for which the power of entry is exercised.

(5)  Subject to subsection (6) below, all the rules of common law under which a constable has power to enter premises without a warrant are hereby abolished.

(6)  Nothing in subsection (5) above affects any power of entry to deal with or prevent a breach of the peace.

In a case where police had been called to an address by an abandoned 999 call, the officers had to move a man away from the front door in order to gain entry under s. 17. The Queen's Bench Divisional Court held that the officers had the power to use reasonable force in order to do so (*Smith (Peter John)* v *DPP* [2001] EWHC Admin 55). The source of the power to use force here is s. 117 of the Police and Criminal Evidence Act 1984.

'Unlawfully at large' does not have a particular statutory meaning; it can apply to someone who is subject to an order under the Mental Health Act 1983, or someone who has escaped from custody. The pursuit of the person must be 'fresh', that is, the power will only be available while the officer is actually 'pursuing' the person concerned (*D'Souza* v *DPP* [1992] 1 WLR 1073).

Force may be used in exercising the power of entry where it is necessary to do so. Generally, the officer should first attempt to communicate with the occupier of the premises, explaining by what authority and for what purpose entry is to be made, before making a forcible entry. Clearly though, there will be occasions where such communication is impossible, impracticable or even unnecessary; in those cases there is no need for the officer to enter into such an explanation (*O'Loughlin* v *Chief Constable of Essex* [1998] 1 WLR 374).

The officer must have reasonable grounds to *believe* that the person is on the premises in all cases except saving life and limb at s. 17(1)(e). This expression is narrower than 'reasonable cause to suspect' and you must be able to justify that belief before using this power (although see *Kynaston* v *DPP* (1988) 87 Cr App R 200, where the court accepted reasonable cause to *suspect*).

Note the requirement for an officer to be in uniform for the purposes of s. 17(1)(c)(ii) and (iv), and the restrictions on the power of search under s. 17(4) (i.e. that any such search is limited to the extent that is reasonably required for the purpose for which you entered the premises in the first place).

The power to enter and search any premises in the relevant police area for the purpose of saving life or limb or preventing serious damage to property above is among those that can be conferred on a designated person under sch. 4 to the Police Reform Act 2002.

## (b) Search of premises where arrest takes place or the arrested person was immediately before arrest

4.2 When a person has been arrested for an indictable offence, a police officer has power under PACE, section 32 to search the premises where the person was arrested or where the person was immediately before being arrested.

1.5.5.2 **KEYNOTE**

### Power to Search after Arrest—s. 32 PACE

The Police and Criminal Evidence Act 1984, s. 32 states:

(1) A constable may search an arrested person, in any case where the person to be searched has been arrested at a place other than a police station, if the constable has reasonable grounds for believing that the arrested person may present a danger to himself or others.

(2) Subject to subsections (3) to (5) below, a constable shall also have power in any such case—

    (a) to search the arrested person for anything—

      (i) which he might use to assist him to escape from lawful custody; or

      (ii) which might be evidence relating to an offence; and

    (b) if the offence for which he has been arrested is an indictable offence, to enter and search any premises in which he was when arrested or immediately before he was arrested for evidence relating to the offence.

(3) The power to search conferred by subsection (2) above is only a power to search to the extent that is reasonably required for the purpose of discovering any such thing or any such evidence.

(4) The powers conferred by this section to search a person are not to be construed as authorising a constable to require a person to remove any of his clothing in public other than an outer coat, jacket or gloves but they do authorise a search of a person's mouth.

(5) A constable may not search a person in the exercise of the power conferred by subsection (2)(a) above unless he has reasonable grounds for believing that the person to be searched may have concealed on him anything for which a search is permitted under that paragraph.

The power to search the arrested person under s. 32(1) is a general one relating to safety.

Section 32(2)(a) then goes on to provide a power to search the person in relation to anything that the arrested person might use to escape from lawful custody and anything that 'might be' evidence relating to *an offence*. There are restrictions placed on the extent and circumstances of the search (s. 32(3) and (4)) and the officer must have reasonable grounds to *believe* (as opposed to mere suspicion) that the person may have such things concealed on him/her (s. 32(5)). Nevertheless, this is still a very wide power. The House of Lords have confirmed that the police have a common law power to search for and seize property after a lawful arrest (*R* v *Governor of Pentonville Prison, ex parte Osman* [1990] 1 WLR 277). This decision was confirmed by the House of Lords in *R (On the Application of Rottman)* v *Commissioner of Police of the Metropolis* [2002] UKHL 20. In *Rottman* the House of Lords held that it was a well-established principle of the common law that an arresting officer had the power to search a room in which a person had been arrested (*per Ghani* v *Jones* [1970] 1 QB 693). This extended power is not limited to purely 'domestic' offences, but also applies to cases involving extradition offences.

Section 32 also provides that a constable shall have the power in such a case to enter and search any premises in which the person was when arrested or immediately before being arrested for an indictable offence (s. 32(2)(b)). The search may be conducted for the purpose of finding evidence relating to the offence for which the person was arrested.

Section 32 also states:

(6) A constable may not search premises in the exercise of the power conferred by subsection (2)(b) above unless he has reasonable grounds for believing that there is evidence for which a search is permitted under that paragraph on the premises.

(7) In so far as the power of search conferred by subsection (2)(b) above relates to premises consisting of two or more separate dwellings, it is limited to a power to search—

    (a) any dwelling in which the arrest took place or in which the person arrested was immediately before his arrest; and

    (b) any parts of the premises which the occupier of any such dwelling uses in common with the occupiers of any other dwellings comprised in the premises.

(8) A constable searching a person in the exercise of the power conferred by subsection (1) above may seize and retain anything he finds, if he has reasonable grounds for believing that the person searched might use it to cause physical injury to himself or to any other person.

(9) A constable searching a person in the exercise of the power conferred by subsection (2)(a) above may seize and retain anything he finds, other than an item subject to legal privilege, if he has reasonable grounds for believing—

(a) that he might use it to assist him to escape from lawful custody; or

(b) that it is evidence of an offence or has been obtained in consequence of the commission of an offence.

(10) Nothing in this section shall be taken to affect the power conferred by section 43 of the Terrorism Act 2000.

Both 'reasonable grounds' and 'immediately' are questions of fact for a court to determine. It has been held that the power under s. 32(2)(b) is one for use at the time of arrest and should not be used to return to the relevant premises some time after the arrest in the way that s. 18 of the 1984 Act may be used (*R* v *Badham* [1987] Crim LR 202).

Officers exercising their power to enter and search under s. 32 must have a genuine belief (i.e. more than mere suspicion) that there is evidence on the premises; it is not a licence for a general fishing expedition (*R* v *Beckford* [1992] 94 Cr App R 43).

The Divisional Court has refused to allow s. 32 to be used in a situation where the arrested person had not been in the relevant premises (where he did not live) for a period of over two hours preceding his arrest and where there were no reasonable grounds for believing that he presented a danger to himself or others (*Hewitson* v *Chief Constable of Dorset Police* [2003] EWHC 3296 (QB)).

## (c) Search of premises occupied or controlled by the arrested person

4.3 The specific powers to search premises which are occupied or controlled by a person arrested for an indictable offence are set out in PACE, section 18. They may not be exercised, except if section 18(5) applies, unless an officer of inspector rank or above has given written authority. That authority should only be given when the authorising officer is satisfied that the premises are occupied or controlled by the arrested person and that the necessary grounds exist. If possible the authorising officer should record the authority on the Notice of Powers and Rights and, subject to paragraph 2.9, sign the Notice. The record of the grounds for the search and the nature of the evidence sought as required by section 18(7) of the Act should be made in:

- the custody record if there is one, otherwise
- the officer's pocket book, or
- the search record.

1.5.5.3    **KEYNOTE**

**Power to Search after Arrest for Indictable Offence—s.18 PACE**

The Police and Criminal Evidence Act 1984, s. 18 states:

(1) Subject to the following provisions of this section, a constable may enter and search any premises occupied or controlled by a person who is under arrest for an indictable offence, if he has reasonable grounds for suspecting that there is on the premises evidence, other than items subject to legal privilege, that relates—

(a) to that offence; or

(b) to some other indictable offence which is connected with or similar to that offence.

(2) A constable may seize and retain anything for which he may search under subsection (1) above.

(3) The power to search conferred by subsection (1) above is only a power to search to the extent that is reasonably required for the purpose of discovering such evidence.

(4) Subject to subsection (5) below, the powers conferred by this section may not be exercised unless an officer of the rank of inspector or above has authorised them in writing.

(5) A constable may conduct a search under subsection (1)—

(a) before the person is taken to a police station or released on bail under section 30A; and

(b) without obtaining an authorisation under subsection (4), if the condition in subsection (5A) is satisfied.

(5A) The condition is that the presence of the person at a place (other than a police station) is necessary for the effective investigation of the offence.

(6) If a constable conducts a search by virtue of subsection (5) above, he shall inform an officer of the rank of inspector or above that he has made the search as soon as practicable after he has made it.

(7) An officer who—

   (a) authorises a search; or

   (b) is informed of a search under subsection (6) above, shall make a record in writing—

      (i) of the grounds for the search; and

      (ii) of the nature of the evidence that was sought.

(8) If the person who was in occupation or control of the premises at the time of the search is in police detention at the time the record is to be made, the officer shall make the record as part of his custody record.

Code B was modified on 6 March 2011: a specific modification was to point out that the power under s. 18 only applies to premises which *are* occupied and controlled by a person under arrest for an indictable offence; *suspicion is not sufficient*.

The search is limited to evidence relating to the indictable offence for which the person has been arrested or another indictable offence which is similar or connected; it does not authorise a general search for anything that might be of use for other purposes (e.g. for intelligence reports). The extent of the search is limited by s. 18(3). If you are looking for a stolen fridge-freezer, you would not be empowered to search through drawers or small cupboards. You would be able to, however, if you were looking for packaging, receipts or other documents relating to the fridge-freezer.

That authority is for a search which is lawful *in all other respects*, that is, the other conditions imposed by s. 18 must be met. An inspector cannot make an otherwise unlawful entry and search lawful simply by authorising it (*Krohn* v *DPP* [1997] COD 345).

Where officers carry out a search under s. 18 they must, so far as is possible in the circumstances, explain to the occupier(s) the reason for it. If officers attempt to carry out an authorised search under s. 18 without attempting to explain to an occupier the reason, it may mean that the officers are not acting in the execution of their duty and their entry may be lawfully resisted (*Lineham* v *DPP* [2000] Crim LR 861).

The provision under s. 18(5) relates to cases where the presence of the person *is in fact necessary* for the effective investigation of the offence. This is a more stringent requirement than merely reasonable suspicion or grounds to believe on the part of the officer concerned. If such a search is made, the searching officer must inform an inspector (or above) as soon as practicable after the search.

If the person is in police detention after the arrest, the facts concerning the search must be recorded in the custody record. Where a person is re-arrested under s. 31 of the 1984 Act for an indictable offence, the powers to search under s. 18 begin again, that is, a new power to search is created in respect of each indictable offence.

## 1.5.6

## 5 Search with consent

5.1 Subject to *paragraph 5.4*, if it is proposed to search premises with the consent of a person entitled to grant entry the consent must, if practicable, be given in writing on the Notice of Powers and Rights before the search. The officer must make any necessary enquiries to be satisfied the person is in a position to give such consent.

5.2 Before seeking consent the officer in charge of the search shall state the purpose of the proposed search and its extent. This information must be as specific as possible, particularly regarding the articles or persons being sought and the parts of the premises to be searched. The person concerned must be clearly informed they are not obliged to consent, that any consent can be withdrawn at any time, including before the search starts or while it is underway and anything seized may be produced in evidence. If at the time the person is not suspected of an offence, the officer shall say this when stating the purpose of the search.

5.3 An officer cannot enter and search or continue to search premises under paragraph 5.1 if consent is given under duress or withdrawn before the search is completed.

5.4 It is unnecessary to seek consent under paragraphs 5.1 and 5.2 if this would cause disproportionate inconvenience to the person concerned.

**1.5.6.1**  **KEYNOTE**

In a lodging house or similar accommodation, every reasonable effort should be made to obtain the consent of the tenant, lodger or occupier. A search should not be made solely on the basis of the landlord's consent.

If the intention is to search premises under the authority of a warrant or a power of entry and search without warrant, and the occupier of the premises cooperates in accordance with para. 6.4, there is no need to obtain written consent.

Paragraph 5.4 is intended to apply when it is reasonable to assume innocent occupiers would agree to, and expect, police to take the proposed action, e.g. if:

- a suspect has fled the scene of a crime or to evade arrest and it is necessary quickly to check surrounding gardens and readily accessible places to see if the suspect is hiding;
- police have arrested someone in the night after a pursuit and it is necessary to make a brief check of gardens along the pursuit route to see if stolen or incriminating articles have been discarded.

**1.5.7**  **6 Searching premises—general considerations**

### (a) Time of searches

6.1    Searches made under warrant must be made within three calendar months of the date of the warrant's issue.

6.2    Searches must be made at a reasonable hour unless this might frustrate the purpose of the search.

6.3    When the extent or complexity of a search mean it is likely to take a long time, the officer in charge of the search may consider using the seize and sift powers referred to in *section 7*.

6.3A    A warrant under PACE, section 8 may authorise entry to and search of premises on more than one occasion if, on the application, the justice of the peace is satisfied that it is necessary to authorise multiple entries in order to achieve the purpose for which the warrant is issued. No premises may be entered or searched on any subsequent occasions without the prior written authority of an officer of the rank of inspector who is not involved in the investigation. All other warrants authorise entry on one occasion only.

6.3B    Where a warrant under PACE section 8, or Schedule 1, paragraph 12 authorises entry to and search of all premises occupied or controlled by a specified person, no premises which are not specified in the warrant may be entered and searched without the prior written authority of an officer of the rank of inspector who is not involved in the investigation.

### (b) Entry other than with consent

6.4    The officer in charge of the search shall first try to communicate with the occupier, or any other person entitled to grant access to the premises, explain the authority under which entry is sought and ask the occupier to allow entry, unless:

(i)    the search premises are unoccupied;

(ii)    the occupier and any other person entitled to grant access are absent;

(iii)    there are reasonable grounds for believing that alerting the occupier or any other person entitled to grant access would frustrate the object of the search or endanger officers or other people.

6.5    Unless sub-paragraph 6.4(iii) applies, if the premises are occupied the officer, subject to paragraph 2.9, shall, before the search begins:

(i)    identify him or herself, show their warrant card (if not in uniform) and state the purpose of and grounds for the search;

(ii) identify and introduce any person accompanying the officer on the search (such persons should carry identification for production on request) and briefly describe that person's role in the process.

6.6 Reasonable and proportionate force may be used if necessary to enter premises if the officer in charge of the search is satisfied the premises are those specified in any warrant, or in exercise of the powers described in paragraphs 4.1 to 4.3, and if:

(i) the occupier or any other person entitled to grant access has refused entry;

(ii) it is impossible to communicate with the occupier or any other person entitled to grant access; or

(iii) any of the provisions of paragraph 6.4 apply.

## (c) Notice of Powers and Rights

6.7 If an officer conducts a search to which this Code applies the officer shall, unless it is impracticable to do so, provide the occupier with a copy of a Notice in a standard format:

(i) specifying if the search is made under warrant, with consent, or in the exercise of the powers described in paragraphs 4.1 to 4.3. Note: the notice format shall provide for authority or consent to be indicated, see paragraphs 4.3 and 5.1;

(ii) summarising the extent of the powers of search and seizure conferred by PACE;

(iii) explaining the rights of the occupier, and the owner of the property seized;

(iv) explaining compensation may be payable in appropriate cases for damages caused entering and searching premises, and giving the address to send a compensation application;

(v) stating this Code is available at any police station.

6.8 If the occupier is:

• present, copies of the Notice and warrant shall, if practicable, be given to them before the search begins, unless the officer in charge of the search reasonably believes this would frustrate the object of the search or endanger officers or other people

• not present, copies of the Notice and warrant shall be left in a prominent place on the premises or appropriate part of the premises and endorsed, subject to paragraph 2.9 with the name of the officer in charge of the search, the date and time of the search

the warrant shall be endorsed to show this has been done.

## (d) Conduct of searches

6.9 Premises may be searched only to the extent necessary to achieve the object of the search, having regard to the size and nature of whatever is sought.

6.9A A search may not continue under:

• a warrant's authority once all the things specified in that warrant have been found

• any other power once the object of that search has been achieved.

6.9B No search may continue once the officer in charge of the search is satisfied whatever is being sought is not on the premises. This does not prevent a further search of the same premises if additional grounds come to light supporting a further application for a search warrant or exercise or further exercise of another power. For example, when, as a result of new information, it is believed articles previously not found or additional articles are on the premises.

6.10 Searches must be conducted with due consideration for the property and privacy of the occupier and with no more disturbance than necessary. Reasonable force may be used only when necessary and proportionate because the cooperation of the occupier cannot be obtained or is insufficient for the purpose.

6.11 A friend, neighbour or other person must be allowed to witness the search if the occupier wishes unless the officer in charge of the search has reasonable grounds for believing the presence of the person asked for would seriously hinder the investigation or endanger officers or other people. A search need not be unreasonably delayed for this purpose. A record of the action taken should be made on the premises search record including the grounds for refusing the occupier's request.

6.12 A person is not required to be cautioned prior to being asked questions that are solely necessary for the purpose of furthering the proper and effective conduct of a search, see Code C, *paragraph 10.1(c)*. For example, questions to discover the occupier of specified premises, to find a key to open a locked drawer or cupboard or to otherwise seek cooperation during the search or to determine if a particular item is liable to be seized.

6.12A If questioning goes beyond what is necessary for the purpose of the exemption in Code C, the exchange is likely to constitute an interview as defined by Code C, *paragraph 11.1A* and would require the associated safeguards included in Code C, *section 10*.

## (e) Leaving premises

6.13 If premises have been entered by force, before leaving the officer in charge of the search must make sure they are secure by:
- arranging for the occupier or their agent to be present
- any other appropriate means.

## (f) Searches under PACE Schedule 1 or the Terrorism Act 2000, Schedule 5

6.14 An officer shall be appointed as the officer in charge of the search, see paragraph 2.10, in respect of any search made under a warrant issued under PACE Act 1984, Schedule 1 or the Terrorism Act 2000, Schedule 5. They are responsible for making sure the search is conducted with discretion and in a manner that causes the least possible disruption to any business or other activities carried out on the premises.

6.15 Once the officer in charge of the search is satisfied material may not be taken from the premises without their knowledge, they shall ask for the documents or other records concerned. The officer in charge of the search may also ask to see the index to files held on the premises, and the officers conducting the search may inspect any files which, according to the index, appear to contain the material sought. A more extensive search of the premises may be made only if:
- the person responsible for them refuses to:
  - produce the material sought, or
  - allow access to the index
- it appears the index is:
  - inaccurate, or
  - incomplete
  - for any other reason the officer in charge of the search has reasonable grounds for believing such a search is necessary in order to find the material sought.

1.5.7.1 **KEYNOTE**

Whether compensation is appropriate depends on the circumstances in each case. Compensation for damage caused when effecting entry is unlikely to be appropriate if the search was lawful, and the force used can be shown to be reasonable, proportionate and necessary to effect entry. If the wrong premises are searched by mistake everything possible should be done at the earliest opportunity to allay any sense of grievance and there should normally be a strong presumption in favour of paying compensation.

It is important that, when possible, all those involved in a search are fully briefed about any powers to be exercised and the extent and limits within which it should be conducted.

In all cases the number of officers and other persons involved in executing the warrant should be determined by what is reasonable and necessary according to the particular circumstances.

# 7 Seizure and retention of property

## (a) Seizure

7.1 Subject to *paragraph 7.2*, an officer who is searching any person or premises under any statutory power or with the consent of the occupier may seize anything:

(a) covered by a warrant

(b) the officer has reasonable grounds for believing is evidence of an offence or has been obtained in consequence of the commission of an offence but only if seizure is necessary to prevent the items being concealed, lost, disposed of, altered, damaged, destroyed or tampered with

(c) covered by the powers in the Criminal Justice and Police Act 2001, Part 2 allowing an officer to seize property from persons or premises and retain it for sifting or examination elsewhere.

7.2 No item may be seized which an officer has reasonable grounds for believing to be subject to legal privilege, as defined in PACE, section 10, other than under the Criminal Justice and Police Act 2001, Part 2.

7.3 Officers must be aware of the provisions in the Criminal Justice and Police Act 2001, section 59, allowing for applications to a judicial authority for the return of property seized and the subsequent duty to secure in section 60, see *paragraph 7.12(iii)*.

7.4 An officer may decide it is not appropriate to seize property because of an explanation from the person holding it but may nevertheless have reasonable grounds for believing it was obtained in consequence of an offence by some person. In these circumstances, the officer should identify the property to the holder, inform the holder of their suspicions and explain the holder may be liable to civil or criminal proceedings if they dispose of, alter or destroy the property.

7.5 An officer may arrange to photograph, image or copy, any document or other article they have the power to seize in accordance with *paragraph 7.1*. This is subject to specific restrictions on the examination, imaging or copying of certain property seized under the Criminal Justice and Police Act 2001, Part 2. An officer must have regard to their statutory obligation to retain an original document or other article only when a photograph or copy is not sufficient.

7.6 If an officer considers information stored in any electronic form and accessible from the premises could be used in evidence, they may require the information to be produced in a form:

• which can be taken away and in which it is visible and legible; or

• from which it can readily be produced in a visible and legible form.

### KEYNOTE

#### General Powers of Seizure—s.19 PACE

The Police and Criminal Evidence Act 1984, s. 19 states:

(1) The powers conferred by subsections (2), (3) and (4) below are exercisable by a constable who is lawfully on any premises.

(2) The constable may seize anything which is on the premises if he has reasonable grounds for believing—

(a) that it has been obtained in consequence of the commission of an offence; and

(b) that it is necessary to seize it in order to prevent it being concealed, lost, damaged, altered or destroyed.

(3) The constable may seize anything which is on the premises if he has reasonable grounds for believing—

(a) that it is evidence in relation to an offence which he is investigating or any other offence; and

(b) that it is necessary to seize it in order to prevent the evidence being concealed, lost, altered or destroyed.

(4) The constable may require any information which is stored in any electronic form and is accessible from the premises to be produced in a form in which it can be taken away and in which it is visible and legible or from which it can readily be produced in a visible and legible form if he has reasonable grounds for believing—

(a) that—

    (i) it is evidence in relation to an offence which he is investigating or any other offence; or

    (ii) it has been obtained in consequence of the commission of an offence; and

(b) that it is necessary to do so in order to prevent it being concealed, lost, or destroyed.

(5) The powers conferred by this section are in addition to any power otherwise conferred.

(6) No power of seizure conferred on a constable under any enactment (including an enactment contained in an Act passed after this Act) is to be taken to authorise the seizure of an item which the constable exercising the power has reasonable grounds for believing to be subject to legal privilege.

For this power to apply, the officers concerned must be on the premises lawfully. If the officers are on the premises only with the consent of the occupier, they become trespassers once that consent has been withdrawn. Once the officers are told to leave, they are no longer 'lawfully' on the premises—even though they must be given a reasonable opportunity to leave—and cannot then seize any property that they may find. For this reason, it is far safer to exercise a power where one exists, albeit that the *cooperation* of the relevant person should be sought.

The power of seizure only applies where the officer has 'reasonable grounds for believing' that:

- the property has been obtained in consequence of the commission of an offence, or
- the property is *evidence* in relation to an offence, *and*

in each case, that its seizure is *necessary* to prevent the property being concealed, lost or destroyed.

Where the 'premises' searched is a vehicle (see s. 23), the vehicle can itself be seized (*Cowan* v *Commissioner of Police for the Metropolis* [2000] 1 WLR 254). In *Cowan* it was argued that the powers given by ss. 18 and 19 authorise the seizure of anything in or on the premises but not the *premises* themselves. The Court of Appeal disagreed, holding that the power to seize 'premises', where it was appropriate and practical to do so, was embodied in both ss. 18 and 19 and also at common law and the defendant's claim for damages following the seizure of his vehicle after his arrest for serious sexual offences was dismissed. Therefore, the powers of seizure conferred by ss. 18(2) and 19(3) of the Police and Criminal Evidence Act 1984 extend to the seizure of the whole premises when it is physically possible to seize and retain the premises in their totality and practical considerations make seizure desirable. The police may remove premises such as tents, vehicles or caravans to a police station for the purpose of preserving evidence.

Unless the elements above are satisfied, the power under s. 19 will not apply. Therefore, the power does not authorise the seizure of property purely for intelligence purposes.

Section 19(5) expressly preserves any common law power of search and seizure; however, in *R (On the Application of Rottman)* v *Commissioner of Police for the Metropolis* [2002] UKHL 20, the House of Lords held that s. 19 was confined to 'domestic' offences (e.g. and did not extend to extradition offences). The same applies to powers under s. 18 of the Police and Criminal Evidence Act 1984.

If the warrant under which entry or seizure was made is invalid, the officers will not be on the premises lawfully.

The power of seizure under s. 19(1), along with the power to require information stored in any electronic form to be made accessible under s. 19(4), are among those that can be conferred on an Investigating Officer designated under sch. 4 to the Police Reform Act 2002. The safeguards provided by s. 19(6) in relation to privileged material also apply to the exercise of these powers by designated Investigating Officers.

**1.5.8.2**    **KEYNOTE**

**Powers of Seizure and Information in Electronic Form**

The Police and Criminal Evidence Act 1984, s. 20 states:

(1) Every power of seizure which is conferred by an enactment to which this section applies on a constable who has entered premises in the exercise of a power conferred by an enactment shall be construed as including a power to require any information stored in any electronic form and accessible from the premises to be produced in a form in which it can be taken away and in which it is visible and legible or from which it can readily be produced in a visible and legible form.

(2) This section applies—

    (a) to any enactment contained in an Act passed before this Act;

    (b) to sections 8 and 18 above;

(c) to paragraph 13 of Schedule 1 to this Act; and

(d) to any enactment contained in an Act passed after this Act.

This provision applies to:

- powers conferred under pre-PACE statutes;
- powers exercised under a s. 8 warrant (for 'indictable offences');
- powers exercised under s. 18 (following arrest for an indictable offence);
- powers under sch. 1 ('excluded' or 'special procedure material');
- powers exercised under s. 19 (officers lawfully on premises);
- powers of seizure exercised by Investigating Officers designated under sch. 4 to the Police Reform Act 2002.

## 1.5.8.3  KEYNOTE

### Supply of Copies of Seized Material

Section 21 of the 1984 Act makes provision for the supplying of copies of records of seizure to certain people after property has been seized. If requested by the person who had custody or control of the seized property immediately before it was seized, the officer in charge of the investigation must allow that person access to it under police supervision. The officer must also make provisions to allow for the property be to photographed or copied by that person or to supply the person with photographs/copies of it within a reasonable time. Such a request need not be complied with if there are reasonable grounds to believe that to do so would prejudice any related investigation or criminal proceedings (s. 21(8)).

## 1.5.8.4  KEYNOTE

### Retention of Seized Material

The provisions for accessing and copying of seized material as set out in ss. 21 and 22 of the Police and Criminal Evidence Act 1984 also apply to powers of seizure exercised by Investigating Officers designated under sch. 4 to the Police Reform Act 2002.

Section 22 of the 1984 Act makes provision for the retention of seized property. Section 22(1) provides that anything seized may be retained for as long as necessary in all the circumstances. However, s. 22(2) allows for property to be retained for use as evidence in a trial, forensic examination or further investigation *unless a photograph or copy would suffice*. Seized property may be retained in order to establish its lawful owner (s. 22(2)(b)). Once this power to retain property is exhausted, a person claiming it can rely on his/her right to possession at the time the property was seized as giving sufficient title to recover the property from the police. This situation was confirmed by the Court of Appeal in a case where the purchaser of a stolen car was allowed to rely upon his possession of the car at the time it was seized. As it could not be established that anyone else was entitled to the vehicle, the court allowed the claimant's action for return of the car to him (*Costello* v *Chief Constable of Derbyshire Constabulary* [2001] EWCA Civ 381). Clearly any claim based on previous possession where it would be unlawful for the police to return the property (e.g. a controlled drug) could not be enforced. Provisions amending this area of legislation are now contained in the Criminal Justice and Police Act 2001. There is no specific provision under s. 22 for the retention of property for purely intelligence purposes.

The importance of police officers being able to point clearly to the need for retaining property either in order to establish its owner or as a necessary part of the investigative or law enforcement process when relying on the above powers, was highlighted by the Court of Appeal in *Gough* v *Chief Constable of the West Midlands Police* [2004] EWCA Civ 206. In that case it was clear that neither of these purposes was being served and therefore the officers could not rely on the statutory power for retaining the property.

Property seized simply to prevent an arrested person from using it to escape or to cause injury, damage etc. cannot be retained for those purposes once the person has been released (s. 22(3)). This includes car keys belonging to someone who is released from police detention having been detained under the relevant drink driving legislation.

**KEYNOTE**

**Prohibitions on Re-use of Information Seized**

Information gained as a result of a lawful search may be passed on to other individuals and organisations for purposes of investigation and prosecution. It must not be used for private purposes (*Marcel* v *Commissioner of Police for the Metropolis* [1992] Ch 225).

**KEYNOTE**

**Disposal of Property in Police Possession**

Any person claiming property seized by the police may apply to a magistrates' court under the Police (Property) Act 1897 for its possession and should, if appropriate, be advised of this procedure.

## (b) Criminal Justice and Police Act 2001: Specific procedures for seize and sift powers

7.7 The Criminal Justice and Police Act 2001, Part 2 gives officers limited powers to seize property from premises or persons so they can sift or examine it elsewhere. Officers must be careful they only exercise these powers when it is essential and they do not remove any more material than necessary. The removal of large volumes of material, much of which may not ultimately be retainable, may have serious implications for the owners, particularly when they are involved in business or activities such as journalism or the provision of medical services. Officers must carefully consider if removing copies or images of relevant material or data would be a satisfactory alternative to removing originals. When originals are taken, officers must be prepared to facilitate the provision of copies or images for the owners when reasonably practicable.

7.8 Property seized under the Criminal Justice and Police Act 2001, sections 50 or 51 must be kept securely and separately from any material seized under other powers. An examination under section 53 to determine which elements may be retained must be carried out at the earliest practicable time, having due regard to the desirability of allowing the person from whom the property was seized, or a person with an interest in the property, an opportunity of being present or represented at the examination.

7.8A All reasonable steps should be taken to accommodate an interested person's request to be present, provided the request is reasonable and subject to the need to prevent harm to, interference with, or unreasonable delay to the investigatory process. If an examination proceeds in the absence of an interested person who asked to attend or their representative, the officer who exercised the relevant seizure power must give that person a written notice of why the examination was carried out in those circumstances. If it is necessary for security reasons or to maintain confidentiality officers may exclude interested persons from decryption or other processes which facilitate the examination but do not form part of it. See Note 7D

7.9 It is the responsibility of the officer in charge of the investigation to make sure property is returned in accordance with sections 53 to 55. Material which there is no power to retain must be:

- separated from the rest of the seized property
- returned as soon as reasonably practicable after examination of all the seized property.

7.9A Delay is only warranted if very clear and compelling reasons exist, e.g. the:

- unavailability of the person to whom the material is to be returned
- need to agree a convenient time to return a large volume of material.

7.9B Legally privileged, excluded or special procedure material which cannot be retained must be returned:

- as soon as reasonably practicable
- without waiting for the whole examination.

7.9C   As set out in section 58, material must be returned to the person from whom it was seized, except when it is clear some other person has a better right to it.

7.10   When an officer involved in the investigation has reasonable grounds to believe a person with a relevant interest in property seized under section 50 or 51 intends to make an application under section 59 for the return of any legally privileged, special procedure or excluded material, the officer in charge of the investigation should be informed as soon as practicable and the material seized should be kept secure in accordance with section 61.

7.11   The officer in charge of the investigation is responsible for making sure property is properly secured. Securing involves making sure the property is not examined, copied, imaged or put to any other use except at the request, or with the consent, of the applicant or in accordance with the directions of the appropriate judicial authority. Any request, consent or directions must be recorded in writing and signed by both the initiator and the officer in charge of the investigation.

7.12   When an officer exercises a power of seizure conferred by sections 50 or 51 they shall provide the occupier of the premises or the person from whom the property is being seized with a written notice:

   (i)   specifying what has been seized under the powers conferred by that section;
   (ii)  specifying the grounds for those powers;
   (iii) setting out the effect of sections 59 to 61 covering the grounds for a person with a relevant interest in seized property to apply to a judicial authority for its return and the duty of officers to secure property in certain circumstances when an application is made;
   (iv)  specifying the name and address of the person to whom:
      - notice of an application to the appropriate judicial authority in respect of any of the seized property must be given;
      - an application may be made to allow attendance at the initial examination of the property.

7.13   If the occupier is not present but there is someone in charge of the premises, the notice shall be given to them. If no suitable person is available, so the notice will easily be found it should either be:

- left in a prominent place on the premises
- attached to the exterior of the premises.

---

**1.5.8.7**   **KEYNOTE**

**Seize and Sift Powers**

These seize and sift powers only extend the scope of *some other existing power*. In other words, they do not provide free-standing powers to seize property—rather, they supplement other powers of search and seizure where the relevant conditions and circumstances apply. The full list of these powers is set out in sch. 1 to the Act and includes all the relevant powers under the Police and Criminal Evidence Act 1984, along with those under other key statutes such as the Firearms Act 1968 and the Misuse of Drugs Act 1971. If there is no existing power of seizure other than the Criminal Justice and Police Act 2001, then there is no power.

The Criminal Justice and Police Act 2001 powers allow officers to remove materials from the premises being searched where there are real practical difficulties in not doing so—e.g. because there will be insufficient time to examine all the material properly, where special equipment is needed to examine it or where the material is stored on a computer.

In summary, s. 50 of the Act provides the extended powers to seize material where it is not reasonably practicable to sort through it at the scene of the search. The factors that can be taken into account in considering whether or not it is reasonably practicable for something to be determined, or for relevant material to be separated from other materials, are set out in s. 50(3); these include the length of time and number of people that would be required to carry out the determination or separation on those premises within a reasonable period, whether that would involve damage to property, any apparatus or equipment that would be needed and (in the case of separation of materials) whether the separation would be likely to prejudice the use of some or all of the separated seizable property. Section 50 also allows for the seizure of material that is reasonably believed to be legally privileged where it is not reasonably practicable to separate it. In some cases, the power to 'seize' will be read as a power to take copies (see s. 63).

Section 51 provides for extended seizure of materials in the same vein as above but where the material is found on people who are being lawfully searched.

### (i) Initial Examination

Where any property has been seized under ss. 50 or 51, the officer in possession of it is under a duty to make sure that a number of things are done (s. 53). These include ensuring that an initial examination of the property is carried out *as soon as reasonably practicable* after the seizure. In determining the earliest practicable time to carry out an initial examination of the seized property, due regard must be had to the desirability of allowing the person from whom it was seized (or a person with an interest in it) an opportunity of being present, or of being represented, at the examination (s. 53(4)). Officers should consider reaching agreement with owners and/or other interested parties on the procedures for examining a specific set of property, rather than awaiting the judicial authority's determination. Agreement can sometimes give a quicker and more satisfactory route for all concerned and minimise costs and legal complexities. What constitutes a relevant interest in specific material may depend on the nature of that material and the circumstances in which it is seized. Anyone with a reasonable claim to ownership of the material and anyone entrusted with its safe keeping by the owner should be considered.

The officer must also ensure that any such examination is confined to whatever is *necessary* for determining how much of the property:

- is property for which the person seizing it had power to search when making the seizure but is not property that has to be returned (by s. 54—see (ii) Protected Material);
- is property authorised to be retained (by s. 56—see (iii) Retention of Property); or
- is something which, in all the circumstances, it will not be reasonably practicable, following the examination, to separate from the property above (see generally s. 53(3)).

The officer must ensure that anything found not to fall within the categories above is separated from the rest of the seized property and *is returned as soon as reasonably practicable* after the examination of all the seized property. That officer is also under a duty to ensure that, until the initial examination of all the seized property has been completed and anything which does not fall within the categories above has been returned, the seized property is kept separate from anything seized under any other power. There are special provisions where the property is inextricably linked to relevant material (e.g. where the 'innocent' material is completely mixed up with or inseparable from the material that is properly the subject of the investigation). However, those provisions place very strict limits on what use can be made of this inextricably linked material (see s. 62).

### (ii) Protected Material

If, at any time, after a seizure of anything has been made in exercise of *any statutory power of seizure*, it appears that the property is subject to legal privilege (or it has such an item comprised in it), s. 54 imposes a general duty on the officer in possession of the property to ensure that the item is returned as soon as reasonably practicable after the seizure. This general duty is subject to some exceptions (e.g. where in all the circumstances it is not reasonably practicable for that item to be separated from the rest of that property without prejudicing the use of the rest of that property—see s. 54(2)) but is otherwise very wide-ranging and absolutely clear. A similar duty is generally imposed in relation to property that appears to be excluded material or special procedure material (s. 55).

### (iii) Retention of Property

The Act authorises the retention of certain seized property by the police. In order to be retained, the property must have been seized on any premises by a constable who was lawfully on the premises, by a person authorised under a relevant statute (see s. 56(5)) who was on the premises accompanied by a constable, or by a constable carrying out a lawful search of any person (s. 56). Generally property so seized will fall within these categories if there are reasonable grounds for believing:

- that it is property obtained in consequence of the commission of an offence; or
- that it is evidence in relation to any offence; *and* (in either case)
- that it is necessary for it to be retained in order to prevent its being concealed, lost, altered or destroyed

(for full details see s. 56(2) and (3)). Note, so far as s. 56(2) is concerned, property may be retained if it is necessary to prevent its being 'damaged', in addition to the other factors listed.

These are fairly wide provisions and, if the property fits the above description, it may be retained even if it was not being searched for. Section 57 goes on to make certain provisions for the retention of property under other statutes such as s. 5(4) of the Knives Act 1997, para. 7(2) of sch. 9 to the Data Protection Act 1998, and sch. 5 to the Human Tissue Act 2004.

### (iv) Notice

Where a person exercises a power of seizure conferred by ss. 50 or 51, that person will be under a duty, on doing so, to give the occupier or person from whom property is seized a written notice (s. 52). That notice will specify:

- what has been seized and the grounds on which the powers have been exercised;
- the effect of the safeguards and rights to apply to a judicial authority for the return of the property (see (v) Return of Property Seized);
- the name and address of the person to whom notice of an application to a judge and an application to be allowed to attend the initial examination should be sent.

Where it appears to the officer exercising a power of seizure under s. 50 that the occupier of the premises is not present at the time of the exercise of the power, but there is some other person present who is in charge of the premises, the officer may give the notice to that other person (s. 52(2)). Where it appears that there is no one present on the premises to whom a notice can be given, the officer must, before leaving the premises, attach a notice in a prominent place to the premises (s. 53(3)).

### (v) Return of Property Seized

There are specific obligations on the police to return property seized under these powers—particularly where the property includes legally privileged, excluded or special procedure material. The general rule is that any extraneous property initially seized under these provisions must be returned—usually—to the person from whom it was seized unless the investigating officer considers that someone else has a better claim to it (see ss. 53 to 58).

Any person with a relevant interest in the seized property may apply to the appropriate judicial authority, on one or more of the grounds in s. 59(3) for the return of the whole or a part of the seized property. Generally those grounds are that there was no power to make the seizure or that the seized property did not fall into one of the permitted categories (see s. 59). Where a person makes such an application, the police must secure the property in accordance with s. 61 (e.g. in a way that prevents investigators from looking at or copying it until the matter has been considered by a judge). There are other occasions where protected material is involved that will give rise to the duty to secure the property under s. 61 too. The mechanics of securing property vary according to the circumstances; 'bagging up', i.e. placing material in sealed bags or containers and strict subsequent control of access is the appropriate procedure in many cases. The 'judicial authority' (at least a Crown Court judge) will be able to make a number of wide-ranging orders in relation to the treatment of the seized property, including its return or examination by a third party. Failure to comply with any such order will amount to a contempt of court (s. 59(9)). Requirements to secure and return property apply equally to all copies, images or other material created because of seizure of the original property.

When material is seized under the powers of seizure conferred by the Police and Criminal Evidence Act 1984, the duty to retain it under the Code of Practice issued under the Criminal Procedure and Investigations Act 1996 is subject to the provisions on retention of seized material in s. 22 of the 1984 Act.

For further details on the extent and use of these powers, see Home Office Circular 19/2003.

## (c) Retention

7.14 Subject to paragraph 7.15, anything seized in accordance with the above provisions may be retained only for as long as is necessary. It may be retained, among other purposes:

  (i) for use as evidence at a trial for an offence;

  (ii) to facilitate the use in any investigation or proceedings of anything to which it is inextricably linked;

  (iii) for forensic examination or other investigation in connection with an offence;

  (iv) in order to establish its lawful owner when there are reasonable grounds for believing it has been stolen or obtained by the commission of an offence.

7.15 Property shall not be retained under paragraph 7.14(i), (ii) or (iii) if a copy or image would be sufficient.

## (d) Rights of owners etc

7.16 If property is retained, the person who had custody or control of it immediately before seizure must, on request, be provided with a list or description of the property within a reasonable time.

7.17 That person or their representative must be allowed supervised access to the property to examine it or have it photographed or copied, or must be provided with a photograph or copy, in either case within a reasonable time of any request and at their own expense, unless the officer in charge of an investigation has reasonable grounds for believing this would:

  (i) prejudice the investigation of any offence or criminal proceedings; or

  (ii) lead to the commission of an offence by providing access to unlawful material such as pornography.

A record of the grounds shall be made when access is denied.

1.5.8.8 **KEYNOTE**

Paragraph 7.14(ii) applies if inextricably linked material is seized under the Criminal Justice and Police Act 2001, ss. 50 or 51. Inextricably linked material is material it is not reasonably practicable to separate from other linked material without prejudicing the use of that other material in any investigation or proceedings. For example, it may not be possible to separate items of data held on computer disk without damaging their evidential integrity. Inextricably linked material must not be examined, imaged, copied or used for any purpose other than for proving the source and/or integrity of the linked material.

1.5.9 ## 8 Action after searches

8.1 If premises are searched in circumstances where this Code applies, unless the exceptions in paragraph 2.3(a) apply, on arrival at a police station the officer in charge of the search shall make or have made a record of the search, to include:

  (i) the address of the searched premises;

  (ii) the date, time and duration of the search;

  (iii) the authority used for the search:

  • if the search was made in exercise of a statutory power to search premises without warrant, the power which was used for the search:

  • if the search was made under a warrant or with written consent;

  - a copy of the warrant and the written authority to apply for it, see paragraph 3.4; or

  - the written consent;

shall be appended to the record or the record shall show the location of the copy warrant or consent.

  (iv) subject to paragraph 2.9, the names of:
- the officer(s) in charge of the search;
- all other officers and any authorised persons who conducted the search;

  (v) the names of any people on the premises if they are known;

  (vi) any grounds for refusing the occupier's request to have someone present during the search, see paragraph 6.11;

  (vii) a list of any articles seized or the location of a list and, if not covered by a warrant, the grounds for their seizure;

  (viii) whether force was used, and the reason;

  (ix) details of any damage caused during the search, and the circumstances;

  (x) if applicable, the reason it was not practicable;
   (a) to give the occupier a copy of the Notice of Powers and Rights, see paragraph 6.7;
   (b) before the search to give the occupier a copy of the Notice, see paragraph 6.8;

  (xi) when the occupier was not present, the place where copies of the Notice of Powers and Rights and search warrant were left on the premises, see paragraph 6.8.

8.2 On each occasion when premises are searched under warrant, the warrant authorising the search on that occasion shall be endorsed to show:

  (i) if any articles specified in the warrant were found and the address where found;

  (ii) if any other articles were seized;

  (iii) the date and time it was executed and if present, the name of the occupier or if the occupier is not present the name of the person in charge of the premises;

  (iv) subject to paragraph 2.9, the names of the officers who executed it and any authorised persons who accompanied them;

  (v) if a copy, together with a copy of the Notice of Powers and Rights was:
- handed to the occupier; or
- endorsed as required by paragraph 6.8; and left on the premises and where.

8.3 Any warrant shall be returned within three calendar months of its issue or sooner on completion of the search(es) authorised by that warrant, if it was issued by a:
- justice of the peace, to the designated officer for the local justice area in which the justice was acting when issuing the warrant; or
- judge, to the appropriate officer of the court concerned.

1.5.10  **9 Search registers**

9.1 A search register will be maintained at each sub-divisional or equivalent police station. All search records required under *paragraph 8.1* shall be made, copied, or referred to in the register.

1.5.10.1  **KEYNOTE**

Paragraph 9.1 also applies to search records made by immigration officers. In these cases, a search register must also be maintained at an immigration office.

1.5.11  **10 Searches under sections 7A, 7B and 7C of the Prevention of Terrorism Act 2005 in connection with control orders**

10.1 Not used.

10.2 Not used.

10.3 Not used.

# Detention and Treatment of Persons by Police Officers

## PACE Code of Practice for the Detention, Treatment and Questioning of Persons by Police Officers (Code C)

> A thick grey line down the margin denotes text that is an extract of the PACE Code itself (i.e. the actual wording of the legislation).

### 1.6.1 Introduction

The powers to detain people who have been arrested and the manner in which they must be dealt with are primarily contained in the Police and Criminal Evidence Act 1984 and the PACE Codes of Practice, whose creation and status come from s. 66 of the Act. These Codes are intended to protect the basic rights of detained people. If these Codes are followed, it is more likely that evidence obtained while people are in custody will be admissible; the provisions of the 1984 Act give guidance in numerous areas. The Human Rights Act 1998 makes it even more important to comply with the 1984 Act and its associated Codes of Practice. This can be seen from the case of *R v Chief Constable of Kent Constabulary, ex parte Kent Police Federation Joint Branch Board* [2000] 2 Cr App R 196, where the court stated that the 1984 Act and the Codes of Practice represented the balance between the important duty of the police to investigate crime and apprehend criminals and the rights of the private citizen. A breach of Code C is fundamental in affecting the fairness of the evidence (*R v Aspinall* [1999] 2 Cr App R 115).

This chapter examines the treatment of persons who have been detained by police. The majority of this is contained within PACE Code C, which was amended on 10 July 2012. Some sections of Code C deal with the interviewing of suspects and as such are included in **Chapter 1.7**. This chapter sets out the actual Code of Practice with keynotes which incorporate the notes of guidance to the Code. Code H is the corresponding Code which applies to persons detained for the purposes of a terrorist investigation; the two Codes are similar and provide further clarity on their application. They also reflect changes to legislation that apply to both these Codes. These include consequential changes to custody records as a result of the reduced stop and search recording requirements in s. 3 of the Police and Criminal Evidence Act 1984, introduced in March 2011. References to terrorism matters, where appropriate, are included in the keynotes to this chapter.

The main responsibility for a detained person lies with the custody officer; however, it is important that all staff, including supervisors involved in investigations or those dealing with detained persons, are aware of the provisions of the Act and the Codes.

As Code C uses terms such as 'custody officer' and 'designated person' (amongst others), it is useful to examine briefly what they mean before examining Code C in detail.

## 1.6.2    Custody Officers

Custody officers are responsible for the reception and treatment of prisoners detained at the police station.

The role of the custody officer is to act independently of those conducting the investigation, thereby ensuring the welfare and rights of the detained person (this requirement is contained in s. 36(5) of the 1984 Act). Section 36 requires that one or more custody officers must be appointed for each designated police station. However, in *Vince v Chief Constable of Dorset* [1993] 1 WLR 415, it was held that a chief constable was under a duty to appoint one custody officer for each designated police station and had a discretionary power to appoint more than one, but this duty did not go so far as to require a sufficient number to ensure that the functions of custody officer were always performed by them. The provision of the facility of a custody officer must be reasonable. Section 36(3) states that a custody officer must be an officer of at least the rank of sergeant. However, s. 36(4) allows officers of any rank to perform the functions of custody officer at a designated police station if a sergeant is not readily available to perform them. The effect of s. 36(3) and (4) is that the practice of allowing officers of any other rank to perform the role of custody officer where a sergeant (*who has no other role to perform*) is in the police station must therefore be unlawful. Should a decision be made to use acting sergeants or untrained custody officers, this may lead to a claim in negligence by the officer or the detained person where there is a breach of the Codes or someone is injured as a result of the failure to manage the custody suite effectively. It could also lead to a prosecution under health and safety legislation.

For cases where arrested people are taken to a non-designated police station, s. 36(7) states that an officer of any rank not involved in the investigation should perform the role of custody officer. If no such person is at the station, the arresting officer (or any other officer involved in the investigation) or the officer that granted him/her bail under s. 30A of the 1984 Act (bail prior to being taken to a police station) should perform the role. In these cases, an officer of at least the rank of inspector at a designated police station must be informed. It is suggested that once informed, that officer should consider the circumstances of the detained person.

Where a custody officer feels that he/she is unable to comply with the minimum standards of detention as required by the 1984 Act, it is suggested that he/she should draw this to the attention of the line manager and/or the superintendent responsible for the custody suite. Custody officers should be mindful of Article 5 of the European Convention on Human Rights in considering whether they are able to manage the number of detained persons in their custody to ensure that their detention is not longer than needed.

## 1.6.3    Designated Support Staff

Sections 38 and 39 of the Police Reform Act 2002 allow persons employed by the police authority or persons employed by a contractor of the police authority (in relation to detention and escort officers) to be designated as investigating officers, detention officers and escort officers.

Designated officers are given powers to carry out certain functions that would up to this time have been carried out by police officers only. Before a person can be given the powers of a designated officer, the chief officer of police must be satisfied that the person is a suitable person to carry out the functions for which he/she is designated, is capable of effectively carrying out those functions, and has received adequate training in the carrying out of those functions and in the exercise and performance of the powers and duties of a designated officer. It should be noted that not all designated officers will be designated with the same range of powers and it will be important to know what powers a particular designated officer has been given and therefore what his/her role will be. Schedule 4 to the Police Reform Act 2002 outlines these powers, some of which are set out below.

### 1.6.3.1 Investigating Officers

- To act as the supervisor of any access to seized material to which a person is entitled, to supervise the taking of a photograph of seized material or to photograph it him/herself.
- To arrest a detainee for a further offence if it appears to him/her that the detainee would be liable to arrest for that further offence if released from his/her initial arrest.
- Power for the custody officer to transfer to a designated civilian investigating officer responsibility for a detainee. This power includes a duty for the person investigating the offence, once the detainee is returned to the custody of the custody officer, to report back to the custody officer on how the Codes were complied with.
- To question an arrested person under ss. 36 and 37 of the Criminal Justice and Public Order Act 1994 about facts which may be attributable to the person's participation in an offence. The designated person may also give the suspect the necessary warning about the capacity of a court to draw inferences from a failure to give a satisfactory account in response to questioning.

### 1.6.3.2 Detention Officers

- Powers to search detained persons, to take fingerprints and certain samples without consent and to take photographs.
- To require certain defined categories of persons who have been convicted, cautioned, reprimanded or warned in relation to recordable offences to attend a police station to have their fingerprints taken.
- To carry out non-intimate searches of persons detained at police stations or elsewhere and to seize items found during such searches.
- To carry out searches and examinations in order to determine the identity of persons detained at police stations. Identifying marks found during such processes may be photographed.
- To carry out intimate searches in the same very limited circumstances that are applicable to constables.
- To take fingerprints without consent in the same circumstances that a constable can.
- To take non-intimate samples without consent and to inform the person from whom the sample is to be taken of any necessary authorisation by a senior officer and of the grounds for that authorisation.
- To require certain defined categories of persons who have been charged with or convicted of recordable offences to attend a police station to have a sample taken.
- To inform a person that intimate samples taken from him/her may be the subject of a speculative search (i.e. this will satisfy the requirement that the person must be informed that the sample will be the subject of a speculative search).
- To photograph detained persons in the same way that constables can.

### 1.6.3.3 Escort Officers

- To transport arrested persons to police stations and escort detained persons from one police station to another or between police stations and other locations specified by the custody officer.
- To carry out the duty of taking a person arrested by a constable to a police station as soon as practicable.
- With the authority of the custody officer, to escort detainees between police stations or between police stations and other specified locations.

- To conduct non-intimate searches of the detainee; and to seize or retain, or cause to be seized or retained, anything found on such a search (restrictions on power to seize personal effects are the same as for police officers, as is the requirement that the search be carried out by a member of the same sex).

Where any of the powers allow for the use of reasonable force when exercised by a police constable, a designated person has the same entitlement to use reasonable force as a constable.

It is important to note that not all support staff will be designated for the purposes of the Police Reform Act 2002 and non-designated staff will not have the additional powers as outlined above.

### 1.6.4 Designated Police Stations

Section 30 of the Police and Criminal Evidence Act 1984 requires that a person who has been arrested must be taken to a police station *as soon as practicable* after arrest, unless the arrested person has been bailed prior to arrival at the police station. Section 30A of the 1984 Act allows a constable to release on bail a person who is under arrest. However, not all police stations have charge rooms or facilities for dealing with prisoners, so the 1984 Act requires that prisoners who will be detained (or who are likely to be detained) for more than six hours must go to a 'designated' police station. A designated police station is one that has enough facilities for the purpose of detaining arrested people. Section 35 requires the Chief Officer of Police to designate sufficient police stations to deal with prisoners. It is for the Chief Officer to decide which stations are to be designated stations and these details are then published. Police stations can be designated permanently or for any specified periods provided that they are not designated for part of a day.

#### PACE Code of Practice for the Detention, Treatment and Questioning of Persons by Police Officers (Code C)

This Code applies to people in police detention after midnight on 10 July 2012, notwithstanding that their period of detention may have commenced before that time.

### 1.6.5  1 General

1.  The powers and procedures in this Code must be used fairly, responsibly, with respect for the people to whom they apply and without unlawful discrimination. The Equality Act 2010 makes it unlawful for police officers to discriminate against, harass or victimise any person on the grounds of the 'protected characteristics' of age, disability, gender reassignment, race, religion or belief, sex and sexual orientation, marriage and civil partnership, pregnancy and maternity when using their powers. When police forces are carrying out their functions, they also have a duty to have regard to the need to eliminate unlawful discrimination, harassment and victimisation and to take steps to foster good relations.

1.1  All persons in custody must be dealt with expeditiously, and released as soon as the need for detention no longer applies.

1.1A  A custody officer must perform the functions in this Code as soon as practicable. A custody officer will not be in breach of this Code if delay is justifiable and reasonable steps are taken to prevent unnecessary delay. The custody record shall show when a delay has occurred and the reason.

1.2  This Code of Practice must be readily available at all police stations for consultation by:

- police officers;
- police staff;
- detained persons;
- members of the public.

1.3    The provisions of this Code:
- include the *Annexes*
- do not include the *Notes for Guidance*.

1.4    If an officer has any suspicion, or is told in good faith, that a person of any age may be mentally disordered or otherwise mentally vulnerable, in the absence of clear evidence to dispel that suspicion, the person shall be treated as such for the purposes of this Code.

1.5    If anyone appears to be under 17, they shall be treated as a juvenile for the purposes of this Code in the absence of clear evidence that they are older.

1.6    If a person appears to be blind, seriously visually impaired, deaf, unable to read or speak or has difficulty orally because of a speech impediment, they shall be treated as such for the purposes of this Code in the absence of clear evidence to the contrary.

1.7    'The appropriate adult' means, in the case of a:

   (a)  juvenile:
   
   (i)   the parent, guardian or, if the juvenile is in the care of a local authority or voluntary organisation, a person representing that authority or organisation;
   
   (ii)  a social worker of a local authority;
   
   (iii) failing these, some other responsible adult aged 18 or over who is not a police officer or employed by the police.

   (b)  person who is mentally disordered or mentally vulnerable:
   
   (i)   a relative, guardian or other person responsible for their care or custody;
   
   (ii)  someone experienced in dealing with mentally disordered or mentally vulnerable people but who is not a police officer or employed by the police;
   
   (iii) failing these, some other responsible adult aged 18 or over who is not a police officer or employed by the police.

1.8    If this Code requires a person be given certain information, they do not have to be given it if at the time they are incapable of understanding what is said, are violent or may become violent or in urgent need of medical attention, but they must be given it as soon as practicable.

1.9    References to a custody officer include any police officer who for the time being, is performing the functions of a custody officer.

1.9A   When this Code requires the prior authority or agreement of an officer of at least inspector or superintendent rank, that authority may be given by a sergeant or chief inspector authorised to perform the functions of the higher rank under the Police and Criminal Evidence Act 1984 (PACE), section 107.

1.10   Subject to *paragraph 1.12*, this Code applies to people in custody at police stations in England and Wales, whether or not they have been arrested, and to those removed to a police station as a place of safety under the Mental Health Act 1983, sections 135 and 136, as a last resort (see paragraph 3.16). *Section 15* applies solely to people in police detention, e.g. those brought to a police station under arrest or arrested at a police station for an offence after going there voluntarily.

1.11   No part of this Code applies to a detained person:

   (a)  to whom PACE Code H applies because:
   - they are detained following arrest under section 41 of the Terrorism Act 2000 (TACT) and not charged; or
   - an authorisation has been given under section 22 of the Counter-Terrorism Act 2008 (CTACT) (post-charge questioning of terrorist suspects) to interview them.

   (b)  to whom the Code of Practice issued under paragraph 6 of Schedule 14 to TACT applies because they are detained for examination under Schedule 7 to TACT.

1.12   This Code does not apply to people in custody:

(i) arrested on warrants issued in Scotland by officers under the Criminal Justice and Public Order Act 1994, section 136(2), or arrested or detained without warrant by officers from a police force in Scotland under section 137(2). In these cases, police powers and duties and the person's rights and entitlements whilst at a police station in England or Wales are the same as those in Scotland;

(ii) arrested under the Immigration and Asylum Act 1999, section 142(3) in order to have their fingerprints taken;

(iii) whose detention is authorised by an immigration officer under the Immigration Act 1971;

(iv) who are convicted or remanded prisoners held in police cells on behalf of the Prison Service under the Imprisonment (Temporary Provisions) Act 1980;

(v) *Not used*

(vi) detained for searches under stop and search powers except as required by Code A. The provisions on conditions of detention and treatment in *sections 8* and *9* must be considered as the minimum standards of treatment for such detainees.

1.13 In this Code:

(a) 'designated person' means a person other than a police officer, designated under the Police Reform Act 2002, Part 4 who has specified powers and duties of police officers conferred or imposed on them;

(b) reference to a police officer includes a designated person acting in the exercise or performance of the powers and duties conferred or imposed on them by their designation.

(c) where a search or other procedure to which this Code applies may only be carried out or observed by a person of the same sex as the detainee, the gender of the detainee and other parties present should be established and recorded in line with Annex L of this Code.

1.14 Designated persons are entitled to use reasonable force as follows:

(a) when exercising a power conferred on them which allows a police officer exercising that power to use reasonable force, a designated person has the same entitlement to use force; and

(b) at other times when carrying out duties conferred or imposed on them that also entitle them to use reasonable force, for example:

- when at a police station carrying out the duty to keep detainees for whom they are responsible under control and to assist any other police officer or designated person to keep any detainee under control and to prevent their escape.

- when securing, or assisting any other police officer or designated person in securing, the detention of a person at a police station.

- when escorting, or assisting any other police officer or designated person in escorting, a detainee within a police station.

- for the purpose of saving life or limb; or

- preventing serious damage to property.

1.15 Nothing in this Code prevents the custody officer, or other officer given custody of the detainee, from allowing police staff who are not designated persons to carry out individual procedures or tasks at the police station if the law allows. However, the officer remains responsible for making sure the procedures and tasks are carried out correctly in accordance with the Codes of Practice). Any such person must be:

(a) a person employed by a police force and under the direction and control of the Chief Officer of that force; or

(b) employed by a person with whom a police force has a contract for the provision of services relating to persons arrested or otherwise in custody.

1.16 Designated persons and other police staff must have regard to any relevant provisions of the Codes of Practice.

1.17 References to pocket books include any official report book issued to police officers or other police staff.

**1.6.5.1**

## KEYNOTE

The revised Codes recognise the importance that detained persons are treated in accordance with the Equality Act 2010. This Code does not affect the principle that all citizens have a duty to help police officers to prevent crime and discover offenders. This is a civic rather than a legal duty; but when a police officer is trying to discover whether, or by whom, an offence has been committed, he/she is entitled to question any person from whom he/she thinks useful information can be obtained, subject to the restrictions imposed by this Code. A person's declaration that he/she is unwilling to reply does not alter this entitlement.

Paragraph 1.1A is intended to cover delays which may occur in processing detainees, e.g. if a large number of suspects are brought into the station simultaneously to be placed in custody, or interview rooms are all being used, or perhaps there are difficulties contacting an appropriate adult, solicitor or interpreter. However, if that delay was not 'justified', it could lead to actions for unlawful detention and false imprisonment, and any evidence obtained as a result may be held to be inadmissible (*Roberts* v *Chief Constable of Cheshire Constabulary* [1999] 1 WLR 662).

Although certain sections of this Code apply specifically to people in custody at police stations, those there voluntarily to assist with an investigation should be treated with no less consideration, e.g. offered refreshments at appropriate times, and enjoy an absolute right to obtain legal advice or communicate with anyone outside the police station.

**1.6.5.2**

## KEYNOTE

### Meaning of Police Detention

Police detention is defined by s. 118 of the Police and Criminal Evidence Act 1984 which states:

(2) Subject to subsection (2A) a person is in police detention for the purposes of this Act if—
  (a) he has been taken to a police station after being arrested for an offence or after being arrested under section 41 of the Terrorism Act 2000, or
  (b) he is arrested at a police station after attending voluntarily at the station or accompanying a constable to it,
  and is detained there or is detained elsewhere in the charge of a constable, except that a person who is at a court after being charged is not in police detention for those purposes.
(2A) Where a person is in another's lawful custody by virtue of paragraph 22, 34(1) or 35(3) of Schedule 4 to the Police Reform Act 2002, he shall be treated as in police detention.

Paragraph 22 of sch. 4 to the Police Reform Act 2002 refers to the power to transfer persons into the custody of investigating officers, para. 34(1) relates to designated escort officers taking an arrested person to a police station and para. 35(3) deals with a designated escort officer transferring a detainee from one police station to another.

**1.6.5.3**

## KEYNOTE

### Mentally Vulnerable/Disordered

'Mentally vulnerable' applies to any detainee who, because of his/her mental state or capacity, may not understand the significance of what is said, of questions or of his/her replies. 'Mental disorder' is defined in the Mental Health Act 1983, s. 1(2) as as 'any disorder or disability of mind'. When the custody officer has any doubt about the mental state or capacity of a detainee, that detainee should be treated as mentally vulnerable and an appropriate adult called.

**1.6.5.4**

## KEYNOTE

### Appropriate Adults

A person, including a parent or guardian, should not be an appropriate adult if he/she is:

- suspected of involvement in the offence;
- the victim;
- a witness;
- involved in the investigation; or
- has received admissions prior to attending to act as the appropriate adult.

If a juvenile's parent is estranged from the juvenile, he/she should not be asked to act as the appropriate adult if the juvenile expressly and specifically objects to his/her presence.

If a juvenile admits an offence to, or in the presence of, a social worker or member of a youth offending team other than during the time that person is acting as the juvenile's appropriate adult, another appropriate adult should be appointed in the interest of fairness.

In the case of people who are mentally disordered or otherwise mentally vulnerable, it may be more satisfactory if the appropriate adult is someone experienced or trained in their care rather than a relative lacking such qualifications. But if the detainee prefers a relative to a better qualified stranger or objects to a particular person, his/her wishes should, if practicable, be respected.

A detainee should always be given an opportunity, when an appropriate adult is called to the police station, to consult privately with a solicitor in the appropriate adult's absence if he/she wants. An appropriate adult is not subject to legal privilege.

A solicitor or independent custody visitor (formerly a lay visitor) present at the police station in that capacity may not be the appropriate adult.

The custody officer must remind the appropriate adult and detainee about the right to legal advice and record any reasons for waiving it in accordance with section 6.

Evidence obtained while a person is in custody where the person called as an appropriate adult does not have that person's best interests in mind or is not capable of assisting that person could be excluded.

An appropriate adult is not required for a 17-year-old (*R v Stratford Youth Court, ex parte Harding* [2001] EWHC 615 (Admin)). However, in the case of *R (on the application of HC) v Secretary of State for the Home Office and the Commissioner for the Metropolitan Police* [2013] EWHC 982 (Admin), the court held that the Home Secretary's refusal to revise Code C of the Code of Practice so as to distinguish the procedures applicable to a 17-year-old detainee in police custody from those applicable to an adult was unlawful. Treating 17-year-olds in detention as adults was contrary to the European Convention on Human Rights 1950 art. 8. It should be noted that the Codes have not been amended and therefore it is suggested that local guidance should be followed.

Whilst an appropriate adult should be given access to a juvenile, this does not mean that he/she has free access to the custody area. In *Butcher* v *DPP* [2003] EWHC 580 (Admin), the custody officer physically escorted the detainee's appropriate adult from the custody suite as she had entered it without being invited and had been verbally abusive and aggressive. The court held that the custody sergeant had not detained the appropriate adult, but had merely used reasonable force to remove her in order to maintain the operational effectiveness of the custody suite. The court held that the custody sergeant was entitled to ask her to leave and to use reasonable force when she failed to comply with that request.

In *R* v *Aspinall* [1999] 2 Cr App R 115, the Court of Appeal emphasised the importance of appropriate adults. There it was held that an appropriate adult played a significant role in respect of a vulnerable person whose condition rendered him/her liable to provide information which was unreliable, misleading or self-incriminating.

It is also important to consider the welfare of the appropriate adult. This is demonstrated by the case of *Leach* v *Chief Constable of Gloucestershire Constabulary* [1999] 1 WLR 1421. Here L was asked by a police officer to attend police interviews of a murder suspect who was also thought to be mentally disordered, as an 'appropriate adult' per the requirement of the Codes. She was told only that the suspect was a 52-year-old male, and was not informed of the nature of the case. The suspect was in fact Frederick West, who was being questioned in connection with murders committed in particularly harrowing and traumatic circumstances. For many weeks L acted as an appropriate adult, accompanying the officer and suspect to murder scenes, and on many occasions being left alone in a locked cell with the suspect. She claimed to be suffering from post-traumatic stress and psychological injury as well as a stroke as a result of her experiences. The Court of Appeal said that the Fred West case was notorious among modern crimes and it was forseeable that psychiatric harm might arise. While there was no requirement to pre-select or warn appropriate adults as to the nature of the case, in some cases counselling or trained help should be offered.

## 2 Custody Records

2.1A When a person is brought to a police station:

- under arrest
- is arrested at the police station having attended there voluntarily or
- attends a police station to answer bail

they must be brought before the custody officer as soon as practicable after their arrival at the station or, if appropriate, following arrest after attending the police station voluntarily. This applies to designated and non-designated police stations. A person is deemed to be 'at a police station' for these purposes if they are within the boundary of any building or enclosed yard which forms part of that police station.

2.1 A separate custody record must be opened as soon as practicable for each person brought to a police station under arrest or arrested at the station having gone there voluntarily or attending a police station in answer to street bail. All information recorded under this Code must be recorded as soon as practicable in the custody record unless otherwise specified. Any audio or video recording made in the custody area is not part of the custody record.

2.2 If any action requires the authority of an officer of a specified rank, subject to *paragraph 2.6A*, their name and rank must be noted in the custody record.

2.3 The custody officer is responsible for the custody record's accuracy and completeness and for making sure the record or copy of the record accompanies a detainee if they are transferred to another police station. The record shall show the:

- time and reason for transfer;
- time a person is released from detention.

2.3A If a person is arrested and taken to a police station as a result of a search in the exercise of any stop and search power to which PACE Code A (Stop and search) or the 'search powers code' issued under TACT applies, the officer carrying out the search is responsible for ensuring that the record of that stop and search, is made as part of the person's custody record. The custody officer must then ensure that the person is asked if they want a copy of the search record and if they do, that they are given a copy as soon as practicable. The person's entitlement to a copy of the search record which is made as part of their custody record is in addition to, and does not affect, their entitlement to a copy of their custody record or any other provisions of section 2 (Custody records) of this Code. (See Code A *paragraph 4.2B* and the TACT search powers code paragraph 5.3.5).

2.4 A solicitor or appropriate adult must be permitted to consult a detainee's custody record as soon as practicable after their arrival at the station and at any other time whilst the person is detained. Arrangements for this access must be agreed with the custody officer and may not unreasonably interfere with the custody officer's duties.

2.4A When a detainee leaves police detention or is taken before a court they, their legal representative or appropriate adult shall be given, on request, a copy of the custody record as soon as practicable. This entitlement lasts for 12 months after release.

2.5 The detainee, appropriate adult or legal representative shall be permitted to inspect the original custody record after the detainee has left police detention provided they give reasonable notice of their request. Any such inspection shall be noted in the custody record.

2.6 Subject to *paragraph 2.6A*, all entries in custody records must be timed and signed by the maker. Records entered on computer shall be timed and contain the operator's identification.

2.6A Nothing in this Code requires the identity of officers or other police staff to be recorded or disclosed:

(a) *Not used*

(b) if the officer or police staff reasonably believe recording or disclosing their name might put them in danger.

In these cases, they shall use their warrant or other identification numbers and the name of their police station.

2.7 The fact and time of any detainee's refusal to sign a custody record, when asked in accordance with this Code, must be recorded.

---

**1.6.6.1**

**KEYNOTE**

The purpose of using warrant or identification numbers instead of names referred to in Code C, para. 2.6A is to protect those involved in serious organised crime investigations or arrests of particularly violent suspects when there is reliable information that those arrested or their associates may threaten or cause harm to those involved. In cases of doubt, an officer of inspector rank or above should be consulted.

---

**1.6.7**

## 3 Initial Action

### (a) Detained persons—normal procedure

3.1 When a person is brought to a police station under arrest or arrested at the station having gone there voluntarily, the custody officer must make sure the person is told clearly about the following continuing rights which may be exercised at any stage during the period in custody:
  (i) the right to have someone informed of their arrest as in *section 5*;
  (ii) the right to consult privately with a solicitor and that free independent legal advice is available;
  (iii) the right to consult these Codes of Practice.

3.2 The detainee must also be given:
  • a written notice setting out:
    • the above three rights;
    • the arrangements for obtaining legal advice;
    • the right to a copy of the custody record as in *paragraph 2.4A*;
    • the caution in the terms prescribed in *section 10*.
  • an additional written notice briefly setting out their entitlements while in custody.
  Note: The detainee shall be asked to sign the custody record to acknowledge receipt of these notices. Any refusal must be recorded on the custody record.

3.3 A citizen of an independent Commonwealth country or a national of a foreign country, including the Republic of Ireland, must be informed as soon as practicable about their rights of communication with their High Commission, Embassy or Consulate. See *section 7*.

3.4 The custody officer shall:
  • record the offence(s) that the detainee has been arrested for and the reason(s) for the arrest on the custody record. See *paragraph 10.3* and Code G *paragraphs 2.2* and *4.3*.
  • note on the custody record any comment the detainee makes in relation to the arresting officer's account but shall not invite comment. If the arresting officer is not physically present when the detainee is brought to a police station, the arresting officer's account must be made available to the custody officer remotely or by a third party on the arresting officer's behalf. If the custody officer authorises a person's detention, subject to paragraph 1.8, that officer must record the grounds for detention in the detainee's presence and at the same time, inform them of the grounds. The detainee must be informed of the ground for their detention before they are questioned about any offence;
  • note any comment the detainee makes in respect of the decision to detain them but shall not invite comment;
  • not put specific questions to the detainee regarding their involvement in any offence, nor in respect of any comments they may make in response to the arresting officer's account or the decision to place them in detention. Such an exchange is likely to constitute an interview as in paragraph 11.1A and require the associated safeguards in *section 11*.

See *paragraph 11.13* in respect of unsolicited comments.

3.5 The custody officer shall:

   (a) ask the detainee, whether at this time, they:

     (i) would like legal advice, see *paragraph 6.5*;

     (ii) want someone informed of their detention, see *section 5*;

   (b) ask the detainee to sign the custody record to confirm their decisions in respect of (a);

   (c) determine whether the detainee:

     (i) is, or might be, in need of medical treatment or attention, see *section 9*;

     (ii) requires:

- an appropriate adult;
- help to check documentation;
- an interpreter;

   (d) record the decision in respect of (c).

Where any duties under this paragraph have been carried out by custody staff at the direction of the custody officer, the outcomes shall, as soon as practicable, be reported to the custody officer who retains overall responsibility for the detainee's care and treatment and ensuring that it complies with this Code.

3.6 When determining these needs the custody officer is responsible for initiating an assessment to consider whether the detainee is likely to present specific risks to custody staff or themselves. Such assessments should always include a check on the Police National Computer, to be carried out as soon as practicable, to identify any risks highlighted in relation to the detainee. Although such assessments are primarily the custody officer's responsibility, it may be necessary for them to consult and involve others, e.g. the arresting officer or an appropriate health care professional, see paragraph 9.13. Reasons for delaying the initiation or completion of the assessment must be recorded.

3.7 Chief Officers should ensure that arrangements for proper and effective risk assessments required by *paragraph 3.6* are implemented in respect of all detainees at police stations in their area.

3.8 Risk assessments must follow a structured process which clearly defines the categories of risk to be considered and the results must be incorporated in the detainee's custody record. The custody officer is responsible for making sure those responsible for the detainee's custody are appropriately briefed about the risks. If no specific risks are identified by the assessment, that should be noted in the custody record.

3.8A The content of any risk assessment and any analysis of the level of risk relating to the person's detention is not required to be shown or provided to the detainee or any person acting on behalf of the detainee. But information should not be withheld from any person acting on the detainee's behalf, for example, an appropriate adult, solicitor or interpreter, if to do so might put that person at risk.

3.9 The custody officer is responsible for implementing the response to any specific risk assessment, e.g.:

- reducing opportunities for self harm;
- calling a health care professional;
- increasing levels of monitoring or observation;
- reducing the risk to those who come into contact with the detainee.

3.10 Risk assessment is an ongoing process and assessments must always be subject to review if circumstances change.

3.11 If video cameras are installed in the custody area, notices shall be prominently displayed showing cameras are in use. Any request to have video cameras switched off shall be refused.

## (b) Detained persons—special groups

3.12 If the detainee appears deaf or there is doubt about their hearing or speaking ability or ability to understand English, and the custody officer cannot establish effective communication, the custody officer must, as soon as practicable, call an interpreter for assistance in the action under *paragraphs 3.1–3.5*. See *section 13*.

3.13   If the detainee is a juvenile, the custody officer must, if it is practicable, ascertain the identity of a person responsible for their welfare. That person

- may be:
  - the parent or guardian;
  - if the juvenile is in local authority or voluntary organisation care, or is otherwise being looked after under the Children Act 1989, a person appointed by that authority or organisation to have responsibility for the juvenile's welfare;
  - any other person who has, for the time being, assumed responsibility for the juvenile's welfare;
- must be informed as soon as practicable that the juvenile has been arrested, why they have been arrested and where they are detained. This right is in addition to the juvenile's right in *section 5* not to be held incommunicado.

3.14   If a juvenile is known to be subject to a court order under which a person or organisation is given any degree of statutory responsibility to supervise or otherwise monitor them, reasonable steps must also be taken to notify that person or organisation (the 'responsible officer'). The responsible officer will normally be a member of a Youth Offending Team, except for a curfew order which involves electronic monitoring when the contractor providing the monitoring will normally be the responsible officer.

3.15   If the detainee is a juvenile, mentally disordered or otherwise mentally vulnerable, the custody officer must, as soon as practicable:

- inform the appropriate adult, who in the case of a juvenile may or may not be a person responsible for their welfare, as in *paragraph 3.13*, of:
  - the grounds for their detention;
  - their whereabouts.
- ask the adult to come to the police station to see the detainee.

3.16   It is imperative that a mentally disordered or otherwise mentally vulnerable person, detained under the Mental Health Act 1983, section 136, be assessed as soon as possible. A police station should only be used as a place of safety as a last resort but if that assessment is to take place at the police station, an approved mental health professional and a registered medical practitioner shall be called to the station as soon as possible to carry it out. The appropriate adult has no role in the assessment process and their presence is not required. Once the detainee has been assessed and suitable arrangements made for their treatment or care, they can no longer be detained under section 136. A detainee must be immediately discharged from detention under section 136 if a registered medical practitioner, having examined them, concludes they are not mentally disordered within the meaning of the Act.

3.17   If the appropriate adult is:

- already at the police station, the provisions of *paragraphs 3.1* to *3.5* must be complied with in the appropriate adult's presence;
- not at the station when these provisions are complied with, they must be complied with again in the presence of the appropriate adult when they arrive.

3.18   The detainee shall be advised that:

- the duties of the appropriate adult include giving advice and assistance;
- they can consult privately with the appropriate adult at any time.

3.19   If the detainee, or appropriate adult on the detainee's behalf, asks for a solicitor to be called to give legal advice, the provisions of *section 6* apply.

3.20   If the detainee is blind, seriously visually impaired or unable to read, the custody officer shall make sure their solicitor, relative, appropriate adult or some other person likely to take an interest in them and not involved in the investigation is available to help check any documentation. When this Code requires written consent or signing the person assisting may be asked to sign instead, if the detainee prefers. This paragraph does not require an appropriate adult to be called solely to assist in checking and signing documentation for a person who is not a juvenile, or mentally disordered or otherwise mentally vulnerable (see *paragraph 3.15*).

## (c) Persons attending a police station or elsewhere voluntarily

3.21 Anybody attending a police station or other location (see *paragraph 3.22*) voluntarily to assist with an investigation may leave at will unless arrested. The person may only be prevented from leaving at will if their arrest on suspicion of committing the offence is necessary in accordance with Code G.

If during an interview it is decided that their arrest is necessary, they must:
- be informed at once that they are under arrest and of the grounds and reasons as required by Code G, and
- be brought before the custody officer at the police station where they are arrested or, as the case may be, at the police station to which they are taken after being arrested elsewhere. The custody officer is then responsible for making sure that a custody record is opened and that they are notified of their rights in the same way as other detainees as required by this Code.

If they are not arrested but are cautioned as in *section 10*, the person who gives the caution must, at the same time, inform them they are not under arrest, they are not obliged to remain at the station or other location but if they agree to remain, they may obtain free and independent legal advice if they want. They shall also be given a copy of the notice explaining the arrangements for obtaining legal advice and told that the right to legal advice includes the right to speak with a solicitor on the telephone and be asked if they want advice. If advice is requested, the interviewer is responsible for securing its provision without delay by contacting the Defence Solicitor Call Centre and for ensuring that the provisions of this Code and Codes E and F concerning the conduct and recording of interviews of suspects are followed insofar as they can be applied to suspects who are not under arrest. See *paragraph 3.2*.

3.22 If the other location mentioned in *paragraph 3.21* is any place or premises for which the interviewer requires the person's informed consent to remain, for example, the person's home, then the references that the person is 'not obliged to remain' and that they 'may leave at will' mean that the person may also withdraw their consent and require the interviewer to leave.

## (d) Documentation

3.23 The grounds for a person's detention shall be recorded, in the person's presence if practicable. See *paragraph 1.8*.

3.24 Action taken under *paragraphs 3.12* to *3.20* shall be recorded.

## (e) Persons answering street bail

3.25 When a person is answering street bail, the custody officer should link any documentation held in relation to arrest with the custody record. Any further action shall be recorded on the custody record in accordance with *paragraphs 3.23* and *3.24* above.

---

**1.6.7.1**    **KEYNOTE**

**Detention of People under Arrest**

Section 37 of the 1984 Act states:

(1) Where—
   (a) a person is arrested for an offence—

           (i)  without a warrant; or
           (ii)  under a warrant not endorsed for bail,
       (b)  repealed,
    the custody officer at each police station where he is detained after his arrest shall determine whether he has before him suf-
    ficient evidence to charge that person with the offence for which he was arrested and may detain him at the police station for
    such period as is necessary to enable him to do so.
     (2)  If the custody officer determines that he does not have such evidence before him, the person arrested shall be released
          either on bail or without bail, unless the custody officer has reasonable grounds for believing that his detention without
          being charged is necessary to secure or preserve evidence relating to an offence for which he is under arrest or to obtain
          such evidence by questioning him.
     (3)  If the custody officer has reasonable grounds for so believing, he may authorise the person arrested to be kept in police
          detention.
     (4)  Where a custody officer authorises a person who has not been charged to be kept in police detention, he shall, as soon
          as is practicable, make a written record of the grounds for the detention.
     (5)  Subject to subsection (6) below, the written record shall be made in the presence of the person arrested who shall at that
          time be informed by the custody officer of the grounds for his detention.

It is suggested that the custody officer record all the reasons for authorising the person's detention. It is suggested that detail of at least minimal level should be included, as it may be necessary in any criminal or civil
proceedings. Indeed, it will be difficult for the custody officer to explain his/her decision without such
information.

  Section 37(6) states:

  Subsection (5) above shall not apply where the person arrested is, at the time when the written record is made—
     (a)  incapable of understanding what is said to him;
     (b)  violent or likely to become violent; or
     (c)  in urgent need of medical attention.

People who have been arrested, returned on bail or have voluntarily given themselves up at a police station,
which includes a person who has attended the police station after having been given street bail, will be
brought before a custody officer who must decide whether the person should be detained at the police station
or released. People who attend police stations voluntarily to assist the police with their investigations are not
subject to this procedure; their treatment is dealt with by s. 29 of the 1984 Act. However, if an officer forms a
view that the person should be arrested at the police station for the purpose of interview and informs the
custody officer of this view, the custody officer can authorise detention for the interview and is entitled
to assume that the arrest by the officer is lawful (*Fayed* v *Metropolitan Police Commissioner* [2004] EWCA
Civ 1579).

  If the grounds were not given at the time of arrest (on justifiable grounds) the custody officer should consider whether the arrested person is now in a position to be given the grounds for the arrest (as being the first
practicable opportunity (s. 28(3) of the 1984 Act)). If the grounds for arrest were not given when they should
have been, the arrest is unlawful regardless of what information is given later (*Wilson* v *Chief Constable of
Lancashire* [2001] Po LR 367).

  Having heard the details of and grounds for the arrest, the custody officer must decide whether or not there
are reasons which justify authorising that person's detention (s. 37 of the 1984 Act deals with the procedures
to be followed before a person is charged). Some commentators have suggested that it is also the role of the
custody officer to establish that the arrest itself was lawful. While good practice, the custody officer's duty is
confined to acting in accordance with the requirements set out in s. 37 of the 1984 Act. These duties do not
appear to include considering whether the arrest was lawful unless this is relevant to the main question of
whether there is sufficient evidence to charge the suspect. The view is supported by the decision of the Divisional Court in *DPP* v *L* [1999] Crim LR 752, where the court held that there was no express or implied requirement imposing a duty on a custody officer to inquire into the legality of an arrest and in that case the custody
officer was therefore entitled to assume that it was lawful. A subsequent finding that the arrest was unlawful
did not invalidate the decision of the custody officer to hold the person in custody. However, where the custody
officer is aware that the arrest is unlawful, he/she will need to consider whether continued detention is justifiable, particularly in light of the Human Rights Act 1998. The Codes allow for the custody officer to delegate
actions to other members of staff; a custody officer or other officer who, in accordance with this Code, allows

or directs the carrying out of any task or action relating to a detainee's care, treatment, rights and entitlements to another officer or any police staff must be satisfied that the officer or police staff concerned is suitable, trained and competent to carry out the task or action in question.

The notice of entitlement, which should also be available in Welsh, the main minority ethnic languages and the principal European languages, whenever they are likely to be helpful, should:

- list the entitlements in this Code, including:
  + visits and contact with outside parties, including special provisions for Commonwealth citizens and foreign nationals;
  + reasonable standards of physical comfort;
  + adequate food and drink;
  + access to toilets and washing facilities, clothing, medical attention, and exercise when practicable;
- mention the:
  + provisions relating to the conduct of interviews;
  + circumstances in which an appropriate adult should be available to assist the detainee and their statutory rights to make representation whenever the period of their detention is reviewed.

Audio versions of the notice should also be made available. Access to 'easy read' illustrated versions should also be provided if they are available.

In cases where a juvenile is in police detention it may be necessary to inform more than one person. For instance, if the juvenile is in local authority or voluntary organisation care but living with his/her parents or other adults responsible for his/her welfare, although there is no legal obligation to inform them, they should normally be contacted, as well as the authority or organisation, unless suspected of involvement in the offence concerned. Even if the juvenile is not living with his/her parents, consideration should be given to informing them.

If the person is arrested on a warrant, any directions given by the court in the warrant must be followed. Consideration can always be given to contacting the court to get a variation on the conditions of the warrant. (If the warrant was issued for the arrest of a person who has not yet been charged or summonsed for an offence, he/she should be dealt with as any other person arrested for an offence without warrant unless there are any additional directions on the warrant that must be followed.)

Where a person who has been bailed under s. 37(7)(a) in order that the DPP can make a case disposal decision answers his/her bail or is arrested for failing to return on bail, detention can only be authorised to allow him/her to be further bailed under s. 37D of the 1984 Act or in order that he/she can be charged or cautioned for offences connected with the original bail. If the person is not in a fit state to be dealt with he/she may be kept in police detention until he/she is (s. 37D of the 1984 Act).

## 1.6.7.2    KEYNOTE

### Authorising a Person's Detention

A custody officer can authorise the detention of a person when there is sufficient evidence to charge and, more commonly, when there is *not* sufficient evidence to charge the suspect. If there is insufficient evidence to charge, the custody officer must decide if the detention is necessary to secure or preserve evidence relating to an offence for which the person is under arrest or to obtain such evidence by questioning him/her.

If a person representing the detained person does not consider that the detention is lawful he/she can apply to the court for the detainee's release (*habeas corpus*). A detainee may also be able to make an application for release or damages following the incorporation of the European Convention on Human Rights (Article 5(4)).

Where a detained person wishes to consult the Codes of Practice, this does not entitle the person concerned to delay unreasonably any necessary investigative or administrative action whilst he/she does so. Examples of action which need not be delayed unreasonably include: procedures requiring the provision of breath, blood or urine specimens under the Road Traffic Act 1988 or the Transport and Works Act 1992; searching detainees at the police station; taking fingerprints, footwear impressions or non-intimate samples without consent for evidential purposes.

**KEYNOTE**

**Risk Assessments**

The custody officer is responsible for initiating a risk assessment to consider whether detainees are likely to present specific risks to custody staff or themselves (Code C, para. 3.6). The risk assessment must follow a structured process which clearly defines the categories of risk to be considered; guidance is given in Home Office Circular 32/2000, *Detainee Risk Assessment and Revised Prisoner Escort (PER) Form*, Annex A. For this reason it is suggested that the risk assessment should be completed prior to the detainee being placed in a cell or detention room.

In addition to considering risk assessments for detained persons, the custody officer also needs to consider the safety of others who are in the custody area. Home Office Circular 34/2007 provides guidance on the arrangements for the safety and security of the custody suite, in particular in respect of solicitors and accredited and probationary representatives working in custody suites. The guidance has been issued following a number of incidents having been brought to the attention of the Home Office and the Health and Safety Executive (HSE), highlighting the actual and potential risks faced by solicitors, particularly when carrying out private consultations with their clients in the custody area, and the Authorised Professional Practice (APP) on Detention and Custody available on POLKA provides more detailed guidance on risk assessments and identifies key risk areas which should always be considered.

## 4 Detainee's Property

### (a) Action

4.1 The custody officer is responsible for:

(a) ascertaining what property a detainee:

(i) has with them when they come to the police station, whether on:

- arrest or re-detention on answering to bail;
- commitment to prison custody on the order or sentence of a court;
- lodgement at the police station with a view to their production in court from prison custody;
- transfer from detention at another station or hospital;
- detention under the Mental Health Act 1983, section 135 or 136;
- remand into police custody on the authority of a court

(ii) might have acquired for an unlawful or harmful purpose while in custody;

(b) the safekeeping of any property taken from a detainee which remains at the police station. The custody officer may search the detainee or authorise their being searched to the extent they consider necessary, provided a search of intimate parts of the body or involving the removal of more than outer clothing is only made as in *Annex A*. A search may only be carried out by an officer of the same sex as the detainee.

4.2 Detainees may retain clothing and personal effects at their own risk unless the custody officer considers they may use them to cause harm to themselves or others, interfere with evidence, damage property, effect an escape or they are needed as evidence. In this event the custody officer may withhold such articles as they consider necessary and must tell the detainee why.

4.3 Personal effects are those items a detainee may lawfully need, use or refer to while in detention but do not include cash and other items of value.

### (b) Documentation

4.4 It is a matter for the custody officer to determine whether a record should be made of the property a detained person has with him or had taken from him on arrest. Any record made is not required to be kept as part of the custody record but the custody record should be noted as to where such a record exists. Whenever a record is made the detainee shall be allowed to check and sign the record of property as correct. Any refusal to sign shall be recorded.

4.5 If a detainee is not allowed to keep any article of clothing or personal effects, the reason must be recorded.

---

**1.6.8.1**

### KEYNOTE

The proper searching of a detained person is very important, it may lead to the discovery of new evidence; it may also avoid people being injured or even escaping from police detention.

Section 54 of the Police and Criminal Evidence Act 1984 places a duty on a custody officer to ascertain what property a person has with him/her when:

- arrested and brought to the station;
- committed to police custody by order or sentence of the court;
- arrested at the station;
- detained after surrendering to bail;
- arrested after failing to surrender to bail.

The custody officer must also consider what property the detained person might have in his/her possession for an unlawful or harmful purpose while in custody. The safekeeping of any property taken from the detained person and kept at the police station is the responsibility of the custody officer.

The Criminal Justice Act 2003 has amended s. 54 of the 1984 Act in that it removes the requirement on the custody officer to record everything a detained person has with him/her. The custody officer will have a discretion as to the nature and detail of any recording and there is no longer any requirement for this to be recorded in the custody record. However, custody officers should be mindful of any force instructions as to what will need to be recorded and where. It is suggested that it will still be necessary to make records, not least to ensure against claims that property has been mishandled or removed. However, it will now be open to the custody officer to make judgements about how to balance the need for recording against the amount of administrative work involved.

Section 54 provides:

(1) The custody officer at a police station shall ascertain everything which a person has with him when he is—
   (a) brought to the station after being arrested elsewhere or after being committed to custody by an order or sentence of a court; or
   (b) arrested at the station or detained there, as a person falling within section 34(7), under section 37 above.

(2) The custody officer may record or cause to be recorded all or any of the things which he ascertains under subsection (1).

(2A) In the case of an arrested person, any such record may be made as part of his custody record.

(3) Subject to subsection (4) below, a custody officer may seize and retain any such thing or cause any such thing to be seized and retained.

(4) Clothes and personal effects may only be seized if the custody officer—
   (a) believes that the person from whom they are seized may use them—
      (i) to cause physical injury to himself or any other person;
      (ii) to damage property;
      (iii) to interfere with evidence; or
      (iv) to assist him to escape; or
   (b) has reasonable grounds for believing that they may be evidence relating to an offence.

(5) Where anything is seized, the person from whom it is seized shall be told the reason for the seizure unless he is—
   (a) violent or likely to become violent; or
   (b) incapable of understanding what is said to him.

(6) Subject to subsection (7) below, a person may be searched if the custody officer considers it necessary to enable him to carry out his duty under subsection (1) above and to the extent that the custody officer considers necessary for that purpose.

(6A) A person who is in custody at a police station or is in police detention otherwise than at a police station may at any time be searched in order to ascertain whether he has with him anything which he could use for any of the purposes specified in subsection (4) (a) above.

(6B) Subject to subsection (6C) below, a constable may seize and retain, or cause to be seized and retained, anything found on such a search.

(6C) A constable may only seize clothes and personal effects in the circumstances specified in subsection (4) above.

(7) An intimate search may not be conducted under this section.

(8) A search under this section shall be carried out by a constable.

(9) The constable carrying out a search shall be of the same sex as the person searched.

## 1.6.8.2 KEYNOTE

### The Search

While the custody officer has a duty to ascertain what property a person has with him/her (often by means of searching the person), there is also a need to consider the rights of the detained person. The custody officer may authorise a constable to search a detained person, or may search the detained person him/herself in order to ascertain what property the detained person has with him/her (s. 54(6)). It should be noted that the custody officer must first authorise any search and the extent of the search; officers should not search a person until this authority has been given. Therefore the custody officer may only authorise a search to the extent that he/she considers necessary to comply with this duty. In order to safeguard the rights of the detained person, there are three levels to which searches can be conducted:

- searches that do not involve the removal of more than the detained person's outer clothing (this includes shoes and socks);
- strip searches;
- intimate searches.

Each of these is examined below.

The extent of the search is determined by the custody officer on the basis of what he/she honestly believes is necessary in order to comply with the above duties. Both the decision to search the detained person and the extent of the search must be decided on the facts of the case in question. It may be important to consider cultural issues that might affect the detained person; for instance, would it be necessary and justifiable to search a Sikh's turban? Force standing orders are not an automatic right to search all detained persons (*Brazil v Chief Constable of Surrey* [1983] 1 WLR 1155). A custody officer can authorise a strip search but an intimate search can only be authorised by an officer of the rank of inspector or above.

## 1.6.8.3 KEYNOTE

### Searches that Do not Involve the Removal of More than the Detained Person's Outer Clothing

In effect, this is any search that does not become a strip search or an intimate search. This type of search applies to almost every person coming before the custody officer. Typically this will involve emptying out all items that are in the person's pockets, removing jewellery and the searching of other areas that can be conducted without the need to remove more than outer garments, such as coats and possibly items such as jumpers. This type of authorisation would also lend itself to a 'pat down' of the detained person. If there is any doubt as to whether the search goes beyond one that falls into this category, it is suggested that it should be treated as a strip search. Where metal detectors are used in custody suites, an indication from the device may give the grounds for authorising a strip search.

Not all detained persons need to be searched; s. 54(1) and para. 4.1 require a detainee to be searched when it is clear the custody officer will have continuing duties in relation to that detainee or when that detainee's behaviour or offence makes an inventory appropriate. They do not require every detainee to be searched, e.g. if it is clear that a person will only be detained for a short period and is not to be placed in a cell, the custody officer may decide not to search him/her. In such a case the custody record will be endorsed 'not searched', para. 4.4 will not apply, and the detainee will be invited to sign the entry. If the detainee refuses, the custody officer will be obliged to ascertain what property he/she has in accordance with para. 4.1.

## 1.6.8.4 KEYNOTE

### Strip Searches

Strip searches are dealt with in Code C, Annex A, paras 9–12.

## 1.6.8.5 KEYNOTE

### Intimate Searches

Intimate searches are dealt with in Code C, Annex A. An intimate search is a search which consists of the physical examination of a person's body orifices other than the mouth.

## 1.6.8.6 KEYNOTE

### Drug Search—X-rays and Ultrasound Scans

Section 55A of the 1984 Act allows detained persons to have an X-ray taken of them or an ultrasound scan to be carried out on them (or both). This is dealt with in Code C, Annex K.

## 1.6.8.7 KEYNOTE

### Conduct of a Search

- Reasonable force may be used (s. 117 of the 1984 Act).
- The custody officer should specify the level of the search to be conducted and this must be recorded in the person's record.
- Reference to Code A, para. 3.1 may be useful when considering how to conduct the search: 'Every reasonable effort must be made to minimise the embarrassment that a person being searched may experience.'
- Annex L should be referred to for guidance when establishing the gender of persons for the purpose of searching.

## 1.6.8.8 KEYNOTE

### What Property can be Retained?

Once a person has been searched and the custody officer has ascertained what property the detained person has with him/her, a decision must be made as to what property will be returned to the detained person and what property will be retained by the police.

It is suggested that the custody officer may authorise the seizure of an article of clothing under s. 54(4)(b) of the 1984 Act, where he/she has reasonable grounds for believing that such clothing may be evidence relating to an offence. For instance, if the detained person is wearing a pair of trainers of the same type as those which are reasonably believed to have made impressions at the scene of a recent burglary and the detained person has a burglary record then, unless the custody officer knows of other facts clearly putting the suspect at some other place at the time of the offence, he/she is plainly justified in having those shoes forensically examined. However, it is submitted that this does not authorise the custody officer to seize footwear on the off-chance that some officer or some other police force may have obtained impressions at a burglary site which might match the trainers of the detained person.

Where property by virtue of its nature, quantity or size in the detainee's possession at the time of arrest has not been brought to the police station the custody officer is not required to record this on the custody record. Only items of clothing worn by the detained person which have been withheld need to be recorded on the custody record.

Unless the property has been seized and retained as evidence under s. 22 of the 1984 Act, it must be returned to the detained person on his/her release. If property has been seized from a third party in the course of the investigation the property can only be retained for so long as is necessary in accordance with s. 22(1) of the 1984 Act; even if it might be needed for another matter it should be returned to the third party unless there was an additional power to seize the item (*Settelen* v *Metropolitan Police Commissioner* [2004] EWHC 2171 (Ch)). If property is rightfully seized but retained unnecessarily this would be unlawful and could lead to a claim for damages (*Martin* v *Chief Constable of Nottinghamshire* (1998) 1 May, unreported). The seizure of a person's property is also protected by the European Convention on Human Rights, First Protocol, Article 1.

## 1.6.9     5 Right not to be Held Incommunicado

### (a) Action

5.1     Subject to paragraph 5.7B, any person arrested and held in custody at a police station or other premises may, on request, have one person known to them or likely to take an interest in their welfare informed at public expense of their whereabouts as soon as practicable. If the person cannot be contacted the detainee may choose up to two alternatives. If they cannot be contacted, the person in charge of detention or the investigation has discretion to allow further attempts until the information has been conveyed.

5.2     The exercise of the above right in respect of each person nominated may be delayed only in accordance with *Annex B*.

5.3     The above right may be exercised each time a detainee is taken to another police station.

5.4     If the detainee agrees, they may at the custody officer's discretion, receive visits from friends, family or others likely to take an interest in their welfare, or in whose welfare the detainee has an interest.

5.5     If a friend, relative or person with an interest in the detainee's welfare enquires about their whereabouts, this information shall be given if the suspect agrees and *Annex B* does not apply.

5.6     The detainee shall be given writing materials, on request, and allowed to telephone one person for a reasonable time. Either or both these privileges may be denied or delayed if an officer of inspector rank or above considers sending a letter or making a telephone call may result in any of the consequences in:

        (a) *Annex B paragraphs 1* and *2* and the person is detained in connection with an indictable offence;

        (b) *Not used*

    Nothing in this paragraph permits the restriction or denial of the rights in paragraphs 5.1 and 6.1.

5.7     Before any letter or message is sent, or telephone call made, the detainee shall be informed that what they say in any letter, call or message (other than in a communication to a solicitor) may be read or listened to and may be given in evidence. A telephone call may be terminated if it is being abused. The costs can be at public expense at the custody officer's discretion.

5.7A     Any delay or denial of the rights in this section should be proportionate and should last no longer than necessary.

5.7B     In the case of a person in police custody for specific purposes and periods in accordance with a direction under the Crime (Sentences) Act 1997, Schedule 1 (productions from prison etc.), the exercise of the rights in this section shall be subject to any additional conditions specified in the direction for the purpose of regulating the detainee's contact and communication with others whilst in police custody.

## (b) Documentation

5.8    A record must be kept of any:

    (a)  request made under this section and the action taken;

    (b)  letters, messages or telephone calls made or received or visit received;

    (c)  refusal by the detainee to have information about them given to an outside enquirer. The detainee must be asked to countersign the record accordingly and any refusal recorded.

**1.6.9.1**

### KEYNOTE

**Right to Have Someone Informed**

Detained people may also be allowed to speak to one person on the telephone for a reasonable time or send letters. A person may request an interpreter to interpret a telephone call or translate a letter. In addition to Code C, this right can be denied or delayed where a person is detained under s. 41 of or sch. 7 to the Terrorism Act 2000 by an officer of the rank of inspector or above (Code H, section 5). The grounds are the same as those regulating the holding of people *incommunicado*. Should there be any delay in complying with a request by a detained person to have someone informed of his/her detention or to communicate with someone, the detained person should be informed of this and told the reason for it and a record kept (s. 56(6) of the 1984 Act). Subject to having sufficient personnel to supervise a visit and any possible hindrance to the investigation, the custody officer also has a discretion to allow visits to the detained person at the police station. This section of Code C allows discretionary visits from family and others in whose welfare the detainee has an interest.

It is suggested that with the Codes of Practice outlining the limited rights for the detained person to make telephone calls and the right to restrict these calls, if the person has a mobile telephone it can be seized for the period of his/her detention. There is no case law on this point and any force policy should be followed. If the detainee does not know anyone to contact for advice or support or cannot contact a friend or relative, the custody officer should bear in mind any local voluntary bodies or other organisations which might be able to help. Paragraph 6.1 applies if legal advice is required.

In some circumstances, it may not be appropriate to use the telephone to disclose information under paras 5.1 and 5.5. So for example there may be occasions when officers wish to conduct a search under s. 18 of the 1984 Act and the detained person has requested to have someone informed. Clearly, if that person is informed before the search is conducted, vital evidence or property may be lost. Often, the custody officer has two methods by which he/she can inform the person requested about the detained person's detention: either in person or on the phone. Contacting the person by telephone is likely to be the quickest; however, there is no requirement to use the quickest method in order to pass on this information. While there is no case law on this point, Code C supports the view that, where the s. 18 search is to be conducted relatively quickly after the request is made by the detained person, it would be permissible to inform that person at the time the s. 18 search is conducted. Where the search is not to be conducted straight away, a lengthy delay may be seen as a breach of this right, which may lead to a stay of proceedings or a claim for damages as a breach of the detained person's human rights.

Paragraph 5.7B exempts persons detained under the Crime (Sentences) Act 1997 from the provisions of Code C, section 5. Prison Service Order 1801 (Production of Prisoners at the Request of Police) provides detailed guidance and instructions for police officers and governors and directors of prisons regarding applications for prisoners to be transferred to police custody and their safe custody and treatment while in police custody.

## 6 Right to Legal Advice

### (a) Action

6.1 Unless Annex B applies, all detainees must be informed that they may at any time consult and communicate privately with a solicitor, whether in person, in writing or by telephone, and that free independent legal advice is available. See *paragraph 3.1*.

6.2 *Not used*

6.3 A poster advertising the right to legal advice must be prominently displayed in the charging area of every police station.

6.4 No police officer should, at any time, do or say anything with the intention of dissuading any person who is entitled to legal advice in accordance with this Code, whether or not they have been arrested and are detained, from obtaining legal advice.

6.5 The exercise of the right of access to legal advice may be delayed only as in *Annex B*. Whenever legal advice is requested, and unless *Annex B* applies, the custody officer must act without delay to secure the provision of such advice. If the detainee has the right to speak to a solicitor in person but declines to exercise the right the officer should point out that the right includes the right to speak with a solicitor on the telephone. If the detainee continues to waive this right, or a detainee whose right to free legal advice is limited to telephone advice from the Criminal Defence Service (CDS) Direct declines to exercise that right, the officer should ask them why and any reasons should be recorded on the custody record or the interview record as appropriate. Reminders of the right to legal advice must be given as in *paragraphs 3.5, 11.2, 15.4, 16.4, 2B of Annex A, 3 of Annex K* and *16.5* of this Code and Code D, *paragraphs 3.17(ii)* and *6.3*. Once it is clear a detainee does not want to speak to a solicitor in person or by telephone they should cease to be asked their reasons.

6.5A In the case of a person who is a juvenile or is mentally disordered or otherwise mentally vulnerable, an appropriate adult should consider whether legal advice from a solicitor is required. If the person indicates that they do not want legal advice, the appropriate adult has the right to ask for a solicitor to attend if this would be in the best interests of the person. However, the person cannot be forced to see the solicitor if they are adamant that they do not wish to do so.

6.6 A detainee who wants legal advice may not be interviewed or continue to be interviewed until they have received such advice unless:

(a) *Annex B* applies, when the restriction on drawing adverse inferences from silence in *Annex C* will apply because the detainee is not allowed an opportunity to consult a solicitor; or

(b) an officer of superintendent rank or above has reasonable grounds for believing that:

   (i) the consequent delay might:
   - lead to interference with, or harm to, evidence connected with an offence;
   - lead to interference with, or physical harm to, other people;
   - lead to serious loss of, or damage to, property;
   - lead to alerting other people suspected of having committed an offence but not yet arrested for it;
   - hinder the recovery of property obtained in consequence of the commission of an offence.

   (ii) when a solicitor, including a duty solicitor, has been contacted and has agreed to attend, awaiting their arrival would cause unreasonable delay to the process of investigation.

   Note: In these cases the restriction on drawing adverse inferences from silence in *Annex C* will apply because the detainee is not allowed an opportunity to consult a solicitor;

(c) the solicitor the detainee has nominated or selected from a list:
  (i) cannot be contacted;
  (ii) has previously indicated they do not wish to be contacted; or
  (iii) having been contacted, has declined to attend; and
    • the detainee has been advised of the Duty Solicitor Scheme but has declined to ask for the duty solicitor;
    • in these circumstances the interview may be started or continued without further delay provided an officer of inspector rank or above has agreed to the interview proceeding.

Note: The restriction on drawing adverse inferences from silence in *Annex C* will not apply because the detainee is allowed an opportunity to consult the duty solicitor;

(d) the detainee changes their mind about wanting legal advice or (as the case may be) about wanting a solicitor present at the interview and states that they no longer wish to speak to a solicitor. In these circumstances, the interview may be started or continued without delay provided that:
  (i) an officer of inspector rank or above:
    • speaks to the detainee to enquire about the reasons for their change of mind, and
    • makes, or directs the making of, reasonable efforts to ascertain the solicitor's expected time of arrival and to inform the solicitor that the suspect has stated that they wish to change their mind and the reason (if given);
  (ii) the detainee's reason for their change of mind (if given) and the outcome of the action in (i) are recorded in the custody record;
  (iii) the detainee, after being informed of the outcome of the action in (i) above, confirms in writing that they want the interview to proceed without speaking or further speaking to a solicitor or (as the case may be) without a solicitor being present and do not wish to wait for a solicitor by signing an entry to this effect in the custody record;
  (iv) an officer of inspector rank or above is satisfied that it is proper for the interview to proceed in these circumstances and:
    • gives authority in writing for the interview to proceed and if the authority is not recorded in the custody record, the officer must ensure that the custody record shows the date and time of the authority and where it is recorded, and
    • takes or directs the taking of, reasonable steps to inform the solicitor that the authority has been given and the time when the interview is expected to commence, and records or causes to be recorded, the outcome of this action in the custody record.
  (v) When the interview starts and the interviewer reminds the suspect of their right to legal advice (see *paragraph 11.2*, Code E *paragraph 4.5* and Code F *paragraph 4.5*), the interviewer shall then ensure that the following is recorded in the written interview record or the interview record made in accordance with Code E or F:
    • confirmation that the detainee has changed their mind about wanting legal advice or (as the case may be) about wanting a solicitor present and the reasons for it if given;
    • the fact that authority for the interview to proceed has been given and, subject to *paragraph 2.6A*, the name of the authorising officer;
    • that if the solicitor arrives at the station before the interview is completed, the detainee will be so informed without delay and a break will be taken to allow them to speak to the solicitor if they wish, unless *paragraph 6.6(a)* applies, and
    • that at any time during the interview, the detainee may again ask for legal advice and that if they do, a break will be taken to allow them to speak to the solicitor, unless *paragraph 6.6(a), (b),* or *(c)* applies.

Note: In these circumstances, the restriction on drawing adverse inferences from silence in *Annex C* will not apply because the detainee is allowed an opportunity to consult a solicitor if they wish.

6.7    If *paragraph 6.6(a)* applies, where the reason for authorising the delay ceases to apply, there may be no further delay in permitting the exercise of the right in the absence of a further authorisation unless *paragraph 6.6(b), (c)* or *(d)* applies. If *paragraph 6.6(b)(i)* applies, once sufficient information has been obtained to avert the risk, questioning must cease until the detainee has received legal advice unless *paragraph 6.6(a), (b)(ii), (c)* or *(d)* applies.

6.8    A detainee who has been permitted to consult a solicitor shall be entitled on request to have the solicitor present when they are interviewed unless one of the exceptions in *paragraph 6.6* applies.

6.9    The solicitor may only be required to leave the interview if their conduct is such that the interviewer is unable properly to put questions to the suspect.

6.10   If the interviewer considers a solicitor is acting in such a way, they will stop the interview and consult an officer not below superintendent rank, if one is readily available, and otherwise an officer not below inspector rank not connected with the investigation. After speaking to the solicitor, the officer consulted will decide if the interview should continue in the presence of that solicitor. If they decide it should not, the suspect will be given the opportunity to consult another solicitor before the interview continues and that solicitor given an opportunity to be present at the interview.

6.11   The removal of a solicitor from an interview is a serious step and, if it occurs, the officer of superintendent rank or above who took the decision will consider if the incident should be reported to the Solicitors Regulation Authority. If the decision to remove the solicitor has been taken by an officer below superintendent rank, the facts must be reported to an officer of superintendent rank or above who will similarly consider whether a report to the Solicitors Regulation Authority would be appropriate. When the solicitor concerned is a duty solicitor, the report should be both to the Solicitors Regulation Authority and to the Legal Services Commission.

6.12   'Solicitor' in this Code means:
       • a solicitor who holds a current practising certificate;
       • an accredited or probationary representative included on the register of representatives maintained by the Legal Services Commission.

6.12A  An accredited or probationary representative sent to provide advice by, and on behalf of, a solicitor shall be admitted to the police station for this purpose unless an officer of inspector rank or above considers such a visit will hinder the investigation and directs otherwise. Once admitted to the police station, *paragraphs 6.6* to *6.10* apply.

6.13   In exercising their discretion under *paragraph 6.12A*, the officer should take into account in particular:
       • whether:
         – the identity and status of an accredited or probationary representative have been satisfactorily established;
         – they are of suitable character to provide legal advice, e.g. a person with a criminal record is unlikely to be suitable unless the conviction was for a minor offence and not recent.
       • any other matters in any written letter of authorisation provided by the solicitor on whose behalf the person is attending the police station.

6.14   If the inspector refuses access to an accredited or probationary representative or a decision is taken that such a person should not be permitted to remain at an interview, the inspector must notify the solicitor on whose behalf the representative was acting and give them an opportunity to make alternative arrangements. The detainee must be informed and the custody record noted.

6.15   If a solicitor arrives at the station to see a particular person, that person must, unless *Annex B* applies, be so informed whether or not they are being interviewed and asked if they would like to see the solicitor. This applies even if the detainee has declined legal advice or, having requested it, subsequently agreed to be interviewed without receiving advice. The solicitor's attendance and the detainee's decision must be noted in the custody record.

## (b) Documentation

6.16 Any request for legal advice and the action taken shall be recorded.

6.17 A record shall be made in the interview record if a detainee asks for legal advice and an interview is begun either in the absence of a solicitor or their representative, or they have been required to leave an interview.

**KEYNOTE**

**Right to Legal Advice**

A poster or posters of the right to legal advice containing translations into Welsh, the main minority ethnic languages and the principal European languages should be displayed wherever they are likely to be helpful and it is practicable to do so.

Section 58 of the Police and Criminal Evidence Act 1984 provides an almost inalienable right for a person arrested and held in custody at a police station or other premises to consult privately with a solicitor free of charge at any time if he/she requests it. In *R* v *Alladice* (1988) 87 Cr App R 380 the Court of Appeal made it clear that:

> no matter how strongly and however justifiably the police may feel that their investigation and detection of crime is being hindered by the presence of a solicitor . . . they are nevertheless confined to the narrow limits imposed by section 58.

A detainee has a right to free legal advice and to be represented by a solicitor. Note for Guidance 6B explains the arrangements which enable detainees to obtain legal advice. An outline of these arrangements is also included in the Notice of Rights and Entitlements given to detainees in accordance with para. 3.2. The arrangements also apply, with appropriate modifications, to persons attending a police station or other location voluntarily who are cautioned prior to being interviewed. See para. 3.21. When a detainee asks for free legal advice, the Defence Solicitor Call Centre (DSCC) must be informed of the request. Free legal advice will be limited to telephone advice provided by CDS Direct if a detainee is:

- detained for a non-imprisonable offence;
- arrested on a bench warrant for failing to appear and being held for production at court (except where the solicitor has clear documentary evidence available that would result in the client being released from custody);
- arrested for drink driving (driving/in charge with excess alcohol, failing to provide a specimen, driving/in charge whilst unfit through drink); or
- detained in relation to breach of police or court bail conditions

unless one or more exceptions apply, in which case the DSCC should arrange for advice to be given by a solicitor at the police station, for example:

- the police want to interview the detainee or carry out an eye-witness identification procedure;
- the detainee needs an appropriate adult;
- the detainee is unable to communicate over the telephone;
- the detainee alleges serious misconduct by the police;
- the investigation includes another offence not included in the list;
- the solicitor to be assigned is already at the police station.

When free advice is not limited to telephone advice, detainees can ask for free advice from a solicitor they know or if they do not know a solicitor or the solicitor they know cannot be contacted, from the duty solicitor.

To arrange free legal advice, the police should telephone the DSCC. The call centre will decide whether legal advice should be limited to telephone advice from CDS Direct, or whether a solicitor known to the detainee or the duty solicitor should speak to the detainee.

When detainees want to pay for legal advice themselves:

- the DSCC will contact a solicitor of their choice on their behalf;
- they may, when free advice is only available by telephone from CDS Direct, still speak to a solicitor of their choice on the telephone for advice, but the solicitor would not be paid by legal aid and may ask the person to pay for the advice;

- they should be given an opportunity to consult a specific solicitor or another solicitor from that solicitor's firm. If this solicitor is not available, they may choose up to two alternatives. If these alternatives are not available, the custody officer has discretion to allow further attempts until a solicitor has been contacted and agreed to provide advice;
- they are entitled to a private consultation with their chosen solicitor on the telephone or the solicitor may decide to come to the police station;
- If their chosen solicitor cannot be contacted, the DSCC may still be called to arrange free legal advice.

Apart from carrying out duties necessary to implement these arrangements, an officer must not advise the suspect about any particular firm of solicitors.

No police officer or police staff shall indicate to any suspect, except to answer a direct question, that the period for which he/she is liable to be detained, or if not detained, the time taken to complete the interview, might be reduced: if the suspect does not ask for legal advice or does not want a solicitor present when he/she is interviewed; or if he/she has asked for legal advice or (as the case may be) asked for a solicitor to be present when he/she is interviewed but changes his/her mind and agrees to be interviewed without waiting for a solicitor.

In *R* v *Aspinall* [1999] 2 Cr App R 115, the court stated that the right to access to legal advice was a fundamental right under Article 6 of the European Convention on Human Rights, and even greater importance had to be attached to advice for a vulnerable person. While the appropriate adult of a juvenile can request legal advice from a solicitor, the detained juvenile cannot be forced to see the solicitor (Code C, para. 6.5A).

A detainee has a right to free legal advice and to be represented by a solicitor. A detainee is not obliged to give reasons for declining legal advice and should not be pressed to do so. The solicitor's only role in the police station is to protect and advance the legal rights of his/her client. On occasions, this may require the solicitor to give advice which has the effect of the client avoiding giving evidence which strengthens a prosecution case. The solicitor may intervene in order to seek clarification, challenge an improper question to the client or the manner in which it is put, advise the client not to reply to particular questions or if he/she wishes to give the client further legal advice. Paragraph 6.9 only applies if the solicitor's approach or conduct prevents or unreasonably obstructs proper questions being put to the suspect or the suspect's response being recorded. Examples of unacceptable conduct include answering questions on a suspect's behalf or providing written replies for the suspect to quote.

If an officer of at least inspector rank considers that a particular solicitor or firm of solicitors is persistently sending probationary representatives who are unsuited to provide legal advice, he/she should inform an officer of at least superintendent rank, who may wish to take the matter up with the Solicitors Regulation Authority.

Whenever a detainee exercises his/her right to legal advice by consulting or communicating with a solicitor, he/she must be allowed to do so in private. This right to consult or communicate in private is fundamental. If the requirement for privacy is compromised because what is said or written by the detainee or solicitor for the purpose of giving and receiving legal advice is overheard, listened to or read by others without the informed consent of the detainee, the right will effectively have been denied. When a detainee chooses to speak to a solicitor on the telephone, he/she should be allowed to do so in private unless this is impractical because of the design and layout of the custody area or the location of telephones. However, the normal expectation should be that facilities will be available, unless they are being used, at all police stations to enable detainees to speak in private to a solicitor either face to face or over the telephone.

Once a person has indicated a wish to have a solicitor, and has not yet been advised by a solicitor, he/she can only be interviewed in limited circumstances as set out in Code C, para. 6.6. In considering whether a detainee can be interviewed or continue to be interviewed under para. 6.6 without having received legal advice which he/she has requested, the officer making this decision should, if practicable, ask the solicitor for an estimate of how long it will take to come to the station and relate this to the time that detention is permitted, the time of day (i.e. whether the rest period under para. 12.2 is imminent) and the requirements of other investigations. Subject to the constraints of Annex B, a solicitor may advise more than one client in an investigation if he/she wishes. Any question of a conflict of interest is for the solicitor under his/her professional code of conduct. If, however, waiting for a solicitor to give advice to one client may lead to unreasonable delay to the interview with another, the provisions of para. 6.6(b) may apply.

Where the solicitor is on the way or is to set off immediately, it will not normally be appropriate to begin an interview before he/she arrives.

Code C, Annex B provides an exception to this right to legal advice. The same exception also applies where the person is held under prevention of terrorism legislation (Terrorism Act 2000, s. 41 or sch. 8) and the conditions in Code H, Annex B apply. In addition, a uniformed officer of at least the rank of inspector not connected with the case may be present if authorised by an Assistant Chief Constable or Commander (Terrorism Act 2000, sch. 8, para. 9 and Code H, paras 6.4, 6.5). The delay can only be for a maximum of 36 hours (48 hours from the time of arrest in terrorism cases) or until the time the person will first appear at court, whichever is the sooner (see below). The 36-hour period is calculated from the 'relevant time'.

This right to have a private consultation also applies to juveniles who, should they wish to have a private consultation without the appropriate adult being present, must be permitted to do so. This point was considered in *R (On the Application of M (A Child)) v Commissioner of the Police of the Metropolis* [2001] EWHC 533 (Admin), where the court said that ideally there ought be a consultation room at every police station and facilities for private telephone calls to be made for legal consultations. However, there was no breach of Article 6(3) of the European Convention on Human Rights where it could not be shown that a detainee had been denied adequate facilities for the preparation of his defence.

Once a person has indicated a wish to have a solicitor, and has not yet been advised by a solicitor, he/she can only be interviewed in limited circumstances as set out in Code C, para. 6.6. In considering whether a detainee can be interviewed or continue to be interviewed under para. 6.6 without having received legal advice which he/she has requested, the officer making this decision should, if practicable, ask the solicitor for an estimate of how long it will take to come to the station and relate this to the time that detention is permitted, the time of day (i.e. whether the rest period under para. 12.2 is imminent) and the requirements of other investigations. A solicitor who represents more than one person which then leads to a delay due to waiting for that solicitor to give advice to one client may lead to unreasonable delay to the interview with another. If the solicitor is on the way or is to set off immediately, it will not normally be appropriate to begin an interview before he/she arrives. If it appears necessary to begin an interview before the solicitor's arrival, he/she should be given an indication of how long the police would be able to wait before starting the interview so that there is an opportunity to make arrangements for someone else to provide legal advice.

Another exception is in relation to the drink-drive procedure for s. 7 of the Road Traffic Act 1988. In *DPP v Noe* [2000] RTR 351 a request to see a solicitor or alternatively to consult a law book to verify the legality of the police request for a specimen of breath was not a reasonable excuse under s. 7. This decision has not been affected by the enactment of the Human Rights Act 1998. This is confirmed by *Campbell v DPP* [2002] EWHC 1314 (Admin), in which it was held that it was entirely proportionate to allow a police officer to require a member of the community to provide a specimen, albeit that legal advice had not been obtained.

Where Code C, para. 6.6 is used it will have to be justified at court if the interview is to be admissible. This power might prove useful in circumstances where there are 'delaying tactics' by legal representatives, particularly where they are aware that the detained person's relevant time is due to expire within a short period.

Subject to the constraints of Annex B, solicitors may advise more than one client in an investigation if they wish. Any question of a conflict of interest is for the solicitor under his/her professional code of conduct.

An officer who takes the decision to exclude a solicitor must be in a position to satisfy the court that the decision was properly made. In order to do this he/she may need to witness what is happening. Exclusion of a solicitor needs to be considered carefully and only where the solicitor's approach or conduct prevents or unreasonably obstructs proper questions being put to the suspect or the suspect's response being recorded. Examples of unacceptable conduct include answering questions on a suspect's behalf or providing written replies for the suspect to quote.

When detainees who wanted legal advice change their mind, an officer of inspector rank or above must authorise the continuation of the interview. It is permissible for such authorisation to be given over the telephone, if the authorising officer is able to satisfy him/herself about the reason for the detainee's change of mind and is satisfied that it is proper to continue the interview in those circumstances.

In terrorism cases a direction may be given by an officer of at least the rank of Commander or Assistant Chief Constable which may provide that a detained person who wishes to exercise the right to consult a solicitor may do so only in the sight and hearing of a qualified officer, this person being a uniformed officer of at least the rank of inspector not connected with the investigation from the authorising officer's force (Code H, para. 6.5).

## 7 Citizens of Independent Commonwealth Countries or Foreign Nationals

### (a) Action

7.1 A detainee who is a citizen of an independent Commonwealth country or a national of a foreign country, including the Republic of Ireland, has the right, upon request, to communicate at any time with the appropriate High Commission, Embassy or Consulate. That detainee must be informed as soon as practicable of this right and asked if they want to have their High Commission, Embassy or Consulate told of their whereabouts and the grounds for their detention. Such a request should be acted upon as soon as practicable.

7.2 A detainee who is a citizen of a country with which a bilateral consular convention or agreement is in force requiring notification of arrest, must also be informed that subject to *paragraph 7.4*, notification of their arrest will be sent to the appropriate High Commission, Embassy or Consulate as soon as practicable, whether or not they request it. Details of the countries to which this requirement currently applies are available from: http://www.fco.gov.uk/en/publications-and-documents/treaties/treaty-texts/prisoner-transfer-agreements.

7.3 Consular officers may, if the detainee agrees, visit one of their nationals in police detention to talk to them and, if required, to arrange for legal advice. Such visits shall take place out of the hearing of a police officer.

7.4 Notwithstanding the provisions of consular conventions, if the detainee claims that they are a refugee or have applied or intend to apply for asylum, the custody officer must ensure that the UK Border Agency (UKBA) is informed as soon as practicable of the claim. UKBA will then determine whether compliance with relevant international obligations requires notification of the arrest to be sent and will inform the custody officer as to what action police need to take.

### (b) Documentation

7.5 A record shall be made:
- when a detainee is informed of their rights under this section and of any requirement in paragraph 7.2;
- of any communications with a High Commission, Embassy or Consulate; and
- of any communications with UKBA about a detainee's claim to be a refugee or to be seeking asylum and the resulting action taken by police.

**KEYNOTE**

The exercise of the rights in this section may not be interfered with even where Code C, Annex B applies.

## 8 Conditions of Detention

### (a) Action

8.1 So far as it is practicable, not more than one detainee should be detained in each cell.

8.2 Cells in use must be adequately heated, cleaned and ventilated. They must be adequately lit, subject to such dimming as is compatible with safety and security to allow people detained overnight to sleep. No additional restraints shall be used within a locked cell unless absolutely necessary and then only restraint equipment, approved for use in that force by the Chief Officer, which is reasonable and necessary in the circumstances having regard to the detainee's demeanour and with a view to ensuring their safety and the safety of others. If a detainee is deaf, mentally disordered or otherwise mentally vulnerable, particular care must be taken when deciding whether to use any form of approved restraints.

8.3   Blankets, mattresses, pillows and other bedding supplied shall be of a reasonable standard and in a clean and sanitary condition.

8.4   Access to toilet and washing facilities must be provided.

8.5   If it is necessary to remove a detainee's clothes for the purposes of investigation, for hygiene, health reasons or cleaning, replacement clothing of a reasonable standard of comfort and cleanliness shall be provided. A detainee may not be interviewed unless adequate clothing has been offered.

8.6   At least two light meals and one main meal should be offered in any 24 hour period. Drinks should be provided at meal times and upon reasonable request between meals. Whenever necessary, advice shall be sought from the appropriate healthcare professional, on medical and dietary matters. As far as practicable, meals provided shall offer a varied diet and meet any specific dietary needs or religious beliefs the detainee may have. The detainee may, at the custody officer's discretion, have meals supplied by their family or friends at their expense.

8.7   Brief outdoor exercise shall be offered daily if practicable.

8.8   A juvenile shall not be placed in a police cell unless no other secure accommodation is available and the custody officer considers it is not practicable to supervise them if they are not placed in a cell or that a cell provides more comfortable accommodation than other secure accommodation in the station. A juvenile may not be placed in a cell with a detained adult.

## (b) Documentation

8.9   A record must be kept of replacement clothing and meals offered.

8.10  If a juvenile is placed in a cell, the reason must be recorded.

8.11  The use of any restraints on a detainee whilst in a cell, the reasons for it and, if appropriate, the arrangements for enhanced supervision of the detainee whilst so restrained, shall be recorded. See *paragraph 3.9*.

**1.6.12.1**

**KEYNOTE**

The provision of bedding, medical and dietary matters are of particular importance in the case of a person likely to be detained for an extended period. In deciding whether to allow meals to be supplied by family or friends, the custody officer is entitled to take account of the risk of items being concealed in any food or package and the officer's duties and responsibilities under food handling legislation. Meals should, so far as practicable, be offered at recognised meal times, or at other times that take account of when the detainee last had a meal.

It is suggested that the custody officer should undertake a further risk assessment which should be recorded in the custody record before more than one person is placed in a cell. Any steps taken to minimise the risk should also be included in the custody record. (Paragraph 2.3 requires the time of release to be recorded; this is relevant in calculating any period of detention which may still be remaining if the person has been bailed, and periods in police detention also count towards the period a person serves in custody.)

Section 117 of the 1984 Act provides that where any provision of the Act confers a power on a constable and does not provide that the power may only be exercised with the consent of some person, other than a police officer, the officer may use reasonable force, if necessary, in the exercise of the power.

This is not a blanket power to use force. In *R* v *Jones* (1999) *The Times*, 21 April, the court said that s. 117 should not be interpreted as giving a right to police to exercise force whenever the consent of a suspect was not required.

A further important duty is placed upon a custody officer where a person is to be handed over to prison custody. The custody officer must complete a form in respect of every prisoner handed over for prison custody who is reasonably suspected of:

- being likely to try to escape;
- being associated with a dangerous gang who may attempt rescue;
- being of a violent nature.

The form should also be completed where:

- other serious charges may be brought;
- any other reason which may help the governor in deciding whether this prisoner represents a special security risk, e.g. having suicidal tendencies, being ill, being liable to take drugs into prison, etc.

(See Home Office Circular 32/2000, *Detainee Risk Assessment and Revised Prisoner Escort (PER) Form*, Annexes B and C, which include this form and fully describe how it should be completed.)

Authorised Professional Practice (APP) on Detention and Custody available on POLKA provides guidance on matters concerning detainee healthcare and treatment and associated forensic issues which should be read in conjunction with ss. 8 and 9 of Code C.

---

**1.6.13**

## 9 Care and Treatment of Detained Persons

### (a) General

9.1 Nothing in this section prevents the police from calling an appropriate healthcare professional to examine a detainee for the purposes of obtaining evidence relating to any offence in which the detainee is suspected of being involved.

9.2 If a complaint is made by, or on behalf of, a detainee about their treatment since their arrest, or it comes to notice that a detainee may have been treated improperly, a report must be made as soon as practicable to an officer of inspector rank or above not connected with the investigation. If the matter concerns a possible assault or the possibility of the unnecessary or unreasonable use of force, an appropriate healthcare professional must also be called as soon as practicable.

9.3 Detainees should be visited at least every hour. If no reasonably foreseeable risk was identified in a risk assessment, see *paragraphs 3.6–3.10*, there is no need to wake a sleeping detainee. Those suspected of being under the influence of drink or drugs or both or of having swallowed drugs, or whose level of consciousness causes concern must, subject to any clinical directions given by the appropriate healthcare professional, see *paragraph 9.13*:
- be visited and roused at least every half hour;
- have their condition assessed as in *Annex H*;
- and clinical treatment arranged if appropriate.

9.4 When arrangements are made to secure clinical attention for a detainee, the custody officer must make sure all relevant information which might assist in the treatment of the detainee's condition is made available to the responsible healthcare professional. This applies whether or not the healthcare professional asks for such information. Any officer or police staff with relevant information must inform the custody officer as soon as practicable.

### (b) Clinical treatment and attention

9.5 The custody officer must make sure a detainee receives appropriate clinical attention as soon as reasonably practicable if the person:
(a) appears to be suffering from physical illness; or
(b) is injured; or
(c) appears to be suffering from a mental disorder; or
(d) appears to need clinical attention.

9.5A   This applies even if the detainee makes no request for clinical attention and whether or not they have already received clinical attention elsewhere. If the need for attention appears urgent, e.g. when indicated as in *Annex H*, the nearest available healthcare professional or an ambulance must be called immediately.

9.5B   The custody officer must also consider the need for clinical attention as set out in *Note 9C* in relation to those suffering the effects of alcohol or drugs.

9.6   *Paragraph 9.5* is not meant to prevent or delay the transfer to a hospital if necessary of a person detained under the Mental Health Act 1983, section 136. When an assessment under that Act is to take place at a police station, see *paragraph 3.16*, the custody officer must consider whether an appropriate healthcare professional should be called to conduct an initial clinical check on the detainee. This applies particularly when there is likely to be any significant delay in the arrival of a suitably qualified medical practitioner.

9.7   If it appears to the custody officer, or they are told, that a person brought to a station under arrest may be suffering from an infectious disease or condition, the custody officer must take reasonable steps to safeguard the health of the detainee and others at the station. In deciding what action to take, advice must be sought from an appropriate healthcare professional. The custody officer has discretion to isolate the person and their property until clinical directions have been obtained.

9.8   If a detainee requests a clinical examination, an appropriate healthcare professional must be called as soon as practicable to assess the detainee's clinical needs. If a safe and appropriate care plan cannot be provided, the appropriate healthcare professional's advice must be sought. The detainee may also be examined by a medical practitioner of their choice at their expense.

9.9   If a detainee is required to take or apply any medication in compliance with clinical directions prescribed before their detention, the custody officer must consult the appropriate healthcare professional before the use of the medication. Subject to the restrictions in *paragraph 9.10*, the custody officer is responsible for the safekeeping of any medication and for making sure the detainee is given the opportunity to take or apply prescribed or approved medication. Any such consultation and its outcome shall be noted in the custody record.

9.10   No police officer may administer or supervise the self-administration of medically prescribed controlled drugs of the types and forms listed in the Misuse of Drugs Regulations 2001, Schedule 2 or 3. A detainee may only self-administer such drugs under the personal supervision of the registered medical practitioner authorising their use or other appropriate healthcare professional. The custody officer may supervise the self-administration of, or authorise other custody staff to supervise the self-administration of drugs listed in Schedule 4 or 5 if the officer has consulted the appropriate healthcare professional authorising their use and both are satisfied self-administration will not expose the detainee, police officers or anyone else to the risk of harm or injury.

9.11   When appropriate healthcare professionals administer drugs or authorise the use of other medications, supervise their self-administration or consult with the custody officer about allowing self-administration of drugs listed in Schedule 4 or 5, it must be within current medicines legislation and the scope of practice as determined by their relevant statutory regulatory body.

9.12   If a detainee has in their possession, or claims to need, medication relating to a heart condition, diabetes, epilepsy or a condition of comparable potential seriousness then, even though *paragraph 9.5* may not apply, the advice of the appropriate healthcare professional must be obtained.

9.13   Whenever the appropriate healthcare professional is called in accordance with this section to examine or treat a detainee, the custody officer shall ask for their opinion about:
- any risks or problems which police need to take into account when making decisions about the detainee's continued detention;
- when to carry out an interview if applicable; and
- the need for safeguards.

9.14 When clinical directions are given by the appropriate healthcare professional, whether orally or in writing, and the custody officer has any doubts or is in any way uncertain about any aspect of the directions, the custody officer shall ask for clarification. It is particularly important that directions concerning the frequency of visits are clear, precise and capable of being implemented.

## (c) Documentation

9.15 A record must be made in the custody record of:
   (a) the arrangements made for an examination by an appropriate healthcare professional under *paragraph 9.2* and of any complaint reported under that paragraph together with any relevant remarks by the custody officer;
   (b) any arrangements made in accordance with *paragraph 9.5*;
   (c) any request for a clinical examination under *paragraph 9.8* and any arrangements made in response;
   (d) the injury, ailment, condition or other reason which made it necessary to make the arrangements in (a) to (c);
   (e) any clinical directions and advice, including any further clarifications, given to police by a healthcare professional concerning the care and treatment of the detainee in connection with any of the arrangements made in (a) to (c);
   (f) if applicable, the responses received when attempting to rouse a person using the procedure in *Annex H*.
9.16 If a healthcare professional does not record their clinical findings in the custody record, the record must show where they are recorded. However, information which is necessary to custody staff to ensure the effective ongoing care and well being of the detainee must be recorded openly in the custody record, see *paragraph 3.8* and *Annex G, paragraph 7*.
9.17 Subject to the requirements of *Section 4*, the custody record shall include:
   • a record of all medication a detainee has in their possession on arrival at the police station;
   • a note of any such medication they claim to need but do not have with them.

---

**1.6.13.1**

**KEYNOTE**

A detainee who appears drunk or behaves abnormally may be suffering from illness, the effects of drugs or may have sustained injury, particularly a head injury which is not apparent. A detainee needing or dependent on certain drugs, including alcohol, may experience harmful effects within a short time of being deprived of his/her supply. In these circumstances, when there is any doubt, police should always act urgently to call an appropriate health care professional or an ambulance. Paragraph 9.5 does not apply to minor ailments or injuries which do not need attention. However, all such ailments or injuries must be recorded in the custody record and any doubt must be resolved in favour of calling the appropriate healthcare professional.

A 'health care professional' means a clinically qualified person working within the scope of practice as determined by his/her relevant professional body. Whether a health care professional is 'appropriate' depends on the circumstances of the duties he/she carries out at the time.

Any information that is available about the detained person should be considered in deciding whether to request a medical examination. In *R* v *HM Coroner for Coventry, ex parte Chief Constable of Staffordshire Police* (2000) 164 JP 665 the detained person had been drunk on arrest and was detained to be interviewed. The detained person made no complaint of his condition but his sister called the police to advise them that he would get the shakes. It was clear at interview and the following morning that he did have the shakes but no complaint was made and no doctor was called. A verdict of accidental death aggravated by neglect was an option in the case as the deceased had died while in police custody. The court considered the facts, such as the deceased's withdrawal and the warning as to his condition, from which a properly directed jury could have concluded that had certain steps been taken it was at least possible that the deceased would not have died.

In this case, a verdict of accidental death aggravated by neglect was left open to the jury, even though a doctor at the inquest gave evidence that he doubted whether calling a doctor would have made any difference to the eventual outcome.

Paragraph 9.3 also applies to a person in police custody by order of a magistrates' court under the Criminal Justice Act 1988, s. 152 (as amended by the Drugs Act 2005, s. 8) to facilitate the recovery of evidence after being charged with drug possession or drug trafficking and suspected of having swallowed drugs. In the case of the healthcare needs of a person who has swallowed drugs, the custody officer, subject to any clinical directions, should consider the necessity for rousing every half hour. This does not negate the need for regular visiting of the suspect in the cell. Whenever possible, juveniles and mentally vulnerable detainees should be visited more frequently. The purpose of recording a person's responses when attempting to rouse them using the procedure in Annex H is to enable any change in the individual's consciousness level to be noted and clinical treatment arranged if appropriate.

Paragraph 9.5 does not apply to minor ailments or injuries which do not need attention. However, all such ailments or injuries must be recorded in the custody record and any doubt must be resolved in favour of calling the appropriate health care professional. The custody officer should always seek to clarify directions that the detainee requires constant observation or supervision and should ask the appropriate health care professional to explain precisely what action needs to be taken to implement such directions.

Whenever practicable, arrangements should be made for persons detained for assessment under s. 136 of the Mental Health Act 1983 to be taken to a hospital. Chapter 10 of the Mental Health Act 1983 Code of Practice (as revised) provides more detailed guidance about arranging assessments under s. 136 of the 1983 Act and transferring detainees from police stations to other places of safety.

1.6.13.2     **KEYNOTE**

**Medical Record Forming Part of the Custody Record**

It is important to respect a person's right to privacy, and information about his/her health must be kept confidential and only disclosed with his/her consent or in accordance with clinical advice when it is necessary to protect the detainee's health or that of others who come into contact with him/her.

A solicitor or appropriate adult must be permitted to consult a detainee's custody record as soon as practicable after his/her arrival at the station and at any other time while the person is detained (Code C, para. 2.4). Therefore details required to be included in the custody record concerning the detainee's injuries and ailments will be accessible to both the solicitor and appropriate adult. However, paras 9.15 and 9.16 do not require any information about the cause of any injury, ailment or condition to be recorded on the custody record if it appears capable of providing evidence of an offence.

As the Codes specify matters which must be included within the custody record, it is suggested that all other matters recorded by the appropriate health care professional do not form part of the custody record and therefore do not need to be made available to the solicitor or appropriate adult under Code C, para. 2.4, i.e. the notes made by the health care professional.

1.6.13.3     **KEYNOTE**

**Independent Custody Visiting (Lay Visitors)**

Section 51 of the Police Reform Act 2002 introduced independent custody visitors on a statutory basis. The arrangements may confer on independent custody visitors such powers as the police authority considers necessary to enable them to carry out their functions under the arrangements and may, in particular, confer on them powers to:

- require access to be given to each police station;
- examine records relating to the detention of persons;
- meet detainees for the purposes of a discussion about their treatment and conditions while detained; and

## 10 Cautions (see chapter 1.8)

## 11 Interviews—general (see chapter 1.8)

## 12 Interviews in police stations (see chapter 1.8)

**1.6.14**

## 13 Interpreters

### (a) General

13.1 Chief officers are responsible for making sure appropriate arrangements are in place for provision of suitably qualified interpreters for people who:
- are deaf;
- do not understand English.

### (b) Foreign languages

13.2 Unless *paragraphs 11.1, 11.18* to *11.20* apply, a person must not be interviewed in the absence of a person capable of interpreting if:
(a) they have difficulty understanding English;
(b) the interviewer cannot speak the person's own language;
(c) the person wants an interpreter present.

13.3 The interviewer shall make sure the interpreter makes a note of the interview at the time in the person's language for use in the event of the interpreter being called to give evidence, and certifies its accuracy. The interviewer should allow sufficient time for the interpreter to note each question and answer after each is put, given and interpreted. The person should be allowed to read the record or have it read to them and sign it as correct or indicate the respects in which they consider it inaccurate. If the interview is audibly recorded or visually recorded, the arrangements in Code E or F apply.

13.4 In the case of a person making a statement to a police officer or other police staff other than in English:
(a) the interpreter shall record the statement in the language it is made;
(b) the person shall be invited to sign it;
(c) official English translation shall be made in due course.

### (c) Deaf people and people with speech difficulties

13.5 If a person appears to be deaf or there is doubt about their hearing or speaking ability, they must not be interviewed in the absence of an interpreter unless they agree in writing to being interviewed without one or *paragraphs 11.1, 11.18* to *11.20* apply.

13.6 An interpreter should also be called if a juvenile is interviewed and the parent or guardian present as the appropriate adult appears to be deaf or there is doubt about their hearing or speaking ability, unless they agree in writing to the interview proceeding without one or *paragraphs 11.1, 11.18* to *11.20* apply.

13.7    The interviewer shall make sure the interpreter is allowed to read the interview record and certify its accuracy in the event of the interpreter being called to give evidence. If the interview is audibly recorded or visually recorded, the arrangements in Code E or F apply.

## (d) Additional rules for detained persons

13.8    All reasonable attempts should be made to make the detainee understand that interpreters will be provided at public expense.

13.9    If *paragraph 6.1* applies and the detainee cannot communicate with the solicitor because of language, hearing or speech difficulties, an interpreter must be called. The interpreter may not be a police officer or any other police staff when interpretation is needed for the purposes of obtaining legal advice. In all other cases a police officer or other police staff may only interpret if the detainee and the appropriate adult, if applicable, give their agreement in writing or if the interview is audibly recorded or visually recorded as in Code E or F.

13.10   When the custody officer cannot establish effective communication with a person charged with an offence who appears deaf or there is doubt about their ability to hear, speak or to understand English, arrangements must be made as soon as practicable for an interpreter to explain the offence and any other information given by the custody officer.

## (e) Documentation

13.11   Action taken to call an interpreter under this section and any agreement to be interviewed in the absence of an interpreter must be recorded.

**1.6.14.1**    **KEYNOTE**

Where the detained person is unable to speak effectively in English, an interpreter must be called to safeguard the rights of the person and to allow him/her to communicate. Whenever possible, interpreters should be provided in accordance with national arrangements approved or prescribed by the Secretary of State. The interpreter is there for the benefit of the detained person and should not be considered to be part of the prosecution team. The case of *R (On the Application of Bozkurt)* v *Thames Magistrates' Court* [2001] EWHC Admin 400, demonstrates the importance of the interpreter's role. In *Bozkurt*, the police arranged for an interpreter to attend the custody suite and interpret for the drink-drive procedure at the police station. The police then arranged for the interpreter to attend court. The interpreter translated for the defendant while he took advice from the duty solicitor at court. The interpreter failed to inform the solicitor that he had translated for the drink-drive procedure at the police station. The court held that an interpreter was under an equal duty to that of the solicitor to keep confidential what he might hear during a conference. In these circumstances, it would have been preferable for a different interpreter to be used, or at least for the interpreter to have obtained the permission of the solicitor to interpret for the conference.

In another drink-drive case, the defendant, who was Polish, had been required to provide breath specimens for analysis under the Road Traffic Act; this had been communicated through a Polish-speaking interpreter, who was present to translate at the police station. The defendant failed to provide the breath specimens and his defence was that he did not understand the requirement. The court held that it was a legitimate inference for the magistrates to draw that the words had been translated accurately. There was no evidence that the interpreter suggested to the officers that the defendant had not understood what was being said. A court could draw the inference, if the evidence supported it, that someone being asked to do something in a police station by a police officer with the assistance of an accredited interpreter of the relevant language had been asked the correct question and understood it and also the consequences of not responding to it (*Bielecki* v *DPP* [2011] EWHC 2245 (Admin)).

## 14 Questioning—Special Restrictions

14.1 If a person is arrested by one police force on behalf of another and the lawful period of detention in respect of that offence has not yet commenced in accordance with PACE, section 41 no questions may be put to them about the offence while they are in transit between the forces except to clarify any voluntary statement they make.

14.2 If a person is in police detention at a hospital they may not be questioned without the agreement of a responsible doctor.

## 15 Reviews and Extensions of Detention

### (a) Persons detained under PACE

15.1 The review officer is responsible under PACE, section 40 for periodically determining if a person's detention, before or after charge, continues to be necessary. This requirement continues throughout the detention period and except as in *paragraph 15.10*, the review officer must be present at the police station holding the detainee.

15.2 Under PACE, section 42, an officer of superintendent rank or above who is responsible for the station holding the detainee may give authority any time after the second review to extend the maximum period the person may be detained without charge by up to 12 hours. Further detention without charge may be authorised only by a magistrates' court in accordance with PACE, sections 43 and 44.

15.2A An authorisation under section 42(1) of PACE extends the maximum period of detention permitted before charge for indictable offences from 24 hours to 36 hours. Detaining a juvenile or mentally vulnerable person for longer than 24 hours will be dependent on the circumstances of the case and with regard to the person's:
   (a) special vulnerability;
   (b) the legal obligation to provide an opportunity for representations to be made prior to a decision about extending detention;
   (c) the need to consult and consider the views of any appropriate adult; and
   (d) any alternatives to police custody.

15.3 Before deciding whether to authorise continued detention the officer responsible under *paragraph 15.1* or *15.2* shall give an opportunity to make representations about the detention to:
   (a) the detainee, unless in the case of a review as in *paragraph 15.1*, the detainee is asleep;
   (b) the detainee's solicitor if available at the time; and
   (c) the appropriate adult if available at the time.

15.3A Other people having an interest in the detainee's welfare may also make representations at the authorising officer's discretion.

15.3B Subject to *paragraph 15.10*, the representations may be made orally in person or by telephone or in writing. The authorising officer may, however, refuse to hear oral representations from the detainee if the officer considers them unfit to make representations because of their condition or behaviour.

15.3C The decision on whether the review takes place in person or by telephone or by video conferencing is a matter for the review officer. In determining the form the review may take, the review officer must always take full account of the needs of the person in custody. The benefits of carrying out a review in person should always be considered, based on the individual circumstances of each case with specific additional consideration if the person is:
   (a) a juvenile (and the age of the juvenile); or
   (b) suspected of being mentally vulnerable; or
   (c) in need of medical attention for other than routine minor ailments; or
   (d) subject to presentational or community issues around their detention.

15.4 Before conducting a review or determining whether to extend the maximum period of detention without charge, the officer responsible must make sure the detainee is reminded of their entitlement to free legal advice, see *paragraph 6.5*, unless in the case of a review the person is asleep.

15.5 If, after considering any representations, the review officer under *paragraph 15.1* decides to keep the detainee in detention or the superintendent under *paragraph 15.2* extends the maximum period for which they may be detained without charge, then any comment made by the detainee shall be recorded. If applicable, the officer shall be informed of the comment as soon as practicable. See also *paragraphs 11.4* and *11.13*.

15.6 No officer shall put specific questions to the detainee:
- regarding their involvement in any offence; or
- in respect of any comments they may make:
  - when given the opportunity to make representations; or
  - in response to a decision to keep them in detention or extend the maximum period of detention.

Such an exchange could constitute an interview as in *paragraph 11.1A* and would be subject to the associated safeguards in *section 11* and, in respect of a person who has been charged, *paragraph 16.5*. See also *paragraph 11.13*.

15.7 A detainee who is asleep at a review, see *paragraph 15.1*, and whose continued detention is authorised must be informed about the decision and reason as soon as practicable after waking.

15.8 *Not used*

## (b) Review of detention by telephone and video conferencing facilities

15.9 PACE, section 40A provides that the officer responsible under section 40 for reviewing the detention of a person who has not been charged, need not attend the police station holding the detainee and may carry out the review by telephone.

15.9A PACE, section 45A(2) provides that the officer responsible under section 40 for reviewing the detention of a person who has not been charged, need not attend the police station holding the detainee and may carry out the review by video conferencing facilities.

15.9B A telephone review is not permitted where facilities for review by video conferencing exist and it is practicable to use them.

15.9C The review officer can decide at any stage that a telephone review or review by video conferencing should be terminated and that the review will be conducted in person. The reasons for doing so should be noted in the custody record.

15.10 When a review is carried out by telephone or by video conferencing facilities, an officer at the station holding the detainee shall be required by the review officer to fulfil that officer's obligations under PACE section 40 and this Code by:
(a) making any record connected with the review in the detainee's custody record;
(b) if applicable, making the record in (a) in the presence of the detainee; and
(c) for a review by telephone, giving the detainee information about the review.

15.11 When a review is carried out by telephone or by video conferencing facilities, the requirement in *paragraph 15.3* will be satisfied:
(a) if facilities exist for the immediate transmission of written representations to the review officer, e.g. fax or email message, by allowing those who are given the opportunity to make representations, to make their representations:
  (i) orally by telephone or (as the case may be) by means of the video conferencing facilities; or
  (ii) in writing using the facilities for the immediate transmission of written representations; and

(b) in all other cases, by allowing those who are given the opportunity to make representations, to make their representations orally by telephone or by means of the video conferencing facilities.

## (c) Documentation

15.12   It is the officer's responsibility to make sure all reminders given under *paragraph 15.4* are
noted in the custody record.

15.13   grounds for, and extent of, any delay in conducting a review shall be recorded.

15.14   When a review is carried out by telephone or video conferencing facilities, a record shall be
made of:

(a) the reason the review officer did not attend the station holding the detainee;

(b) the place the review officer was;

(c) the method representations, oral or written, were made to the review officer, see *paragraph 15.11*.

15.15   Any written representations shall be retained.

15.16   A record shall be made as soon as practicable of:

(a) the outcome of each review of detention before or after charge, and if *paragraph 15.7*
applies, of when the person was informed and by whom;

(b) the outcome of any determination under PACE, section 42 by a superintendent whether
to extend the maximum period of detention without charge beyond 24 hours from the
relevant time. If an authorisation is given, the record shall state the number of hours
and minutes by which the detention period is extended or further extended.

(c) the outcome of each application under PACE, section 43, for a warrant of further
detention or under section 44, for an extension or further extension of that warrant. If
a warrant for further detention is granted under section 43 or extended or further
extended under 44, the record shall state the detention period authorised by the warrant and the date and time it was granted or (as the case may be) the period by which
the warrant is extended or further extended.

Note: Any period during which a person is released on bail does not count towards the maximum period of detention without charge allowed under PACE, sections 41 to 44.

---

**1.6.16.1**   **KEYNOTE**

**Relevant Time**

There are limits on how long a person can be detained. The Police and Criminal Evidence Act 1984 and the
Codes of Practice talk of the 'relevant time'. This is the time from which the limits of detention are calculated.
The relevant time of a person's detention starts in accordance with s. 41(2)–(5) of the 1984 Act. Section 41
states:

(2) The time from which the period of detention of a person is to be calculated (in this Act referred to as 'the relevant time')—

(a) in the case of a person to whom this paragraph applies, shall be—

(i) the time at which that person arrives at the relevant police station; or

(ii) the time 24 hours after the time of that person's arrest,

whichever is the earlier;

(b) in the case of a person arrested outside England and Wales, shall be—

(i) the time at which that person arrives at the first police station to which he is taken in the police area in England
or Wales in which the offence for which he was arrested is being investigated; or

(ii) the time 24 hours after the time of that person's entry into England and Wales,

whichever is the earlier;

(c) in the case of a person who—

(i) attends voluntarily at a police station; or

(ii) accompanies a constable to a police station without having been arrested, and is arrested at the police station, the time of his arrest;

    (ca) in the case of a person who attends a police station to answer to bail granted under section 30A, the time he arrives at the police station;

    (d) in any other case, except where subsection (5) below applies, shall be the time at which the person arrested arrives at the first police station to which he is taken after his arrest.

(3) Subsection (2)(a) above applies to a person if—

    (a) his arrest is sought in one police area in England and Wales;

    (b) he is arrested in another police area; and

    (c) he is not questioned in the area in which he is arrested in order to obtain evidence in relation to an offence for which he is arrested;

and in sub-paragraph (i) of that paragraph 'the relevant police station' means the first police station to which he is taken in the police area in which his arrest was sought.

(4) Subsection (2) above shall have effect in relation to a person arrested under section 31 above as if every reference in it to his arrest or his being arrested were a reference to his arrest or his being arrested for the offence for which he was originally arrested.

(5) If—

    (a) a person is in police detention in a police area in England and Wales ('the first area'); and

    (b) his arrest for an offence is sought in some other police area in England and Wales ('the second area'); and

    (c) he is taken to the second area for the purposes of investigating that offence, without being questioned in the first area in order to obtain evidence in relation to it,

the relevant time shall be—

        (i) the time 24 hours after he leaves the place where he is detained in the first area; or

        (ii) the time at which he arrives at the first police station to which he is taken in the second area, whichever is the earlier.

Note that under s. 41(5) the relevant time may vary, depending on whether the detainee is interviewed in relation to the offence while still in the first police area.

For those detained under the Terrorism Act 2000 the detention clock starts from the time the person is arrested, not the time he/she arrives at the police station.

The Criminal Justice Act 2003 inserted s. 41(2)(ca) into the Police and Criminal Evidence Act 1984. This allows for a person who has been arrested to be bailed before being taken to a police station. When the person attends the police station to which he/she has been bailed the relevant time starts when he/she arrives at the police station.

Some situations occur where a person is arrested at one police station and has been circulated as wanted by another police station in the same force area. In these cases, where the person is not wanted on warrant, the detention clock for the second offence starts at the same time as for the original offence for which he/she was arrested. Consideration will need to be given as to how to protect the detention period for the second offence while officers are dealing with the first matter. Options that might be considered would include bailing the person for one of the offences or conducting both investigations at the same station. Here there may be a risk of 'confusing' the suspect, which may allow him/her to retract or qualify any confession he/she might make.

In *Henderson* v *Chief Constable of Cleveland* [2001] EWCA Civ 335 the court considered the policy of not executing a court warrant until after other matters for which the person had been detained were completed. The court held that, once a warrant was executed, there was a requirement to follow the directions of the warrant. The police, however, had a discretion as to *when* to execute the warrant. This may be relevant where a person has been arrested for one offence and it is discovered that he/she is also wanted for another offence or where there are warrants in existence for that person at more than one court. In such cases, if the warrant is executed immediately, the direction on the warrant tells officers to take the person before the next available court, an action which could interfere with the investigation. If *Henderson* is followed there is no requirement to execute the warrant straight away and the other matters can be dealt with before the requirement to produce the person at court under the warrant applies.

**KEYNOTE**

**Limits on Detention and Review**

Once detention has been authorised this does not mean that a person can be detained indefinitely. Section 34 of the Police and Criminal Evidence Act 1984 requires the custody officer to release a person if he/she becomes aware that the grounds for detention no longer apply and that no other grounds exist for the continuing detention (unless the person appears to have been unlawfully at large when he/she was arrested). Failure to comply with this could also lead to a breach of Article 5 of the European Convention on Human Rights. If there are additional grounds, these should be recorded in the custody record and the person informed of these additional grounds in the same way as when a person is first detained. For example, this could be for new offences or it could be that it becomes necessary to preserve evidence by questioning the detained person.

It is only the *custody officer* who can authorise the release of a detained person (s. 34(3)). In addition to the requirement to release a person should the grounds for detention no longer exist, there are also maximum time limits for which a person can be detained without charge. Once this limit has been reached any prosecution will need to proceed by summons or by warrant.

**KEYNOTE**

**Time Limits: Without Charge**

While a person is in police detention there is a requirement that his/her continuing detention is reviewed. There are minimum time requirements for when these reviews must be conducted, with the timing of the first review being calculated from the time detention is authorised. This time can be considered as the 'review time'. The question of whether a person should be kept in custody is a continuous one and the review process is intended as an added protection to the detained person.

The maximum period that a person can be detained without charge is 96 hours (with the exception of suspected acts of terrorism, in which case it is 14 days). The necessity for the continued detention of the person must be reviewed throughout this time. The period of detention is calculated from the 'relevant time' which can be calculated from Table A below (do not confuse the relevant time with the time from which reviews are due). The relevant time 'clock' will always start before, or at the same time as, the review 'clock'. This is because the review clock does not start until detention has been authorised, which clearly cannot happen until the person is brought before the custody officer which, as can be seen from the table below, is at the very latest the time the prisoner walks into the custody suite (with the exception of where the person has been under arrest for 24 hours but has not yet been taken to a police station).

This relevant time period (that is, the maximum period a person can be detained for) relates to the actual time spent in custody and not a 24-hour period in time. This means that every time the person is bailed the clock stops and usually continues from the time that the person returns to custody for the offence(s) for which he/she was bailed. The case of *R (on the application of Chief Constable of Greater Manchester Police)* v *Salford Magistrates' Court and Hookway* [2011] EWHC 1578 (Admin) created concern in that the decision of the court was that the detention clock for warrants of further detention did not stop when the person was bailed, the effect of which was there would be no time left on the detention clock when the person returned to answer their bail. The issue caused by this decision has been rectified by the Police (Detention and Bail) Act 2011. The Act amends ss. 34 and 47 of PACE so that any time during which a person is on bail does not count when calculating how long a detained person has been in police detention. This legislation applies retrospectively and therefore the changes to ss. 34 and 47 brought about by this Act are deemed always to have had effect.

Where a person has been released and re-arrested for an offence, it is possible that the relevant time will start again. This is covered by s. 47 of the 1984 Act:

(7) Where a person who was released on bail under this Part subject to a duty to attend at a police station is re-arrested, the provisions of this Part of this Act shall apply to him/her as they apply to a person arrested for the first time but this subsection does not apply to a person who is arrested under section 46A above or has attended a police station in accordance with the grant of bail (and who accordingly is deemed by section 34(7) above to have been arrested for an offence).

In cases where this subsection applies, the relevant time starts again and a fresh clock starts. This will apply where the person has been re-arrested for the same offence because of some new evidence (except at such time as when he/she is returning on bail at the appointed time) under s. 30C(4), 41(9) or 47(2).

Section 41 states:

(9) A person released under subsection (7) [i.e. where his/her relevant time period had expired] above shall not be re-arrested without a warrant for the offence for which he was previously arrested unless new evidence justifying a further arrest has come to light since his release; but this subsection does not prevent an arrest under section 46A below.

Section 47 states:

(2) Nothing in the Bail Act 1976 shall prevent the re-arrest without warrant of a person released on bail subject to a duty to attend at a police station if new evidence justifying a further arrest has come to light since his release.

Section 30C states:

(4) Nothing in section 30A or 30B or in this section prevents the re-arrest without warrant of a person released on bail under section 30A (bail by a constable elsewhere than a police station) if new evidence justifying a further arrest has come to light since his release.

The issue will be whether new evidence has come to light since the grant of bail and it will be a question of fact as to what the new evidence is. It is suggested that this must be evidence which was not available at the time the person was last in detention or which would not have been available even if all reasonable inquiries had been conducted.

It will always be important to check how much time is left on the person's 'relevant time' and when his/her next review is due.

## 1.6.16.4  KEYNOTE

### The Three Stages of Pre-charge Detention

After the custody officer has authorised detention but before a person has been charged there are three distinct stages of detention. These are distinguished by the level at which authorisation for continuing detention is required.

The three stages of detention under the 1984 Act are:

- the basic period of detention, which is the period of detention up to 24 hours, as first authorised by the custody officer;
- those authorised by an officer of the rank of superintendent or above (s. 42) up to 36 hours (indictable offences only);
- those authorised by a magistrates' court (ss. 43 and 44) up to a maximum of 96 hours.

Each of these is examined in detail below.

## 1.6.16.5  KEYNOTE

### The Basic Period of Detention

The majority of people detained by the police are detained for less than six hours; most other cases are dealt with within 24 hours. If a person's continued detention is not authorised beyond 24 hours and the person is not charged with an offence, he/she *must* be released (with or without bail) and cannot be re-arrested for the offence unless new evidence comes to light (s. 41(7) and (9) of the 1984 Act). New evidence is not defined by the 1984 Act but it is suggested that it covers evidence which was not available at the time the person was detained, or which would not have been available if the investigating officers had conducted reasonable inquiries.

During this period of detention the custody officer has a responsibility to monitor whether the grounds for detention still exist. An officer of at least the rank of inspector not directly involved in the investigation (s. 40(1)(b)) must review the person's detention *at least once in the first six hours* and then, after the first review, *within nine hours of that review*. Further reviews must then be conducted *no later than nine hours after the last review* was conducted, until the person is either charged or released.

Further reviews must then be conducted no later than nine hours after the last review was conducted, until the person is either charged or released. Review officer for the purposes of ss. 40, 40A and 45A of the 1984 Act means, in the case of a person arrested but not charged, an officer of at least inspector rank not directly involved in the investigation and, if a person has been arrested and charged, the custody officer.

The detention of persons in police custody not subject to the statutory review requirement should still be reviewed periodically as a matter of good practice.

Such reviews can be carried out by an officer of the rank of sergeant or above. The purpose of such reviews is to check that the particular power under which a detainee is held continues to apply, any associated conditions are complied with, and to make sure that appropriate action is taken to deal with any changes. This includes the detainee's prompt release when the power no longer applies, or his/her transfer if the power requires the detainee be taken elsewhere as soon as the necessary arrangements are made. Examples include persons: arrested on warrant because they failed to answer bail to appear at court; arrested under the Bail Act 1976, s. 7(3) for breaching a condition of bail granted after charge and in police custody for specific purposes and periods under the Crime (Sentences) Act 1997, sch. 1; convicted or remand prisoners, held in police stations on behalf of the Prison Service under the Imprisonment (Temporary Provisions) Act 1980, s. 6; being detained to prevent them causing a breach of the peace; detained at police stations on behalf of the Immigration Service or detained by order of a magistrates' court under the Criminal Justice Act 1988, s. 152 (as amended by the Drugs Act 2005, s. 8) to facilitate the recovery of evidence after being charged with drug possession or drug trafficking and suspected of having swallowed drugs.

The detention of persons remanded into police detention by order of a court under the Magistrates' Courts Act 1980, s. 128 is subject to a statutory requirement to review that detention. This is to make sure that the detainee is taken back to court no later than the end of the period authorised by the court or when the need for his/her detention by police ceases, whichever is the sooner.

In the case of a review of detention, but not an extension, the detainee need not be woken for the review. However, if the detainee is likely to be asleep, e.g. during a period of rest, at the latest time a review or authorisation to extend detention may take place, the officer should, if the legal obligations and time constraints permit, bring forward the procedure to allow the detainee to make representations. A detainee not asleep during the review must be present when the grounds for his/her continued detention are recorded and must at the same time be informed of those grounds unless the review officer considers that the person is incapable of understanding what is said, is violent or likely to become violent or is in urgent need of medical attention. In relation to the detainee's solicitor or appropriate adult being 'available' to make representations, this includes being contactable in time to enable him/her to make representations remotely by telephone or other electronic means or in person by attending the station. Reasonable efforts should therefore be made to give the solicitor and appropriate adult sufficient notice of the time the decision is expected to be made so that they can make themselves available.

If a detained person is taken to hospital for medical treatment, the time at hospital and the period spent travelling to and from the hospital does not count towards the relevant time unless the person is asked questions for the purpose of obtaining evidence about an offence. Where questioning takes place, this period would count towards the relevant time and therefore the custody officer must be informed of it (s. 41(6)).

### 1.6.16.6 KEYNOTE

#### Detention Authorised by an Officer of the Rank of Superintendent or Above

Under s. 42(1) of the Police and Criminal Evidence Act 1984, detention can only be authorised beyond 24 hours and up to a maximum of 36 hours from the relevant time if:

- an offence being investigated is an 'indictable offence'; *and*
- an officer of the rank of superintendent or above is responsible for the station at which the person is detained (referred to here as the authorising officer); *and*
- that senior officer is satisfied that:
    + there is not sufficient evidence to charge; *and*
    + the investigation is being conducted diligently and expeditiously; *and*
    + the person's detention is necessary to secure or preserve evidence relating to the offence or to obtain such evidence by questioning that person.

Where a person has been arrested under s. 41 of the Terrorism Act 2000 he/she can be kept in police detention (in this case, this is generally from the time of the arrest) up to 48 hours without the court authorising an extension of time. If the authorising officer considers that there is sufficient evidence to charge, he/she cannot authorise further detention beyond 24 hours unless the detained person is in custody for another indictable offence for which further detention can be authorised (*R* v *Samuel* [1988] QB 615 and Code H, para. 14.3). It is suggested that in considering the strength of evidence the authorising officer may wish to consult with any readily accessible CPS representative.

The grounds for this continuing detention are the same as those when the custody officer made the initial decision to detain, with the additional requirements that the case has been conducted diligently and expeditiously. To be able to satisfy the senior officer of this, it will be necessary for the custody record to be available for inspection and also details of what inquiries have been made and evidence that the investigation has been moving at a pace that will satisfy the senior officer that the inquiries should not already have been completed.

The authorising officer (which here must be an officer of the rank of superintendent or above who is responsible for the station at which the person is detained) can authorise detention up to a maximum of 36 hours from the 'relevant time' of detention. The period can be shorter than this and can then be further authorised by that officer or any other officer of the rank of superintendent or above who is responsible for the station at which the person is detained to allow the period to be further extended up to the maximum 36-hour period (s. 42(2)). The officer responsible for the station holding the detainee includes a superintendent or above who, in accordance with their force operational policy or police regulations, is given that responsibility on a temporary basis whilst the appointed long-term holder is off duty or otherwise unavailable.

Section 42(5)–(8) mirrors the responsibility on the authorising officer at this stage with those of the review officer during the 'general period' of detention with regard to allowing representations, informing the detained person of the decision to authorise further detention and the need to record the decision. The main difference here is that the authorising officer must look into how the case is being investigated and whether this is being done diligently and expeditiously. Consequently, the authorising officer must also consider any representations on these points and these points should also be covered in any record as to whether detention should continue. When considering whether to authorise further detention the authorising officer must check whether the detained person has exercised his/her right to have someone informed and to consult with a legal representative.

If it is proposed to transfer a detained person from one police area to another for the purpose of investigating the offences for which he/she is detained, the authorising officer may take into consideration the period it will take to get to the other police area when deciding whether detention can go beyond 24 hours (s. 42(3)).

**Table A Maximum Periods of Detention for Non-terrorism Act Offences**

| Arrest | Relevant time starts | Review clock relevant time | 24 hours from detention | 24 to 36 hours' detention | 36 to 42 hours' detention | 42 to 78 hours' detention | up to 96 hours |
|---|---|---|---|---|---|---|---|
| Arrested locally. | 24 hours from arrest or arrival at police station, whichever earliest. | | All offences other than indictable offences where the detention period has been extended by superintendent or above. | Only indictable offences. | Only indictable offences. | Only indictable offences. | Only indictable offences. |
| Arrested outside England and Wales. | Time first arrives at police station in police area where matter being investigated or 24 hours after first entered England or Wales, whichever is earliest. | Time custody officer authorises detention. | Release unless s. 41(1) applies. | Detention authorised by superintendent or above (s. 42). | Where delay in applying for warrant of further detention is reasonable (s. 43(5)). **see para. 1.6.16.10** for the dangers of not applying within the 36-hour period. | First warrant for further detention issued by magistrates' court (s. 42). Remember the warrant can be applied for at any stage of detention. | Further warrants of detention issued by magistrates' court (s. 43). |
| Arrested for an offence in one police area in England or Wales then transferred to another police area for separate offence in that second police area, which is also in England or Wales. Arrested and bailed at a place other than a police station. Voluntarily attends police station or accompanies constable to station but not under arrest. | 24 hours from time he/she leaves the police station in the first police area or the time he/she arrives at the first police station in second police area where the crime is being investigated, provided not interviewed about the offence while detained in the first police area, whichever is the earliest. Time of arrival at the police station to which the notice of bail states he/she must attend. Time of arrest. | This timing applies where the person was in detention for an offence in the first police area (s. 41(5)). | | | | | |
| Arrested in one police area in England or Wales for an offence in another police area in England or Wales, there being no 'local' offence(s) for which he/she has been arrested. | From time the suspect arrives at the first police station in the area he/she is being sought or from 24 hours after the time he/she is arrested or if questioned about the offence while in the first police area, the relevant time starts from the time he/she first arrived at a police station in the first police area, whichever is the earliest. | | | | | | |

**1.6.16.7**

**KEYNOTE**

**Detention Authorised by a Magistrates' Court**

Once the 36-hour limit has been reached, a person's detention can only continue with the authority of the courts through the issuing of a warrant of further detention and this power only applies to indictable offences. If a person's continued detention is not authorised beyond 36 hours by a court and the person is not charged with an offence, he/she must be released with or without bail and cannot be re-arrested for the offence unless new evidence comes to light.

**1.6.16.8**

**KEYNOTE**

**Warrants of Further Detention**

Applications for warrants of further detention are made at the magistrates' court. Initially, the magistrates can issue a warrant for further detention for a period of up to 36 hours. This can be extended by the courts on further applications by police up to a maximum total period of detention of 96 hours. The warrant will specify what period of further detention the court has authorised. If detention of the person is required for any longer period, further applications can be made to the court up to a maximum of 96 hours' detention. The grounds on which the court must decide whether to grant a warrant, authorising further detention are the same as those that must be considered by a 'superintendent's review'.

Should it be necessary to apply for a warrant, it is important that the time restraints are kept in mind at all times and the application procedure followed closely.

**1.6.16.9**

**KEYNOTE**

**Procedure**

The application is made in the magistrates' court and both the detained person and the police must be in attendance (s. 43(1) and (2) of the Police and Criminal Evidence Act 1984). The application is made by laying an information before the court. The officer making the application does so on oath and is subject to cross-examination. Under s. 43(14) the information must set out:

- the nature of the offence (this must be an indictable offence);
- the general nature of the evidence on which the person was arrested;
- what inquiries have been made;
- what further inquiries are proposed; and
- the reasons for believing that continuing detention is necessary for such further inquiries.

It will be important to be able to demonstrate why the person needs to remain in detention while additional inquiries are made, for instance that further facts need to be verified before further questioning of the suspect can continue and that this cannot be done effectively if the person is released. The detained person must be provided with a copy of the information before the matter can be heard (s. 43(2)). He/she is also entitled to be legally represented. If the person is not legally represented but then requests legal representation at court, the case must be adjourned to allow representation (s. 43(3)). In cases where the person is not represented it may be prudent to remind the person of his/her right to legal representation prior to the court hearing and to make a record of this in the custody record. Should the detained person choose to be legally represented at court, and thereby try to delay the police investigation, s. 43(3)(b) allows the person to be taken back into police detention during the adjournment.

## 1.6.16.10 KEYNOTE

### Timing of the Application

In monitoring a person's detention, officers should be mindful of whether a warrant for further detention may be required. If it appears likely that the investigation of the indictable offence requires the person's detention to go beyond 36 hours, then thought must be given as to when to make the application to the magistrates' court; whether a court will be available to hear the application. If a court will not be available, then consideration should be given to making an earlier application. Section 43(5) allows the application to be made before the expiry of the 36-hour period (calculated from the relevant time) or, where it has not been practicable for the court to sit within the 36-hour period, the application can be made within the next six hours. There are dangers in applying outside the 36-hour period in that if the court feels that it would have been reasonable to make the application within the 36-hour period it must refuse the application for the warrant regardless of the merits of the case (s. 43(7)). If the court is not satisfied that there are reasonable grounds for believing that further detention is justified, the court may either refuse the application or adjourn the hearing until such time as it specifies up to the end of the 36-hour period of detention (s. 43(8)). If the application is refused, the person must be charged or released with or without bail at the expiry of the current permissible period of detention (s. 43(15)).

The application for the warrant can be made at any time, *even before a superintendent's review has been carried out*. If the application is made within the 36-hour period and it is refused, it does not mean that the person must be released straight away. Section 43(16) allows the person to be detained until the end of the current detention period (24 hours or 36 hours). The benefit of an early application has to be set against the risk that, once the court has refused an application, it is not allowed to hear any further applications for a warrant of further detention unless new evidence has come to light since the application was refused (s. 43(17)). An application to a magistrates' court should be made between 10 am and 9 pm, and if possible during normal court hours. It will not usually be practicable to arrange for a court to sit specially outside the hours of 10 am to 9 pm. If it appears that a special sitting may be needed outside normal court hours but between 10 am and 9 pm, the clerk to the justices should be given notice and informed of this possibility, while the court is sitting if possible.

In *R* v *Slough Justices, ex parte Stirling* [1987] Crim LR 576, the 36-hour period expired at 12.53 pm. The case was not heard by the justices until 2.45 pm. The Divisional Court held that the police should have made their application between 10.30 am and 11.30 am, even though this was before the 36-hour time limit had been reached.

## 1.6.16.11 KEYNOTE

### Applying to Extend Warrants of Further Detention

Under s. 44 of the 1984 Act, the process for applying to extend the warrant follows the same procedure as for the initial warrant, with the exception that the application *must be* made before the expiry of the extension given in the previous warrant. Once the period of detention that has been authorised has expired, and no other applications have been made, the detained person must be charged or released with or without bail.

## 1.6.16.12 KEYNOTE

### Terrorism Cases

The court can extend the period of detention of a person up to a total of 14 days. In the case of those arrested under s. 41 this starts at the time of arrest or, if the person was being detained under sch. 7 when he/she was arrested under s. 41, at the time his/her examination under that schedule began (Terrorism Act 2000, sch. 8, para. 36(3)).

A person detained in these circumstances may only be held for a maximum of 48 hours without charge before an application must be made to a court to issue or extend a warrant of further detention. At the end of that period, the detained person must either be released or an application to a court for a warrant for an extension to that detention must have been made and granted prior to the expiry of the initial 48-hour period. Extensions by the court will normally be for a seven-day period unless the application for a warrant of further detention requests a shorter period or the court is satisfied that it would be inappropriate for the period to be as long as seven days.

If detention is required beyond the first seven days, further applications are required to be made to the court as it is not possible for the court to issue a warrant authorising the full 14 days' detention on the first occasion a warrant for detention is sought (Code H, Note 14C).

The application to the court must be made by a superintendent or a Crown Prosecutor. Usually applications that cover a period of detention that does not extend beyond 14 days are heard by a district judge in the magistrates' court (unless an application in that case has already been considered by a High Court judge) and those that cover the period beyond 14 days are heard by a High Court judge. Paragraph 37 of sch. 8 to the Terrorism Act 2000 states that if at any time the police officer or person in charge of the case considers that the grounds on which the warrant of further detention authorised by the court no longer apply the detained person must be released. Paragraph 33 of sch. 8 to the Terrorism Act 2000 allows for these applications to be conducted by live television links. The person who makes the application may also apply to the court for an order that specified information upon which he/she intends to rely should be withheld from the person to whom the application relates and anyone representing him/her. The order to withhold information can only be made if one of the following applies:

- evidence of an offence under any of the provisions mentioned in s. 40(1)(a) of the Terrorism Act 2000 would be interfered with or harmed;
- the recovery of property obtained as a result of an offence under any of those provisions would be hindered;
- the recovery of property in respect of which a forfeiture order could be made under s. 23 of the Terrorism Act 2000 would be hindered;
- the apprehension, prosecution or conviction of a person who is suspected of committing offences under the Terrorism Act 2000 would be made more difficult as a result of his/her being alerted;
- the prevention of an act of terrorism would be made more difficult as a result of the person being alerted;
- the gathering of information about the commission, preparation or instigation of an act of terrorism would be interfered with;
- a person would be interfered with or physically injured;
- the detained person has benefited from his criminal conduct and the recovery of the value of the property constituting the benefit would be hindered if the information were disclosed.

(sch. 8, part III to the Terrorism Act 2000)

Where a warrant is issued which authorises detention beyond a period of 14 days from the time of arrest the detainee must be transferred from detention in a police station to detention in a designated prison as soon as practicable, unless:

(a) the detainee specifically requests to remain in detention at a police station and that request can be accommodated; or
(b) there are reasonable grounds to believe that transferring a person to a prison would:
  (i) significantly hinder a terrorism investigation;
  (ii) delay charging of the detainee or his/her release from custody; or
  (iii) otherwise prevent the investigation from being conducted diligently and expeditiously.

(Code H, para. 14.5)

If any of the grounds in (b)(i)–(iii) are relied upon, these must be presented to the judicial authority as part of the application for the warrant that would extend detention beyond a period of 14 days from the time of arrest. After grounds (b)(i)–(iii) cease to apply, the person must be transferred to a prison as soon as practicable.

**KEYNOTE**

**The Review**

While a person is in police detention before charge, his/her detention must be reviewed by an officer of the rank of inspector or above (inspector reviews). This review acts as another safeguard to protect the detained person's right to be detained for only such periods as are necessary to allow for the investigation of an offence. Reviews of police detention are covered by s. 40 of the Police and Criminal Evidence Act 1984.

Section 40 sets out the times when reviews must be conducted:

(3) Subject to subsection (4) . . .

    (a) the first review shall be not later than six hours after the detention was first authorised;

    (b) the second review shall be not later than nine hours after the first;

    (c) subsequent reviews shall be at intervals of not more than nine hours.

The periods set out in s. 40(3) are the *maximum* periods that a review can be left; should the review officer wish to review before this time for operational reasons, etc. the review could be brought forward. The first review must be made within six hours of the custody officer authorising detention (this, it must be remembered, is not the time from which the 24-hour clock starts, i.e. the time the detainee came into the station, but the time at which the custody officer authorised detention). Thereafter, each review must be made within nine hours of the last review.

Section 40(4)(b) does allow reviews to be delayed if it is not practicable to carry out the review. Conducting late reviews should be avoided where at all possible (see *Roberts* v *Chief Constable of Cheshire Constabulary* [1999] 1 WLR 662).

Review officer for the purposes of ss. 40, 40A and 45A of the 1984 Act means, in the case of a person arrested but not charged, an officer of at least inspector rank not directly involved in the investigation and, if a person has been arrested and charged, the custody officer.

It is suggested that even where a detainee is not in police detention as defined by s. 118 of the 1984 Act, consideration should be given to reviewing his/her detention; this can be conducted by the custody officer. A case that supports this view is *Chief Constable of Cleveland Police* v *McGrogan* [2002] EWCA Civ 86, which involved a person detained at a police station overnight after having been arrested for breach of the peace. The Court of Appeal held that the need regularly to review the person's detention was required even though breach of the peace was not an 'offence' for the purpose of s. 118.

Section 40(4) provides two other occasions where it may be justified to delay the review if at that time:

- the person in detention is being questioned by a police officer and the review officer is satisfied that an interruption of the questioning for the purpose of carrying out the review would prejudice the investigation in connection with which he/she is being questioned (s. 40(4)(b)(i));
- no review officer is readily available (s. 40(4)(b)(ii)).

It is suggested that it will be necessary to justify why no review officer was available and that where it is known that a review may fall during an interview, the review is conducted prior to the interview where appropriate. It is suggested that with the ability to undertake reviews by telephone or video link, a delay to a review is likely to need greater justification.

In *Roberts*, the defendant had his first review conducted 8 hours 20 minutes after his detention had been authorised. The Court of Appeal held that under s. 40(1)(b) of the 1984 Act a review of his detention should have been carried out by an officer of the rank of inspector or above six hours after detention was first authorised. Section 34(1) was mandatory and provided that a person must not be kept in police detention except in accordance with the relevant provisions of the Act. Therefore, the respondent's detention had been unlawful unless some event occurred to have made it lawful. Video conferencing facilities means any facilities (whether a live television link or other facilities) by means of which the review can be carried out with the review officer, the detainee concerned and the detainee's solicitor all being able to both see and hear each other.

The court made it clear that the 1984 Act existed in order to ensure that members of the public were not detained except in certain defined circumstances. In the absence of a review, the time spent in detention between 5.25 am and 7.45 am, meant that for that period the defendant's detention was unlawful and amounted to a false imprisonment. When video conferencing is not required, the use of a telephone to carry out a review of detention before charge is allowed. The procedure under PACE, s. 42 must be done in person.

Section 45A of the 1984 Act allows for pre-charge reviews to be conducted by video-conferencing facilities and provision for video conferencing is included within Code C; however, there are currently no regulations allowing such remote reviews.

Where a review is due under s. 40 and the detainee has not been charged, the review may be carried out by means of a discussion, conducted by telephone, with one or more persons at the police station where the arrested person is held. The provisions of s. 40A of the 1984 Act allowing telephone reviews do not apply to reviews of detention after charge by the custody officer.

If the review is delayed, then it must still be conducted as soon as practicable and the reason for the delay must be recorded in the custody record by the review officer. In these circumstances the nine-hour period until the next review is calculated from the latest time the review should have been carried out and not from the time it was actually carried out. For instance, if the review was due at 3.15 pm and was delayed until 4 pm, the next review would have to be conducted no later than 12.15 am and not 1 am. When the review is conducted the review officer does not have to authorise detention for the full nine-hour period; he/she could decide that the case should be reviewed again within a shorter period and the review decision would reflect this.

When reviewing the detention of a person the review officer goes through the same process as the custody officer did when detention was first authorised (ss. 40(8) and 37(1)–(6)), namely by asking:

- Is there sufficient evidence to charge? If 'yes', charge or release the person with or without bail. If 'no', then:
- Is detention necessary in order to secure or preserve evidence or is it necessary to detain the person in order to obtain such evidence by questioning him/her? If 'yes', authorise continued detention. If 'no', release the person with or without bail.

It is suggested that in order to consider whether there is sufficient evidence to charge, the review officer should have consideration for the Code for Crown Prosecutors and the Threshold Test. The situation may arise where the review officer considers that there is sufficient evidence to charge and only authorises continued detention to charge even though the custody officer disagrees. In this case, it is suggested that the custody officer must either charge or release the person with or without bail in line with s. 37B of the Police and Criminal Evidence Act 1984. Where bailed this may be in order to submit papers to the CPS in order for a decision to be made as to whether to charge and for what offence. There may also be situations where the custody officer has concluded that there is sufficient evidence to charge but the review officer disagrees; in these cases the review officer cannot overrule the custody officer's decision under s. 37(7). In any case where the decision has been made that there is sufficient evidence to charge, the review officer should confirm that the referral has been made, note the custody record to this effect and, thereafter, check to ensure that the decision is made within a *reasonable time*.

It is suggested that the reviewing officer (or any other officer other than a superintendent or above) cannot tell the custody officer what he/she must do. The reviewing officer may wish to give advice but it will be for the custody officer to decide whether to take that advice. Clearly failure to do so could lead to internal criticism, but legally there is no requirement to follow that advice.

If there is not sufficient evidence to charge, the review officer may want to consider the question: 'If this person is bailed, what evidence will be lost?' If the answer is none, continued detention would seem unlawful.

In cases where it has been decided that a person should be charged but he/she has been detained because he/she is not in a fit state to be charged (s. 37(9)), the review officer must determine whether the person is yet in a fit state. If the detainee is in a fit state, the custody officer should be informed that the person should be charged or released. If the detainee is not in a fit state, detention can be authorised for a further period (s. 40(9)). In such cases, if the person is still unfit, it may be prudent to consider his/her welfare.

It is important to understand the difference between the action of authorising an extension to the 'detention clock' and the role of the review officer. These are two distinct roles and both need to be carried out. When an officer of the rank of superintendent or above extends the 'relevant time' period, this is not automatically a review (although there is nothing to stop that officer from conducting the review). This means that the 'reviewing' officer may still have to conduct a review even though the relevant time has only recently been extended, unless the officer of the rank of superintendent or above extending the relevant time has shown the review as having been conducted in the custody record.

**1.6.16.14**

## KEYNOTE

**Terrorism Act Reviews**

In cases where the person has been detained under the Terrorism Act 2000, the first review should be conducted as soon as reasonably practicable after his/her arrest and then at least every 12 hours; after 24 hours it must be conducted by an officer of the rank of superintendent or above. Once a warrant of further detention has been obtained there is no requirement to conduct further reviews. If an officer of higher rank than the review officer gives directions relating to the detained person, and those directions are at variance with the performance by the review officer of a duty imposed on him/her, then he/she must refer the matter at once to an officer of at least the rank of superintendent.

A review officer may only authorise a person's continued detention if he/she is satisfied that it is necessary:

- in order to obtain relevant evidence whether by questioning the person or otherwise;
- to preserve relevant evidence;
- pending a decision whether to apply to the Secretary of State for a deportation notice to be served on the detained person.

A review officer may authorise a person's continued detention if satisfied that detention is necessary:

(a)  to obtain relevant evidence whether by questioning the person or otherwise;

(b)  to preserve relevant evidence;

(c)  while awaiting the result of an examination or analysis of relevant evidence;

(d)  for the examination or analysis of anything with a view to obtaining relevant evidence;

(e)  pending a decision to apply to the Secretary of State for a deportation notice to be served on the detainee, the making of any such application, or the consideration of any such application by the Secretary of State;

(f)  pending a decision to charge the detainee with an offence.

Section 14 of Code H provides guidance on terrorism reviews and extensions of detention. In all cases the review officer must be satisfied that the matter is being dealt with diligently and expeditiously. Where the detained person's rights to a solicitor have been withheld or he/she is being held *incommunicado* at the time of the review, the review officer must consider whether the reason or reasons for which the delay was authorised continue to exist. If in his/her opinion the reason or reasons no longer exist, he/she must inform the officer who authorised the delay of his/her opinion. When recording the grounds for the review the officer must also include his/her conclusion on whether there is a continuing need to withhold the detained person's rights.

In cases where the person is detained under the Terrorism Act 2000 and the review officer does not authorise continued detention, the person does not have to be released if an application for a warrant for further detention is going to be applied for or if an application has been made and the result is pending (s. 41 and sch. 8).

**1.6.17**

## 16 Charging Detained Persons

## (a) Action

16.1  When the officer in charge of the investigation reasonably believes there is sufficient evidence to provide a realistic prospect of conviction for the offence (see *paragraph 11.6*), they shall without delay, and subject to the following qualification, inform the custody officer who will be responsible for considering whether the detainee should be charged. When a person is detained in respect of more than one offence it is permissible to delay informing the custody officer until the above conditions are satisfied in respect of all the offences, but see *paragraph 11.6*. If the detainee is a juvenile, mentally disordered or otherwise mentally vulnerable, any resulting action shall be taken in the presence of the appropriate adult if they are present at the time.

16.1A    Where guidance issued by the Director of Public Prosecutions under PACE, section 37A is in force the custody officer must comply with that Guidance in deciding how to act in dealing with the detainee.

16.1B    Where in compliance with the DPP's Guidance the custody officer decides that the case should be immediately referred to the CPS to make the charging decision, consultation should take place with a Crown Prosecutor as soon as is reasonably practicable. Where the Crown Prosecutor is unable to make the charging decision on the information available at that time, the detainee may be released without charge and on bail (with conditions if necessary) under section 37(7)(a). In such circumstances, the detainee should be informed that they are being released to enable the Director of Public Prosecutions to make a decision under section 37B.

16.2    When a detainee is charged with or informed they may be prosecuted for an offence , they shall, unless the restriction on drawing adverse inferences from silence applies, see *Annex C*, be cautioned as follows:

*'You do not have to say anything. But it may harm your defence if you do not mention now something which you later rely on in court. Anything you do say may be given in evidence.'*

Where the use of the Welsh Language is appropriate, a constable may provide the caution directly in Welsh in the following terms:

*'Does dim rhaid i chi ddweud dim byd. Ond gall niweidio eich amddiffyniad os na fyddwch chi'n sôn, yn awr, am rywbeth y byddwch chi'n dibynnu arno nes ymlaen yn y llys. Gall unrhyw beth yr ydych yn ei ddweud gael ei roi fel tystiolaeth.'*

*Annex C, paragraph 2* sets out the alternative terms of the caution to be used when the restriction on drawing adverse inferences from silence applies.

16.3    When a detainee is charged they shall be given a written notice showing particulars of the offence and, subject to *paragraph 2.6A*, the officer's name and the case reference number. As far as possible the particulars of the charge shall be stated in simple terms, but they shall also show the precise offence in law with which the detainee is charged. The notice shall begin:

*'You are charged with the offence(s) shown below.'* Followed by the caution.

If the detainee is a juvenile, mentally disordered or otherwise mentally vulnerable, a copy of the notice should also be given to the appropriate adult.

16.4    If, after a detainee has been charged with or informed they may be prosecuted for an offence, an officer wants to tell them about any written statement or interview with another person relating to such an offence, the detainee shall either be handed a true copy of the written statement or the content of the interview record brought to their attention. Nothing shall be done to invite any reply or comment except to:

(a)    caution the detainee, '*You do not have to say anything, but anything you do say may be given in evidence.*';

Where the use of the Welsh Language is appropriate, caution the detainee in the following terms:

*Does dim rhaid i chi ddweud dim byd, ond gall unrhyw beth yr ydych yn ei ddweud gael ei roi fel tystiolaeth.*

and

(b)    remind the detainee about their right to legal advice.

16.4A    If the detainee:

- cannot read, the document may be read to them
- is a juvenile, mentally disordered or otherwise mentally vulnerable, the appropriate adult shall also be given a copy, or the interview record shall be brought to their attention.

16.5    A detainee may not be interviewed about an offence after they have been charged with, or informed they may be prosecuted for it, unless the interview is necessary:

- to prevent or minimise harm or loss to some other person, or the public
- to clear up an ambiguity in a previous answer or statement
- in the interests of justice for the detainee to have put to them, and have an opportunity to comment on, information concerning the offence which has come to light since they were charged or informed they might be prosecuted

Before any such interview, the interviewer shall:

(a) caution the detainee, '*You do not have to say anything, but anything you do say may be given in evidence.*'

Where the use of the Welsh Language is appropriate, the interviewer shall caution the detainee: '*Does dim rhaid i chi ddweud dim byd, ond gall unrhyw beth yr ydych yn ei ddweud gael ei roi fel tystiolaeth.*'

(b) remind the detainee about their right to legal advice.

16.6 The provisions of *paragraphs 16.2* to *16.5* must be complied with in the appropriate adult's presence if they are already at the police station. If they are not at the police station then these provisions must be complied with again in their presence when they arrive unless the detainee has been released.

16.7 When a juvenile is charged with an offence and the custody officer authorises their continued detention after charge, the custody officer must make arrangements for the juvenile to be taken into the care of a local authority to be detained pending appearance in court unless the custody officer certifies in accordance with PACE, section 38(6), that:

(a) for any juvenile; it is impracticable to do so; or,

(b) in the case of a juvenile of at least 12 years old, no secure accommodation is available and other accommodation would not be adequate to protect the public from serious harm from that juvenile.

## (b) Documentation

16.8 A record shall be made of anything a detainee says when charged.

16.9 Any questions put in an interview after charge and answers given relating to the offence shall be recorded in full during the interview on forms for that purpose and the record signed by the detainee or, if they refuse, by the interviewer and any third parties present. If the questions are audibly recorded or visually recorded the arrangements in Code E or F apply.

16.10 If arrangements for a juvenile's transfer into local authority care as in *paragraph 16.7* are not made, the custody officer must record the reasons in a certificate which must be produced before the court with the juvenile.

1.6.17.1 **KEYNOTE**

**Charging**

**The Decision Whether or Not to Charge**

Section 37 of the Police and Criminal Evidence Act 1984 states:

(7) Subject to section 41(7) below [expiry of 24 hours after the relevant time], if the custody officer determines that he has before him sufficient evidence to charge the person arrested with the offence for which he was arrested, the person arrested—

(a) shall be—

(i) released without charge and on bail, or

(ii) kept in police detention,

for the purpose of enabling the Director of Public Prosecutions to make a decision under section 37B below,

(b) shall be released without charge and on bail but not for that purpose,

(c) shall be released without charge and without bail, or

(d) shall be charged.

(7A) The decision as to how a person is to be dealt with under subsection (7) above shall be that of the custody officer.

(7B) Where a person is released under subsection (7)(a) above, it shall be the duty of the custody officer to inform him that he is being released or (as the case may be) detained, to enable the Director of Public Prosecutions to make a decision under section 37B below.

(8) Where—

(a) a person is released under subsection (7)(b) or (c) above; and

(b) at the time of his release a decision whether he should be prosecuted for the offence for which he was arrested has not been taken,

it shall be the duty of the custody officer so to inform him/her.

Section 37A of the Police and Criminal Evidence Act 1984 states:

(1) The Director of Public Prosecutions may issue guidance—

(a) for the purpose of enabling custody officers to decide how persons should be dealt with under section 37(7) above or 37(C) or 37CA(2) below, and

(b) as to the information to be sent to the Director of Public Prosecutions under section 37B(1) below.

. . .

(3) Custody officers are to have regard to guidance under this section in deciding how persons should be dealt with under section 37(7) above or 37C(2) or 37CA(2) below.

Unless officers are still investigating other offences for which the person is in police detention, s. 37(7) requires the custody officer to review the evidence in order to determine whether there is sufficient evidence to charge the detained person. When a person is arrested under the provisions of the Criminal Justice Act 2003 which allow a person to be retried after being acquitted of a serious offence, provided a further prosecution has not been precluded by the Court of Appeal, an officer of the rank of superintendent or above who has not been directly involved in the investigation is responsible for determining whether the evidence is sufficient to charge. If the custody officer decides that there is sufficient evidence to charge the detained person that person must be charged or, if not charged, released in relation to that matter, in any of the following ways:

- without charge on bail for the purpose of enabling the DPP to make a decision under s. 37B (in this case the custody officer must inform the person that he/she is being released to enable the DPP to make a decision as to case disposal);
- without charge on bail but not for the case to be referred to the DPP; or
- without charge and without bail (in either of these last two bullet points if at the time of his/her release a decision whether he/she should be prosecuted has not been made it shall be the duty of the custody officer to inform the detained person of this).

Under s. 37A(1) guidance has been issued to enable custody officers to decide whether there is sufficient evidence to charge and for which offences the police may charge without reference to the CPS. Where in accordance with the guidance the case is referred to the CPS for decision, the custody officer should ensure that an officer involved in the investigation sends to the CPS such information as is specified in the guidance.

Charging decisions in cases will be made following a review of evidence and in accordance with the Code for Crown Prosecutors (<http://www.cps.gov.uk/publications/docs/code2013english_v2.pdf>). This requires that the custody officer or Crown Prosecutor making the decision is satisfied that there is enough evidence for there to be a realistic prospect of conviction and that it is in the public interest to prosecute (Full Code Test). In order to allow the matter to have full consideration, often the time needed to consider the matter will require the detained person to be bailed. However, there will clearly be occasions when it will not be desirable to bail the detained person but the evidence required to permit the Full Code Test to be applied is not available. In such a case, the Threshold Test should be applied; this requires there to be reasonable suspicion that the suspect has committed an offence and it is in the public interest to charge that suspect. The evidential considerations include:

- there is insufficient evidence currently available to apply the evidential stage of the Full Code Test; and
- there are reasonable grounds for believing that further evidence will become available within a reasonable period; and
- the seriousness or the circumstances of the case justifies the making of an immediate charging decision; and
- there are continuing substantial grounds to object to bail in accordance with the Bail Act 1976 and in all the circumstances of the case it is proper to do so.

(para. 5.2 of the Code for Crown Prosecutors)

The Code for Crown Prosecutors advises that a prosecution will automatically take place once the evidential stage is met. A prosecution will usually take place unless the prosecutor is satisfied that there are public interest factors tending against prosecution which outweigh those tending in favour (para. 4.8).

Paragraph 12 sets out the public interest factors to be considered. These are:

- How serious is the offence committed?
- What is the level of culpability of the suspect?
- What are the circumstances of and the harm caused to the victim?
- Was the suspect under the age of 18 at the time of the offence?
- What is the impact on the community?
- Is prosecution a proportionate response?
- Do sources of information require protecting?

It is quite possible that one public interest factor alone may outweigh a number of other factors (Code for Crown Prosecutors, para. 4.11).

1.6.17.2    **KEYNOTE**

**Sufficient Evidence to Charge**

Here the custody officer is looking at the evidence in order to satisfy him/herself that no further investigation is needed before the person can be charged. If this is the case, detention may be authorised for the purpose of charging the detained person.

Where Guidance issued by the DPP under s. 37B is in force, a custody officer who determines in accordance with that Guidance that there is sufficient evidence to charge the detainee may detain that person for no longer than is reasonably necessary to decide how that person is to be dealt with under PACE, s. 37(7)(a)–(d), including, where appropriate, consultation with the Duty Prosecutor. The period is subject to the maximum period of detention before charge determined by PACE, ss. 41–44. Where in accordance with the Guidance the case is referred to the CPS for decision, the custody officer should ensure that an officer involved in the investigation sends to the CPS such information as is specified in the Guidance.

Where there is sufficient evidence to charge, a delay in bringing charges may be seen to be unreasonable under Article 6 of the European Convention on Human Rights (*D* v *HM Advocate* [2000] HRLR 389). In deciding whether there is sufficient evidence to charge for the purposes of authorising detention or when a person's detention is reviewed, where there is a conflict between the detained person's account and victims' or witnesses' accounts it is reasonable to be in possession of at least one witness statement in the English language before preferring charges (*R (On the Application of Wiles)* v *Chief Constable of Hertfordshire* [2002] EWHC 387 (Admin)). There is no breach of PACE in keeping the detained person in police detention while a statement is translated. It is suggested that the translation needs to be completed expeditiously.

A detained person should not be kept in custody just for the sole purpose of seeking advice from the CPS as to what offences the offender should be charged with (*R (On the Application of G)* v *Chief Constable of West Yorkshire Police and DPP* [2008] EWCA Civ 28).

There is no power under PACE to detain a person and delay action under paras 16.2 to 16.5 solely to await the arrival of the appropriate adult. Reasonable efforts should therefore be made to give the appropriate adult sufficient notice of the time the decision (charge etc.) is to be implemented so that he/she can be present. If the appropriate adult is not, or cannot be, present at that time, the detainee should be released on bail to return for the decision to be implemented when the adult is present, unless the custody officer determines that the absence of the appropriate adult makes the detainee unsuitable for bail for this purpose. After charge, bail cannot be refused, or release on bail delayed, simply because an appropriate adult is not available, unless the absence of that adult provides the custody officer with the necessary grounds to authorise detention after charge under s. 38 of the 1984 Act.

Except as in para. 16.7, neither a juvenile's behaviour nor the nature of the offence provides grounds for the custody officer to decide it is impracticable to arrange the juvenile's transfer to local authority care. Impracticability concerns the transport and travel requirements, and the lack of secure accommodation which is provided for the purposes of restricting liberty does not make it impracticable to transfer the juvenile. The availability of secure accommodation is only a factor in relation to a juvenile aged 12 or over when other local authority accommodation would not be adequate to protect the public from serious harm from the juvenile. The obligation to transfer a juvenile to local authority accommodation applies as much to a juvenile charged during the daytime as to a juvenile to be held overnight, subject to a requirement to bring the juvenile before a court under s. 46 of the 1984 Act.

Under s. 37(9) of the 1984 Act release can be delayed if the person is not in a fit state to be released (e.g. he/she is drunk), until he/she is fit.

**1.6.17.3**   **KEYNOTE**

**Insufficient Evidence to Charge**

This creates two separate criteria for detention, that is to say, where detention is necessary to:

- secure and preserve evidence relating to an offence for which the person is arrested; or
- obtain such evidence by questioning the detained person.

If the custody officer has determined that there is not sufficient evidence to charge the person, the person must be released unless the custody officer has *reasonable grounds* for believing that the person's detention is necessary to preserve or obtain such evidence by questioning the person and the custody officer must be able to justify any decision not to release a person from detention.

When deciding if detention should be authorised in order to obtain evidence by questioning, the case of *R* v *McGuinness* [1999] Crim LR 318 should be considered. There the court held that the words 'sufficient evidence to prosecute' and 'sufficient evidence for a prosecution to succeed', in Code C, para. 16.1 (this was the wording under the previous PACE Code of Practice), had to involve some consideration of any explanation, or lack of one, from the suspect. While an interview may not be needed in all cases, questioning of detained people before they are charged may be necessary, particularly where intention or dishonesty is involved or where there may be a defence. It may also be important to put questions to the person about the offence or his/her explanation, as this may be important to negate any defence the person raises at court (see s. 34 of the Criminal Justice and Public Order Act 1994).

Where initial suspicion rests on several people, it may be appropriate to hold all suspects until they all are interviewed before deciding whether there is enough evidence to warrant a charge against any of them. Detention for questioning where there are reasonable grounds for suspecting that an offence has been committed is lawful so long as the suspicion has not been dispelled in the interim and the questioning is not unnecessarily delayed (*Clarke* v *Chief Constable of North Wales* [2000] Po LR 83).

The mere fact that a person needs to be interviewed about the offence is not of itself justification for authorising detention. The question that has to be asked is whether the person can be bailed prior to the interview or even bailed before being taken to the police station (s. 30A of the 1984 Act). Factors which might be relevant in making this decision include:

- whether the person may interfere with witnesses;
- whether he/she is likely to return if bailed;
- where there is more than one suspect, that they would have an opportunity to confer before their interviews;
- whether there is outstanding property;
- whether the person's name and address are verified.

The fact that the officers and any legal representative will be ready to start the interview shortly may also be relevant when making this decision.

**1.6.17.4**  **KEYNOTE**

**Cases where the Detained Person is Bailed to Allow Consultation with the CPS**

Section 37B of the Police and Criminal Evidence Act 1984 states:

(1)  Where a person is dealt with under section 37(7)(a) above, an officer involved in the investigation of the offence shall, as soon as is practicable, send to the Director of Public Prosecutions such information as may be specified in guidance under section 37A above.

(2)  The Director of Public Prosecutions shall decide whether there is sufficient evidence to charge the person with an offence.

(3)  If he decides that there is sufficient evidence to charge the person with an offence, he shall decide—

    (a)  whether or not the person should be charged and, if so, the offence with which he should be charged, and

    (b)  whether or not the person should be given a caution and, if so, the offence in respect of which he should be given a caution.

(4)  The Director of Public Prosecutions shall give notice of his decision to an officer involved in the investigation of the offence.

(4A)  Notice under subsection (4) above shall be in writing, but in the case of a person kept in police detention under section 37(7)(a) above it may be given orally in the first instance and confirmed in writing subsequently.

(5)  If his decision is—

    (a)  that there is not sufficient evidence to charge the person with an offence, or

    (b)  that there is sufficient evidence to charge the person with an offence but that the person should not be charged with an offence or given a caution in respect of an offence,

    a custody officer shall give the person notice in writing that he is not to be prosecuted.

Where a person has been bailed under s. 37(7)(a) with or without bail conditions, the CPS must be consulted in order to determine what case disposal decision will be made (this may itself require further inquiries to gather further evidence). This referral should be made using forms MG3 (Report to Crown Prosecutor for a Charging Decision), and MG3A (Further Report to Crown Prosecutor for a Charging Decision). The pre-charge advice file can be a pre-charge expedited report (straightforward and guilty plea cases) or a pre-charge evidential report (contested/Crown Court cases) and must also include other relevant information, including:

Pre-charge Expedited Report

- MG3;
- MG11(s)—Witness statement or Index notes (if offence is witnessed by more than one officer and up to four, use the statement of one officer and summarise the others);
- MG15—Record of interview;
- Phoenix print of suspect(s)' previous convictions/cautions/reprimands/final warnings. If there is any other information that may be relevant, include it on form MG6—Case File Information.

Pre-charge Evidential Report

- MG3;
- MG5—Case summary (unless the statements cover all elements of the case);
- MG6—Case file information;
- MG11—Key witness statement(s), or Index notes (if offence is witnessed by police use the statement of one officer and summarise the others);
- MG12—Exhibit list;
- MG15—Interview record;
- Crime report and incident log;
- Unused material likely to undermine the case;
- Copies of key documentary exhibits;
- Phoenix print of suspect(s)' pre-cons/cautions/reprimands/final warnings.

The prosecutor will decide whether there is sufficient evidence to charge or caution the person and shall give written notice of the decision to an officer involved in the investigation of the details of the offence. This decision must be followed (s. 37B(6)) if the decision was for the person to be cautioned (this includes conditional cautions), and if the person refuses, or for some other reason a caution cannot be given, he/she must be charged with the offence (s. 37B(7)).

In cases where the prosecutor decides that there is not sufficient evidence to charge the person with an offence, or that there is sufficient evidence to charge the person with an offence but that the person should not be charged with an offence or given a caution in respect of an offence, the custody officer must inform the person in writing of the decision. Similarly the person must be informed of those cases where there is insufficient evidence to charge him/her, but if further evidence or information comes to light in the future the case may be reconsidered under the Code for Crown Prosecutors.

In cases where further time is needed to obtain evidence or for the prosecutor to make a case disposal decision, the person can be further bailed. In these cases the custody officer must give the person notice in writing. This does not affect any bail conditions that were included when the detained person was bailed (s. 37D(1)–(3)).

---

**1.6.17.5**  **KEYNOTE**

### Bail to Allow Referral to the CPS

Section 47 of the Police and Criminal Evidence Act 1984 states:

> (1A)  The normal powers to impose conditions of bail shall be available to him where a custody officer releases a person on bail under section 37 above or section 38(1) above (including that subsection as applied by section 40(10) above) but not in any other cases.

In this subsection, 'the normal powers to impose conditions of bail' has the meaning given in s. 3(6) of the Bail Act 1976.

Where the person is bailed after charge or bailed without charge and on bail for the purpose of enabling the CPS to make a decision regarding case disposal, the custody officer may impose conditions on that bail (**see para. 1.9.7**). In cases where a person is bailed without being charged under s. 37(7)(b) or (c), that is to say bail is not given for the purposes of a CPS referral, the custody officer cannot impose conditions on that bail (s. 47(1A)).

---

**1.6.17.6**  **KEYNOTE**

### Cautioning, Reprimands and Final Warnings and Conditional Cautioning

In considering whether to charge a detained person the custody officer must take into account alternatives to prosecution under the Crime and Disorder Act 1998, reprimands and warning applicable to persons under 18, and national guidance on the cautioning of offenders, for persons aged 18 and over.

---

**1.6.17.7**  **KEYNOTE**

### Police Caution

There are occasions where a person for whom there is sufficient evidence to charge may be cautioned as an alternative method of disposing with the case. *R v Chief Constable of Lancashire Constabulary, ex parte Atkinson* (1998) 162 JP 275 is a case which considered the level of evidence required before a caution can be considered. There the court said that, provided it was clear that there had been an admission of guilt, it was not necessary, for the purposes of administering a caution, to show that the admission had been obtained in circumstances which satisfied the Codes of Practice. That was not to say that police authorities would not be well advised to take precautions which would satisfy the Code, but it did not follow that in every case there had to be a formal interview. However, police officers would be well advised to take precautions that would satisfy Code C. It would be both fairer and more reliable for a formal interview to take place.

Before making a case disposal decision it is essential that the matter has been fully investigated in order to reach an informed decision. In *Omar* v *Chief Constable of Bedfordshire Constabulary* [2002] EWHC 3060 (Admin), the Divisional Court quashed a caution that had been administered in order to allow a prosecution to be pursued. The court held that a number of reasonable lines of inquiry had not been made; for instance, the police had failed to take a statement from the victim's friend or obtain CCTV footage that was available or fully investigate the victim's injuries. Further, the length of time in custody (17 hours) should not have been a relevant consideration and also the suspect's admission was ambiguous. Therefore, it was in the public interest that a decision to caution rather than to charge should not prevent the subsequent pursuit of the prosecution of the offender.

While there is no general obligation on the police to disclose material prior to charge, there may be a need to make some disclosure to a suspect's legal representative in order that he/she can advise on whether a caution should be accepted (*DPP* v *Ara* [2001] EWHC Admin 493). In *Ara*, the suspect had been interviewed without a legal representative being present but the officers refused to disclose the terms of the interview.

Guidance as to the use of cautioning is provided by Home Office Circular 16/2008, *Simple Cautioning of Adult Offenders*. The guidelines should be considered carefully in all cases as any decision can be challenged by judicial review.

In cases where the case has been referred to the CPS under s. 37B of the 1984 Act and a decision has been made that the suspect should receive a caution, an officer involved in the investigation of the offence will be informed in writing. The notification will include the offence in respect of which a caution should be administered. If it is not possible to give the suspect such a caution then he/she must be charged with the offence (s. 37B(7)).

---

**1.6.17.8**    **KEYNOTE**

**Reprimands and Warnings**

Sections 65 and 66 of the Crime and Disorder Act 1998 made provisions for reprimands and warnings for children and young persons (**see chapter 2.5**) which the custody officer must take into account as alternatives to prosecution.

It should be noted that while the *Final Warning Scheme: Guidance for the Police and Youth Offending Teams* indicates when a final warning should be given, the case of *R (On the Application of A)* v *(1) South Yorkshire Police (2) CPS* [2007] EWHC 1261 (Admin) acknowledges that where there are aggravating factors, in exceptional circumstances it may justify the person's being charged. *M* v *Leicester Constabulary* [2009] EWHC 3640 (Admin) emphasises the need for a clear and unambiguous admission of guilt. The court stated that for a warning to be imposed, the evidence had to meet the required standard, namely that it was reliable and that the alleged offence was more likely than not to have happened.

There is only one exception to the rule that reprimands and warnings replace cautions, and that is in respect of prostitutes' cautions. This approach to dealing with child prostitutes recognises that they are victims of abuse, and do not consent freely to prostitution. Joint guidance issued by the Home Office and the Department of Health sets out the appropriate way to deal with children in prostitution. That treatment aims to divert children away from prostitution, rather than to prosecute them.

---

**1.6.17.9**    **KEYNOTE**

**Conditional Cautioning**

Sections 22–27 of the Criminal Justice Act 2003 introduced conditional cautioning, the aim being to deal with offenders without the involvement of the usual court processes.

Section 24A of the Criminal Justice Act 2003 allows a constable to arrest without warrant any person who the officer has reasonable grounds for believing has failed, without reasonable excuse, to comply with any of the conditions attached to the conditional caution. Certain provisions of the Police and Criminal Evidence Act 1984 relating to detention, reviews, searches, and searches and examinations to ascertain identity apply, with modifications, to a person arrested under s. 24A of the Criminal Justice Act 2003.

**1.6.18**

## 17 Testing Persons for the Presence of Specified Class A Drugs

### (a) Action

17.1   This section of Code C applies only in selected police stations in police areas where the provisions for drug testing under section 63B of PACE (as amended by section 5 of the Criminal Justice Act 2003 and section 7 of the Drugs Act 2005) are in force and in respect of which the Secretary of State has given a notification to the relevant chief officer of police that arrangements for the taking of samples have been made. Such a notification will cover either a police area as a whole or particular stations within a police area. The notification indicates whether the testing applies to those arrested or charged or under the age of 18 as the case may be and testing can only take place in respect of the persons so indicated in the notification. Testing cannot be carried out unless the relevant notification has been given and has not been withdrawn.

17.2   A sample of urine or a non-intimate sample may be taken from a person in police detention for the purpose of ascertaining whether they have any specified Class A drug in their body only where they have been brought before the custody officer and:

(a)   either the arrest condition, see *paragraph 17.3*, or the charge condition, see *paragraph 17.4* is met;

(b)   the age condition, see *paragraph 17.5*, is met;

(c)   the notification condition is met in relation to the arrest condition, the charge condition, or the age condition, as the case may be. (Testing on charge and/or arrest must be specifically provided for in the notification for the power to apply. In addition, the fact that testing of under 18s is authorised must be expressly provided for in the notification before the power to test such persons applies.). See *paragraph 17.1*; and

(d)   a police officer has requested the person concerned to give the sample (the request condition).

17.3   The arrest condition is met where the detainee:

(a)   has been arrested for a trigger offence, but not charged with that offence; or

(b)   has been arrested for any other offence but not charged with that offence and a police officer of inspector rank or above, who has reasonable grounds for suspecting that their misuse of any specified Class A drug caused or contributed to the offence, has authorised the sample to be taken.

17.4   The charge condition is met where the detainee:

(a)   has been charged with a trigger offence, or

(b)   has been charged with any other offence and a police officer of inspector rank or above, who has reasonable grounds for suspecting that the detainee's misuse of any specified Class A drug caused or contributed to the offence, has authorised the sample to be taken.

17.5   The age condition is met where:

(a)   in the case of a detainee who has been arrested but not charged as in *paragraph 17.3*, they are aged 18 or over;

(b)   in the case of a detainee who has been charged as in *paragraph 17.4*, they are aged 14 or over.

17.6    Before requesting a sample from the person concerned, an officer must:
   (a) inform them that the purpose of taking the sample is for drug testing under PACE. This is to ascertain whether they have a specified Class A drug present in their body;
   (b) warn them that if, when so requested, they fail without good cause to provide a sample they may be liable to prosecution;
   (c) where the taking of the sample has been authorised by an inspector or above in accordance with *paragraph 17.3(b)* or *17.4(b)* above, inform them that the authorisation has been given and the grounds for giving it;
   (d) remind them of the following rights, which may be exercised at any stage during the period in custody:
      (i)   the right to have someone informed of their arrest [see section 5];
      (ii)  the right to consult privately with a solicitor and that free independent legal advice is available [see section 6]; and
      (iii) the right to consult these Codes of Practice [see section 3].
17.7    In the case of a person who has not attained the age of 17 —
   (a) the making of the request for a sample under *paragraph 17.2(d)* above;
   (b) the giving of the warning and the information under *paragraph 17.6* above; and
   (c) the taking of the sample,
   may not take place except in the presence of an appropriate adult.
17.8    Authorisation by an officer of the rank of inspector or above within *paragraph 17.3(b)* or *17.4(b)* may be given orally or in writing but, if it is given orally, it must be confirmed in writing as soon as practicable.
17.9    If a sample is taken from a detainee who has been arrested for an offence but not charged with that offence as in *paragraph 17.3*, no further sample may be taken during the same continuous period of detention. If during that same period the charge condition is also met in respect of that detainee, the sample which has been taken shall be treated as being taken by virtue of the charge condition, see *paragraph 17.4*, being met.
17.10   A detainee from whom a sample may be taken may be detained for up to six hours from the time of charge if the custody officer reasonably believes the detention is necessary to enable a sample to be taken. Where the arrest condition is met, a detainee whom the custody officer has decided to release on bail without charge may continue to be detained, but not beyond 24 hours from the relevant time (as defined in section 41(2) of PACE), to enable a sample to be taken.
17.11   A detainee in respect of whom the arrest condition is met, but not the charge condition, see *paragraphs 17.3* and *17.4*, and whose release would be required before a sample can be taken had they not continued to be detained as a result of being arrested for a further offence which does not satisfy the arrest condition, may have a sample taken at any time within 24 hours after the arrest for the offence that satisfies the arrest condition.

## (b) Documentation

17.12   The following must be recorded in the custody record:
   (a) if a sample is taken following authorisation by an officer of the rank of inspector or above, the authorisation and the grounds for suspicion;
   (b) the giving of a warning of the consequences of failure to provide a sample;
   (c) the time at which the sample was given; and
   (d) the time of charge or, where the arrest condition is being relied upon, the time of arrest and, where applicable, the fact that a sample taken after arrest but before charge is to be treated as being taken by virtue of the charge condition, where that is met in the same period of continuous detention. See *paragraph 17.9*.

## (c) General

17.13 A sample may only be taken by a prescribed person.

17.14 Force may not be used to take any sample for the purpose of drug testing.

17.15 The terms 'Class A drug' and 'misuse' have the same meanings as in the Misuse of Drugs Act 1971. 'Specified' (in relation to a Class A drug) and 'trigger offence' have the same meanings as in Part III of the Criminal Justice and Court Services Act 2000.

17.16 Any sample taken:
    (a) may not be used for any purpose other than to ascertain whether the person concerned has a specified Class A drug present in his body; and
    (b) can be disposed of as clinical waste unless it is to be sent for further analysis in cases where the test result is disputed at the point when the result is known, including on the basis that medication has been taken, or for quality assurance purposes.

## (d) Assessment of misuse of drugs

17.17 Under the provisions of Part 3 of the Drugs Act 2005, where a detainee has tested positive for a specified Class A drug under section 63B of PACE a police officer may, at any time before the person's release from the police station, impose a requirement on the detainee to attend an initial assessment of their drug misuse by a suitably qualified person and to remain for its duration. Where such a requirement is imposed, the officer must, at the same time, impose a second requirement on the detainee to attend and remain for a follow-up assessment. The officer must inform the detainee that the second requirement will cease to have effect if, at the initial assessment they are informed that a follow-up assessment is not necessary. These requirements may only be imposed on a person if:
    (a) they have reached the age of 18
    (b) notification has been given by the Secretary of State to the relevant chief officer of police that arrangements for conducting initial and follow-up assessments have been made for those from whom samples for testing have been taken at the police station where the detainee is in custody.

17.18 When imposing a requirement to attend an initial assessment and a follow-up assessment the police officer must:
    (a) inform the person of the time and place at which the initial assessment is to take place;
    (b) explain that this information will be confirmed in writing; and
    (c) warn the person that they may be liable to prosecution if they fail without good cause to attend the initial assessment and remain for it's duration and if they fail to attend the follow-up assessment and remain for its duration (if so required).

17.19 Where a police officer has imposed a requirement to attend an initial assessment and a follow-up assessment in accordance with *paragraph 17.17*, he must, before the person is released from detention, give the person notice in writing which:
    (a) confirms their requirement to attend and remain for the duration of the assessments; and
    (b) confirms the information and repeats the warning referred to in *paragraph 17.18*.

17.20 The following must be recorded in the custody record:
    (a) that the requirement to attend an initial assessment and a follow-up assessment has been imposed; and
    (b) the information, explanation, warning and notice given in accordance with *paragraphs 17.17* and *17.19*.

17.21 Where a notice is given in accordance with *paragraph 17.19*, a police officer can give the person a further notice in writing which informs the person of any change to the time or place at which the initial assessment is to take place and which repeats the warning referred to in *paragraph 17.18(c)*.

17.22 Part 3 of the Drugs Act 2005 also requires police officers to have regard to any guidance issued by the Secretary of State in respect of the assessment provisions.

**1.6.18.1**

**KEYNOTE**

The power to take samples is subject to notification by the Secretary of State that appropriate arrangements for the taking of samples have been made for the police area as a whole or for the particular police station concerned for whichever of the following is specified in the notification: persons in respect of whom the arrest condition is met; persons in respect of whom the charge condition is met; and/or persons who have not attained the age of 18.

A sample has to be sufficient and suitable. A sufficient sample is sufficient in quantity and quality to enable drug-testing analysis to take place. A suitable sample is one which by its nature is suitable for a particular form of drug analysis. It can only be taken by a prescribed person as defined in regulations made by the Secretary of State under s. 63B(6) of the Police and Criminal Evidence Act 1984. The regulations are currently contained in the Police and Criminal Evidence Act 1984 (Drug Testing Persons in Police Detention) (Prescribed Persons) Regulations 2001 (SI 2001/2645). Samples, and the information derived from them, may not subsequently be used in the investigation of any offence or in evidence against the persons from whom they were taken.

When warning a person who is asked to provide a urine or non-intimate sample in accordance with para. 17.6(b), the following form of words may be used:

You do not have to provide a sample, but I must warn you that if you fail or refuse without good cause to do so, you will commit an offence for which you may be imprisoned, or fined, or both.

Where the Welsh language is appropriate, the following form of words may be used:

Does dim rhaid i chi roi sampl, ond mae'n rhaid i mi eich rhybuddio y byddwch chi'n cyflawni trosedd os byddwch chi'n methu neu yn gwrthod gwneud hynny heb reswm da, ac y gellir, oherwydd hynny, eich carcharu, eich dirwyo, neu'r ddau.

The trigger offences referred to in the section are:

1. Offences under the following provisions of the Theft Act 1968:

| | |
|---|---|
| section 1 | (theft) |
| section 8 | (robbery) |
| section 9 | (burglary) |
| section 10 | (aggravated burglary) |
| section 12 | (taking a motor vehicle or other conveyance without authority) |
| section 12A | (aggravated vehicle-taking) |
| section 22 | (handling stolen goods) |
| section 25 | (going equipped for stealing, etc.) |

2. Offences under the following provisions of the Misuse of Drugs Act 1971, if committed in respect of a specified Class A drug:

| | |
|---|---|
| section 4 | (restriction on production and supply of controlled drugs) |
| section 5(2) | (possession of a controlled drug) |
| section 5(3) | (possession of a controlled drug with intent to supply) |

3. Offences under the following provisions of the Fraud Act 2006:

| | |
|---|---|
| section 1 | (fraud) |
| section 6 | (possession, etc. of articles for use in frauds) |
| section 7 | (making or supplying articles for use in frauds) |

3A. An offence under s. 1(1) of the Criminal Attempts Act 1981 if committed in respect of an offence under:
   (a) any of the following provisions of the Theft Act 1968:

| | |
|---|---|
| section 1 | (theft) |
| section 8 | (robbery) |
| section 9 | (burglary) |
| section 22 | (handling stolen goods) |

(b) s. 1 of the Fraud Act 2006 (fraud)

4. Offences under the following provisions of the Vagrancy Act 1824:

| | |
|---|---|
| section 3 | (begging) |
| section 4 | (persistent begging) |

For the purposes of needing the presence of an appropriate adult for Code C, para. 17.7, an appropriate adult in para. 17.7 means the person's:

(a) parent or guardian or, if he/she is in the care of a local authority or voluntary organisation, a person representing that authority or organisation; or

(b) a social worker of a local authority; or

(c) if no person falling within (a) or (b) above is available, any responsible person aged 18 or over who is not a police officer or a person employed by the police.

## 1.6.19 Annex A—Intimate and Strip Searches

### A Intimate search

1. An intimate search consists of the physical examination of a person's body orifices other than the mouth. The intrusive nature of such searches means the actual and potential risks associated with intimate searches must never be underestimated.

### (a) Action

2. Body orifices other than the mouth may be searched only:
   (a) if authorised by an officer of inspector rank or above who has reasonable grounds for believing that the person may have concealed on themselves:
      (i) anything which they could and might use to cause physical injury to themselves or others at the station; or
      (ii) a Class A drug which they intended to supply to another or to export; and the officer has reasonable grounds for believing that an intimate search is the only means of removing those items; and
   (b) if the search is under *paragraph 2(a)(ii)* (a drug offence search), the detainee's appropriate consent has been given in writing.

2A. Before the search begins, a police officer or designated detention officer, must tell the detainee:
   (a) that the authority to carry out the search has been given;
   (b) the grounds for giving the authorisation and for believing that the article cannot be removed without an intimate search.

2B. Before a detainee is asked to give appropriate consent to a search under *paragraph 2(a)(ii)* (a drug offence search) they must be warned that if they refuse without good cause their refusal may harm their case if it comes to trial. This warning may be given by a police officer or member of police staff. In the case of juveniles, mentally vulnerable or mentally disordered suspects the seeking and giving of consent must take place in the presence of the appropriate adult. A juvenile's consent is only valid if their parent's or guardian's consent is also obtained unless the juvenile is under 14, when their parent's or guardian's consent is sufficient in its own right. A detainee who is not legally represented must be reminded of their entitlement to have free legal advice, see Code C, *paragraph 6.5*, and the reminder noted in the custody record.

3. An intimate search may only be carried out by a registered medical practitioner or registered nurse, unless an officer of at least inspector rank considers this is not practicable and the search is to take place under *paragraph 2(a)(i)*, in which case a police officer may carry out the search.

3A. Any proposal for a search under *paragraph 2(a)(i)* to be carried out by someone other than a registered medical practitioner or registered nurse must only be considered as a last resort and when the authorising officer is satisfied the risks associated with allowing the item to remain with the detainee outweigh the risks associated with removing it.

4. An intimate search under:
   - *paragraph 2(a)(i)* may take place only at a hospital, surgery, other medical premises or
   - *paragraph 2(a)(ii)* may take place only at a hospital, surgery or other medical premises and must be carried out by a registered medical practitioner or a registered nurse.

5. An intimate search at a police station of a juvenile or mentally disordered or otherwise mentally vulnerable person may take place only in the presence of an appropriate adult of the same sex (see *Annex L*), unless the detainee specifically requests a particular adult of the opposite sex who is readily available. In the case of a juvenile the search may take place in the absence of the appropriate adult only if the juvenile signifies in the presence of the appropriate adult they do not want the adult present during the search and the adult agrees. A record shall be made of the juvenile's decision and signed by the appropriate adult.

6. When an intimate search under *paragraph 2(a)(i)* is carried out by a police officer, the officer must be of the same sex as the detainee (see *Annex L*). A minimum of two people, other than the detainee, must be present during the search. Subject to *paragraph 5*, no person of the opposite sex who is not a medical practitioner or nurse shall be present, nor shall anyone whose presence is unnecessary. The search shall be conducted with proper regard to the sensitivity and vulnerability of the detainee.

## (b) Documentation

7. In the case of an intimate search, the following shall be recorded as soon as practicable, in the detainee's custody record:
   (a) for searches under paragraphs 2(a)(i) and (ii);
      - the authorisation to carry out the search;
      - the grounds for giving the authorisation;
      - the grounds for believing the article could not be removed without an intimate search;
      - which parts of the detainee's body were searched;
      - who carried out the search;
      - who was present;
      - the result.
   (b) for searches under paragraph 2(a)(ii):
      - the giving of the warning required by *paragraph 2B*;
      - the fact that the appropriate consent was given or (as the case may be) refused, and if refused, the reason given for the refusal (if any).

8. If an intimate search is carried out by a police officer, the reason why it was impracticable for a registered medical practitioner or registered nurse to conduct it must be recorded.

## B  Strip search

9.	A strip search is a search involving the removal of more than outer clothing. In this Code, outer clothing includes shoes and socks.

## (a)  Action

10.	A strip search may take place only if it is considered necessary to remove an article which a detainee would not be allowed to keep, and the officer reasonably considers the detainee might have concealed such an article. Strip searches shall not be routinely carried out if there is no reason to consider that articles are concealed.

## The conduct of strip searches

11.	When strip searches are conducted:
	(a)	a police officer carrying out a strip search must be the same sex as the detainee (see *Annex L*);
	(b)	the search shall take place in an area where the detainee cannot be seen by anyone who does not need to be present, nor by a member of the opposite sex (see *Annex L*) except an appropriate adult who has been specifically requested by the detainee;
	(c)	except in cases of urgency, where there is risk of serious harm to the detainee or to others, whenever a strip search involves exposure of intimate body parts, there must be at least two people present other than the detainee, and if the search is of a juvenile or mentally disordered or otherwise mentally vulnerable person, one of the people must be the appropriate adult. Except in urgent cases as above, a search of a juvenile may take place in the absence of the appropriate adult only if the juvenile signifies in the presence of the appropriate adult that they do not want the adult to be present during the search and the adult agrees. A record shall be made of the juvenile's decision and signed by the appropriate adult. The presence of more than two people, other than an appropriate adult, shall be permitted only in the most exceptional circumstances;
	(d)	the search shall be conducted with proper regard to the sensitivity and vulnerability of the detainee in these circumstances and every reasonable effort shall be made to secure the detainee's co-operation and minimise embarrassment. Detainees who are searched shall not normally be required to remove all their clothes at the same time, e.g. a person should be allowed to remove clothing above the waist and redress before removing further clothing;
	(e)	if necessary to assist the search, the detainee may be required to hold their arms in the air or to stand with their legs apart and bend forward so a visual examination may be made of the genital and anal areas provided no physical contact is made with any body orifice;
	(f)	if articles are found, the detainee shall be asked to hand them over. If articles are found within any body orifice other than the mouth, and the detainee refuses to hand them over, their removal would constitute an intimate search, which must be carried out as in *Part A*;
	(g)	a strip search shall be conducted as quickly as possible, and the detainee allowed to dress as soon as the procedure is complete.

## (b)  Documentation

12.	A record shall be made on the custody record of a strip search including the reason it was considered necessary, those present and any result.

**1.6.19.1**

**KEYNOTE**

Before authorising any intimate search, the authorising officer must make every reasonable effort to persuade the detainee to hand the article over without a search. If the detainee agrees, a registered medical practitioner or registered nurse should whenever possible be asked to assess the risks involved and, if necessary, attend to assist the detainee.

If the detainee does not agree to hand the article over without a search, the authorising officer must carefully review all the relevant factors before authorising an intimate search. In particular, the officer must consider whether the grounds for believing that an article may be concealed are reasonable.

If authority is given for a search for anything which the detained person could and might use to cause physical injury to him/herself or others at the station, a registered medical practitioner or registered nurse shall be consulted whenever possible. The presumption should be that the search will be conducted by the registered medical practitioner or registered nurse and the authorising officer must make every reasonable effort to persuade the detainee to allow the medical practitioner or nurse to conduct the search. A constable should only be authorised to carry out a search as a last resort and when all other approaches have failed. In these circumstances, the authorising officer must be satisfied that the detainee might use the article to cause physical injury to him/herself and/or others at the station and the physical injury likely to be caused is sufficiently severe to justify authorising a constable to carry out the search. If an officer has any doubts whether to authorise an intimate search by a constable, the officer should seek advice from an officer of superintendent rank or above. Annex L should be referred to for guidance when establishing the gender of persons for the purpose of searching.

The following form of words should be used when asking a detained person to consent to an intimate drug offence search:

> You do not have to allow yourself to be searched, but I must warn you that if you refuse without good cause, your refusal may harm your case if it comes to trial.

Where the use of the Welsh language is appropriate, the following form of words may be used:

> Nid oes rhaid i chi roi caniatâd i gael eich archwilio, ond mae'n rhaid i mi eich rhybuddio os gwrthodwch heb reswm da, y gallai eich penderfyniad i wrthod wneud niwed i'ch achos pe bai'n dod gerbron llys.

**1.6.20**

## Annex B—Delay in Notifying Arrest or Allowing Access to Legal Advice

### A  Persons detained under PACE

1.  The exercise of the rights in *Section 5* or *Section 6*, or both, may be delayed if the person is in police detention, as in PACE, section 118(2), in connection with an indictable offence, has not yet been charged with an offence and an officer of superintendent rank or above, or inspector rank or above only for the rights in Section 5, has reasonable grounds for believing their exercise will:
    (i)  lead to:
        • interference with, or harm to, evidence connected with an indictable offence; or
        • interference with, or physical harm to, other people; or
    (ii)  lead to alerting other people suspected of having committed an indictable offence but not yet arrested for it; or
    (iii)  hinder the recovery of property obtained in consequence of the commission of such an offence.
2.  These rights may also be delayed if the officer has reasonable grounds to believe that:
    (i)  the person detained for an indictable offence has benefited from their criminal conduct (decided in accordance with Part 2 of the Proceeds of Crime Act 2002); and
    (ii)  the recovery of the value of the property constituting that benefit will be hindered by the exercise of either right.

3. Authority to delay a detainee's right to consult privately with a solicitor may be given only if the authorising officer has reasonable grounds to believe the solicitor the detainee wants to consult will, inadvertently or otherwise, pass on a message from the detainee or act in some other way which will have any of the consequences specified under *paragraphs 1* or *2*. In these circumstances the detainee must be allowed to choose another solicitor.

4. If the detainee wishes to see a solicitor, access to that solicitor may not be delayed on the grounds they might advise the detainee not to answer questions or the solicitor was initially asked to attend the police station by someone else. In the latter case the detainee must be told the solicitor has come to the police station at another person's request, and must be asked to sign the custody record to signify whether they want to see the solicitor.

5. The fact the grounds for delaying notification of arrest may be satisfied does not automatically mean the grounds for delaying access to legal advice will also be satisfied.

6. These rights may be delayed only for as long as grounds exist and in no case beyond 36 hours after the relevant time as in PACE, section 41. If the grounds cease to apply within this time, the detainee must, as soon as practicable, be asked if they want to exercise either right, the custody record must be noted accordingly, and action taken in accordance with the relevant section of the Code.

7. A detained person must be permitted to consult a solicitor for a reasonable time before any court hearing.

## B  Not used

## C  Documentation

13. The grounds for action under this Annex shall be recorded and the detainee informed of them as soon as practicable.

14. Any reply given by a detainee under *paragraphs 6* or *11* must be recorded and the detainee asked to endorse the record in relation to whether they want to receive legal advice at this point.

## D  Cautions and special warnings

15. When a suspect detained at a police station is interviewed during any period for which access to legal advice has been delayed under this Annex, the court or jury may not draw adverse inferences from their silence.

1.6.20.1

**KEYNOTE**

Even if Annex B applies in the case of a juvenile, or a person who is mentally disordered or otherwise mentally vulnerable, action to inform the appropriate adult and the person responsible for a juvenile's welfare if that is a different person, must nevertheless be taken as in paras 3.13 and 3.15. Similarly, for detained persons who are citizens of independent Commonwealth countries or foreign nationals the exercise of the rights in Code C, section 7 may not be interfered with.

In cases where the person is detained under the Terrorism Act 2000 an officer of the rank of superintendent or above may delay the exercise of either right or both if he/she has reasonable grounds for believing that the exercise of the right will lead to any of the consequences of:

- interference with or harm to evidence of a serious offence;
- interference with or physical injury to any person;
- the alerting of persons who are suspected of having committed a serious offence but who have not been arrested for it;

- the hindering of the recovery of property obtained as a result of a serious offence or in respect of which a forfeiture order could be made under s. 23;
- interference with the gathering of information about the commission, preparation or instigation of acts of terrorism;
- the alerting of a person and thereby making it more difficult to prevent an act of terrorism;
- the alerting of a person and thereby making it more difficult to secure a person's apprehension, prosecution or conviction in connection with the commission, preparation or instigation of an act of terrorism;
- the detained person having benefited from his/her criminal conduct, and the recovery of the value of the property constituting the benefit will be hindered by informing the named person of the detained person's detention or access to legal advice. For these purposes whether a person has benefited from his/her criminal conduct is to be decided in accordance with part 2 of the Proceeds of Crime Act 2002. Briefly, criminal conduct is conduct which constitutes an offence in England and Wales, or would constitute such an offence if it occurred in England and Wales. A person benefits from conduct if he/she obtains property as a result of or in connection with the conduct (Code H, Annex B, paras 1 and 2).

When considering the delay of access to a solicitor the authorising officer must bear in mind that access to a solicitor is 'a fundamental right of a citizen' (*R* v *Samuel* [1988] QB 615). The authorising officer must actually believe that by allowing access to the solicitor he/she will intentionally or inadvertently alert other suspects.

Occasions where delay will be authorised in such circumstances will be rare and only when it can be shown that the suspect is capable of misleading that particular solicitor and there is more than a substantial risk that the suspect will succeed in causing information to be conveyed which will lead to one or more of the specified consequences. In deciding whether such an interview will be admissible the court will consider how reliable it is and will consider how the refusal to allow that particular detained person access to a solicitor affected his/her decision to make a confession. One such case where the confession was excluded is *R* v *Sanusi* [1992] Crim LR 43, where a person from another country was denied access to a solicitor and the court held that his right to advice was particularly significant due to his lack of familiarity with police procedures.

### Annex C—Restriction on Drawing Adverse Inferences from Silence and Terms of the Caution when the Restriction Applies (see chapter 1.7)

### Annex D—Written Statements Under Caution (see chapter 1.7)

1.6.21

### Annex E—Summary of Provisions Relating to Mentally Disordered and Otherwise Mentally Vulnerable People

1.  If an officer has any suspicion, or is told in good faith, that a person of any age may be mentally disordered or otherwise mentally vulnerable, or mentally incapable of understanding the significance of questions or their replies that person shall be treated as mentally disordered or otherwise mentally vulnerable for the purposes of this Code.

2.  In the case of a person who is mentally disordered or otherwise mentally vulnerable, 'the appropriate adult' means:
    (a) a relative, guardian or other person responsible for their care or custody;
    (b) someone experienced in dealing with mentally disordered or mentally vulnerable people but who is not a police officer or employed by the police;
    (c) failing these, some other responsible adult aged 18 or over who is not a police officer or employed by the police.

3.  If the custody officer authorises the detention of a person who is mentally vulnerable or appears to be suffering from a mental disorder, the custody officer must as soon as practicable

inform the appropriate adult of the grounds for detention and the person's whereabouts, and ask the adult to come to the police station to see them. If the appropriate adult:

- is already at the station when information is given as in *paragraphs 3.1* to *3.5* the information must be given in their presence;
- is not at the station when the provisions of *paragraph 3.1* to *3.5* are complied with these provisions must be complied with again in their presence once they arrive.

See *paragraphs 3.15* to *3.17*.

4. If the appropriate adult, having been informed of the right to legal advice, considers legal advice should be taken, the provisions of *section 6* apply as if the mentally disordered or otherwise mentally vulnerable person had requested access to legal advice. See *paragraph 3.19*.

5. The custody officer must make sure a person receives appropriate clinical attention as soon as reasonably practicable if the person appears to be suffering from a mental disorder or in urgent cases immediately call the nearest appropriate healthcare professional or an ambulance. It is not intended these provisions delay the transfer of a detainee to a place of safety under the Mental Health Act 1983, section 136 if that is applicable. If an assessment under that Act is to take place at a police station, the custody officer must consider whether an appropriate healthcare professional should be called to conduct an initial clinical check on the detainee. See *paragraph 9.5* and *9.6*.

6. It is imperative a mentally disordered or otherwise mentally vulnerable person detained under the Mental Health Act 1983, section 136 be assessed as soon as possible. A police station should only be used as a place of safety as a last resort but if that assessment is to take place at the police station, an approved social worker and registered medical practitioner shall be called to the station as soon as possible to carry it out. Once the detainee has been assessed and suitable arrangements been made for their treatment or care, they can no longer be detained under section 136. A detainee should be immediately discharged from detention if a registered medical practitioner having examined them, concludes they are not mentally disordered within the meaning of the Act. See *paragraph 3.16*.

7. If a mentally disordered or otherwise mentally vulnerable person is cautioned in the absence of the appropriate adult, the caution must be repeated in the appropriate adult's presence. See *paragraph 10.12*.

8. A mentally disordered or otherwise mentally vulnerable person must not be interviewed or asked to provide or sign a written statement in the absence of the appropriate adult unless the provisions of *paragraphs 11.1* or *11.18* to *11.20* apply. Questioning in these circumstances may not continue in the absence of the appropriate adult once sufficient information to avert the risk has been obtained. A record shall be made of the grounds for any decision to begin an interview in these circumstances. See *paragraphs 11.1, 11.15* and *11.18* to *11.20*.

9. If the appropriate adult is present at an interview, they shall be informed they are not expected to act simply as an observer and the purposes of their presence are to:

- advise the interviewee;
- observe whether or not the interview is being conducted properly and fairly;
- facilitate communication with the interviewee.

See *paragraph 11.17*.

10. If the detention of a mentally disordered or otherwise mentally vulnerable person is reviewed by a review officer or a superintendent, the appropriate adult must, if available at the time, be given an opportunity to make representations to the officer about the need for continuing detention. See *paragraph 15.3*.

11. If the custody officer charges a mentally disordered or otherwise mentally vulnerable person with an offence or takes such other action as is appropriate when there is sufficient evidence for a prosecution this must be carried out in the presence of the appropriate adult if they are at the police station. A copy of the written notice embodying any charge must also be given to the appropriate adult. See *paragraphs 16.1* to *16.4A*.

12. An intimate or strip search of a mentally disordered or otherwise mentally vulnerable person may take place only in the presence of the appropriate adult of the same sex, unless the

detainee specifically requests the presence of a particular adult of the opposite sex. A strip search may take place in the absence of an appropriate adult only in cases of urgency when there is a risk of serious harm to the detainee or others. See *Annex A, paragraphs 5* and *11(c)*.

13. Particular care must be taken when deciding whether to use any form of approved restraints on a mentally disordered or otherwise mentally vulnerable person in a locked cell. See *paragraph 8.2*.

---

**1.6.21.1**     **KEYNOTE**

The purpose of allowing the detained person's appropriate adult on the detainee's behalf to ask for a solicitor to be called to give legal advice is to protect the rights of a mentally disordered or otherwise mentally vulnerable detained person who does not understand the significance of what is said to him/her. If the detained person wants to exercise the right to legal advice, the appropriate action should be taken and not delayed until the appropriate adult arrives. A mentally disordered or otherwise mentally vulnerable detained person should always be given an opportunity, when an appropriate adult is called to the police station, to consult privately with a solicitor in the absence of the appropriate adult if he/she wants.

Although people who are mentally disordered or otherwise mentally vulnerable are often capable of providing reliable evidence, they may, without knowing or wanting to do so, be particularly prone in certain circumstances to provide information that may be unreliable, misleading or self-incriminating. Special care should always be taken when questioning such a person, and the appropriate adult should be involved if there is any doubt about a person's mental state or capacity. Because of the risk of unreliable evidence, it is important to obtain corroboration of any facts admitted whenever possible. For these reasons officers of superintendent rank or above should exercise their discretion to authorise the commencement of an interview in the appropriate adult's absence only in exceptional cases, if it is necessary to avert an immediate risk of serious harm.

There is no requirement for an appropriate adult to be present if a person is detained under s. 136 of the Mental Health Act 1983 for assessment.

---

**1.6.22**     **Annex F—No longer in use, see Code C, section 7**

**1.6.23**     **Annex G—Fitness to be Interviewed**

1. This Annex contains general guidance to help police officers and healthcare professionals assess whether a detainee might be at risk in an interview.

2. A detainee may be at risk in a interview if it is considered that:
   (a) conducting the interview could significantly harm the detainee's physical or mental state;
   (b) anything the detainee says in the interview about their involvement or suspected involvement in the offence about which they are being interviewed might be considered unreliable in subsequent court proceedings because of their physical or mental state.

3. In assessing whether the detainee should be interviewed, the following must be considered:
   (a) how the detainee's physical or mental state might affect their ability to understand the nature and purpose of the interview, to comprehend what is being asked and to appreciate the significance of any answers given and make rational decisions about whether they want to say anything;
   (b) the extent to which the detainee's replies may be affected by their physical or mental condition rather than representing a rational and accurate explanation of their involvement in the offence;
   (c) how the nature of the interview, which could include particularly probing questions, might affect the detainee.

4. It is essential healthcare professionals who are consulted consider the functional ability of the detainee rather than simply relying on a medical diagnosis, e.g. it is possible for a person with severe mental illness to be fit for interview.

5. Healthcare professionals should advise on the need for an appropriate adult to be present, whether reassessment of the person's fitness for interview may be necessary if the interview lasts beyond a specified time, and whether a further specialist opinion may be required.

6. When healthcare professionals identify risks they should be asked to quantify the risks. They should inform the custody officer:
   - whether the person's condition:
     – is likely to improve;
     – will require or be amenable to treatment; and
   - indicate how long it may take for such improvement to take effect.

7. The role of the healthcare professional is to consider the risks and advise the custody officer of the outcome of that consideration. The healthcare professional's determination and any advice or recommendations should be made in writing and form part of the custody record.

8. Once the healthcare professional has provided that information, it is a matter for the custody officer to decide whether or not to allow the interview to go ahead and if the interview is to proceed, to determine what safeguards are needed. Nothing prevents safeguards being provided in addition to those required under the Code. An example might be to have an appropriate healthcare professional present during the interview, in addition to an appropriate adult, in order constantly to monitor the person's condition and how it is being affected by the interview.

## 1.6.24   Annex H—Detained Person: Observation List

1. If any detainee fails to meet any of the following criteria, an appropriate healthcare professional or an ambulance must be called.

2. When assessing the level of rousability, consider:
   *Rousability*—can they be woken?
   - go into the cell
   - call their name
   - shake gently
   
   *Response to questions*—can they give appropriate answers to questions such as:
   - What's your name?
   - Where do you live?
   - Where do you think you are?
   
   *Response to commands*—can they respond appropriately to commands such as:
   - Open your eyes!
   - Lift one arm, now the other arm!

3. Remember to take into account the possibility or presence of other illnesses, injury, or mental condition, a person who is drowsy and smells of alcohol may also have the following:
   - Diabetes
   - Epilepsy
   - Head injury
   - Drug intoxication or overdose
   - Stroke

## Annex I—NOT USED

## Annex J—NOT USED

## 1.6.25   Annex K—X-rays and Ultrasound Scans

### (a) Action

1. PACE, section 55A allows a person who has been arrested and is in police detention to have an X-ray taken of them or an ultrasound scan to be carried out on them (or both) if:
   (a) authorised by an officer of inspector rank or above who has reasonable grounds for believing that the detainee:
      (i) may have swallowed a Class A drug; and
      (ii) was in possession of that Class A drug with the intention of supplying it to another or to export; and
   (b) the detainee's appropriate consent has been given in writing.
2. Before an x-ray is taken or an ultrasound scan carried out, a police officer, designated detention officer or staff custody officer must tell the detainee:
   (a) that the authority has been given; and
   (b) the grounds for giving the authorisation.
3. Before a detainee is asked to give appropriate consent to an x-ray or an ultrasound scan, they must be warned that if they refuse without good cause their refusal may harm their case if it comes to trial. This warning may be given by a police officer or member of police staff. In the case of juveniles, mentally vulnerable or mentally disordered suspects the seeking and giving of consent must take place in the presence of the appropriate adult. A juvenile's consent is only valid if their parent's or guardian's consent is also obtained unless the juvenile is under 14, when their parent's or guardian's consent is sufficient in its own right. A detainee who is not legally represented must be reminded of their entitlement to have free legal advice, see Code C, *paragraph 6.5*, and the reminder noted in the custody record.
4. An x-ray may be taken, or an ultrasound scan may be carried out, only by a registered medical practitioner or registered nurse, and only at a hospital, surgery or other medical premises.

## (b) Documentation

5. The following shall be recorded as soon as practicable in the detainee's custody record:
   (a) the authorisation to take the x-ray or carry out the ultrasound scan (or both);
   (b) the grounds for giving the authorisation;
   (c) the giving of the warning required by *paragraph 3*; and
   (d) the fact that the appropriate consent was given or (as the case may be) refused, and if refused, the reason given for the refusal (if any); and
   (e) if an x-ray is taken or an ultrasound scan carried out:
      • where it was taken or carried out;
      • who took it or carried it out;
      • who was present;
      • the result.
6. Paragraphs 1.4–1.7 of this Code apply and an appropriate adult should be present when consent is sought to any procedure under this Annex.

<table>
<tr><td>1.6.25.1</td><td>

**KEYNOTE**

If authority is given for an x-ray to be taken or an ultrasound scan to be carried out (or both), consideration should be given to asking a registered medical practitioner or registered nurse to explain to the detainee what is involved and to allay any concerns that the detainee might have about the effect on him/her of taking an x-ray or carrying out an ultrasound scan. If appropriate consent is not given, evidence of the explanation may, if the case comes to trial, be relevant to determining whether the detainee had a good cause for refusing.

The following form of words may be used to warn a detainee who is asked to consent to an X-ray being taken or an ultrasound scan being carried out (or both):

You do not have to allow an x-ray of you to be taken or an ultrasound scan to be carried out on you, but I must warn you that if you refuse without good cause, your refusal may harm your case if it comes to trial.
</td></tr>
</table>

Where the use of the Welsh language is appropriate, the following form of words may be provided in Welsh:

Does dim rhaid i chi ganiatáu cymryd sgan uwchsain neu belydr-x (neu'r ddau) arnoch, ond mae'n rhaid i mi eich rhybuddio os byddwch chi'n gwrthod gwneud hynny heb reswm da, fe allai hynny niweidio eich achos pe bai'n dod gerbron llys.

## 1.6.26 Annex L—Establishing Gender of Persons for the Purpose of Searching

1. Certain provisions of this and other PACE Codes explicitly state that searches and other procedures may only be carried out by, or in the presence of, persons of the same sex as the person subject to the search or other procedure.

2. All searches and procedures must be carried out with courtesy, consideration and respect for the person concerned. Police officers should show particular sensitivity when dealing with transgender individuals (including transsexual persons) and transvestite persons.

### (a) Consideration

3. In law, the gender (and accordingly the sex) of an individual is their gender as registered at birth unless they have been issued with a Gender Recognition Certificate (GRC) under the Gender Recognition Act 2004 (GRA), in which case the person's gender is their acquired gender. This means that if the acquired gender is the male gender, the person's sex becomes that of a man and, if it is the female gender, the person's sex becomes that of a woman and they must be treated as their acquired gender.

4. When establishing whether the person concerned should be treated as being male or female for the purposes of these searches and procedures, the following approach which is designed to minimise embarrassment and secure the person's co-operation should be followed:

   (a) The person must not be asked whether they have a GRC (see *paragraph 8*);

   (b) If there is no doubt as to as to whether the person concerned should be treated as being male or female, they should be dealt with as being of that sex.

   (c) If at any time (including during the search or carrying out the procedure) there is doubt as to whether the person should be treated, or continue to be treated, as being male or female:

      (i) the person should be asked what gender they consider themselves to be. If they express a preference to be dealt with as a particular gender, they should be asked to indicate and confirm their preference by signing the custody record or, if a custody record has not been opened, the search record or the officer's notebook. Subject to (ii) below, the person should be treated according to their preference;

      (ii) if there are grounds to doubt that the preference in (i) accurately reflects the person's predominant lifestyle, for example, if they ask to be treated as a woman but documents and other information make it clear that they live predominantly as a man, or vice versa, they should be treated according to what appears to be their predominant lifestyle and not their stated preference;

      (iii) If the person is unwilling to express a preference as in (i) above, efforts should be made to determine their predominant lifestyle and they should be treated as such. For example, if they appear to live predominantly as a woman, they should be treated as being female; or

      (iv) if none of the above apply, the person should be dealt with according to what reasonably appears to have been their sex as registered at birth.

5. Once a decision has been made about which gender an individual is to be treated as, each officer responsible for the search or procedure should where possible be advised before the search or procedure starts of any doubts as to the person's gender and the person informed that the doubts have been disclosed. This is important so as to maintain the dignity of the person and any officers concerned.

## (b) Documentation

6. The person's gender as established under *paragraph 4(c)(i)* to (*iv*) above must be recorded in the person's custody record, or if a custody record has not been opened, on the search record or in the officer's notebook.
7. Where the person elects which gender they consider themselves to be under *paragraph 4(b)(i)* but following *4(b)(ii)* is not treated in accordance with their preference, the reason must be recorded in the search record, in the officer's notebook or, if applicable, in the person's custody record.

## (c) Disclosure of information

8. Section 22 of the GRA defines any information relating to a person's application for a GRC or to a successful applicant's gender before it became their acquired gender as 'protected information'. Nothing in this Annex is to be read as authorising or permitting any police officer or any police staff who has acquired such information when acting in their official capacity to disclose that information to any other person in contravention of the GRA. Disclosure includes making a record of 'protected information' which is read by others.

1.6.26.1

**KEYNOTE**

Provisions to which paragraph 1 applies include:

- in Code C: para. 4.1 and Annex A, paras 5, 6 and 11 (searches, strip and intimate searches of detainees under ss. 54 and 55 of the 1984 Act);
- in Code A: paras 2.8 and 3.6 and Note 4;
- in Code D: para. 5.5 and Note 5F (searches, examinations and photographing of detainees under s. 54A of the 1984 Act) and para. 6.9 (taking samples);
- in Code H: para. 4.1 and Annex A, paras 6, 7 and 12 (searches, strip and intimate searches under ss. 54 and 55 of the 1984 Act of persons arrested under s. 41 of the Terrorism Act 2000).

While there is no agreed definition of transgender (or trans), it is generally used as an umbrella term to describe people whose gender identity (self-identification as being a woman, man, neither or both) differs from the sex they were registered as at birth. The term includes, but is not limited to, transsexual people. Transsexual means a person who is proposing to undergo, is undergoing or has undergone a process (or part of a process) for the purpose of gender reassignment which is a protected characteristic under the Equality Act 2010 by changing physiological or other attributes of their sex. This includes aspects of gender such as dress and title. It would apply to a woman making the transition to being a man and a man making the transition to being a woman, as well as to a person who has only just started out on the process of gender reassignment and to a person who has completed the process. Both would share the characteristic of gender reassignment with each having the characteristics of one sex, but with certain characteristics of the other sex. Transvestite means a person of one gender who dresses in the clothes of a person of the opposite gender. However, transvestites do not live permanently in the gender opposite to their birth sex.

It is important to check the force guidance and instructions for the deployment of transgender officers and staff under their direction and control to duties which involve carrying out, or being present at, any of the searches and procedures described in para. 1. Force guidance which must be provided by each force's Chief Officer must comply with the Equality Act 2010.

# Interviews

PACE Code of Practice for the Detention, Treatment and Questioning of Persons by Police Officers (Code C)

PACE Code of Practice on Audio Recording Interviews with Suspects (Code E)

PACE Code of Practice on Visual Recording with Sound of Interviews with Suspects (Code F)

> A thick grey line down the margin denotes text that is an extract of the PACE Code itself (i.e. the actual wording of the legislation).

### 1.7.1 Introduction

The PACE Codes of Practice C, E and F are intended to provide some protection to people being interviewed by the police and lay down guidelines as to how interviews should be conducted. This chapter examines the treatment of suspects when they are interviewed. The chapter includes the relevant sections of Code C and all of Code E and F. The chapter sets out the actual Codes of Practice with keynotes, which incorporate the notes of guidance to the Code.

Please **see chapter 1.6** regarding designated officers carrying out some functions of police officers.

Code C was amended 10 July 2012. Code H applies to persons detained for the purposes of a terrorist investigation; references to terrorism matters, where appropriate, are included in the keynotes to this chapter.

**PACE Code of Practice for the Detention, Treatment and Questioning of Persons by Police Officers (Code C)**

### 1.7.2 10 Cautions

#### (a) When a caution must be given

10.1 A person whom there are grounds to suspect of an offence, must be cautioned before any questions about an offence, or further questions if the answers provide the grounds for suspicion, are put to them if either the suspect's answers or silence, (i.e. failure or refusal to *answer* or answer satisfactorily) may be given in evidence to a court in a prosecution. A person need not be cautioned if questions are for other necessary purposes, e.g.:

(a) solely to establish their identity or ownership of any vehicle;

(b) to obtain information in accordance with any relevant statutory requirement, see *paragraph 10.9*;

(c) in furtherance of the proper and effective conduct of a search, e.g. to determine the need to search in the exercise of powers of stop and search or to seek co-operation while carrying out a search;

(d) to seek verification of a written record as in *paragraph 11.13*;

(e) *Not used*

10.2 Whenever a person not under arrest is initially cautioned, or reminded they are under caution, that person must at the same time be told they are not under arrest and are free to leave if they want to.

10.3 A person who is arrested, or further arrested, must be informed at the time if practicable, or if not, or as soon it becomes as practicable thereafter, that they are under arrest and the grounds and reasons for their arrest, see *paragraph 3.4* and Code G, *paragraphs 2.2* and *4.3*.

10.4 As required by Code G, *section 3*, a person who is arrested, or further arrested, must also be cautioned unless:

(a) it is impracticable to do so by reason of their condition or behaviour at the time;

(b) they have already been cautioned immediately prior to arrest as in *paragraph 10.1*.

## (b) Terms of the cautions

10.5 The caution which must be given on:

(a) arrest;

(b) all other occasions before a person is charged or informed they may be prosecuted, see *section 16*,

should, unless the restriction on drawing adverse inferences from silence applies, see *Annex C*, be in the following terms:

*'You do not have to say anything. But it may harm your defence if you do not mention when questioned something which you later rely on in Court. Anything you do say may be given in evidence.'*

Where the use of the Welsh Language is appropriate, a constable may provide the caution directly in Welsh in the following terms:

*'Does dim rhaid i chi ddweud dim byd. Ond gall niweidio eich amddiffyniad os na fyddwch chi'n sôn, wrth gael eich holi, am rywbeth y byddwch chi'n dibynnu arno nes ymlaen yn y Llys. Gall unrhyw beth yr ydych yn ei ddweud gael ei roi fel tystiolaeth.'*

10.6 *Annex C, paragraph 2* sets out the alternative terms of the caution to be used when the restriction on drawing adverse inferences from silence applies.

10.7 Minor deviations from the words of any caution given in accordance with this Code do not constitute a breach of this Code, provided the sense of the relevant caution is preserved.

10.8 After any break in questioning under caution, the person being questioned must be made aware they remain under caution. If there is any doubt the relevant caution should be given again in full when the interview resumes.

10.9 When, despite being cautioned, a person fails to co-operate or to answer particular questions which may affect their immediate treatment, the person should be informed of any relevant consequences and that those consequences are not affected by the caution. Examples are when a person's refusal to provide:

• their name and address when charged may make them liable to detention;

• particulars and information in accordance with a statutory requirement, e.g. under the Road Traffic Act 1988, may amount to an offence or may make the person liable to a further arrest.

### (c) Special warnings under the Criminal Justice and Public Order Act 1994, sections 36 and 37

10.10 When a suspect interviewed at a police station or authorised place of detention after arrest fails or refuses to answer certain questions, or to answer satisfactorily, after due warning, a court or jury may draw such inferences as appear proper under the Criminal Justice and Public Order Act 1994, sections 36 and 37. Such inferences may only be drawn when:

(a) the restriction on drawing adverse inferences from silence, see *Annex C*, does not apply; and

(b) the suspect is arrested by a constable and fails or refuses to account for any objects, marks or substances, or marks on such objects found:

- on their person;
- in or on their clothing or footwear;
- otherwise in their possession; or
- in the place they were arrested;

(c) the arrested suspect was found by a constable at a place at or about the time the offence for which that officer has arrested them is alleged to have been committed, and the suspect fails or refuses to account for their presence there.

When the restriction on drawing adverse inferences from silence applies, the suspect may still be asked to account for any of the matters in (*b*) or (*c*) but the special warning described in *paragraph 10.11* will not apply and must not be given.

10.11 For an inference to be drawn when a suspect fails or refuses to answer a question about one of these matters or to answer it satisfactorily, the suspect must first be told in ordinary language:

(a) what offence is being investigated;

(b) what fact they are being asked to account for;

(c) this fact may be due to them taking part in the commission of the offence;

(d) a court may draw a proper inference if they fail or refuse to account for this fact;

(e) a record is being made of the interview and it may be given in evidence if they are brought to trial.

### (d) Juveniles and persons who are mentally disordered or otherwise mentally vulnerable

10.11A The information required in paragraph 10.11 must not be given to a suspect who is a juvenile or who is mentally disordered or otherwise mentally vulnerable unless the appropriate adult is present.

10.12 If a juvenile or a person who is mentally disordered or otherwise mentally vulnerable is cautioned in the absence of the appropriate adult, the caution must be repeated in the adult's presence.

### (e) Documentation

10.13 A record shall be made when a caution is given under this section, either in the interviewer's pocket book or in the interview record.

---

**1.7.2.1**

**KEYNOTE**

In considering whether there are grounds to suspect a person of committing an offence there must be some reasonable, objective grounds for the suspicion, based on known facts or information which are/is relevant to the likelihood that the offence has been committed and that the person to be questioned committed it.

An arrested person must be given sufficient information to enable him/her to understand that he/she has been deprived of his/her liberty and the reason for the arrest, e.g. when a person is arrested on suspicion of committing an offence he/she must be informed of the suspected offence's nature, and when and where it was committed. The suspect must also be informed of the reason or reasons why the arrest is considered necessary. Vague or technical language should be avoided. If it appears that a person does not understand the caution, the person giving it should explain it in his/her own words.

The Criminal Justice and Public Order Act 1994, ss. 36 and 37 apply only to suspects who have been arrested by a constable or Customs and Excise officer and are given the relevant warning by the police or customs officer who made the arrest or who is investigating the offence. They do not apply to any interviews with suspects who have not been arrested. Further, a person who is not in police detention is not prevented from seeking legal advice if he/she wants; therefore the restrictions on drawing inferences from silence set out in Code C, Annex C, para. 1, do not apply.

As well as considering whether to administer the caution again after a break in questioning or at the beginning of a subsequent interview, the interviewing officer should summarise the reason for the break and confirm this with the suspect. This may help to show to the court that nothing occurred during an interview break or between interviews which influenced the suspect's recorded evidence.

Nothing in this Code requires a caution to be given or repeated when informing a person not under arrest that he/she may be prosecuted for an offence. However, a court will not be able to draw any inferences under the Criminal Justice and Public Order Act 1994, s. 34, if the person was not cautioned.

The giving of a warning or the service of the Notice of Intended Prosecution required by the Road Traffic Offenders Act 1988, s. 1 does not amount to informing a detainee that he/she may be prosecuted for an offence and so does not preclude further questioning in relation to that offence.

1.7.2.2     **KEYNOTE**

**Inferences from Silence when Questioned or Charged**

Section 34 of the Criminal Justice and Public Order Act 1994 provides that inferences can be drawn if, when questioned by the police under caution, charged or officially informed that he/she may be prosecuted, the accused fails to mention a fact on which he/she later relies in his/her defence, and which he/she could reasonably have been expected to mention at the time.

Section 34 states:

(1)  Where, in any proceedings against a person for an offence, evidence is given that the accused—
   (a)  at any time before he was charged with the offence, on being questioned under caution by a constable trying to discover whether or by whom the offence had been committed, failed to mention any fact relied on in his defence in those proceedings; or
   (b)  on being charged with the offence or officially informed that he might be prosecuted for it, failed to mention any such fact, or
   (c)  at any time after being charged with the offence, on being questioned under section 22 of the Counter-Terrorism Act 2008 (post-charge questioning), failed to mention any such fact,
   being a fact which in the circumstances existing at the time the accused could reasonably have been expected to mention when so questioned, charged or informed, as the case may be, subsection (2) below applies.
(2)  Where this subsection applies—
   (a)  a magistrates' court inquiring into the offence as examining justices in deciding whether to grant an application for dismissal made by the accused under section 6 of the Magistrates' Courts Act 1980 (application for dismissal of charge in course of proceedings with a view to transfer for trial);
   (b)  a judge, in deciding whether to grant an application made by the accused under—
      (i)  section 6 of the Criminal Justice Act 1987 (application for dismissal of charge of serious fraud in respect of which notice of transfer has been given under section 4 of that Act); or
      (ii)  paragraph 5 of schedule 6 to the Criminal Justice Act 1991 (application for dismissal of charge of violent or sexual offence involving child in respect of which notice of transfer has been given under section 53 of that Act);
   (c)  the court, in determining whether there is a case to answer; and
   (d)  the court or jury, in determining whether the accused is guilty of the offence charged,
   may draw such inferences from the failure as appear proper.
(2A)  Where the accused was at an authorised place of detention at the time of the failure, subsections (1) and (2) above do not apply if he had not been allowed an opportunity to consult a solicitor prior to being questioned, charged or informed as mentioned in subsection (1) above.

(3) Subject to any directions by the court, evidence tending to establish the failure may be given before or after evidence tending to establish the fact which the accused is alleged to have failed to mention.

(4) This section applies in relation to questioning by persons (other than constables) charged with the duty of investigating offences or charging offenders as it applies in relation to questioning by constables; and in subsection (1) above 'officially informed' means informed by a constable or any such person.

(5) This section does not—

    (a) prejudice the admissibility in evidence of the silence or other reaction of the accused in the face of anything said in his presence relating to the conduct in respect of which he is charged, in so far as evidence thereof would be admissible apart from this section; or

    (b) preclude the drawing of any inference from any such silence or other reaction of the accused which could properly be drawn apart from this section.

Although judges have discretion in individual cases it has been recommended that in relation to s. 34 they should closely follow the Judicial Studies Board specimen direction. This direction was followed in *Beckles* v *United Kingdom* (2003) 36 EHRR 13 and accepted by the European Court of Human Rights. However, failure to give proper direction does not necessarily involve a breach of Article 6 (right to a fair trial).

Section 34 deals with the 'failure to mention any fact' and the word 'fact' is given its normal dictionary definition of 'something that is actually the case' (*R* v *Milford* [2001] Crim LR 330). Where an accused alleges that he/she did mention the relevant fact when being questioned it is for the prosecution to prove the contrary before any adverse inference can be drawn.

There have been numerous domestic and European case decisions about failure to advance facts following legal advice to remain silent, and more recent cases have attempted to unravel the difficulties experienced in this area. These cases have accepted that a genuine reliance by a defendant on his/her solicitor's advice to remain silent is not in itself enough to preclude adverse comment. The real question to be answered is whether the defendant remained silent, not because of legal advice, but because there was no satisfactory explanation to give (*R* v *Beckles* [2004] EWCA Crim 2766, *R* v *Bresa* [2005] EWCA Crim 1414 and *R* v *Loizou* [2006] EWCA Crim 1719).

In assessing whether to draw an inference from a failure to mention facts later relied on as part of the defence, the court may look at the validity of the waiver to legal advice. In *R* v *Saunders* [2012] EWCA Crim 1380, the suspect declined the offer of legal representation, and in interview she either made no comment or denied the allegations put to her. At trial she blamed her cousin who she said had been staying at her flat at the time. The prosecution sought to rely on her interview to show that she had made no mention of her cousin at that stage. In accepting the prosecution's submission the court considered the extent of her knowledge and the extent to which her decision caused her disadvantage. As to the first factor, S had particular experience and understanding of the interview procedure having experienced it before and was well-fitted to decide whether she wanted legal advice. She was neither unintelligent nor vulnerable and could be expected to be well aware of the benefit of legal advice.

In relation to s. 34, the accused cannot be convicted solely on an inference drawn from silence. The European Court of Human Rights, although accepting that there are cases which clearly call for an accused to provide an explanation, stated that the court is required to apply 'particular caution' before invoking the accused's silence against him (*Condron* v *United Kingdom* (2001) 31 EHRR 1). In *R* v *Miah* [2009] EWCA Crim 2368, Hughes LJ said: 'Section 34 bites not on silence in interview but upon the late advancing of a case which could have been made earlier. What it does is to permit the jury to ask why, if there is an explanation for the evidence, or a defence to the accusation, the defendant did not advance it when he could have done, providing only that it was reasonable to expect him to have done so then.'

In *R* v *Argent* [1997] 2 Cr App R 27, the court stated that personal factors which might be relevant to an assessment of what an individual could reasonably have been expected to mention were age, experience, mental capacity, state of health, sobriety, tiredness and personality.

In *R* v *Flynn* [2001] EWCA Crim 1633, the court held that the police are entitled to conduct a second interview with a suspect, having obtained evidence from their witnesses which was not available in the first interview, and adverse inference could be drawn from the suspect's silence.

Where an accused, following legal advice, fails to answer questions during interview but presents a prepared statement, no adverse inference can be drawn where the accused's defence does not rely on any facts not mentioned in the interview (*R* v *Campbell* [2005] EWCA Crim 1249). However, this would not be the case when evidence of facts relied on during the trial was not contained within the pre-prepared statement (*R* v *Turner* [2003] EWCA Crim 3108).

Section 34 differs from the other 'inference' sections in that the questioning need not occur at a police station and therefore the presence of a legal representative is not required. However, it appears clear that, should the prosecution seek to draw any inferences of an accused's silence where such questioning has occurred, the questions would need to be asked of the suspect again once he/she had access to legal advice.

A requirement to caution the person is contained in s. 34(1)(a) in order to make clear the risks connected with a failure to mention facts which later form part of the defence.

In certain justice areas the Criminal Justice Act 2003 repeals s. 34(2)(a) and (b)(i) and (ii) and replaces them with sch. 3, para. 2 to the Crime and Disorder Act 1998 (these amendments are not yet in force in other areas). Section 22(9) of the Counter Terrorism Act 2008 adds s. 34(1)(c) to the Criminal Justice and Public Order Act 1994, which extends inferences from silence to post-charge questioning which has been authorised by a judge of the Crown Court if the offence is a terrorism offence or it appears to the judge that the offence has a terrorist connection. The post-charge questioning provisions of the 2008 Act require the issue of a mandatory code for the video recording with sound of such questioning.

## 1.7.2.3 KEYNOTE

### Inferences from Silence: Failure to Account for Objects, Substances and Marks

Section 36 of the Criminal Justice and Public Order Act 1994 provides that inferences can be drawn from an accused's failure to give evidence or refusal to answer any question about any object, substance or mark which may be attributable to the accused in the commission of an offence.

Section 36 states:

(1) Where—
    (a) a person is arrested by a constable, and there is—
      (i) on his person; or
      (ii) in or on his clothing or footwear; or
      (iii) otherwise in his possession; or
      (iv) in any place in which he is at the time of his arrest,
      any object, substance or mark, or there is any mark on any such object; and
    (b) that or another constable investigating the case reasonably believes that the presence of the object, substance or mark may be attributable to the participation of the person arrested in the commission of an offence specified by the constable; and
    (c) the constable informs the person arrested that he so believes, and requests him to account for the presence of the object, substance or mark; and
    (d) the person fails or refuses to do so,
    then if, in any proceedings against the person for the offence so specified, evidence of those matters is given, subsection (2) below applies.
(2) Where this subsection applies—
    (a) a magistrates' court inquiring into the offence as examining justices; in deciding whether to grant an application for dismissal made by the accused under section 6 of the Magistrates' Courts Act 1980 (application for dismissal of charge in course of proceedings with a view to transfer for trial);
    (b) a judge, in deciding whether to grant an application made by the accused under—
      (i) section 6 of the Criminal Justice Act 1987 (application for dismissal of charge of serious fraud in respect of which notice of transfer has been given under section 4 of that Act); or
      (ii) paragraph 5 of schedule 6 to the Criminal Justice Act 1991 (application for dismissal of charge of violent or sexual offence involving a child in respect of which notice of transfer has been given under section 53 of that Act);
    (c) the court, in determining whether there is a case to answer; and
    (d) the court or jury, in determining whether the accused is guilty of the offence charged, may draw such inferences from the failure or refusal as appear proper.

(3) Subsections (1) and (2) above apply to the condition of clothing or footwear as they apply to a substance or mark thereon.

(4) Subsections (1) and (2) above do not apply unless the accused was told in ordinary language by the constable when making the request mentioned in subsection (1)(c) above what the effect of this section would be if he failed or refused to comply with the request.

(4A) Where the accused was at an authorised place of detention at the time of the failure or refusal, subsections (1) and (2) do not apply if he had not been allowed an opportunity to consult a solicitor prior to the request being made.

(5) This section applies in relation to officers of customs and excise as it applies in relation to constables.

(6) This section does not preclude the drawing of any inference from a failure or refusal of the accused to account for the presence of an object, substance or mark or from the condition of clothing or footwear which could properly be drawn apart from this section.

As with s. 37 below, an inference may only be drawn where four conditions are satisfied:

- the accused has been arrested;
- a constable reasonably believes that the object, substance or mark (or the presence of the accused (s. 37)) may be attributable to the accused's participation in a crime (s. 36 (an offence 'specified by the constable') or s. 37 (the offence for which he/she was arrested));
- the constable informs the accused of his/her belief and requests an explanation (by giving a special warning (see below));
- the constable tells the suspect (in ordinary language) the effect of a failure or refusal to comply with the request.

The request for information under both s. 36 and s. 37 is a form of questioning and should be undertaken during the interview at the police station. The request for such information prior to this would be an exception to the rule.

The interviewing officer is required to give the accused a 'special warning' for an inference to be drawn from a suspect's failure or refusal to answer a question about one of these matters or to answer it satisfactorily. This 'special warning' is provided by PACE Code C, para. 10.11 which states that the interviewing officer must first tell the suspect *in ordinary language*:

- what offence is being investigated;
- what fact the suspect is being asked to account for;
- that the interviewing officer believes this fact may be due to the suspect's taking part in the commission of the offence in question;
- that a court may draw a proper inference if the suspect fails or refuses to account for the fact about which he/she is being questioned;
- that a record is being made of the interview and that it may be given in evidence at any subsequent trial.

As with s. 34, in relation to s. 36 the accused cannot be convicted solely on an inference drawn from a failure or refusal (s. 38(3)).

When the provisions of the Criminal Justice Act 2003 are in force s. 36(2)(a) and (2)(b)(i) and (ii) will be repealed and replaced by sch. 3, para. 2 to the Crime and Disorder Act 1998.

1.7.2.4   **KEYNOTE**

**Inferences from Silence: Failure to Account for Presence**

Section 37 of the Criminal Justice and Public Order Act 1994 provides that inferences can be drawn from an accused's failure to give evidence or refusal to answer any question about his/her presence at a place or time when the offence for which he/she was arrested was committed.

Section 37 states:

(1) Where—
 (a) a person arrested by a constable was found by him at a place at or about the time the offence for which he was arrested is alleged to have been committed; and

(b) that or another constable investigating the offence reasonably believes that the presence of the person at that place and at that time may be attributable to his participation in the commission of the offence; and

(c) the constable informs the person that he so believes, and requests him to account for that presence; and

(d) the person fails or refuses to do so,

then if, in any proceedings against the person for the offence, evidence of those matters is given, subsection (2) below applies.

(2) Where this subsection applies—

(a) a magistrates' court inquiring into the offence as examining justices; in deciding whether to grant an application for dismissal made by the accused under section 6 of the Magistrates' Courts Act 1980 (application for dismissal of charge in course of proceedings with a view to transfer for trial);

(b) a judge, in deciding whether to grant an application made by the accused under—

(i) section 6 of the Criminal Justice Act 1987 (application for dismissal of charge of serious fraud in respect of which notice of transfer has been given under section 4 of that Act); or

(ii) paragraph 5 of schedule 6 to the Criminal Justice Act 1991 (application for dismissal of charge of violent or sexual offence involving child in respect of which notice of transfer has been given under section 53 of that Act);

(c) the court, in determining whether there is a case to answer; and

(d) the court or jury, in determining whether the accused is guilty of the offence charged,

may draw such inferences from the failure or refusal as appear proper.

(3) Subsections (1) and (2) do not apply unless the accused was told in ordinary language by the constable when making the request mentioned in subsection (1)(c) above what the effect of this section would be if he failed or refused to comply with the request.

(3A) Where the accused was at an authorised place of detention at the time of the failure or refusal, subsections (1) and (2) do not apply if he had not been allowed an opportunity to consult a solicitor prior to the request being made.

(4) This section applies in relation to officers of customs and excise as it applies in relation to constables.

(5) This section does not preclude the drawing of any inference from a failure or refusal of the accused to account for his presence at a place which could properly be drawn apart from this section.

Section 37 appears somewhat restrictive in that it is only concerned with the suspect's location at the time of arrest and applies only when he/she was found at that location at or about the time of the offence.

PACE Code C also applies to s. 37 in relation to the 'special warning' required to be given by the interviewing officer.

Unlike s. 36, here the officer that sees the person at or near the scene of the alleged offence must be the arresting officer.

As with ss. 34 and 36, in relation to s. 37 the accused cannot be convicted solely on an inference drawn from a failure or refusal (s. 38(3)).

When the provisions of the Criminal Justice Act 2003 are in force s. 37(2)(a) and (2)(b)(i) and (ii) will be repealed and replaced by sch. 3, para. 2 to the Crime and Disorder Act 1998.

---

**1.7.2.5**   **KEYNOTE**

**Inferences from Silence at Trial**

Section 35 of the Criminal Justice and Public Order Act 1994 provides that inferences can be drawn from an accused's failure to give evidence or refusal to answer any question, without good cause, where the person has been sworn. Section 35 states:

(1) At the trial of any person for an offence, subsections (2) and (3) below apply unless—

(a) the accused's guilt is not in issue; or

(b) it appears to the court that the physical or mental condition of the accused makes it undesirable for him to give evidence; but subsection (2) below does not apply if, at the conclusion of the evidence for the prosecution, his legal representative informs the court that the accused will give evidence or, where he is unrepresented, the court ascertains from him that he will give evidence.

(2) Where this subsection applies, the court shall, at the conclusion of the evidence for the prosecution, satisfy itself (in the case of proceedings on indictment with a jury, in the presence of the jury) that the accused is aware that the stage has been reached at which evidence can be given for the defence and that he can, if he wishes, give evidence and that, if he chooses not to give evidence, or having been sworn, without good cause refuses to answer any question, it will be permissible for the court or jury to draw such inferences as appear proper from his failure to give evidence or his refusal, without good cause, to answer any question.

(3) Where this subsection applies, the court or jury, in determining whether the accused is guilty of the offence charged, may draw such inferences as appear proper from the failure of the accused to give evidence or his refusal, without good cause, to answer any question.

(4) This section does not render the accused compellable to give evidence on his own behalf, and he shall accordingly not be guilty of contempt of court by reason of a failure to do so.

(5) For the purposes of this section a person who, having been sworn, refuses to answer any question shall be taken to do so without good cause unless—

    (a) he is entitled to refuse to answer the question by virtue of any enactment, whenever passed or made, or on the ground of privilege; or

    (b) the court in the exercise of its general discretion excuses him from answering it.

(6) [repealed]

In *R* v *Friend* [1997] 1 WLR 1433 (in considering s. 35(1)(b) of the Act), the accused was aged 15 with a mental age of nine and an IQ of 63. It was held that the accused's mental condition did not make it 'undesirable' for him to give evidence and it was right that inferences be drawn under s. 35(3).

As with s. 34, in relation to s. 35 the accused cannot be convicted solely on an inference drawn from a failure or refusal (s. 38(3)).

It must be made clear to the accused that when the prosecution case has finished he/she may give evidence if he/she so wishes. The court must inform the accused that if he/she fails to give evidence or, being sworn, refuses to answer any question without good cause, then the jury may infer such inferences that appear proper from such a failure to give evidence or a refusal to answer any question. In *R* v *Gough* [2001] EWCA Crim 2545, it was held that it is mandatory for the court to inform the accused of his/her right to give or not to give evidence even where the accused has absconded.

In *Murray* v *United Kingdom* (1996) 22 EHRR 29 it was held that it would be incompatible with the rights of an accused to base a conviction 'solely or mainly' on their silence, or on their refusal to answer questions or give evidence in person. The Court of Appeal also held that in cases involving directions under s. 34, the burden of proof remained on the Crown despite the fact that the accused chose to make no comment (*R* v *Gowland-Wynn* [2001] EWCA Crim 2715).

## 1.7.3  11 Interviews—General

### (a) Action

11.1A An interview is the questioning of a person regarding their involvement or suspected involvement in a criminal offence or offences which, under paragraph 10.1, must be carried out under caution. Whenever a person is interviewed they must be informed of the nature of the offence, or further offence. Procedures under the Road Traffic Act 1988, section 7 or the Transport and Works Act 1992, section 31 do not constitute interviewing for the purpose of this Code.

11.1 Following a decision to arrest a suspect, they must not be interviewed about the relevant offence except at a police station or other authorised place of detention, unless the consequent delay would be likely to:

    (a) lead to:

- interference with, or harm to, evidence connected with an offence;
- interference with, or physical harm to, other people; or
- serious loss of, or damage to, property;

    (b) lead to alerting other people suspected of committing an offence but not yet arrested for it; or

    (c) hinder the recovery of property obtained in consequence of the commission of an offence.

Interviewing in any of these circumstances shall cease once the relevant risk has been averted or the necessary questions have been put in order to attempt to avert that risk.

11.2 Immediately prior to the commencement or re-commencement of any interview at a police station or other authorised place of detention, the interviewer should remind the suspect of their entitlement to free legal advice and that the interview can be delayed for legal advice to be obtained, unless one of the exceptions in *paragraph 6.6* applies. It is the interviewer's responsibility to make sure all reminders are recorded in the interview record.

11.3 *Not used*

11.4 At the beginning of an interview the interviewer, after cautioning the suspect, see *section 10*, shall put to them any significant statement or silence which occurred in the presence and hearing of a police officer or other police staff before the start of the interview and which have not been put to the suspect in the course of a previous interview. The interviewer shall ask the suspect whether they confirm or deny that earlier statement or silence and if they want to add anything.

11.4A A significant statement is one which appears capable of being used in evidence against the suspect, in particular a direct admission of guilt. A significant silence is a failure or refusal to answer a question or answer satisfactorily when under caution, which might, allowing for the restriction on drawing adverse inferences from silence, see *Annex C*, give rise to an inference under the Criminal Justice and Public Order Act 1994, Part III.

11.5 No interviewer may try to obtain answers or elicit a statement by the use of oppression. Except as in *paragraph 9.9*, no interviewer shall indicate, except to answer a direct question, what action will be taken by the police if the person being questioned answers questions, makes a statement or refuses to do either. If the person asks directly what action will be taken if they answer questions, make a statement or refuse to do either, the interviewer may inform them what action the police propose to take provided that action is itself proper and warranted.

11.6 The interview or further interview of a person about an offence with which that person has not been charged or for which they have not been informed they may be prosecuted, must cease when:

(a) the officer in charge of the investigation is satisfied all the questions they consider relevant to obtaining accurate and reliable information about the offence have been put to the suspect, this includes allowing the suspect an opportunity to give an innocent explanation and asking questions to test if the explanation is accurate and reliable, e.g. to clear up ambiguities or clarify what the suspect said;

(b) the officer in charge of the investigation has taken account of any other available evidence; and

(c) the officer in charge of the investigation, or in the case of a detained suspect, the custody officer, see *paragraph 16.1*, reasonably believes there is sufficient evidence to provide a realistic prospect of conviction for that offence.

This paragraph does not prevent officers in revenue cases or acting under the confiscation provisions of the Criminal Justice Act 1988 or the Drug Trafficking Act 1994 from inviting suspects to complete a formal question and answer record after the interview is concluded.

## (b) Interview records

11.7

(a) An accurate record must be made of each interview, whether or not the interview takes place at a police station.

(b) The record must state the place of interview, the time it begins and ends, any interview breaks and, subject to *paragraph 2.6A*, the names of all those present; and must be made on the forms provided for this purpose or in the interviewer's pocket book or in accordance with the Codes of Practice E or F.

(c) Any written record must be made and completed during the interview, unless this would not be practicable or would interfere with the conduct of the interview, and must constitute either a verbatim record of what has been said or, failing this, an account of the interview which adequately and accurately summarises it.

11.8 If a written record is not made during the interview it must be made as soon as practicable after its completion.

11.9 Written interview records must be timed and signed by the maker.

11.10 If a written record is not completed during the interview the reason must be recorded in the interview record.

11.11 Unless it is impracticable, the person interviewed shall be given the opportunity to read the interview record and to sign it as correct or to indicate how they consider it inaccurate. If the person interviewed cannot read or refuses to read the record or sign it, the senior interviewer present shall read it to them and ask whether they would like to sign it as correct or make their mark or to indicate how they consider it inaccurate. The interviewer shall certify on the interview record itself what has occurred.

11.12 If the appropriate adult or the person's solicitor is present during the interview, they should also be given an opportunity to read and sign the interview record or any written statement taken down during the interview.

11.13 A written record shall be made of any comments made by a suspect, including unsolicited comments, which are outside the context of an interview but which might be relevant to the offence. Any such record must be timed and signed by the maker. When practicable the suspect shall be given the opportunity to read that record and to sign it as correct or to indicate how they consider it inaccurate.

11.14 Any refusal by a person to sign an interview record when asked in accordance with this Code must itself be recorded.

## (c) Juveniles and mentally disordered or otherwise mentally vulnerable people

11.15 A juvenile or person who is mentally disordered or otherwise mentally vulnerable must not be interviewed regarding their involvement or suspected involvement in a criminal offence or offences, or asked to provide or sign a written statement under caution or record of interview, in the absence of the appropriate adult unless *paragraphs 11.1, 11.18 to 11.20* apply.

11.16 Juveniles may only be interviewed at their place of education in exceptional circumstances and only when the principal or their nominee agrees. Every effort should be made to notify the parent(s) or other person responsible for the juvenile's welfare and the appropriate adult, if this is a different person, that the police want to interview the juvenile and reasonable time should be allowed to enable the appropriate adult to be present at the interview. If awaiting the appropriate adult would cause unreasonable delay, and unless the juvenile is suspected of an offence against the educational establishment, the principal or their nominee can act as the appropriate adult for the purposes of the interview.

11.17 If an appropriate adult is present at an interview, they shall be informed:
- they are not expected to act simply as an observer; and
- the purpose of their presence is to:
  - advise the person being interviewed;
  - observe whether the interview is being conducted properly and fairly;
  - facilitate communication with the person being interviewed.

## (d) Vulnerable suspects—urgent interviews at police stations

11.18   The following persons may not be interviewed unless an officer of superintendent rank or above considers delay will lead to the consequences in *paragraph 11.1(a)* to *(c)*, and is satisfied the interview would not significantly harm the person's physical or mental state (see Annex G):

(a)   a juvenile or person who is mentally disordered or otherwise mentally vulnerable if at the time of the interview the appropriate adult is not present;

(b)   anyone other than in (*a*) who at the time of the interview appears unable to:
- appreciate the significance of questions and their answers; or
- understand what is happening because of the effects of drink, drugs or any illness, ailment or condition;

(c)   a person who has difficulty understanding English or has a hearing disability, if at the time of the interview an interpreter is not present.

11.19   These interviews may not continue once sufficient information has been obtained to avert the consequences in *paragraph 11.1(a)* to *(c)*.

11.20   A record shall be made of the grounds for any decision to interview a person under *paragraph 11.18*.

1.7.3.1   **KEYNOTE**

Whether an interaction between a police officer and a member of the public is defined as an interview by the court can be crucial as to whether it will be admissible in evidence. It is therefore essential to understand the definition of an interview for the purposes of the Police and Criminal Evidence Act 1984 and when a caution must be given and which caution must be given.

If a person is asked questions for reasons *other than obtaining evidence about his/her involvement or suspected involvement in an offence*, this is not an interview (and a caution need not be given). This point is confirmed in the case of *R v McGuinness* [1999] Crim LR 318, where the court confirmed that it was only when a person was suspected of an offence that the caution must be administered before questioning. Consequently, in *R v Miller* [1998] Crim LR 209 the court held that asking a person the single question, 'Are these ecstasy tablets?' criminally implicated the person and therefore the conversation was an interview (i.e. it would not be necessary to ask such a question if there were no suspicion that the tablets were a controlled substance).

Guidance on when questions do not amount to an interview is given by Code C, para. 10.1.

This is not an exhaustive list, and officers may have other valid reasons to speak to a person before it becomes an interview.

Before a person can be interviewed about his/her involvement in an offence, that person must be cautioned. So it might be said that an interview is any questioning of a person after such time as a caution has been or should have been administered. Where a person is arrested for an offence, he/she must also be cautioned, as any questioning will amount to an interview.

Where the questions relate to the issue of guilt, this is likely to be an interview for the purposes of the Police and Criminal Evidence Act 1984. In *CPS v O'Shea* (1998) 11 May, unreported, police were called to a road traffic accident. O'Shea, the owner of the vehicle, was near the car, exhibiting signs of drunkenness and there was no one else in the vicinity who might have been driving the vehicle. The officer said to O'Shea: 'An accident has just happened that is alleged was your fault.' The court held that it was clear that when the officer had asked O'Shea whether he was driving his vehicle at the time of the accident, the officer had known that he was the owner of the vehicle and therefore the question was not solely to establish whether he was the owner. Accordingly, the thrust of the question was whether he had committed an offence. The defendant's subsequent answer was held to be inadmissible as the PACE Codes of Practice had not been complied with. *O'Shea* can be contrasted with *R v Maguire* [1989] Crim LR 815 where the court held that Code C does not prevent a police officer from asking questions at or near the scene of the crime to elicit an explanation which, if true or accepted, would clear the suspect. The giving of a warning or the service of the Notice of Intended Prosecution required by the Road Traffic Offenders Act 1988, s. 1 does not amount to informing a detainee that he/she may be prosecuted for an offence and so does not preclude further questioning in relation to that offence.

If a person has not been arrested then he/she can be interviewed almost anywhere (but an officer intending to interview a person on private property must consider whether he/she is trespassing). If the interview with a person not under arrest takes place in a police station, Code C, para. 3.21 applies. Juveniles should not be arrested at their place of education unless this is unavoidable. When a juvenile is arrested at his/her place of education, the principal or his/her nominee must be informed.

Code C, para. 11.1 deals with when an interview should be held. By itself this might suggest that an interview is not needed when there is other strong evidence. However, the Criminal Procedure and Investigations Act 1996 Code of Practice, para. 3.4 states: 'In conducting an investigation, the investigator should pursue all reasonable lines of enquiry, whether these point towards or away from the suspect. What is reasonable will depend on the particular circumstances.' Interviewers should keep this in mind when deciding what questions to ask in an interview. Although juveniles or people who are mentally disordered or otherwise mentally vulnerable are often capable of providing reliable evidence, they may, without knowing or wishing to do so, be particularly prone in certain circumstances to provide information that may be unreliable, misleading or self-incriminating. Special care should always be taken when questioning such a person, and the appropriate adult should be involved if there is any doubt about a person's age, mental state or capacity. Because of the risk of unreliable evidence it is also important to obtain corroboration of any facts admitted whenever possible.

Significant statements described in paras 11.4 and 11.4A will always be relevant to the offence and must be recorded. When a suspect agrees to read records of interviews and other comments and sign them as correct, he/she should be asked to endorse the record with, for example, 'I agree that this is a correct record of what was said' and add his/her signature. If the suspect does not agree with the record, the interviewer should record the details of any disagreement and ask the suspect to read these details and sign them to the effect that they accurately reflect his/her disagreement. Any refusal to sign should be recorded. Even where, as required by para. 11.4, at the beginning of an interview the interviewer puts to the detainee any significant statement or silence which occurred in the presence and hearing of a police officer or other police staff, this does not prevent the interviewer from putting significant statements and silences to a suspect again at a later stage or a further interview.

1.7.3.2    **KEYNOTE**

**Statements from Suspects**

Statements made by an accused under caution to the police are confidential in the sense that they may be used against the suspect in proceedings, not that they could be used for any purpose of the police. It is clearly implicit in the relationship between the police and the accused that the information, before being used in open court, is used only for the purposes for which it is provided and not for extraneous purposes, such as the media. However, the obligation of confidentiality (which is now included in the Police Code of Conduct) in respect of such a statement will be brought to an end where the contents of the statement are already in the public domain (*Bunn* v *British Broadcasting Corporation* [1998] 3 All ER 552).

1.7.4    ## 12 Interviews in Police Stations

### (a)  Action

12.1    If a police officer wants to interview or conduct enquiries which require the presence of a detainee, the custody officer is responsible for deciding whether to deliver the detainee into the officer's custody. An investigating officer who is given custody of a detainee takes over responsibility for the detainee's care and safe custody for the purposes of this Code until they return the detainee to the custody officer when they must report the manner in which they complied with the Code whilst having custody of the detainee.

12.2    Except as below, in any period of 24 hours a detainee must be allowed a continuous period of at least 8 hours for rest, free from questioning, travel or any interruption in connection with the investigation concerned. This period should normally be at night or other appropriate time which takes account of when the detainee last slept or rested. If a detainee is arrested at a police station after going there voluntarily, the period of 24 hours runs from the time of their arrest and not the time of arrival at the police station. The period may not be interrupted or delayed, except:

(a) when there are reasonable grounds for believing not delaying or interrupting the period would:

    (i) involve a risk of harm to people or serious loss of, or damage to, property;

    (ii) delay unnecessarily the person's release from custody;

    (iii) otherwise prejudice the outcome of the investigation;

(b) at the request of the detainee, their appropriate adult or legal representative;

(c) when a delay or interruption is necessary in order to:

    (i) comply with the legal obligations and duties arising under *section 15*;

    (ii) to take action required under *section 9* or in accordance with medical advice.

If the period is interrupted in accordance with *(a)*, a fresh period must be allowed. Interruptions under *(b)* and *(c)*, do not require a fresh period to be allowed.

12.3 Before a detainee is interviewed the custody officer, in consultation with the officer in charge of the investigation and appropriate healthcare professionals as necessary, shall assess whether the detainee is fit enough to be interviewed. This means determining and considering the risks to the detainee's physical and mental state if the interview took place and determining what safeguards are needed to allow the interview to take place. *See Annex G.* The custody officer shall not allow a detainee to be interviewed if the custody officer considers it would cause significant harm to the detainee's physical or mental state. Vulnerable suspects listed at *paragraph 11.18* shall be treated as always being at some risk during an interview and these persons may not be interviewed except in accordance with *paragraphs 11.18* to *11.20*.

12.4 As far as practicable interviews shall take place in interview rooms which are adequately heated, lit and ventilated.

12.5 A suspect whose detention without charge has been authorised under PACE, because the detention is necessary for an interview to obtain evidence of the offence for which they have been arrested, may choose not to answer questions but police do not require the suspect's consent or agreement to interview them for this purpose. If a suspect takes steps to prevent themselves being questioned or further questioned, e.g. by refusing to leave their cell to go to a suitable interview room or by trying to leave the interview room, they shall be advised their consent or agreement to interview is not required. The suspect shall be cautioned as in *section 10*, and informed if they fail or refuse to co-operate, the interview may take place in the cell and that their failure or refusal to co-operate may be given in evidence. The suspect shall then be invited to co-operate and go into the interview room.

12.6 People being questioned or making statements shall not be required to stand.

12.7 Before the interview commences each interviewer shall, subject to *paragraph 2.6A*, identify themselves and any other persons present to the interviewee.

12.8 Breaks from interviewing should be made at recognised meal times or at other times that take account of when an interviewee last had a meal. Short refreshment breaks shall be provided at approximately two hour intervals, subject to the interviewer's discretion to delay a break if there are reasonable grounds for believing it would:

(i) involve a:

    • risk of harm to people;

    • serious loss of, or damage to, property;

(ii) unnecessarily delay the detainee's release;

(iii) otherwise prejudice the outcome of the investigation.

12.9 If during the interview a complaint is made by or on behalf of the interviewee concerning the provisions of any of the Codes, or it comes to the interviewer's notice that the interviewee may have been treated improperly, the interviewer should:

(i) record it in the interview record;

(ii) inform the custody officer, who is then responsible for dealing with it as in *section 9*.

## (b) Documentation

12.10    A record must be made of the:
- time a detainee is not in the custody of the custody officer, and why;
- reason for any refusal to deliver the detainee out of that custody.

12.11    A record shall be made of:

(a) the reasons it was not practicable to use an interview room; and

(b) any action taken as in *paragraph 12.5*.

The record shall be made on the custody record or in the interview record for action taken whilst an interview record is being kept, with a brief reference to this effect in the custody record.

12.12    Any decision to delay a break in an interview must be recorded, with reasons, in the interview record.

12.13    All written statements made at police stations under caution shall be written on forms provided for the purpose.

12.14    All written statements made under caution shall be taken in accordance with *Annex D*. Before a person makes a written statement under caution at a police station they shall be reminded about the right to legal advice.

---

**1.7.4.1**

**KEYNOTE**

When deciding whether to hand over a detained person to the interviewing officer under para. 12.1 the custody officer should be mindful of whether there is sufficient relevant time remaining for the detained person to be interviewed (see Code C, para. 15).

Statements under caution, particularly of a detained person, are less common than interviews. If a person has been interviewed and it has been audio or visually recorded or an interview has been recorded contemporaneously in writing, statements under caution should normally be taken in these circumstances only at the person's express wish. See Code C, Annex C for restrictions on drawing inferences and Annex D for the variable declarations the person must include in his/her statements.

Meal breaks should normally last at least 45 minutes and shorter breaks after two hours should last at least 15 minutes. If the interviewer prolongs the interview to avoid the risk of harm to people, serious loss of, or damage to, property, to delay the detainee's release or otherwise prejudice the outcome of the investigation, a longer break should be provided. If there is a short interview, and another short interview is contemplated, the length of the break may be reduced if there are reasonable grounds to believe that this is necessary to avoid any of the consequences in para. 12.8(i)–(iii).

---

**1.7.4.2**

**KEYNOTE**

**Solicitors and Legal Advice**

Code C, section 6 provides guidance with regard to legal advice and access to solicitors during interview. Where a solicitor is available at the time the interview begins or while it is in progress, the solicitor must be allowed to be present while the person is interviewed (Code C, para. 6.8).

If the investigating officer considers that a solicitor is acting in such a way that he/she is unable properly to put questions to the suspect, he/she will stop the interview and consult an officer not below the rank of superintendent, if one is readily available, otherwise an officer not below the rank of inspector who is not connected with the investigation, to decide whether that solicitor should be excluded from the interview. The interview may also have to be stopped in order to allow another solicitor to be instructed (Code C, para. 6.10).

If a request for legal advice is made during an interview, the interviewing officer must stop the interview immediately and arrange for legal advice to be provided. If the suspect changes his/her mind again, the interview can continue provided Code C, para. 6.6 is complied with.

**KEYNOTE**

**What should be Disclosed to the Solicitor?**

It is important not to confuse the duty of disclosure to a person once charged with the need to disclose evidence to suspects before interviewing them. After a person has been charged, and before trial, the rules of disclosure are clear (**see chapter 1.10**) and almost all material must be disclosed to the defence.

However, this is not necessarily the case at the interview stage of the investigation. There is no specific provision within the Police and Criminal Evidence Act 1984 or the Codes of Practice for the disclosure of *any* information by the police at the police station, *with the exception of the custody record* and, generally in identification procedures, the initial description given by the witnesses. In respect of the provision of a copy of the 'first description' of a suspect it should be noted that Code D (para. 3.1) states that a copy of the 'first description' shall, where practicable, be given to the suspect or his/her solicitor before any procedures under paras 3.5–3.10, 3.21 or 3.23 are carried out. In other words, the disclosure requirement is that a copy of the 'first description' shall, where practicable, be given to the suspect or his/her solicitor before a video identification, an identification parade, a group identification or confrontation takes place. Therefore, an officer disclosing information to a solicitor at the interview stage (which is taking place in advance of any identification procedures) need not provide the 'first description' of a suspect at that time.

Further, there is nothing within the Criminal Justice and Public Order Act 1994 that states that information must be disclosed before an inference from silence can be made. Indeed, in *R* v *Imran* [1997] Crim LR 754, the court held that it is totally wrong to submit that a defendant should be prevented from lying by being presented with the whole of the evidence against him/her prior to the interview.

In *R* v *Argent* [1997] Crim LR 346, the court dismissed the argument that an inference could not be drawn under s. 34 of the Criminal Justice and Public Order Act 1994 because there had not been full disclosure at the interview. However, the court did recognise that it may be a factor to take into account for the jury to decide whether the failure to answer questions was reasonable.

In *R* v *Roble* [1997] Crim LR 449, the court suggested that an inference would not be drawn where a solicitor gave advice to remain silent where, for example, the interviewing officer had disclosed too little of the case for the solicitor usefully to advise his/her client, or where the nature of the offence, or the material in the hands of the police, was so complex or related to matters so long ago that no sensible immediate response was feasible.

It was not uncommon in the past for solicitors to advise on no comment interviews and this has been relied on by defendants to avoid adverse inferences being drawn from their silence. The courts and legal advisers are now very aware of the consequences of advising a suspect to offer no comment. In *R* v *Morgan* [2001] EWCA Crim 445, the Court of Appeal stated that a court was entitled to assume that a solicitor would advise his/her client about the adverse inferences rule. In *R* v *Ali* [2001] EWCA Crim 683, the court stated that the question was not whether the advice to remain silent was good advice but whether it provided an adequate reason for failing to answer questions.

In *R* v *Hoare* [2004] EWCA Crim 784, the Court of Appeal held that the purpose of s. 34 was to qualify a defendant's right to silence, rather than to exclude a jury from drawing an adverse inference against a defendant merely because he/she had been advised by his/her solicitor to remain silent, whether or not he/she genuinely or reasonably relied on that advice. Where a defendant had an explanation to give that was consistent with his/her innocence it was not 'reasonable', within the meaning of s. 34(1), for him/her to fail to give that explanation in interview even where he/she had been advised by his/her solicitor to remain silent. Legal advice by itself could not preclude the drawing of an adverse inference.

There is a balance to be struck between providing the solicitor with enough information to understand the nature of the case against his/her client and keeping back material which, if disclosed, may allow the suspect the opportunity to avoid implicating him/herself. For instance in *R* v *Thirlwell* [2002] EWCA Crim 286, the Court of Appeal agreed that the solicitor had not been entitled to provisional medical evidence as to possible causes of death in a murder case.

**1.7.5**　　**Annex C—Restriction on Drawing Adverse Inferences from Silence and Terms of the Caution when the Restriction Applies**

### (a) The restriction on drawing adverse inferences from silence

1. The Criminal Justice and Public Order Act 1994, sections 34, 36 and 37 as amended by the Youth Justice and Criminal Evidence Act 1999, section 58 describe the conditions under which adverse inferences may be drawn from a person's failure or refusal to say anything about their involvement in the offence when interviewed, after being charged or informed they may be prosecuted. These provisions are subject to an overriding restriction on the ability of a court or jury to draw adverse inferences from a person's silence. This restriction applies:

    (a) to any detainee at a police station who, before being interviewed, see *section 11* or being charged or informed they may be prosecuted, see *section 16*, has:
    
    　(i) asked for legal advice, see *section 6, paragraph 6.1*;
    
    　(ii) not been allowed an opportunity to consult a solicitor, including the duty solicitor, as in this Code; and
    
    　(iii) not changed their mind about wanting legal advice, see *section 6, paragraph 6.6(d)*.
    　Note the condition in (ii) will:
    
    　　~ apply when a detainee who has asked for legal advice is interviewed before speaking to a solicitor as in *section 6, paragraph 6.6(a)* or *(b)*;
    
    　　~ not apply if the detained person declines to ask for the duty solicitor, see *section 6, paragraphs 6.6(c)* and *(d)*.
    
    (b) to any person charged with, or informed they may be prosecuted for, an offence who:
    
    　(i) has had brought to their notice a written statement made by another person or the content of an interview with another person which relates to that offence, see *section 16, paragraph 16.4*;
    
    　(ii) is interviewed about that offence, see *section 16, paragraph 16.5*; or
    
    　(iii) makes a written statement about that offence, see *Annex D paragraphs 4* and *9*.

### (b) Terms of the caution when the restriction applies

2. When a requirement to caution arises at a time when the restriction on drawing adverse inferences from silence applies, the caution shall be:

    *'You do not have to say anything, but anything you do say may be given in evidence.'*
    Where the use of the Welsh Language is appropriate, the caution may be used directly in Welsh in the following terms:

    *'Does dim rhaid i chi ddweud dim byd, ond gall unrhyw beth yr ydych chi'n ei ddweud gael ei roi fel tystiolaeth.'*

3. Whenever the restriction either begins to apply or ceases to apply after a caution has already been given, the person shall be re-cautioned in the appropriate terms. The changed position on drawing inferences and that the previous caution no longer applies shall also be explained to the detainee in ordinary language.

---

**1.7.5.1**　　**KEYNOTE**

The restriction on drawing inferences from silence does not apply to a person who has not been detained and who therefore cannot be prevented from seeking legal advice if he/she wants to (see Code C, paras 10.2 and 3.15).

　The following is suggested as a framework to help explain changes in the position on drawing adverse inferences if the restriction on drawing adverse inferences from silence applies. Annex C, para. 2 sets out the alternative terms of the caution to be used when the restriction on drawing adverse inferences from silence applies. The situation is likely to occur during a detainee's detention where it will be necessary to administer both of these cautions at various times during his/her detention. As there is a significant difference between them in relation to the right to silence, it will be important to make it clear which caution applies to the detainee during any interview or charge procedure. Guidance as to what the detainee should be told is provided by Code C, Annex C, Note C2; this paragraph gives sample explanations that need to be explained to the detainee before the change in caution is given.

| | | | |
|---|---|---|---|
| Full caution already given (in most cases given when arrested) | → Detainee's access to legal advice restricted as per Code C, Annex C, para. 1. Need to give alternative caution. | → Explain change in caution as set out at Code C, Annex C, Note C2(a)(i). | → Give caution as set out at Annex C, para. 2. |
| Full caution already given | → Detainee has been charged but is further interviewed (Code C, Annex C, para. 1). Need to give alternative caution. | → Explain change in caution as set out at Code C, Annex C, Note C2(a)(ii). | → Give caution as set out at Annex C, para. 2. |
| Caution as set out at Annex C, para. 2, given | → Detainee has now had access to a solicitor or changed his/her mind. Need to give alternative caution. | → Explain change in caution as set out at Code C, Annex C, Note C2(b). | → Give caution as set out at Code C, para. 10.5. |

Where Code C, Annex C, para. 1 applies (i.e. the detainee has not been given access to a solicitor) and the detainee is charged with an offence or informed that he/she may be prosecuted, the caution at Annex C, para. 2 should be used; on all other occasions the caution at Code C, para. l6.2 should be used.

When the circumstances of the detained person changes and restrictions on drawing adverse inferences now apply the following form of words, where applicable, can be used:

The caution you were previously given no longer applies. This is because after that caution:

(i) you asked to speak to a solicitor but have not yet been allowed an opportunity to speak to a solicitor; or

(ii) you have been charged with/informed you may be prosecuted.

See para. 1(b).

Followed by:

This means that from now on, adverse inferences cannot be drawn at court and your defence will not be harmed just because you choose to say nothing. Please listen carefully to the caution I am about to give you because it will apply from now on. You will see that it does not say anything about your defence being harmed.

The following form of words should be used where the circumstances set out in Annex C, para. 1(a) that a restriction on drawing adverse inferences ceases to apply before or at the time the person is charged or informed that he/she may be prosecuted apply:

The caution you were previously given no longer applies. This is because after that caution you have been allowed an opportunity to speak to a solicitor. Please listen carefully to the caution I am about to give you because it will apply from now on. It explains how your defence at court may be affected if you choose to say nothing.

## 1.7.6    Annex D—Written Statements under Caution

### (a)  Written by a person under caution

1.    A person shall always be invited to write down what they want to say.

2. A person who has not been charged with, or informed they may be prosecuted for, any offence to which the statement they want to write relates, shall:

(a) unless the statement is made at a time when the restriction on drawing adverse inferences from silence applies, see Annex C, be asked to write out and sign the following before writing what they want to say:

   *'I make this statement of my own free will. I understand that I do not have to say anything but that it may harm my defence if I do not mention when questioned something which I later rely on in court. This statement may be given in evidence.';*

(b) if the statement is made at a time when the restriction on drawing adverse inferences from silence applies, be asked to write out and sign the following before writing what they want to say;

   *'I make this statement of my own free will. I understand that I do not have to say anything. This statement may be given in evidence.'*

3. When a person, on the occasion of being charged with or informed they may be prosecuted for any offence, asks to make a statement which relates to any such offence and wants to write it they shall:

(a) unless the restriction on drawing adverse inferences from silence, see *Annex C*, applied when they were so charged or informed they may be prosecuted, be asked to write out and sign the following before writing what they want to say:

   *'I make this statement of my own free will. I understand that I do not have to say anything but that it may harm my defence if I do not mention when questioned something which I later rely on in court. This statement may be given in evidence.';*

(b) if the restriction on drawing adverse inferences from silence applied when they were so charged or informed they may be prosecuted, be asked to write out and sign the following before writing what they want to say:

   *'I make this statement of my own free will. I understand that I do not have to say anything. This statement may be given in evidence.'*

4. When a person, who has already been charged with or informed they may be prosecuted for any offence, asks to make a statement which relates to any such offence and wants to write it they shall be asked to write out and sign the following before writing what they want to say:

   *'I make this statement of my own free will. I understand that I do not have to say anything. This statement may be given in evidence.'*

5. Any person writing their own statement shall be allowed to do so without any prompting except a police officer or other police staff may indicate to them which matters are material or question any ambiguity in the statement.

## (b) Written by a police officer or other police staff

6. If a person says they would like someone to write the statement for them, a police officer, or other police staff shall write the statement.

7. If the person has not been charged with, or informed they may be prosecuted for, any offence to which the statement they want to make relates they shall, before starting, be asked to sign, or make their mark, to the following:

(a) unless the statement is made at a time when the restriction on drawing adverse inferences from silence applies, see Annex C:

   *'I,..........................., wish to make a statement. I want someone to write down what I say. I understand that I do not have to say anything but that it may harm my defence if I do not mention when questioned something which I later rely on in court. This statement may be given in evidence.';*

(b) if the statement is made at a time when the restriction on drawing adverse inferences from silence applies:

*'I,..........................., wish to make a statement. I want someone to write down what I say. I understand that I do not have to say anything. This statement may be given in evidence.'*

8. If, on the occasion of being charged with or informed they may be prosecuted for any offence, the person asks to make a statement which relates to any such offence they shall before starting be asked to sign, or make their mark to, the following:

(a) unless the restriction on drawing adverse inferences from silence applied, see Annex C, when they were so charged or informed they may be prosecuted:

*'I,..........................., wish to make a statement. I want someone to write down what I say. I understand that I do not have to say anything but that it may harm my defence if I do not mention when questioned something which I later rely on in court. This statement may be given in evidence.';*

(b) if the restriction on drawing adverse inferences from silence applied when they were so charged or informed they may be prosecuted:

*'I,..........................., wish to make a statement. I want someone to write down what I say. I understand that I do not have to say anything. This statement may be given in evidence.'*

9. If, having already been charged with or informed they may be prosecuted for any offence, a person asks to make a statement which relates to any such offence they shall before starting, be asked to sign, or make their mark to:

*'I,..........................., wish to make a statement. I want someone to write down what I say. I understand that I do not have to say anything. This statement may be given in evidence.'*

10. The person writing the statement must take down the exact words spoken by the person making it and must not edit or paraphrase it. Any questions that are necessary, e.g. to make it more intelligible, and the answers given must be recorded at the same time on the statement form.

11. When the writing of a statement is finished the person making it shall be asked to read it and to make any corrections, alterations or additions they want. When they have finished reading they shall be asked to write and sign or make their mark on the following certificate at the end of the statement:

*'I have read the above statement, and I have been able to correct, alter or add anything I wish. This statement is true. I have made it of my own free will.'*

12. If the person making the statement cannot read, or refuses to read it, or to write the above mentioned certificate at the end of it or to sign it, the person taking the statement shall read it to them and ask them if they would like to correct, alter or add anything and to put their signature or make their mark at the end. The person taking the statement shall certify on the statement itself what has occurred.

The sections of Code C above need to be read in conjunction with Code E where the interview of a suspect is to be audio recorded.

## PACE Code of Practice on Audio Recording Interviews with Suspects (Code E)

This code applies to interviews carried out after midnight on 1 May 2010, notwithstanding that the interview may have commenced before that time.

1.7.7

## 1 General

1.1 This Code of Practice must be readily available for consultation by:

- police officers
- police staff
- detained persons
- members of the public.

1.2 The *Notes for Guidance* included are not provisions of this Code.

1.3 Nothing in this Code shall detract from the requirements of Code C, the Code of Practice for the detention, treatment and questioning of persons by police officers.

1.4 This Code does not apply to those people listed in Code C, *paragraph 1.12*.

1.5 The term:
- 'appropriate adult' has the same meaning as in Code C, paragraph 1.7;
- 'solicitor' has the same meaning as in Code C, *paragraph 6.12*.

1.5A Recording of interviews shall be carried out openly to instil confidence in its reliability as an impartial and accurate record of the interview.

1.6 In this Code:

(aa) 'recording media' means any removable, physical audio recording medium (such as magnetic tape, optical disc or solid state memory) which can be played and copied;

(a) 'designated person' means a person other than a police officer, designated under the Police Reform Act 2002, Part 4 who has specified powers and duties of police officers conferred or imposed on them;

(b) any reference to a police officer includes a designated person acting in the exercise or performance of the powers and duties conferred or imposed on them by their designation;

(c) 'secure digital network' is a computer network system which enables an original interview recording to be stored as a digital multi media file or a series of such files, on a secure file server which is accredited by the National Accreditor for Police Information Systems in the National Police Improvement Agency (NPIA) in accordance with the UK Government Protective Marking Scheme (see section 7 of this Code).

1.7 Sections 2 to 6 of this Code set out the procedures and requirements which apply to all interviews together with the provisions which apply only to interviews recorded using removable media. Section 7 sets out the provisions which apply to interviews recorded using a secure digital network and specifies the provisions in sections 2 to 6 which do not apply to secure digital network recording.

1.8 Nothing in this Code prevents the custody officer, or other officer given custody of the detainee, from allowing police staff who are not designated persons to carry out individual procedures or tasks at the police station if the law allows. However, the officer remains responsible for making sure the procedures and tasks are carried out correctly in accordance with this Code. Any such police staff must be:

(a) a person employed by a police authority maintaining a police force and under the control and direction of the Chief Officer of that force; or

(b) employed by a person with whom a police authority has a contract for the provision of services relating to persons arrested or otherwise in custody.

1.9 Designated persons and other police staff must have regard to any relevant provisions of the Codes of Practice.

1.10 References to pocket book include any official report book issued to police officers or police staff.

1.11 References to a custody officer include those performing the functions of a custody officer as in *paragraph 1.9* of Code C.

## 2 Recording and Sealing Master Recordings

**1.7.8**

2.1 *Not used.*

2.2 One recording, the master recording, will be sealed in the suspect's presence. A second recording will be used as a working copy. The master recording is either of the two recordings used in a twin deck/drive machine or the only recording in a single deck/drive machine. The working copy is either the second/third recording used in a twin/triple deck/drive machine or a copy of the master recording made by a single deck/drive machine. *[This paragraph does not apply to interviews recorded using a secure digital network, see paragraphs 7.4 to 7.6.]*

2.3 Nothing in this Code requires the identity of officers or police staff conducting interviews to be recorded or disclosed:

(a) in the case of enquiries linked to the investigation of terrorism (see paragraph 3.2); or

(b) if the interviewer reasonably believes recording or disclosing their name might put them in danger.

In these cases interviewers should use warrant or other identification numbers and the name of their police station.

### 1.7.8.1      KEYNOTE

The purpose of sealing the master recording in the suspect's presence is to show that the recording's integrity is preserved. If a single deck/drive machine is used, the working copy of the master recording must be made in the suspect's presence and without the master recording leaving his/her sight. The working copy shall be used for making further copies if needed.

The reason for the interviewer using his/her warrant number or other identification numbers and the name of his/her police station is to protect those involved in serious organised crime investigations or arrests of particularly violent suspects when there is reliable information that those arrested or their associates may threaten or cause harm to those involved. The interviewer must hold a reasonable belief that by recording or disclosing his/her name it might put him/her in danger. In these cases interviewers should use warrant or other identification numbers and the name of their police station.

### 1.7.9      3 Interviews to be Audio Recorded

3.1 Subject to *paragraphs 3.3* and *3.4*, audio recording shall be used at police stations for any interview:

(a) with a person cautioned under Code C, *section 10* in respect of any indictable offence, including an offence triable either way;

(b) which takes place as a result of an interviewer exceptionally putting further questions to a suspect about an offence described in *paragraph 3.1(a)* after they have been charged with, or told they may be prosecuted for, that offence, see Code C, *paragraph 16.5*;

(c) when an interviewer wants to tell a person, after they have been charged with, or informed they may be prosecuted for, an offence described in *paragraph 3.1(a)*, about any written statement or interview with another person, see Code C, *paragraph 16.4*.

3.2 The Terrorism Act 2000 makes separate provision for a Code of Practice for the audio recording of interviews of those arrested under Section 41 of detained under Schedule 7 to the Act. The provisions of this Code do not apply to such interviews.

3.3 The custody officer may authorise the interviewer not to audio record the interview when it is:

(a) not reasonably practicable because of equipment failure or the unavailability of a suitable interview room or recording equipment and the authorising officer considers, on reasonable grounds, that the interview should not be delayed; or

(b) clear from the outset there will not be a prosecution.

Note: In these cases the interview should be recorded in writing in accordance with Code C, *section 11*. In all cases the custody officer shall record the specific reasons for not audio recording.

3.4 If a person refuses to go into or remain in a suitable interview room, see Code C, *paragraph 12.5*, and the custody officer considers, on reasonable grounds, that the interview should not be delayed the interview may, at the custody officer's discretion, be conducted in a cell using portable recording equipment or, if none is available, recorded in writing as in Code C, section 11. The reasons for this shall be recorded.

3.5 The whole of each interview shall be audio recorded, including the taking and reading back of any statement.

3.6 An Sign or indicator which is visible to the suspect must show when the recording equipment is recording.

**1.7.9.1**

> **KEYNOTE**
>
> The interviewing of suspects is governed by PACE Code of Practice E. These requirements do not preclude other interviews being audio recorded. Investigators may well be advised to audio record interviews concerning summary only offences as it may be more difficult for the defence to suggest that any confession was fabricated.
>
> A decision not to audio record an interview for any reason may be the subject of comment in court. The authorising officer should be prepared to justify that decision.
>
> If, during the course of an interview under this Code, it becomes apparent that the interview should be conducted under one of the terrorism codes for video recording of interviews, the interview should only continue in accordance with the relevant code.
>
> For cases where:
>
> - a person detained under s. 41 of the Terrorism Act 2000 is interviewed in a police station in England, Wales or Scotland; or
> - any questioning by a constable of a person detained for examination under sch. 7 to the Terrorism Act 2000 takes place in a police station in England, Wales or Scotland;
> - any interview by a constable of a person which takes place in accordance with an authorisation under s. 22 of the Counter-Terrorism Act 2008 (post-charge questioning) anywhere in England and Wales; and
> - any interview by a constable of a person which takes place in accordance with an authorisation under s. 23 of the Counter-Terrorism Act 2008 (post-charge questioning) anywhere in Scotland,
>
> the Code of Practice for the video recording with sound of interviews of persons detained under s. 41 of, or sch. 7 to, the Terrorism Act 2000 and post-charge questioning of persons authorised under ss. 22 or 23 of the Counter-Terrorism Act 2008 must be followed.

**1.7.10**

## 4 The Interview

### (a) General

4.1 The provisions of Code C:
- *sections 10 and 11*, and the applicable *Notes for Guidance* apply to the conduct of interviews to which this Code applies
- *paragraphs 11.7 to 11.14* apply only when a written record is needed.

4.2 Code C, *paragraphs 10.10, 10.11* and Annex C describe the restriction on drawing adverse inferences from a suspect's failure or refusal to say anything about their involvement in the offence when interviewed or after being charged or informed they may be prosecuted, and how it affects the terms of the caution and determines if and by whom a special warning under sections 36 and 37 of the Criminal Justice and Public Order Act 1994 can be given.

### (b) Commencement of interviews

4.3 When the suspect is brought into the interview room the interviewer shall, without delay but in the suspect's sight, load the recorder with new recording media and set it to record.

The recording media must be unwrapped or opened in the suspect's presence. *[This paragraph does not apply to interviews recorded using a secure digital network, see paragraphs 7.4 and 7.5.]*

4.4 The interviewer should tell the suspect about the recording process and point out the sign or indicator which shows that the recording equipment is activated and recording. See paragraph 3.6. The interviewer shall:

(a) say the interview is being audibly recorded

(b) subject to *paragraph 2.3*, give their name and rank and that of any other interviewer present

(c) ask the suspect and any other party present, e.g. a solicitor, to identify themselves

(d) state the date, time of commencement and place of the interview

(e) state the suspect will be given a notice about what will happen to the copies of the recording. *[This sub-paragraph does not apply to interviews recorded using a secure digital network, see paragraphs 7.4 and 7.6 to 7.7.]*

4.5 The interviewer shall:

• caution the suspect, see Code C, *section 10*

• remind the suspect of their entitlement to free legal advice, see Code C, *paragraph 11.2.*

4.6 The interviewer shall put to the suspect any significant statement or silence; see Code C, *paragraph 11.4.*

## (c) Interviews with deaf persons

4.7 If the suspect is deaf or is suspected of having impaired hearing, the interviewer shall make a written note of the interview in accordance with Code C, at the same time as audio recording it in accordance with this Code.

## (d) Objections and complaints by the suspect

4.8 If the suspect objects to the interview being audibly recorded at the outset, during the interview or during a break, the interviewer shall explain that the interview is being audibly recorded and that this Code requires the suspect's objections to be recorded on the audio recording. When any objections have been audibly recorded or the suspect has refused to have their objections recorded, the interviewer shall say they are turning off the recorder, give their reasons and turn it off. The interviewer shall then make a written record of the interview as in Code C, section 11. If, however, the interviewer reasonably considers they may proceed to question the suspect with the audio recording still on, the interviewer may do so. This procedure also applies in cases where the suspect has previously objected to the interview being visually recorded, see Code F, *paragraph 4.8*, and the investigating officer has decided to audibly record the interview.

4.9 If in the course of an interview a complaint is made by or on behalf of the person being questioned concerning the provisions of this Code or Code C, the interviewer shall act as in Code C, *paragraph 12.9.*

4.10 If the suspect indicates they want to tell the interviewer about matters not directly connected with the offence and they are unwilling for these matters to be audio recorded, the suspect should be given the opportunity to tell the interviewer at the end of the formal interview.

## (e) Changing recording media

4.11 When the recorder shows the recording media only has a short time left, the interviewer shall tell the suspect the recording media are coming to an end and round off that part of the interview. If the interviewer leaves the room for a second set of recording media, the suspect shall not be left unattended. The interviewer will remove the recording media from the recorder and insert the new recording media which shall be unwrapped or opened in the suspect's presence. The recorder should be set to record on the new media. To avoid confusion between the recording media, the interviewer shall mark the media with an identification number immediately after they are removed from the recorder. *[This paragraph does not apply to interviews recorded using a secure digital network as this does not use removable media, see paragraphs 1.6(c), 7.4 and 7.14 to 7.15.]*

## (f) Taking a break during interview

4.12    When a break is taken, the fact that a break is to be taken, the reason for it and the time shall be recorded on the audio recording.

4.12A    When the break is taken and the interview room vacated by the suspect, the recording media shall be removed from the recorder and the procedures for the conclusion of an interview followed, see *paragraph 4.18.*

4.13    When a break is a short one and both the suspect and an interviewer remain in the interview room, the recording may be stopped. There is no need to remove the recording media and when the interview recommences the recording should continue on the same recording media. The time the interview recommences shall be recorded on the audio recording.

4.14    After any break in the interview the interviewer must, before resuming the interview, remind the person being questioned that they remain under caution or, if there is any doubt, give the caution in full again. *[Paragraphs 4.12 to 4.14 do not apply to interviews recorded using a secure digital network, see paragraphs 7.4 and 7.8 to 7.10.]*

## (g) Failure of recording equipment

4.15    If there is an equipment failure which can be rectified quickly, e.g. by inserting new recording media, the interviewer shall follow the appropriate procedures as in *paragraph 4.11.* When the recording is resumed the interviewer shall explain what happened and record the time the interview recommences. If, however, it will not be possible to continue recording on that recorder and no replacement recorder is readily available, the interview may continue without being audibly recorded. If this happens, the interviewer shall seek the custody officer's authority as in *paragraph 3.3. [This paragraph does not apply to interviews recorded using a secure digital network, see paragraphs 7.4 and 7.11.]*

## (h) Removing recording media from the recorder

4.16    When recording media is removed from the recorder during the interview, they shall be retained and the procedures in *paragraph 4.18* followed. *[This paragraph does not apply to interviews recorded using a secure digital network as this does not use removable media, see paragraphs 1.6(c), 7.4 and 7.14 to 7.15.]*

## (i) Conclusion of interview

4.17    At the conclusion of the interview, the suspect shall be offered the opportunity to clarify anything he or she has said and asked if there is anything they want to add.

4.18    At the conclusion of the interview, including the taking and reading back of any written statement, the time shall be recorded and the recording shall be stopped. The interviewer shall seal the master recording with a master recording label and treat it as an exhibit in accordance with force standing orders. The interviewer shall sign the label and ask the suspect and any third party present during the interview to sign it. If the suspect or third party refuse to sign the label an officer of at least inspector rank, or if not available the custody officer, shall be called into the interview room and asked, subject to *paragraph 2.3*, to sign it.

4.19 The suspect shall be handed a notice which explains:

- how the audio recording will be used
- the arrangements for access to it
- that if the person is charged or informed they will be prosecuted, a copy of the audio recording will be supplied as soon as practicable or as otherwise agreed between the suspect and the police or on the order of a court.

*[Paragraphs 4.17 to 4.19 do not apply to interviews recorded using a secure digital network, see paragraphs 7.4 and 7.12 to 7.13.]*

---

**1.7.10.1** **KEYNOTE**

**Preparation before Interview at Police Station**

Preparation is essential before any interview (indeed it is the first step in the PACE interviewing model). This preparation should include the following points:

- Decide where the interview will be conducted. Consider the availability of a room and the timing of the interview.
- The location must have a seat for the person being interviewed (Code C, para. 12.6) and should be adequately lit, heated and ventilated (Code C, para. 12.4). The detained person must also have clothing of a reasonable standard of comfort and cleanliness (Code C, para. 8.5). (It will be a question of fact as to what amounts to adequate clothing and it is suggested that if the clothing is such as to degrade the detained person or make him/her uncomfortable, it may lead to the confession being held to be unreliable.)
- If the interview is being audio recorded (this is not relevant to interviews being recorded on a secure digital network), ensure that there are sufficient recording media for the anticipated length of the interview (or at least until the first break period). If the interview is being recorded in writing, ensure that there are enough forms.
- In deciding the timing of the interview, consideration must be given to the detainee's rest period, which should not be interrupted or delayed unless Code C, para. 12.2 applies. Where the interview goes ahead during the rest period under Code C, para. 12.2(a), a fresh rest period must be allowed. Before a detainee is interviewed, the custody officer, in consultation with the officer in charge of the investigation and appropriate health care professionals as necessary, shall assess whether the detainee is fit enough to be interviewed (Code C, para. 12.3 and Annex G).
- If legal advice has been requested you must arrange for the legal representative to be present at the interview unless Code C, para. 6.6 applies.
- If a person has asked for legal advice and an interview is initiated in the absence of a legal adviser (e.g. where the person has agreed to be interviewed without his/her legal adviser being present or because of the urgent need to interview under Code C, para. 11.1), a record must be made in the interview record (Code C, para. 6.17).
- If an appropriate adult should be present, arrange for his/her attendance. (For the definition of appropriate adult, see Code C, para. 1.7.)
- If an interpreter is needed for the interview, arrange for his/her attendance. The provisions of Code C, section 13 on interpreters for deaf persons or for interviews with suspects who have difficulty understanding English apply to these interviews.
- The reason for the interviewer making a written note of the interview where a person is deaf or has impaired hearing is to give the equivalent rights of access to the full interview record as far as this is possible using audio recording. The interview notes must be in accordance with Code C.

It is also important to draw up an interview plan and to include any relevant areas that may provide a general or specific defence.

- Look at the evidence available and identify any significant statement or silence by the suspect in order that it can be put to him/her in interview (Code C, para. 11.4).

**KEYNOTE**

### Conduct During Interview

- Code C, para. 11.5 reiterates the fact that officers must not act oppressively.
- For the purpose of voice identification, at the start of the interview, or when persons enter the interview room the interviewer should ask the suspect and any other people present to identify themselves.
- If the suspect asks for the audio recording to be stopped and the interviewer decides to continue recording against the wishes of the suspect the decision may be the subject of comment in court. That said, it should be noted that in any case where the custody officer is called to deal with the complaint, the recorder should, if possible, be left on until the custody officer has entered the room and spoken to the person being interviewed. Continuation or termination of the interview should be at the interviewer's discretion pending action by an inspector under Code C, para. 9.2. If the complaint is about a matter not connected with this Code or Code C, the decision to continue is at the interviewer's discretion. When the interviewer decides to continue the interview, he/she shall tell the suspect that the complaint will be brought to the custody officer's attention at the conclusion of the interview. When the interview is concluded the interviewer must, as soon as practicable, inform the custody officer about the existence and nature of the complaint made.

At the start of the interview the investigating officer should put to the suspect any significant statement or silence which occurred before his/her arrival at the police station and ask the suspect whether he/she confirms the earlier statement or silence and whether he/she wishes to add anything. Code C, para. 11.4A defines a 'significant' statement or silence. This aspect of the interview is very important in terms of establishing whether the facts are disputed. If they are not disputed at this stage, it is unlikely that they will be challenged at any later court hearing and, if challenged, the defence will have to explain why this was not done at the time of the interview. The courts may also view this failure to put the statement to the suspect in a more sinister light. In *R v Allen* [2001] EWCA Crim 1607, the court was concerned that the police failed to put the admission to the suspect in interview, despite thorough questioning, which it felt clearly placed a question mark over the admission's reliability. If the suspect remains silent in relation to a 'significant silence', that silence may give rise to an adverse inference being drawn under s. 34 of the Criminal Justice and Public Order Act 1994 if the person raises it in his/her defence at court. (As this is a very important issue, it may be necessary to delay the interview until the arrest notes are completed or the officers witnessing the offence/arrest have been consulted to ensure that all matters are put to the suspect at this stage.) Consideration should be given to putting questions to a suspect who makes no comment, or even where the legal representative has stated that the suspect will make no comment, as this may allow the court to draw inferences against a defence that the suspect raises at court. The interviewer may wish to go through any significant statement or silence again if during earlier interviews adverse inferences could not be drawn.

The interviewer should remember that it may be necessary to show to the court that nothing occurred during a break or between interviews which influenced the suspect's recorded evidence. After a break or at the beginning of a subsequent interview, the interviewer should consider summarising on the record the reason for the break and confirming this with the suspect.

Where the interview is being recorded and the media or the recording equipment fails, the officer conducting the interview should stop the interview immediately. Where part of the interview is unaffected by the error and is still accessible on the media, that media shall be copied and sealed in the suspect's presence and the interview recommenced using new equipment/media as required. Where the content of the interview has been lost in its entirety the media should be sealed in the suspect's presence and the interview begun again. If the recording equipment cannot be fixed or no replacement is immediately available the interview should be recorded in accordance with Code C, section 11.

Guidance is provided by Code C, para. 11.6 as to when an interview should be concluded. It is important to remember that the interview should not be concluded at the point when there is sufficient evidence to prosecute but when there is sufficient evidence to provide a realistic prospect of conviction. (In *Prouse* v *DPP* [1999] All ER (D) 748 the question was said to be not how much evidence there is but the quality of it.) Once there is enough evidence to prosecute, it may still be necessary to cover those other points in the interview that may be relevant to the defence case.

**1.7.10.3**   **KEYNOTE**

**Special Groups**

As a confession can be very damning evidence against a defendant, it is important to provide safeguards that give all suspects the same level of protection. The PACE Codes of Practice recognise certain groups as being in need of additional protection. These groups include juveniles, people who do not speak English, those suffering from a mental impairment and those who are deaf. Such suspects must not be interviewed without the relevant person being present. See Code C, section 13.

The Criminal Justice Act 2003 introduces a code of practice for police officers interviewing a witness notified by the accused (which would include an alibi witness), **see para. 1.10.10.7.**

**1.7.10.4**   **KEYNOTE**

**Special Warnings**

Now that inferences can be drawn from a suspect's silence (albeit in limited circumstances), it is necessary to warn the person of the dangers of remaining silent. For this reason, the 'special warning' was introduced where there is potentially incriminating evidence relating to objects, marks or substances; or relating to the accused's presence at a particular place. If the special warning is not given, inferences from silence will not be allowed to boost the prosecution case but the potentially incriminating evidence may still be admissible. Code C, paras 10.10–10.11 must be followed.

These provisions also apply to any questions about why the suspect was at any place, at or about the time the offence for which he/she was arrested was committed, and has failed to or refuses to account for his/her presence at that place (see s. 37 of the Criminal Justice and Public Order Act 1994).

See Code C, Annex C for occasions when special warnings and adverse inferences do not apply.

**1.7.11**   **5 After the Interview**

5.1   The interviewer shall make a note in their pocket book that the interview has taken place, was audibly recorded, its time, duration and date and the master recording's identification number.

5.2   If no proceedings follow in respect of the person whose interview was recorded, the recording media must be kept securely as in *paragraph 6.1.*
*[This section (paragraphs 5.1, 5.2) does not apply to interviews recorded using a secure digital network, see paragraphs 7.4 and 7.14 to 7.15.]*

**1.7.11.1**   **KEYNOTE**

Any written record of an audibly recorded interview should be made in accordance with national guidelines approved by the Secretary of State, and with regard to the advice contained in the Manual of Guidance for the preparation, processing and submission of prosecution files.

## 6 Media Security

6.1 The officer in charge of each police station at which interviews with suspects are recorded shall make arrangements for master recordings to be kept securely and their movements accounted for on the same basis as material which may be used for evidential purposes, in accordance with force standing orders.

6.2 A police officer has no authority to break the seal on a master recording required for criminal trial or appeal proceedings. If it is necessary to gain access to the master recording, the police officer shall arrange for its seal to be broken in the presence of a representative of the Crown Prosecution Service. The defendant or their legal adviser should be informed and given a reasonable opportunity to be present. If the defendant or their legal representative is present they shall be invited to reseal and sign the master recording. If either refuses or neither is present this should be done by the representative of the Crown Prosecution Service.

6.3 If no criminal proceedings result or the criminal trial and, if applicable, appeal proceedings to which the interview relates have been concluded, the chief officer of police is responsible for establishing arrangements for breaking the seal on the master recording, if necessary.

6.4 When the master recording seal is broken, a record must be made of the procedure followed, including the date, time, place and persons present.

*[This section (paragraphs 6.1 to 6.4) does not apply to interviews recorded using a secure digital network, see paragraphs 7.4 and 7.14 to 7.15.]*

**KEYNOTE**

This section is concerned with the security of the master recording sealed at the conclusion of the interview. Care must be taken of working copies of recordings because their loss or destruction may lead to the need to access master recordings.

If the recording has been delivered to the Crown Court for its keeping after committal for trial the Crown Prosecutor will apply to the Chief Clerk of the Crown Court centre for the release of the recording for unsealing by the Crown Prosecutor.

Reference to the CPS or to the Crown Prosecutor in this part of the Code should be taken to include any other body or person with a statutory responsibility for prosecution for whom the police conduct any audibly recorded interviews.

## 7 Recording of Interviews by Secure Digital Network

7.1 A secure digital network does not use removable media and this section specifies the provisions which will apply when a secure digital network is used.

7.2 *Not used*

7.3 The following requirements are solely applicable to the use of a secure digital network for the recording of interviews.

### (a) Application of section 1 to 6 of Code E

7.4 Sections 1 to 6 of Code E above apply except for the following paragraphs:
- Paragraph 2.2 under 'Recording and sealing of master recordings'
- Paragraph 4.3 under '(b) Commencement of interviews'
- Paragraph 4.4 (e) under '(b) Commencement of interviews'
- Paragraphs 4.11–4.19 under '(e) Changing recording media', '(f) Taking a break during interview', '(g) Failure of recording equipment', '(h) Removing recording media from the recorder' and '(i) Conclusion of interview'
- Paragraphs 6.1–6.4 under 'Media security'

## (b) Commencement of Interview

7.5    When the suspect is brought into the interview room, the interviewer shall without delay and in the sight of the suspect, switch on the recording equipment and enter the information necessary to log on to the secure network and set it to record.

7.6    The interviewer must then inform the suspect that the interview is being recorded via a secure digital network and that recording has commenced.

7.7    In addition to the requirements of paragraph 4.4 (a–d) above, the interviewer must inform the person that:

- they will be given access to the recording of the interview in the event that they are charged or informed that they will be prosecuted but if they are not charged or informed that they will be prosecuted, they will only be given access as agreed with the police or on the order of the court;
- they will be given a written notice at the end of the interview setting out their rights to access the recording and what will happen to the recording.

## (c) Taking a break during interview

7.8    When a break is taken, the fact that a break is to be taken, the reason for it and the time shall be recorded on the audio recording. The recording shall be stopped and the procedures for the conclusion of an interview followed.

7.9    When the interview recommences the procedures in paragraphs 7.5 to 7.7 for commencing an interview shall be followed to create a new file to record the continuation of the interview. The time the interview recommences shall be recorded on the audio recording.

7.10   After any break in the interview the interviewer must, before resuming the interview, remind the person being questioned that they remain under caution or, if there is any doubt, give the caution in full again.

## (d) Failure of recording equipment

7.11   If there is an equipment failure which can be rectified quickly, e.g. by commencing a new secure digital network recording, the interviewer shall follow the appropriate procedures as in *paragraphs 7.8 and 7.10*. When the recording is resumed the interviewer shall explain what happened and record the time the interview recommences. If, however, it is not possible to continue recording on the secure digital network the interview should be recorded on removable media as in *paragraph 4.3* unless the necessary equipment is not available. If this happens the interview may continue without being audibly recorded and the interviewer shall seek the custody officer's authority as in *paragraph 3.3*.

## (e) Conclusion of interview

7.12   At the conclusion of the interview, the suspect shall be offered the opportunity to clarify anything he or she has said and asked if there is anything they want to add.

7.13   At the conclusion of the interview, including the taking and reading back of any written statement:

(a) the time shall be orally recorded.

(b) the suspect shall be handed a notice which explains:
- how the audio recording will be used
- the arrangements for access to it

- that if they are charged or informed that they will be prosecuted, they will be given access to the recording of the interview either electronically or by being given a copy on removable recording media, but if they are not charged or informed they will be prosecuted, they will only be given access as agreed with the police or on the order of a court.

(c) the suspect must be asked to confirm that he or she has received a copy of the notice at *paragraph 7.13(b)* above. If the suspect fails to accept or to acknowledge receipt of the notice, the interviewer will state for the recording that a copy of the notice has been provided to the suspect and that he or she has refused to take a copy of the notice or has refused to acknowledge receipt.

(d) the time shall be recorded and the interviewer shall notify the suspect that the recording is being saved to the secure network. The interviewer must save the recording in the presence of the suspect. The suspect should then be informed that the interview is terminated.

## (f) After the interview

7.14 The interviewer shall make a note in their pocket book that the interview has taken place, was audibly recorded, its time, duration and date and the original recording's identification number.

7.15 If no proceedings follow, in respect of the person whose interview was recorded, the recordings must be kept securely as in paragraphs 7.16 and 7.17.

## (g) Security of secure digital network interview records

7.16 Interview record files are stored in read only format on non-removable storage devices, for example, hard disk drives, to ensure their integrity. The recordings are first saved locally to a secure non-removable device before being transferred to the remote network device. If for any reason the network connection fails, the recording remains on the local device and will be transferred when the network connections are restored.

7.17 Access to interview recordings, including copying to removable media, must be strictly controlled and monitored to ensure that access is restricted to those who have been given specific permission to access for specified purposes when this is necessary. For example, police officers and CPS lawyers involved in the preparation of any prosecution case, persons interviewed if they have been charged or informed they may be prosecuted and their legal representatives.

**1.7.13.1**

**KEYNOTE**

The notice given to the suspect at the conclusion of the interview (see Code E, para. 7.13) should provide a brief explanation of the secure digital network and how access is strictly limited to the recording. The notice should also explain the access rights of the suspect, his or her legal representative, the police and the prosecutor to the recording of the interview. Space should be provided on the form to insert the date and the file reference number for the interview.

## PACE Code of Practice on Visual Recording with Sound of Interviews with Suspects (Code F)

The contents of this code should be considered if an interviewing officer decides to make a visual recording with sound of an interview with a suspect after midnight 1 May 2010.

There is no statutory requirement under PACE to visually record interviews.

**1.7.14**

## 1 General

1.1 This code of practice must be readily available for consultation by police officers and other police staff, detained persons and members of the public.

1.2 The notes for guidance included are not provisions of this code. They form guidance to police officers and others about its application and interpretation.

1.3 Nothing in this code shall be taken as detracting in any way from the requirements of the Code of Practice for the Detention, Treatment and Questioning of Persons by Police Officers (Code C).

1.4 The interviews to which this Code applies are set out in paragraphs 3.1–3.3.

1.5 In this code, the term 'appropriate adult', 'solicitor' and 'interview' have the same meaning as those set out in Code C. The corresponding provisions and Notes for Guidance in Code C applicable to those terms shall also apply where appropriate.

1.5A The visual recording of interviews shall be carried out openly to instil confidence in its reliability as an impartial and accurate record of the interview.

1.6 Any reference in this code to visual recording shall be taken to mean visual recording with sound and in this code:

(a) 'recording media' means any removable, physical audio recording medium (such as magnetic tape, optical disc or solid state memory) which can be played and copied;

(b) 'designated person' means a person other than a police officer, designated under the Police Reform Act 2002, Part 4 who has specified powers and duties of police officers conferred or imposed on them;

(c) any reference to a police officer includes a designated person acting in the exercise or performance of the powers and duties conferred or imposed on them by their designation;

(d) 'secure digital network' is a computer network system which enables an original interview recording to be stored as a digital multi media file or a series of such files, on a secure file server which is accredited by the National Accreditor for Police Information Systems in the National Police Improvement Agency (NPIA) in accordance with the UK Government Protective Marking Scheme. (See section 7 of this Code.)

1.7 References to 'pocket book' in this Code include any official report book issued to police officers.

**1.7.15**

## 2 Recording and Sealing of Master Recordings

2.1 *Not used*

2.2 The camera(s) shall be placed in the interview room so as to ensure coverage of as much of the room as is practicably possible whilst the interviews are taking place.

2.3 The certified recording medium will be of a high quality, new and previously unused. When the certified recording medium is placed in the recorder and switched on to record, the correct date and time, in hours, minutes and seconds, will be superimposed automatically, second by second, during the whole recording. See section 7 regarding the use of a secure digital network to record the interview.

2.4 One copy of the certified recording medium, referred to in this code as the master copy, will be sealed before it leaves the presence of the suspect. A second copy will be used as a working copy.

2.5 Nothing in this code requires the identity of an officer to be recorded or disclosed if:
 (a) the interview or record relates to a person detained under the Terrorism Act 2000; or
 (b) otherwise where the officer reasonably believes that recording or disclosing their name might put them in danger.

In these cases, the officer will have their back to the camera and shall use their warrant or other identification number and the name of the police station to which they are attached. Such instances and the reasons for them shall be recorded in the custody record.

---

**1.7.15.1**

**KEYNOTE**

The certified recording media should be capable of having an image of the date and time superimposed upon them as they record the interview. Interviewing officers will wish to arrange that, as far as possible, visual recording arrangements are unobtrusive. It must be clear to the suspect, however, that there is no opportunity to interfere with the recording equipment or the recording media. The purpose of sealing the master copy before it leaves the presence of the suspect is to establish his/her confidence that the integrity of the copy is preserved.

In cases where a suspect is not available for an identification as set out in Code D, para. 3.21, the recording of the interview may be used for identification procedures.

The purpose of the interviewer having his/her back to the camera and using his/her warrant number or other identification numbers and the name of his/her police station is to protect police officers and others involved in the investigation of serious organised crime or the arrest of particularly violent suspects when there is reliable information that those arrested or their associates may threaten or cause harm to the officers, their families or their personal property.

---

**1.7.16**

## 3 Interviews to be Visually Recorded

3.1 Subject to paragraph 3.2 below, if an interviewing officer decides to make a visual recording these are the areas where it might be appropriate:
 (a) with a suspect in respect of an indictable offence (including an offence triable either way);
 (b) which takes place as a result of an interviewer exceptionally putting further questions to a suspect about an offence described in sub-paragraph (a) above after they have been charged with, or informed they may be prosecuted for, that offence;
 (c) in which an interviewer wishes to bring to the notice of a person, after that person has been charged with, or informed they may be prosecuted for an offence described in sub-paragraph (a) above, any written statement made by another person, or the content of an interview with another person;
 (d) with, or in the presence of, a deaf or deaf/blind or speech impaired person who uses sign language to communicate;
 (e) with, or in the presence of anyone who requires an 'appropriate adult'; or
 (f) in any case where the suspect or their representative requests that the interview be recorded visually.

3.2 The Terrorism Act 2000 makes separate provision for a code of practice for the video recording of interviews in a police station of those detained under Schedule 7 or section 41 of the Act. The provisions of this code do not therefore apply to such interviews.

3.3 The custody officer may authorise the interviewing officer not to record the interview visually:

(a) where it is not reasonably practicable to do so because of failure of the equipment, or the non-availability of a suitable interview room, or recorder, and the authorising officer considers on reasonable grounds that the interview should not be delayed until the failure has been rectified or a suitable room or recorder becomes available. In such cases the custody officer may authorise the interviewing officer to audio record the interview in accordance with the guidance set out in Code E;

(b) where it is clear from the outset that no prosecution will ensue; or

(c) where it is not practicable to do so because at the time the person resists being taken to a suitable interview room or other location which would enable the interview to be recorded, or otherwise fails or refuses to go into such a room or location, and the authorising officer considers on reasonable grounds that the interview should not be delayed until these conditions cease to apply.

3.4   When a person who is voluntarily attending the police station is required to be cautioned in accordance with Code C prior to being interviewed, the subsequent interview shall be recorded, unless the custody officer gives authority in accordance with the provisions of paragraph 3.3 above for the interview not to be so recorded.

3.5   The whole of each interview shall be recorded visually, including the taking and reading back of any statement.

3.6   A sign or indicator which is visible to the suspect must show when the visual recording equipment is recording.

1.7.16.1   **KEYNOTE**

A decision not to record an interview visually for any reason may be the subject of comment in court. The authorising officer should therefore be prepared to justify his/her decision in each case. Nothing in the Code is intended to preclude visual recording at police discretion of interviews at police stations with people cautioned in respect of offences not covered by para. 3.1, or responses made by interviewees after they have been charged they may be prosecuted for, an offence, provided that this Code is complied with.

As stated, Code F needs to be read in conjunction with the relevant sections of Code C. For instance, attention is drawn to the provisions set out in Code C about the matters to be considered when deciding whether a detained person is fit to be interviewed. Code C also sets out the circumstances in which a suspect may be questioned about an offence after being charged with it, as well as the procedures to be followed when a person's attention is drawn, after charge, to a statement made by another person. One method of bringing the content of an interview with another person to the notice of a suspect may be to play him/her a recording of that interview.

If, during the course of an interview under this Code, it becomes apparent that the interview should be conducted under one of the terrorism codes for video recording of interviews, the interview should only continue in accordance with the relevant code (see Code H).

1.7.17   **4 The Interview**

**(a) General**

4.1   The provisions of Code C in relation to cautions and interviews and the Notes for Guidance applicable to those provisions shall apply to the conduct of interviews to which this Code applies.

4.2   Particular attention is drawn to those parts of Code C that describe the restrictions on drawing adverse inferences from a suspect's failure or refusal to say anything about their involvement in the offence when interviewed, or after being charged or informed they may be prosecuted and how those restrictions affect the terms of the caution and determine whether a special warning under Sections 36 and 37 of the Criminal Justice and Public Order Act 1994 can be given.

## (b) Commencement of interviews

4.3 When the suspect is brought into the interview room the interviewer shall without delay, but in sight of the suspect, load the recording equipment and set it to record and point out the sign or indicator which shows that the recording equipment is activated and recording. See *paragraph 3.6*. The recording media must be unwrapped or otherwise opened in the presence of the suspect.

4.4 The interviewer shall then tell the suspect formally about the visual recording. The interviewer shall:
   (a) explain the interview is being visually recorded;
   (b) subject to paragraph 2.5, give his or her name and rank, and that of any other interviewer present;
   (c) ask the suspect and any other party present (e.g. his solicitor) to identify themselves;
   (d) state the date, time of commencement and place of the interview; and
   (e) state that the suspect will be given a notice about what will happen to the recording.

4.5 The interviewer shall then caution the suspect, which should follow that set out in Code C, and remind the suspect of their entitlement to free and independent legal advice and that they can speak to a solicitor on the telephone.

4.6 The interviewer shall then put to the suspect any significant statement or silence (i.e. failure or refusal to answer a question or to answer it satisfactorily) which occurred before the start of the interview, and shall ask the suspect whether they wish to confirm or deny that earlier statement or silence or whether they wish to add anything. The definition of a 'significant' statement or silence is the same as that set out in Code C.

## (c) Interviews with the deaf

4.7 If the suspect is deaf or there is doubt about their hearing ability, the provisions of Code C on interpreters for the deaf or for interviews with suspects who have difficulty in understanding English continue to apply.

## (d) Objections and complaints by the suspect

4.8 If the suspect raises objections to the interview being visually recorded either at the outset or during the interview or during a break in the interview, the interviewer shall explain the fact that the interview is being visually recorded and that the provisions of this code require that the suspect's objections shall be recorded on the visual recording. When any objections have been visually recorded or the suspect has refused to have their objections recorded, the interviewer shall say that they are turning off the recording equipment, give their reasons and turn it off. If a separate audio recording is being maintained, the officer shall ask the person to record the reasons for refusing to agree to visual recording of the interview. Paragraph 4.8 of Code E will apply if the person objects to audio recording of the interview. The officer shall then make a written record of the interview. If the interviewer reasonably considers they may proceed to question the suspect with the visual recording still on, the interviewer may do so.

4.9 If in the course of an interview a complaint is made by the person being questioned, or on their behalf, concerning the provisions of this code or of Code C, then the interviewer shall act in accordance with Code C, record it in the interview record and inform the custody officer.

4.10 If the suspect indicates that they wish to tell the interviewer about matters not directly connected with the offence of which they are suspected and that they are unwilling for these matters to be recorded, the suspect shall be given the opportunity to tell the interviewer about these matters after the conclusion of the formal interview.

### (e) Changing the recording media

4.11 In instances where the recording medium is not of sufficient length to record all of the interview with the suspect, further certified recording medium will be used. When the recording equipment indicates that the recording medium has only a short time left to run, the interviewer shall advise the suspect and round off that part of the interview. If the interviewer wishes to continue the interview but does not already have further certified recording media with him, they shall obtain a set. The suspect should not be left unattended in the interview room. The interviewer will remove the recording media from the recording equipment and insert the new ones which have been unwrapped or otherwise opened in the suspect's presence. The recording equipment shall then be set to record. Care must be taken, particularly when a number of sets of recording media have been used, to ensure that there is no confusion between them. This could be achieved by marking the sets of recording media with consecutive identification numbers.

### (f) Taking a break during the interview

4.12 When a break is to be taken during the course of an interview and the interview room is to be vacated by the suspect, the fact that a break is to be taken, the reason for it and the time shall be recorded. The recording equipment must be turned off and the recording media removed. The procedures for the conclusion of an interview set out in paragraph 4.19, below, should be followed.

4.13 When a break is to be a short one, and both the suspect and a police officer are to remain in the interview room, the fact that a break is to be taken, the reasons for it and the time shall be recorded on the recording media. The recording equipment may be turned off, but there is no need to remove the recording media. When the interview is recommenced the recording shall continue on the same recording media and the time at which the interview recommences shall be recorded.

4.14 When there is a break in questioning under caution, the interviewing officer must ensure that the person being questioned is aware that they remain under caution. If there is any doubt, the caution must be given again in full when the interview resumes.

### (g) Failure of recording equipment

4.15 If there is a failure of equipment which can be rectified quickly, the appropriate procedures set out in paragraph 4.12 shall be followed. When the recording is resumed the interviewer shall explain what has happened and record the time the interview recommences. If, however, it is not possible to continue recording on that particular recorder and no alternative equipment is readily available, the interview may continue without being recorded visually. In such circumstances, the procedures set out in paragraph 3.3 of this Code for seeking the authority of the custody officer will be followed.

## (h) Removing used recording media from recording equipment

4.16 Where used recording media are removed from the recording equipment during the course of an interview, they shall be retained and the procedures set out in paragraph 4.18 below followed.

## (i) Conclusion of interview

4.17 Before the conclusion of the interview, the suspect shall be offered the opportunity to clarify anything he or she has said and asked if there is anything that they wish to add.

4.18 At the conclusion of the interview, including the taking and reading back of any written statement, the time shall be recorded and the recording equipment switched off. The master recording shall be removed from the recording equipment, sealed with a master recording label and treated as an exhibit in accordance with the force standing orders. The interviewer shall sign the label and also ask the suspect and any third party present during the interview to sign it. If the suspect or third party refuses to sign the label, an officer of at least the rank of inspector, or if one is not available, the custody officer, shall be called into the interview room and asked subject to *paragraph 2.5*, to sign it.

4.19 The suspect shall be handed a notice which explains the use which will be made of the recording and the arrangements for access to it. The notice will also advise the suspect that a copy of the tape shall be supplied as soon as practicable if the person is charged or informed that he will be prosecuted.

**1.7.17.1**  **KEYNOTE**

**Preparation before Interview at Police Station**

Preparation is essential before any interview (indeed it is the first step in the PACE interviewing model). This preparation should include the following points:

- Decide where the interview will be conducted. Consider the availability of a room and the timing of the interview.
- The location must have a seat for the person being interviewed (Code C, para. 12.6) and should be adequately lit, heated and ventilated (Code C, para. 12.4). The detained person must also have clothing of a reasonable standard of comfort and cleanliness (Code C, para. 8.5). (It will be a question of fact as to what amounts to adequate clothing and it is suggested that if the clothing is such as to degrade the detained person or make him/her uncomfortable, it may lead to the confession being held to be unreliable.)
- The interviewer should attempt to estimate the likely length of the interview and ensure that an appropriate quantity of certified recording media and labels with which to seal the master copies are available in the interview room.
- In deciding the timing of the interview, consideration must be given to the detainee's rest period, which should not be interrupted or delayed unless Code C, para. 12.2 applies. Where the interview goes ahead during the rest period under Code C, para. 12.2(a), a fresh rest period must be allowed. Before a detainee is interviewed, the custody officer, in consultation with the officer in charge of the investigation and appropriate health care professionals as necessary, shall assess whether the detainee is fit enough to be interviewed (Code C, para. 12.3 and Annex G).
- If legal advice has been requested you must arrange for the legal representative to be present at the interview unless Code C, para. 6.6 applies.
- If a person has asked for legal advice and an interview is initiated in the absence of a legal adviser (e.g. where the person has agreed to be interviewed without his/her legal adviser being present or because of the urgent need to interview under Code C, para. 11.1), a record must be made in the interview record (Code C, para. 6.17).

- If an appropriate adult should be present, arrange for his/her attendance. (For the definition of appropriate adult, see Code C, para. 1.7.)
- If an interpreter is needed for the interview, arrange for his/her attendance. The provisions of Code C, section 13 on interpreters for deaf persons or for interviews with suspects who have difficulty understanding English apply to these interviews. The reason for the interviewer making a written note of the interview where a person is deaf or has impaired hearing is to give the equivalent rights of access to the full interview record as far as this is possible using audio recording. The interview notes must be in accordance with Code C.

It is also important to draw up an interview plan and to include any relevant areas that may provide a general or specific defence.

- Look at the evidence available and identify any significant statement or silence by the suspect in order that it can be put to him/her in interview (Code C, para. 11.4).

**1.7.17.2**  **KEYNOTE**

**Conduct During Interview**

Code C, para. 11.5 reiterates the fact that officers must not act oppressively.

If the suspect asks for the audio recording to be stopped and the interviewer decides to continue recording against the wishes of the suspect, the decision may be the subject of comment in court. That said, it should be noted that in any case where the custody officer is called to deal with the complaint, the recorder should, if possible, be left on until the custody officer has entered the room and spoken to the person being interviewed. Continuation or termination of the interview should be at the interviewer's discretion pending action by an inspector under Code C, para. 9.2. If the complaint is about a matter not connected with this Code or Code C, the decision to continue is at the interviewer's discretion. When the interviewer decides to continue the interview, they shall tell the suspect that the complaint will be brought to the custody officer's attention at the conclusion of the interview. When the interview is concluded the interviewer must, as soon as practicable, inform the custody officer about the existence and nature of the complaint made.

At the start of the interview, the investigating officer should put to the suspect any significant statement or silence which occurred before his/her arrival at the police station and ask the suspect whether he/she confirms the earlier statement or silence and whether he/she wishes to add anything. Code C, para. 11.4A defines a 'significant' statement or silence. This aspect of the interview is very important in terms of establishing whether the facts are disputed. If they are not disputed at this stage, it is unlikely that they will be challenged at any later court hearing and, if challenged, the defence will have to explain why this was not done at the time of the interview. The courts may also view this failure to put the statement to the suspect in a more sinister light. In *R v Allen* [2001] EWCA Crim 1607, the court was concerned that the police failed to put the admission to the suspect in interview, despite thorough questioning, which it felt clearly placed a question mark over the admission's reliability. If the suspect remains silent in relation to a 'significant silence', that silence may give rise to an adverse inference being drawn under s. 34 of the Criminal Justice and Public Order Act 1994 if the person raises it in his/her defence at court. (As this is a very important issue, it may be necessary to delay the interview until the arrest notes are completed or the officers witnessing the offence/arrest have been consulted to ensure that all matters are put to the suspect at this stage.) Consideration should be given to putting questions to a suspect who makes no comment, or even where the legal representative has stated that the suspect will make no comment, as this may allow the court to draw inferences against a defence that the suspect raises at court. The interviewer may wish to go through any significant statement or silence again if during earlier interviews adverse inferences could not be drawn.

The interviewer should remember that it may be necessary to show to the court that nothing occurred during a break or between interviews which influenced the suspect's recorded evidence. After a break or at the beginning of a subsequent interview, the interviewer should consider summarising on the record the reason for the break and confirming this with the suspect. In considering whether to caution again after a break, the officer should bear in mind that he/she may have to satisfy a court that the person understood that he/she was still under caution when the interview resumed.

If any part of the recording media breaks or is otherwise damaged during the interview, it should be sealed as a master copy in the presence of the suspect and the interview resumed where it left off. The undamaged part should be copied and the original sealed as a master tape in the suspect's presence, if necessary after the interview. If equipment for copying is not readily available, both parts should be sealed in the suspect's presence and the interview begun again.

Guidance is provided by Code C, para. 11.6 as to when an interview should be concluded. It is important to remember that the interview should not be concluded at the point when there is sufficient evidence to prosecute but when there is sufficient evidence to provide a realistic prospect of conviction. (In *Prouse* v *DPP* [1999] All ER (D) 748 the question was said to be not how much evidence there is but the quality of it.) Once there is enough evidence to prosecute, it may still be necessary to cover those other points in the interview that may be relevant to the defence case.

## 1.7.18    5 After the Interview

5.1    The interviewer shall make a note in his or her pocket book of the fact that the interview has taken place and has been recorded, its time, duration and date and the identification number of the master copy of the recording media.

5.2    Where no proceedings follow in respect of the person whose interview was recorded, the recording media must nevertheless be kept securely in accordance with paragraph 6.1.

## 1.7.18.1    KEYNOTE

Any written record of an audibly recorded interview should be made in accordance with national guidelines approved by the Secretary of State, and with regard to the advice contained in the Manual of Guidance for the preparation, processing and submission of prosecution files.

## 1.7.19    6 Master Copy Security

### (a) General

6.1    The officer in charge of the police station at which interviews with suspects are recorded shall make arrangements for the master copies to be kept securely and their movements accounted for on the same basis as other material which may be used for evidential purposes, in accordance with force standing orders.

### (b) Breaking master copy seal for criminal proceedings

6.2    A police officer has no authority to break the seal on a master copy which is required for criminal trial or appeal proceedings. If it is necessary to gain access to the master copy, the police officer shall arrange for its seal to be broken in the presence of a representative of the Crown Prosecution Service. The defendant or their legal adviser shall be informed and given a reasonable opportunity to be present. If the defendant or their legal representative is present they shall be invited to reseal and sign the master copy. If either refuses or neither is present, this shall be done by the representative of the Crown Prosecution Service.

## (c) Breaking master copy seal: other cases

6.3 The chief officer of police is responsible for establishing arrangements for breaking the seal of the master copy where no criminal proceedings result, or the criminal proceedings, to which the interview relates, have been concluded and it becomes necessary to break the seal. These arrangements should be those which the chief officer considers are reasonably necessary to demonstrate to the person interviewed and any other party who may wish to use or refer to the interview record that the master copy has not been tampered with and that the interview record remains accurate.

6.4 Subject to paragraph 6.6, a representative of each party must be given a reasonable opportunity to be present when the seal is broken, the master copy copied and re-sealed.

6.5 If one or more of the parties is not present when the master copy seal is broken because they cannot be contacted or refuse to attend or paragraph 6.6 applies, arrangements should be made for an independent person such as a custody visitor, to be present. Alternatively, or as an additional safeguard, arrangement should be made for a film or photographs to be taken of the procedure.

6.6 Paragraph 6.5 does not require a person to be given an opportunity to be present when:
   (a) it is necessary to break the master copy seal for the proper and effective further investigation of the original offence or the investigation of some other offence; and
   (b) the officer in charge of the investigation has reasonable grounds to suspect that allowing an opportunity might prejudice any such an investigation or criminal proceedings which may be brought as a result or endanger any person.

## (d) Documentation

6.7 When the master copy seal is broken, copied and re-sealed, a record must be made of the procedure followed, including the date, time and place and persons present.

1.7.19.1

**KEYNOTE**

This section is concerned with the security of the master copy, which will have been sealed at the conclusion of the interview. Care should, however, be taken of working copies since their loss or destruction may lead unnecessarily to the need to have access to master copies.

If the master copy has been delivered to the Crown Court for its keeping after committal for trial the Crown Prosecutor will apply to the Chief Clerk of the Crown Court Centre for its release for unsealing by the Crown Prosecutor.

Reference to the CPS or to the Crown Prosecutor in this part of the Code shall be taken to include any other body or person with a statutory responsibility for prosecution for whom the police conduct any recorded interviews.

The most common reasons for needing access to master copies that are not required for criminal proceedings arise from civil actions and complaints against police and civil actions between individuals arising out of allegations of crime investigated by police.

Breaking the master seal in the absence of the suspect as set out in Code F, para. 6.6 could apply, for example, when one or more of the outcomes or likely outcomes of the investigation might be: (i) the prosecution of one or more of the original suspects; (ii) the prosecution of someone previously not suspected, including someone who was originally a witness; and (iii) any original suspect being treated as a prosecution witness and when premature disclosure of any police action, particularly through contact with any parties involved, could lead to a real risk of compromising the investigation and endangering witnesses.

# 7 Visual Recording of Interviews by Secure Digital Network

7.1   Sections 1 to 6 of this code apply when an interviewing officer wishes to make a visual recording of an interview with sound on removable media. This section applies if an officer wishes to make a visual recording with sound of an interview mentioned in section 3 of this Code using a secure digital network which does not use removable media (see Code E, paragraph 1.6(c)).

7.2   The provisions of sections 1 to 6 of this Code which relate or apply only to removable media will not apply to a secure digital network recording.

7.3   The statutory requirement and provisions the audio recording of interviews using a secure digital network set out in section 7 of Code E should be applied to the visual recording with sound of interviews mentioned in section 3 of this code as if references to audio recordings of interviews include visual recordings with sound.

**KEYNOTE**

**Miscellaneous Matters**

The Criminal Justice Act 2003 introduces a code of practice for police officers interviewing a witness notified by the accused (which would include an alibi witness), see para. 1.10.10.7.

**KEYNOTE**

**Interviews on Behalf of Scottish Forces and *vice versa***

The CPS, in consultation with the Scottish Crown Office, has produced guidelines in relation to the potential admissibility of interview evidence when officers from England and Wales conduct interviews on behalf of Scottish forces and *vice versa*. These interviews relate to people subject to cross-border arrest as provided by ss. 136–140 of the Criminal Justice and Public Order Act 1994.

**KEYNOTE**

**Suspects in Scotland: Interview Evidence Required for Prosecutions in England and Wales**

Under the legislation governing prosecutions in Scotland, the suspect is not entitled to legal representation during an interview. Suspects are not warned that a failure to answer questions may harm their defence. Failure to answer questions cannot harm their defence. Interviews under caution are, however, subject to guidelines which incorporate judicial precedent fairness to the accused.

In investigations of any great seriousness, English/Welsh constables should attend in Scotland, arrest the suspect and bring him/her back to their jurisdiction for interview. If such an arrest is made, the arrested person must be taken either to the nearest designated police station in England or a designated police station in a police area in England and Wales in which the offence is being investigated (s. 137(1) and (7)(a) of the Criminal Justice and Public Order Act 1994).

Scottish officers do not have any statutory or common law powers to detain or arrest a suspect without warrant who is believed to have committed an offence in England and Wales. If there is insufficient evidence for the issue of a warrant, and the case is not sufficiently serious to justify officers travelling to Scotland, Scottish officers can be requested to invite the suspect to attend a police station on a voluntary basis for interview under caution.

When it has not been practicable for an English/Welsh constable to make an arrest, but a constable has gone to Scotland to interview a suspect following arrest or detention by a Scottish constable for Scottish offences, or a person has voluntarily agreed to be interviewed, the English/Welsh constable should comply, in so far as it is practical, with the PACE Codes of Practice, in particular:

- A suspect not under arrest or detention should be told that he/she is not under arrest or detention and that he/she is free to leave.
- A suspect should be told that he/she may seek legal advice and that arrangements are made for legal representation when required. An appropriate adult should also be present when interviewing a youth or a mentally disordered or mentally handicapped person.
- An English/Welsh law caution should be administered. When appropriate, officers should warn arrested suspects of the consequences of failure or refusal to account for objects, substances or marks (s. 36 of the 1994 Act) and the failure or refusal to account for their presence in a particular place (s. 37).
- The interview should be audio recorded if possible.
- If it is not possible to audio record the interview, a contemporaneous written record of the interview should be made. The suspect must be given the opportunity to read the record and to sign it.

Scottish constables interviewing suspects in Scotland when they are aware that the interview is required for a prosecution in England and Wales, should comply with Scottish law. In addition, in so far as it is practical:

- A suspect should be told that he/she may seek legal advice and that arrangements are made for legal representation when required. A solicitor may be present during any subsequent interview if the suspect requires. An appropriate adult should also be present when interviewing a youth or a mentally disordered or mentally vulnerable person.
- When it is certain that the interview evidence will only be used in English/Welsh courts, the appropriate English/Welsh caution should be used.
- The interview should be audio recorded if possible.
- If it is not possible to audio record the interview, a written contemporaneous record of the interview should be made. The suspect must be given the opportunity to read the record and to sign it.

English/Welsh officers should assist interviewing Scottish officers by providing a schedule of points to be covered in an interview. This could include a list of appropriate questions.

1.7.20.4     **KEYNOTE**

**Suspects in England and Wales: Interview Evidence Required for Prosecutions in Scotland**

- English officers do not have any statutory or common law powers to detain or arrest a suspect without warrant who is believed to have committed an offence in Scotland. If there is insufficient evidence for the issue of a warrant, and the case is not sufficiently serious to justify Scottish officers travelling to England or Wales to exercise their cross-border powers under the Act, English or Welsh officers can be requested to invite the suspect to attend an interview on a voluntary basis for interview under caution.
- Where a Scottish officer has attended to interview the suspect, the Scottish form of caution should be given.
- English and Welsh constables interviewing suspects in England/Wales when they are aware that the interview is required for a prosecution in Scotland, should comply with the PACE Codes of Practice, save that a Scottish caution should be used in the following terms:

  You are not obliged to say anything but anything you do say will be noted and may be used in evidence.

The use of an English/Welsh caution may render the interview inadmissible in Scotland.

Scottish officers should assist the interviewing officers by providing a schedule of points to be covered in an interview and a possible list of appropriate questions.

In all circumstances, officers should ensure that suspects fully understand the significance of a caution or warning.

# Identification

## PACE Code of Practice for the Identification of Persons by Police Officers (Code D)

A thick grey line down the margin denotes text that is an extract of the PACE Code itself (i.e. the actual wording of the legislation).

### 1.8.1 Introduction

A critical issue in the investigation and prosecution of offences is the identification of the offender. Many different methods of identification exist but the main feature which must be considered in relation to each is its *reliability*. The Police and Criminal Evidence Act 1984 Code of Practice, Code D provides guidance for the identification of persons by police officers. This chapter sets out the actual Codes of Practice with keynotes which incorporate the notes of guidance to the Code.

Generally, the methods of identification covered by Code D can be divided into two:

- occasions where the identity of the suspect is known; and
- occasions where the identity of the suspect is not known.

Where the identity of the suspect is known this can be further divided into those cases where the suspect is available and those where he/she is not available.

Although a breach of Code D (or any of the other Codes of Practice) will not automatically result in the evidence being excluded (*R v Khan* (1999) 19 July, CA, unreported), the judge or magistrate(s) will consider the effects of any breach on the fairness of any subsequent proceedings. The Codes are intended to provide protection to suspects and, if it is felt that the breach of Code D has resulted in unfairness or other prejudicial effect on the defendant, the court may exclude the related evidence under s. 78 of the Police and Criminal Evidence Act 1984.

The Police Reform Act 2002 has introduced designated support staff who have some of the powers that police officers have (**see chapter 1.6**).

Code D was revised on 7 March 2011 to bring in the effects of the Equality Act 2010, ss. 1–7 of the Crime and Security Act 2010 and s. 117 of the Serious Organised Crime Police Act 2005 in relation to powers to take fingerprints and DNA. Changes have also been made to reflect the current case law in relation to identification for recognition cases.

**PACE Code of Practice for the Identification of Persons by Police Officers (Code D)**

This code has effect in relation to any identification procedure carried out after midnight on 06 March 2011.

**1.8.2**

# 1 Introduction

1.1 This Code of Practice concerns the principal methods used by police to identify people in connection with the investigation of offences and the keeping of accurate and reliable criminal records. The powers and procedures in this code must be used fairly, responsibly, with respect for the people to whom they apply and without unlawful discrimination. The Equality Act 2010 makes it unlawful for police officers to discriminate against, harass or victimise any person on the grounds of the 'protected characteristics' of age, disability, gender reassignment, race, religion or belief, sex and sexual orientation, marriage and civil partnership, pregnancy and maternity when using their powers. When police forces are carrying out their functions they also have a duty to have regard to the need to eliminate unlawful discrimination, harassment and victimisation and to take steps to foster good relations.

1.2 Identification by witnesses arises, e.g., if the offender is seen committing the crime and a witness is given an opportunity to identify the suspect in a video identification, identification parade or similar procedure. The procedures are designed to:
- test the witness' ability to identify the person they saw on a previous occasion
- provide safeguards against mistaken identification.

While this Code concentrates on visual identification procedures, it does not preclude the police making use of aural identification procedures such as a 'voice identification parade', where they judge that appropriate.

1.2A In this code, separate provisions in Part B of section 3 below apply when any person, including a police officer, is asked if they recognise anyone they see in an image as being someone they know and to test their claim that they recognise that person as someone who is known to them. Except where stated, these separate provisions are not subject to the eye-witnesses identification procedures described in paragraph 1.2.

1.3 Identification by fingerprints applies when a person's fingerprints are taken to:
- compare with fingerprints found at the scene of a crime
- check and prove convictions
- help to ascertain a person's identity.

1.3A Identification using footwear impressions applies when a person's footwear impressions are taken to compare with impressions found at the scene of a crime.

1.4 Identification by body samples and impressions includes taking samples such as blood or hair to generate a DNA profile for comparison with material obtained from the scene of a crime, or a victim.

1.5 Taking photographs of arrested people applies to recording and checking identity and locating and tracing persons who:
- are wanted for offences
- fail to answer their bail.

1.6 Another method of identification involves searching and examining detained suspects to find, e.g., marks such as tattoos or scars which may help establish their identity or whether they have been involved in committing an offence.

1.7 The provisions of the Police and Criminal Evidence Act 1984 (PACE) and this Code are designed to make sure fingerprints, samples, impressions and photographs are taken, used and retained, and identification procedures carried out, only when justified and necessary for preventing, detecting or investigating crime. If these provisions are not observed, the application of the relevant procedures in particular cases may be open to question.

**1.8.3**

# 2 General

2.1 This Code must be readily available at all police stations for consultation by:
- police officers and police staff
- detained persons
- members of the public

2.2 The provisions of this Code:
- include the *Annexes*
- do not include the *Notes for guidance*.

2.3 Code C, paragraph 1.4, regarding a person who may be mentally disordered or otherwise mentally vulnerable and the *Notes for guidance* applicable to those provisions apply to this Code.

2.4 Code C, paragraph 1.5, regarding a person who appears to be under the age of 17 applies to this Code.

2.5 Code C, paragraph 1.6, regarding a person who appears blind, seriously visually impaired, deaf, unable to read or speak or has difficulty orally because of a speech impediment applies to this Code.

2.6 In this Code:
- 'appropriate adult' means the same as in Code C, paragraph 1.7,
- 'solicitor' means the same as in Code C, paragraph 6.12
  and the *Notes for guidance* applicable to those provisions apply to this Code.
- where a search or other procedure under this code may only be carried out or observed by a person of the same sex as the person to whom the search or procedure applies, the gender of the detainee and other persons present should be established and recorded in line with Annex F of Code A.

2.7 References to custody officers include those performing the functions of custody officer, see *paragraph 1.9* of Code C.

2.8 When a record of any action requiring the authority of an officer of a specified rank is made under this Code, subject to *paragraph 2.18*, the officer's name and rank must be recorded.

2.9 When this Code requires the prior authority or agreement of an officer of at least inspector or superintendent rank, that authority may be given by a sergeant or chief inspector who has been authorised to perform the functions of the higher rank under PACE, section 107.

2.10 Subject to *paragraph 2.18*, all records must be timed and signed by the maker.

2.11 Records must be made in the custody record, unless otherwise specified. References to 'pocket book' include any official report book issued to police officers or police staff.

2.12 If any procedure in this Code requires a person's consent, the consent of a:
- mentally disordered or otherwise mentally vulnerable person is only valid if given in the presence of the appropriate adult
- juvenile, is only valid if their parent's or guardian's consent is also obtained unless the juvenile is under 14, when their parent's or guardian's consent is sufficient in its own right. If the only obstacle to an identification procedure in *section 3* is that a juvenile's parent or guardian refuses consent or reasonable efforts to obtain it have failed, the identification officer may apply the provisions of *paragraph 3.21*.

2.13 If a person is blind, seriously visually impaired or unable to read, the custody officer or identification officer shall make sure their solicitor, relative, appropriate adult or some other person likely to take an interest in them and not involved in the investigation is available to help check any documentation. When this Code requires written consent or signing, the person assisting may be asked to sign instead, if the detainee prefers. This paragraph does not require an appropriate adult to be called solely to assist in checking and signing documentation for a person who is not a juvenile, or mentally disordered or otherwise mentally vulnerable (see Code C *paragraph 3.15*).

2.14 If any procedure in this Code requires information to be given to or sought from a suspect, it must be given or sought in the appropriate adult's presence if the suspect is mentally disordered, otherwise mentally vulnerable or a juvenile. If the appropriate adult is not present when the information is first given or sought, the procedure must be repeated in the presence of the appropriate adult when they arrive. If the suspect appears deaf or there is doubt about their hearing or speaking ability or ability to understand English, and effective communication cannot be established, the information must be given or sought through an interpreter.

2.15 Any procedure in this Code involving the participation of a suspect who is mentally disordered, otherwise mentally vulnerable or a juvenile must take place in the presence of the appropriate adult. See Code C *paragraph 1.4*.

2.15A Any procedure in this Code involving the participation of a witness who is or appears to be mentally disordered, otherwise mentally vulnerable or a juvenile should take place in the presence of a pre-trial support person. However, the support-person must not be allowed to prompt any identification of a suspect by a witness.

2.16 References to:
- 'taking a photograph', include the use of any process to produce a single, still or moving, visual image
- 'photographing a person', should be construed accordingly
- 'photographs', 'films', 'negatives' and 'copies' include relevant visual images recorded, stored, or reproduced through any medium
- 'destruction' includes the deletion of computer data relating to such images or making access to that data impossible.

2.17 Except as described, nothing in this Code affects the powers and procedures:
  (i) for requiring and taking samples of breath, blood and urine in relation to driving offences, etc, when under the influence of drink, drugs or excess alcohol under the:
    - Road Traffic Act 1988, sections 4 to 11
    - Road Traffic Offenders Act 1988, sections 15 and 16
    - Transport and Works Act 1992, sections 26 to 38;
  (ii) under the Immigration Act 1971, Schedule 2, paragraph 18, for taking photographs and fingerprints from persons detained under that Act, Schedule 2, paragraph 16 (Administrative Controls as to Control on Entry etc.); for taking fingerprints in accordance with the Immigration and Asylum Act 1999; sections 141 and 142(3), or other methods for collecting information about a person's external physical characteristics provided for by regulations made under that Act, section 144;
  (iii) under the Terrorism Act 2000, Schedule 8, for taking photographs, fingerprints, skin impressions, body samples or impressions from people:
    - arrested under that Act, section 41,
    - detained for the purposes of examination under that Act, Schedule 7, and to whom the Code of Practice issued under that Act, Schedule 14, paragraph 6, applies ('the terrorism provisions')
  (iv) for taking photographs, fingerprints, skin impressions, body samples or impressions from people who have been:
    - arrested on warrants issued in Scotland, by officers exercising powers under the Criminal Justice and Public Order Act 1994, section 136(2)
    - arrested or detained without warrant by officers from a police force in Scotland exercising their powers of arrest or detention under the Criminal Justice and Public Order Act 1994, section 137(2), (Cross Border powers of arrest etc.).
  Note: In these cases, police powers and duties and the person's rights and entitlements whilst at a police station in England and Wales are the same as if the person had been arrested in Scotland by a Scottish police officer.

2.18 Nothing in this Code requires the identity of officers or police staff to be recorded or disclosed:
  (a) in the case of enquiries linked to the investigation of terrorism;
  (b) if the officers or police staff reasonably believe recording or disclosing their names might put them in danger.
  In these cases, they shall use warrant or other identification numbers and the name of their police station.

2.19 In this Code:
  (a) 'designated person' means a person other than a police officer, designated under the Police Reform Act 2002, Part 4, who has specified powers and duties of police officers conferred or imposed on them;

     (b) any reference to a police officer includes a designated person acting in the exercise or performance of the powers and duties conferred or imposed on them by their designation.

2.20   If a power conferred on a designated person:

     (a) allows reasonable force to be used when exercised by a police officer, a designated person exercising that power has the same entitlement to use force;

     (b) includes power to use force to enter any premises, that power is not exercisable by that designated person except:

      (i) in the company, and under the supervision, of a police officer; or

      (ii) for the purpose of:

        • saving life or limb; or

        • preventing serious damage to property.

2.21   Nothing in this Code prevents the custody officer, or other officer given custody of the detainee, from allowing police staff who are not designated persons to carry out individual procedures or tasks at the police station if the law allows. However, the officer remains responsible for making sure the procedures and tasks are carried out correctly in accordance with the Codes of Practice. Any such person must be:

     (a) a person employed by a police authority maintaining a police force and under the control and direction of the Chief Officer of that force;

     (b) employed by a person with whom a police authority has a contract for the provision of services relating to persons arrested or otherwise in custody.

2.22   Designated persons and other police staff must have regard to any relevant provisions of the Codes of Practice.

### 1.8.3.1   KEYNOTE

For the purposes of any procedures within this Code which require an appropriate adult's consent, where a juvenile is in the care of a local authority or voluntary organisation the consent may be given by that authority or organisation. Where a parent, guardian or representative of a local authority or voluntary organisation is not acting as the appropriate adult under para. 2.14 or 2.15 he/she does not have to be present to give consent. However, it is important that a parent or guardian not present is fully informed before being asked to consent. He/she must be given the same information about the procedure and the juvenile's suspected involvement in the offence as the juvenile and appropriate adult. The parent or guardian must also be allowed to speak to the juvenile and the appropriate adult if he/she wishes. Provided the consent is fully informed and is not withdrawn, it may be obtained at any time before the procedure takes place.

Examples of when it would not be practicable to obtain a detainee's consent, under para. 2.12, to a search, examination or the taking of a photograph of an identifying mark include:

• when the person is drunk or otherwise unfit to give consent;

• when there are reasonable grounds to suspect that if the person became aware that a search or examination was to take place or an identifying mark was to be photographed, he/she would take steps to prevent this happening, e.g. by violently resisting, covering or concealing the mark, etc. and it would not otherwise be possible to carry out the search or examination or to photograph any identifying mark;

• in the case of a juvenile, if the parent or guardian cannot be contacted in sufficient time to allow the search or examination to be carried out or the photograph to be taken.

Examples of when it would not be practicable to obtain the person's consent to a photograph being taken include:

• when the person is drunk or otherwise unfit to give consent;

• when there are reasonable grounds to suspect that if the person became aware a photograph suitable to be used or disclosed for the use and disclosure described in para. 5.6 was to be taken, he/she would take steps to prevent it being taken, e.g. by violently resisting, covering or distorting his/her face etc., and it would not otherwise be possible to take a suitable photograph;

- when, in order to obtain a suitable photograph, it is necessary to take it covertly; and
- in the case of a juvenile, if the parent or guardian cannot be contacted in sufficient time to allow the photograph to be taken.

People who are seriously visually impaired or unable to read may be unwilling to sign police documents. The alternative, i.e. the representative signing on his/her behalf, seeks to protect the interests of both police and suspects.

The Youth Justice and Criminal Evidence Act 1999 guidance 'Achieving Best Evidence in Criminal Proceedings: Guidance on interviewing victims and witnesses, and guidance on using special measures' indicates that a pre-trial support person should accompany a vulnerable witness during any identification procedure. It states that this support person should not be (or not be likely to be) a witness in the investigation.

In relation to terrorism cases, photographs, fingerprints, samples and impressions may be taken from a person detained under the terrorism provisions to help determine whether he/she is, or has been, involved in terrorism, as well as when there are reasonable grounds for suspecting his/her involvement in a particular offence (see Code H, appendix 2.1).

The purpose of using warrant or identification numbers instead of names referred to in Code D, para. 2.18(b) is to protect those involved in serious organised crime investigations or arrests of particularly violent suspects when there is reliable information that those arrested or their associates may threaten or cause harm to those involved. In cases of doubt, an officer of inspector rank or above should be consulted.

## 1.8.4      3 Identification by Witnesses

### (A) Identification of a suspect by an eye-witness

3.0    This part applies when an eye-witness has seen the offender committing the crime or in any other circumstances which tend to prove or disprove the involvement of the person they saw in the crime, for example, close to the scene of the crime, immediately before or immediately after it was committed. It sets out the procedures to be used to test the ability of that eye-witness to identify a person suspected of involvement in the offence as the person they saw on the previous occasion. Except where stated, this part does not apply to the procedures described in Part B and *Note 3AA*.

3.1    A record shall be made of the suspect's description as first given by a potential witness. This record must:

(a) be made and kept in a form which enables details of that description to be accurately produced from it, in a visible and legible form, which can be given to the suspect or the suspect's solicitor in accordance with this Code; and

(b) unless otherwise specified, be made before the witness takes part in any identification procedures under *paragraphs 3.5* to *3.10*, *3.21* or *3.23*.

A copy of the record shall where practicable, be given to the suspect or their solicitor before any procedures under *paragraphs 3.5* to *3.10*, *3.21* or *3.23* are carried out.

### (a) Cases when the suspect's identity is not known

3.2    In cases when the suspect's identity is not known, a witness may be taken to a particular neighbourhood or place to see whether they can identify the person they saw. Although the number, age, sex, race, general description and style of clothing of other people present at the location and the way in which any identification is made cannot be controlled, the principles applicable to the formal procedures under *paragraphs 3.5* to *3.10* shall be followed as far as practicable. For example:

(a) where it is practicable to do so, a record should be made of the witness' description of the suspect, as in *paragraph 3.1(a)*, before asking the witness to make an identification;

(b) care must be taken not to direct the witness' attention to any individual unless, taking into account all the circumstances, this cannot be avoided. However, this does not prevent a witness being asked to look carefully at the people around at the time or to look towards a group or in a particular direction, if this appears necessary to make sure that the witness does not overlook a possible suspect simply because the witness is looking in the opposite direction and also to enable the witness to make comparisons between any suspect and others who are in the area;

(c) where there is more than one witness, every effort should be made to keep them separate and witnesses should be taken to see whether they can identify a person independently;

(d) once there is sufficient information to justify the arrest of a particular individual for suspected involvement in the offence, e.g., after a witness makes a positive identification, the provisions set out from *paragraph 3.4* onwards shall apply for any other witnesses in relation to that individual. Subject to *paragraphs 3.12* and *3.13*, it is not necessary for the witness who makes such a positive identification to take part in a further procedure;

(e) the officer or police staff accompanying the witness must record, in their pocket book, the action taken as soon as, and in as much detail, as possible. The record should include: the date, time and place of the relevant occasion the witness claims to have previously seen the suspect; where any identification was made; how it was made and the conditions at the time (e.g., the distance the witness was from the suspect, the weather and light); if the witness's attention was drawn to the suspect; the reason for this; and anything said by the witness or the suspect about the identification or the conduct of the procedure.

3.3 A witness must not be shown photographs, computerised or artist's composite likenesses or similar likenesses or pictures (including 'E-fit' images) if the identity of the suspect is known to the police and the suspect is available to take part in a video identification, an identification parade or a group identification. If the suspect's identity is not known, the showing of such images to a witness to obtain identification evidence must be done in accordance with *Annex E*.

## (b) Cases when the suspect is known and available

3.4 If the suspect's identity is known to the police and they are available, the identification procedures set out in paragraphs 3.5 to 3.10 may be used. References in this section to a suspect being 'known' mean there is sufficient information known to the police to justify the arrest of a particular person for suspected involvement in the offence. A suspect being 'available' means they are immediately available or will be within a reasonably short time and willing to take an effective part in at least one of the following which it is practicable to arrange:

- video identification;
- identification parade; or
- group identification.

### Video identification

3.5 A 'video identification' is when the witness is shown moving images of a known suspect, together with similar images of others who resemble the suspect. Moving images must be used unless:

- the suspect is known but not available (see *paragraph 3.21* of this Code); or
- in accordance with *paragraph 2A of Annex A* of this Code, the identification officer does not consider that replication of a physical feature can be achieved or that it is not possible to conceal the location of the feature on the image of the suspect.

The identification officer may then decide to make use of video identification but using still images.

3.6 Video identifications must be carried out in accordance with *Annex A*.

## Identification parade

3.7  An 'identification parade' is when the witness sees the suspect in a line of others who resemble the suspect.

3.8  Identification parades must be carried out in accordance with *Annex B*.

## Group identification

3.9  A 'group identification' is when the witness sees the suspect in an informal group of people.

3.10  Group identifications must be carried out in accordance with *Annex C*.

## Arranging eye-witness identification procedures

3.11  Except for the provisions in *paragraph 3.19*, the arrangements for, and conduct of, the identification procedures in paragraphs 3.5 to 3.10 and circumstances in which an identification procedure must be held shall be the responsibility of an officer not below inspector rank who is not involved with the investigation, 'the identification officer'. Unless otherwise specified, the identification officer may allow another officer or police staff, see *paragraph 2.21*, to make arrangements for, and conduct, any of these identification procedures. In delegating these procedures, the identification officer must be able to supervise effectively and either intervene or be contacted for advice. No officer or any other person involved with the investigation of the case against the suspect, beyond the extent required by these procedures, may take any part in these procedures or act as the identification officer. This does not prevent the identification officer from consulting the officer in charge of the investigation to determine which procedure to use. When an identification procedure is required, in the interest of fairness to suspects and witnesses, it must be held as soon as practicable.

## Circumstances in which an eye-witness identification procedure must be held

3.12  Whenever:
   (i)  a witness has identified a suspect or purported to have identified them prior to any identification procedure set out in paragraphs 3.5 to 3.10 having been held; or
   (ii) there is a witness available, who expresses an ability to identify the suspect, or where there is a reasonable chance of the witness being able to do so, and they have not been given an opportunity to identify the suspect in any of the procedures set out in paragraphs 3.5 to 3.10, and the suspect disputes being the person the witness claims to have seen, an identification procedure shall be held unless it is not practicable or it would serve no useful purpose in proving or disproving whether the suspect was involved in committing the offence, for example:
   • where the suspect admits being at the scene of the crime and gives an account of what took place and the eye-witness does not see anything which contradicts that;
   • when it is not disputed that the suspect is already known to the witness who claims to have recognised them when seeing them commit the crime.

3.13  An eye-witness identification procedure may also be held if the officer in charge of the investigation considers it would be useful.

## Selecting an eye-witness identification procedure

3.14 If, because of paragraph 3.12, an identification procedure is to be held, the suspect shall initially be offered a video identification unless:

(a) a video identification is not practicable; or

(b) an identification parade is both practicable and more suitable than a video identification; or

(c) paragraph 3.16 applies.

The identification officer and the officer in charge of the investigation shall consult each other to determine which option is to be offered. An identification parade may not be practicable because of factors relating to the witnesses, such as their number, state of health, availability and travelling requirements. A video identification would normally be more suitable if it could be arranged and completed sooner than an identification parade. Before an option is offered the suspect must also be reminded of their entitlement to have free legal advice, see Code C, *paragraph 6.5*.

3.15 A suspect who refuses the identification procedure first offered shall be asked to state their reason for refusing and may get advice from their solicitor and/or if present, their appropriate adult. The suspect, solicitor and/or appropriate adult shall be allowed to make representations about why another procedure should be used. A record should be made of the reasons for refusal and any representations made. After considering any reasons given, and representations made, the identification officer shall, if appropriate, arrange for the suspect to be offered an alternative which the officer considers suitable and practicable. If the officer decides it is not suitable and practicable to offer an alternative identification procedure, the reasons for that decision shall be recorded.

3.16 A group identification may initially be offered if the officer in charge of the investigation considers it is more suitable than a video identification or an identification parade and the identification officer considers it practicable to arrange.

## Notice to suspect

3.17 Unless *paragraph 3.20* applies, before a video identification, an identification parade or group identification is arranged, the following shall be explained to the suspect:

(i) the purposes of the video identification, identification parade or group identification;

(ii) their entitlement to free legal advice; see Code C, *paragraph 6.5*;

(iii) the procedures for holding it, including their right to have a solicitor or friend present;

(iv) that they do not have to consent to or co-operate in a video identification, identification parade or group identification;

(v) that if they do not consent to, and co-operate in, a video identification, identification parade or group identification, their refusal may be given in evidence in any subsequent trial and police may proceed covertly without their consent or make other arrangements to test whether a witness can identify them, see *paragraph 3.21*;

(vi) whether, for the purposes of the video identification procedure, images of them have previously been obtained, see *paragraph 3.20*, and if so, that they may co-operate in providing further, suitable images to be used instead;

(vii) if appropriate, the special arrangements for juveniles;

(viii) if appropriate, the special arrangements for mentally disordered or otherwise mentally vulnerable people;

(ix) that if they significantly alter their appearance between being offered an identification procedure and any attempt to hold an identification procedure, this may be given in evidence if the case comes to trial, and the identification officer may then consider other forms of identification, see *paragraph 3.21*;

(x) that a moving image or photograph may be taken of them when they attend for any identification procedure;

(xi) whether, before their identity became known, the witness was shown photographs, a computerised or artist's composite likeness or similar likeness or image by the police;

(xii) that if they change their appearance before an identification parade, it may not be practicable to arrange one on the day or subsequently and, because of the appearance change, the identification officer may consider alternative methods of identification;

(xiii) that they or their solicitor will be provided with details of the description of the suspect as first given by any witnesses who are to attend the video identification, identification parade, group identification or confrontation, see *paragraph 3.1*.

3.18 This information must also be recorded in a written notice handed to the suspect. The suspect must be given a reasonable opportunity to read the notice, after which, they should be asked to sign a second copy to indicate if they are willing to co-operate with the making of a video or take part in the identification parade or group identification. The signed copy shall be retained by the identification officer.

3.19 The duties of the identification officer under *paragraphs 3.17* and *3.18* may be performed by the custody officer or other officer not involved in the investigation if:

(a) it is proposed to release the suspect in order that an identification procedure can be arranged and carried out and an inspector is not available to act as the identification officer, see *paragraph 3.11*, before the suspect leaves the station; or

(b) it is proposed to keep the suspect in police detention whilst the procedure is arranged and carried out and waiting for an inspector to act as the identification officer, see *paragraph 3.11*, would cause unreasonable delay to the investigation.

The officer concerned shall inform the identification officer of the action taken and give them the signed copy of the notice.

3.20 If the identification officer and officer in charge of the investigation suspect, on reasonable grounds that if the suspect was given the information and notice as in *paragraphs 3.17* and *3.18*, they would then take steps to avoid being seen by a witness in any identification procedure, the identification officer may arrange for images of the suspect suitable for use in a video identification procedure to be obtained before giving the information and notice. If suspects' images are obtained in these circumstances, the suspect may, for the purposes of a video identification procedure, co-operate in providing new images which if suitable, would be used instead, see *paragraph 3.17(vi)*.

## (c) Cases when the suspect is known but not available

3.21 When a known suspect is not available or has ceased to be available, see *paragraph 3.4*, the identification officer may make arrangements for a video identification (see *Annex A*). If necessary, the identification officer may follow the video identification procedures but using *still* images. Any suitable moving or still images may be used and these may be obtained covertly if necessary. Alternatively, the identification officer may make arrangements for a group identification. These provisions may also be applied to juveniles where the consent of their parent or guardian is either refused or reasonable efforts to obtain that consent have failed (see *paragraph 2.12*).

3.22 Any covert activity should be strictly limited to that necessary to test the ability of the witness to identify the suspect.

3.23 The identification officer may arrange for the suspect to be confronted by the witness if none of the options referred to in paragraphs 3.5 to 3.10 or 3.21 are practicable. A 'confrontation' is when the suspect is directly confronted by the witness. A confrontation does not require the suspect's consent. Confrontations must be carried out in accordance with Annex D.

3.24 Requirements for information to be given to, or sought from, a suspect or for the suspect to be given an opportunity to view images before they are shown to a witness, do not apply if the suspect's lack of co-operation prevents the necessary action.

## (d) Documentation

3.25 A record shall be made of the video identification, identification parade, group identification or confrontation on forms provided for the purpose.

3.26 If the identification officer considers it is not practicable to hold a video identification or identification parade requested by the suspect, the reasons shall be recorded and explained to the suspect.

3.27 A record shall be made of a person's failure or refusal to co-operate in a video identification, identification parade or group identification and, if applicable, of the grounds for obtaining images in accordance with *paragraph 3.20*.

## (e) Showing films and photographs of incidents and information released to the media

3.28 Nothing in this Code inhibits showing films, photographs or other images to the public through the national or local media, or to police officers for the purposes of recognition and tracing suspects. However, when such material is shown to obtain evidence of recognition, the procedures in Part B will apply.

3.29 When a broadcast or publication is made, see *paragraph 3.28*, a copy of the relevant material released to the media for the purposes of recognising or tracing the suspect, shall be kept. The suspect or their solicitor shall be allowed to view such material before any eye-witness identification procedures under *paragraphs 3.5* to *3.10, 3.21 or 3.23* of Part A are carried out, provided it is practicable and would not unreasonably delay the investigation. Each eye-witness involved in the procedure shall be asked, after they have taken part, whether they have seen any film, photograph or image relating to the offence or any description of the suspect which has been broadcast or published in any national or local media or on any social networking site and if they have, they should be asked to give details of the circumstances, such as the date and place, as relevant. Their replies shall be recorded. This paragraph does not affect any separate requirement under the Criminal Procedure and Investigations Act 1996 to retain material in connection with criminal investigations.

## (f) Destruction and retention of photographs taken or used in eye-witness identification procedures

3.30 PACE, section 64A, see *paragraph 5.12*, provides powers to take photographs of suspects and allows these photographs to be used or disclosed only for purposes related to the prevention or detection of crime, the investigation of offences or the conduct of prosecutions by, or on behalf of, police or other law enforcement and prosecuting authorities inside and outside the United Kingdom or the enforcement of a sentence. After being so used or disclosed, they may be retained but can only be used or disclosed for the same purposes.

3.31 Subject to *paragraph 3.33*, the photographs (and all negatives and copies), of suspects not taken in accordance with the provisions in *paragraph 5.12* which are taken for the purposes of, or in connection with, the identification procedures in *paragraphs 3.5* to *3.10, 3.21* or *3.23* must be destroyed unless the suspect:

(a) is charged with, or informed they may be prosecuted for, a recordable offence;

(b) is prosecuted for a recordable offence;

(c) is cautioned for a recordable offence or given a warning or reprimand in accordance with the Crime and Disorder Act 1998 for a recordable offence; or

(d) gives informed consent, in writing, for the photograph or images to be retained for purposes described in *paragraph 3.30*.

3.32 When *paragraph 3.31* requires the destruction of any photograph, the person must be given an opportunity to witness the destruction or to have a certificate confirming the destruction if they request one within five days of being informed that the destruction is required.

3.33 Nothing in *paragraph 3.31* affects any separate requirement under the Criminal Procedure and Investigations Act 1996 to retain material in connection with criminal investigations.

## (B) Evidence of recognition by showing films, photographs and other images

3.34 This Part of this section applies when, for the purposes of obtaining evidence of recognition, any person, including a police officer:
(a) views the image of an individual in a film, photograph or any other visual medium; and
(b) is asked whether they recognise that individual as someone who is known to them.

3.35 The films, photographs and other images shall be shown on an individual basis to avoid any possibility of collusion and to provide safeguards against mistaken recognition, the showing shall as far as possible follow the principles for video identification if the suspect is known, see *Annex A*, or identification by photographs if the suspect is not known, see *Annex E*.

3.36 A record of the circumstances and conditions under which the person is given an opportunity to recognise the individual must be made and the record must include:
(a) Whether the person knew or was given information concerning the name or identity of any suspect.
(b) What the person has been told *before* the viewing about the offence, the person(s) depicted in the images or the offender and by whom.
(c) How and by whom the witness was asked to view the image or look at the individual.
(d) Whether the viewing was alone or with others and if with others, the reason for it.
(e) The arrangements under which the person viewed the film or saw the individual and by whom those arrangements were made.
(f) Whether the viewing of any images was arranged as part of a mass circulation to police and the public or for selected persons.
(g) The date time and place images were viewed or further viewed or the individual was seen.
(h) The times between which the images were viewed or the individual was seen.
(i) How the viewing of images or sighting of the individual was controlled and by whom.
(j) Whether the person was familiar with the location shown in any images or the place where they saw the individual and if so, why.
(k) Whether or not on this occasion, the person claims to recognise any image shown, or any individual seen, as being someone known to them, and if they do:
(i) the reason
(ii) the words of recognition
(iii) any expressions of doubt
(iv) what features of the image or the individual triggered the recognition.

3.37 The record under paragraph 3.36 may be made by:
• the person who views the image or sees the individual and makes the recognition.
• the officer or police staff in charge of showing the images to the person or in charge of the conditions under which the person sees the individual.

---

**1.8.4.1**    **KEYNOTE**

**Visual Identification**

Section 3 is now split into Part A and Part B, thereby distinguishing eye-witness identification procedures such as video identification from procedures for obtaining recognition evidence by viewing CCTV and similar images.

The visual identification of suspects by witnesses is one of the most common forms of identification; it is also one of the most unreliable. Even under research conditions, the recall of eye witnesses is inconsistent; where the witness sees or experiences the spontaneous commission of a crime, that reliability is reduced even further.

It was for these reasons that the *Turnbull* guidelines were set out, together with the provisions of Code D. If there is no identification evidence, the *Turnbull* guidelines will not apply. It should be remembered that a witness who does not identify the suspect may still be able to provide other valuable evidence to the case, for instance a description of the person who committed the offence, or a description of what he/she was wearing. Again it is not uncommon for witnesses to qualify their identification of the suspect by indicating that they 'cannot be quite certain'. While a defendant cannot be convicted on such a qualified identification alone, it may be admissible to support the case where other evidence is also available (*R* v *George* [2002] EWCA Crim 1923).

A lot will depend on the individual circumstances of each case, but it is essential that these issues are covered in any interview or other evidence-gathering process.

'Dock identifications', where the witness's first identification of the accused involves pointing out the person in the dock, are often dramatised by filmmakers but, in practice, are generally disallowed as being unreliable and unfair.

The rules for identification differ between cases where the suspect *is known* and those where the suspect is *not known*.

**1.8.4.2**

**KEYNOTE**

**Identification Where there is a Known Suspect**

It is crucial that once the person becomes a known suspect, any witnesses, *including police officers*, who might be used at an identification parade, are kept apart from the suspect, as any contact could jeopardise a conviction. In *R* v *Lennon* (1999) 28 June, unreported, a suspect was arrested for public order offences after his description was circulated by the police officers that witnessed the offence. The suspect was placed in a van and the officers accidentally went in the van and identified the suspect. The court held that the person was a known suspect and the identification evidence should have been excluded.

Where a suspect is identified by witnesses, other evidence should still be sought to strengthen the case (or to prove the person's innocence) as identification evidence is often challenged at court. Such supporting evidence may include admissions by the suspect that links him/her to the identification evidence; e.g. that he/she owns the vehicle that was driven at the time of the offence (*R* v *Ward* [2001] Crim LR 316).

**1.8.4.3**

**KEYNOTE**

**When Must an Identification Procedure be Held?**

Identification procedures should be held for the benefit of the defence as well as the prosecution (*R* v *Wait* [1998] Crim LR 68). The *key factor* to consider when deciding whether to hold an identification parade is whether *a failure to hold a parade could be a matter of genuine potential prejudice to the suspect*. In *R* v *SBC (A Juvenile)* [2001] EWCA Crim 885 the defence was one of duress but the appeal was based on the failure of the police to hold identification parades. The Court of Appeal stated that this was not a case about identification, as none of the defendants denied their presence at the scene. What they denied was their criminal participation in the activities that took place. It followed, therefore, that Code D did not apply. Other examples would be where it is not in dispute that the suspect is already well known to the witness who claims to have seen the suspect commit the crime or where there is no reasonable possibility that a witness would be able to make an identification.

Any decision to proceed without an identification parade must be capable of justification later to the relevant court. The courts have taken different approaches to justification based on practical difficulties. In an early case, the submissions of the identification officer that it was impracticable to find enough people who sufficiently resembled the defendant were treated fairly dismissively by the trial judge (*R* v *Gaynor* [1988] Crim LR

242). In later cases, however, the courts have been more lenient, accepting that the timescales involved in arranging identification parades may render them 'impracticable' (see *R* v *Jamel* [1993] Crim LR 52, where the court refused an objection by the defence to a group identification). A group identification was used in *Jamel* because a parade using mixed-race volunteers would have taken too long to arrange. All reasonable steps must be taken to investigate the possibility of one identification option before moving on to an alternative, and an offer from a suspect's solicitor to find volunteers to stand on a parade is such a 'reasonable' step (*R* v *Britton & Richards* [1989] Crim LR 144).

There have been a number of Court of Appeal cases concerning the requirement to hold identification parades. It is suggested that these should be applied to the revised Code regardless of which form of identification procedure is used. The leading case is *R* v *Forbes* [2001] 1 AC 473, which was based on earlier versions of the Code of Practice. The House of Lords held that if the police are in possession of sufficient evidence to justify the arrest of a suspect, and that suspect's identification depends on eye-witness identification evidence, even in part, then if the identification is disputed, the Code requires that an identification parade should be held with the suspect's consent, unless one of the exceptions applies.

The House of Lords went on to say that this mandatory obligation to hold an identification parade ('parade' at the time of judgment was right, but this applies equally to any identification procedure) applies even if there has been a 'fully satisfactory', 'actual and complete' or 'unequivocal' identification of the suspect.

Despite the wording of Code D, it has been held that a suspect's right to have an identification [procedure] is not confined to cases where a dispute over identity has already arisen; that right also applies where such a dispute might reasonably be anticipated (*R* v *Rutherford and Palmer* (1994) 98 Cr App R 191). Similarly, a suspect's failure to request an identification [procedure] does not mean that the police may proceed without one (*R* v *Graham* [1994] Crim LR 212).

It is important to consider the distinction between identification of a suspect and the suspect's clothing or other features. In *D* v *DPP* (1998) *The Times*, 7 August, a witness had observed two youths for a continuous period of five to six minutes and then informed the police of what he had seen, describing the age of the youths and the clothes that they were wearing. The court held that there had not been an identification within the terms of the Codes of Practice because the witness had at no stage identified the defendant or the co-accused. He had described only their clothing and their approximate ages, and the police, acting on that information, had made the arrests. An identification parade could have served no useful purpose, since the clothing would have been changed and those persons used for the parade would have been the same approximate age. This point was further supported in *R* v *Haynes* [2004] EWCA Crim 390, where the Court of Appeal held that as a practical point the identification parade, whether or not the suspect was regarded as a known or unknown suspect, was of little value where the witness identified the suspect by clothing and not by recognition of the suspect's features. An identification parade would have provided little assistance.

The question for the court will be whether it is fair to admit the identification evidence. When looking at this issue the court will consider how reliable that identification evidence is.

1.8.4.4    **KEYNOTE**

**Recognition Cases**

Recognition cases, that is to say, those cases where the witness states that he/she knows the person who committed the offence as opposed to only being able to give a description, need to be carefully considered and Part B of this section of the Code adhered to. The eye-witness identification procedures in Part A should not be used to test whether a witness can recognise a person as someone he/she knows and would be able to give evidence of recognition along the lines of 'On (describe date, time location) I saw an image of an individual who I recognised as XY'. In these cases, the procedures in Part B shall apply. The admissibility and value of evidence of recognition obtained when carrying out the procedures in Part B may be compromised if before the person is recognised, the witness who has claimed to know him/her is given or is made, or becomes, aware of, information about the person which was not previously known to the witness personally but which he/she has purported to rely on to support his/her claim that the person is in fact known to him/her.

In *R* v *Ridley* (1999) *The Times*, 13 October, the Court of Appeal stated that there has never been a rule that an identification parade had to be held in all recognition cases and that it will be a question of fact in each case whether or not there is a need to do so. The view that an identification procedure is not required in these cases is supported by para. 3.12(ii).

The facts in *Ridley*, which it is suggested are not uncommon among patrolling officers, were that two police officers in a marked police vehicle noticed a car, which had been stolen earlier that day, drive past them. Both officers said that they recognised the defendant driving the car. The officers gave chase and gave evidence that the car was speeding and being driven dangerously. They decided that it was unsafe to continue pursuit, but arrested the suspect six days later. One of the officers claimed to have recognised the suspect because she had interviewed him for some 20 minutes five months previously and had seen him about town. She gave evidence that she had a view of the suspect in the car for about nine seconds. The other officer said that he recognised the suspect from a photograph but could not say when he had seen that photograph. He said that he had seen the suspect in the car for about two seconds. The court found that the female police officer's identification had been complete and there was no requirement for her to have further identified the suspect.

*Ridley* can be contrasted with *R* v *Conway* (1990) 91 Cr App R 143, where the witnesses' evidence was not as strong. There the witnesses stated that they recognised the accused simply because they knew him. The defence argument was that the witnesses did not actually know the accused and so could not have recognised him at the time of the offence. His conviction was quashed because of the prejudice caused by the absence of a parade. In *R* v *Davies* [2004] EWCA Crim 2521 a witness identified a masked attacker from his voice and eyes. The court in this case held that this identification evidence coupled with other circumstantial evidence was sufficient for a conviction.

A case can still amount to one of recognition, even where the witness does not know the name of the suspect but later obtained those details from a third party, for example where the witness and the suspect went to the same school and the witness became aware of the suspect's full names from other pupils at the school (*R* v *C*; *R* v *B* [2003] EWCA Crim 718).

In *R (On the Application of H)* v *DPP* [2003] EWHC 133 (Admin), the court accepted that it was reasonable for the police not to undertake an identification procedure. In the circumstances of the case the police had every reason to believe that the claimant and the victim were well known to each other. The claimant had accepted that the victim knew her. There was no question of doubt as to the victim's ability to recognise the claimant and as such this was a case of pure recognition where it was futile to hold an identification parade.

Care must be taken in cases where it is believed that the case is one of recognition not requiring an identification procedure. In *R* v *Harris* [2003] EWCA Crim 174 the witness stated that he recognised the suspect as being someone he went to school with. The suspect gave a prepared statement in which he disputed the suggestion that he was well known to the witness. Here the court held that an identification procedure should have been undertaken, as the circumstances of the case did not fall within the general exception of the Code, i.e. that an identification procedure would serve no useful purpose in proving or disproving whether the suspect had been involved in committing the offence. It is suggested therefore that where a suspect disputes that a witness knows him/her, an identification procedure should be considered.

When a suspect is filmed committing an offence, it may be admissible to give evidence of identification by way of recognition from a witness not present at the scene. In *Attorney-General's Ref (No. 2 of 2002)* [2002] EWCA Crim 2373 the Court reviewed the previous case law and concluded that there are at least four circumstances in which a jury could be invited to conclude that a defendant committed an offence on the basis of photographic evidence from the scene:

- where the photographic image was sufficiently clear the jury could compare it with the defendant sitting in the dock;
- where a witness knew the defendant sufficiently well to recognise him as the offender depicted in the photographic image;
- where a witness who did not know the defendant spent substantial time viewing and analysing photographic images from the scene, thereby acquiring special knowledge which the jury did not have, evidence of identification based on comparison between them and a reasonably contemporary photo of the defendant could be given so long as the image and photograph were available to the jury. Further, in

*R* v *Savalia*[2011] EWCA Crim 1334 the Court held that this did not just apply to facial features but could properly be extended to apply to identification of a defendant from closed-circuit television footage based on a combination of factors, including build and gait;

- a suitably qualified expert with facial mapping skills giving opinion evidence of identification based on a comparison between images from the scene and a reasonably contemporary photograph of the defendant could be given so long as the image and photograph were available to the jury.

*R* v *McCullough* [2011] EWCA Crim 1413 is a case where the victim of a robbery identified the suspect from a photograph on Facebook and then later identified the suspect on a video identification parade. The Court of Appeal found that the Facebook identification was far from ideal and it was capable of having a substantial effect on the weight of the witness's subsequent identification of the defendant in the formal identification procedure. The key here is that the formal identification procedure is still required.

---

**1.8.4.5**

### KEYNOTE

#### Identification of Disqualified Drivers

Another common identification problem is that of disqualified drivers and being able to satisfy the court that the person charged with disqualified driving is the same person who was disqualified by the court. This is because s. 73 of the Police and Criminal Evidence Act 1984 requires proof that the person named in a certificate of conviction as having been convicted is the person whose conviction is to be proved. There has been some guidance from the courts as to how this can be achieved. In *R* v *Derwentside Justices, ex parte Heaviside* [1996] RTR 384, the court stated that this could be done by:

- fingerprints under s. 39 of the Criminal Justice Act 1948;
- the evidence of a person who was present in court when the disqualification order was made;
- admission of the defendant (preferably in interview) (*DPP* v *Mooney* (1997) RTR 434);
- requiring the suspect's solicitor who was present when he/she was disqualified on the earlier occasion to give evidence (such a summons is a last resort when there was no other means of identifying whether an individual had been disqualified from driving) (*R (On the Application of Howe) and Law Society (Interested Party)* v *South Durham Magistrates' Court and CPS (Interested Party)* [2004] EWHC 362 (Admin)).

The methods outlined in *ex parte Heaviside* are not exhaustive, but just suggested methods (*DPP* v *Mansfield* [1997] RTR 96).

---

**1.8.4.6**

### KEYNOTE

#### Which Identification Procedure should be Used?

Where a known suspect is not available (or has ceased to be available for any reason), the identification officer has a discretion to make arrangements for a video identification to be conducted. For cases when a known suspect deliberately makes him/herself 'unavailable' in order to delay or frustrate arrangements for obtaining identification evidence see Code D, para. 3.21. This paragraph also apples where a suspect refuses or fails to take part in a video identification, an identification parade or a group identification, or refuses or fails to take part in the only practicable options from that list. It enables any suitable images of the suspect, moving or still, which are available or can be obtained, to be used in an identification procedure. Examples include images from custody and other CCTV systems and from visually recorded interview records.

It is only if none of the other options are practicable that the identification officer may arrange for the suspect to be confronted by the witness. A confrontation does not require the suspect's consent. In *R* v *McCulloch, Smith & Wheeler* (1999) 6 May, unreported, the Court of Appeal made it clear that confrontations between suspects and witnesses should only be carried out if no other procedure is practicable (see paras 1.8.4.7 to 1.8.4.9).

---

**KEYNOTE**

**Conduct of Identification Parades**

Identification evidence can be crucial to the success of a prosecution. There are clear guidelines that must be followed. Where such guidelines are not followed it is likely that the defence will argue strongly to have the identification evidence excluded. In *R* v *Jones* (1999) *The Times*, 21 April, identification evidence was excluded as the officers told the suspect that if he did not comply with the procedure, force would be used against him.

The purpose of allowing the custody officer or other officer not involved in the investigation to undertake the role of the identification officer at Code D, paras 3.17 and 3.18 is to avoid or reduce delays in arranging identification procedures by enabling the required information and warning to be given at the earliest opportunity.

Annexes A–F of Code D set out in detail the procedures and requirements which must be followed in conducting identification procedures.

Although the courts are aware of the many practical difficulties involved in organising and running identification procedures (see e.g. *R* v *Jamel* [1993] Crim LR 52), any flaws in the procedure will be considered in the light of their potential impact on the defendant's trial. Serious or deliberate breaches (such as the showing of photographs to witnesses before the parade), will invariably lead to any evidence so gained being excluded (*R* v *Finley* [1993] Crim LR 50). The key question for the court will be whether the breach of the Codes is likely to have made the identification less reliable.

Breaches which appear to impact on the safeguards imposed by Annexes A–F to separate the functions of investigation and identification (e.g. where the investigating officer becomes involved with the running of the parade in a way which allows him/her to talk to the witnesses (*R* v *Gall* (1989) 90 Cr App R 64)) will also be treated seriously by the court.

The case of *R* v *Marrin* [2002] EWCA Crim 251, provides some guidance as to methods that could be used to get a suitable pool of participants for an identification parade. The court held that there was nothing inherently unfair or objectionable in some colouring or dye being used on the facial stubble of some volunteers to make them look more like the suspect. However, care needed to be taken with such measures because the procedure would be undermined if it was obvious to the witness that make-up had been used. Another point raised was that it may sometimes be appropriate for those on parade to wear hats, but if possible the wearing of hats should be avoided if hats had not been worn during the offence because this would make it more difficult for a witness to make an identification. However, there could be circumstances where the wearing of hats could help to achieve a resemblance and might be desirable to minimise differences. Finally, an identification of a suspect was not invalidated by the witness's request for the removal of a hat. There was nothing unfair in that taking place and there was no breach of any Code either.

It is important to follow the guidance in the Codes regardless of what agreement is obtained from the suspect or his/her solicitor. In *R* v *Hutton* [1999] Crim LR 74, at the suggestion of the suspect's solicitor, all the participants in the identification parade wore back-to-front baseball caps and had the lower part of their faces obscured by material. That identification was the only evidence against the defendant on that count. The court excluded the evidence and did not accept the fact that the decision had been agreed by the defence.

It will be essential that any photographs, photofits or other such material is stored securely in a manner that restricts access so as to be able to demonstrate to the court that the material cannot have been viewed by any of the witnesses and that copies have not been made that have not been accounted for. Where a witness attending an identification procedure has previously been shown photographs, or been shown or provided with computerised or artist's composite likenesses, or similar likenesses or pictures, it is the officer in charge of the investigation's responsibility to make the identification officer aware of this.

**KEYNOTE**

**Identification Where there is No Suspect**

Where the police have no suspect, Code D provides for witnesses (including police officers) to be shown photographs. If photographs are to be shown, the procedure set out at Annex E must be followed. When it is proposed to show photographs to a witness in accordance with Annex E, it is the responsibility of the officer in charge of the investigation to confirm to the officer responsible for supervising and directing the showing, that the first description of the suspect given by that witness has been recorded. If this description has not been recorded, the procedure under Annex E must be postponed. Except for the provisions of Annex E, para. 1, a police officer who is a witness for the purposes of this part of the Code is subject to the same principles and procedures as a civilian witness.

Using photographs from police criminal records can affect the judgment of a jury and nothing should be done to draw their attention to the fact that the defendant's photograph was already held by the police (*R* v *Lamb* (1980) 71 Cr App R 198). This rule does not apply if the jury are already aware of the defendant's previous convictions (*R* v *Allen* [1996] Crim LR 426).

If a film which has been shown to a witness is later lost or unavailable, the witness may give evidence of what he/she saw on that film but the court will have to consider all the relevant circumstances in deciding whether to admit that evidence *and* what weight to attach to it. (For a discussion of those circumstances, see *Taylor* v *Chief Constable of Cheshire* [1986] 1 WLR 1479.)

It is important that where pictures or film are shown to specific police officers to try to identify suspects this must be done in a controlled way. In *R* v *Smith (Dean)* [2008] EWCA Crim 1342, the court held that a police officer who was asked to view a CCTV recording to see if he could recognise any suspects involved in a robbery was not in the same shoes as a witness asked to identify someone he/she had seen committing a crime. However, safeguards that Code D was designed to put in place were equally important in cases where a police officer was asked to see whether he/she could recognise anyone in a CCTV recording. Whether or not Code D applied, there had to be in place some record that assisted in gauging the reliability of the assertion that the police officer recognised an individual. It was important that a police officer's initial reactions to viewing a CCTV recording were set out and available for scrutiny. Thus if the police officer failed to recognise anyone on first viewing but did so subsequently, those circumstances ought to be noted. If a police officer failed to pick anybody else out, that also should be recorded, as should any words of doubt. Furthermore, it was necessary that if recognition took place a record was made of what it was about the image that was said to have triggered the recognition. The case of *R* v *JD* [2012] EWCA Crim 2637 further highlights the need to keep records and comply with the Codes. As there was no record of how the police officer in this case viewed the CCTV, the court held that the defence could not test the officer's account that he watched the footage alone and no records had been made as to what features of the image triggered the recognition and other aspects of the recognition. It had been highly suggestive of the investigating constable to tell C that she believed D to feature in the CCTV footage rather than simply asking him to watch it and waiting to see if he recognised anybody. Another case is *R* v *McCook* [2012] EWCA Crim 2817 where the court commented on some of the process required by Code D, for example, the witness's statement did not reveal the nature of the viewing equipment, the number of times the footage was played, how the viewing arrangements were made, what the witness had been told prior to the viewing and whether or not he was alone.

Other types of identification are also coming before the courts. In *R* v *Alexander and McGill* [2012] EWCA Crim 2768 the victim identified the suspects through their Facebook account pictures. The court observed that identifications done in this way, through the use of Facebook, were likely to rise and it was therefore incumbent upon investigators to take steps to obtain, in as much detail as possible, evidence in relation to the initial identification. In this case, before trial requests were made by the defence for photographs of the other Facebook pages that had been considered by victim and his sister so that defendants could consider how their identifications might have been made.

---

1.8.4.9    **KEYNOTE**

**Identification at the Scene**

The need for 'scene identifications' was recognised by Lord Lane CJ in *R* v *Oscar* [1991] Crim LR 778 and by the Court of Appeal in *R* v *Rogers* [1993] Crim LR 386.

In *Oscar*, the court held that there had been no requirement for an identity parade in that case and Lord Lane pointed out that, in any case, a later parade where the suspect was dressed differently would be of no value at all. In *Rogers*, the suspect was found near a crime scene and was confronted by a witness who positively identified him. The court held that the identification in that case was necessary for an arrest to be made, although the court considered that a later parade could have been carried out.

The admissibility of identification evidence obtained when carrying out a 'scene identification' may be compromised if before a person is identified, the witness's attention is specifically drawn to that person.

Careful consideration must be given before a decision to identify a suspect in this manner is used. If there is sufficient evidence to arrest the suspect without using a witness's identification, then it is likely that the courts will find that an identification method outlined at Code D, para. 3.4 should have been used and the evidence may be excluded. Confrontations between witnesses and suspects on the street can be useful at times, but where this takes place it defeats the formal identification process and needs to be carefully considered. The reason for this is that, even if the suspect is picked out on the identification parade by that witness, the defence will be able to argue that the identification was from the confrontation after the incident and not at the time of the commission of the offence. If there is more than one witness available and a decision is taken to use a witness to try to identify a suspect at the scene, other witnesses should be moved away, so as to reduce the possibility of a chance encounter with the suspect. Where possible, these witnesses should be kept apart until the identification parade and ideally should not discuss the matter between themselves.

An example where a street identification was appropriate is *R* v *El-Hinnachi* [1998] 2 Cr App R 226. Here an affray took place in the car park of a public house. A witness had seen the man earlier in the pub and she had had an unobstructed view in good light before the attack. The witness described the attacker's clothing to the police and then identified a group of men who had been stopped by other officers a short distance away. The court accepted that this was the correct approach. The defendants were not known suspects when they were stopped by the police prior to the witness's identification. The court also accepted that it had not been practicable for a record to have been made of the witness's description, as required by Code D, para. 3.1, prior to the identification.

A not uncommon situation is where police officers chase a suspect who is arrested by other officers on the description circulated by the chasing officer, who then attends the scene to confirm the person's identity. The case of *R* v *Nunes* [2001] EWCA Crim 2283, covers this point and points out the dangers of this practice. The facts of the case were that a police officer saw a man inside a house and circulated a description on his radio. A person fitting the description was seen and arrested. The first officer arrived on the scene and identified the arrested person as the man he had earlier seen in the house. The Court of Appeal held that on the particular facts of this case the identification amounted to a breach of the Code. By the time of the identification, the man had been arrested for suspected involvement in the offence and, on his arrest, the identity of the suspect was known to the police. Therefore, by the time the witnessing officer arrived on the scene, the case involved 'disputed identification evidence' because the suspect had said that he had not done anything while the police had told him he matched the description of a suspected burglar. That said, the court did go on to hold that the judge had the discretion to allow the identification evidence to be adduced notwithstanding the breach of the Codes, but a full and careful direction regarding the breaches, together with a warning about the shortcomings in the procedure, would have been necessary.

| 1.8.4.10 | **KEYNOTE** |

**Photographs, Image and Sound Reproduction Generally**

The use of photographic and computer-generated images (such as E-Fit) to identify suspects has increased considerably over the past few years. Although the courts will exercise considerable caution when admitting such evidence (see *R* v *Blenkinsop* [1995] 1 Cr App R 7), these methods of identification are particularly useful. Expert evidence may be admitted to interpret images on film (see e.g. *R* v *Stockwell* (1993) 97 Cr App R 260) and police officers who are very familiar with a particular film clip (e.g. of crowd violence at a football match) may be allowed to assist the court in interpreting and explaining events shown within it (see *R* v *Clare* [1995] 2 Cr App R 333).

Logically E-Fit and other witness-generated images would be treated as 'visual statements', in that they represent the witness's recollection of what he/she saw. However, the Court of Appeal has decided that they are not to be so treated (*R* v *Cook* [1987] QB 417) and therefore the restrictions imposed by the rule against hearsay will not apply (see also *R* v *Constantinou* (1990) 91 Cr App R 74, where this ruling was followed in relation to a photofit image).

**KEYNOTE**

**Voice Identification**

The Codes do not preclude the police making use of aural identification procedures such as a 'voice identification parade', where they judge that appropriate.

Generally, a witness may give evidence identifying the defendant's voice (*R* v *Robb* (1991) 93 Cr App R 161), while expert testimony may be admitted in relation to tape recordings of a voice which is alleged to belong to the defendant. In the latter case, the jury should be allowed to hear the recording(s) so that they can draw their own conclusions (*R* v *Bentum* (1989) 153 JP 538).

In *R* v *Flyn*; *R* v *St John* [2008] EWCA Crim 970 the Court of Appeal held that where the voice identification is from a recording a prerequisite for making a speaker identification was that there should be a sample of an adequate size from the disputed recording that could confidently be attributed to a single speaker. The court also recognised that expert evidence showed that lay listeners with considerable familiarity with a voice and listening to a clear recording could still make mistakes. It is therefore suggested that other supporting evidence will be needed for a conviction to succeed.

Home Office Circular 57/2003, *Advice on the Use of Voice Identification Parades*, provides guidance on the use of voice identification parades.

## 4 Identification by Fingerprints and Footwear Impressions

## (A) Taking fingerprints in connection with a criminal investigation

### (a) General

4.1 References to 'fingerprints' means any record, produced by any method, of the skin pattern and other physical characteristics or features of a person's:

(i) fingers; or

(ii) palms.

### (b) Action

4.2 A person's fingerprints may be taken in connection with the investigation of an offence only with their consent or if *paragraph 4.3* applies. If the person is at a police station consent must be in writing.

4.3 PACE, section 61, provides powers to take fingerprints without consent from any person over the age of ten years:

(a) under section 61(3), from a person detained at a police station in consequence of being arrested for a recordable offence, if they have not had their fingerprints taken in the course of the investigation of the offence unless those previously taken fingerprints are not a complete set or some or all of those fingerprints are not of sufficient quality to allow satisfactory analysis, comparison or matching;

(b) under section 61(4), from a person detained at a police station who has been charged with a recordable offence, or informed they will be reported for such an offence if they have not had their fingerprints taken in the course of the investigation of or all of those fingerprints are not of sufficient quality to allow satisfactory analysis, comparison or matching;

(c) under section 61(4A), from a person who has been bailed to appear at a court or police station if the person:

    (i)  has answered to bail for a person whose fingerprints were taken previously and there are reasonable grounds for believing they are not the same person; or

    (ii)  who has answered to bail claims to be a different person from a person whose fingerprints were previously taken;

and in either case, the court or an officer of inspector rank or above, authorises the fingerprints to be taken at the court or police station (an inspector's authority may be given in writing or orally and confirmed in writing as soon as practicable);

(ca)  under section 61(5A) from a person who has been arrested for a recordable offence and released if the person:

    (i)  is on bail and has not had their fingerprints taken in the course of the investigation of the offence, or;

    (ii)  has had their fingerprints taken in the course of the investigation of the offence, but they do not constitute a complete set or some, or all, of the fingerprints are not of sufficient quality to allow satisfactory analysis, comparison or matching;

(cb)  under section 61(5B) from a person not detained at a police station who has been charged with a recordable offence or informed they will be reported for such an offence if they have not had their fingerprints taken in the course of the investigation or their fingerprints have been taken in the course of the investigation of the offence, but they do not constitute a complete set or some, or all, of the fingerprints are not of sufficient quality to allow satisfactory analysis, comparison or matching.

(d)  under section 61(6), from a person who has been:

    (i)  convicted of a recordable offence;

    (ii)  given a caution in respect of a recordable offence which, at the time of the caution, the person admitted; or

    (iii)  warned or reprimanded under the Crime and Disorder Act 1998, section 65, for a recordable offence,

if, since their conviction, caution, warning or reprimand their fingerprints have not been taken or their fingerprints which have been taken since then do not constitute a complete set or some, or all, of the fingerprints are not of sufficient quality to allow satisfactory analysis, comparison or matching, and in either case, an officer of inspector rank or above, is satisfied that taking the fingerprints is necessary to assist in the prevention or detection of crime and authorises the taking;

(e)  under section 61(6A) from a person a constable reasonably suspects is committing or attempting to commit, or has committed or attempted to commit, any offence if either:

• the person's name is unknown and cannot be readily ascertained by the constable; or

• the constable has reasonable grounds for doubting whether a name given by the person is their real name.

Note: fingerprints taken under this power are not regarded as having been taken in the course of the investigation of an offence.

(f)  under section 61(6D) from a person who has been convicted outside England and Wales of an offence which if committed in England and Wales would be a qualifying offence as defined by PACE, section 65A if:

    (i)  the person's fingerprints have not been taken previously under this power or their fingerprints have been so taken on a previous occasion but they do not constitute a complete set or some, or all, of the fingerprints are not of sufficient quality to allow satisfactory analysis, comparison or matching; and

    (ii)  a police officer of inspector rank or above is satisfied that taking fingerprints is necessary to assist in the prevention or detection of crime and authorises them to be taken.

4.4    PACE, section 63A(4) and Schedule 2A provide powers to:

(a)  make a requirement (in accordance with Annex G) for a person to attend a police station to have their fingerprints taken in the exercise of certain powers in paragraph 4.3 above when that power applies at the time the fingerprints would be taken in accordance with the requirement. Those powers are:

(i) section 61(5A) – Persons arrested for a recordable offence and released, see paragraph 4.3(ca): The requirement may not be made more than six months from the day the investigating officer was informed that the fingerprints previously taken were incomplete or below standard.

(ii) section 61(5B) – Persons charged etc. with a recordable offence, see paragraph 4.3(cb): The requirement may not be made more than six months from:

- the day the person was charged or reported if fingerprints have not been taken since then; or
- the day the investigating officer was informed that the fingerprints previously taken were incomplete or below standard.

(iii) section 61(6) – Person convicted, cautioned, warned or reprimanded for a recordable offence in England and Wales, see paragraph 4.3(d): Where the offence for which the person was convicted etc is also a qualifying offence, there is no time limit for the exercise of this power. Where the conviction etc. is for a recordable offence which is not a qualifying offence, the requirement may not be made more than two years from:

- the day the person was convicted, cautioned, warned or reprimanded, or the day Schedule 2A comes into force (if later), if fingerprints have not been taken since then; or
- the day an officer from the force investigating the offence was informed that the fingerprints previously taken were incomplete or below standard or the day Schedule 2A comes into force (if later).

(iv) section 61(6D) – A person who has been convicted of a qualifying offence outside England and Wales, see paragraph 4.3(g): There is no time limit for making the requirement.

Note: A person who has had their fingerprints taken under any of the powers in section 61 mentioned in paragraph 4.3 on two occasions in relation to any offence may not be required under Schedule 2A to attend a police station for their fingerprints to be taken again under section 61 in relation to that offence, unless authorised by an officer of inspector rank or above. The fact of the authorisation and the reasons for giving it must be recorded as soon as practicable.

**(b) arrest, without warrant, a person who fails to comply with the requirement.**

4.5 A person's fingerprints may be taken, as above, electronically.

4.6 Reasonable force may be used, if necessary, to take a person's fingerprints without their consent under the powers as in *paragraphs 4.3* and *4.4*.

4.7 Before any fingerprints are taken:

(a) without consent under any power mentioned in *paragraphs 4.3* and *4.4* above, the person must be informed of:

(i) the reason their fingerprints are to be taken;

(ii) the power under which they are to be taken; and

(iii) the fact that the relevant authority has been given if any power mentioned in *paragraph 4.3(c), (d)* or *(f)* applies;

(b) with or without consent at a police station or elsewhere, the person must be informed:

(i) that their fingerprints may be subject of a speculative search against other fingerprints and

(ii) that their fingerprints may be retained in accordance with *Annex F, Part (a)* unless they were taken under the power mentioned in paragraph 4.3(e) when they must be destroyed after they have being checked.

## (c) Documentation

4.8A A record must be made as soon as practicable after the fingerprints are taken, of:

- the matters in paragraph 4.7(a)(i) to (iii) and the fact that the person has been informed of those matters; and

- the fact that the person has been informed of the matters in paragraph 4.7(b)(i) and (ii).

The record must be made in the person's custody record if they are detained at a police station when the fingerprints are taken.

4.8 If force is used, a record shall be made of the circumstances and those present.

4.9 *Not used*

## (B) Taking fingerprints in connection with immigration enquiries

## (a) Action

4.10 A person's fingerprints may be taken and retained for the purposes of immigration law enforcement and control in accordance with powers and procedures other than under PACE and for which the UK Border Agency (not the police) are responsible. Details of these powers and procedures which are under the Immigration Act 1971, Schedule 2 and Immigration and Asylum Act 1999, section 141, including modifications to the PACE Codes of Practice are contained in Chapter 24 of the Operational Instructions and Guidance manual which is published by the UK Border Agency.

4.11 *Not used*

4.12 *Not used*

4.13 *Not used*

4.14 *Not used*

4.15 *Not used*

## (C) Taking footwear impressions in connection with a criminal investigation

## (a) Action

4.16 Impressions of a person's footwear may be taken in connection with the investigation of an offence only with their consent or if *paragraph 4.17* applies. If the person is at a police station consent must be in writing.

4.17 PACE, section 61A, provides power for a police officer to take footwear impressions without consent from any person over the age of ten years who is detained at a police station:

(a) in consequence of being arrested for a recordable offence or if the detainee has been charged with a recordable offence, or informed they will be reported for such an offence; and

(b) the detainee has not had an impression of their footwear taken in the course of the investigation of the offence unless the previously taken impression is not complete or is not of sufficient quality to allow satisfactory analysis, comparison or matching (whether in the case in question or generally).

4.18 Reasonable force may be used, if necessary, to take a footwear impression from a detainee without consent under the power in *paragraph 4.17*.

4.19 Before any footwear impression is taken with, or without, consent as above, the person must be informed:

(a) of the reason the impression is to be taken;

(b) that the impression may be retained and may be subject of a speculative search against other impressions, unless destruction of the impression is required in accordance with *Annex F, Part (a)*; and

(c) that if their footwear impressions are required to be destroyed, they may witness their destruction as provided for in *Annex F, Part (a)*.

## (b) Documentation

4.20 A record must be made as soon as possible, of the reason for taking a person's footwear impressions without consent. If force is used, a record shall be made of the circumstances and those present.

4.21 A record shall be made when a person has been informed under the terms of *paragraph 4.19(b)*, of the possibility that their footwear impressions may be subject of a speculative search

### 1.8.5.1    KEYNOTE

References to 'recordable offences' in this Code relate to those offences for which convictions, cautions, reprimands and warnings may be recorded in national police records. See the Police and Criminal Evidence Act 1984, s. 27(4). The recordable offences current at the time when this Code was prepared are any offences which carry a sentence of imprisonment on conviction (irrespective of the period, or the age of the offender or actual sentence passed) as well as the non-imprisonable offences under the Vagrancy Act 1824, ss. 3 and 4 (begging and persistent begging), the Street Offences Act 1959, s. 1 (loitering or soliciting for purposes of prostitution), the Road Traffic Act 1988, s. 25 (tampering with motor vehicles), the Criminal Justice and Public Order Act 1994, s. 167 (touting for hire car services) and others listed in the National Police Records (Recordable Offences) Regulations 2000 (SI 2000/1139) as amended.

When dealing with a person convicted of an offence outside England and Wales, a qualifying offence is one of the offences specified in s. 65A of the 1984 Act. These indictable offences which concern the use or threat of violence or unlawful force against persons, sexual offences and offences against children include, for example, murder, manslaughter, false imprisonment, kidnapping and other offences such as:

- ss. 4, 16, 18, 20 to 24 or 47 of the Offences Against the Person Act 1861;
- ss. 16–18 of the Firearms Act 1968;
- ss. 9 or 10 of the Theft Act 1968 or under s. 12A of that Act involving an accident which caused a person's death;
- s. 1 of the Criminal Damage Act 1971 required to be charged as arson;
- s. 1 of the Protection of Children Act 1978; and
- ss. 1–19, 25, 26, 30–41, 47–50, 52, 53, 57 to 59, 61–67, 69–70 of the Sexual Offences Act 2003.

Whether fingerprint evidence is admissible as evidence tending to prove guilt, depends on:

- the experience and expertise of the witness: this requires at least three years' experience;
- the number of similar ridge characteristics (if there are fewer than eight ridge characteristics matching the fingerprints of the accused with those found by the police, it is unlikely that a judge would exercise his/her discretion to admit such evidence);
- whether there are dissimilar characteristics;
- the size of print relied on; and
- the quality and clarity of print relied on.

The jury should be warned that expert evidence is not conclusive in itself and that guilt has to be proved in the light of all evidence (*R* v *Buckley* [1999] EWCA Crim 1191).

### 1.8.5.2    KEYNOTE

**Before Conviction**

This means that the fingerprints, footwear impressions or DNA sample may be checked against other fingerprints, footwear impressions and DNA records held by, or on behalf of, the police and other law enforcement authorities in, or outside, the United Kingdom, or held in connection with, or as a result of, an investigation of an offence inside or outside the United Kingdom. Fingerprints, footwear impressions and samples taken from a person suspected of committing a recordable offence but not arrested, charged or informed that he/she will be reported for it, may be subject to a speculative search only if the person consents in writing. The following is an example of a basic form of words:

I consent to my fingerprints, footwear impressions and DNA sample and information derived from it being retained and used only for purposes related to the prevention and detection of a crime, the investigation of an offence or the conduct of a prosecution either nationally or internationally.

I understand that my fingerprints, footwear impressions or DNA sample may be checked against other fingerprint, footwear impressions and DNA records held by or on behalf of relevant law enforcement authorities, either nationally or internationally.

I understand that once I have given my consent for my fingerprints, footwear impressions or DNA sample to be retained and used I cannot withdraw this consent.

The power under s. 61(6A) of the 1984 Act described in para. 4.3(e) allows fingerprints of a suspect who has not been arrested to be taken in connection with any offence (whether recordable or not) using a mobile device and then checked on the street against the database containing the national fingerprint collection. Fingerprints taken under this power cannot be retained after they have been checked. The results may make an arrest for the suspected offence based on the name condition unnecessary (see Code G, para. 2.9(a)) and enable the offence to be disposed of without arrest, e.g. by summons/charging by post, penalty notice or words of advice. If arrest for a non-recordable offence is necessary for any other reasons, this power may also be exercised at the station. Before the power is exercised, the officer should:

- inform the person of the nature of the suspected offence and why he/she is suspected of committing it;
- give the person a reasonable opportunity to establish his/her real name before deciding that his/her name is unknown and cannot be readily ascertained or that there are reasonable grounds to doubt that a name that he/she has given is his/her real name;
- as applicable, inform the person of the reason why his/her name is not known and cannot be readily ascertained or of the grounds for doubting that a name he/she has given is his/her real name, including, for example, the reason why a particular document the person has produced to verify his/her real name is not sufficient.

Powers to take fingerprints without consent for immigration purposes are given to police and immigration officers under the:

(a) Immigration Act 1971, sch. 2, para. 18(2), when it is reasonably necessary for the purposes of identifying a person detained under the Immigration Act 1971, sch. 2, para. 16 (Detention of person liable to examination or removal); and

(b) Immigration and Asylum Act 1999, s. 141(7) when a person:
  - fails without reasonable excuse to produce, on arrival, a valid passport with a photograph or some other document satisfactorily establishing his/her identity and nationality;
  - is refused entry to the United Kingdom but is temporarily admitted if an immigration officer reasonably suspects that the person might break a residence or reporting condition;
  - is subject to directions for removal from the United Kingdom;
  - has been arrested under the Immigration Act 1971, sch. 2, para. 17;
  - has made a claim for asylum;
  - is a dependant of any of the above.

The Immigration and Asylum Act 1999, s. 142(3) also gives police and immigration officers power to arrest without warrant a person who fails to comply with a requirement imposed by the Secretary of State to attend a specified place for fingerprinting.

1.8.5.3   **KEYNOTE**

**Power to Require Persons to Attend a Police Station to Provide Samples**

Code D, Annex G deals with the requirement for a person to attend a police station for fingerprints and samples.

**KEYNOTE**

**Retention of Fingerprints**

Code D, Annex F deals with the destruction and the speculative searches of fingerprints and samples and speculative searches of footwear impressions. It is important that the Annex is followed particularly in relation to obtaining consent and explaining to volunteers what they are consenting to.

**1.8.5.5**

**KEYNOTE**

**Criminal Record and Conviction Certificates**

Under s. 118 of the Police Act 1997, in certain circumstances the Secretary of State issues certificates concerning an individual's previous convictions. In some cases the Secretary of State will not do this until it has been possible to verify the person's identity, which can be done through the taking of his/her fingerprints. Where this is the case, the Secretary of State may require the police officer in charge of the specified police station, or any other police station the Secretary of State reasonably determines, to take the applicant's fingerprints at the specified station at such reasonable time as the officer may direct and notify the applicant.

If fingerprints are taken in these circumstances they must be destroyed as soon as is practicable after the identity of the applicant is established to the satisfaction of the Secretary of State. The destruction can be witnessed by the person giving the fingerprints if he/she requests and/or the person can ask for a certificate stating that the fingerprints have been destroyed. The certificate must be issued within three months of the request.

In the case of an individual under the age of 18 years the consent of the applicant's parent or guardian to the taking of the applicant's fingerprints is also required.

**1.8.5.6**

**KEYNOTE**

**Other Body Prints**

While the more established and convincing body marks are fingerprints it is possible for other body prints to be used as evidence to identify a suspect. In *R* v *Kempster* [2008] EWCA Crim 975 the police recovered an ear print from the fixed window pane to the side of the window that had been forced in order to gain entry to the property. In this case the conviction was not successful, but it was recognised that an ear print comparison was capable of providing information that could identify a person who had left an ear print on a surface. This would only be achieved with certainty where the minutiae of the ear structure could be identified and matched.

Fingerprints etc. and non-intimate samples may be taken from an arrested or detained person with the authority of an officer of a rank no lower than inspector.

**1.8.6**

## 5 Examinations to Establish Identity and the Taking of Photographs

### (A)  Detainees at police stations

### (a)  Searching or examination of detainees at police stations

5.1  PACE, section 54A(1), allows a detainee at a police station to be searched or examined or both, to establish:

(a) whether they have any marks, features or injuries that would tend to identify them as a person involved in the commission of an offence and to photograph any identifying marks, see *paragraph 5.5*; or

(b) their identity.

A person detained at a police station to be searched under a stop and search power, see Code A, is not a detainee for the purposes of these powers.

5.2 A search and/or examination to find marks under section 54A(1)(a) may be carried out without the detainee's consent, see *paragraph 2.12*, only if authorised by an officer of at least inspector rank when consent has been withheld or it is not practicable to obtain consent.

5.3 A search or examination to establish a suspect's identity under section 54A(1)(b) may be carried out without the detainee's consent, see *paragraph 2.12*, only if authorised by an officer of at least inspector rank when the detainee has refused to identify themselves or the authorising officer has reasonable grounds for suspecting the person is not who they claim to be.

5.4 Any marks that assist in establishing the detainee's identity, or their identification as a person involved in the commission of an offence, are identifying marks. Such marks may be photographed with the detainee's consent, see *paragraph 2.12*; or without their consent if it is withheld or it is not practicable to obtain it.

5.5 A detainee may only be searched, examined and photographed under section 54A, by a police officer of the same sex.

5.6 Any photographs of identifying marks, taken under section 54A, may be used or disclosed only for purposes related to the prevention or detection of crime, the investigation of offences or the conduct of prosecutions by, or on behalf of, police or other law enforcement and prosecuting authorities inside, and outside, the UK. After being so used or disclosed, the photograph may be retained but must not be used or disclosed except for these purposes.

5.7 The powers, as in *paragraph 5.1*, do not affect any separate requirement under the Criminal Procedure and Investigations Act 1996 to retain material in connection with criminal investigations.

5.8 Authority for the search and/or examination for the purposes of *paragraphs 5.2* and *5.3* may be given orally or in writing. If given orally, the authorising officer must confirm it in writing as soon as practicable. A separate authority is required for each purpose which applies.

5.9 If it is established a person is unwilling to co-operate sufficiently to enable a search and/or examination to take place or a suitable photograph to be taken, an officer may use reasonable force to:
   (a) search and/or examine a detainee without their consent; and
   (b) photograph any identifying marks without their consent.

5.10 The thoroughness and extent of any search or examination carried out in accordance with the powers in section 54A must be no more than the officer considers necessary to achieve the required purpose. Any search or examination which involves the removal of more than the person's outer clothing shall be conducted in accordance with Code C, Annex A, paragraph 11.

5.11 An intimate search may not be carried out under the powers in section 54A.

## (b) Photographing detainees at police stations and other persons elsewhere than at a police station

5.12 Under PACE, section 64A, an officer may photograph:
   (a) any person whilst they are detained at a police station; and
   (b) any person who is elsewhere than at a police station and who has been:
      (i) arrested by a constable for an offence;
      (ii) taken into custody by a constable after being arrested for an offence by a person other than a constable;
      (iii) made subject to a requirement to wait with a community support officer under paragraph 2(3) or (3B) of Schedule 4 to the Police Reform Act 2002;
      (iiia) given a direction by a constable under section 27 of the Violent Crime Reduction Act 2006;

(iv) given a penalty notice by a constable in uniform under Chapter 1 of Part 1 of the Criminal Justice and Police Act 2001, a penalty notice by a constable under section 444A of the Education Act 1996, or a fixed penalty notice by a constable in uniform under section 54 of the Road Traffic Offenders Act 1988;

(v) given a notice in relation to a relevant fixed penalty offence (within the meaning of paragraph 1 of Schedule 4 to the Police Reform Act 2002) by a community support officer by virtue of a designation applying that paragraph to him;

(vi) given a notice in relation to a relevant fixed penalty offence (within the meaning of paragraph 1 of Schedule 5 to the Police Reform Act 2002) by an accredited person by virtue of accreditation specifying that that paragraph applies to him; or

(vii) given a direction to leave and not return to a specified location for up to 48 hours by a police constable (under section 27 of the Violent Crime Reduction Act 2006).

5.12A  Photographs taken under PACE, section 64A:

(a) may be taken with the person's consent, or without their consent if consent is withheld or it is not practicable to obtain their consent, and

(b) may be used or disclosed only for purposes related to the prevention or detection of crime, the investigation of offences or the conduct of prosecutions by, or on behalf of, police or other law enforcement and prosecuting authorities inside and outside the United Kingdom or the enforcement of any sentence or order made by a court when dealing with an offence. After being so used or disclosed, they may be retained but can only be used or disclosed for the same purposes.

5.13  The officer proposing to take a detainee's photograph may, for this purpose, require the person to remove any item or substance worn on, or over, all, or any part of, their head or face. If they do not comply with such a requirement, the officer may remove the item or substance.

5.14  If it is established the detainee is unwilling to co-operate sufficiently to enable a suitable photograph to be taken and it is not reasonably practicable to take the photograph covertly, an officer may use reasonable force:

(a) to take their photograph without their consent; and

(b) for the purpose of taking the photograph, remove any item or substance worn on, or over, all, or any part of, the person's head or face which they have failed to remove when asked.

5.15  For the purposes of this Code, a photograph may be obtained without the person's consent by making a copy of an image of them taken at any time on a camera system installed anywhere in the police station.

## (c) Information to be given

5.16  When a person is searched, examined or photographed under the provisions as in *paragraph 5.1* and *5.12*, or their photograph obtained as in *paragraph 5.15*, they must be informed of the:

(a) purpose of the search, examination or photograph;

(b) grounds on which the relevant authority, if applicable, has been given; and

(c) purposes for which the photograph may be used, disclosed or retained.

This information must be given before the search or examination commences or the photograph is taken, except if the photograph is:

(i) to be taken covertly;

(ii) obtained as in *paragraph 5.15*, in which case the person must be informed as soon as practicable after the photograph is taken or obtained.

## (d) Documentation

5.17 A record must be made when a detainee is searched, examined, or a photograph of the person, or any identifying marks found on them, are taken. The record must include the:
   (a) identity, subject to paragraph 2.18, of the officer carrying out the search, examination or taking the photograph;
   (b) purpose of the search, examination or photograph and the outcome;
   (c) detainee's consent to the search, examination or photograph, or the reason the person was searched, examined or photographed without consent;
   (d) giving of any authority as in *paragraphs 5.2* and *5.3*, the grounds for giving it and the authorising officer.

5.18 If force is used when searching, examining or taking a photograph in accordance with this section, a record shall be made of the circumstances and those present.

## (B) Persons at police stations not detained

5.19 When there are reasonable grounds for suspecting the involvement of a person in a criminal offence, but that person is at a police station **voluntarily** and not detained, the provisions of *paragraphs 5.1* to *5.18* should apply, subject to the modifications in the following paragraphs.

5.20 References to the 'person being detained' and to the powers mentioned in *paragraph 5.1* which apply only to detainees at police stations shall be omitted.

5.21 Force may not be used to:
   (a) search and/or examine the person to:
      (i) discover whether they have any marks that would tend to identify them as a person involved in the commission of an offence; or
      (ii) establish their identity;
   (b) take photographs of any identifying marks, see *paragraph 5.4*; or
   (c) take a photograph of the person.

5.22 Subject to *paragraph 5.24*, the photographs of persons or of their identifying marks which are not taken in accordance with the provisions mentioned in *paragraphs 5.1* or *5.12*, must be destroyed (together with any negatives and copies) unless the person:
   (a) is charged with, or informed they may be prosecuted for, a recordable offence;
   (b) is prosecuted for a recordable offence;
   (c) is cautioned for a recordable offence or given a warning or reprimand in accordance with the Crime and Disorder Act 1998 for a recordable offence; or
   (d) gives informed consent, in writing, for the photograph or image to be retained as in *paragraph 5.6*.

5.23 When *paragraph 5.22* requires the destruction of any photograph, the person must be given an opportunity to witness the destruction or to have a certificate confirming the destruction provided they so request the certificate within five days of being informed the destruction is required.

5.24 Nothing in *paragraph 5.22* affects any separate requirement under the Criminal Procedure and Investigations Act 1996 to retain material in connection with criminal investigations.

1.8.6.1 **KEYNOTE**

The conditions under which fingerprints may be taken to assist in establishing a person's identity, are described in section 4.

A photograph taken under s. 54A of the Police and Criminal Evidence Act 1984 may be used by, or disclosed to, any person for any purpose related to the prevention or detection of crime, the investigation of an offence or the conduct of a prosecution. The use of the photograph is for any conduct which constitutes a criminal offence (whether under UK law or in another country). Examples of purposes related to the prevention or detection of crime, the investigation of offences or the conduct of prosecutions include:

- checking the photograph against other photographs held in records or in connection with, or as a result of, an investigation of an offence to establish whether the person is liable to arrest for other offences;
- when the person is arrested at the same time as other people, or at a time when it is likely that other people will be arrested, using the photograph to help establish who was arrested, at what time and where;
- when the real identity of the person is not known and cannot be readily ascertained or there are reasonable grounds for doubting that a name and other personal details given by the person, are his/her real name and personal details. In these circumstances, using or disclosing the photograph to help to establish or verify the person's real identity or determine whether he/she is liable to arrest for some other offence, e.g. by checking it against other photographs held in records or in connection with, or as a result of, an investigation of an offence;
- when it appears that any identification procedure in section 3 may need to be arranged for which the person's photograph would assist;
- when the person's release without charge may be required, and if the release is:
- on bail to appear at a police station, using the photograph to help verify the person's identity when he/she answers bail and if the person does not answer bail, to assist in arresting him/her; or
- without bail, using the photograph to help verify the person's identity or assist in locating him/her for the purposes of serving him/her with a summons to appear at court in criminal proceedings;
- when the person has answered to bail at a police station and there are reasonable grounds for doubting that he/she is the person who was previously granted bail, using the photograph to help establish or verify his/her identity;
- when the person has been charged with, reported for, or convicted of, a recordable offence and his/her photograph is not already on record as a result of any of the circumstances set out in the bullet points above or his/her photograph is on record but his/her appearance has changed since it was taken and the person has not yet been released or brought before a court;
- when the person arrested on a warrant claims to be a different person from the person named on the warrant and a photograph would help to confirm or disprove this claim.

There is no power to arrest a person convicted of a recordable offence solely to take his/her photograph. The power to take photographs in this section applies only where the person is in custody as a result of the exercise of another power, e.g. arrest for fingerprinting under s. 27 of the 1984 Act.

The use of reasonable force to take the photograph of a suspect elsewhere than at a police station must be carefully considered. In order to obtain a suspect's consent and co-operation to remove an item of religious headwear to take his/her photograph, a constable should consider whether in the circumstances of the situation the removal of the headwear and the taking of the photograph should be by an officer of the same sex as the person. It would be appropriate for these actions to be conducted out of public view.

## 1.8.7 | 6 Identification by Body Samples and Impressions

### (A) General

6.1 References to:
   (a) an 'intimate sample' mean a dental impression or sample of blood, semen or any other tissue fluid, urine, or pubic hair, or a swab taken from any part of a person's genitals or from a person's body orifice other than the mouth;
   (b) a 'non-intimate sample' means:
      (i) a sample of hair, other than pubic hair, which includes hair plucked with the root;
      (ii) a sample taken from a nail or from under a nail;
      (iii) a swab taken from any part of a person's body other than a part from which a swab taken would be an intimate sample;
      (iv) saliva;
      (v) a skin impression which means any record, other than a fingerprint, which is a record, in any form and produced by any method, of the skin pattern and other physical characteristics or features of the whole, or any part of, a person's foot or of any other part of their body.

## (B) Action

### (a) Intimate samples

6.2 PACE, section 62, provides that intimate samples may be taken under:

(a) section 62(1), from a person in police detention only:

    (i) if a police officer of inspector rank or above has reasonable grounds to believe such an impression or sample will tend to confirm or disprove the suspect's involvement in a recordable offence, and gives authorisation for a sample to be taken; and

    (ii) with the suspect's written consent;

(b) section 62(1A), from a person not in police detention but from whom two or more non-intimate samples have been taken in the course of an investigation of an offence and the samples, though suitable, have proved insufficient if:

    (i) a police officer of inspector rank or above authorises it to be taken; and

    (ii) the person concerned gives their written consent;

(c) section 62(2A), from a person convicted outside England and Wales of an offence which if committed in England and Wales would be qualifying offence as defined by PACE, section 65A from whom two or more non intimate samples taken under section 63(3E) (see paragraph 6.6(h)) have proved insufficient if:

    (i) a police officer of inspector rank or above is satisfied that taking the sample is necessary to assist in the prevention or detection of crime and authorises it to be taken; and

    (ii) the person concerned gives their written consent.

6.2A PACE, section 63A(4) and Schedule 2A provide powers to:

(a) make a requirement (in accordance with Annex G) for a person to attend a police station to have an intimate sample taken in the exercise of one of the following powers in paragraph 6.2 when that power applies at the time the sample is to be taken in accordance with the requirement or after the person's arrest if they fail to comply with the requirement:

    (i) section 62(1A) – Persons from whom two or more non-intimate samples have been taken and proved to be insufficient, see paragraph 6.2(b): There is no time limit for making the requirement.

    (ii) section 62(2A) – Persons convicted outside England and Wales from whom two or more non-intimate samples taken under section 63(3E) (see paragraph 6.6(h)) have proved insufficient, see *paragraph 6.2(c)*: There is no time limit for making the requirement.

6.3 Before a suspect is asked to provide an intimate sample, they must be:

(a) informed:

    (i) of the reason, including the nature of the suspected offence (except if taken under paragraph 6.2(c) from a person convicted outside England and Wales;

    (ii) that authorisation has been given and the provisions under which given;

    (iii) that a sample taken at a police station may be subject of a speculative search;

(b) warned that if they refuse without good cause their refusal may harm their case if it comes to trial. If the suspect is in police detention and not legally represented, they must also be reminded of their entitlement to have free legal advice, see Code C, *paragraph 6.5*, and the reminder noted in the custody record. If *paragraph 6.2(b)* applies and the person is attending a station voluntarily, their entitlement to free legal advice as in Code C, *paragraph 3.21* shall be explained to them.

6.4 Dental impressions may only be taken by a registered dentist. Other intimate samples, except for samples of urine, may only be taken by a registered medical practitioner or registered nurse or registered paramedic.

## (b) Non-intimate samples

6.5 A non-intimate sample may be taken from a detainee only with their written consent or if *paragraph 6.6* applies.

6.6 a non-intimate sample may be taken from a person without the appropriate consent in the following circumstances:

(a) Under section 63(2A) from a person who is in police detention as a consequence of being arrested for a recordable offence and who has not had a non-intimate sample of the same type and from the same part of the body taken in the course of the investigation of the offence by the police or they have had such a sample taken but it proved insufficient.

(b) Under section 63(3) from a person who is being held in custody by the police on the authority of a court if an officer of at least the rank of inspector authorises it to be taken. An authorisation may be given:

   (i) if the authorising officer has reasonable grounds for suspecting the person of involvement in a recordable offence and for believing that the sample will tend to confirm or disprove that involvement, and

   (ii) in writing or orally and confirmed in writing, as soon as practicable;

   but an authorisation may not be given to take from the same part of the body a further non-intimate sample consisting of a skin impression unless the previously taken impression proved insufficient.

(c) Under section 63(3ZA) from a person who has been arrested for a recordable offence and released if the person:

   (i) is on bail and has not had a sample of the same type and from the same part of the body taken in the course of the investigation of the offence, or;

   (ii) has had such a sample taken in the course of the investigation of the offence, but it proved unsuitable or insufficient.

(d) Under section 63(3A), from a person (whether or not in police detention or held in custody by the police on the authority of a court) who has been charged with a recordable offence or informed they will be reported for such an offence if the person:

   (i) has not had a non-intimate sample taken from them in the course of the investigation of the offence;

   (ii) has had a sample so taken, but it proved unsuitable or insufficient or

   (iii) has had a sample taken in the course of the investigation of the offence and the sample has been destroyed and in proceedings relating to that offence there is a dispute as to whether a DNA profile relevant to the proceedings was derived from the destroyed sample.

(e) Under section 63(3B), from a person who has been:

   (i) convicted of a recordable offence;

   (ii) given a caution in respect of a recordable offence which, at the time of the caution, the person admitted; or

   (iii) warned or reprimanded under the Crime and Disorder Act 1998, section 65, for a recordable offence,

   if, since their conviction, caution, warning or reprimand a non-intimate sample has not been taken from them or a sample which has been taken since then has proved to be unsuitable or insufficient and in either case, an officer of inspector rank or above, is satisfied that taking the fingerprints is necessary to assist in the prevention or detection of crime and authorises the taking.

(f) Under section 63(3C) from a person to whom section 2 of the Criminal Evidence (Amendment) Act 1997 applies (persons detained following acquittal on grounds of insanity or finding of unfitness to plead).

(g) Under section 63(3E) from a person who has been convicted outside England and Wales of an offence which if committed in England and Wales would be a qualifying offence as defined by PACE, section 65A if:

      (i)  a non-intimate sample has not been taken previously under this power or unless a sample was so taken but was unsuitable or insufficient; and

      (ii)  a police officer of inspector rank or above is satisfied that taking a sample is necessary to assist in the prevention or detection of crime and authorises it to be taken.

6.6A   PACE, section 63A(4) and Schedule 2A provide powers to:

(a)  make a requirement (in accordance with Annex G) for a person to attend a police station to have a non-intimate sample taken in the exercise of one of the following powers in paragraph 6.6 when that power applies at the time the sample would be taken in accordance with the requirement:

      (i)  section 63(3ZA) – Persons arrested for a recordable offence and released, see paragraph 6.6(c): The requirement may not be made more than six months from the day the investigating officer was informed that the sample previously taken was unsuitable or insufficient.

      (ii)  section 63(3A) – Persons charged etc. with a recordable offence, see paragraph 6.6(d): The requirement may not be made more than six months from:

- the day the person was charged or reported if a sample has not been taken since then; or
- the day the investigating officer was informed that the sample previously taken was unsuitable or insufficient.

      (iii)  section 63(3B) – Person convicted, cautioned, warned or reprimanded for a recordable offence in England and Wales, see paragraph 6.6(e): Where the offence for which the person was convicted etc is also a qualifying offence, there is no time limit for the exercise of this power. Where the conviction etc was for a recordable offence that is not a qualifying offence, the requirement may not be made more than two years from:

- the day the person was convicted, cautioned, warned or reprimanded, or the day Schedule 2A comes into force (if later), if a samples has not been taken since then; or
- the day an officer from the force investigating the offence was informed that the sample previously taken was unsuitable or insufficient or the day Schedule 2A comes into force (if later).

      (iv)  section 63(3E) – A person who has been convicted of qualifying offence outside England and Wales, see paragraph 6.6(h): There is no time limit for making the requirement.

Note: A person who has had a non-intimate sample taken under any of the powers in section 63 mentioned in paragraph 6.6 on two occasions in relation to any offence may not be required under Schedule 2A to attend a police station for a sample to be taken again under section 63 in relation to that offence, unless authorised by an officer of inspector rank or above. The fact of the authorisation and the reasons for giving it must be recorded as soon as practicable.

(b)  arrest, without warrant, a person who fails to comply with the requirement.

6.7    Reasonable force may be used, if necessary, to take a non-intimate sample from a person without their consent under the powers mentioned in *paragraph 6.6.*

6.8    Before any non-intimate sample is taken:

(a)  without consent under any power mentioned in paragraphs 6.6 and 6.6A, the person must be informed of:

      (i)  the reason for taking the sample;

      (ii)  the power under which the sample is to be taken;

      (iii)  the fact that the relevant authority has been given if any power mentioned in *paragraph 6.6(b), (e)* or *(h)* applies;

(b)  with or without consent at a police station or elsewhere, the person must be informed:

      (i)  that their sample or information derived from it may be subject of a speculative search against other samples and information derived from them; and

      (ii)  that their sample and the information derived from it may be retained in accordance with Annex F, Part (a).

### (c) Removal of clothing

6.9 When clothing needs to be removed in circumstances likely to cause embarrassment to the person, no person of the opposite sex who is not a registered medical practitioner or registered health care professional shall be present (unless in the case of a juvenile, mentally disordered or mentally vulnerable person, that person specifically requests the presence of an appropriate adult of the opposite sex who is readily available) nor shall anyone whose presence is unnecessary. However, in the case of a juvenile, this is subject to the overriding proviso that such a removal of clothing may take place in the absence of the appropriate adult only if the juvenile signifies, in their presence, that they prefer the adult's absence and they agree.

### (C) Documentation

6.10 A record of the reasons for taking a sample or impression and, if applicable, of its destruction must be made as soon as practicable. If force is used, a record shall be made of the circumstances and those present. If written consent is given to the taking of a sample or impression, the fact must be recorded in writing.

6.11 A record must be made of a warning given as required by *paragraph 6.3*.

6.12 *Not used*

1.8.7.1 **KEYNOTE**

**Intimate and Non-intimate Samples**

The analysis of intimate and non-intimate samples may provide essential evidence in showing or refuting a person's involvement in an offence. However, the courts have made it clear that DNA evidence alone will not be sufficient for a conviction and that there needs to be supporting evidence to link the suspect to the crime.

The purpose behind the taking of many samples is to enable the process of DNA profiling. Very basically, this involves an analysis of the sample taken from the suspect (the first sample), an analysis of samples taken from the crime scene or victim (the second sample) and then a comparison of the two. Both the process and the conclusions which might be drawn from the results are set out by Lord Taylor CJ in *R v Deen* (1994) *The Times*, 10 January.

The matching process involves creating 'bands' from each sample and then comparing the number of those bands which the two samples share. The more 'matches' that exist between the first and second samples, the less probability there is of that happening by pure chance. A 'good match' between the two samples does not of itself prove that the second sample came from the defendant. In using such samples to prove identification the prosecution will give evidence of:

- the *probability* of such a match happening by chance; and
- the *likelihood* that the person responsible was in fact the defendant.

While DNA evidence is often portrayed in the media as conclusive evidence of guilt, the question for the courts remains 'How reliable is this piece of evidence in proving or disproving the person's involvement in the offence?'

In most cases there will be other evidence against the defendant which clearly increases the likelihood of his/her having committed the offence. Such evidence may include confessions, or may show that the suspect was near the crime scene at the time of the offence or that the suspect lived in the locality or had connections in the area.

It will be for the prosecution to produce other facts to the court which reduce the 'chance' of the DNA sample belonging to someone other than the defendant. This may require further inquiries linking the suspect to the area or circumstances of the crime or may come from questions put to the suspect during interview. In

*R* v *Lashley* (2000) 25 February, unreported, the sole evidence against the defendant for a robbery was DNA evidence from a half-smoked cigarette found behind the counter of the post office. The DNA matched a sample obtained from the suspect and would have matched the profile of seven to 10 other males in the United Kingdom. The court held that the significance of DNA evidence depended critically upon what else was known about the suspect. Had there been evidence that the suspect was in the area, or normally lived there, or had connections there, at the material time, then the jury could have found that the case was compelling. This, the court said, would be because it may have been almost incredible that two out of seven men in the United Kingdom were in the vicinity at the relevant time. The courts are willing to allow the jury to consider partial or incomplete DNA profiles in some circumstances. In *R* v *Bates* [2006] EWCA Crim 1395, DNA evidence at the scene produced a partial profile that was interpreted as providing a 1 in 610,000 probability that Bates was the killer. The Court of Appeal held that there was no reason why partial-profile DNA evidence should not be admissible provided that the jury were made aware of its inherent limitations and were given a sufficient explanation to enable them to evaluate it.

If there is a decision to charge on partial DNA profile basis of such a match, the supporting evidence needs to be all the stronger. The amount of supporting evidence required will depend on the value of the DNA evidence in the context of the case. A scientist should be consulted where the value of the DNA evidence requires clarification.

It is also important to ensure that there is no cross-contamination of DNA evidence between crime scenes, victims and suspects, as was seen in the infamous American case of OJ Simpson's murder trial. It will be important to ensure that any allegations that officers may have contaminated evidence through handling/being present at several crime scenes can be successfully challenged. It is suggested that the best evidence here will be through records of crime scene logs and, where suspects have been or are being held in custody, records of who visited the custody suite. It will also be important that suspects and victims are kept apart. The integrity and continuity of DNA samples will be important evidence and likely to be challenged by the defence if not managed properly.

Speculative searches may be carried out of the National DNA Database and a suspect may now be charged on the basis of a match between a profile from DNA from the scene of the crime and a profile on the National DNA Database from an individual, so long as there is further supporting evidence (Home Office Circular 58/2004, *Charges on Basis of Speculative Search Match on the National DNA Database*).

It should also be noted that the databases can also now be used for the purpose of identifying a deceased person or a person from whom a body part came (Serious Organised Crime and Police Act 2005, s. 117(7) amending s. 64 of the 1984 Act).

An insufficient sample is one which is not sufficient either in quantity or quality to provide information for a particular form of analysis, such as DNA analysis. A sample may also be insufficient if enough information cannot be obtained from it by analysis because of loss, destruction, damage or contamination of the sample or as a result of an earlier, unsuccessful attempt at analysis. An unsuitable sample is one which, by its nature, is not suitable for a particular form of analysis.

---

**1.8.7.2**      **KEYNOTE**

**Intimate Samples**

Taking a sample without the relevant authority may amount to inhuman or degrading treatment under Article 3 of the European Convention on Human Rights. It may also amount to a criminal offence of assault and give rise to liability at civil law.

Nothing in para. 6.2 prevents intimate samples being taken for elimination purposes with the consent of the person concerned, but the provisions of para. 2.12, relating to the role of the appropriate adult, should be applied. Paragraph 6.2(b) does not, however, apply where the non-intimate samples were previously taken under the Terrorism Act 2000, sch. 8, para. 10.

In warning a person who is asked to provide an intimate sample, the following form of words may be used:

You do not have to provide this sample/allow this swab or impression to be taken, but I must warn you that if you refuse without good cause, your refusal may harm your case if it comes to trial.

**1.8.7.3**

**KEYNOTE**

**Taking a Non-intimate Sample**

Where a non-intimate sample consisting of a skin impression is taken electronically from a person, it must be taken only in such manner, and using such devices, as the Secretary of State has approved for the purpose of the electronic taking of such an impression (s. 63(9A) of PACE). No such devices are currently approved.

When hair samples are taken for the purpose of DNA analysis (rather than for other purposes, such as making a visual match), the suspect should be permitted a reasonable choice as to what part of the body the hairs are taken from. When hairs are plucked, they should be plucked individually, unless the suspect prefers otherwise and no more should be plucked than the person taking them reasonably considers necessary for a sufficient sample.

Fingerprints or a DNA sample and the information derived from it taken from a person arrested on suspicion of being involved in a recordable offence, or charged with such an offence, or informed that he/she will be reported for such an offence, may be the subject of a speculative search. This means that they may be checked against other fingerprints and DNA records held by, or on behalf of, the police and other law enforcement authorities in or outside the United Kingdom or held in connection with, or as a result of, an investigation of an offence inside or outside the United Kingdom. Fingerprints and samples taken from any other person, e.g. a person suspected of committing a recordable offence but who has not been arrested, charged or informed that he/she will be reported for it, may be subject to a speculative search only if the person consents in writing to his/her fingerprints being the subject of such a search. The following is an example of a basic form of words:

> I consent to my fingerprints/DNA sample and information derived from it being retained and used only for purposes related to the prevention and detection of a crime, the investigation of an offence or the conduct of a prosecution either nationally or internationally.
>
> I understand that this sample may be checked against other fingerprint/DNA records held by or on behalf of relevant law enforcement authorities, either nationally or internationally.
>
> I understand that once I have given my consent for the sample to be retained and used I cannot withdraw this consent.

Urine and non-intimate samples and the information derived from testing detained persons for the presence of specified Class A drugs, may not be subsequently used in the investigation of any offence or in evidence against the persons from whom they were taken.

---

**1.8.7.4**

**KEYNOTE**

**Power to Require Persons to Attend a Police Station to Provide Samples**

Code D, Annex G deals with the requirement for a person to attend a police station for fingerprints and samples.

---

**1.8.7.5**

**KEYNOTE**

**Destruction of Samples**

Code D, Annex F deals with the destruction and the speculative searches of fingerprints and samples and speculative searches of footwear impressions. It is important that the Annex is followed, particularly in relation to obtaining consent and explaining to volunteers what they are consenting to.

---

**1.8.8**

## Annex A—Video Identification

### (a) General

1. The arrangements for obtaining and ensuring the availability of a suitable set of images to be used in a video identification must be the responsibility of an identification officer, who has no direct involvement with the case.

2. The set of images must include the suspect and at least eight other people who, so far as possible, resemble the suspect in age, general appearance and position in life. Only one suspect shall appear in any set unless there are two suspects of roughly similar appearance, in which case they may be shown together with at least twelve other people.

2A If the suspect has an unusual physical feature, e.g., a facial scar, tattoo or distinctive hairstyle or hair colour which does not appear on the images of the other people that are available to be used, steps may be taken to:

(a) conceal the location of the feature on the images of the suspect and the other people; or

(b) replicate that feature on the images of the other people.

For these purposes, the feature may be concealed or replicated electronically or by any other method which it is practicable to use to ensure that the images of the suspect and other people resemble each other. The identification officer has discretion to choose whether to conceal or replicate the feature and the method to be used. If an unusual physical feature has been described by the witness, the identification officer should, if practicable, have that feature replicated. If it has not been described, concealment may be more appropriate.

2B If the identification officer decides that a feature should be concealed or replicated, the reason for the decision and whether the feature was concealed or replicated in the images shown to any witness shall be recorded.

2C If the witness requests to view an image where an unusual physical feature has been concealed or replicated without the feature being concealed or replicated, the witness may be allowed to do so.

3. The images used to conduct a video identification shall, as far as possible, show the suspect and other people in the same positions or carrying out the same sequence of movements. They shall also show the suspect and other people under identical conditions unless the identification officer reasonably believes:

(a) because of the suspect's failure or refusal to co-operate or other reasons, it is not practicable for the conditions to be identical; and

(b) any difference in the conditions would not direct a witness' attention to any individual image.

4. The reasons identical conditions are not practicable shall be recorded on forms provided for the purpose.

5. Provision must be made for each person shown to be identified by number.

6. If police officers are shown, any numerals or other identifying badges must be concealed. If a prison inmate is shown, either as a suspect or not, then either all, or none of, the people shown should be in prison clothing.

7. The suspect or their solicitor, friend, or appropriate adult must be given a reasonable opportunity to see the complete set of images before it is shown to any witness. If the suspect has a reasonable objection to the set of images or any of the participants, the suspect shall be asked to state the reasons for the objection. Steps shall, if practicable, be taken to remove the grounds for objection. If this is not practicable, the suspect and/or their representative shall be told why their objections cannot be met and the objection, the reason given for it and why it cannot be met shall be recorded on forms provided for the purpose.

8. Before the images are shown in accordance with *paragraph 7*, the suspect or their solicitor shall be provided with details of the first description of the suspect by any witnesses who are to attend the video identification. When a broadcast or publication is made, as in *paragraph 3.28*, the suspect or their solicitor must also be allowed to view any material released to the media by the police for the purpose of recognising or tracing the suspect, provided it is practicable and would not unreasonably delay the investigation.

9. The suspect's solicitor, if practicable, shall be given reasonable notification of the time and place the video identification is to be conducted so a representative may attend on behalf of the suspect. If a solicitor has not been instructed, this information shall be given to the suspect. The suspect may not be present when the images are shown to the witness(es). In the absence of the suspect's representative, the viewing itself shall be recorded on video. No unauthorised people may be present.

## (b) Conducting the video identification

10. The identification officer is responsible for making the appropriate arrangements to make sure, before they see the set of images, witnesses are not able to communicate with each other about the case, see any of the images which are to be shown, see, or be reminded of, any photograph or description of the suspect or be given any other indication as to the suspect's identity, or overhear a witness who has already seen the material. There must be no discussion with the witness about the composition of the set of images and they must not be told whether a previous witness has made any identification.

11. Only one witness may see the set of images at a time. Immediately before the images are shown, the witness shall be told that the person they saw on a specified earlier occasion may, or may not, appear in the images they are shown and that if they cannot make a positive identification, they should say so. The witness shall be advised that at any point, they may ask to see a particular part of the set of images or to have a particular image frozen for them to study. Furthermore, it should be pointed out to the witness that there is no limit on how many times they can view the whole set of images or any part of them. However, they should be asked not to make any decision as to whether the person they saw is on the set of images until they have seen the whole set at least twice.

12. Once the witness has seen the whole set of images at least twice and has indicated that they do not want to view the images, or any part of them, again, the witness shall be asked to say whether the individual they saw in person on a specified earlier occasion has been shown and, if so, to identify them by number of the image. The witness will then be shown that image to confirm the identification, see *paragraph 17*.

13. Care must be taken not to direct the witness' attention to any one individual image or give any indication of the suspect's identity. Where a witness has previously made an identification by photographs, or a computerised or artist's composite or similar likeness, the witness must not be reminded of such a photograph or composite likeness once a suspect is available for identification by other means in accordance with this Code. Nor must the witness be reminded of any description of the suspect.

14. After the procedure, each witness shall be asked whether they have seen any broadcast or published films or photographs, or any descriptions of suspects relating to the offence and their reply shall be recorded.

## (c) Image security and destruction

15. Arrangements shall be made for all relevant material containing sets of images used for specific identification procedures to be kept securely and their movements accounted for. In particular, no-one involved in the investigation shall be permitted to view the material prior to it being shown to any witness.

16. As appropriate, *paragraph 3.30* or *3.31* applies to the destruction or retention of relevant sets of images.

## (d) Documentation

17. A record must be made of all those participating in, or seeing, the set of images whose names are known to the police.

18. A record of the conduct of the video identification must be made on forms provided for the purpose. This shall include anything said by the witness about any identifications or the conduct of the procedure and any reasons it was not practicable to comply with any of the provisions of this Code governing the conduct of video identifications.

## 1.8.9 Annex B—Identification Parades

### (a) General

1. A suspect must be given a reasonable opportunity to have a solicitor or friend present, and the suspect shall be asked to indicate on a second copy of the notice whether or not they wish to do so.

2. An identification parade may take place either in a normal room or one equipped with a screen permitting witnesses to see members of the identification parade without being seen. The procedures for the composition and conduct of the identification parade are the same in both cases, subject to *paragraph 8* (except that an identification parade involving a screen may take place only when the suspect's solicitor, friend or appropriate adult is present or the identification parade is recorded on video).

3. Before the identification parade takes place, the suspect or their solicitor shall be provided with details of the first description of the suspect by any witnesses who are attending the identification parade. When a broadcast or publication is made as in *paragraph 3.28*, the suspect or their solicitor should also be allowed to view any material released to the media by the police for the purpose of recognising or tracing the suspect, provided it is practicable to do so and would not unreasonably delay the investigation.

### (b) Identification parades involving prison inmates

4. If a prison inmate is required for identification, and there are no security problems about the person leaving the establishment, they may be asked to participate in an identification parade or video identification.

5. An identification parade may be held in a Prison Department establishment but shall be conducted, as far as practicable under normal identification parade rules. Members of the public shall make up the identification parade unless there are serious security, or control, objections to their admission to the establishment. In such cases, or if a group or video identification is arranged within the establishment, other inmates may participate. If an inmate is the suspect, they are not required to wear prison clothing for the identification parade unless the other people taking part are other inmates in similar clothing, or are members of the public who are prepared to wear prison clothing for the occasion.

### (c) Conduct of the identification parade

6. Immediately before the identification parade, the suspect must be reminded of the procedures governing its conduct and cautioned in the terms of Code C, paragraphs 10.5 or 10.6, as appropriate.

7. All unauthorised people must be excluded from the place where the identification parade is held.

8. Once the identification parade has been formed, everything afterwards, in respect of it, shall take place in the presence and hearing of the suspect and any interpreter, solicitor, friend or appropriate adult who is present (unless the identification parade involves a screen, in which case everything said to, or by, any witness at the place where the identification parade is held, must be said in the hearing and presence of the suspect's solicitor, friend or appropriate adult or be recorded on video).

9. The identification parade shall consist of at least eight people (in addition to the suspect) who, so far as possible, resemble the suspect in age, height, general appearance and position in life. Only one suspect shall be included in an identification parade unless there are two suspects of roughly similar appearance, in which case they may be paraded together with at least twelve other people. In no circumstances shall more than two suspects be included in one identification parade and where there are separate identification parades, they shall be made up of different people.

10. If the suspect has an unusual physical feature, e.g., a facial scar, tattoo or distinctive hairstyle or hair colour which cannot be replicated on other members of the identification parade, steps may be taken to conceal the location of that feature on the suspect and the other members of the identification parade if the suspect and their solicitor, or appropriate adult, agree. For example, by use of a plaster or a hat, so that all members of the identification parade resemble each other in general appearance.

11. When all members of a similar group are possible suspects, separate identification parades shall be held for each unless there are two suspects of similar appearance when they may appear on the same identification parade with at least twelve other members of the group who are not suspects. When police officers in uniform form an identification parade any numerals or other identifying badges shall be concealed.

12. When the suspect is brought to the place where the identification parade is to be held, they shall be asked if they have any objection to the arrangements for the identification parade or to any of the other participants in it and to state the reasons for the objection. The suspect may obtain advice from their solicitor or friend, if present, before the identification parade proceeds. If the suspect has a reasonable objection to the arrangements or any of the participants, steps shall, if practicable, be taken to remove the grounds for objection. When it is not practicable to do so, the suspect shall be told why their objections cannot be met and the objection, the reason given for it and why it cannot be met, shall be recorded on forms provided for the purpose.

13. The suspect may select their own position in the line, but may not otherwise interfere with the order of the people forming the line. When there is more than one witness, the suspect must be told, after each witness has left the room, that they can, if they wish, change position in the line. Each position in the line must be clearly numbered, whether by means of a number laid on the floor in front of each identification parade member or by other means.

14. Appropriate arrangements must be made to make sure, before witnesses attend the identification parade, they are not able to:
    (i) communicate with each other about the case or overhear a witness who has already seen the identification parade;
    (ii) see any member of the identification parade;
    (iii) see, or be reminded of, any photograph or description of the suspect or be given any other indication as to the suspect's identity; or
    (iv) see the suspect before or after the identification parade.

15. The person conducting a witness to an identification parade must not discuss with them the composition of the identification parade and, in particular, must not disclose whether a previous witness has made any identification.

16. Witnesses shall be brought in one at a time. Immediately before the witness inspects the identification parade, they shall be told the person they saw on a specified earlier occasion may, or may not, be present and if they cannot make a positive identification, they should say so. The witness must also be told they should not make any decision about whether the person they saw is on the identification parade until they have looked at each member at least twice.

17. When the officer or police staff (see paragraph 3.11) conducting the identification procedure is satisfied the witness has properly looked at each member of the identification parade, they shall ask the witness whether the person they saw on a specified earlier occasion is on the identification parade and, if so, to indicate the number of the person concerned, see *paragraph 28*.

18. If the witness wishes to hear any identification parade member speak, adopt any specified posture or move, they shall first be asked whether they can identify any person(s) on the identification parade on the basis of appearance only. When the request is to hear members of the identification parade speak, the witness shall be reminded that the participants in the identification parade have been chosen on the basis of physical appearance only. Members of the identification parade may then be asked to comply with the witness' request to hear them speak, see them move or adopt any specified posture.

19. If the witness requests that the person they have indicated remove anything used for the purposes of *paragraph 10* to conceal the location of an unusual physical feature, that person may be asked to remove it.

20. If the witness makes an identification after the identification parade has ended, the suspect and, if present, their solicitor, interpreter or friend shall be informed. When this occurs, consideration should be given to allowing the witness a second opportunity to identify the suspect.

21. After the procedure, each witness shall be asked whether they have seen any broadcast or published films or photographs or any descriptions of suspects relating to the offence and their reply shall be recorded.

22. When the last witness has left, the suspect shall be asked whether they wish to make any comments on the conduct of the identification parade.

## (d) Documentation

23. A video recording must normally be taken of the identification parade. If that is impracticable, a colour photograph must be taken. A copy of the video recording or photograph shall be supplied, on request, to the suspect or their solicitor within a reasonable time.

24. As appropriate, *paragraph 3.30* or *3.31*, should apply to any photograph or video taken as in *paragraph 23*.

25. If any person is asked to leave an identification parade because they are interfering with its conduct, the circumstances shall be recorded.

26. A record must be made of all those present at an identification parade whose names are known to the police.

27. If prison inmates make up an identification parade, the circumstances must be recorded.

28. A record of the conduct of any identification parade must be made on forms provided for the purpose. This shall include anything said by the witness or the suspect about any identifications or the conduct of the procedure, and any reasons it was not practicable to comply with any of this Code's provisions.

## 1.8.10 Annex C—Group Identification

## (a) General

1. The purpose of this Annex is to make sure, as far as possible, group identifications follow the principles and procedures for identification parades so the conditions are fair to the suspect in the way they test the witness' ability to make an identification.

2. Group identifications may take place either with the suspect's consent and cooperation or covertly without their consent.

3. The location of the group identification is a matter for the identification officer, although the officer may take into account any representations made by the suspect, appropriate adult, their solicitor or friend.

4. The place where the group identification is held should be one where other people are either passing by or waiting around informally, in groups such that the suspect is able to join them and be capable of being seen by the witness at the same time as others in the group. For example people leaving an escalator, pedestrians walking through a shopping centre, passengers on railway and bus stations, waiting in queues or groups or where people are standing or sitting in groups in other public places.

5. If the group identification is to be held covertly, the choice of locations will be limited by the places where the suspect can be found and the number of other people present at that time. In these cases, suitable locations might be along regular routes travelled by the suspect, including buses or trains or public places frequented by the suspect.

6. Although the number, age, sex, race and general description and style of clothing of other people present at the location cannot be controlled by the identification officer, in selecting the location the officer must consider the general appearance and numbers of people likely to be present. In particular, the officer must reasonably expect that over the period the witness observes the group, they will be able to see, from time to time, a number of others whose appearance is broadly similar to that of the suspect.

7. A group identification need not be held if the identification officer believes, because of the unusual appearance of the suspect, none of the locations it would be practicable to use satisfy the requirements of *paragraph 6* necessary to make the identification fair.

8. Immediately after a group identification procedure has taken place (with or without the suspect's consent), a colour photograph or video should be taken of the general scene, if practicable, to give a general impression of the scene and the number of people present. Alternatively, if it is practicable, the group identification may be video recorded.

9. If it is not practicable to take the photograph or video in accordance with *paragraph 8*, a photograph or film of the scene should be taken later at a time determined by the identification officer if the officer considers it practicable to do so.

10. An identification carried out in accordance with this Code remains a group identification even though, at the time of being seen by the witness, the suspect was on their own rather than in a group.

11. Before the group identification takes place, the suspect or their solicitor shall be provided with details of the first description of the suspect by any witnesses who are to attend the identification. When a broadcast or publication is made, as in *paragraph 3.28*, the suspect or their solicitor should also be allowed to view any material released by the police to the media for the purposes of recognising or tracing the suspect, provided that it is practicable and would not unreasonably delay the investigation.

12. After the procedure, each witness shall be asked whether they have seen any broadcast or published films or photographs or any descriptions of suspects relating to the offence and their reply recorded.

## (b) Identification with the consent of the suspect

13. A suspect must be given a reasonable opportunity to have a solicitor or friend present. They shall be asked to indicate on a second copy of the notice whether or not they wish to do so.

14. The witness, the person carrying out the procedure and the suspect's solicitor, appropriate adult, friend or any interpreter for the witness, may be concealed from the sight of the individuals in the group they are observing, if the person carrying out the procedure considers this assists the conduct of the identification.

15. The person conducting a witness to a group identification must not discuss with them the forthcoming group identification and, in particular, must not disclose whether a previous witness has made any identification.

16. Anything said to, or by, the witness during the procedure about the identification should be said in the presence and hearing of those present at the procedure.

17. Appropriate arrangements must be made to make sure, before witnesses attend the group identification, they are not able to:
    (i) communicate with each other about the case or overhear a witness who has already been given an opportunity to see the suspect in the group;
    (ii) see the suspect; or
    (iii) see, or be reminded of, any photographs or description of the suspect or be given any other indication of the suspect's identity.

18. Witnesses shall be brought one at a time to the place where they are to observe the group. Immediately before the witness is asked to look at the group, the person conducting the procedure shall tell them that the person they saw may, or may not, be in the group and that if they cannot make a positive identification, they should say so. The witness shall be asked to

observe the group in which the suspect is to appear. The way in which the witness should do this will depend on whether the group is moving or stationary.

## Moving group

19. When the group in which the suspect is to appear is moving, e.g. leaving an escalator, the provisions of *paragraphs 20* to *24* should be followed.
20. If two or more suspects consent to a group identification, each should be the subject of separate identification procedures. These may be conducted consecutively on the same occasion.
21. The person conducting the procedure shall tell the witness to observe the group and ask them to point out any person they think they saw on the specified earlier occasion.
22. Once the witness has been informed as in *paragraph 21* the suspect should be allowed to take whatever position in the group they wish.
23. When the witness points out a person as in *paragraph 21* they shall, if practicable, be asked to take a closer look at the person to confirm the identification. If this is not practicable, or they cannot confirm the identification, they shall be asked how sure they are that the person they have indicated is the relevant person.
24. The witness should continue to observe the group for the period which the person conducting the procedure reasonably believes is necessary in the circumstances for them to be able to make comparisons between the suspect and other individuals of broadly similar appearance to the suspect as in *paragraph 6*.

## Stationary groups

25. When the group in which the suspect is to appear is stationary, e.g. people waiting in a queue, the provisions of *paragraphs 26* to *29* should be followed.
26. If two or more suspects consent to a group identification, each should be subject to separate identification procedures unless they are of broadly similar appearance when they may appear in the same group. When separate group identifications are held, the groups must be made up of different people.
27. The suspect may take whatever position in the group they wish. If there is more than one witness, the suspect must be told, out of the sight and hearing of any witness, that they can, if they wish, change their position in the group.
28. The witness shall be asked to pass along, or amongst, the group and to look at each person in the group at least twice, taking as much care and time as possible according to the circumstances, before making an identification. Once the witness has done this, they shall be asked whether the person they saw on the specified earlier occasion is in the group and to indicate any such person by whatever means the person conducting the procedure considers appropriate in the circumstances. If this is not practicable, the witness shall be asked to point out any person they think they saw on the earlier occasion.
29. When the witness makes an indication as in *paragraph 28*, arrangements shall be made, if practicable, for the witness to take a closer look at the person to confirm the identification. If this is not practicable, or the witness is unable to confirm the identification, they shall be asked how sure they are that the person they have indicated is the relevant person.

## All cases

30. If the suspect unreasonably delays joining the group, or having joined the group, deliberately conceals themselves from the sight of the witness, this may be treated as a refusal to co-operate in a group identification.

31. If the witness identifies a person other than the suspect, that person should be informed what has happened and asked if they are prepared to give their name and address. There is no obligation upon any member of the public to give these details. There shall be no duty to record any details of any other member of the public present in the group or at the place where the procedure is conducted.

32. When the group identification has been completed, the suspect shall be asked whether they wish to make any comments on the conduct of the procedure.

33. If the suspect has not been previously informed, they shall be told of any identifications made by the witnesses.

### (c) Identification without the suspect's consent

34. Group identifications held covertly without the suspect's consent should, as far as practicable, follow the rules for conduct of group identification by consent.

35. A suspect has no right to have a solicitor, appropriate adult or friend present as the identification will take place without the knowledge of the suspect.

36. Any number of suspects may be identified at the same time.

### (d) Identifications in police stations

37. Group identifications should only take place in police stations for reasons of safety, security or because it is not practicable to hold them elsewhere.

38. The group identification may take place either in a room equipped with a screen permitting witnesses to see members of the group without being seen, or anywhere else in the police station that the identification officer considers appropriate.

39. Any of the additional safeguards applicable to identification parades should be followed if the identification officer considers it is practicable to do so in the circumstances.

### (e) Identifications involving prison inmates

40. A group identification involving a prison inmate may only be arranged in the prison or at a police station.

41. When a group identification takes place involving a prison inmate, whether in a prison or in a police station, the arrangements should follow those in *paragraphs 37* to *39*. If a group identification takes place within a prison, other inmates may participate. If an inmate is the suspect, they do not have to wear prison clothing for the group identification unless the other participants are wearing the same clothing.

### (f) Documentation

42. When a photograph or video is taken as in *paragraph 8* or *9*, a copy of the photograph or video shall be supplied on request to the suspect or their solicitor within a reasonable time.

43. *Paragraph 3.30* or *3.31*, as appropriate, shall apply when the photograph or film taken in accordance with *paragraph 8* or *9* includes the suspect.

44. A record of the conduct of any group identification must be made on forms provided for the purpose. This shall include anything said by the witness or suspect about any identifications or the conduct of the procedure and any reasons why it was not practicable to comply with any of the provisions of this Code governing the conduct of group identifications.

**1.8.11** | **Annex D—Confrontation by a Witness**

1. Before the confrontation takes place, the witness must be told that the person they saw may, or may not, be the person they are to confront and that if they are not that person, then the witness should say so.

2. Before the confrontation takes place the suspect or their solicitor shall be provided with details of the first description of the suspect given by any witness who is to attend. When a broadcast or publication is made, as in *paragraph 3.28*, the suspect or their solicitor should also be allowed to view any material released to the media for the purposes of recognising or tracing the suspect, provided it is practicable to do so and would not unreasonably delay the investigation.

3. Force may not be used to make the suspect's face visible to the witness.

4. Confrontation must take place in the presence of the suspect's solicitor, interpreter or friend unless this would cause unreasonable delay.

5. The suspect shall be confronted independently by each witness, who shall be asked 'Is this the person?'. If the witness identifies the person but is unable to confirm the identification, they shall be asked how sure they are that the person is the one they saw on the earlier occasion.

6. The confrontation should normally take place in the police station, either in a normal room or one equipped with a screen permitting a witness to see the suspect without being seen. In both cases, the procedures are the same except that a room equipped with a screen may be used only when the suspect's solicitor, friend or appropriate adult is present or the confrontation is recorded on video.

7. After the procedure, each witness shall be asked whether they have seen any broadcast or published films or photographs or any descriptions of suspects relating to the offence and their reply shall be recorded.

**1.8.12** | **Annex E—Showing Photographs**

**(a) Action**

1. An officer of sergeant rank or above shall be responsible for supervising and directing the showing of photographs. The actual showing may be done by another officer or police staff, see *paragraph 3.11*.

2. The supervising officer must confirm the first description of the suspect given by the witness has been recorded before they are shown the photographs. If the supervising officer is unable to confirm the description has been recorded they shall postpone showing the photographs.

3. Only one witness shall be shown photographs at any one time. Each witness shall be given as much privacy as practicable and shall not be allowed to communicate with any other witness in the case.

4. The witness shall be shown not less than twelve photographs at a time, which shall, as far as possible, all be of a similar type.

5. When the witness is shown the photographs, they shall be told the photograph of the person they saw may, or may not, be amongst them and if they cannot make a positive identification, they should say so. The witness shall also be told they should not make a decision until they have viewed at least twelve photographs. The witness shall not be prompted or guided in any way but shall be left to make any selection without help.

6. If a witness makes a positive identification from photographs, unless the person identified is otherwise eliminated from enquiries or is not available, other witnesses shall not be shown photographs. But both they, and the witness who has made the identification, shall be asked to attend a video identification, an identification parade or group identification unless there is no dispute about the suspect's identification.

7. If the witness makes a selection but is unable to confirm the identification, the person showing the photographs shall ask them how sure they are that the photograph they have indicated is the person they saw on the specified earlier occasion.

8. When the use of a computerised or artist's composite or similar likeness has led to there being a known suspect who can be asked to participate in a video identification, appear on an identification parade or participate in a group identification, that likeness shall not be shown to other potential witnesses.

9. When a witness attending a video identification, an identification parade or group identification has previously been shown photographs or computerised or artist's composite or similar likeness (and it is the responsibility of the officer in charge of the investigation to make the identification officer aware that this is the case), the suspect and their solicitor must be informed of this fact before the identification procedure takes place.

10. None of the photographs shown shall be destroyed, whether or not an identification is made, since they may be required for production in court. The photographs shall be numbered and a separate photograph taken of the frame or part of the album from which the witness made an identification as an aid to reconstituting it.

### (b) Documentation

11. Whether or not an identification is made, a record shall be kept of the showing of photographs on forms provided for the purpose. This shall include anything said by the witness about any identification or the conduct of the procedure, any reasons it was not practicable to comply with any of the provisions of this Code governing the showing of photographs and the name and rank of the supervising officer.

12. The supervising officer shall inspect and sign the record as soon as practicable.

1.8.13    ## Annex F—Fingerprints, Footwear Impressions and Samples—Destruction and Speculative Searches

### (a) Fingerprints, footwear impressions and samples taken in connection with a criminal investigation from a person suspected of committing the offence under investigation

1. The retention and destruction of fingerprints, footwear impressions and samples taken in connection with a criminal investigation from a person suspected of committing the offence under investigation is subject to PACE, section 64.

### (b) Fingerprints, footwear impressions and samples taken in connection with a criminal investigation from a person not suspected of committing the offence under investigation

2. When fingerprints, footwear impressions or DNA samples are taken from a person in connection with an investigation and the person is not suspected of having committed the offence, they must be destroyed as soon as they have fulfilled the purpose for which they were taken unless:
   (a) they were taken for the purposes of an investigation of an offence for which a person has been convicted; and
   (b) fingerprints, footwear impressions or samples were also taken from the convicted person for the purposes of that investigation.
   However, subject to *paragraph 2*, the fingerprints, footwear impressions and samples, and the information derived from samples, may not be used in the investigation of any offence or in evidence against the person who is, or would be, entitled to the destruction of the fingerprints, footwear impressions and samples.

3. The requirement to destroy fingerprints, footwear impressions and DNA samples, and information derived from samples, and restrictions on their retention and use in paragraph 1 do not apply if the person gives their written consent for their fingerprints, footwear impressions or sample to be retained and used after they have fulfilled the purpose for which they were taken.

4. When a person's fingerprints, footwear impressions or sample are to be destroyed:
   (a) any copies of the fingerprints and footwear impressions must also be destroyed;
   (b) the person may witness the destruction of their fingerprints, footwear impressions or copies if they ask to do so within five days of being informed destruction is required;
   (c) access to relevant computer fingerprint data shall be made impossible as soon as it is practicable to do so and the person shall be given a certificate to this effect within three months of asking; and
   (d) neither the fingerprints, footwear impressions, the sample, or any information derived from the sample, may be used in the investigation of any offence or in evidence against the person who is, or would be, entitled to its destruction.

5. Fingerprints, footwear impressions or samples, and the information derived from samples, taken in connection with the investigation of an offence which are not required to be destroyed, may be retained after they have fulfilled the purposes for which they were taken but may be used only for purposes related to the prevention or detection of crime, the investigation of an offence or the conduct of a prosecution in, as well as outside, the UK and may also be subject to a speculative search. This includes checking them against other fingerprints, footwear impressions and DNA records held by, or on behalf of, the police and other law enforcement authorities in, as well as outside, the UK.

## (c) Fingerprints taken in connection with Immigration Service enquiries

6. See *paragraph 4.10*.

**1.8.13.1**

**KEYNOTE**

The rules around the retention and use of DNA samples, fingerprints and associated data is likely to change with the passing of the Protection of Freedoms Bill. In *Goggins and Others* v *United Kingdom* [2011] ECHR 1121 the European Court, whilst acknowledging the current position was not compatible with Human Rights law, recognised proposals to amend the scheme of retention of DNA data along the lines of the Scottish model and that it is the intention of the government to bring this legislation into force. Acting on the basis that this is likely to occur, the majority granted a declaration that the present ACPO guidelines were unlawful. However, since Parliament had the matter under examination the court did not consider it appropriate to make an order requiring a change in the legislation, nor was it appropriate to make an order for the destruction of data which it was possible it would be lawful to retain under the new scheme contained in the Protection of Freedoms Bill. (The bill is now enacted, but not yet in force.)

Fingerprints, footwear impressions and samples given voluntarily for the purposes of elimination play an important part in many police investigations. It is, therefore, important to make sure that innocent volunteers are not deterred from participating and their consent to their fingerprints, footwear impressions and DNA being used for the purposes of a specific investigation is fully informed and voluntary. If the police seek to have the fingerprints, footwear impressions or samples of a volunteer retained for use after the specific investigation ends, it is important that the volunteer's consent to this is also fully informed and voluntary.

The two types of consent are to allow DNA/fingerprints/footwear impressions to be used only for the purposes of a specific investigation or for specific investigation *and* retained by the police for future use.

To minimise the risk of confusion, each consent should be physically separate and the volunteer should be asked to sign *each consent*. For example:

For a DNA sample taken for the purposes of elimination or as part of an intelligence-led screening and to be used only for the purposes of that investigation and destroyed afterwards:

I consent to my DNA/mouth swab being taken for forensic analysis. I understand that the sample will be destroyed at the end of the case and that my profile will only be compared to the crime stain profile from this enquiry. I have been advised that the person taking the sample may be required to give evidence and/or provide a written statement to the police in relation to the taking of it.

Where the person agrees to the DNA sample to be retained on the National DNA database and used in the future:

I consent to my DNA sample and information derived from it being retained and used only for purposes related to the prevention and detection of a crime, the investigation of an offence or the conduct of a prosecution either nationally or internationally.

I understand that this sample may be checked against other DNA records held by, or on behalf of, relevant law enforcement authorities, either nationally or internationally.

I understand that once I have given my consent for the sample to be retained and used I cannot withdraw this consent.

For fingerprints taken for the purposes of elimination or as part of an intelligence-led screening and to be used only for the purposes of that investigation and destroyed afterwards:

I consent to my fingerprints being taken for elimination purposes. I understand that the fingerprints will be destroyed at the end of the case and that my fingerprints will only be compared to the fingerprints from this enquiry. I have been advised that the person taking the fingerprints may be required to give evidence and/or provide a written statement to the police in relation to the taking of it.

For cases where the person agrees to fingerprints to be retained for future use:

I consent to my fingerprints being retained and used only for purposes related to the prevention and detection of a crime, the investigation of an offence or the conduct of a prosecution either nationally or internationally.

I understand that my fingerprints may be checked against other records held by, or on behalf of, relevant law enforcement authorities, either nationally or internationally.

I understand that once I have given my consent for my fingerprints to be retained and used I cannot withdraw this consent.

For footwear impressions taken for the purposes of elimination or as part of an intelligence-led screening and to be used only for the purposes of that investigation and destroyed afterwards:

I consent to my footwear impressions being taken for elimination purposes. I understand that the footwear impressions will be destroyed at the end of the case and that my footwear impressions will only be compared to the footwear impressions from this enquiry. I have been advised that the person taking the footwear impressions may be required to give evidence and/or provide a written statement to the police in relation to the taking of it.

For cases where the person agrees to footwear impressions to be retained for future use:

I consent to my footwear impressions being retained and used only for purposes related to the prevention and detection of a crime, the investigation of an offence or the conduct of a prosecution, either nationally or internationally.

I understand that my footwear impressions may be checked against other records held by, or on behalf of, relevant law enforcement authorities, either nationally or internationally.

I understand that once I have given my consent for my footwear impressions to be retained and used I cannot withdraw this consent.

The provisions for the retention of fingerprints, footwear impressions and samples taken from a person in connection to an investigation need to be retained to allow all fingerprints, footwear impressions and samples in a case to be available for any subsequent miscarriage of justice investigation.

## 1.8.14    Annex G—Requirement for a Person to Attend a Police Station for Fingerprints and Samples

1. A requirement under Schedule 2A for a person to attend a police station to have fingerprints or samples taken:
   (a) must give the person a period of at least seven days within which to attend the police station; and

(b) may direct them to attend at a specified time of day or between specified times of day.

2. When specifying the period and times of attendance, the officer making the requirements must consider whether the fingerprints or samples could reasonably be taken at a time when the person is required to attend the police station for any other reason.

3. An officer of the rank of inspector or above may authorise a period shorter than 7 days if there is an urgent need for person's fingerprints or sample for the purposes of the investigation of an offence. The fact of the authorisation and the reasons for giving it must be recorded as soon as practicable.

4. The constable making a requirement and the person to whom it applies may agree to vary it so as to specify any period within which, or date or time at which, the person is to attend. However, variation shall not have effect for the purposes of enforcement, unless it is confirmed by the constable in writing.

**1.8.14.1**

**KEYNOTE**

The specified period within which the person is to attend need not fall within the period allowed (if applicable) for making the requirement. To justify the arrest without warrant of a person who fails to comply with a requirement (**see section 4.4 at para. 1.8.5**), the officer making the requirement, or confirming a variation, should be prepared to explain how, when and where the requirement was made or the variation was confirmed and what steps were taken to ensure that the person understood what to do and the consequences of not complying with the requirement.

# 1.9 Bail

## 1.9.1 Introduction

The Bail Act 1976 is the primary source of legislation in relation to bail in criminal proceedings granted by the police and courts. Other legislation also impacts upon bail, in particular the Police and Criminal Evidence Act 1984 and the Criminal Justice and Public Order Act 1994.

The meaning of 'bail in criminal proceedings' is contained in s. 1 of the Bail Act 1976 which states:

(1) In this Act 'bail in criminal proceedings' means—
   (a) bail grantable in or in connection with proceedings for an offence to a person who is accused or convicted of the offence, or
   (b) bail grantable in connection with an offence to a person who is under arrest for the offence or for whose arrest for the offence a warrant (endorsed for bail) is being issued, or
   (c) bail grantable in connection with extradition proceedings in respect of an offence.

> **KEYNOTE**
>
> This section provides that bail can be granted immaterial of whether the offence was committed in 'England or Wales or elsewhere', and immaterial as to which country's law the offence relates (s. 1(5)).
>
> In R (*On the Application of Thompson*) v *Central Criminal Court* [2005] EWHC 2345 (Admin) it was held that the approach under the Bail Act complied with Article 5 of the European Convention on Human Rights (right to liberty and security), i.e. that bail must be granted unless there is good reason to refuse it. (A *R (On the Application of Fergus)* v *Southampton Crown Court* [2008] EWHC 3273 (Admin) and *R (On the Application of Shehzad)* v *Newcastle Crown Court* [2012] EWHC 1453 (Admin)).

## 1.9.2 Police Bail

Bail can either be granted by a custody officer at a police station or by a constable elsewhere than at a police station (known as 'street bail').

### 1.9.2.1 Street Bail

The Police and Criminal Evidence Act 1984, s. 30A provides for persons arrested elsewhere than at a police station to be released on bail without being required to attend a police station.

### 1.9.2.2 Release on Bail

| | |
|---|---|
| Section 30A(1) | A constable may release on bail a person who is arrested or taken into custody in the circumstances mentioned in s. 30(1). |
| Section 30A(2) | A person may be released on bail under subs. (1) at any time before he arrives at a police station. |
| Section 30A(3) | A person released on bail under subs. (1) must be required to attend a police station. |

Section 30A(3A)  Where a constable releases a person on bail under subs. (1)—
(a) no recognisance for the person's surrender to custody shall be taken from the person,
(b) no security for the person's surrender to custody shall be taken from the person or from anyone else on the person's behalf,
(c) the person shall not be required to provide a surety or sureties for his surrender to custody, and
(d) no requirement to reside in a bail hostel may be imposed as a condition of bail.

Section 30A(3B)  Subject to subs. (3A), where a constable releases a person on bail under subs. (1) the constable may impose, as conditions of the bail, such requirements as appear to the constable to be necessary—
(a) to secure that the person surrenders to custody,
(b) to secure that the person does not commit an offence while on bail,
(c) to secure that the person does not interfere with witnesses or otherwise obstruct the course of justice, whether in relation to him or any other person, or
(d) for the person's own protection or, if the person is under the age of 17, for the person's own welfare or in the person's own interests.

Section 30A(4)  Where a person is released on bail under subs. (1), a requirement may be imposed on the person as a condition of bail only under the preceding provisions of this section.

Section 30A(5)  The police station which the person is required to attend may be any police station.

**KEYNOTE**

Section 30A(3B) enables the officer granting bail to consider attaching conditions relevant and proportionate to the suspect and the offence. The conditions that may be considered are the same as those available to a custody officer as contained in s. 3A(5) of the 1976 Act, except for those specified in s. 30A(3A) above.

Guidance on street bail is contained in Home Office Circular 61/2003, *Bail Elsewhere than at a Police Station*. Although there is no limit on the time for which 'street' bail may be granted, the Circular suggests a normal maximum time of six weeks.

1.9.2.3  **Notice in Writing**

Section 30B(1)  Where a constable grants bail to a person under s. 30A, he must give that person a notice in writing before he is released.

Section 30B(2)  The notice must state:
(a) the offence for which he was arrested, and
(b) the grounds on which he was arrested.

Section 30B(3)  The notice must inform him that he is required to attend a police station.

Section 30B(4)  It may also specify the police station which he is required to attend and the time when he is required to attend.

Section 30B(4A)  If the person is granted bail subject to conditions under s. 30A(3B), the notice also—
(a) must specify the requirements imposed by those conditions,
(b) must explain the opportunities under ss. 30CA(1) and 30CB(1) for variation of those conditions, and
(c) if it does not specify the police station at which the person is required to attend, must specify a police station at which the person may make a request under s. 30CA(1)(b),

Section 30B(5)  If the notice does not include the information mentioned in subs. (4), the person must subsequently be given a further notice in writing which contains that information.

| Section 30B(6) | The person may be required to attend a different police station from that specified in the notice under subs. (1) or (5) or to attend at a different time. |
|---|---|
| Section 30B(7) | He must be given notice in writing of any such change as is mentioned in subs. (6) but more than one such notice may be given to him. |

---

**KEYNOTE**

This section requires that the person bailed be given a written notice identifying the offence and grounds for arrest and informing the person that he/she is required to attend a police station. The notice may specify a police station and a time to attend, but if not, or where the person is required to attend a different police station, a further notice must be issued detailing the rearranged place and time. The notice must also include details of how the person bailed may apply for variation to any conditions (s. 30CA(1)(b)).

---

### 1.9.2.4 Release, Attendance and Re-arrest

| Section 30C(1) | A person who has been required to attend a police station is not required to do so if he is given notice in writing that his attendance is no longer required. |
|---|---|
| Section 30C(2) | If a person is required to attend a police station which is not a designated police station he must be:<br>(a) released, or<br>(b) taken to a designated police station, not more than six hours after his arrival. |
| Section 30C(3) | Nothing in the Bail Act 1976 applies in relation to bail under s. 30A. |
| Section 30C(4) | Nothing in s. 30A or 30B or in this section prevents the re-arrest without warrant of a person released on bail under s. 30A if new evidence justifying a further arrest has come to light since his release. |

### 1.9.2.5 Variation of Bail Conditions: Police

| Section 30CA(1) | Where a person released on bail under s. 30A(1) is on bail subject to conditions—<br>(a) a relevant officer at the police station at which the person is required to attend, or<br>(b) where no notice under s. 30B specifying that police station has been given to the person, a relevant officer at the police station specified under s. 30B(4A)(c),<br>may, at the request of the person but subject to subs. (2), vary the conditions. |
|---|---|
| Section 30CA(2) | On any subsequent request made in respect of the same grant of bail, subs. (1) confers power to vary the conditions of the bail only if the request is based on information that, in the case of the previous request or each previous request, was not available to the relevant officer considering that previous request when he/she was considering it. |
| Section 30CA(3) | Where conditions of bail granted to a person under s. 30A(1) are varied under subs. (1)—<br>(a) paragraphs (a) to (d) of s. 30A(3A) apply,<br>(b) requirements imposed by the conditions as so varied must be requirements that appear to the relevant officer varying the conditions to be necessary for any of the purposes mentioned in paragraphs (a) to (d) of s. 30A(3B), and<br>(c) the relevant officer who varies the conditions must give the person notice in writing of the variation. |
| Section 30CA(4) | Power under subs. (1) to vary conditions is, subject to subs. (3)(a) and (b), power—<br>(a) to vary or rescind any of the conditions, and<br>(b) to impose further conditions. |

## 1.9.2.6 Variation of Bail Conditions: Court

Section 30CB(1)     Where a person released on bail under s. 30A(1) is on bail subject to conditions, a magistrates' court may, on an application by or on behalf of the person, vary the conditions if—
(a) the conditions have been varied under s. 30CA(1) since being imposed under s. 30A(3B),
(b) a request for variation under s. 30CA(1) of the conditions has been made and refused, or
(c) a request for variation under s. 30CA(1) of the conditions has been made and the period of 48 hours beginning with the day when the request was made has expired without the request having been withdrawn or the conditions having been varied in response to the request.

## 1.9.2.7 Power of Arrest for Non-attendance and Breach of Bail Conditions

Section 30D(1)     A constable may arrest without warrant a person who:
(a) has been released on bail under s. 30A subject to a requirement to attend a specified police station, but
(b) fails to attend the police station at the specified time.

Section 30D(2)     A person arrested under subs. (1) must be taken to a police station (which may be the specified police station or any other police station) as soon as practicable after the arrest.

Section 30D(2A)     A person who has been released on bail under s. 30A may be arrested without a warrant by a constable if the constable has reasonable grounds for suspecting that the person has broken any of the conditions of bail.

Section 30D(2B)     A person arrested under subs. (2A) must be taken to a police station (which may be the specified police station mentioned in subs. (1) or any other police station) as soon as practicable after the arrest.

Section 30D(3)     In subs. (1), 'specified' means specified in a notice under subs. (1) or (5) of s. 30B or, if notice of change has been given under subs. (7) of that section, in that notice.

### 1.9.3  Pre-charge Bail

Broadly, the Police and Criminal Evidence Act 1984 provides the following pre-charge scenario. The custody officer may decide to grant bail, with or without conditions, or withhold bail altogether where:

- there is as insufficient evidence to charge with an offence suspects whom it is necessary to continue to investigate without their having to be held in custody (s. 37(2));
- the police consider there is sufficient evidence to charge but the case has been referred to the CPS for a charging decision (s. 37(7)(a));
- there is sufficient evidence to charge but not for the purposes outlined in s. 37(7)(a) above (this would usually be where further inquiries are to be made) (s. 37(7)(b));
- there is sufficient evidence and the person is charged with an offence (s. 37(7)(d));
- the officer conducting the review concludes that the detention without charge can no longer be justified (s. 40(8));
- at the end of 24 hours' detention without charge, unless the detained person is suspected of committing an indictable offence and continued detention up to 36 hours is authorised by a superintendent (s. 41(7)).

### 1.9.4 Bail After Charge

Where a person is charged at the police station (otherwise than a warrant backed for bail) the custody officer must make a decision to keep the person in custody until they can be brought before a magistrates' court, or to release the person either on bail or without bail, unless one or more conditions in the Police and Criminal Evidence Act 1984, s. 38, are satisfied (s. 38(1)).

Where the custody officer decides to bail a person who has been charged, s. 47(3) of the 1984 Act provides they may do so:

(a) to appear before a magistrates' court at such time and such place as the custody officer may appoint;

(b) to attend at such police station as the custody officer may appoint at such time as he may appoint for the purposes of—

    (i) proceedings in relation to a live link direction under section 57C of the Crime and Disorder Act 1998 (use of live link direction at preliminary hearings where accused is at police station); and

    (ii) any preliminary hearing in relation to which such a direction is given; or

(c) to attend at such police station as the custody officer may appoint at such time as he may appoint for purposes other than those mentioned in paragraph (b).

---

**KEYNOTE**

Where a custody officer grants bail to a person to appear before a magistrates' court, he must appoint for the appearance a date which is not later than the first sitting of the court after the person is charged with the offence. If informed by the court that the appearance cannot be accommodated until a later date, that later date. For a person subject to a duty to appear at a police station, the custody officer may give notice in writing to that person that his/her attendance at the police station is not required (s.47(3A)).

In *Williamson* v *Chief Constable of West Midlands* [2003] EWCA Civ 337, it was clarified that the Bail Act 1976 does not apply to 'breach of the peace' as it is not a criminal offence.

---

### 1.9.5 Bail Restrictions

The Criminal Justice and Public Order Act 1994 provides for those occasions when bail may only be granted in *exceptional circumstances* where a person is charged with certain specified offences. Section 25 of the 1994 Act states:

(1) A person who in any proceedings has been charged with or convicted of an offence to which this section applies in circumstances to which it applies shall be granted bail in those proceedings only if the court or, as the case may be, the constable considering the grant of bail is of the opinion that there are exceptional circumstances which justify it.

(2) This section applies, subject to subsection (3) below, to the following offences, that is to say—

    (a) murder;

    (b) attempted murder;

    (c) manslaughter;

    (d) rape under the law of Scotland;

    (e) an offence under section 1 of the Sexual Offences Act 1956 (rape);

    (f) an offence under section 1 of the Sexual Offences Act 2003 (rape);

    (g) an offence under section 2 of that Act (assault by penetration);

    (h) an offence under section 4 of that Act (causing a person to engage in sexual activity without consent) where the activity caused involved penetration within subsection (4)(a) to (d) of that section;

    (i) an offence under section 5 of that Act (rape of a child under 13);

    (j) an offence under section 6 of that Act (assault of a child under 13 by penetration);

(k) an offence under section 8 of that Act (causing or inciting a child under 13 to engage in sexual activity), where an activity involving penetration within subsection (3)(a) to (d) of that section was caused;

(l) an offence under section 30 of that Act (sexual activity with a person with a mental disorder impeding choice), where the touching involved penetration within subsection (3)(a) to (d) of that section;

(m) an offence under section 31 of that Act (causing or inciting a person, with a mental disorder impeding choice, to engage in sexual activity), where an activity involving penetration within subsection (3)(a) to (d) of that section was caused;

(n) an attempt to commit an offence within any of paragraphs (d) to (m).

(3) This section applies in the circumstances described in subsection (3A) or (3B) only.

(3A) This section applies where—

(a) the person has been previously convicted by or before a court in any part of the United Kingdom of any offence within subsection (2) or of culpable homicide, and

(b) if that previous conviction is one of manslaughter or culpable homicide—

(i) the person was then a child or young person, and was sentenced to long-term detention under any of the relevant enactments, or

(ii) the person was not then a child or young person, and was sentenced to imprisonment or detention.

(3B) This section applies where—

(a) the person has been previously convicted by or before a court in another member State of any relevant foreign offence corresponding to an offence within subsection (2) or to culpable homicide, and

(b) if the previous conviction is of a relevant foreign offence corresponding to the offence of manslaughter or culpable homicide—

(i) the person was then a child or young person, and was sentenced to detention for a period in excess of 2 years, or

(ii) the person was not then a child or young person, and was sentenced to detention.

(4) This section applies whether or not an appeal is pending against conviction or sentence.

(5) In this section—

'conviction' includes—

(a) a finding that a person is not guilty by reason of insanity;

(b) a finding under section 4A(3) of the Criminal Procedure (Insanity) Act 1964 (cases of unfitness to plead) that a person did the act or made the omission charged against him; and

(c) a conviction of an offence for which an order is made discharging the offender absolutely or conditionally;

and 'convicted' shall be construed accordingly;

'relevant foreign offence', in relation to a member State other than the United Kingdom, means an offence under the law in force in that member State; and

'the relevant enactments' means—

(a) as respects England and Wales, section 91 of the Powers of Criminal Courts (Sentencing) Act 2000;

(b) as respects Scotland, sections 205(1) to (3) and 208 of the Criminal Procedure (Scotland) Act 1995;

(c) ...

(5A) For the purposes of subsection (3B), a relevant foreign offence corresponds to another offence if the relevant foreign offence would have constituted that other offence if it had been done in any part of the United Kingdom at the time when the relevant foreign offence was committed.

## KEYNOTE

Section 25 provides that bail may not be granted where a person is charged with murder, attempted murder, manslaughter, rape or attempted rape if he/she has been convicted of any of these offences *unless* there are exceptional circumstances. A person charged with murder may not be granted bail except by order of a Crown Court judge (s. 115 of the Coroners and Justice Act 2009). This does not apply to attempted murder or conspiracy to murder.

In *R (On the Application of O)* v *Crown Court at Harrow* [2006] UKHL 42 it was held that s. 25 was compatible with the European Convention on Human Rights, Article 5(3)—presumption of an individual's right to liberty. Even where a person's custody time limit had expired, s. 25 could still be applied and the evidential burden was on the defence to demonstrate that exceptional circumstances existed. Also, in the case of *Hurnam* v *State of*

*Mauritius* [2005] UKPC 49, the Privy Council stated that the seriousness of the offence is not a conclusive reason for refusing bail and the court must consider whether or not the accused is likely to abscond if released on bail.

In all other cases the custody officer must consider the issue of bail and s. 38(1) of the 1984 Act sets out the occasions where bail can be refused. Where bail is refused, the custody officer must inform the detained person of the reasons why and make an entry as to these reasons in the custody record (s. 38(3) and (4)).

### 1.9.5.1 Condition of Detained Person and Communication of Refused Bail

A detained person should be informed of the bail decision as soon as it is made. This can be delayed if the conditions set out in PACE Code C, para. 1.8 apply, in which case the detainee should be informed as soon as practicable.

In reaching a decision as to whether a person should be refused bail the custody officer should consider whether the same objective can be achieved by imposing conditions to the bail, that is, for the person to appear at an appointed place at an appointed time. If conditions attached to a person's bail are likely to achieve the same objective as keeping the person in detention, bail must be given.

In *Gizzonio* v *Chief Constable of Derbyshire* (1998) *The Times*, 29 April, Gizzonio had been remanded in custody in respect of certain charges which had not ultimately been pursued. Damages (for the wrongful exercise of lawful authority) were sought on the basis that the police had wrongly opposed the grant of bail. It was held that the decision regarding bail is part of the process of investigation of crime with a view to prosecution and so the police enjoyed immunity in that respect.

### 1.9.6 Grounds for Refusing Bail

The Police and Criminal Evidence Act 1984, s. 38(1) provides that where an arrested person is charged with an offence, the custody officer, subject to s. 25 of the Criminal Justice and Public Order Act 1994, need not grant bail if the person arrested *is not an arrested juvenile* and one or more of the following grounds apply:

(a) the person's name or address cannot be ascertained or the custody officer has reasonable grounds for doubting whether a name or address furnished is his/her real name or address;

(b) the custody officer has reasonable grounds for believing that the person arrested will fail to appear in court to answer to bail;

(c) in the case of a person arrested for an imprisonable offence, the custody officer has reasonable grounds for believing that the detention of the person arrested is necessary to prevent him/her from committing an offence;

(d) in a case of a person aged 18 or over, where a sample may be taken from the person under s. 63B (where there is a provision for drug testing in force for that police area and station), the custody officer has reasonable grounds for believing that the detention of the person is necessary to enable the sample to be taken;

(e) in the case of a person arrested for an offence which is not an imprisonable offence, the custody officer has reasonable grounds for believing that the detention of the person arrested is necessary to prevent him/her from causing physical injury to any other person or from causing loss of or damage to property;

(f) the custody officer has reasonable grounds for believing that the detention of the person arrested is necessary to prevent him/her from interfering with the administration of justice or with the investigation of offences or of a particular offence; or

(g) the custody officer has reasonable grounds for believing that the detention of the person arrested is necessary for his/her own protection;

(h) the offence with which the person is charged is murder.

If the person arrested is *an arrested juvenile* and one or more of the following grounds apply:

(a)  any of the requirements of paras (a) to (h) above, but in the case of para. (d) only if the arrested juvenile has attained the minimum age;

(b)  the custody officer has reasonable grounds for believing that the arrested juvenile ought to be detained in his/her own interests.

---

**KEYNOTE**

Juveniles being detained 'in their own interests' means for their own welfare. The expression 'welfare' has a wider meaning than just 'protection' and might apply to juveniles who, if released, might be homeless or become involved in prostitution or vagrancy (Bail Act 1976, sch. 1, part I, para. (3)).

In taking the decisions required by s. 38(1), except where a defendant's name and address cannot be ascertained, detention is necessary for the person's own protection, or a juvenile is detained in his/her own interests, the custody officer is required to have regard to the same considerations as those which a court is required to have regard to in taking corresponding decisions under the Bail Act 1976, sch. 1, part I, para. 2(1) (s. 38(2A)).

Schedule 1, part I, para. 2(1) provides that the defendant need not be granted bail if the court (custody officer) is satisfied that there are substantial grounds for believing that the defendant, if released on bail (whether subject to conditions or not) would:

- fail to surrender to custody, or
- commit an offence while on bail, or
- interfere with witnesses or otherwise obstruct the course of justice, whether in relation to him/herself or any other person.

In *R (On the Application of Ajaib)* v *Birmingham Magistrates' Court* [2009] EWHC 2127 (Admin), it was held that a police officer's opinion that the accused is a 'flight risk' was sufficient even though the source of information giving rise to the officer's opinion was not disclosed.

Schedule 1, part I, para. 9 provides that in taking the decisions required by para. 2(1), the court (custody officer) will have regard to such of the following considerations as appear to be relevant:

(a)  the nature and seriousness of the offence or default (and the probable method of dealing with the defendant for it);

(b)  the character, antecedents, associations and community ties of the defendant;

(c)  the defendant's record as respects the fulfilment of his/her obligations under previous grants of bail in criminal proceedings;

(d)  except in the case of a defendant whose case is adjourned for inquiries or a report, the strength of the evidence of his/her having committed the offence or having defaulted;

(e)  if the court is satisfied that there are substantial grounds for believing that the defendant, if released on bail (whether subject to conditions or not), would commit an offence while on bail, the risk that the defendant may do so by engaging in conduct that would, or would be likely to, cause physical or mental injury to any person other than the defendant, as well as to any others which appear to be relevant.

In relation to juveniles, Article 37(b) of the United Nations Convention on the Rights of the Child 1989 requires that the arrest, detention or imprisonment of a child shall be in conformity with the law and shall be used as a measure of last resort and for the shortest appropriate period of time.

---

### 1.9.7  Bail Consideration by the Custody Officer

The granting of bail in criminal proceedings is provided by s. 3 of the Bail Act 1976 and this section examines the general provisions in relation to bail granted by a custody officer, the conditions that may be attached and applications to vary or remove those conditions.

### 1.9.7.1 General Provisions

The general provisions as to bail in criminal proceedings are provided by s. 3 of the 1976 Act, but this is modified by s. 3A, which relates specifically to a custody officer. Section 3 states:

(1) A person granted bail in criminal proceedings shall be under a duty to surrender to custody, and that duty is enforceable in accordance with section 6 of this Act.

(2) No recognisance for his surrender to custody shall be taken from him.

(3) Except as provided by this section—
    (a) no security for his surrender to custody shall be taken from him,
    (b) he shall not be required to provide a surety or sureties for his surrender to custody, and
    (c) no other requirement shall be imposed on him as a condition of bail.

(4) He may be required, before release on bail, to provide a surety or sureties to secure his surrender to custody.

(5) He may be required, before release on bail, to give security for his surrender to custody. The security may be given by him or on his behalf.

(6) He may be required to comply, before release on bail or later, with such requirements as appear to the court to be necessary to secure that—
    (a)  he surrenders to custody,
    (b)  he does not commit an offence while on bail,
    (c)  he does not interfere with witnesses or otherwise obstruct the course of justice whether in relation to himself or any other person,
    (ca) for his own protection or, if he is a child or young person, for his own welfare or in his own interests.

(7) If a parent or guardian of a person under the age of seventeen consents to be surety for the person for the purposes of this subsection, the parent or guardian may be required to secure that the person complies with any requirement imposed on him by virtue of subsection (6) . . . above but—
    (a) no requirement shall be imposed on the parent or the guardian by virtue of this subsection where it appears that the person will attain the age of 17 before the time to be appointed for him to surrender to custody, and
    (b) the parent or guardian shall not be required to secure compliance with any requirement to which his consent does not extend and shall not, in respect of those requirements to which his consent does extend, be bound in a sum greater than £50.

> **KEYNOTE**
>
> Guidance to courts, applicable also to a custody officer, when approaching the decision to grant bail was given in *R v Mansfield Justices, ex parte Sharkey* [1985] QB 613, where it was held that any relevant risk, for example, absconding, must be a 'real' risk, not just a fanciful one.
>
> Where a custody officer grants bail there is a requirement for a record to be made of the decision in the prescribed manner and containing the prescribed particulars. If requested, a copy of the record of the decision must, as soon as practicable, be given to the person in relation to whom the decision was taken (s. 5(1)).

### 1.9.7.2 Bail Conditions

The power of a custody officer to impose bail conditions is provided by s. 3A of the 1976 Act, which states:

(5) Where a constable grants bail to a person no conditions shall be imposed under subsections (4), (5), (6) or (7) of section 3 of this Act unless it appears to the constable that it is necessary to do so—
    (a) for the purpose of preventing that person from failing to surrender to custody, or
    (b) for the purpose of preventing that person from committing an offence while on bail, or
    (c) for the purpose of preventing that person from interfering with witnesses or otherwise obstructing the course of justice, whether in relation to himself or any other person, or
    (d) for that person's own protection, or if he is a child or young person, for his own welfare or in his own interests.

Where a custody officer decides to grant bail and considers one or more of the requirements in s. 3A(5)(a)–(d) apply, one or more of the following conditions can be imposed:

- the accused is to live and sleep at a specified address;
- the accused is to notify any changes of address;
- the accused is to report periodically (daily, weekly or at other intervals) to his/her local police station;
- the accused is restricted from entering a certain area or building or to go within a specified distance of a specified address;
- the accused is not to contact (whether directly or indirectly) the victim of the alleged offence and/or any other probable prosecution witness;
- the accused is to surrender his/her passport;
- the accused's movements are restricted by an imposed curfew between set times (i.e. when it is thought the accused might commit offences or come into contact with witnesses);
- the accused is required to provide a surety or security.

In *McDonald* v *Dickson* [2003] SLT 476, it was held that a condition for an accused to remain in his dwelling at all times except between 10 am and 12 noon did not amount to detention or deprivation of his liberty and did not constitute an infringement of his right to liberty under the European Convention on Human Rights, Article 5.

In *R (On the Application of Carson)* v *Ealing Magistrates' Court* [2012] EWHC 1456 (Admin) the defendant was subject to pre-charge bail conditions, one of which was not to reside at her home address. The police investigation was in relation to racially aggravated harassment, the complainants being her neighbours. The condition that the claimant cease to reside at her home address was held to be disproportionate as it is a serious matter to exclude a person from her own home.

In relation to non-imprisonable offences it has been held that a hunt protester who was arrested for an offence under s. 5 of the Public Order Act 1986 was rightly required as a condition of his bail not to attend another hunt meeting before his next court appearance (*R* v *Bournemouth Magistrates' Court, ex parte Cross* [1989] Crim LR 207).

The conditions outlined in this section can also be imposed by a constable granting bail elsewhere than at a police station under s. 30A(3B) of the Police and Criminal Evidence Act 1984.

### 1.9.7.3    Applications to Vary or Remove Bail Conditions

The power to vary or remove conditions is provided by s. 3A of the Bail Act 1976. Section 3A(4) substitutes s. 3(8) and states:

> Where a custody officer has granted bail in criminal proceedings he or another custody officer serving at the same police station may, at the request of the person to whom it was granted, vary the conditions of bail and in doing so he may impose conditions or more onerous conditions.

---

**KEYNOTE**

Section 3A(5) above also applies on any request to a custody officer to vary or remove conditions of bail.

There is a requirement that a custody officer either imposing or varying the conditions of bail must include a note of the reasons in the custody record and give a copy of that note to the person in relation to whom the decision was taken (s. 5A(3)).

An accused may also apply to the magistrates' court under s. 43B(1) of the Magistrates' Courts Act 1980, to vary conditions of police bail. Details of the procedure to be followed are contained in the Criminal Procedure Rules 2012, part 19.

---

### 1.9.7.4    Police Bail: Surety

The Bail Act 1976, s. 8 states:

(1) This section applies where a person is granted bail in criminal proceedings on condition that he provides one or more surety or sureties for the purpose of securing that he surrenders to custody.

(2) In considering the suitability for that purpose of a proposed surety, regard may be had (amongst other things) to—

    (a) the surety's financial resources;

    (b) his character and any previous convictions of his; and

    (c) his proximity (whether in point of kinship, place of residence or otherwise) to the person for whom he is to be surety.

---

**KEYNOTE**

The question as to whether or not sureties are necessary is at the discretion of the custody officer (or court). However, this condition can only be used where the custody officer believes it is necessary to secure that the person surrenders to custody; does not commit an offence while on bail; or does not interfere with witnesses or otherwise obstruct the course of justice whether in relation to him/herself or any other person (s. 3(6)(a)–(c)). A person cannot stand as his/her own surety (s. 3(2)).

The decision as to the suitability of individual sureties is a matter for the custody officer. Where no surety, or suitable surety, is available, the custody officer can fix the amount of cash or security in which the surety is to be bound for the purpose of enabling the recognisance of the surety to be entered into subsequently (s. 8(3)).

The normal consequence for a surety, where an accused fails to answer bail, is that he/she is required to forfeit the entire cash or security in which he/she stood surety. The power to forfeit recognisances is a matter for a court (Magistrates' Courts Act 1980, s. 120).

It is not necessary to prove that the surety had any involvement in the accused's non-appearance (*R v Warwick Crown Court, ex parte Smalley* [1987] 1 WLR 237). However, in *R v York Crown Court, ex parte Coleman* (1988) 86 Cr App R 151, it was held that where a surety had taken all reasonable steps to ensure the accused's appearance the recognisance ought not to be forfeited.

The Bail Act 1976 provides that a surety may notify a constable *in writing* that the accused is unlikely to surrender to custody and for that reason he/she wishes to be relieved of his/her obligations as surety. This written notification provides a constable with the power to arrest the accused without warrant (s. 7(3)).

---

### 1.9.7.5 Security

A person granted bail may be required to give security for his/her surrender to custody (Bail Act 1976, s. 3(5)). The security can be money or some other valuable item which will be liable to forfeiture in the event of non-attendance in answer to bail.

A security may be required as a condition of bail but only if it is considered necessary to prevent the person absconding.

A third party may make an asset available to an accused to enable him/her to provide it as security for his/her release on bail (*R (On the Application of Stevens)* v *Truro Magistrates' Court* [2001] EWHC Admin 558).

### 1.9.7.6 Acknowledging Bail

OFFENCE: **Acknowledging Bail in the Name of Another—*Forgery Act 1861, s. 34***

    • Triable on indictment • Seven years' imprisonment

The Forgery Act 1861, s. 34 states:

Whosoever, without lawful authority or excuse (the proof whereof shall lie on the party accused), shall in the name of any other person acknowledge any recognisance or bail,...or judgment or any deed or other instrument, before any court, judge, or other person lawfully authorised in that behalf, shall be guilty of felony...

## 1.9.8 Juveniles Refused Bail

The Children (Secure Accommodation) Regulations 1991 (SI 1991/1505 as amended by SI 2012/3134) provide that a child who is detained by the police under s. 38(6) of the Police and Criminal Evidence Act 1984, and who is aged 12 or over but under the age of 17, must be moved to local authority accommodation unless this is impracticable or there is no secure accommodation available and local authority accommodation would be inadequate to protect the child or public from serious harm. Where no secure accommodation is available and the serious harm criterion is met, the child can be kept in police detention.

Where the detained child is aged 10 or 11, the police must move the child to local authority accommodation unless this is impracticable, e.g. in extreme weather conditions. The type of accommodation in which the local authority proposes to place the youth is not a factor which the custody officer may take into account in considering whether the transfer is acceptable.

The obligation to transfer a child to local authority accommodation applies equally to a child charged during the daytime as it does to a child to be held overnight, subject to a requirement to bring the child before a court in accordance with s. 46 of the 1984 Act.

## 1.9.9 Failure to Comply with Police Bail

The Police and Criminal Evidence Act 1984, s. 46A states:

(1) A constable may arrest without a warrant any person who, having been released on bail under this Part of this Act subject to a duty to attend at a police station, fails to attend at that police station at the time appointed for him to do so.

(1ZA) The reference in subsection (1) to a person who fails to attend at a police station at the time appointed for him to do so includes a reference to a person who—

    (a) attends at a police station to answer to bail granted subject to the duty mentioned in section 47(3)(b), but (b) leaves the police station at any time before the beginning of proceedings in relation to a live link direction under section 57C of the Crime and Disorder Act 1998 in relation to him.

(1ZB) The reference in subsection (1) to a person who fails to attend at a police station at the time appointed for the person to do so includes a reference to a person who—

    (a) attends at a police station to answer to bail granted subject to the duty mentioned in section 47(3)(b), but

    (b) refuses to be searched under section 54B.

(1A) A person who has been released on bail under section 37, 37C(2)(b) or 37CA(2)(b) above may be arrested without warrant by a constable if the constable has reasonable grounds for suspecting that the person has broken any of the conditions of bail.

(2)   A person who is arrested under this section shall be taken to the police station appointed as the place at which he is to surrender to custody as soon as practicable after the arrest.

(3)   For the purposes of—

(a)  section 30 above (subject to the obligation in subsection (2) above), and

(b)  section 31 above,

an arrest under this section shall be treated as an arrest for an offence.

---

**KEYNOTE**

Breach of conditions of bail is not a Bail Act offence, nor is it a contempt of court unless there is some additional feature (*R* v *Ashley* [2003] EWCA Crim 2571).

The offence for which a person is arrested under subs. (1) is the offence for which he/she was granted bail (s. 34(7)).

Section 46A(1) provides a power of arrest only where a person *fails to attend at that police station at the time appointed*. This should be contrasted with s. 46A(1A) where a person released on bail under s. 37 (release on bail without charge), s. 37C(2)(b) (breach of bail following release under s. 37(7)(a)) or s. 37CA(2)(b) (breach of bail following release under s. 37(7)(b)), may be arrested if there are *reasonable grounds for suspecting that the person has broken any of the conditions of bail*.

---

1.9.10      **Failure to Appear at Court**

The Bail Act 1976, s. 7 states:

(1)   If a person who has been released on bail in criminal proceedings and is under a duty to surrender into the custody of a court fails to surrender to custody at the time appointed for him to do so the court may issue a warrant for his arrest.

(1A)  Subsection (1B) applies if—

(a)  a person has been released on bail in connection with extradition proceedings;

(b)  the person is under a duty to surrender into the custody of a constable; and

(c)  the person fails to surrender to custody at the time appointed for him to do so.

(1B)  A magistrates' court may issue a warrant for the person's arrest.

(2)   If a person who has been released on bail in criminal proceedings absents himself from the court at any time after he has surrendered into the custody of the court and before the court is ready to begin or to resume the hearing of the proceedings, the court may issue a warrant for his arrest but no warrant shall be issued under this subsection where that person is absent in accordance with leave given to him by or on behalf of the court.

(3)   A person who has been released on bail in criminal proceedings and is under a duty to surrender into the custody of a court may be arrested without warrant by a constable—

(a)  if the constable has reasonable grounds for believing that person is not likely to surrender to custody;

(b)  if the constable has reasonable grounds for believing that that person is likely to break any of the conditions of his bail or has reasonable grounds for suspecting that that person has broken any of those conditions; or

(c)  in a case where that person was released on bail with one or more surety or sureties, if a surety notifies a constable in writing that that person is unlikely to surrender to custody and that for that reason the surety wishes to be relieved of his obligations as a surety.

---

**KEYNOTE**

Where a person is arrested under s. 7 he/she shall be brought before a magistrate as soon as practicable and in any event within 24 hours (s. 7(4)(a)). However, in the case of a person charged with murder, or with murder and one or more other offences, he/she must be brought before a judge of the Crown Court (s. 7(8)).

This section requires that a detainee not merely be brought to the court precincts or cells but actually be dealt with by a justice within 24 hours of being arrested (*R (On the Application of Culley)* v *Dorchester Crown Court* [2007] EWHC 109 (Admin)).

---

In *R* v *Evans* [2011] EWCA Crim 2842, the Court of Appeal stated:

> The general practice of accepting surrender by way of entry into the dock accords not only with common experience and general practice but also with principle…Crown Court surrender may also be accomplished by the commencement of any hearing before the judge where the defendant is formally identified and whether he enters the dock or not.

The word 'court' includes a judge of the court or a justice of the peace. Also a bail notice stating a particular time of attendance is a notice that may happen at any time from 9.30 am onwards. Mere arrival at the Crown Court building does not constitute surrender, neither does reporting to an advocate. Surrender has to be accomplished personally by the defendant.

Section 7 does not create an offence, it merely confers a power of arrest (*R* v *Gangar* [2008] EWCA Crim 2987).

## 1.9.11 Offence of Absconding

The Bail Act 1976 s. 6 creates two offences in relation to absconding and states:

(1) If a person who has been released on bail in criminal proceedings fails without reasonable cause to surrender to custody he shall be guilty of an offence.

(2) If a person who—

    (a) has been released on bail in criminal proceedings, and

    (b) having reasonable cause therefor, has failed to surrender to custody, fails to surrender to custody at the appointed place as soon after the appointed time as is reasonably practicable he shall be guilty of an offence.

---

**KEYNOTE**

Section 6 applies where:

- the police grant bail to a suspect to appear at the police station;
- the police grant bail to a defendant to appear at court on the first appearance;
- the court grants bail to the defendant to return to court at a later date.

The burden of proof in relation to showing 'reasonable cause' (s. 6(1)) is a matter for the accused (s. 6(3)).

A person who has 'reasonable cause' still commits the offence if he/she fails to surrender 'as soon after the appointed time as is reasonably practicable'. Where an accused was half an hour late in appearing at court it was held that he/she had absconded (*R* v *Scott* [2007] EWCA Crim 2757). In *Laidlaw* v *Atkinson* (1986) *The Times*, 2 August, it was held that being mistaken about the day on which one should have appeared was not a reasonable excuse. Also, there is no requirement on the court to inquire as to whether a person arrested for failing to comply with bail conditions had any reasonable excuse for breaching bail (*R (On the Application of Vickers)* v *West London Magistrates' Court* (2003) EWHC 1809 (Admin)).

Failure to give to a person granted bail in criminal proceedings a copy of the record of the decision does not constitute reasonable cause for that person's failure to surrender to custody (s. 6(4)).

The procedure for prosecuting offences where bail has been granted by a police officer for a person to attend court and subsequently fails to surrender to custody is contained in the *Consolidated Criminal Practice Direction*, part I.13.6 and 7: Initiating proceedings—bail granted by a police officer (see *Blackstone's Criminal Practice 2013*, Supplement 2).

The offence in this form is a summary offence and the decision to initiate proceedings is for the police/prosecutor using the written charge and requisition procedure. Such an offence may not be tried unless proceedings are commenced either within six months of the commission of the offence, or within three months: (a) after the person surrenders to custody at the appointed place; (b) is arrested, or attends at a police station, in connection with the bail offence or the offence for which he/she was granted bail; or (c) the person appears or is brought before a court in connection with the bail offence or the offence for which he/she was granted bail (s. 6(12)–(14)).

---

## 1.9.12 Remands in Police Custody

Where a person is remanded in custody it normally means detention in prison. However, s. 128 of the Magistrates' Courts Act 1980 provides that a magistrates' court may remand a person to police custody:

* for a period not exceeding three clear days (24 hours for persons under 18 (s. 91(5) of the Legal Aid, Sentencing and Punishment of Offenders Act 2012) (s. 128(7));
* for the purpose of inquiries into offences (other than the offence for which he/she appears before the court) (s. 128(8)(a));
* as soon as the need ceases he/she must be brought back before the magistrates (s. 128 (8)(b));
* the conditions of detention and periodic review apply as if the person was arrested without warrant on suspicion of having committed an offence (s. 128(8)(c) and (d)).

# 1.10 Disclosure of Evidence
## Criminal Procedure and Investigations Act 1996 and Code of Practice

> A thick grey line down the margin denotes text that is an extract of the Code itself (i.e. the actual wording of the legislation).

### 1.10.1 Introduction

The need for the prosecution to provide the defence with material relating to the charge(s) in a case has been recognised by the courts and the government to be crucial in ensuring that defendants get a fair trial. Such disclosure can be grouped under two main areas: the material the prosecution will use in court to prove the case against the defendant, and all other material not forming part of the prosecution case which might have a bearing on the decision the court makes.

The Criminal Procedure and Investigations Act 1996, as amended by the Criminal Justice Act 2003, sets out the requirements for disclosure of unused material, i.e. the material that will not be used by the prosecution to prove the case. The 1996 Act is made up of seven parts. It is the first two parts which are of interest to the police:

- part I sets out the procedures for disclosure and the effects of failing to comply with the Act; and
- part II sets out the duties of police officers in relation to the disclosure provisions.

The 1996 Act introduced a Code of Practice which sets out the manner in which police officers are to record, retain and reveal to the prosecutor material obtained in a criminal investigation and which may be relevant to the investigation, and related matters. The Code assumes that the defence have already been informed of the details of the prosecution case; the Code is included within this chapter.

### 1.10.2 Disclosing the Prosecution Case—Advanced Information

This refers to the material that the defence are entitled to have in order to consider whether to plead guilty or not guilty. In some cases, it is not a question of whether the defendant committed the crime but whether the prosecution are in a position to prove the offence and, in order to consider this, the defence are unlikely to agree to plead or decide on the mode of trial without knowing the strength of the prosecution case. It is clearly in the public interest that guilty pleas are entered or indicated as soon as possible (*R* v *Calderdale Magistrates' Court, ex parte Donahue* [2001] Crim LR 141) and often this cannot be achieved unless advanced information has been provided. The need to know as early as possible whether a defendant is going to plead not guilty can be particularly important as there are time limits by which the courts have to set trials and committals. Often these can be delayed because the prosecution have not complied with their disclosure duties.

Ensuring that all defendants receive copies of any advanced information (or any later disclosure) is also important. In *R* v *Tompkins* [2005] EWCA Crim 3035 the court held that where there has been non-disclosure at the time a plea had been entered, a defendant who had pleaded guilty should not in any way be in a worse position than a defendant who had pleaded not guilty.

### 1.10.2.1 Obligations on Prosecution Regarding Disclosing the Prosecution Case—Advanced Information

In magistrates' courts, part 21 of the Criminal Procedure Rules 2012 provides that where the offence is one that can be tried in a magistrates' court the prosecutor must provide initial details of the prosecution case to the Court and the defendant at, or before, the beginning of the day of the first hearing. These initial details must include:

- a summary of the evidence on which that case will be based; or
- any statement, document or extract setting out facts or other matters on which that case will be based; or
- any combination of such a summary, statement, document or extract; and
- the defendant's previous convictions.

The Attorney-General's Guidelines: Disclosure of Information in Criminal Proceedings provide that the prosecutor should, in addition to complying with the obligations under the 1996 Act, provide to the defence all evidence upon which the Crown proposes to rely in a summary trial. Such provision should allow the accused and their legal advisers sufficient time properly to consider the evidence before it is called (A-G's Guidelines, para. 3).

For trials at the Crown Court, the defence will receive the majority of the prosecution case through the disclosure of witness statements or depositions. If the prosecution wish to use any additional evidence after committal they must serve this on the defence.

It is suggested that Article 6 of the European Convention on Human Rights supports the need to provide advanced information to the defence and that this should be done as soon as possible. Article 6(3)(a) states that a person is:

...to be informed promptly...and in detail, of the nature and cause of the accusation against him;

Article 6(3)(b) states that an accused is entitled to:

...have adequate time...for the preparation of his defence.

The point concerning advanced information in summary cases was considered in *R* v *Stratford Justices, ex parte Imbert* [1999] 2 Cr App R 276, where the court gave its opinion that Article 6 does not give an absolute right to pre-trial disclosure; it will be a question of whether the defendant can have a fair trial. Clearly, it will be easier to satisfy this test where advanced information has been provided to the defence.

Advanced information might also include the following and so consideration should be had to providing this material to the prosecutor so that he/she can forward it to the defence where appropriate (ensuring that the addresses and other details of witnesses and victims are protected):

- a copy of the custody record;
- copies of any interview tape(s);
- a copy of any first descriptions where relevant;
- significant information that might affect a bail decision or enable the defence to contest the committal proceedings (A-G's Guidelines, para. 55);
- any material which is relevant to sentence (e.g. information which might mitigate the seriousness of the offence or assist the accused to lay blame in whole or in part upon a co-accused or another person) (A-G's Guidelines, para. 58);

- statements and/or a summary of the prosecution cases;
- a copy of any video evidence.

Where a person has made several statements but all the relevant evidence for the prosecution case is contained in one statement, it is only that one statement which needs to be disclosed. In order to comply with advanced information the defence need to be either given a copy of the document or allowed to inspect the document (or a copy of it). In *R v Lane and Lane* [2011] EWCA Crim 2745 one of the witnesses refused to put incriminating evidence into their statement due to fear of repercussions. The police had notified the prosecution of the witness's increased knowledge, but the prosecution failed to notify the defence that the statement had been a partial account. The Court of Appeal held that the statement was untruthful as it did not disclose all the information that it should have done. The witness should have been told to make a full statement or he should have been abandoned as a witness, but he should never have been allowed to make a partial statement.

The following sections set out the Disclosure Code of Practice issued under the Criminal Procedure and Investigations Act 1996.

## 1.10.3 Disclosure Code of Practice—1 Introduction

1.1 This Code of Practice applies in respect of criminal investigations conducted by police officers which begin on or after the day on which this Code comes into effect. Persons other than police officers who are charged with the duty of conducting an investigation as defined in the Act are to have regard to the relevant provisions of the Code, and should take these into account in applying their own operating procedures.

1.2 This Code does not apply to persons who are not charged with the duty of conducting an investigation as defined in the Act.

1.3 Nothing in this Code applies to material intercepted in obedience to a warrant issued under section 2 of the Interception of Communications Act 1985 or section 5 of the Regulation of Investigatory Powers Act 2000, or to any copy of that material as defined in section 10 of the 1985 Act or section 15 of the 2000 Act.

1.4 This Code extends only to England and Wales.

### 1.10.3.1 KEYNOTE

**Disclosure and the Criminal Procedure and Investigations Act 1996**

In most investigations there will be material that has come to the attention of the police which will not be used as evidence to prove the prosecution case but which might be useful to the defence. It is through the disclosure rules that this information will be provided to the defendant. The 1996 Act put the prosecution duty to disclose information to the defence on a statutory footing, and also introduced a concept in criminal law where the defence have a duty to advise the prosecution of certain matters relating to their case. This is also supported by the 1996 Act Code of Practice, the Attorney-General's Guidelines on Disclosure and the CPS Disclosure Manual.

### 1.10.3.2 KEYNOTE

**Aims of the 1996 Act**

The aim of the disclosure rules within the Criminal Procedure and Investigations Act 1996 is to make sure that a defendant gets a fair trial and speeds up the whole trial process. This was confirmed by *R v Stratford Justices, ex parte Imbert* [1999] 2 Cr App R 276, where the court said that the legislation was to try to ensure that nothing which might assist the defence was kept from the accused.

The Act originally placed a responsibility on the prosecution to make *primary* disclosure of material to the defence; a responsibility for the defence—under certain conditions—to disclose their case to the prosecution with a further responsibility on the prosecution to make a *secondary* disclosure to the defence. As a 'catch all' the prosecution also have a continuing duty to review the material they have disclosed.

The changes introduced by the Criminal Justice Act 2003 removed the concept of primary and secondary disclosure and provided for an initial duty to disclose with a continuing duty to disclose until the accused is acquitted or convicted or the prosecutor decides not to proceed with the case.

One of the effects of this change is that under the pre-April 2005 position the prosecution only had to provide disclosure of material that was relevant to the prosecution case. Now disclosure from the start has to consider any material that might undermine the prosecution case or assist the defence (s. 3 of the 1996 Act). It is submitted that this requires the prosecution to consider in more detail the types of defence that might be used at trial. Once the prosecution has provided their initial disclosure the defence in some cases are obliged to provide a defence statement and in other cases this is optional (**see para. 1.10.10.1**). Once the defence have provided their defence statement it may provide greater focus to the prosecution as to what other unused material may need to be disclosed.

While the duty of disclosure is placed on the prosecutor, the police have a responsibility to assist in this process. It is therefore vital that police officers understand, not only the statutory requirements made of them, but also the extent of their role within the whole disclosure process

## 1.10.3.3    KEYNOTE

### Failure to Comply

Compliance with the rules of disclosure, by both the defence and prosecution, is essential if the 1996 Act is to have any real value. First, in cases where the defence are obliged to make disclosure to the prosecution, failure to do so may lead to the court or jury drawing such inferences as appear proper in deciding the guilt or innocence of the accused (s. 11(5) of the 1996 Act). Should the prosecution fail to comply with their obligations then an accused does not have to make defence disclosure and no such inference can be made. Secondly, failure by the prosecution to comply with the rules could lead to the court staying the proceedings on the grounds that there has been an abuse of process (s. 10). It could also lead to an action for damages or such other relief as the court sees fit under the Human Rights Act 1998, particularly in relation to Article 6 of the European Convention on Human Rights and the right to a fair trial.

Additionally, where the prosecution have not made disclosure on time or fully, a stay on the proceedings or a further adjournment is possible. It is suggested that the more adjournments in a case, the more likely that witnesses will get fed up with the delays and will fail to attend on the next occasion and the case could therefore be lost!

Even if there has been a failure to comply with disclosure the case will not automatically be stayed and therefore any failings should be brought to the attention of the CPS so that the matter can be considered. In *R (On the Application of Ebrahim)* v *Feltham Magistrates' Court* [2001] EWHC Admin 130 the court stated that:

> It must be remembered that it is a commonplace in criminal trial for the defendant to rely on holes in the prosecution case. If in such a case, there is sufficient credible evidence, apart from the missing evidence, which, if believed, would justify safe conviction then the trial should proceed, leaving the defendant to seek to persuade the jury or magistrates not to convict because evidence that might otherwise have been available was not before the court through no fault of the defendant.

Further guidance was provided in *R* v *Brooks* [2004] EWCA Crim 3537, a case where the prosecution failed to comply with the disclosure requirements. The Court of Appeal held that if the court was satisfied that the prosecution had deliberately withheld evidence from the court or frustrated the defence, the court did have the power to stay the prosecution. If the court was not so satisfied it would consider whether, despite all that had gone wrong, a fair trial was possible.

Failure to disclose may result in convictions being overturned; for instance in *R* v *Poole* [2003] EWCA Crim 1753, the Court of Appeal overturned convictions for murder because the non-disclosure of prosecution evidence influenced the jury's assessment of the reliability of the evidence of a key eye-witness. In this case the witness gave an account that was false in a material particular. However, the police did not follow up those inconsistencies and they failed to inform the CPS that his evidence was unreliable. The level of disclosure that is required will be a question of fact in each case. In *Filmer* v *DPP* [2006] EWHC 3450 (Admin) the court held that the extent of disclosure required from the prosecution depends on the evidence and issue in a particular case. The prosecution are required to provide sufficient disclosure to enable a defendant to present his/her case. The court went on to say that this has to be the approach otherwise the prosecution would have to second guess every question the defence may want to ask (this is where the defence disclosure becomes relevant, see para. 1.10.10.1).

## 1.10.4 | Disclosure Code of Practice—2 Definitions

2.1 In this Code:
- *a criminal investigation* is an investigation conducted by police officers with a view to it being ascertained whether a person should be charged with an offence, or whether a person charged with an offence is guilty of it. This will include:
  - investigations into crimes that have been committed;
  - investigations whose purpose is to ascertain whether a crime has been committed, with a view to the possible institution of criminal proceedings; and
  - investigations which begin in the belief that a crime may be committed, for example when the police keep premises or individuals under observation for a period of time, with a view to the possible institution of criminal proceedings;
- charging a person with an offence includes prosecution by way of summons;
- *an investigator* is any police officer involved in the conduct of a criminal investigation. All investigators have a responsibility for carrying out the duties imposed on them under this Code, including in particular recording information, and retaining records of information and other material;
- the *officer in charge of an investigation* is the police officer responsible for directing a criminal investigation. He is also responsible for ensuring that proper procedures are in place for recording information, and retaining records of information and other material, in the investigation;
- the *disclosure officer* is the person responsible for examining material retained by the police during the investigation; revealing material to the prosecutor during the investigation and any criminal proceedings resulting from it, and certifying that he has done this; and disclosing material to the accused at the request of the prosecutor;
- the *prosecutor* is the authority responsible for the conduct, on behalf of the Crown, of criminal proceedings resulting from a specific criminal investigation;
- *material* is material of any kind, including information and objects, which is obtained in the course of a criminal investigation and which may be relevant to the investigation. This includes not only material coming into the possession of the investigator (such as documents seized in the course of searching premises) but also material generated by him (such as interview records);
- material may be *relevant to an investigation* if it appears to an investigator, or to the officer in charge of an investigation, or to the disclosure officer, that it has some bearing on any offence under investigation or any person being investigated, or on the surrounding circumstances of the case, unless it is incapable of having any impact on the case;
- *sensitive material* is material, the disclosure of which, the disclosure officer believes, would give rise to a real risk of serious prejudice to an important public interest;
- references to *prosecution disclosure* are to the duty of the prosecutor under sections 3 and 7A of the Act to disclose material which is in his possession or which he has inspected in pursuance of this Code, and which might reasonably be considered capable of undermining the case against the accused, or of assisting the case for the accused;

- references to the disclosure of material to a person accused of an offence include references to the disclosure of material to his legal representative;
- references to police officers and to the chief officer of police include those employed in a police force as defined in section 3(3) of the Prosecution of Offences Act 1985.

**1.10.4.1**

## KEYNOTE

### Application of the Disclosure Provisions

Section 1 of the Criminal Procedure and Investigations Act 1996 defines in which type of cases the disclosure provisions apply. In reality, this applies to all cases other than those where the defendant pleads guilty at the magistrates' court. These rules only apply where no criminal investigation into the alleged offence took place before 1 April 1997. If an investigation began before 1 April 1997, then it will be necessary to refer to the common law rules; however, ACPO has stated that the 1996 Act should be followed in all cases when considering disclosure. For those investigations that started after 4 April 2005, the amendments introduced by the Criminal Justice Act 2003 will apply.

Some guidance is given by the case of *R* v *Uxbridge Magistrates' Court, ex parte Patel* (2000) 164 JP 209, as to the time an investigation begins. There it was said that the phrase 'criminal investigation' in s. 1(3) of the 1996 Act means that a criminal investigation could begin into an offence before it was committed. This could be so in a surveillance case or where a series of cases was committed, some before and some after the appointed day. Whether in any given case that was the correct view would be a question of fact for the court to determine.

Section 1 also defines a criminal investigation and states:

(4) For the purposes of this section a criminal investigation is an investigation which police officers or other persons have a duty to conduct with a view to it being ascertained—
  (a) whether a person should be charged with an offence, or
  (b) whether a person charged with an offence is guilty of it.

Consequently, this part of the Act also applies to other people, besides the police, who carry out investigations where they have a duty to ascertain whether criminal offences have been committed (e.g. HM Revenue and Customs; Benefits Agency investigators). It does not apply to those whose primary responsibility does not relate to criminal offences (e.g. local authorities and schools).

**1.10.4.2**

## KEYNOTE

### Disclosure Officer

If not appointed at the start of an investigation, a disclosure officer must be appointed in sufficient time to be able to prepare the unused material schedules for inclusion in the full file submitted to the CPS (Disclosure Manual, para. 3.11).

**1.10.4.3**

## KEYNOTE

### Duties of Investigators

An officer who is classed as an investigator must pursue all reasonable lines of inquiry (Code, para. 3.5) and having done so retain all material which is relevant to the case (**see para. 1.10.5.2**), whether or not it is helpful to the prosecution (Code, para. 5.1). Failure to do so could lead to a miscarriage of justice.

**1.10.4.4**

**KEYNOTE**

**Prosecutor**

This role is defined by s. 2(3) of the 1996 Act as being 'any person acting as prosecutor whether an individual or a body'. In other words, the person who will be taking the case to court. On most occasions, this will be the CPS. It would also apply to the Serious Fraud Office or the Data Protection Registrar. In the case of private prosecutions, the prosecutor is obliged to comply with the disclosure provisions of the 1996 Act but does not have to comply with the Code of Practice. The prosecutor is responsible for ensuring that primary initial disclosure is made to the defence and, where appropriate, secondary disclosure. The prosecutor should also be available to advise the OIC, disclosure officer and investigators on matters relating to the relevance of material recorded and retained by police, sensitive material and any other disclosure issues that might arise.

Should there need to be an application to the court to withhold material because of public interest (**see para. 1.10.8.3**), this will be done through the prosecutor.

A more detailed explanation of the roles and responsibilities of the prosecutor are set out in the CPS/Police Joint Operational Instructions (JOPI) Guidelines (2004).

---

**1.10.4.5**

**KEYNOTE**

**Relevant Material**

The material will be *relevant* whether or not it is beneficial to the prosecution case, weakens the prosecution case or assists the defence case. It is not only material that will become 'evidence' in the case that should be considered; any information, record or thing which may have a bearing on the case can be material for the purposes of disclosure. The way in which evidence has been obtained may in itself be relevant.

What is relevant to the offence is once again a question of fact, and will not include everything. In *DPP* v *Metten* (1999) 22 January, unreported, it was claimed that the constables who had arrested the defendant had known the identities of potential witnesses to the arrest and these had not been disclosed. The court said that this was not relevant to the case as it did not fall within the definition of an investigation in s. 2(1) of the 1996 Act in that it concerned the time of arrest, and not what happened at the time the *offence* was committed. Paragraphs 5.4 and 5.5 of the Code give guidance on items that might be considered to be relevant material in a case.

Relevant material may relate to the credibility of witnesses, such as previous convictions, the fact that they have a grudge against the defendant or even the weather conditions for the day if relevant to the issue of identification. It may include information that house-to-house inquiries were made and that no one witnessed anything.

Particularly at the early stages of an investigation (sometimes not until the defence statement is provided outlining the defence case), it may not be possible to know whether material is relevant. If in doubt, it should be recorded and placed on the schedule of undisclosed material. Throughout the case, investigators and all others involved should continually review the material in the light of the investigation.

---

**1.10.5**

## Disclosure Code of Practice—3 General Responsibilities

3.1 The functions of the investigator, the officer in charge of an investigation and the disclosure officer are separate. Whether they are undertaken by one, two or more persons will depend on the complexity of the case and the administrative arrangements within each police force. Where they are undertaken by more than one person, close consultation between them is essential to the effective performance of the duties imposed by this Code.

3.2 In any criminal investigation, one or more deputy disclosure officers may be appointed to assist the disclosure officer, and a deputy disclosure officer may perform any function of a disclosure officer as defined in paragraph 2.1.

3.3 The chief officer of police for each police force is responsible for putting in place arrangements to ensure that in every investigation the identity of the officer in charge of an investigation and the disclosure officer is recorded. The chief officer of police for each police force shall ensure that disclosure officers and deputy disclosure officers have sufficient skills and authority, commensurate with the complexity of the investigation, to discharge their functions effectively. An individual must not be appointed as disclosure officer, or continue in that role, if that is likely to result in a conflict of interest, for instance, if the disclosure officer is the victim of the alleged crime which is the subject of the investigation. The advice of a more senior officer must always be sought if there is doubt as to whether a conflict of interest precludes an individual acting as disclosure officer. If thereafter the doubt remains, the advice of a prosecutor should be sought.

3.4 The officer in charge of an investigation may delegate tasks to another investigator, to civilians employed by the police force, or to other persons participating in the investigation under arrangements for joint investigations, but he remains responsible for ensuring that these have been carried out and for accounting for any general policies followed in the investigation. In particular, it is an essential part of his duties to ensure that all material which may be relevant to an investigation is retained, and either made available to the disclosure officer or (in exceptional circumstances) revealed directly to the prosecutor.

3.5 In conducting an investigation, the investigator should pursue all reasonable lines of inquiry, whether these point towards or away from the suspect. What is reasonable in each case will depend on the particular circumstances. For example, where material is held on computer, it is a matter for the investigator to decide which material on the computer it is reasonable to inquire into, and in what manner.

3.6 If the officer in charge of an investigation believes that other persons may be in possession of material that may be relevant to the investigation, and if this has not been obtained under paragraph 3.5 above, he should ask the disclosure officer to inform them of the existence of the investigation and to invite them to retain the material in case they receive a request for its disclosure. The disclosure officer should inform the prosecutor that they may have such material. However, the officer in charge of an investigation is not required to make speculative enquiries of other persons; there must be some reason to believe that they may have relevant material. That reason may come from information provided to the police by the accused or from other inquiries made or from some other source.

3.7 If, during a criminal investigation, the officer in charge of an investigation or disclosure officer for any reason no longer has responsibility for the functions falling to him, either his supervisor or the police officer in charge of criminal investigations for the police force concerned must assign someone else to assume that responsibility. That person's identity must be recorded, as with those initially responsible for these functions in each investigation.

---

**1.10.5.1**  **KEYNOTE**

**Disclosure Officer**

The disclosure officer creates the link between the investigation team and the prosecutor (CPS) and is therefore very important to the disclosure process. For investigations carried out by the police, generally speaking there is no restriction on who performs this role; however, they must be suitably trained and experienced. The role and responsibility of the disclosure officer is set out in the Disclosure Manual at para. 3.9:

- examine, inspect, view or listen to all relevant material that has been retained by the investigator and that does not form part of the prosecution case
- create schedules that fully describe the material
- identify all material which satisfies the disclosure test using the MG6E
- submit the schedules and copies of disclosable material to the prosecutor
- at the same time, supply to the prosecutor a copy of material falling into any of the categories described in paragraph 7.3 of the Code and copies of all documents required to be routinely revealed and which have not previously been revealed to the prosecutor

- consult with and allow the prosecutor to inspect the retained material
- review the schedules and the retained material continually, particularly after the defence statement has been received, identify to the prosecutor material that satisfies the disclosure test using the MG6E and supply a copy of any such material not already provided
- schedule and reveal to the prosecutor any relevant additional unused material pursuant to the continuing duty of disclosure
- certify that all retained material has been revealed to the prosecutor in accordance with the Code
- where the prosecutor requests the disclosure officer to disclose any material to the accused, give the accused a copy of the material or allow the accused to inspect it.

**1.10.5.2**

## KEYNOTE

### Reasonable Lines of Inquiry

An officer who is classed as an investigator must pursue all reasonable lines of inquiry (Code, para. 3.5) and having done so retain all material which is relevant to the case (see para. 1.10.7.1), whether or not it is helpful to the prosecution (Code, para. 5.1). Failure to do so could lead to a miscarriage of justice. In *R* v *Poole* [2003] EWCA Crim 1753, Y provided a statement to police in a murder case. It transpired that N had been with Y at the relevant time and this cast doubt over Y's evidence. The police did not follow up the inconsistencies. The Court of Appeal held that the failure to disclose N's evidence was a material irregularity which in part led to a successful appeal by the defendant. The investigator also has a responsibility to identify material that could be sensitive and bring this to the attention of the CPS. This need to be proactive was reinforced in *R* v *Joof* [2012] EWCA Crim 1475 where the court held that the responsibilities imposed by the Criminal Procedure and Investigations Act 1996 and the A-G's Guidelines could not be circumvented by not making inquiries. An officer who believed that a person might have information which might undermine the prosecution case or assist the defence could not decline to make inquiries in order to avoid the need to disclose what might be said. Where material is identified steps must be taken to record and retain the material. For information recorded on computers, see the JOPI Guidelines from para. 2.29 onwards.

Section 3 of the Criminal Procedure and Investigations Act 1996 talks about material which *'might undermine the prosecution case against the accused or which might assist'* the case for the accused. The courts are likely to consider this to include material which has an adverse effect on the strength of the prosecution case. Clearly, there is a need to guess what the defence case may be in considering what should be disclosed but this can be further reviewed after the defence disclosure.

**1.10.5.3**

## KEYNOTE

### Material that Undermines the Prosecution Case

There is only limited case law in this area but it is likely that such material will consist mainly of material which raises question marks over the strength of the prosecution case, the value of evidence given by witnesses and issues relating to identification. If officers feel that the material is not relevant to the prosecution case but may be useful to the defence in cross-examination, it may well come within the category of material which undermines the prosecution case. In *Tucker* v *CPS* [2008] EWCA Crim 3063, the prosecution did not reveal to the defence a record containing important information as to a possible motive for a witness lying about the defendant's involvement in the offence. This led to the conviction being overturned. It was clearly material that undermined the prosecution case as it raised questions over the value of the witness's evidence.

Disclosure of previous convictions and other matters that might affect the credibility of a witness may 'undermine the prosecution case' as it may limit the value of the witness's testimony. This factor may not be apparent at the time but may come to light after the initial disclosure, such as where it becomes known that the witness has a grudge against the defendant. This is one reason why the 1996 Act requires the decision as to whether material undermines the prosecution case to be continuously monitored throughout the case.

In *R (On the Application of Ebrahim)* v *Feltham Magistrates' Court* [2001] EWHC Admin 130 the court stated that the extent of the investigation should be proportionate to the seriousness of the matter being investigated. What is reasonable in a case may well depend on such factors as the staff and resources available, the seriousness of the case, the strength of evidence against the suspect and the nature of the line of inquiry to be pursued. If in doubt it is suggested that the CPS is contacted for guidance.

Paragraph 5.16 of the Disclosure Manual makes important observations concerning negative results: when making inquiries, 'negative results can sometimes be as significant to an investigation as positive ones'. It is impossible to define precisely when a negative result may be significant, as every case is different. However, it will include the result of any inquiry that differs from what might be expected, given the prevailing circumstances. Not only must material or information which points towards a fact or an individual be retained, but also that which casts doubt on the suspect's guilt, or implicates another person. Examples of negative information include:

- a CCTV camera that did not record the crime/location/suspect in a manner which is consistent with the prosecution case (the fact that a CCTV camera did not function or have videotape loaded will not usually be considered relevant negative information);
- where a number of people present at a particular location at the particular time that an offence is alleged to have taken place state that they saw nothing unusual;
- where a finger-mark from a crime scene cannot be identified as belonging to a known suspect;
- any other failure to match a crime scene sample with one taken from the accused.

1.10.5.4   **KEYNOTE**

**Complaints against Police Officers Involved in a Case**

Not only might the credibility of witnesses undermine the prosecution case, but so too might complaints against officers involved in the case, together with any occasions where officers have not been believed in court in the past. In these cases, it will be necessary to decide whether this information should be disclosed to the defence and, if disclosed, in how much detail. This question is probably best answered by the following extract from advice given to prosecutors by the DPP:

> It is, of course, necessary in the first instance for the police to bring such matters to the notice of the prosecutor, but it is submitted that the prosecutor should have a greater element of discretion than with the disclosure of previous convictions. With convictions against prosecution witnesses, disclosure normally follows, whereas in relation to disciplinary findings regard should be had to the nature of the finding and its likely relevance to the matters in issue. Findings which involve some element of dishonesty should invariably be disclosed, while matters such as disobedience to orders, neglect of duty and discreditable conduct will often have no relevance to the officer's veracity or the guilt or otherwise of a defendant. Certainly, there should be no duty on the prosecution to disclose details of unsubstantiated complaints even though this is a popular type of inquiry from some defence representatives. The imposition of such a duty would only encourage the making of false complaints in the hope that they might be used to discredit an officer in the future.

Detailed guidance is provided in chapter 18 of the Disclosure Manual.

The prosecutor should be informed if officers involved in a case have discipline matters on their record. This may well appear on the schedule in order that the prosecutor can consider the matter and amend the schedule if necessary. It is suggested that advice should be sought from the prosecutor as to what information is included on the schedule and, if disclosure is to be made, advice on what information to be included should also be sought.

Some guidance is given by the courts. In *R* v *Edwards* [1991] 1 WLR 207 the court held that a disciplinary finding and reprimand of a DCI for countersigning interview notes which had been wrongly re-written in another case should have been disclosed to the defence. *R* v *Guney* [1998] 2 Cr App R 242 followed *Edwards*. In *Guney* six police officers went to the defendant's home with a warrant to search for drugs. Three of the officers had formerly been members of a squad which had been subject to 'considerable internal police interest'. The court held that the defence were not entitled to be informed of every occasion when any officer had given evidence 'unsuccessfully' or whenever allegations were made against him/her. In this case, the information should have been disclosed. The court went on to say that the records available to the CPS should include transcripts of any decisions of the Court of Appeal Criminal Division where convictions were quashed because of the misconduct or lack of veracity of identified police officers as well as cases stopped by the trial judge or discontinued on the same basis. The systematic collection of such material was preferable to the existing haphazard arrangement.

If in doubt advice should be sought from the CPS.

## 1.10.6    Disclosure Code of Practice—4 Recording of Information

4.1   If material which may be relevant to the investigation consists of information which is not recorded in any form, the officer in charge of an investigation must ensure that it is recorded in a durable or retrievable form (whether in writing, on video or audio tape, or on computer disk).

4.2   Where it is not practicable to retain the initial record of information because it forms part of a larger record which is to be destroyed, its contents should be transferred as a true record to a durable and more easily-stored form before that happens.

4.3   Negative information is often relevant to an investigation. If it may be relevant it must be recorded. An example might be a number of people present in a particular place at a particular time who state that they saw nothing unusual.

4.4   Where information which may be relevant is obtained, it must be recorded at the time it is obtained or as soon as practicable after that time. This includes, for example, information obtained in house-to-house enquiries, although the requirement to record information promptly does not require an investigator to take a statement from a potential witness where it would not otherwise be taken.

## 1.10.6.1    KEYNOTE

**Contemporaneous Records**

The need for contemporaneous records is also required under the Police and Criminal Evidence Act 1984 and if not complied with could affect the admissibility of important evidence (see s. 78 of the 1984 Act).

## 1.10.7    Disclosure Code of Practice—5 Retention of Material

### (a) Duty to retain material

5.1   The investigator must retain material obtained in a criminal investigation which may be relevant to the investigation. Material may be photographed, video-recorded, captured digitally or otherwise retained in the form of a copy rather than the original at any time, if the original is perishable; the original was supplied to the investigator rather than generated by him and is to be returned to its owner; or the retention of a copy rather than the original is reasonable in all the circumstances.

5.2   Where material has been seized in the exercise of the powers of seizure conferred by the Police and Criminal Evidence Act 1984, the duty to retain it under this Code is subject to the provisions on the retention of seized material in section 22 of that Act.

5.3   If the officer in charge of an investigation becomes aware as a result of developments in the case that material previously examined but not retained (because it was not thought to be relevant) may now be relevant to the investigation, he should, wherever practicable, take steps to obtain it or ensure that it is retained for further inspection or for production in court if required.

5.4   The duty to retain material includes in particular the duty to retain material falling into the following categories, where it may be relevant to the investigation:

- crime reports (including crime report forms, relevant parts of incident report books or police officer's notebooks);
- custody records;
- records which are derived from tapes of telephone messages (for example, 999 calls) containing descriptions of an alleged offence or offender;
- final versions of witness statements (and draft versions where their content differs from the final version), including any exhibits mentioned (unless these have been returned to their owner on the understanding that they will be produced in court if required);
- interview records (written records, or audio or video tapes, of interviews with actual or potential witnesses or suspects);
- communications between the police and experts such as forensic scientists, reports of work carried out by experts, and schedules of scientific material prepared by the expert for the investigator, for the purposes of criminal proceedings;
- records of the first description of a suspect by each potential witness who purports to identify or describe the suspect, whether or not the description differs from that of subsequent descriptions by that or other witnesses;
- any material casting doubt on the reliability of a witness.

5.5    The duty to retain material, where it may be relevant to the investigation, also includes in particular the duty to retain material which may satisfy the test for prosecution disclosure in the Act, such as:
- information provided by an accused person which indicates an explanation for the offence with which he has been charged;
- any material casting doubt on the reliability of a confession;
- any material casting doubt on the reliability of a prosecution witness.

5.6    The duty to retain material falling into these categories does not extend to items which are purely ancillary to such material and possess no independent significance (for example, duplicate copies of records or reports).

## (b)  Length of time for which material is to be retained

5.7    All material which may be relevant to the investigation must be retained until a decision is taken whether to institute proceedings against a person for an offence.

5.8    If a criminal investigation results in proceedings being instituted, all material which may be relevant must be retained at least until the accused is acquitted or convicted or the prosecutor decides not to proceed with the case.

5.9    Where the accused is convicted, all material which may be relevant must be retained at least until:
- the convicted person is released from custody, or discharged from hospital, in cases where the court imposes a custodial sentence or a hospital order;
- six months from the date of conviction, in all other cases.

If the court imposes a custodial sentence or hospital order and the convicted person is released from custody or discharged from hospital earlier than six months from the date of conviction, all material which may be relevant must be retained at least until six months from the date of conviction.

5.10   If an appeal against conviction is in progress when the release or discharge occurs, or at the end of the period of six months specified in paragraph 5.9, all material which may be relevant must be retained until the appeal is determined. Similarly, if the Criminal Cases Review Commission is considering an application at that point in time, all material which may be relevant must be retained at least until the Commission decides not to refer the case to the Court.

**1.10.7.1**

**Retention of Material**

In order to disclose material to the defence, there is a need first to find it and secondly retain it. Retention of material applies to documents and other evidence, including videos. Failure to retain material could lead to the prosecution losing the case, particularly where the court considers that its absence will lead to the defendant not being able to receive a fair trial (Article 6 of the European Convention on Human Rights). In *Mouat* v *DPP* [2001] EWHC Admin 130 the defendant had been charged with speeding. Police officers had recorded a video of the defendant driving at speed and had shown the video to the defendant prior to charge but had later recorded over it. The defendant contended that he had been intimidated by the unmarked police car being driven only inches from his rear bumper. The policy of the force was to keep videos for 28 days, unless they recorded an offence, in which case they were kept for 12 months. The court held that the police were under a duty to retain the video tapes at least until the end of the suspended enforcement period, during which time the defendant was entitled to consider whether he wished to contest his liability in court.

In deciding what material should be retained in an investigation, consideration should be given to any force orders, what powers there are to seize and retain the said material, as well as the Disclosure Code and the A-G's Guidelines. Where an investigator discovers material that is relevant to the case, he/she must record that information or retain the material (Code, para. 5.1).

When deciding if the material should be retained the A-G's Guidelines provide that: 'investigators should always err on the side of recording and retaining material where they have any doubt as to whether it may be relevant' (A-G's Guidelines, para. 24).

It is important to note that the material itself does not have to be admissible in court for it to undermine the prosecution case. This point was made in *R* v *Preston* [1994] 2 AC 130, where it was said that:

> In the first place, the fact that an item of information cannot be put in evidence by a party does not mean that it is worthless. Often, the train of inquiry which leads to the discovery of evidence which is admissible at a trial may include an item which is not admissible, and this may apply, although less frequently, to the defence as well as the prosecution.

If, during the lifetime of a case, the OIC becomes aware that material which has been examined during the course of an investigation, but not retained, becomes relevant as a result of new developments, para. 5.3 of the Code will apply. That officer should take steps to recover the material wherever practicable, or ensure that it is preserved by the person in possession of it (Disclosure Manual, para. 5.25).

In some of these cases the investigation may well have started some time before the defendant became a suspect. In such cases all the material from the investigation/operation would have to be reviewed to see if it is relevant to the defence case. In cases where there is a surveillance operation or observation point, it may be that the details of the observation point and the surveillance techniques would not be revealed but it would be necessary to retain material generating from it (see para. 1.10.8.3).

**1.10.7.2**

**CCTV**

The likelihood of an incident being caught on CCTV can be quite strong, which raises the question as to the responsibility of the police to investigate the possibility of there being a recording and retaining the recording tape. This point was considered in *R (On the Application of Ebrahim)* v *Feltham Magistrates' Court* [2001] EWHC Admin 130. These cases related to the obliteration of video evidence. In coming to its judgment, the court considered a number of previous decisions where the police were not required to retain CCTV evidence. The general question for the court was whether the prosecution had been under a duty to obtain or retain video evidence. If there was no such duty, the prosecution could not have abused the process of the court simply because the material was no longer available, i.e. it was a reasonable line of inquiry (as to whether they were under a duty to obtain the evidence, see para. 1.10.5.2). *Ebrahim* shows that CCTV footage does not necessarily have to be retained in all cases. *R* v *Dobson* [2001] EWCA Crim 1606 followed *Ebrahim*. Dobson had been convicted of arson with intent to endanger life, his defence being that he was elsewhere at the time.

There had been a strong possibility that the route that Dobson claimed to have taken would have been covered by CCTV but it would have depended on which side of the road he had been using and which way the cameras were pointing at the time. Dobson's solicitors had not asked for the tapes to be preserved at interview and the police confirmed that the possibility of investigating the tapes had been overlooked. The tapes had been overwritten after 31 days. In following the principles set down in *Ebrahim*, the police, by their own admissions, had failed in their duty to obtain and retain the relevant footage. While there was plainly a degree of prejudice in Dobson being deprived of the opportunity of checking the footage in the hope that it supported his case, that prejudice was held not to have seriously prejudiced his case given the uncertainty of the likelihood that it would assist and the fact that Dobson had equally been in a position to appreciate the possible existence and significance of the tapes. The fact that there was no suggestion of malice or intentional omission by the police was also an important consideration for the court.

## 1.10.7.3    KEYNOTE

### Third Party Material

Third party material can be considered in two categories:

(a) that which is or has been in the possession of the police or which has been inspected by the police;

(b) all other material not falling under (a).

Material which falls into the first category is covered by the same rules of disclosure as any other material the police have. Where police do not have material that they believe may be relevant to the case, para. 3.6 of the Code provides direction.

In the vast majority of cases the third party will make the material available to the investigating officer. However, there may be occasions where the third party refuses to hand over the material and/or allow it to be examined.

If the OIC, the investigator or the disclosure officer believes that a third party holds material that may be relevant to the investigation, that person or body should be told of the investigation. They should be alerted to the need to preserve relevant material. Consideration should be given as to whether it is appropriate to seek access to the material and, if so, steps should be taken to obtain such material. It will be important to do so if the material or information is likely to undermine the prosecution case, or to assist a known defence. A letter should be sent to the third party together with the explanatory leaflet, specimens of which are provided in the Disclosure Manual at Annex B.

Where access to the material is declined or refused by the third party and it is believed that it is reasonable to seek production of the material before a suspect is charged, the investigator should consider making an application under sch. 1 to the Police and Criminal Evidence Act 1984 (special procedure material).

Where the suspect has been charged and the third party refuses to produce the material, application will have to be made to the court for a witness summons. In the magistrates' court this is covered by s. 97 of the Magistrates' Courts Act 1980 and in the Crown Court it is covered by ss. 2(2) and 2A–2D of the Criminal Procedure (Attendance of Witnesses) Act 1965. The third party may still wish to resist the requirement to produce the material and the point was considered in *R* v *Brushett* [2001] Crim LR 471 (this was a case that concerned Social Services Department files relating to a children's home). The court considered a number of earlier cases and established some central principles as follows:

- To be material evidence documents must be not only relevant to the issues arising in the criminal proceedings, but also documents admissible as such in evidence.
- Documents which are desired merely for the purpose of possible cross-examination are not admissible in evidence and, thus, are not material for the purposes of s. 97.
- Whoever seeks production of documents must satisfy the justices with some evidence that the documents are 'likely to be material' in the sense indicated, likelihood for this purpose involving a real possibility, although not necessarily a probability.

- It is not sufficient that the applicant merely wants to find out whether or not the third party has such material documents. This procedure must not be used as a disguised attempt to obtain discovery.
- Where social services documents are supplied to the prosecution, the prosecution should retain control of such material as part of the disclosure regime. That is envisaged by the rules. It cannot be acceptable to return material to social services to avoid the obligations arising under the rules. In any event, the obligation would arise in relation to the notes taken and retained.
- The obligation laid on the prosecution by statute and rules cannot be avoided by a third party making an agreement with the prosecution that the prosecution will abrogate any duties laid upon it by either common law or statute.
- If circumstances arise where it would be unjust not to allow disclosure of certain other material, so a defendant would not receive a fair trial in the sense that he/she could not establish his innocence where he/she might otherwise do so, then that material must be disclosed.
- The fact that the prosecution have knowledge of the third party material may be a relevant factor to allow the defence access.
- Material concerning false allegations in the past may be relevant material (*R* v *Bourimech* [2002] EWCA Crim 2089).
- If the disputed material might prove the defendant's innocence or avoid a miscarriage of justice, the weight came down resoundingly in favour of disclosing it (*R* v *Reading Justices, ex parte Berkshire County Council* (1996) 1 Cr App R 239).

In *R* v *Alibhai* [2004] EWCA Crim 681 the Court of Appeal held that under the Criminal Procedure and Investigations Act 1996 the prosecutor was only under a duty to disclose material in the hands of third parties if that material had come into the prosecutor's hands and the prosecutor was of the opinion that such material undermined the case. However, the A-G's Guidelines went further by requiring a prosecutor to take steps pursuing third party disclosure if there was a suspicion that documents would be detrimental to the prosecution or of assistance to the defence. However, in such circumstances, the prosecutor enjoyed a margin of consideration as to what steps were appropriate. The provisions for disclosure are not intended to create duties for third parties to follow. The disclosure duties under the 1996 Act were created in respect of material that the prosecution or the police had and which the prosecution had inspected. Material was not prosecution material unless it was held by the investigator or by the disclosure officer (*DPP* v *Wood and McGillicuddy* [2006] EWHC 32 (Admin)).

The A-G's Guidelines also deal with materials held by third parties (including government agencies) in paras 47–54. Paragraphs 47–50 deal with material held by government departments or other Crown bodies and suggest that reasonable steps should be taken to identify and consider material that may be relevant to an issue in the case. Paragraph 51 examines the circumstances in which the prosecution should take steps to obtain access to material or information in the possession of other third parties. In such cases, consideration should be given to take steps to obtain such material or information. It will be important to do so if the material or information is likely to undermine the prosecution case, or assist a known defence. Paragraph 52 deals with the situation where the police or prosecutor meet with a refusal by the third party to supply such material or information. If, despite the reasons put forward for refusal by the third party, it still appears reasonable to seek its production, a witness summons requiring the third party to produce the material should be applied for (such an application can also be made by the defence). The third party can then argue at court that it is not material, or that it should not be disclosed on grounds of public interest immunity.

## 1.10.8    Disclosure Code of Practice—6 Preparation of Material for Prosecutor

### (a) Introduction

6.1    The officer in charge of the investigation, the disclosure officer or an investigator may seek advice from the prosecutor about whether any particular item of material may be relevant to the investigation.

6.2 Material which may be relevant to an investigation, which has been retained in accordance with this Code, and which the disclosure officer believes will not form part of the prosecution case, must be listed on a schedule.

6.3 Material which the disclosure officer does not believe is sensitive must be listed on a schedule of non-sensitive material. The schedule must include a statement that the disclosure officer does not believe the material is sensitive.

6.4 Any material which is believed to be sensitive must be either listed on a schedule of sensitive material or, in exceptional circumstances, revealed to the prosecutor separately. If there is no sensitive material, the disclosure officer must record this fact on a schedule of sensitive material.

6.5 Paragraphs 6.6 to 6.11 below apply to both sensitive and non-sensitive material. Paragraphs 6.12 to 6.14 apply to sensitive material only.

## (b) Circumstances in which a schedule is to be prepared

6.6 The disclosure officer must ensure that a schedule is prepared in the following circumstances:
- the accused is charged with an offence which is triable only on indictment;
- the accused is charged with an offence which is triable either way, and it is considered either that the case is likely to be tried on indictment or that the accused is likely to plead not guilty at a summary trial;
- the accused is charged with a summary offence, and it is considered that he is likely to plead not guilty.

6.7 In respect of either way and summary offences, a schedule may not be needed if a person has admitted the offence, or if a police officer witnessed the offence and that person has not denied it.

6.8 If it is believed that the accused is likely to plead guilty at a summary trial, it is not necessary to prepare a schedule in advance. If, contrary to this belief, the accused pleads not guilty at a summary trial, or the offence is to be tried on indictment, the disclosure officer must ensure that a schedule is prepared as soon as is reasonably practicable after that happens.

## (c) Way in which material is to be listed on schedule

6.9 The disclosure officer should ensure that each item of material is listed separately on the schedule, and is numbered consecutively. The description of each item should make clear the nature of the item and should contain sufficient detail to enable the prosecutor to decide whether he needs to inspect the material before deciding whether or not it should be disclosed.

6.10 In some enquiries it may not be practicable to list each item of material separately. For example, there may be many items of a similar or repetitive nature. These may be listed in a block and described by quantity and generic title.

6.11 Even if some material is listed in a block, the disclosure officer must ensure that any items among that material which might satisfy the test for prosecution disclosure are listed and described individually.

## (d) Treatment of sensitive material

6.12 Subject to paragraph 6.13 below, the disclosure officer must list on a sensitive schedule any material, the disclosure of which he believes would give rise to a real risk of serious prejudice to an important public interest, and the reason for that belief. The schedule must include a statement that the disclosure officer believes the material is sensitive. Depending on the circumstances, examples of such material may include the following among others:

- material relating to national security;
- material received from the intelligence and security agencies;
- material relating to intelligence from foreign sources which reveals sensitive intelligence gathering methods;
- material given in confidence;
- material relating to the identity or activities of informants, or undercover police officers, or witnesses, or other persons supplying information to the police who may be in danger if their identities are revealed;
- material revealing the location of any premises or other place used for police surveillance, or the identity of any person allowing a police officer to use them for surveillance;
- material revealing, either directly or indirectly, techniques and methods relied upon by a police officer in the course of a criminal investigation, for example covert surveillance techniques, or other methods of detecting crime;
- material whose disclosure might facilitate the commission of other offences or hinder the prevention and detection of crime;
- material upon the strength of which search warrants were obtained;
- material containing details of persons taking part in identification parades;
- material supplied to an investigator during a criminal investigation which has been generated by an official of a body concerned with the regulation or supervision of bodies corporate or of persons engaged in financial activities, or which has been generated by a person retained by such a body;
- material supplied to an investigator during a criminal investigation which relates to a child or young person and which has been generated by a local authority social services department, an Area Child Protection Committee or other party contacted by an investigator during the investigation;
- material relating to the private life of a witness.

6.13   In exceptional circumstances, where an investigator considers that material is so sensitive that its revelation to the prosecutor by means of an entry on the sensitive schedule is inappropriate, the existence of the material must be revealed to the prosecutor separately. This will apply only where compromising the material would be likely to lead directly to the loss of life, or directly threaten national security.

6.14   In such circumstances, the responsibility for informing the prosecutor lies with the investigator who knows the detail of the sensitive material. The investigator should act as soon as is reasonably practicable after the file containing the prosecution case is sent to the prosecutor. The investigator must also ensure that the prosecutor is able to inspect the material so that he can assess whether it is disclosable and, if so, whether it needs to be brought before a court for a ruling on disclosure.

1.10.8.1   **KEYNOTE**

**Initial Disclosure**

Under s. 3 of the 1996 Act, all previously undisclosed material that might undermine the prosecution case must be disclosed to the defence. If there is no such material, then the accused must be given a written statement to that effect. This applies to all material in possession of the police or that has been inspected under the provisions of the Disclosure Code of Practice. This therefore requires the disclosure officer to know what material exists and what material has already been made available to the defence.

In *R* v *Olu, Wilson and Brooks* [2010] EWCA Crim 2975 the Court of Appeal said that the disclosure regime would not work in practice unless a disclosure officer was directed by the Crown Prosecutor as to what was likely to be most relevant and important so that the disclosure officer approached the matter through the exercise of judgement and not simply as a schedule-completing exercise. It was the task of a CPS lawyer to identify the issues in the case and the police officer who was not trained in that skill to act under the guidance of the CPS.

The prosecution only have to disclose material relevant to the prosecution in question. For instance, surveillance logs concerning another matter would not need to be disclosed (*R v Dennis* (2000) 13 April, unreported). It is up to the prosecutor to decide on the format in which material is disclosed to the accused. If material is to be copied, s. 3(3) of the 1996 Act leaves open the question of whether this should be done by the prosecutor or by the police. The prosecutor must also provide the defence with a schedule of all non-sensitive material (s. 4(2) of the 1996 Act). This includes all other information in police possession, or material that has been examined by the police other than 'sensitive material' (this is disclosed to the prosecutor separately). 'Sensitive material' is material which it is not in the public interest to disclose. At this stage, the defence are not entitled to inspect items on the schedule that have not been disclosed (s. 3(6) and (7)).

Material must not be disclosed to the extent that the court concludes that it is not in the public interest to disclose it and orders accordingly or it is material whose disclosure is prohibited by s. 17 of the Regulation of Investigatory Powers Act 2000 unless it falls within the exception provided by s. 18 of the Act.

## 1.10.8.2    KEYNOTE

### Completing the Schedules

It is important that the schedules themselves are completed fully. Guidance is given by paras 6.9–6.11 of the Code and in detail in the Disclosure Manual, chapters 6–8. While items should be listed separately, there may be occasions where items are similar or the same, in which case these may be listed together (Disclosure Manual, para. 7.4). This also applies to sensitive schedules, in so far as is possible without compromising the confidentiality of the information (see also the Disclosure Manual, para. 7.4). Paragraph 27 of the A-G's Guidelines also allows in some circumstances, because of the large volumes of material, not to examine all the material. If such material is not examined by the investigator or disclosure officer, and it is not intended to examine it, its existence should be made known to the accused in general terms.

The following items should also be considered when deciding on initial disclosure in cases where the disclosure is in the public interest (that is where they are not *'sensitive material'*). The material is (A-G's Guidelines, para. 12) (see also Disclosure Manual, para. 10.1):

- any material casting doubt upon the accuracy of any prosecution evidence;
- any material which may point to another person, whether charged or not (including a co-accused) having involvement in the commission of the offence;
- any material which may cast doubt upon the reliability of a confession;
- any material that might go to the credibility of a prosecution witness;
- any material that might support a defence that is either raised by the defence or apparent from the prosecution papers;
- any material which may have a bearing on the admissibility of any prosecution evidence.

The disclosure officer should be mindful of the need to demonstrate that he/she has taken all reasonable steps should it transpire that full disclosure had not been made.

It should be remembered that the prosecutor is required to advise the disclosure officer of any omissions or amendments or where there are insufficient or unclear descriptions, or where there has been a failure to provide schedules at all. The disclosure officer must then take all necessary remedial action and provide properly completed schedules to the prosecutor. Failure to do so may result in the matter being raised with a senior officer. There may also be occasions where schedules need to be edited; this is covered in the Disclosure Manual at paras 7.7 and 7.8.

**1.10.8.3**

## KEYNOTE

### Sensitive Material

This is material which the disclosure officer believes it is not in the public interest to disclose. While the general principle that governs the 1996 Act and Article 6 of the European Convention is that material should not be withheld from the defence, sensitive material is an exception to this. In *Van Mechelen* v *Netherlands* (1998) 25 EHRR 647, the court stated that in some cases it may be necessary to withhold certain evidence from the defence so as to preserve the fundamental rights of another individual or to safeguard an important public interest. However, only such measures restricting the rights of the defence which are strictly necessary are permissible under Article 6. It should be noted that the court did recognise that the entitlement of disclosure of relevant evidence was not an absolute right but could only be restricted as was strictly necessary. In *R* v *Keane* [1994] 1 WLR 746 Lord Taylor CJ stated that 'the judge should carry out a balancing exercise, having regard both to the weight of the public interest in non-disclosure and to the importance of the documents to the issues of interest, present and potential, to the defence, and if the disputed material might prove a defendant's innocence or avoid a miscarriage of justice, the balance came down resoundingly in favour of disclosure'.

Decisions as to what should be withheld from the defence are a matter for the court and, where necessary, an application to withhold the material must be made to the court (*R* v *Ward* [1993] 1 WLR 619). The application of public interest immunity was considered by the House of Lords in *R* v *H* [2004] UKHL 3. In this case, the defendants were charged with conspiracy to supply a Class A drug following a covert police investigation, and sought disclosure of material held by the prosecution relating to the investigation. The prosecution resisted the disclosure on grounds of public interest immunity. The court held that if the material did not weaken the prosecution case or strengthen the defence, there would be no requirement to disclose it. Only in truly borderline cases should the prosecution seek a judicial ruling on the disclosability of material in their hands. In considering any disclosure issue the trial judge has constantly to bear in mind the overriding principle that derogation from the principle of full disclosure has always to be the minimum necessary to protect the public interest in question and must never imperil the overall fairness of the trial. Once material is considered to be sensitive then it should be disclosed only if the public interest application fails (unless abandoning the case is considered more appropriate) or with the express written approval of the Treasury Solicitor (Disclosure Manual, chapters 33–34). Such material is not as wide as it seems; for instance it does not mean evidence which might harm the prosecution case. This category is limited and the Code of Practice, at para. 6.12, gives a number of examples of such material. It will be for the disclosure officer to decide what material, if any, falls into this category. Guidance is provided in chapters 13 and 18 of the Disclosure Manual.

Paragraph 6.12 of the Code provides examples of sensitive material. Many of these items are included within the common law principles of public interest immunity. The case law in this area will still apply to decisions regarding the disclosure of such material. These groups are not exclusive and the areas most likely to apply will be those concerning the protection of intelligence and intelligence methods. In any consideration as to what should be withheld, the provisions of part II of the Regulation of Investigatory Powers Act 2000 should be referred to. Part II of the Act will make provision, not only for the gathering and recording of intelligence, but also disclosure of any material gained and methods used. Claims to withhold material may be made by parties other than the prosecutor (who would do so on behalf of the police). In some cases, the relevant minister or the Attorney-General may intervene to claim immunity. Alternatively, the claim to immunity may be made by the party seeking to withhold the evidence, either on its own initiative or at the request of the relevant government department.

Guidance is also provided in paras 20–22 of the A-G's Guidelines: even where an application is made to the court to withhold material a prosecutor should aim to disclose as much of the material as he/she properly can (by giving the defence redacted or edited copies of summaries).

In deciding whether material attracts public interest immunity the court will have to be satisfied that the material in no way helps the defence or undermines the prosecution case. Where the material related to secret or confidential systems it should not be revealed as this would aid serious criminal enterprise in the future (*R* v *Templar* [2003] EWCA Crim 3186).

Where police consider that material should not be disclosed due to its sensitive nature, the Disclosure Manual should be followed. This is covered at paras 8.5–8.27. Some of the key points from these paragraphs include the following:

- Consultation should take place at a senior level, and a senior officer (who may be independent of the investigation) should be involved.
- The consultation should cover:
  + the reasons why the material is said to be sensitive;
  + the degree of sensitivity said to attach to the material, i.e. why it is considered that disclosure will create a real risk of serious prejudice to an important public interest;
  + the consequences of revealing to the defence:
    — the material itself,
    — the category of the material,
    — the fact that an application is being made;
  + the apparent significance of the material to the issues in the trial;
  + the involvement of any third parties in bringing the material to the attention of the police;
  + where the material is likely to be the subject of an order for disclosure, what police views are regarding continuance of the prosecution.
- Any submission that is to be made to the court will be signed by the prosecutor, and by the senior officer, who will state that to the best of his/her knowledge and belief the assertions of fact on which the submission is based are correct. In applications for public interest immunity the CPS has an obligation to ensure that all such material is in its possession and the police have a duty to pass the material on (*R v Menga and Marshalleck* [1998] Crim LR 58.
- Whether it is possible to disclose the material without compromising its sensitivity.

Care must be taken to safeguard material that is sensitive and keep it separate from other material because if the material subject to a public interest immunity order for nondisclosure is inadvertently disclosed by the prosecution to lawyers for the defendants, those lawyers cannot be ordered not to further disseminate that material to any third party, including their own clients (*R v G* [2004] EWCA Crim 1368).

The investigator also has a responsibility to identify material that could be sensitive and bring this to the attention of the CPS. Where material is identified steps must be taken to record and retain the material. For information recorded on computers, see the JOPI Guidelines from para. 2.29 onwards.

---

## 1.10.8.4   KEYNOTE

### Informants

The courts recognise the need to protect the identity of informants to ensure that the supply of information about criminal activities does not dry up and to ensure the informants' own safety. However, there may be occasions where if the case is to continue the identity of an informant will have to be disclosed.

This is particularly so where there is a suggestion that an informant has participated in the events constituting, surrounding or following the crime; the judge must consider whether this role so impinges on an issue of interest to the defence, present or potential, as to make disclosure necessary (*R v Turner* [1995] 1 WLR 264).

In *R v Agar* [1990] 2 All ER 442 the court held that if a defence was manifestly frivolous and doomed to failure, a trial judge might conclude that it must be sacrificed to the general public interest in the protection of informers. But if there was a tenable defence the rule of public policy protecting informants was outweighed by the stronger public interest in allowing a defendant to put forward a case. In this case, the defendant alleged that the police had arranged with an informer to ask the accused to go to the informer's house, where drugs allegedly found on him had been planted by the police. The court ruled that the disclosure of the informant should have been made.

The need to disclose details of informants has been considered by the Court of Appeal in two cases. The first case, *R v Denton* [2002] EWCA Crim 272, concerned a defendant who was a police informer. The defendant was charged with murder and alleged that he had been told by his police handlers not to tell his lawyers about his status. The court held that there was no duty for the Crown to disclose to the defence, or to seek a ruling from the judge, as to any information regarding an accused being a police informer. On any common sense view, the material had already been disclosed to the defendant, and the Crown had no duty to supply the defendant with information with which he was already familiar. This last point may also be relevant to other situations. The second case, *R v Dervish* [2001] EWCA Crim 2789, concerned an undercover operation that was commenced after an informant gave information. The court held in this case that the public interest in protecting the identification of an informant had to be balanced against the right of the defendant to a fair trial; if there was material that might assist the defence, the necessity for the defendant to have a fair trial would outweigh the other interests in the case and the material would have to be disclosed or the prosecution discontinued. There had been no such material in this case. In *R v Edwards (formerly Steadman)* [2012] EWCA Crim 5, a murder case, the prosecution failed to disclose the fact that they were seeking one of the witness's registration as an informant, and that this witness was willing to give information if he did not receive any additional custodial sentence in respect of the offences with which he had been charged. The Court stated that these were factors which should have been made available to the jury in deciding the credibility of the witness. However, in the circumstances of the case, even with full and proper disclosure, the task of assessing this witness's reliability would have changed neither the landscape of the trial nor the jury's deliberations upon the evidence. The circumstantial case was compelling, and the verdict was safe.

Where an informant who has participated in the crime is called to give evidence at the trial there would have to be very strong reasons for this fact not to be disclosed (*R v Patel* [2001] EWCA Crim 2505).

There are strong links between the principles of informants and undercover police officers. In *R v Barkshire* [2011] EWCA Crim 1885 the Court of Appeal, upholding the appeal, held that recordings and the statement of an undercover police officer contained information which assisted the defence. They showed that the undercover officer had been involved in activities which went much further than the authorisation that he had been given. They appeared to show him as an enthusiastic supporter of criminal activity, arguably, as an *agent provocateur*. Further, the recordings supported the defendant's contentions that their intended activities were directed to the saving of life and avoidance of injury, and that they proposed to conduct the occupation in a careful and proportionate manner. This material was pertinent to a potential submission of abuse of process by way of entrapment and in any event had the capacity to support B's defence.

| 1.10.8.5 | **KEYNOTE** |
|---|---|

**Observation Points and the *Johnson* Ruling**

*R v Rankine* [1986] 2 WLR 1075, considering previous cases, stated that it was the rule that police officers should not be required to disclose sources of their information, whether those sources were paid informers or public spirited citizens, subject to a discretion to admit to avoid a miscarriage of justice and that observation posts were included in this rule.

In *R v Johnson* [1988] 1 WLR 1377, the appellant was convicted of supplying drugs. The only evidence against him was given by police officers, who testified that, while stationed in private premises in a known drug-dealing locality, they had observed him selling drugs. The defence applied to cross-examine the officers on the exact location of the observation posts, in order to test what they could see, having regard to the layout of the street and the objects in it. In the jury's absence, the prosecution called evidence as to the difficulty of obtaining assistance from the public, and the desire of the occupiers, who were also occupiers at the time of the offence, that their names and addresses should not be disclosed because they feared for their safety.

The judge ruled that the exact location of the premises need not be revealed. The appeal was dismissed; although the conduct of the defence was to some extent affected by the restraints placed on it, this led to no injustice. The jury were well aware of the restraints, and were most carefully directed about the very special care they had to give to any disadvantage they may have brought to the defence. *Johnson* was applied and approved in *R v Hewitt* (1992) 95 Cr App R 81 (see also *R v Grimes* [1994] Crim LR 213).

In *Johnson*, Watkins LJ at pp. 1385–6 gave the following guidance as to the minimum evidential requirements needed if disclosure is to be protected:

a) The police officer in charge of the observations to be conducted, no one of lower rank than a sergeant should usually be acceptable for this purpose, must be able to testify that beforehand he visited all observation places to be used and ascertained the attitude of occupiers of premises, not only to the use to be made of them, but to the possible disclosure thereafter of the use made and facts which could lead to the identification of the premises thereafter and of the occupiers. He may of course in addition inform the court of difficulties, if any, usually encountered in the particular locality of obtaining assistance from the public.

b) A police officer of no lower rank than a chief inspector must be able to testify that immediately prior to the trial he visited the places used for observations, the results of which it is proposed to give in evidence, and ascertained whether the occupiers are the same as when the observations took place and whether they are or are not, what the attitude of those occupiers is to the possible disclosure of the use previously made of the premises and of facts which could lead at the trial to identification of premises and occupiers.

Such evidence will of course be given in the absence of the jury when the application to exclude the material evidence is made. The judge should explain to the jury, as this judge did, when summing up or at some appropriate time before that, the effect of his ruling to exclude, if he so rules.

The guidelines in *Johnson* do not require a threat of violence before protection can be afforded to the occupier of an observation post; it suffices that the occupier is in fear of harassment (*Blake* v *DPP* (1993) 97 Cr App R 169).

This extended the rules established in *R* v *Rankine* [1986] QB 861 and is based on the protection of the owner or occupier of the premises, and not on the identity of the observation post. Thus, where officers have witnessed the commission of an offence as part of a surveillance operation conducted from an unmarked police vehicle, information relating to the surveillance and the colour, make and model of the vehicle should not be withheld (*R* v *Brown and Daley* (1988) 87 Cr App R 52).

## 1.10.9 | Disclosure Code of Practice—7 Revelation of Material to Prosecutor

7.1 The disclosure officer must give the schedules to the prosecutor. Wherever practicable this should be at the same time as he gives him the file containing the material for the prosecution case (or as soon as is reasonably practicable after the decision on mode of trial or the plea, in cases to which paragraph 6.8 applies).

7.2 The disclosure officer should draw the attention of the prosecutor to any material an investigator has retained (including material to which paragraph 6.13 applies) which may satisfy the test for prosecution disclosure in the Act, and should explain why he has come to that view.

7.3 At the same time as complying with the duties in paragraphs 7.1 and 7.2, the disclosure officer must give the prosecutor a copy of any material which falls into the following categories (unless such material has already been given to the prosecutor as part of the file containing the material for the prosecution case):

- information provided by an accused person which indicates an explanation for the offence with which he has been charged;
- any material casting doubt on the reliability of a confession;
- any material casting doubt on the reliability of a prosecution witness;
- any other material which the investigator believes may satisfy the test for prosecution disclosure in the Act.

7.4 If the prosecutor asks to inspect material which has not already been copied to him, the disclosure officer must allow him to inspect it. If the prosecutor asks for a copy of material which has not already been copied to him, the disclosure officer must give him a copy. However, this does not apply where the disclosure officer believes, having consulted the officer in charge of the investigation, that the material is too sensitive to be copied and can only be inspected.

7.5 If material consists of information which is recorded other than in writing, whether it should be given to the prosecutor in its original form as a whole, or by way of relevant extracts recorded in the same form, or in the form of a transcript, is a matter for agreement between the disclosure officer and the prosecutor.

1.10.9.1     **KEYNOTE**

**What Satisfies the Test for Prosecution Disclosure**

Paragraph 7.2 of the Code creates a catchall provision and presumably requires the disclosure officer to make inquiries of the other officers in the case to ensure that all material is included.

This would include any material individually or when viewed with other factors. Examples are material which:

- casts doubt upon the accuracy of any prosecution evidence;
- may point to another person, whether charged or not (including a co-accused) having involvement in the commission of the offence;
- casts doubt upon the reliability of a confession;
- might go to the credibility of a prosecution witness;
- might support a defence that is either raised by the defence or apparent from the prosecution papers;
- may have a bearing on the admissibility of any prosecution evidence;
- relates to the defendant's mental or physical health, or his/her intellectual capacity;
- relates to any ill-treatment which the defendant may have suffered when in the investigator's custody.

(A-G's Guidelines, paras 12 and 14)

However, what needs to be disclosed should be balanced by A-G's Guidelines:

Disclosure must not be an open-ended trawl of unused material. A critical element to fair and proper disclosure is that the defence play their role to ensure that the prosecution are directed to material which might reasonably be considered capable of undermining the prosecution case or assisting the case for the accused. This process is key to ensuring prosecutors make informed determinations about disclosure of unused material.

Fairness does recognise that there are other interests that need to be protected, including those of victims and witnesses who might otherwise be exposed to harm. The scheme of the Act protects those interests. It should also ensure that material is not disclosed which overburdens the participants in the trial process, diverts attention from the relevant issues, leads to unjustifiable delay, and is wasteful of resources. (A-G's Guidelines, paras 5 and 6)

The case of *R* v *Hadley* [2006] EWCA Crim 2544, it is suggested, shows that the courts will err on the side of caution when deciding if material should be disclosed as possibly undermining the prosecution case and that this approach should be considered prior to trial to avoid later appeals. In this case, the court held that, given the importance of disclosure in ensuring a fair trial, the court is likely to be slow to accept that the safety of a conviction is unaffected if it was satisfied that a substantial volume of disclosable material is wrongly withheld from the accused, unless the court could be satisfied that the evidence tending to establish guilt is so strong that the undisclosed material could have made no difference to the outcome of the case.

There will occasionally be cases where the police investigation has been intelligence-led; there may be a deputy disclosure officer appointed just to deal with intelligence material which, by its very nature, is likely to be sensitive (see para. 1.10.8.3). In cases where more than one disclosure officer has been appointed to deal with different aspects of the case, a lead disclosure officer should be identified as the single point of contact for the prosecutor. Where an officer other than the lead disclosure officer submits a disclosure schedule to the prosecutor, that officer should inform the lead disclosure officer (A-G's Guidelines, para. 26).

It should be noted that where material is available to police from a particular source, e.g. local authority records, a decision that some of the material is relevant does not mean that it all has to be disclosed. This point was reinforced by the case of *R* v *Abbott* [2003] EWCA Crim 350, where the Court of Appeal held that the defendant was not entitled to blanket disclosure of all the files. He was certainly not entitled to documents which were not relevant to the case.

**KEYNOTE**

**Time Period for Initial Disclosure**

While there are provisions to set specific time periods by which initial/primary disclosure must be met, none currently exist. Until such time, disclosure at this stage must be made as soon as practicable after the duty arises. Where disclosure is not made within a reasonable period it could lead to the case being lost. In *R* v *Bourimech* [2002] EWCA Crim 2089, the defendant sought disclosure following the service of his defence statement of a previous crime report made by the victim. One day before the trial was scheduled to begin, the crime report relating to that incident was served among other papers on the defence. This report escaped the notice of the defence until the final day of the trial. The court held that the defect in disclosure amounted to unfairness in the proceedings and the court could not be confident that if the victim had been cross-examined in relation to the previous allegation the jury might have been influenced by the credit and credibility of the witness.

The 1996 Act in effect only applies once the defendant has been committed/transferred to the Crown Court or is proceeding to trial in the magistrates'/youth court. In most cases prosecution disclosure can wait until after this time without jeopardising the defendant's right to a fair trial. However, the prosecutor must always be alive to the need to make advance disclosure of material that should be disclosed at an earlier stage (*R* v *DPP, ex parte Lee* [1999] 1 WLR 1950). Examples include:

- previous convictions of a complainant or a deceased if that information could reasonably be expected to assist the defence when applying for bail;
- material that might enable a defendant to make a pre-committal application to stay the proceedings as an abuse of process;
- material that might enable a defendant to submit that he/she should only be committed for trial on a lesser charge, or perhaps that he/she should not be committed for trial at all;
- depending on what the defendant chooses to reveal about his/her case at this early stage, material that would enable the defendant and his/her legal advisers to make preparations for trial that would be significantly less effective if disclosure were delayed; for example, names of eye-witnesses whom the prosecution did not intend to use.

It should be noted that any disclosure by the prosecution prior to committal would not normally exceed the initial disclosure which, after committal, would be required by s. 3 of the 1996 Act.

## 1.10.10 Disclosure Code of Practice—8 Subsequent Action by Disclosure Officer

8.1 At the time a schedule of non-sensitive material is prepared, the disclosure officer may not know exactly what material will form the case against the accused, and the prosecutor may not have given advice about the likely relevance of particular items of material. Once these matters have been determined, the disclosure officer must give the prosecutor, where necessary, an amended schedule listing any additional material:
  - which may be relevant to the investigation,
  - which does not form part of the case against the accused,
  - which is not already listed on the schedule, and
  - which he believes is not sensitive,

  unless he is informed in writing by the prosecutor that the prosecutor intends to disclose the material to the defence.

8.2 Section 7A of the Act imposes a continuing duty on the prosecutor, for the duration of criminal proceedings against the accused, to disclose material which satisfies the test for disclosure (subject to public interest considerations). To enable him to do this, any new material coming to light should be treated in the same way as the earlier material.

8.3 In particular, after a defence statement has been given, the disclosure officer must look again at the material which has been retained and must draw the attention of the prosecutor to any material which might reasonably be considered capable of undermining the case for the prosecution against the accused or of assisting the case for the accused; and he must reveal it to him in accordance with paragraphs 7.4 and 7.5 above.

**KEYNOTE**

**Disclosure by the Defence**

The duty on the defence to make disclosure only arises *after* the prosecution has made the initial disclosure (s. 5(1) of the 1996 Act). This duty falls into two categories: compulsory and voluntary. The disclosure required by the defence is limited to material that they intend to use at trial.

The defence statement should set out the nature of the defendant's defence, including any particular defences on which he/she intends to rely, particulars of the matters of fact on which the defendant intends to rely; this means the defence will need to disclose a factual narrative of their case. In addition, those issues, relevant to the case, which the accused disputes with the prosecution must be set out with reasons. Additionally, from 4 April 2005 the defence statement must indicate any point of law (including any point as to the admissibility of evidence or an abuse of process) which the defendant wishes to raise, and any authority on which he/she intends to rely for that purpose (s. 6A of the 1996 Act). This requirement to give reasons is intended to stop the defence going on a 'fishing expedition' to speculatively look at material in order to find some kind of defence.

Where the defence case involves an alibi, the statement must give details of the alibi, including the name and address of any alibi witness. In cases where there are co-accused, there is no duty to disclose this information to the other defendants, although this could be done voluntarily.

An alibi for the purposes of the defence statement is defined as evidence tending to show that by reason of the presence of the accused at a particular place or in a particular area at a particular time, he/she was not, or was unlikely to have been, at the place where the offence is alleged to have been committed at the time of its alleged commission. Where this applies, the defence must provide details including the name, address and date of birth of any witness the accused believes is able to give evidence in support of the alibi, or as many of those details as are known to the accused when the statement is given. Where such details are not known, the statement must include any information in the accused's possession which might be of material assistance in identifying or finding any such witness (s. 6A(2) of the 1996 Act).

The defence must also give to the court and the prosecutor notice of any other witnesses other than the defendant who will be called to give evidence. If any other witness is to be called then the name, address and date of birth of each such proposed witness, or as many of those details as are known to the accused must be provided. If any of this information is not available the defence must provide any information in their possession which might be of material assistance in identifying or finding any such proposed witness (s. 6C of the 1996 Act), see para. 1.10.10.7.

There may be occasions where the defence statement is allowed to be used in cross-examination when it is alleged that the defendant has changed his/her defence or in re-examination to rebut a suggestion of recent invention (*R* v *Lowe* [2003] EWCA Crim 3182).

**KEYNOTE**

**Compulsory Disclosure by Defence (s. 5)**

The duty for the defence to make disclosure does not apply to cases being tried summarily. Where there are other accused in the proceedings and the court so orders, the accused must also give a defence statement to each of the other accused specified by the court, and a request for a copy of the defence statement may be made by any co-accused.

Once a defence statement has been provided (whether compulsorily or voluntarily), the prosecution must disclose any prosecution material that:

- might be reasonably expected to assist the accused's defence; and
- has not already been disclosed.

It will be a question of fact whether material in police possession might be reasonably expected to assist the defence case. If the court feels that material that was not disclosed would to any reasonable person have been expected to help the defence case, the case may fail.

If there is no additional material to be disclosed then the prosecutor must give a written statement to this effect. It is not the responsibility of the prosecutor or the police to examine material held by third parties which the defence have stated they wish to examine (the defence can request this from the third party or apply for a witness summons). However, there may be occasions where matters disclosed in the defence statement lead investigators to look at material held by third parties as it might impact on the prosecution case. This stage of the disclosure process may require further inquiries prompted by the defence statement. The result of those inquiries may then have to be disclosed because it either undermines the prosecution case or it assists the accused's defence.

Where the defence statement points the prosecution to other lines of inquiry, e.g. the investigation of an alibi, or where forensic expert evidence is involved, the disclosure officer should inform the officer in charge of the investigation and copy the defence statement to him/her, together with any CPS advice provided if appropriate (Disclosure Manual, para. 15.17).

---

**1.10.10.3**    **KEYNOTE**

**Voluntary Disclosure by Accused (s. 6)**

The purpose of s. 6 of the 1996 Act is to allow the defence, in cases where the case is being tried summarily as a not guilty plea, to obtain further disclosure from the prosecution after the initial/primary disclosure. This is only likely to happen where:

- the defence are not satisfied with the material disclosed at the initial/primary disclosure stage or where they wish to examine items listed in the schedule of non-sensitive material;
- the defence wish to show the strength of their case in order to persuade the prosecution not to proceed.

If the defence decide to make a defence statement they must comply with the same conditions imposed on compulsory defence disclosure.

---

**1.10.10.4**    **KEYNOTE**

**Time Period for the Defence Statement**

Once the prosecution provides the initial disclosure, the defence have 14 days in respect of summary proceedings, or 28 days in respect of Crown Court proceedings within which the accused in criminal proceedings must give: a compulsory defence statement under s. 5 of the Act; a voluntary defence statement under s. 6 of the Act; or a notice of his/her intention to call any person, other than him/herself, as a witness at trial under s. 6C of the Act (Alibi witness). The court can only grant an extension if satisfied that the accused could not reasonably have given a defence statement or given notification within the relevant period. There is no limit on the number of days by which the relevant period may be extended or the number of applications for extensions that may be made (Criminal Procedure and Investigations Act 1996 (Defence Disclosure Time Limits) Regulations 2011 (SI 2011/209)).

---

**1.10.10.5**    **KEYNOTE**

**Effect of Failure in Defence Disclosure**

If the defence fail to give a defence statement under s. 5 or, where a defence statement is provided, they:

- are outside the time limits;
- set out inconsistent defences in a defence statement or at trial put forward a different defence; or
- at trial adduce evidence in support of an alibi without having given particulars of the alibi in a defence statement, or call a witness in support of an alibi without providing details of the witness or information that might help trace the witness;

then the following sanctions may apply:

- the court or, with the leave of the court, any other party may make such comment as appears appropriate;
- the court or jury may draw such inferences as appear proper in deciding whether the accused is guilty of the offence concerned (but there must also be other evidence to convict the defendant);
- even if the defence serve the defence statement outside the time limits, the prosecution must still consider the impact of the statement in terms of the need for any further disclosure (*Murphy* v *DPP* [2006] EWHC 1753 (Admin)).

---

**1.10.10.6**        **KEYNOTE**

**Continuing Duty of Prosecutor to Disclose (s. 7A)**

For investigations commencing after 4 April 2005, ss. 7 and 9 are repealed and replaced by s. 7A, which places a continuing duty on the prosecutor at any time between the initial disclosure and the accused being acquitted or convicted or the prosecutor deciding not to proceed with the case concerned, to keep under review the question of further disclosure. In considering the need for further disclosure the prosecutor must consider whether material might reasonably be considered capable of undermining the case for the prosecution against the accused or of assisting the case for the accused. If there is any such material, it must be disclosed to the accused as soon as is reasonably practicable. Consideration of what might need to be disclosed could change depending on the state of affairs at that time (including the case for the prosecution as it then stands) and so should be reviewed on a continuing basis (s. 7A(4)).

In *R* v *Tyrell* [2004] EWCA Crim 3279 this responsibility was clearly outlined. The court held that there was an obligation to consider whether there was any material in the hands of the prosecution which might undermine the case against the applicants or might reasonably be expected to assist the disclosed defences. In addition, the Crown had to consider whether there was any material which might be relevant to an issue which might feature in the trial; this clearly required a continuing duty. In this case, the court found that disclosure had been considered many times as the case progressed in relation to a variety of issues as they arose and ensured a fair trial.

Material must not be disclosed to the extent that the court concludes that it is not in the public interest to disclose it and orders accordingly or it is material whose disclosure is prohibited by s. 17 of the Regulation of Investigatory Powers Act 2000.

There is a duty on the prosecution to continue to review the disclosure of prosecution material right up until the case is completed (acquittal, conviction or discontinuance of the case). This point was reinforced in *R* v *Joof* [2012] EWCA Crim 1475 where the court held that the responsibilities imposed by the Criminal Procedure and Investigations Act 1996 and the A-G's Guidelines could not be circumvented by not making inquiries. An officer who believed that a person might have information which might undermine the prosecution case or assist the defence could not decline to make inquiries in order to avoid the need to disclose what might be said.

If the defence are not satisfied that the prosecution have disclosed all they should have, s. 8 of the 1996 Act allows for the defence to apply to the court for further disclosure.

---

**1.10.10.7**        **KEYNOTE**

**Interviewing Defence Witnesses or Alibi Witnesses**

Section 21A of the Criminal Procedure and Investigations Act 1996 introduced a Code of Practice for Arranging and Conducting Interviews of Witnesses Notified by the Accused. The Code sets out guidance that police officers and other persons charged with investigating offences must follow if they arrange or conduct interviews of proposed witnesses whose details are disclosed to the prosecution under the 1996 Act. These are set out below:

## Arrangement of the interview

*Information to be provided to the witness before any interview may take place*

3.1 If an investigator wishes to interview a witness, the witness must be asked whether he consents to being interviewed and informed that:

- an interview is being requested following his identification by the accused as a proposed witness under section 6A(2) or section 6C of the Act,
- he is not obliged to attend the proposed interview,
- he is entitled to be accompanied by a solicitor at the interview (but nothing in this Code of Practice creates any duty on the part of the Legal Services Commission to provide funding for any such attendance), and
- a record will be made of the interview and he will subsequently be sent a copy of the record.

3.2 If the witness consents to being interviewed, the witness must be asked:

- whether he wishes to have a solicitor present at the interview,
- whether he consents to a solicitor attending the interview on behalf of the accused, as an observer, and
- whether he consents to a copy of the record being sent to the accused. If he does not consent, the witness must be informed that the effect of disclosure requirements in criminal proceedings may nevertheless require the prosecution to disclose the record to the accused (and any co-accused) in the course of the proceedings.

*Information to be provided to the accused before any interview may take place*

4.1 The investigator must notify the accused or, if the accused is legally represented in the proceedings, the accused's representatives:

- that the investigator requested an interview with the witness,
- whether the witness consented to the interview, and
- if the witness consented to the interview, whether the witness also consented to a solicitor attending the interview on behalf of the accused, as an observer.

4.2 If the accused is not legally represented in the proceedings, and if the witness consents to a solicitor attending the interview on behalf of the accused, the accused must be offered the opportunity, a reasonable time before the interview is held, to appoint a solicitor to attend it.

*Identification of the date, time and venue for the interview*

5 The investigator must nominate a reasonable date, time and venue for the interview and notify the witness of them and any subsequent changes to them.

*Notification to the accused's solicitor of the date, time and venue of the interview*

6 If the witness has consented to the presence of the accused's solicitor, the accused's solicitor must be notified that the interview is taking place, invited to observe, and provided with reasonable notice of the date, time and venue of the interview and any subsequent changes.

## Conduct of the interview

*The investigator conducting the interview*

7 The identity of the investigator conducting the interview must be recorded. That person must have sufficient skills and authority, commensurate with the complexity of the investigation, to discharge his functions effectively. That person must not conduct the interview if that is likely to result in a conflict of interest, for instance, if that person is the victim of the alleged crime which is the subject of the proceedings. The advice of a more senior officer must always be sought if there is doubt as to whether a conflict of interest precludes an individual conducting the interview. If thereafter the doubt remains, the advice of a prosecutor must be sought.

*Attendance of the accused's solicitor*

8.1 The accused's solicitor may only attend the interview if the witness has consented to his presence as an observer. Provided that the accused's solicitor was given reasonable notice of the date, time and place of the interview, the fact that the accused's solicitor is not present will not prevent the interview from being conducted. If the witness at any time withdraws consent to the accused's solicitor being present at the interview, the interview may continue without the presence of the accused's solicitor.

8.2 The accused's solicitor may attend only as an observer.

*Attendance of the witness's solicitor*

9 Where a witness has indicated that he wishes to appoint a solicitor to be present, that solicitor must be permitted to attend the interview.

*Attendance of any other appropriate person*

10 A witness under the age of 18 or a witness who is mentally disordered or otherwise mentally vulnerable must be interviewed in the presence of an appropriate person.

*Recording of the interview*

11.1 An accurate record must be made of the interview, whether it takes place at a police station or elsewhere. The record must be made, where practicable, by audio recording or by visual recording with sound, or otherwise in writing. Any written record must be made and completed during the interview, unless this would not be practicable or would interfere with the conduct of the interview, and must constitute either a verbatim record of what has been said or, failing this, an account of the interview which adequately and accurately summarises it. If a written record is not made during the interview it must be made as soon as practicable after its completion. Written interview records must be timed and signed by the maker.

11.2 A copy of the record must be given, within a reasonable time of the interview, to:

(a) the witness, and

(b) if the witness consents, to the accused or the accused's solicitor.

## 1.10.11   Disclosure Code of Practice—9 Certification by Disclosure Officer

9.1 The disclosure officer must certify to the prosecutor that to the best of his knowledge and belief, all relevant material which has been retained and made available to him has been revealed to the prosecutor in accordance with this Code. He must sign and date the certificate. It will be necessary to certify not only at the time when the schedule and accompanying material is submitted to the prosecutor, and when relevant material which has been retained is reconsidered after the accused has given a defence statement, but also whenever a schedule is otherwise given or material is otherwise revealed to the prosecutor.

## 1.10.12   Disclosure Code of Practice—10 Disclosure of Material to Accused

10.1 If material has not already been copied to the prosecutor, and he requests its disclosure to the accused on the ground that:

- it satisfies the test for prosecution disclosure, or
- the court has ordered its disclosure after considering an application from the accused,

the disclosure officer must disclose it to the accused.

10.2 If material has been copied to the prosecutor, and it is to be disclosed, whether it is disclosed by the prosecutor or the disclosure officer is a matter of agreement between the two of them.

10.3 The disclosure officer must disclose material to the accused either by giving him a copy or by allowing him to inspect it. If the accused person asks for a copy of any material which he has been allowed to inspect, the disclosure officer must give it to him, unless in the opinion of the disclosure officer that is either not practicable (for example because the material consists of an object which cannot be copied, or because the volume of material is so great), or not desirable (for example because the material is a statement by a child witness in relation to a sexual offence).

10.4 If material which the accused has been allowed to inspect consists of information which is recorded other than in writing, whether it should be given to the accused in its original form or in the form of a transcript is matter for the discretion of the disclosure officer. If the material is transcribed, the disclosure officer must ensure that the transcript is certified to the accused as a true record of the material which has been transcribed.

10.5 If a court concludes that an item of sensitive material satisfies the prosecution disclosure test and that the interests of the defence outweigh the public interest in withholding disclosure, it will be necessary to disclose the material if the case is to proceed. This does not mean that sensitive documents must always be disclosed in their original form: for example, the court may agree that sensitive details still requiring protection should be blocked out, or that documents may be summarised, or that the prosecutor may make an admission about the substance of the material under section 10 of the Criminal Justice Act 1967.

**1.10.12.1**

## KEYNOTE

### Disclosing Material to the Defence

The court can order disclosure of material which the prosecution contend is sensitive. In such cases it may be appropriate to seek guidance on whether to disclose the material or offer no evidence, thereby protecting the sensitive material or the source of that material (e.g. where informants or surveillance techniques are involved).

For further guidance, see the Disclosure Manual, paras 10.16, 10.17 and 12.25. Forces may have instructions as to providing further copies when requested by the defence in relation to procedures and costs. It is suggested that where copies are provided, some proof of delivery should be obtained.

**1.10.12.2**

## KEYNOTE

### Disclosure of Statements in Cases of Complaints against the Police

Statements made by witnesses during an investigation of a complaint against a police officer are disclosable; however, the timing of the disclosure may be controlled. In *R v Police Complaints Authority, ex parte Green* [2002] EWCA Civ 389, the Court of Appeal stated that there is no requirement to disclose witness statements to eye-witness complainants during the course of an investigation. The evidence of such complainants could be contaminated and, therefore, disclosure would risk hindering or frustrating the very purpose of the investigation. A complainant's legitimate interests were appropriately and adequately safeguarded by his/her right to a thorough and independent investigation, to contribute to the evidence, to be kept informed of the progress of the investigation and to be given reasoned conclusions on completion of the investigation. However, a complainant had no right to participate in the investigation as though he/she were supervising it. The general rule was that complainants, whether victims or next of kin, were not entitled to the disclosure of witness statements used in the course of a police investigation until its conclusion at the earliest.

Police complaints and disciplinary files may also fall within sensitive material that does not have to be disclosed (*Halford v Sharples* [1992] 1 WLR 736). This would not apply to written complaints against the police prompting investigations or the actual statements obtained during the investigations, although immunity may be claimed in the case of a particular document by reason of its contents (*R v Chief Constable of the West Midlands Police, ex parte Wiley* [1995] 1 AC 274). However, the working papers and reports prepared by the investigating officers do form a class which is entitled to immunity and therefore production of such material should be ordered only where the public interest in disclosure of their contents outweighs the public interest in preserving confidentiality (*Taylor v Anderton* [1995] 1 WLR 447).

**1.10.12.3**

## KEYNOTE

### Confidentiality

The defence may only use material disclosed to them under the 1996 Act for purposes related to the defence case; any other use will be a contempt of court. Once evidence has been given in open court, however, the material is available for other purposes.

# 1.11 Issues in Evidence

### 1.11.1 Introduction

Evidence can be described as information that may be presented to a court so that it may decide on the probability of some facts asserted before it, that is information by which facts in issue tend to be proved or disproved. There are several types of evidence by which facts are open to proof—or disproof—and these are discussed below.

### 1.11.2 Weight and Admissibility of Evidence

The two questions that need to be applied to any evidence are:

- admissibility; and
- weight.

The question of admissibility, to be decided by the judge in all cases, is whether the evidence is relevant to a fact in issue. All evidence of facts in issue and all evidence which is sufficiently relevant to prove (or disprove) facts in issue are potentially admissible.

The admissibility of evidence is very important to the outcome of any trial as it is from this that a person's guilt is decided. When collecting evidence in a case it should always be a consideration whether the evidence being collected is the best available and whether it will be admissible.

Once it is established that the evidence is admissible, it is put before the court to determine what weight it will attach to the evidence, that is, how much effect does it have on proving or disproving the case.

#### 1.11.2.1 Evidence Gathering

The word evidence must not be confused with information. In relation to preparing an offence file, the investigation of the offence will result in the collection of information. What is and what is not evidence can be decided at a later stage with the help of the CPS. The importance of this distinction is that rules of evidence should not restrict the initial collection of information, otherwise a fact vital to the outcome of the case may be disregarded as irrelevant and/or inadmissible.

#### 1.11.2.2 Reasons for Excluding Admissible Evidence

Even though evidence may be admissible in criminal cases, at common law, the trial judge has a general discretion to exclude legally admissible evidence tendered by the prosecution. This can be seen in *R* v *Sang* [1980] AC 402, where it was held that:

- A trial judge, as part of his/her duty to ensure that an accused receives a fair trial, always has a discretion to exclude evidence tendered by the prosecution if in his/her opinion its prejudicial effect outweighs its probative value. In deciding if the evidence should be admitted, the question the judge asks him/herself is whether it is fair to allow the evidence, not whether it is obtained fairly or by unfair means.

- With the exception of admissions and confessions (here s. 76 of the Police and Criminal Evidence Act 1984 applies) and generally with regard to evidence obtained from the accused after the commission of the offence, the judge generally has no discretion whether to exclude relevant admissible evidence on the ground that this was obtained by improper or unfair means.

If the evidence is relevant to the matters in issue then it is admissible and the court is not concerned with how the evidence was obtained *(Kuruma, Son of Kaniu* v *The Queen* [1955] AC 197). This proposition was upheld in *Jeffrey* v *Black* [1978] QB 490 where evidence was admissible concerning the unlawful search of premises.

Evidence may also be excluded for the following reasons:

- the incompetence of the witness;
- it relates to previous convictions, the character or disposition of the accused;
- it falls under hearsay;
- it is non-expert opinion evidence;
- it is privileged information;
- it is withheld as a matter of public policy.

There are also powers to exclude evidence under ss. 76 and 78 of the Police and Criminal Evidence Act 1984.

## 1.11.3 Facts in Issue

In a criminal case, facts in issue are those facts which must be proved by the prosecution in order to establish the defendant's guilt, or in exceptional cases those facts which are the essential elements of a defence, where the burden of proof is on the defendant to prove the defence.

Such facts will include:

- the identity of the defendant;
- the *actus reus;*
- the *mens rea.*

The relevant criminal conduct (*actus reus*) and state of mind (*mens rea*) will always be facts in issue, and it is therefore essential that these features are understood, both as general concepts and also in relation to the particular offence being investigated.

## 1.11.4 Burden of Proof

In *Re B* (*Children*) [2008] UKHL 35 Lord Hoffmann commented:

> If a legal rule requires a fact to be proved (a 'fact in issue'), a judge or jury must decide whether or not it happened. There is no room for a finding that it might have happened. The law operates a binary system in which the only values are 0 and 1. The fact either happened or it did not. If the tribunal is left in doubt, the doubt is resolved by a rule that one party or the other carries the burden of proof. If the party who bears the burden of proof falls to discharge it, a value of 0 is returned and the fact is treated as not having happened. If he does discharge it, a value of 1 is returned and the fact is treated as having happened.

The facts in issue fall into two distinct categories:

- the facts that the *prosecution* bear the burden of proving or disproving in order to establish the defendant's guilt;
- the facts which, in exceptional circumstances, the *defence* need to prove to show that the defendant is not guilty.

### 1.11.4.1 Duty of the Prosecution

'Throughout the web of the English criminal law one golden thread is always to be seen; that is the duty of the prosecution to prove the prisoner's guilt.' This famous passage is taken from the House of Lords' decision in *Woolmington* v *DPP* [1935] AC 462. The underlying principle was perhaps best explained by Geoffrey Lawrence QC in an address to the jury in a murder trial:

> The possibility of guilt is not enough, suspicion is not enough, probability is not enough, likelihood is not. A criminal matter is not a question of balancing probabilities and deciding in favour of probability.
>
> If the accusation is not proved beyond reasonable doubt against the man accused in the dock, then by the law he is entitled to be acquitted, because that is the way our rules work. It is no concession to give him the benefit of the doubt. He is entitled by law to a verdict of not guilty.

(See Brian Harris, *The Literature of the Law,* Blackstone Press, 1998.)

Therefore the general rule is that the prosecution have the legal (or persuasive) burden of proving all the elements of the offence in order to prove guilt.

In *Evans* v *DPP* [2001] EWHC Admin 369, it was held that the justices had wrongly applied *the balance of probabilities* in finding the defendant guilty rather than the full criminal standard of proof.

Where the defendant enters a plea of not guilty to the charge, the onus is on the prosecution to prove the whole of their case. This includes the 'identity of the accused, the nature of the act and the existence of any necessary knowledge or intent' (*R* v *Sims* [1946] KB 531).

Generally the onus is on the prosecution in the first instance to establish particular facts to prove the accused's guilt beyond all reasonable doubt. However, once a *prima facie* case is made out, the defence have to establish particular facts in order to rebut the prosecution evidence. Here there is a shift of the onus to establish particular facts.

### 1.11.4.2 Duty of the Defence

Exceptionally, the defence may have the burden of proof. In such circumstances the standard of proof for the defence is less rigorous than for the prosecution when establishing guilt (beyond all reasonable doubt). The defence will succeed if the court or jury are satisfied that the defence evidence is more probably true than false. This standard of proof is referred to as *the balance of probabilities,* the same standard of proof as operates in a civil trial.

Generally the prosecution bear the duty of proving or disproving certain facts and, if they fail to do so, the defence need say nothing; the prosecution fails and the defendant is acquitted.

Exceptionally, the common law (e.g. the defence of insanity), or a statute (e.g. diminished responsibility (s. 2 of the Homicide Act 1957)), may impose a burden on the defence to prove the defence.

The law relating to the carrying of weapons is a good illustration of where the defence may have a burden of proof. Once the prosecution have proved (beyond a reasonable doubt) that a defendant was carrying an offensive weapon, the burden then shifts to the defence to prove (on the balance of probabilities) that the defendant had lawful authority or reasonable excuse.

There will also be occasions where the defence have what is called an *evidential burden* in relation to certain specific defences they intend to rely on. Common examples of defences that only place an evidential burden on the defence are defences relating to alibis, self-defence, accident and provocation. In contrast to the evidential burden borne by the prosecution (to show that there is a case to answer by the end of the prosecution evidence), the defence's evidential burden arises somewhat differently. Unlike those defences that place a full legal burden of proof on the defence, the defence do not have to satisfy the judge of anything as such. All that the defence have to do is to ensure that there is enough evidence relating to the defence that is to be raised to enable the judge to direct the jury upon that defence as a live issue.

Section 101 of the Magistrates' Courts Act 1980 places a legal burden of proof on the accused either expressly or by implication. The section provides that where the accused relies for his/her defence on any *exemption, proviso, excuse* or *qualification*, the burden of proving this is on the accused.

---

**KEYNOTE**

An example of a summary offence where the burden of proof is on the defence is driving without insurance where the accused is required to prove he/she is insured (*Williams* v *Russell* (1933) 149 LT 190). An example of an indictable offence is where the accused was convicted on indictment of selling intoxicating liquor without a licence and the Court of Appeal held that it was for the accused to prove that he was the holder of a licence (*R* v *Edwards* [1975] QB 27).

---

# 1.12 | Offences Against the Administration of Justice and Public Interest

## 1.12.1 Perjury

OFFENCE: **Perjury in Judicial Proceeding—*Perjury Act 1911, s. 1***
- Triable on indictment • Seven years' imprisonment

The Perjury Act 1911, s. 1 states:

(1) If any person lawfully sworn as a witness or as an interpreter in a judicial proceedings wilfully makes a statement material in that proceeding, which he knows to be false or does not believe to be true, he shall be guilty of perjury...

(2) The expression 'judicial proceeding' includes a proceeding before any court, tribunal, or person having by law power to hear, receive, and examine evidence on oath.

(3) Where a statement made for the purposes of a judicial proceeding is not made before the tribunal itself, but is made on oath before a person authorised by law to administer an oath to the person who makes the statement, and to record or authenticate the statement, it shall, for the purposes of this section, be treated as having been made in a judicial proceeding.

---

**KEYNOTE**

To commit this offence a defendant must have been *lawfully sworn* (see the Evidence Act 1851, s. 16). The statement made in 'judicial proceeding' can be one given orally before the court or tribunal, or it can be given in the form of an affidavit (sworn statement). If a witness tenders a false statement used under s. 89 of the Criminal Justice Act 1967, he/she commits a separate, lesser offence.

'Wilful' in this case means deliberate or intentional and it must be proved that any alleged perjury was not the result of a misunderstanding or an accidental slip of the tongue (*R v Millward* [1985] QB 519).

A 'statement material in that proceeding' means that the content of the evidence tendered in that case must have some importance to it and not just be of passing relevance. Whether something is material to a case is a question of law for a judge to decide. Whether a motorist had taken a drink between the time of having a road traffic accident and being breathalysed would be such a material issue, and to get a witness to provide false evidence about that matter would be a 'statement material in that proceeding' (*R v Lewins* (1979) 1 Cr App R (S) 246).

To prove perjury you must also show that the defendant *knew* the statement to be false or *did not believe it to be true*.

Evidence of an opinion provided by a witness who does not genuinely hold such an opinion may also be perjury.

Perjury may be proved by using a court transcript or the evidence of others who were present at the proceeding in question (see Perjury Act 1911, s. 14).

Corroboration is required in cases of perjury (see Perjury Act 1911, s. 13). The requirement for corroboration is solely in relation to the *falsity* of the defendant's statement. There is no requirement under s. 13 for corroboration of the fact that the defendant *actually made* the alleged statement, nor that he/she knew or believed it to be untrue. However, as that corroboration can be documentary and may even come from the defendant's earlier conduct (*R v Threlfall* (1914) 10 Cr App R 112) this requirement does not appear to present much of a hurdle to the prosecution.

Evidence given by live TV link under the provisions of the Criminal Justice Act 1988, s. 32 is also subject to the offence of perjury.

---

### 1.12.1.1 Aiding and Abetting

OFFENCE: **Aiding and Abetting Perjury—*Perjury Act 1911, s. 7***
- If principal offence is contrary to s.1 triable on indictment • Seven years' imprisonment • Otherwise either way • Two years' imprisonment on indictment
- Six months' imprisonment and/or a fine summarily

The Perjury Act 1911, s. 7 states:

(1) Every person who aids, abets, counsels, procures, or suborns another person to commit an offence against this Act shall be liable to be proceeded against, indicted, tried and punished as if he were a principal offender.

(2) Every person who incites...another person to commit an offence against this Act shall be guilty of a misdemeanour.

---

**KEYNOTE**

'Subornation' is the same as procuring. This specific section does not appear to add anything to the general offences of aiding and abetting principal offenders (see chapter 1.2).

---

## 1.12.2 Perverting the Course of Justice

OFFENCE: **Perverting the Course of Justice—*Common Law***
- Triable on indictment • Life imprisonment and/or a fine

It is an offence at common law to do an act tending and intended to pervert the course of public justice.

---

**KEYNOTE**

'The course of public justice' includes the process of criminal investigation (see *R* v *Rowell* (1978) 1 WLR 132).

Although traditionally referred to—and charged—as 'attempting' to pervert the course of justice, it is recognised that behaviour which is *aimed* at perverting the course of public justice does just that and the substantive offence should be charged (see *R* v *Williams* (1991) 92 Cr App R 158).

One way in which this offence is commonly committed is where a prisoner uses a false identity when arrested. Although the offence of perverting the course of justice may be made out in these—or similar—circumstances in connection with a number of other substantive offences, the Court of Appeal has held that, in many cases, the addition of such a charge is unnecessary and only serves to complicate the sentencing process (*R* v *Sookoo* [2002] EWCA Crim 800). Whereas, in *Sookoo*, a defendant makes an unsophisticated attempt to hide his/her identity and fails, the court felt that a specific separate count of perverting the course of justice should not be laid. If it was shown that there were serious aggravating features, for instance where a lot of police time and resources had been involved or innocent members of the public had been arrested as a result, a specific charge may be appropriate and could be justified.

Perverting the course of justice requires positive acts by the defendant, not merely standing by and allowing an injustice to take place, i.e. omissions. The offence will include cases where evidence is deliberately destroyed, concealed or falsified as well as cases where witnesses and jurors are intimidated.

Admitting to a crime to enable the true offender to avoid prosecution would fall under this offence (*R* v *Devito* [1975] Crim LR 175), as would abusing your authority as a police officer to excuse someone of a criminal charge (*R* v *Coxhead* [1986] RTR 411). Other examples include:

- making a false allegation of an offence (*R* v *Goodwin* (1989) 11 Cr App R (S) 194 (rape);
- giving another person's personal details when being reported for an offence (*R* v *Hurst* (1990–91) 12 Cr App R (S) 373);
- destroying and concealing evidence of a crime (*R* v *Kiffin* [1994] Crim LR 449).

---

It is important that the requisite intention is proved in every case as that intention cannot be implied, even from admitted facts (*R* v *Lalani* [1999] 1 Cr App R 481).

Where a person makes a false allegation to the police justifying a criminal investigation with the possible consequences of detention, arrest, charge or prosecution and that person intends that the allegation be taken seriously, the offence of perverting the course of justice is *prima facie* made out—whether or not the allegation is capable of identifying specific individuals. This is clear from *R* v *Cotter* [2002] EWCA Crim 1033, a case involving the boyfriend of a black Olympic athlete who claimed to have been attacked as part of a racist campaign.

### 1.12.3 Considerations Affecting Witnesses, Jurors and Others

There are several significant areas of common and statute law to consider when considering witnesses. The main legislative provisions are set out below.

The Serious Organised Crime and Police Act 2005 sets out specific provisions relating to witness protection arrangements. In fact these arrangements stretch beyond witnesses and extend to a series of people involved in the criminal justice process, including people who are *or have been*:

- constables
- employees accredited under the Police Reform Act 2002
- jurors
- magistrates (or their equivalent outside the United Kingdom)
- holders of judicial office (whether in the United Kingdom or elsewhere)
- the DPP, criminal prosecutors and staff of the Crown Prosecution Service

(see the Serious Organised Crime and Police Act 2005, sch. 5).

Chapter 4 of the Act allows for the making of arrangements to protect these and other relevant people ordinarily resident in the United Kingdom where the 'protection provider' (usually the Chief Officer of Police or the Director General of the Serious Organised Crime Agency) considers that the person's safety is at risk by virtue of being a witness, constable, juror etc. (s. 82(1)). A protection provider may vary or cancel any arrangements made by him/her under subs. (1) if the provider considers it appropriate to do so. Joint arrangements (e.g. between police forces) can be made where appropriate, and public authorities (other than courts and tribunals or parliament) are under a duty to take reasonable steps to assist protection providers where requested to do so (see ss. 83 and 85).

#### 1.12.3.1 Witnesses or Jurors in Investigation or Proceedings for an Offence

The first measure can be found in the Criminal Justice and Public Order Act 1994.

OFFENCE: **Intimidating Witnesses and Jurors—*Criminal Justice and Public Order Act 1994, s. 51***
- Triable either way • Five years' imprisonment and/or a fine on indictment
- Six months' imprisonment and/or a fine summarily

The Criminal Justice and Public Order Act 1994, s. 51 states:

(1) A person commits an offence if—
   (a) he does an act which intimidates, and is intended to intimidate, another person ('the victim'),
   (b) he does the act knowing or believing that the victim is assisting in the investigation of an offence or is a witness or potential witness or a juror or potential juror in proceedings for an offence, and
   (c) he does it intending thereby to cause the investigation or the course of justice to be obstructed, perverted or interfered with.

(2) A person commits an offence if—
  (a) he does an act which harms, and is intended to harm, another person or, intending to cause another person to fear harm, he threatens to do an act which would harm that other person,
  (b) he does or threatens to do the act knowing or believing that the person harmed or threatened to be harmed ('the victim'), or some other person, has assisted in an investigation into an offence or has given evidence or particular evidence in proceedings for an offence, or has acted as a juror or concurred in a particular verdict in proceedings for an offence, and
  (c) he does or threatens to do it because of that knowledge or belief.
(3) For the purposes of subsections (1) and (2) it is immaterial that the act is or would be done, or that the threat is made—
  (a) otherwise than in the presence of the victim, or
  (b) to a person other than the victim.
(4) The harm that may be done or threatened may be financial as well as physical (whether to the person or a person's property) and similarly as respects an intimidatory act which consists of threats.
(5) The intention required by subsection (1)(c) and the motive required by subsection (2)(c) above need not be the only or the predominating intention or motive with which the act is done or, in the case of subsection (2), threatened.

---

### KEYNOTE

These offences are designed to exist alongside the common-law offence of perverting the course of justice, and there will be circumstances which may fall under both the statutory and the common-law offences.

This is an offence of 'specific intent' as it must be shown that the act was done with the intentions set out in s. 51(1)(a) and (c). It must also be shown that the defendant knew or believed the other person to be assisting in the investigation of an offence or that the person was going to testify/appear on the jury in proceedings for an offence.

In a decision which appears to contradict the specific wording of the statute (s. 51(1)(a), 'he does an act which intimidates, and is intended to intimidate, another person') the Court of Appeal has confirmed that 'an act which intimidates' does not have to result in the victim *actually* being intimidated; so no intimidation 'result' from the defendant's actions is required even though the statute appears to require one. Therefore if a defendant seeks to deter a witness from giving evidence by means of intimidation, the offence could be made out even if the victim was not actually in fear.

In *R* v *Patrascu* [2004] EWCA Crim 2417, the court provided further detail with regard to interpretation of the term 'intimidation'. The court held that a person did an act which intimidated another within the meaning of s. 51(1) if he/she put that other person in fear, or sought by threat or violence to deter that person from some relevant action such as giving evidence. However, mere pressure which did not put the victim in fear or contained no element of threat or violence was insufficient. In other words, whilst not requiring an intimidation 'result', the defendant must do something more than just pressurising a victim to be guilty of the offence.

'Harm' for the purposes of s. 51(2) means physical harm and not simply an assault or battery. Therefore spitting at a person does not amount to 'harm' for these purposes (*R* v *Normanton* [1998] Crim LR 220).

Section 51(2) provides a similar offence for acts done or threatened in the knowledge or belief that the person, *or another person*, has so assisted or taken part in proceedings. Doing acts to third parties in order to intimidate or harm the relevant person is also covered by this offence (s. 51(3)). Making threats by telephone will amount to 'doing an act to another' (*DPP* v *Mills* [1997] QB 300).

Section 51(8) creates a statutory presumption under certain circumstances that the defendant had the required motive at the time of the actions or threats.

Making a *threat* via a third person knowing it will be passed on and that the ultimate recipient would be intimidated by it amounts to an offence under s. 51(1) (*Attorney-General's Reference (No. 1 of 1999)* [2000] QB 365).

The intention to obstruct, pervert or interfere with the course of justice need not be the only or even the main intention (s. 51(5)).

### 1.12.3.2    Intimidation of Witnesses in Other Proceedings

In addition to the measures aimed at protecting those involved in the investigation and trial of criminal offences, there are further statutory measures designed to protect witnesses and others who are (or may become) involved in other proceedings.

OFFENCE:  **Intimidation of Witnesses—*Criminal Justice and Police Act 2001, s. 39***
- Triable either way • Five years' imprisonment on indictment • Six months' imprisonment and/or a fine summarily

The Criminal Justice and Police Act 2001, s. 39 states:

(1) A person commits an offence if—
  (a) he does an act which intimidates, and is intended to intimidate, another person ('the victim');
  (b) he does the act—
   (i) knowing or believing that the victim is or may be a witness in any relevant proceedings; and
   (ii) intending, by his act, to cause the course of justice to be obstructed, perverted or interfered with;
  and
  (c) the act is done after the commencement of those proceedings.

---

**KEYNOTE**

This offence has some similarities to the Criminal Justice and Public Order Act 1994 offence at **para. 1.12.3.1**. References to doing an act include threats—against people and/or their property—and the making of any other statement (s. 39(6)). The key difference is that this offence is concerned with protecting people who are in some way connected with 'relevant proceedings' which are 'any proceedings in or before the Court of Appeal, the High Court, the Crown Court or any county or magistrates' court which are not proceedings for an offence' (s. 41(1)). This means that the offence will be relevant if the proceedings involved are civil proceedings in the higher courts or the county court or if they are non-offence proceedings in the Crown Court or magistrates' court. Examples of the latter would be a hearing to deal with a breach of a community order or an application for an anti-social behaviour order. You must show that the relevant proceedings had already commenced by the time of the offence.

Note that some proceedings, such as inquests or police conduct hearings, will not be covered by the s. 41 definition and therefore the offences above.

As with the Criminal Justice and Public Order Act offence, this requires proof of intent in that, as well as showing the intimidatory act, it must also be shown that the elements set out at s. 39(1)(a)–(c) are present. However, if you can prove that the defendant:

- did any act that intimidated, and was intended to intimidate, another person, and
- that the defendant did that act knowing or believing that that other person was or might be a 'witness' in any relevant proceedings that had already commenced,

there will be a presumption that the defendant did the act with the intention of causing the course of justice to be obstructed, perverted or interfered with (s. 39(3)). This presumption is, however, rebuttable. 'Witness' here is a very wide expression and extends to anyone who provides, or is able to provide, any information, document or other thing which might be used in evidence in those proceedings (see s. 39(5)).

In proving the offence it is immaterial whether the act:

- is done in the presence of the victim
- is done to the victim him/herself or to another person

or whether or not the intention to obstruct, pervert or interfere with the course of justice is the main intention of the person doing it (s. 39(2)).

This offence is intended to exist alongside the common law offence of perverting the course of justice.

---

### 1.12.4 Harming Witnesses

OFFENCE: **Harming Witnesses—*Criminal Justice and Police Act 2001, s. 40***
  • Triable either way • Five years' imprisonment on indictment • Six months' imprisonment and/or a fine summarily

The Criminal Justice and Police Act 2001, s. 40 states:

(1) A person commits an offence if in circumstances falling within subsection (2)—
  (a) he does an act which harms, and is intended to harm, another person; or
  (b) intending to cause another person to fear harm, he threatens to do an act which would harm that other person.
(2) The circumstances fall within this subsection if—
  (a) the person doing or threatening to do the act does so knowing or believing that some person (whether or not the person harmed or threatened or the person against whom harm is threatened) has been a witness in relevant proceedings; and
  (b) he does or threatens to do that act because of that knowledge or belief.

---

**KEYNOTE**

A distinction between this and the s. 39 offence is that the offence above refers to someone who *has been* (or is believed to *have been*) a witness in relevant proceedings. Again, 'witness' is very wide and extends to anyone who has provided any information, document, etc. which was (or might have been) used in evidence in those proceedings (see s. 40(7)). For 'relevant proceedings' see the s. 39 offence. This offence is aimed at the general protection of people who have been involved in relevant proceedings. Therefore there is no requirement here for any intention to pervert or interfere with the course of justice. The harm caused or threatened does not have to be directed towards the witness him/herself; the key element is the motivation of the defendant. In relation to that motivation, the Act creates a presumption that if you can prove that, between the start of the proceedings and one year after they are concluded, the defendant:

• did an act which harmed, and was intended to harm, another person, or
• threatened to do an act which would harm another person intending to cause that person to fear harm

with the knowledge or belief required by s. 40(2)(a) above, the defendant will be presumed to have acted because of that knowledge or belief (s. 40(3)). Again, this is rebuttable. It is immaterial whether the act or threat is made (or would be carried out) in the presence of the person who is or would be harmed, or of the person threatened or whether the motive mentioned in s. 40(2)(b) is the main motive. The harm done or threatened can be physical or financial and can be made to a person or property (s. 40(4)).

---

### 1.12.5 Assisting Offenders

OFFENCE: **Assisting Offenders—*Criminal Law Act 1967, s. 4***
  • Triable on indictment; either way if original offence is either way • Where sentence for original offence is fixed by law, ten years' imprisonment and/or a fine on indictment; six months' imprisonment and/or a fine summarily • Where sentence for original offence is 14 years' imprisonment, seven years' imprisonment and/or a fine on indictment; six months' imprisonment and/or a fine summarily • Where sentence for original offence is ten years imprisonment, five years' imprisonment and/or a fine on indictment; six months' imprisonment and/or a fine summarily • Otherwise three years' imprisonment and/or a fine on indictment; six months' imprisonment and/or a fine summarily

The Criminal Law Act 1967, s. 4 states:

(1) Where a person has committed a relevant offence, any other person who, knowing or believing him to be guilty of the offence or of some other relevant offence, does without lawful authority or reasonable excuse any act with intent to impede his apprehension or prosecution shall be guilty of an offence.

(1A) In this section and section 5 below, 'relevant offence' means—

(a) an offence for which the sentence is fixed by law,

(b) an offence for which a person of 18 years or over (not previously convicted) may be sentenced to imprisonment for a term of five years (or might be so sentenced but for the restrictions imposed by section 33 of the Magistrates' Courts Act 1980).

---

**KEYNOTE**

This offence must involve some positive act by the defendant; simply doing or saying nothing will not suffice.

Although there is no duty on people to assist the police in their investigations generally, this offence and the one below create a negative duty not to interfere with investigations after an offence has taken place.

For there to be an offence under ss. 4 or 5 there must first have been a relevant offence committed by someone. That relevant offence must, in the case of the above offence, have been committed by the 'assisted' person.

The defendant can commit the offence before the person assisted is convicted of committing the relevant offence.

It must be shown that the defendant knew or believed the person to be guilty of that, *or some other* relevant offence. Therefore, if the defendant believed that the 'assisted' person had committed a robbery when in fact he/she had committed a theft, that mistaken part of the defendant's belief will not prevent a conviction for this offence.

Mere *suspicion*, however strong, that the 'assisted' person had committed a relevant offence will not be enough.

This offence requires the consent of the DPP before a prosecution is brought (s. 4(4)).

This offence cannot be 'attempted' (Criminal Attempts Act 1981, s. 1(4)).

---

## 1.12.6 Concealing Relevant Offences

OFFENCE: **Concealing Relevant Offences—*Criminal Law Act 1967, s. 5***

• Triable on indictment; either way if original offence is triable either way • Two years' imprisonment on indictment • Six months' imprisonment and/or a fine summarily

The Criminal Law Act 1967, s. 5 states:

(1) Where a person has committed a relevant offence, any other person who, knowing or believing that the offence or some other relevant offence has been committed, and that he has information which might be of material assistance in securing the prosecution or conviction of an offender for it, accepts or agrees to accept for not disclosing that information any consideration other than the making good of loss or injury caused by the offence, or the making of reasonable compensation for that loss or injury, shall be liable...

---

**KEYNOTE**

This offence also requires the consent of the DPP before a prosecution can be brought (s. 5(3)).

It is also excluded from the provisions of the Criminal Attempts Act 1981 (s. 1(4)).

Again, someone must have committed a relevant offence before this particular offence can be committed. The main focus of this offence is:

• the acceptance of, or agreement to accept 'consideration' (i.e. anything of value)

• beyond reasonable compensation for loss/injury *caused by the relevant offence*

• in exchange for not disclosing material information.

---

'Disclosure' does not appear to be confined to information passed to the police. It would probably extend to other agencies with a duty to investigate offences but is perhaps even wider than that.

This offence requires proof, not only of the defendant's knowledge or belief that a relevant offence had been committed, but also that the defendant has information that might be of material assistance in securing the *prosecution or conviction* of *an offender* for it. Given this very broad wording, the possession of information that might provide useful intelligence in an investigation into relevant offences may meet the requirements of s. 5, although *proving* that the defendant had the required knowledge or belief presents considerable practical problems.

## 1.12.7 Miscellaneous Offences Relating to Offenders

OFFENCE: **Escaping—*Common Law***

> • Triable on indictment • Unlimited punishment

It is an offence at common law to escape from legal custody.

### KEYNOTE

The 'custody' from which a person escapes must be shown to have been lawful. The offence applies to both police custody (or police detention—see the Police and Criminal Evidence Act 1984, s. 118) or custody following conviction.

Whether a person was 'in custody' is a question of fact and the word 'custody' is to be given its ordinary and natural meaning—*E* v *DPP* [2002] EWHC 433 (Admin). (See also *Richards* v *DPP* [1988] QB 701.) In proving that a person was in custody at a particular time it should be shown that his/her liberty was restricted in a way that meant that he/she was confined by another and that his/her freedom of movement was controlled; it is not necessary, however, to show that the person's actual ability to move around was physically impeded, e.g. in secure accommodation (*E* v *DPP* above).

People may be in lawful custody even if not directly in the custody of a sworn police officer, for example those people who are being dealt with by an investigating officer or escort officers under sch. 4 to the Police Reform Act 2002.

People detained under the Mental Health Act 1983, s. 136, are also in lawful custody.

If a defendant uses force to *break out* of a prison or a police station, he/she commits an offence of prison breach, again at common law and attracting the same punishment and mode of trial as escaping.

Under the Prisoners (Return to Custody) Act 1995, s. 1, a person who has been temporarily released under the Prison Act 1952 commits a summary offence if he/she remains unlawfully at large or fails to respond to an order of recall to prison.

Escort officers designated under sch. 4 to the Police Reform Act 2002 have a duty to prevent the escape of people in their charge whom they are escorting in accordance with their statutory powers (see the Police Reform Act 2002, sch. 4, part 4, para. 35).

OFFENCE: **Assisting Escape—*Prison Act 1952, s. 39***

> • Triable on indictment • Ten years' imprisonment

The Prison Act 1952, s. 39 states:

(1) Any person who
    (a) assists a prisoner in escaping or attempting to escape from a prison, or
    (b) intending to facilitate the escape of a prisoner—
        (i) brings, throws or otherwise conveys anything into prison,
        (ii) causes another person to bring, throw or otherwise convey anything into prison, or
        (iii) gives anything to a prisoner or leaves anything in any place (whether inside or outside a prison),
is guilty of an offence.

OFFENCE: **Harbouring Offenders—*Criminal Justice Act 1961, s. 22(2)***
- Triable either way • Ten years' imprisonment and/or a fine on indictment
- Six months' imprisonment and/or a fine summarily

The Criminal Justice Act 1961, s. 22 states:

(2) If any person knowingly harbours a person who has escaped from a prison or other institution to which the said section thirty-nine applies, or who, having been sentenced in any part of the United Kingdom or in any of the Channel Islands or the Isle of Man to imprisonment or detention, is otherwise unlawfully at large, or gives to any such person any assistance with intent to prevent, hinder or interfere with his being taken into custody, he shall be liable...

---

**KEYNOTE**

The offences under s. 39 of the 1952 Act and s. 22 of the 1961 Act do not apply to a prisoner who escapes while in transit to or from prison (*R* v *Moss and Harte* (1986) 82 Cr App R 116).

---

## 1.12.8 Contempt of Court

Acts which amount to contempt of court can be divided into criminal and civil contempt. Criminal contempt is defined at common law as 'behaviour involving interference with the due administration of justice' (*Attorney-General* v *Newspaper Publishing plc* [1988] Ch 333 and see *Blackstone's Criminal Practice 2013*, section B14.78).

Contempt can be committed in many different ways including misbehaviour in court, publication of matters prejudicial to a trial and taking photographs inside a court building.

Any behaviour that is seen as interfering with witnesses (or potential witnesses) by promises of favours and rewards or by threats will be a contempt of court (see *R* v *Kellett* [1976] QB 372). Trying to restrict the way in which defendants and/or their legal advisers obtain evidence for their defence—e.g. by properly approaching witnesses—can also amount to a contempt of court (see *Connolly* v *Dale* [1996] QB 120).

For a full explanation of the subject together with the extensive powers of courts to deal with contempt, see *Blackstone's Criminal Practice 2013*, para. B14.78 *et seq.*

# Property Offences

# 2.1 | Theft

### 2.1.1 Theft

OFFENCE: **Theft—*Theft Act 1968, s. 1***
  • Triable either way • Seven years' imprisonment on indictment • Six months' imprisonment and/or a fine summarily

The Theft Act 1968, s. 1 states:

  (1) A person is guilty of theft if he dishonestly appropriates property belonging to another with the intention of permanently depriving the other of it; and 'thief' and 'steal' shall be construed accordingly.

---

**KEYNOTE**

In order for an offence of theft to exist, each element of the definition must be proved and those elements are considered in detail below.

The final line of s. 1 is important and tells us that the words '"thief" and "steal" shall be construed accordingly'. This means that in any Theft Act 1968 offence where the words 'thief' and/or 'steal' are used (such as in the Theft Act 1968 offences of burglary (s. 9(1)(a)), robbery (s. 8) or handling stolen goods (s. 22)), the 'thief' is the person who commits the theft offence and 'steal' means to commit theft. All of the elements of the theft offence must be present to 'steal'. So, for example, the definition of robbery (s. 8) tells us that 'A person is guilty of robbery if he steals'. If the entire definition of theft has not been satisfied by the actions of the defendant then he/she cannot have committed theft and will not 'steal'—if he/she does not 'steal' he/she cannot commit robbery. This is the origin of the often heard statement that 'without theft there can be no robbery'.

Note that offences of theft from businesses (classed as 'theft from a shop') involving first-time offenders who are not substance mis-users and where the value of the goods stolen is less than £100 can be dealt with by way of fixed penalty notice.

---

As described by s.1 of the Act, there are five key elements to the offence of theft. These are:

• dishonesty (s.2)
• appropriation (s.3)
• property (s.4)
• belonging to another (s.5)
• intention of permanently depriving (s.6).

### 2.1.2 Dishonestly

Each element of the offence of theft must be proved. Therefore, if a person cannot be shown to have acted 'dishonestly', he/she is not guilty of theft. The decision as to whether or not a defendant was dishonest is a question of fact for the jury or magistrate(s) to decide. Whilst there is no statutory definition of the term 'dishonestly', the 1968 Act does deal with the issue by setting out a number of specific circumstances where the relevant person will *not* be treated as dishonest and one circumstance where a person *may* be dishonest.

The Theft Act 1968, s. 2 states:

(1) A person's appropriation of property belonging to another is not to be regarded as dishonest—
   (a) if he appropriates the property in the belief that he has in law the right to deprive the other of it, on behalf of himself or of a third person; or
   (b) if he appropriates the property in the belief that he would have the other's consent if the other knew of the appropriation and the circumstances of it; or
   (c) (except where the property came to him as trustee or personal representative) if he appropriates the property in the belief that the person to whom the property belongs cannot be discovered by taking reasonable steps.

## KEYNOTE

In all three instances it is the person's *belief* that is important.

### Right in Law

- X is owed £100 by Y. Y tells X that he will not give him the money so X, *honestly believing that he has a right in law to do so*, takes property belonging to Y (to the value of £100) as payment for the debt. It does not matter that there is no actual right in law for X to behave in this way—the honestly held belief by X that he does have a right in law means that he is not dishonest. The belief need not even be reasonable, only honestly held, and could be based on a 'mistake' (contrast the general defence of mistake). This would also include the situation where the person acts on the basis of belief in the legal right of another. So if X, acting for the benefit of Y, took property from Z (wrongly but honestly believing that Y was entitled to it), X would not be dishonest.

### Consent

- Under s. 2(1)(b) the person appropriating the property must believe both elements, i.e. that the other person would have *consented* had he/she known of the appropriation *and the circumstances of it*. For example, a person is about to run out of time on a street parking meter and needs £5 to park for the next hour or risk incurring a £60 fine. Believing that a work colleague would consent in this situation, the person takes £5 belonging to the colleague from a change jar on the colleague's desk. If the person *honestly believes the work colleague would consent to the taking and the circumstances of it*, this would not be dishonest. If the person knew that the work colleague would not approve, this would be dishonest.

### Lost

- Under s. 2(1)(c), the belief has to be in relation to the likelihood of *discovering* the 'owner' by taking reasonable steps. Both the nature and value of the property, together with the attendant circumstances, will be relevant. The chances of finding the owner of a valuable, monogrammed engagement ring found after a theatre performance would be considerably greater than those of discovering the owner of a can of beer found outside Twickenham stadium following a Six Nations match between England and Wales. Again, it is the defendant's *honest belief* at the time of the appropriation that is important here, not that the defendant went on to take reasonable steps to discover the person to whom the property belongs.
- This section highlights the fact that trustees or personal representatives cannot rely on s. 2(1)(c). This is because a trustee or personal representative can never be personally entitled to the property in question (unless the trust or will states that is the case) as if the beneficiary cannot be found, the person entitled to the property in question (now effectively 'ownerless goods') is the Crown.

The Theft Act 1968, s. 2 states:

(2) A person's appropriation of property belonging to another may be dishonest notwithstanding that he is willing to pay for the property.

**KEYNOTE**

Under s. 2(2), if a person appropriates another's property, leaving money or details of where he/she can be contacted to make restitution, this will not of itself negate dishonesty (see *Boggeln* v *Williams* [1978] 1 WLR 873). The wording of s. 2(2) gives latitude to a court where the defendant was willing to pay for the property. The subsection says that such an appropriation *may* be dishonest, not that it *will always* be dishonest.

EXAMPLE

X wants to buy a pint of milk and sees an unattended milk float displaying a sign, 'Milk—60p a pint'. X waits for several minutes but nobody in charge of the milk float appears so X leaves 60p on the float and takes a pint of milk. The fact that the milk is for sale and X left payment would be convincing evidence to suggest that X is not dishonest.

Y wants to own a painting that is on display in a museum. Y has made several approaches to buy the painting but has been told that the painting is not for sale. Y knows the painting is worth £10,000 and decides to take the painting from the museum, leaving a cheque for £10,000 in its place. Just because Y is willing to pay the market value for the painting does not mean to say that he is not dishonest.

### 2.1.3 Dishonesty: The Ruling in *Ghosh*

Section 2 will not cater for every circumstance and indeed ss. 2–6 only affect the interpretation of the basic elements of theft as set out in s. 1 unless the Act says otherwise (s. 1(3)). Since the case of *R* v *Ghosh* [1982] QB 1053 there has been a requirement for juries to be given some form of direction where the issue of dishonesty is raised and s. 2 is of no assistance. As well as clarifying that the defendant's dishonesty is a matter for a jury to decide, the Court of Appeal in *Ghosh* also identified two aspects which the jury should consider when so deciding. If s. 2 is not applicable or helpful then a jury must ask two questions:

- Was what was done dishonest according to the ordinary standards of reasonable and honest people? If the answer to that question is 'no' then the defendant is not guilty of theft but if it is 'yes' then the second question is asked.
- Did the defendant realise that what was done was dishonest *by those standards*?

This test against the standards of reasonable and honest people means that defendants who have a purely *subjective* belief that they are doing what is morally right although it is legally wrong (e.g. an anti-vivisectionist taking animals from a laboratory) can still be 'dishonest'. Taking the animals from the laboratory is dishonest according to the ordinary standards or reasonable and honest people and the anti-vivisectionist knows that to be the case. The *Ghosh* test is probably the source of the questions so loved by some interviewing officers: 'But what would an *honest* person have done?' or 'What would have been the *honest* thing to do?'.

### 2.1.4 Appropriates

The Theft Act 1968, s. 3 states:

(1) Any assumption by a person of the rights of an owner amounts to an appropriation, and this includes, where he has come by the property (innocently or not) without stealing it, any later assumption of a right to it by keeping or dealing with it as owner.

**KEYNOTE**

The owner of property has many rights in relation to it—the right to sell it, to give it away, to damage it or to destroy it are just *some* examples. 'Appropriation' does not envisage that a person assumes *all* of those rights—just *one* of them would suffice for 'appropriation' to occur.

While damaging or destroying property is clearly an act of 'appropriation' (*R* v *Graham* [1997] 1 Cr App R 302) it does not follow that an act of destruction of property is also thereby automatically theft of that property. *Dishonestly* causing the destruction of property can itself amount to an offence of theft (*R* v *Kohn* (1979) 69 Cr App R 395) but this does not make theft an appropriate charge where D merely smashes V's car window by throwing a brick through it—criminal damage would be the appropriate charge on such facts as there is clearly no 'dishonesty' present in such an act.

It is important to note that there can be an 'appropriation' without any criminal liability and appropriation itself does not amount to an offence; it describes one of the elements of the criminal conduct that must exist before a charge of theft can be made out. An appropriation requires no mental state on the part of the appropriator. It is an objective act.

Where an appropriation takes place and is accompanied by the required dishonesty and intention to deprive permanently, there will be a theft.

Appropriation under s. 3(1) envisages a *physical* act—*Biggs* v *R* (2003) 12 December, unreported.

When and where the particular act amounting to an appropriation took place is therefore of critical importance when bringing a charge of theft; it is also vital when establishing other offences such as robbery, aggravated burglary and handling stolen goods.

The decision of the House of Lords in *R* v *Gomez* [1993] AC 442 significantly developed the meaning of 'appropriation'. Following an earlier case (*Lawrence* v *Metropolitan Police Commissioner* [1972] AC 626), Lord Keith disagreed with the argument (made in *Gomez*) that an act expressly or impliedly authorised by the owner of the property in question can never amount to an 'appropriation' and pointed out that the decision in *Lawrence* was a direct contradiction of that proposition. The House of Lords upheld the convictions for theft in *Gomez* and accepted that there are occasions where property can be 'appropriated' for the purposes of the Theft Act 1968, *even though the owner has given his/her consent or authority*.

**A number of issues come from this decision:**

• *Taking or depriving*. First, it is not necessary that the property be 'taken' in order for there to be an appropriation, neither need the owner be 'deprived' of the property. Similarly, there is no need for the defendant to 'gain' anything by an appropriation.

• *Consent*. Secondly, it is irrelevant to the issue of appropriation whether or not the owner consented to that appropriation. This is well illustrated in *Lawrence*, the decision followed by the House of Lords in *Gomez*. In *Lawrence* a tourist gave his wallet full of unfamiliar English currency to a taxi driver for the latter to remove the correct fare. The driver in fact helped himself to ('appropriated') far more than the amount owed. It was held that the fact that the wallet and its contents were handed over freely (with consent) by the owner did not prevent the taxi driver's actions from amounting to an 'appropriation' of it. The Court of Appeal appears—at least on one occasion—to have interpreted *Gomez* as deciding that consent *obtained by fraud* is irrelevant to the issue of appropriation (see *R* v *Mazo* [1997] 2 Cr App R 518). However, there is no such restriction placed on the decision in *Gomez* and it seems safe to assume that consent given by the owner will not prevent an 'appropriation' of property for the purposes of the Theft Act 1968.

• *Interfering with goods*. A third point that is now clear from the decision in *Gomez* is that simply swapping the price labels on items displayed for sale in a shop *would* amount to an 'appropriation'. This is because to do so, irrespective of any further intention, involves an assumption of one of the owner's rights in relation to the property (the right to put a price on property). If that appropriation were accompanied by the required circumstances of dishonesty and intention to deprive, then there would be a *prima facie* case of theft.

• *More than one appropriation*. A fourth point apparent from *Gomez* is that there may be an appropriation of the same property on more than one occasion. However, once property has been *stolen* (as opposed to merely appropriated), that same property cannot be stolen again by the same thief (*R* v *Atakpu* [1994] QB 69).

Appropriation can also be a continuing act, that is, it can include the whole episode of entering and ransacking a house and the subsequent removal of property (*R* v *Hale* (1979) 68 Cr App R 415). Therefore identifying the exact point at which property was appropriated with the requisite intention and accompanying dishonesty can cause practical difficulties.

In *R* v *Hinks* [2001] 2 AC 24, the House of Lords was asked to rule on whether a person could 'appropriate' property belonging to another where the other person made her an absolute gift of property, retaining no proprietary interest in the property or any right to resume or recover it. In that case the defendant had befriended a middle-aged man of limited intelligence who had given her some £60,000 over a period of time. The defendant was charged with five counts of theft and, after conviction, eventually appealed to the House of Lords. Their lordships held that:

- in a prosecution for theft it was unnecessary to prove that the taking was without the owner's consent (as in *Lawrence* above);
- it was immaterial whether the act of appropriation was done with the owner's consent or authority (as in *Gomez*); and
- *Gomez* therefore gave effect to s. 3(1) by treating 'appropriation' as a neutral word covering 'any assumption by a person of the rights of an owner'.

This finding is consistent with earlier cases.

If a person, having come by property—innocently or not—without stealing it, later assumes any rights to it by keeping it or treating it as his/her own, then he/she 'appropriates' that property (s. 3(1)).

**KEYNOTE**

A later assumption of the rights of an owner amounts to 'appropriation' and could lead to an offence of theft.

. . . . . . . . . . . . . . . . . . . . . . . . . . . . . . . . . . . . . . . . . . . . . . . . . . . . . . . . . . . . . . . . . . . . . . . . . . . . . . . . . . . . . .

EXAMPLE

X is shopping in a large department store and has placed several items in his shopping basket. Thinking about other things, X absent-mindedly walks out of the store without paying for the goods. Once outside the store X realises what he has done but as the store alarm has not activated and nobody seems to have noticed X leaving the store without paying, X decides to keep the goods and walks away from the store. X initially came by the goods innocently but his later assumption of the rights of an owner means he has now 'appropriated' the goods and in the circumstances would commit theft.

An exception to these circumstances is provided by the Theft Act 1968, s. 3 which states:

(2) Where property or a right or interest in property is or purports to be transferred for value to a person acting in good faith, no later assumption by him of rights which he believed himself to be acquiring shall, by reason of any defect in the transferor's title, amount to theft of the property.

**KEYNOTE**

If a person buys a car in good faith and gives value for it (i.e. a reasonable price) but then discovers it has been stolen, a refusal to return it to the original owner would not, without more, *attract liability for theft*. Without s. 3(2) the retention of the vehicle would be caught by s. 3(1). This narrow exemption does not mean however that the innocent purchaser gets good title to the car (see *National Employers' Mutual Insurance Association Ltd* v *Jones* [1990] 1 AC 24), nor would it provide a defence if the stolen goods are a gift and the 'donee' (recipient) subsequently discovers that they had been stolen (the 'donee' will not have given 'value' for the property).

## 2.1.5 Property

The Theft Act 1968, s. 4 states:

(1) 'Property' includes money and all other property, real or personal, including things in action and other intangible property.

(2) A person cannot steal land, or things forming part of land and severed from it by him or by his directions, except in the following cases, that is to say—

   (a) when he is a trustee or personal representative, or is authorised by power of attorney, or as liquidator of a company, or otherwise, to sell or dispose of land belonging to another, and he appropriates the land or anything forming part of it by dealing with it in breach of the confidence reposed in him; or

   (b) when he is not in possession of the land and appropriates anything forming part of the land by severing it or causing it to be severed, or after it has been severed; or

   (c) when, being in possession of the land under a tenancy, he appropriates the whole or part of any fixture or structure let to be used with the land.

For purposes of this subsection 'land' does not include incorporeal hereditaments; 'tenancy' means a tenancy for years or any less period and includes an agreement for such a tenancy, but a person who after the end of a tenancy remains in possession as statutory tenant or otherwise is to be treated as having possession under the tenancy, and 'let' shall be construed accordingly.

(3) A person who picks mushrooms growing wild on any land, or who picks flowers, fruit or foliage from a plant growing wild on any land, does not (although not in possession of the land) steal what he picks unless he does it for reward or for sale or other commercial purpose. For purposes of this subsection 'mushroom' includes any fungus, and 'plant' includes any shrub or tree.

(4) Wild creatures, tamed or untamed, shall be regarded as property; but a person cannot steal a wild creature not tamed nor ordinarily kept in captivity, or the carcase of any such creature, unless either it has been reduced into possession by or on behalf of another person and possession of it has not since been lost or abandoned, or another person is in course of reducing it into possession.

---

**KEYNOTE**

**Money**

Coins and banknotes are property (see *R* v *Davis* (1989) 88 Cr App R 347). 'Money' does not include cheques or credit balances held in banks and building societies (but see below).

**Cheques and Credit Balances**

Cheques will be property as they are pieces of paper ('personal' property albeit of very little intrinsic value). The contents of a bank or building society account, however, are also a 'thing in action' that can be stolen provided the account is in credit or within the limits of an agreed overdraft facility (*R* v *Kohn* (1979) 69 Cr App R 395). Therefore reducing the credit balance in one account, and transferring a like sum into your own account amounts to an 'appropriation' of property within the meaning of s. 1. This principle (set out in *Kohn*) was reaffirmed in *R* v *Williams (Roy)* [2001] 1 Cr App R 23 by the Court of Appeal.

**Personal Property**

Personal property includes tangible personal property which might be described as 'things in possession'. The TV in your house, the settee you sit on, the wallet or purse you keep your money in are all examples of 'personal' property.

**Things in Action and Other Intangible Property**

Under s. 4(1) 'things in action' would include patents and trademarks and other things which can only be enforced by legal action as opposed to physical possession. Other intangible property would include software programs and perhaps credits accumulated on 'smart cards'. Confidential information—such as the contents of an examination paper—is not intangible property *per se* (see *Oxford* v *Moss* (1979) 68 Cr App R 183). However, the document itself would be 'real' property. It has been accepted by the Court of Appeal that contractual rights obtained by buying a ticket for the London Underground may amount to a 'thing in action' (see *R* v *Marshall* [1998] 2 Cr App R 282).

An area of criminal activity causing concern (and cost) is that of so-called 'identity theft'. This is a somewhat misleading description as adopting another person's characteristics and using his/her administrative data (such as national insurance number) is not theft of the information—this 'confidential information' is not 'property' for the purposes of the Theft Act 1968 (see para. 2.1.6).

## Land

Under s. 4(2) you cannot generally steal land even though it is 'property' for the purposes of criminal damage (see chapter 1.16). However, there are three exceptions to this general rule:

(1) Trustees or personal representatives or someone in a position of trust to dispose of land belonging to another, can be guilty of stealing it if, in such circumstances, they dishonestly dispose of it.

........................................................................................................................

EXAMPLE

Two company employees are asked by the company directors to sell land belonging to the company. The value of the land is £10,000 an acre. The company employees sell the land to each other for £1,000 an acre. The company employees are in a position of trust and have 'breached the confidence reposed in them' and commit theft of the land.

........................................................................................................................

(2) Persons not in possession of the land may commit theft in a variety of ways. This may be accomplished by severing fixtures, plants, topsoil, etc. from the land or by appropriating such property after it has been severed. If X decides to take an established and cultivated rose bush from the garden of his neighbour by ripping it out of the ground and then planting it in his own garden, this would be theft as the rose bush has been severed from the land (see below for wild plants). This would not however, for example, include a person who dishonestly moves a boundary fence so as to appropriate some part of a neighbouring property—the land has not been 'severed'.

(3) Tenants can steal land but only fixtures and structures let to be used with the land. Examples of 'fixtures' would be a fireplace or the kitchen sink; a structure might be a greenhouse or a garden shed which is fixed to the land. Therefore a tenant cannot steal land such as topsoil or a rosebush growing in the garden of the rented premises—these things are not 'fixtures or structures'.

## Things Growing Wild

Things growing wild on any land are 'property' and could be stolen by a person not in possession of the land if he severed and appropriated them. However, s. 4(3) of the Act tells us that a person who picks mushrooms, flowers, fruit and foliage growing wild on any land will not commit theft by so doing, unless the picking is done for reward, sale or other commercial purpose. Except in the case of a mushroom, if the whole plant is removed this is theft as it is not 'picking'. Likewise, sawing through the trunk of a Christmas tree growing wild is not picking and would be theft. It is arguable that, if the person does not have such a purpose at the time of the picking, any later intention to sell the fruit, etc. may not bring it within the provisions of s. 4(3). If the mushroom, flower etc. is cultivated it will be theft to pick it wherever it is growing.

## Wild Creatures

Section 4(4) acknowledges that all wild creatures are 'property' whether they are tamed (your dog or your cat) or untamed but ordinarily kept in captivity (a lion in a zoo). Wild creatures that are not tamed or ordinarily kept in captivity are not classed as property unless they have been reduced into possession or in the process of being so reduced. For example, X shoots a rabbit on land belonging to Y (with Y's permission to be there and shoot). Z takes the rabbit from X—Z commits theft. If the rabbit is lost or abandoned after it has been reduced into possession or killed then it cannot be 'stolen'.

## 2.1.6  **What is not Property?**

Confidential information is not property—so an Ospre Part I student who reads and makes a copy of the examination paper may not be convicted of stealing intangible property, namely the confidential information belonging to the Examinations and Assessment Unit of the College of Policing.

Human bodies (dead or alive) are not property ('there is no property in a corpse' *Doodeward v Spence* (1908) 6 CLR 406). However, a body or body parts are capable of being stolen if they have been subject to a special application of human skill (an Egyptian mummy would be the property of the museum it was kept in). This principle was upheld by the Court of Appeal in *R v Kelly* [1999] QB 621, after the conviction of two people involved in the theft of body parts from the Royal College of Surgeons. The court upheld the convictions for theft on the grounds that the process of *alteration* (amputation, dissection and preservation) which the body parts had undergone did make them 'property' for the purposes of the 1968 Act.

Fluids taken from a living body are property so a motorist has been convicted of stealing a specimen of his own urine provided by him for analysis (*R v Welsh* [1971] RTR 478). The same rule would clearly apply to a blood sample.

Electricity is the subject of a specific offence.

## 2.1.7 Belonging to Another

The Theft Act 1968, s. 5 states:

(1) Property shall be regarded as belonging to any person having possession or control of it, or having in it any proprietary right or interest (not being an equitable interest arising only from an agreement to transfer or grant an interest).
(2) Where property is subject to a trust, the persons to whom it belongs shall be regarded as including any person having a right to enforce the trust, and an intention to defeat the trust shall be regarded accordingly as an intention to deprive of the property any person having that right.

---

**KEYNOTE**

Property can be 'stolen' from any person who has possession or control or a proprietary right or interest in that property. In one case where the defendant recovered his own recently repaired car from a street outside the garage where the repairs had taken place, he was convicted of stealing the car which at the time 'belonged to' the garage proprietor who had possession of it (*R v Turner (No. 2)* [1971] 1 WLR 901). In determining whether or not a person had 'possession' of property for the purposes of s. 5(1), the period of possession can be finite (i.e. for a given number of hours, days, etc.) or infinite (*R v Kelly* [1999] QB 621).

It is not necessary to show who does own the property—only that it 'belongs to' someone other than the defendant.

A good example of how this principle operates can be seen in a case before the Court of Appeal where the two defendants went diving in a lake on a golf course, recovering sacks of 'lost' balls which it was believed they were going to sell. This activity was carried out without the permission of the golf club who owned the course. Although the defendants argued that the balls had been abandoned by their owners, the Crown had shown that they were 'property belonging to another' (the golf club) and therefore the convictions were safe (*R v Rostron; R v Collinson* [2003] EWCA Crim 2206).

Where money is given by members of the public to charity collectors it becomes the property of the relevant charitable trustees at the moment it goes into the collecting tin (*R v Dyke* [2001] EWCA Crim 2184). But if s. 5(2) did not exist, those charitable trustees could take the donation to the charity and do what they wished with it, including placing the charitable funds in their own bank account. Charitable trusts are enforceable by the Attorney-General, and an appropriation of the trust property by a charitable trustee will amount to theft from the Attorney-General.

When a cheque is written, that will create a 'thing in action'. That thing in action belongs only to the payee. Therefore a payee of a cheque cannot 'steal' the thing in action which it creates (*R v Davis* (1989) 88 Cr App R 347).

In proving theft, you must show that the property belonged to another *at the time of the appropriation*. This requirement has caused some difficulty where a defendant's decision not to pay for goods has been made *after* property passed to him/her. In such cases (e.g. people refusing to pay for meals after they have eaten or deciding to drive off having filled their car with petrol), the proper charge is found under the Fraud Act 2006 or by charging with the offence of making off without payment. The House of Lords' ruling in *Gomez* raises some questions over such cases (**see para. 2.1.4**). As the consent of the owner is irrelevant to the issue of 'appropriation', the key element in such cases is whether the property 'belonged to another' at the time of the act of appropriation. If ownership of the property had passed to the defendant *before* he/she appropriated it (e.g. by virtue of the Sale of Goods Act 1979; see *Edwards* v *Ddin* [1976] 1 WLR 942) then this element of theft would not be made out and an alternative charge should be considered.

## 2.1.8 Obligations Regarding Another's Property

The Theft Act 1968, s. 5 states:

(3) Where a person receives property from or on account of another, and is under an obligation to the other to retain and deal with that property or its proceeds in a particular way, the property or proceeds shall be regarded (as against him) as belonging to the other.

### KEYNOTE

'Obligation' means a legal obligation, not simply a moral one (*R* v *Hall* [1973] QB 126). Whether or not such an obligation exists is a matter of law for a trial judge to decide (*R* v *Dubar* [1994] 1 WLR 1484).

Instances under s. 5(3) most commonly involve receiving money from others to retain and use in a certain way (e.g. travel agents taking deposits; solicitors holding funds for mortgagees; or pension fund managers collecting contributions (*R* v *Clowes (No. 2)* [1994] 2 All ER 316)). The Court of Appeal has held that one effect of s. 5(3) is that property can be regarded as belonging to another even where it does not 'belong' to that person on a strict interpretation of civil law (*R* v *Klineberg* [1999] 1 Cr App R 427). In that case the defendants collected money from customers in their timeshare business.

Although the customers were told that their deposits would be placed with an independent trustee, the defendants paid the sums into their company account, thereby breaching the 'obligation' under s. 5(3) to deal with the money in a particular way. Section 5(3) would also include, say, the owners of shopping centres where coins thrown into a fountain are to be donated to charity; if the owners did not deal with those coins in the way intended, the provisions of s. 5(3) may well apply.

## 2.1.9 Obligation to Restore Another's Property

The Theft Act 1968, s. 5 states:

(4) Where a person gets property by another's mistake, and is under an obligation to make restoration (in whole or in part) of the property or its proceeds or of the value thereof, then to the extent of that obligation the property or proceeds shall be regarded (as against him) as belonging to the person entitled to restoration, and an intention not to make restoration shall be regarded accordingly as an intention to deprive that person of the property or proceeds.

### KEYNOTE

Where extra money is mistakenly credited into an employee's bank account, the employee will be liable for stealing the extra money if he/she dishonestly keeps it (see *Attorney-General's Reference (No. 1 of 1983)* [1985] QB 182 where a police officer's account was credited with money representing overtime which she had not actually worked).

Section 5(4) only applies where someone *other than the defendant* has made a mistake. It is clear that such a mistake can be a mistake as to a material fact; whether or not a mistake as to *law* would be covered is unclear.

Again, the obligation to make restoration is a *legal* one and, as with s. 5(3), an unenforceable or moral obligation will not be covered by s. 5(4). (See *R v Gilks* [1972] 1 WLR 1341 where a betting shop mistakenly paid out winnings against the wrong horse. As gambling debts are not legally enforceable the defendant was not under 'an obligation' to restore the money and therefore s. 5(4) did not apply.)

## 2.1.10 Intention of Permanently Depriving

If you cannot prove an intention permanently to deprive you cannot prove theft (see *R v Warner* (1970) 55 Cr App R 93).

If there is such an intention at the time of the appropriation, giving the property back later will not alter the fact and the charge will be made out (*R v McHugh* (1993) 97 Cr App R 335).

In certain circumstances s. 6 may help in determining the presence or absence of such an intention.

The Theft Act 1968, s. 6 states:

(1) A person appropriating property belonging to another without meaning the other permanently to lose the thing itself is nevertheless to be regarded as having the intention of permanently depriving the other of it if his intention is to treat the thing as his own to dispose of regardless of the other's rights; and a borrowing or lending of it may amount to so treating it if, but only if, the borrowing or lending is for a period and in circumstances making it equivalent to an outright taking or disposal.

### KEYNOTE

The key feature of s. 6(1) is the intention to treat 'the thing' as one's own to dispose of regardless of the other's rights. An example of such a case would be where property is 'held to ransom' (*R v Coffey* [1987] Crim LR 498). The borrowing or lending of another's property is specifically caught within s. 6(1). If a person takes property from his/her employer (e.g. carpet tiles) and uses it in a way which makes restoration unlikely or impossible (e.g. by laying them in his/her living room), s. 6(1) will apply (see *R v Velumyl* [1989] Crim LR 299).

Similarly, if X is given a football season ticket by Y to use for one match but then X holds on to the season ticket for several matches knowing that this was not part of the arrangement and against the wishes of Y, s. 6(1) would help prove the required intention to permanently deprive because the circumstances of the borrowing make it equivalent to an outright taking.

In a case involving robbery, the defendants took the victim's personal stereo headphones from him and broke them in two, rendering them useless before returning them to him. The Administrative Court held that a person who took something and dealt with it for the purpose of rendering it useless in this way demonstrated the intention of treating that article as his/her own to dispose of. The court did not accept the argument that the property had to be totally exhausted before s. 6 applied (see also *R v Fernandes* [1996] 1 Cr App R 175) and held that the magistrates had been wrong to accept the submission of no case to answer on this point (*DPP v J* [2002] EWHC 291 (Admin)). Therefore, the deliberate breaking of an item of property will amount to the 'intention to permanently deprive'; however, unless this action is accompanied by the other theft elements it will be criminal damage. Note that in this case the offence dealt with was robbery so that the other elements of theft were plainly satisfied when the defendant initially took the property.

The Theft Act 1968, s. 6 states:

(2) Without prejudice to the generality of subsection (1) above, where a person, having possession or control (lawfully or not) of property belonging to another, parts with the property under a condition as to its return which he may not be able to perform, this (if done for purposes of his own and without the other's authority) amounts to treating the property as his own to dispose of regardless of the other's rights.

**KEYNOTE**

Section 6(2) deals with occasions such as pawning another's property. If there is a likelihood that the defendant will be unable to meet the conditions under which he/she parted with another person's property, s. 6(2) would help in proving an intention permanently to deprive.

# 2.2 Burglary

The main offence of burglary is split into two—s. 9(1)(a) and s. 9(1)(b). These are discussed below.

## 2.2.1 Section 9(1)(a)

OFFENCE: **Burglary—*Theft Act 1968, s. 9***
   - Triable on indictment if 'ulterior offence' is so triable, or if committed in dwelling and violence used; otherwise triable either way • 14 years' imprisonment if building/part of building is dwelling • Otherwise ten years' imprisonment on indictment
   - Six months' imprisonment and/or a fine summarily

The Theft Act 1968, s. 9 states:

(1) A person is guilty of burglary if—
   (a) he enters any building or part of a building as a trespasser and with intent to commit any such offence as is mentioned in subsection (2) below; or...
(2) The offences referred to in subsection (1)(a) above are offences of stealing anything in the building or part of a building in question, of inflicting on any person therein any grievous bodily harm and of doing unlawful damage to the building or anything therein.

---

**KEYNOTE**

**Enters**

What action on the part of the defendant constitutes 'entry' into a building or part of a building? The Theft Act 1968 does not define the term 'entry' and so we are left to resolve the meaning of this term by reference to case law and the decisions of the courts. The common law rule was that the insertion of any part of the body, *however small*, was sufficient to be considered an 'entry'. So where D pushed in a window pane and the forepart of his finger was observed in the building that was enough (*R v Davis* (1823) Russ & Ry 499). This approach was narrowed considerably in *R v Collins* [1973] QB 100, where it was said that entry needed to be 'effective and substantial'. The ruling in *Collins* was rejected by the Court of Appeal in *R v Brown* [1985] Crim LR 212, where it was stated that the 'substantial' element was surplus to requirements and that entry need only be 'effective'. Whether an entry was 'effective' or not was for the jury to decide. So the decision of the court in *Brown* appears to be the current accepted approach to defining the term; entry must therefore be 'effective'.

An 'effective' entry does not mean that the defendant has to enter a building or part of a building to such a degree that the ulterior offence, which he/she is entering with the intention to commit (the theft, GBH or criminal damage), can be committed (*R v Ryan* [1996] Crim LR 320). Nor does it mean that the defendant must get his/her whole body into the building. In *Brown*, the defendant had his feet on the ground outside the building with the upper half inside the building as he searched for goods to steal; this was held to be an entry. In *Ryan*, the defendant, who had become trapped by his neck with only his head and right arm inside the window, was held to have 'entered' the building. In *Brown*, the Court of Appeal stated that it would be astounding if a smash-and-grab raider, who inserted his hand through a shop window to grab goods, was not considered to have 'entered' the building.

At common law, the insertion of an instrument would constitute entry as long as the instrument was inserted to enable the ulterior offence to take place, e.g. a hook inserted into premises to steal property or the muzzle of a gun pushed through a letterbox with a view to cause GBH. Insertion of an instrument merely to facilitate entry, e.g. using a coat hanger to open a window lock, *would not* be entry. Although there is no recent authority on the issue, it is likely that this line of reasoning in relation to the use of instruments in burglary is still acceptable.

Entry must be deliberate and not accidental.

Ultimately, whether the defendant has entered a building or not will be a question of fact for the jury or magistrate(s).

### Trespasser

To be guilty of the offence of burglary people must know that they are entering as a trespasser (i.e. they must know they are entering without a right by law or with express or implied permission to do so) or be reckless as to that fact. Sometimes a defendant may have a general permission to enter a building or part of a building for a legitimate purpose; however, the true intention of the defendant when entering is not for that legitimate purpose but in order to steal or commit grievous bodily harm or to cause criminal damage. As these intentions invariably form no part of the permission to enter the building or part of it, any entry in such circumstances means that the defendant becomes a trespasser the moment he/she enters the building or part of the building. In such circumstances the exceeding of the granted permission places the defendant in a position of being a trespasser from the outset. In *R* v *Jones and Smith* [1976] 1 WLR 672, the defendant was convicted of burglary when he took two televisions from his father's home. He had a key to the premises and was free to come and go as he liked but when he entered his father's house (using the key) accompanied by a friend at 3am and stole the television sets, he committed burglary as it was his intention to steal—such an intent voids the general permission to enter.

## 2.2.2   Building

The Theft Act 1968 s. 9 states:

(4) References in subsections (1) and (2) above to a building, . . . and the reference in subsection (3), above, to a building which is a dwelling, shall apply also to an inhabited vehicle or vessel, and shall apply to any such vehicle or vessel at times when the person having a habitation in it is not there as well as at times when he is.

### KEYNOTE

#### Building

A building is generally considered to be a structure of a permanent nature (*Norfolk Constabulary* v *Seekings and Gould* [1986] Crim LR 167), although a substantial portable structure with most of the attributes of a building can be a 'building' for the purposes of burglary. For example, in *B & S* v *Leathley* [1979] Crim LR 314, a portable container measuring 25ft by 7ft by 7ft and weighing three tons, which had occupied the same position for three years, was connected to mains electricity, and which was due to remain in the same position for the foreseeable future, was considered to be a building for the purposes of burglary. An unfinished house can be a building for the purposes of burglary (*R* v *Manning* (1871) LR 1 CCR 338), although at what precise point a pile of building materials becomes an 'unfinished house' and therefore a building or part of a building would be a question of fact for the jury to decide. Tents and marquees are considered to fall outside the term, even if the tent is someone's home (the Criminal Law Revision Committee intended tents to be outside the protection of burglary).

The effect of s. 9(4) is to include *inhabited* vehicles and vessels (such as house boats or motor homes) within the term. A canal boat that is not inhabited is not a building as whilst it may be capable of habitation, it is not being lived in.

### 2.2.3 Intentions at the Time of Entry

The intentions must be as follows:

- Stealing—this means an intention to commit theft under s. 1 (and 'thief' and 'steal' will be construed accordingly). It will not include abstracting electricity because abstracting under s. 13 is not stealing as electricity is not 'property' for the purposes of theft (*Low* v *Blease* [1975] Crim LR 513), neither will it include taking a conveyance (as there is no intention to permanently deprive). The property which the defendant intends to steal must be in a building or part of a building.
- Inflicting grievous bodily harm—if grievous bodily harm is inflicted, then the second offence under s. 9(1)(b) below would apply. In proving an intention to commit grievous bodily harm under s. 9(1)(a), it is not necessary to prove that a wounding/grievous bodily harm offence was actually committed (*Metropolitan Police Commissioner* v *Wilson* [1984] AC 242). The offence in question in respect of a burglary under s. 9(1)(a) is of grievous bodily harm contrary to s. 18 of the Offences Against the Person Act 1861.
- Causing unlawful damage—this includes damage, not only to the building but to anything in it.

### 2.2.4 Conditional Intent

Provided the required intention can be proved, it is immaterial whether or not there is anything 'worth stealing' within the building (*R* v *Walkington* [1979] 1 WLR 1169). The same will be true if the person whom the defendant intends to cause serious harm is not in the building or part of the building at the time (**see also para. 1.3.4**).

### 2.2.5 Section 9(1)(b)

OFFENCE: **Burglary—*Theft Act 1968, s. 9***
- Triable on indictment if 'ulterior offence' is so triable, or if committed in dwelling and violence used; otherwise triable either way • 14 years' imprisonment if building/ part of building is a dwelling • Otherwise ten years' imprisonment on indictment
- Six months' imprisonment and/or a fine summarily

The Theft Act 1968, s. 9 states:

(1) A person is guilty of burglary if—

...

(b) having entered any building or part of a building as a trespasser he steals or attempts to steal anything in the building or that part of it or inflicts or attempts to inflict on any person therein any grievous bodily harm.

---

**KEYNOTE**

The second type of burglary involves a defendant's behaviour *after* entering a building or part of a building as a trespasser.

The defendant must have entered the building or part of a building as a trespasser; it is not enough that the defendant subsequently became a trespasser by exceeding a condition of entry (e.g. hiding in the public area of a shop during open hours until the shop closes). However, where a person has entered a particular building (such as a shop or a pub) lawfully and without trespassing, if he/she later moves to *another part* of the building as a trespasser, this element of the offence will be made out.

. . . . . . . . . . . . . . . . . . . . . . . . . . . . . . . . . . . . . . . . . . . . . . . . . . . . . . . . . . . . . . . . . . . . . . . . . . . . . . . . . . . . . . . . . . . . . . . . . . . . . . . . . . . . . . .

EXAMPLE

D enters a public house near closing time with a friend who buys him a drink from the bar. D's entry onto that part of the premises has been authorised by the implied licence extended to members of the adult public by the publican and therefore D is not a trespasser. D then goes into the lavatories to use them as such. At this point he has entered another part of a building but again his entry is made under the implied licence to customers wishing to use the lavatories. While inside the lavatory area, D decides to hide until closing time in order to avoid buying his friend a drink. At this point, although D's intention in hiding may be considered a little mean-spirited, he has none of the required intentions for the purposes of s. 9(1)(a).

Once the publican has shut the pub for the night, D becomes a trespasser in the lavatory. This is because he is not supposed to be there—he has no express or implied permission or lawful right to be in the lavatory after the pub has closed. While D is a trespasser at this point in time, if he went on to steal from the lavatory he *would not* commit burglary because he did not enter the lavatory as a trespasser—he became one at a later stage by exceeding a condition of entry. It is essential, for an offence of burglary to occur, that the defendant *has entered the building or part of a building as a trespasser*. D then leaves the lavatory and walks into the bar area. Now D has entered *a part of a building as a trespasser*. Having no particular intention at this point, however, D has still not committed an offence of burglary.

On seeing the gaming machines in the public bar, D decides to break into them and steal the money inside. At this point, although he has *two* of the required intentions for s. 9(1)(a) (an intention to steal and an intention to cause unlawful damage), those intentions were formed *after* his entry. Therefore, D has not committed burglary under s. 9(1)(a). Because he has not stolen/attempted to steal or inflicted/attempted to inflict grievous bodily harm on any person therein, D has not committed burglary under s. 9(1)(b) either.

D then breaks open a gaming machine. At this point he commits burglary under s. 9(1)(b). This is because, having entered a part of a building (the public bar area) as a trespasser (because the pub is closed and D knows that to be the case), he *attempts to steal*. If he simply damaged the machine without an intention of stealing the contents, D would not commit this offence because causing unlawful damage is only relevant to the offence under s. 9(1)(a).

. . . . . . . . . . . . . . . . . . . . . . . . . . . . . . . . . . . . . . . . . . . . . . . . . . . . . . . . . . . . . . . . . . . . . . . . . . . . . . . . . . . . . . . . . . . . . . . . . . . . . . . . . . . . . . .

Unlike s. 9(1)(a), there are only two further elements to the offence under s. 9(1)(b)—the subsequent theft/ attempted theft of anything in the building or part of it, and the subsequent inflicting/attempted inflicting of grievous bodily harm to any person therein. The offence in question in respect of a burglary under s. 9(1)(b) is of grievous bodily harm contrary to s. 18 or s. 20 of the Offences Against the Person Act 1861.

It has been suggested that if, having entered a building or part of a building as a trespasser, the defendant commits an offence of criminal damage, this will be an offence under s. 9(1)(b) of the Act as to damage or destroy something is also to steal it. *This is not the case.* If a person enters in such circumstances and causes criminal damage, there is little argument that such an activity would satisfy part of the offence of theft, i.e. appropriating property (see para. 2.1.4)—but where is the 'dishonesty'? In addition, this would clearly be an unwarranted extension of the burglary offence under s. 9(1)(b)of the Theft Act 1968. If Parliament wanted such activity to be caught by the legislation, it would have included the offence of criminal damage within the definition of burglary under s. 9(1)(b).

# 2.3 Aggravated Burglary

## 2.3.1 Aggravated Burglary

OFFENCE: **Aggravated Burglary—*Theft Act 1968, s. 10***
- Triable on indictment • Life imprisonment

The Theft Act 1968, s. 10 states:

(1) A person is guilty of aggravated burglary if he commits any burglary and at the time has with him any firearm or imitation firearm, any weapon of offence, or any explosive;...

---

**KEYNOTE**

An aggravated burglary is committed when a person commits an offence of burglary (either a s. 9(1)(a) or a s. 9(1)(b)) and at the time he/she has with him/her a **WIFE**.

W – Weapon of offence
I – Imitation firearm
F – Firearm
E – Explosive

Two points in the definition merit further discussion: (i) *at the time* and (ii) *has with him/her.*

**At the time**

These words require consideration of the type of burglary the defendant is charged with. The moment at which a burglary under s. 9(1)(a) is committed is at the point of entry, therefore it is essential that the defendant has the WIFE with him/her when entering a building or part of a building with the intention of committing one of the trigger offences under s. 9(1)(a). If that is the case, the defendant commits aggravated burglary. The moment at which a burglary under s. 9(1)(b) is committed is when the defendant steals, inflicts grievous bodily harm on any person or attempts to do either. If the defendant has the WIFE with him/her when committing or attempting to commit either offence, an aggravated burglary is committed.

...........................................................................................................

EXAMPLE·

A person (X) enters the kitchen of a house as a trespasser intending to steal property. At the point of entry X does not have any WIFE item with him, so at this point in time X has committed a s. 9(1)(a) burglary. While X is in the kitchen the occupier of the house enters the kitchen and disturbs him. X picks up a carving knife (not intending to steal it but to hurt the occupier with it if necessary) and threatens the occupier with it. At this point the carving knife becomes a weapon of offence (intended to cause injury and because of the concept of 'instant arming' (see below)) but this is not an aggravated burglary as X has not committed or attempted to commit theft or to inflict GBH. The occupier rushes towards X who stabs the occupier, inflicting GBH in the process. This is a s. 9(1)(b) burglary and at the time of its commission X has a WIFE item with him; as a result this becomes an aggravated burglary.

**Has with him**

'Has with him' is more restrictive than the term 'possession'. It will require the defendant to have some degree of *immediate control* of the item (*R v Pawlicki* [1992] 1 WLR 827) and will normally (but not exclusively) be the same as 'carrying' (*R v Klass* [1998] 1 Cr App R 453) although the defendant need not actually

---

have the WIFE item *on his/her person* to be in *immediate control* of it. It is also essential that the individual has knowledge of the presence of the WIFE item. So if a burglary is committed by a single offender who knows he/she has a bayonet in his/her coat pocket when the offence is committed, the issue of aggravated burglary is clear. However, what of the situation where two offenders commit such a burglary? Liability depends on knowledge.

EXAMPLE

X and Y decide to commit a burglary together. X is concerned about being disturbed during the burglary and decides to take a flick-knife (a weapon of offence as it is made for causing injury) along with him when the burglary takes place; he does not tell Y about the flick-knife. When X and Y enter the building they intend to burgle, both commit a s. 9(1)(a) burglary. As X has a flick-knife with him at the time, X commits an aggravated burglary. However, Y does not commit the aggravated offence because he has no knowledge of the existence of the WIFE item. If X had told Y about the flick-knife then Y would have the required knowledge and would be deemed to have it with him so both would be guilty under s. 10 (*R* v *Jones* [1979] CLY 411).

Therefore, if the defendant has no knowledge of the WIFE item he/she does not commit the aggravated offence. If several people are charged with the offence of aggravated burglary, it must be shown that one of the defendants who actually entered the building or part of a building had the weapon with him/her (*R* v *Klass* [1998] 1 Cr App R 453).

It is important to note that the aggravated offence is committed due to the presence of the WIFE when the s. 9(1)(a) or s. 9(1)(b) burglary is carried out. It is irrelevant that the defendant had the item with him/her for some other purpose unconnected with the burglary offence. The thought process underpinning this point is that if a burglar has the WIFE item with him/her during the course of a domestic burglary and is confronted by the householder, there would be a strong temptation to make use of it regardless of why the burglar had the WIFE in the first place.

**Instant Arming**

Ordinary items can, instantaneously, change into weapons of offence; it is the intention of the person to use an item in a particular way that allows this to take place. A good illustration of this concept is the case of *R* v *Kelly* (1993) 97 Cr App R 245. The defendant entered a building using a screwdriver to facilitate entry. When he was confronted he prodded the person confronting him in the stomach with the screwdriver. At that moment the screwdriver instantly became a weapon of offence and the defendant was later convicted of aggravated burglary.

## 2.3.2 Firearm/Weapon of Offence/Explosive

The Theft Act 1968, s. 10 goes on to state:

(1) ... and for this purpose—
   (a) 'firearm' includes an airgun or pistol, and 'imitation firearm' means anything which has the appearance of being a firearm, whether capable of being discharged or not, and
   (b) 'weapon of offence' means any article made or adapted for use for causing injury to or incapacitating a person, or intended by the person having it with him for such use; and
   (c) 'explosive' means any article manufactured for the purpose of producing a practical effect by explosion, or intended by the person having it with him for that purpose.

### Weapon of Offence

This is a wider definition than that under the Prevention of Crime Act 1953. It includes:

- Items *made* for causing injury, e.g. a bayonet or a flick-knife (as above).
- Items *adapted* for causing injury, e.g. a screwdriver that has been sharpened at the tip.

- Items *intended* for causing injury, e.g. an ordinary cutlery knife. The cutlery knife is certainly inoffensive in everyday use but if the defendant *intends* to use it to injure, it will fall into this category.
- Items *made, adapted or intended* to incapacitate a person, e.g. handcuffs, rope, CS spray and chloroform.

The defendant must not only know of the presence of the weapon but also that it is a weapon of offence.

### Imitation Firearm

This includes anything which has the appearance of being a firearm, whether capable of being discharged or not (but note that this will not include the defendant's fingers pointed at someone under a coat to resemble a firearm (*R* v *Bentham* [2005] UKHL 18)).

### Firearm

This does not relate to the definition under the Firearms Act 1968. Indeed, the term is not defined other than to include airguns and air pistols.

### Explosive

This would cover explosives such as TNT and items such as grenades—both manufactured to produce a practical effect by explosion. It also covers an item intended by the person having it with him/her for such a purpose, potentially bringing home-made devices or substances into the equation. The issue in relation to fireworks has yet to be firmly resolved by the courts, although they may well be excluded from the definition as fireworks are, by and large, manufactured to produce a pyrotechnic rather than practical effect by explosion and have been described as 'things that are made for amusement' (*Bliss* v *Lilley* (1862) 32 LJMC 3)).

# 2.4 Robbery

## 2.4.1 Robbery

OFFENCE: **Robbery—*Theft Act 1968, s. 8***
  • Triable on indictment • Life imprisonment

The Theft Act 1968, s. 8 states:

> (1) A person is guilty of robbery if he steals, and immediately before or at the time of doing so, and in order to do so, he uses force on any person or puts or seeks to put any person in fear of being then and there subjected to force.

---

**KEYNOTE**

### The Theft Element of the Offence

For there to be a robbery, there must be a theft; so if there is no theft, then there can be no robbery. The word 'steal' in the offence relates to the offence under s. 1 of the Theft Act 1968 and, therefore, if *any* element of theft cannot be proved the offence of robbery will not be made out. For example, in *R* v *Robinson* [1977] Crim LR 173, D, who was owed £7 by P's wife, approached P, brandishing a knife. A fight followed, during which P dropped a £5 note. D picked it up and demanded the remaining £2 owed to him. Allowing D's appeal against a conviction for robbery, the Court of Appeal held that the prosecution had to prove that D was guilty of theft, and that he would not be (under the Theft Act 1968, s. 2(1)(a)) if he believed that he had a right in law to deprive P of the money, even though he knew that he was not entitled to use the knife to get it, i.e. there was no dishonesty.

### The Robbery Time Frame

Section 8(1) requires that the force must be used or the threat made 'immediately before or at the time' of the theft. There is no guidance as to what 'immediately before' means. Clearly, if the force used or threatened is *after* the offence of theft has taken place, there will be no robbery; however theft can be a continuing offence. This was decided in *R* v *Hale* (1979) 68 Cr App Rep 415, where the Court of Appeal stated that appropriation is a continuing act and whether it has finished or not is a matter for the jury to decide. From the robbery perspective, *Hale* decides that where D had assumed ownership of goods in a house, the 'time' of stealing is a continuing process. It does not end as soon as the property is picked up by the defendant and can be a continuing act so long as he/she is in the course of removing it from the premises. So, if D uses or threatens force to get away with the property (while still in the house for example), a robbery is committed. This would not be the case if the defendant used force outside the house as there must come a time when the appropriation ends. The issue may be resolved by asking the question, 'Was D still on the job?' (*R* v *Atakpu* [1994] QB 69).

### In Order to Do So

The use or threat of force must be 'in order' to carry out the theft. Force used in any other context means the offence is not committed, for example:

• Two men have an argument outside a pub and begin fighting each other. One man punches the other in the face and the force of the blow knocks the man out. As the injured man falls to the floor, his wallet drops out of his jacket pocket and onto the pavement. His opponent decides that he will steal the wallet. *No robbery is committed in these circumstances because the force is used for a purpose other than to steal.*

The question to ask in such circumstances is 'Why has the force been used and/or threatened?' If the answer is anything other than 'To enable the defendant to commit theft' then there is no offence of robbery.

---

## Force

A small amount of force used in order to accomplish a theft may change that theft into a robbery. An illustration can be found in the case of *R* v *Dawson* (1977) 64 Cr App R 170, where the defendant and two others surrounded their victim. One of the attackers 'nudged' the victim and while he was unbalanced another stole his wallet. In *Dawson*, the court declined to define 'force' any further than to say that juries would understand it readily enough. In line with general principles of *actus reus* (criminal conduct), the force used by the defendant must be used voluntarily. Therefore, the accidental use of force such as when a pickpocket, in the process of stealing a wallet from his victim on a train, is pushed into his victim by the train jolting on the railway line would not be a robbery.

### On Any Person

The force used to accomplish a robbery need not be used against the owner or possessor of the property. For example, a gang of armed criminals use force against a security guard in order to overpower him and steal cash from the bank he is standing outside and guarding.

### Use of Force on Property

Force does not actually have to be used 'on' the *person,* i.e. on the actual body of the victim. It may be used indirectly, for example on something that the victim is carrying and thereby transferring the force to the person. This was the case in *R* v *Clouden* [1987] Crim LR 65, where the Court of Appeal dismissed an appeal against a conviction for robbery when the defendant had wrenched the victim's shopping basket from her hand and ran off with it. However, in *P* v *DPP* [2012] EWHC 1657 (Admin), it was held that snatching a cigarette from the hand of the victim was incapable of amounting to robbery. Mitting J stated 'It cannot be said that the minimum use of force required to remove a cigarette from between the fingers suffices to amount to the use of force against that person'. In this case there was no evidence of direct physical contact between the victim and the thief.

### The Fear of Force

Where only the *threat* of force is involved the intention must be to put a person in fear for *himself*; an intention to put someone in fear for another is not enough (*R* v *Taylor* [1996] 10 Archbold News 2). This may seem at odds with the approach to the actual *use* of force in the offence of robbery (in that force *can* be used against a third party who is unconnected with the property subject to the theft). For example:

- A man enters a betting shop and approaches the cashier. Without saying a word he passes a note to the cashier that simply says, 'Look to your left'. The cashier looks to her left and sees the man's accomplice standing several feet away and pointing a knife at the back of one of the betting shop customers. The customer is oblivious to the actions of the man's accomplice. The man passes a second note to the cashier that says, 'Give me the money in the till or else he gets it!' The cashier, fearing for the customer, hands over the contents of the betting shop till. *This would not be an offence of robbery as the cashier cannot fear force for the betting shop customer. However, whilst there is no robbery there would be an offence of blackmail (Theft Act 1968, s. 21).* Let us say that instead of handing the contents of the betting shop till over to the offender, the cashier shakes her head and refuses to hand over any money. At this point, the man signals to his accomplice who pulls the customer's head backwards and drags the knife across the side of the customer's throat causing a small cut. The customer screams in terror and at this point the cashier concedes to the man's demand and hands over the till contents. *At this point in time a robbery is committed as force is actually being used (albeit on a third party).*

### General Points

Any threats to use force at some time in the future (even by a matter of minutes) would constitute an offence of blackmail. Threats to use force at some place other than the location of the offence fall into the same category. This effectively excludes threats made via the telephone in all but the most improbable of situations.

# 2.5 | Blackmail

## 2.5.1 Blackmail

OFFENCE: **Blackmail—*Theft Act 1968, s. 21***

- Triable on indictment • 14 years' imprisonment

The Theft Act 1968, s. 21 states:

(1) A person is guilty of blackmail if, with a view to gain for himself or another or with intent to cause loss to another, he makes any unwarranted demand with menaces; and for this purpose a demand with menaces is unwarranted unless the person making it does so in the belief—
   (a) that he has reasonable grounds for making the demand; and
   (b) that the use of the menaces is a proper means of reinforcing the demand.

(2) The nature of the act or omission demanded is immaterial, and it is also immaterial whether the menaces relate to action to be taken by the person making the demand.

### KEYNOTE

In proving this offence you must show that the defendants acted either with a view to gain for themselves or another or with intent to cause loss to another. The distinction here is important. The phrase 'with a view to' has been held (albeit under a different criminal statute) by the Court of Appeal to be less than 'with intent to' (*R v Zaman* [2002] EWCA Crim 1862). In *Zaman*, the court accepted that a lesser degree of *mens rea* was required to prove that the defendant acted 'with a view to' something and that this phrase meant simply that the defendant had something in his contemplation as *something that realistically might occur*, not that he necessarily intended or even wanted it to happen. Clearly this is a very different test from 'intent'. In the above offence then, it appears that the state of mind needed to prove the first element is that the defendant contemplated some gain for himself or for another as being realistically likely to flow from his actions. The alternative is an 'intent' to cause loss.

There is no requirement for dishonesty or theft and the offence is aimed at the making of the demands rather than the consequences of them.

## 2.5.2 Meaning of Gain and Loss

Section 34 of the 1968 Act states:

(2) For the purposes of this Act—
   (a) 'gain' and 'loss' are to be construed as extending only to gain or loss in money or other property, but as extending to any such gain or loss whether temporary or permanent; and—
      (i) 'gain' includes a gain by keeping what one has, as well as a gain by getting what one has not; and
      (ii) 'loss' includes a loss by not getting what one might get, as well as a loss by parting with what one has; ...

### KEYNOTE

Keeping what you already have can amount to a 'gain'. Similarly, not getting something that you might expect to get can be a 'loss'.

A person makes unwarranted demands with menaces with a view to getting a sports fixture cancelled and thereby to avoid losing money that he/she has bet on the outcome of that fixture. Here the intention of keeping what the defendant already had (the money at risk on the bet) amounts to 'gain' as defined under s. 34(2). Similarly, the intention of preventing others getting what they might have got (their winnings or the club's earnings) could amount to a 'loss'.

A blackmailer need not be seeking any kind of material profit. In *R* v *Bevans* (1988) 87 Cr App R 64, D used menaces in order to obtain a pain-killing injection from a doctor; this was held to be blackmail as the drug involved was a form of property.

### 2.5.3 Criminal Conduct

The offence of blackmail is complete when the demand with menaces is made. As a result it is extremely difficult, if not impossible, to have an offence of attempted blackmail as the defendant will either be preparing to make the demand or will have made it. It does not matter whether the demands bring about the desired consequences or not. If a demand is made by letter, the act of making it is complete when the letter is posted. The letter does not have to be received (*Treacy* v *DPP* [1971] AC 537).

The Court of Appeal has held that words or conduct which would not intimidate or influence anyone to respond to the demand would not be 'menaces'. As such, the term requires threats and conduct of such a nature and extent that a person of normal stability and courage might be influenced or made apprehensive so as to give in to the demands (see *R* v *Clear* [1968] 1 QB 670).

Menaces will therefore include threats but these must be significant *to the victim*. If a threat bears a particular significance for a victim (such as being locked in the boot of a car to someone who is claustrophobic) that will be enough, provided the defendant was aware of that fact. If a victim is particularly timid and the defendant knows it, that timidity may be taken into account when assessing whether or not the defendant's conduct was 'menacing' (*R* v *Garwood* [1987] 1 WLR 319).

### 2.5.4 Unwarranted?

If a defendant raises the issue that his/her demand was reasonable and proper, you will have to prove that he/she did not believe:

- that he/she had reasonable grounds for making the demand; and
- that the use of the particular menaces employed was not a proper means of reinforcing it.

The defendant's *belief* will be a subjective one and therefore could be entirely unreasonable. However, if the threatened action would itself be unlawful (such as a threat to rape the victim) then it is unlikely that the courts would accept any claim by a defendant that he/she believed such a demand to be 'proper' (see *R* v *Harvey* (1981) 72 Cr App R 139).

# 2.6 Fraud

## 2.6.1 Introduction

The Fraud Act 2006 provides a general offence of fraud which can be committed in three ways (by false representation, by failing to disclose information, and by abuse of position). It also deals with offences of obtaining services dishonestly, and possessing, making, and supplying articles for use in fraud.

## 2.6.2 Fraud

OFFENCE: **Fraud—*Fraud Act 2006, s. 1***
- Triable either way • Ten years' imprisonment and/or a fine on indictment
- 12 months' imprisonment and/or a fine summarily

The Fraud Act 2006, s. 1 states:

(1) A person is guilty of fraud if he is in breach of any of the sections listed in subsection (2) (which provide for different ways of committing the offence).
(2) The sections are—
(a) section 2 (fraud by false representation),
(b) section 3 (fraud by failing to disclose information), and
(c) section 4 (fraud by abuse of position).

---

**KEYNOTE**

The heart of all three methods of committing the offence of fraud is in the *conduct and ulterior intent* of the defendant. The effect of this approach is that a defendant's unsuccessful 'attempt' to commit the offence of fraud may amount to the commission of the substantive offence, effectively excluding the possibility of an offence under the Criminal Attempts Act 1981.

---

## 2.6.3 Fraud by False Representation

The Fraud Act 2006, s. 2 states:

(1) A person is in breach of this section if he—
(a) dishonestly makes a false representation, and
(b) intends, by making the representation—
(i) to make a gain for himself or another, or
(ii) to cause loss to another or to expose another to the risk of loss.
(2) A representation is false if—
(a) it is untrue or misleading, and
(b) the person making it knows that it is, or might be, untrue or misleading.
(3) 'Representation' means any representation as to fact or law, including a representation as to the state of mind of—
(a) the person making the representation, or
(b) any other person.
(4) A representation may be express or implied.

(5) For the purposes of this section a representation may be regarded as made if it (or anything implying it) is submitted in any form to any system or device designed to receive, convey or respond to communications (with or without human intervention).

---

KEYNOTE

### Dishonestly

The 'dishonestly' referred to in s. 2(1)(a) is a reference to the test of dishonesty established in *R* v *Ghosh* [1982] QB 1053. The same test applies to ss. 3 and 4 of the Act.

### Gain and Loss

Section 2(1)(b) refers to 'gain' and 'loss' and that the person making the representation must do so with the intention of making a gain or causing a loss or risk of loss to another. *The gain or loss does not actually have to take place*.

### Representation

A representation is false if it is untrue or misleading *and* the person making it knows this is or knows this might be the case. Therefore, an untrue statement made in the honest belief that it is in fact true, would not suffice. The words 'or might be' must involve a subjective belief on the part of the person making the representation. Where a defendant makes a false representation knowing that it is false or might be, the offence of fraud is complete.

The representation may be express or implied and can be communicated in words or conduct. There is no limitation on the way in which the representation must be expressed, so it could be written, spoken or posted on a website.

A representation may be implied by conduct. For example, a person dishonestly misusing a credit card to pay for items hands the card to a cashier without saying a word. By handing the card to the cashier the person is falsely representing that he has the authority to use it for that transaction. It is immaterial whether that the cashier accepting the card for payment is deceived by the representation as the cashier's state of mind plays no part in the commission of the offence.

Any representation made must be one as to fact or law, so a broken promise is not in itself a false representation. However, a statement may be false if it misrepresents the current intentions or state of mind of the person making it or anyone else. For example, D visits V's house and tells V that he needs emergency work carried out on his roof. D states that he is in a position to do the work immediately but only if V pays him £1,000 there and then. V gives D the money and D then leaves without carrying out the work; the truth of the matter was that D had never intended to carry out the work. Such a 'promise' by D would amount to an offence as it involved a false representation i.e. he never intended to keep the promise.

A representation may be *proved* by inference. Where an elderly or other vulnerable person has paid D vastly more for a job or product (such as gardening work) than it was worth, it may be open to a court or jury to *infer* that D must dishonestly have misrepresented the value of that job or product, even if there is no direct evidence of any such misrepresentation (*R* v *Greig* [2010] EWCA Crim 1183). When an unidentified imposter presented himself to take a driving test in D's name, it could be inferred that D was complicit in any false representations made by that person with a view to gaining a pass certificate in his name (*Idrees* v *DPP* [2011] EWHC 624 (Admin)).

The offence is complete the moment the false representation is made. The representation need never be heard nor communicated to the recipient and if carried out by post, would be complete when the letter is posted (*Treacy* v *DPP* [1971] AC 537).

### Phishing

The offence would also be committed by someone who engages in 'phishing'. This is the practice of sending out e-mails in bulk, purporting to represent a well-known brand in the hope of sending victims to a bogus website that tricks them into disclosing bank account details. 'Phishing kits' have long been available on the Internet; the offence under s. 2 covers such activity.

### Machines

Section 2(5) of the Fraud Act enables the offence of fraud to apply to cases where the representation is made to a machine (for example where a person enters a number into a 'Chip and PIN' machine).

### 2.6.4 Fraud by Failing to Disclose

The Fraud Act 2006, s. 3 states:

A person is in breach of this section if he—
- (a) dishonestly fails to disclose to another person information which he is under a legal duty to disclose, and
- (b) intends, by failing to disclose the information—
    - (i) to make a gain for himself or another, or
    - (ii) to cause loss to another or to expose another to a risk of loss.

---

**KEYNOTE**

Section 3 creates an offence of dishonestly failing to disclose information where there is a legal duty to do so. The term 'legal duty' has not been defined but will include duties under oral contracts as well as written contracts. The Law Commission's *Report on Fraud* dealt with the concept of legal duty and stated that duties might arise:

- from statute
- where the transaction is one of the utmost good faith
- from the express or implied terms of a contract
- from the custom of a particular trade or market, or
- from the existence of a fiduciary relationship between parties.

The legal duty to disclose information will exist if:

- the defendant's actions give the victim a cause in action for damages or
- if the law gives the victim the right to set aside any change in his/her legal position to which he or she may have consented as a result of the non-disclosure.

A fiduciary relationship is one relating to the responsibility of looking after someone else's money in a correct way. Examples of such behaviour would include solicitors failing to share vital information with a client in the context of their work relationship, in order to carry out a fraud upon that client, or if a person intentionally failed to disclose information relating to a heart condition when making an application for life insurance. Where recipients of benefits dishonestly fail to disclose income etc. that they are legally required to disclose, fraud by failing to disclose is an appropriate charge (*R* v *El-Mashta* [2010] EWCA Crim 2595).

---

### 2.6.5 Fraud by Abuse of Position

The Fraud Act 2006, s. 4 states:

- (1) A person is in breach of this section if he—
    - (a) occupies a position in which he is expected to safeguard, or not to act against, the financial interests of another person,
    - (b) dishonestly abuses that position, and
    - (c) intends, by means of the abuse of that position—
        - (i) to make a gain for himself or another, or
        - (ii) to cause loss to another or to expose another to a risk of loss.
- (2) A person may be regarded as having abused his position even though his conduct consisted of an omission rather than an act.

---

**KEYNOTE**

The crux of this offence is the financial and dishonest abuse of a privileged position of trust. An offence under s. 4 may be committed in a variety of ways as the 'position' that the defendant occupies may be the result of an assortment of relationships. The Law Commission explained the meaning of 'position' at para. 7.38:

The necessary relationship will be present between trustee and beneficiary, director and company, professional person and client, agent and principle, employee and employer, or between partners. It may arise otherwise, for example within a family, or in the context of voluntary work, or in any context where the parties are not at arm's length.

The term 'abuse' is not defined by the Act.

Liability for the offence could develop from a wide range of conduct, for example:

- An employee of a software company uses his position to clone software products with the intention of selling the products on.
- An estate agent values a house belonging to an elderly person at an artificially low price and then arranges for the agent's brother to purchase the house.
- A person who is employed to care for a disabled person and has access to that person's bank account, abuses that position by transferring funds to invest in a high-risk business venture of his own.

The offence can also be committed by omission, for example:

- An employee fails to take up the chance of a crucial contract in order that an associate or rival company can take it up instead of and at the expense of the employer.

## 2.6.6  Gain and Loss

The Fraud Act 2006, s. 5 states:

(1) The references to gain and loss in sections 2 to 4 are to be read in accordance with this section.
(2) 'Gain' and 'loss'—
   (a) extend only to gain and loss in money or other property;
   (b) include any such gain or loss whether temporary or permanent;
   and 'property' means any property whether real or personal (including things in action and other intangible property).
(3) 'Gain' includes a gain by keeping what one has, as well as getting what one does not have.
(4) 'Loss' includes a loss by not getting what one might get, as well as a loss by parting with what one has.

### KEYNOTE

It is important to note that the 'gain' and 'loss' relates only to *money and other property*. The definition of property covers all forms of property including intellectual property.

## 2.6.7  Possession or Control of Articles for Use in Frauds

OFFENCE:  **Possession or Control of Articles for Use in Frauds—*Fraud Act 2006, s. 6***
- Triable either way • Five years' imprisonment and/or a fine on indictment
- 12 months' imprisonment and/or a fine summarily

The Fraud Act 2006, s. 6 states:

(1) A person is guilty of an offence if he has in his possession or under his control any article for use in the course of or in connection with any fraud.

### KEYNOTE

The offence under s. 6 can be committed *anywhere at all*, including the home of the defendant. The offence is not only committed when the defendant has articles in his/her possession but also when the defendant has them in his/her control—a term that indicates that the defendant may be some distance away from the articles and yet still commit the offence. The offence under s. 6 applies to *all fraud offences* under the 2006 Act.

However, much like the offence of 'going equipped' the offence is only committed in respect of *future* offences and not offences that have already taken place. The offence can be committed if possession, or control is to enable *another* to commit an offence of fraud. The definition of the term 'article' is discussed at **para. 2.6.9.**

## 2.6.8 Making or Supplying Articles for Use in Frauds

OFFENCE: **Making or Supplying Articles for Use in Frauds—*Fraud Act 2006, s. 7***
- • Triable either way • Ten years' imprisonment on indictment and/or a fine
- • 12 months' imprisonment and/or a fine summarily

The Fraud Act 2006, s. 7 states:

(1) A person is guilty of an offence if he makes, adapts, supplies or offers to supply any article—
  (a) knowing that it is designed or adapted for use in the course of or in connection with fraud, or
  (b) intending it to be used to commit, or assist in the commission of, fraud.

---

**KEYNOTE**

The broad terms of the offence ensure that any activity in respect of the making, supplying etc. of any 'article' for use in fraud offences is an offence. Making an 'offer to supply' would not require the defendant to be in possession of the 'article' (a similar situation to offering to supply a controlled drug, see para. 3.8.4). Examples of such behaviour include:

- A person makes a viewing card for a satellite TV system, enabling him/her to view all satellite channels for free.
- The same person then offers to sell similar cards to work colleagues although he/she has only made the one prototype card and does not actually have further cards to sell.
- A number of the person's work colleagues express an interest in buying the cards, so the person makes a dozen more cards and then actually supplies them to those work colleagues.

---

## 2.6.9 'Article'

The Fraud Act 2006, s. 8 states:

(1) For the purposes of—
  (a) sections 6 and 7, and
  (b) the provisions listed in subsection (2), so far as they relate to articles for use in the course of or in connection with fraud,
  'article' includes any program or data held in electronic form.
(2) The provisions are—
  (a) section 1(7)(b) of the Police and Criminal Evidence Act 1984 (c 60),
  (b) ...
  (c) ...

Section 8 extends the meaning of 'article' for the purposes of ss. 6 and 7 of the Act to include any program or data held in electronic form. Examples of cases where electronic programs or data could be used in fraud are:

- a computer program that generates credit card numbers
- a computer template that can be used for producing blank utility bills
- a computer file that contains lists of other people's credit card details.

### 2.6.10    Obtaining Services Dishonestly

OFFENCE:   **Obtaining Services Dishonestly—*Fraud Act 2006, s. 11***
  - Triable either way  • Five years' imprisonment and/or a fine on indictment
  - 12 months' imprisonment and/or a fine summarily

The Fraud Act 2006, s. 11 states:

(1) A person is guilty of an offence under this section if he obtains services for himself or another—
  - (a) by a dishonest act, and
  - (b) in breach of subsection (2).
(2) A person obtains services in breach of this subsection if—
  - (a) they are made available on the basis that payment has been, is being or will be made for or in respect of them,
  - (b) he obtains them without any payment having been made for or in respect of them or without payment having been made in full, and
  - (c) when he obtains them, he knows—
    - (i) that they are being made available on the basis described in paragraph (a), or
    - (ii) that they might be,

but intends that payment will not be made, or will not be made in full.

---

**KEYNOTE**

It is important to note that unlike the other Fraud Act 2006 offences, the offence under s. 11 is not a conduct crime; it is a *result crime* and requires the *actual obtaining* of the service. However, the offence does not require a fraudulent representation or deception. Someone would commit this offence if, intending to avoid payment, she slipped into a concert hall to watch a concert without paying for the privilege. The offence can be committed where the defendant intends to avoid payment or payment in full but the defendant must know that the services are made available on the basis that they are chargeable, i.e. services provided for free are not covered by the offence. The terms 'service' and 'obtaining' are not defined by the Act.

---

### 2.6.11    Falsification of Documents and Other Instruments

In addition to the offence of fraud, there are a series of closely-related offences which deal with falsification of documents or other 'instruments'.

### 2.6.11.1    False Accounting

OFFENCE:   **False Accounting—*Theft Act 1968, s. 17***
  - Triable either way  • Seven years' imprisonment on indictment
  - Six months' imprisonment and/or a fine summarily

The Theft Act 1968, s. 17 states:

(1) Where a person dishonestly, with a view to gain for himself or another or with intent to cause loss to another,—
  - (a) destroys, defaces, conceals or falsifies any account or any record or document made or required for any accounting purpose; or
  - (b) in furnishing information for any purpose produces or makes use of any account, or any such record or document as aforesaid, which to his knowledge is or may be misleading, false or deceptive in a material particular;
he shall [commit an offence].
(2) For purposes of this section a person who makes or concurs in making in an account or other document an entry which is or may be misleading, false or deceptive in a material particular, or who omits or concurs in omitting a material particular from an account or other document, is to be treated as falsifying the account or document.

This section creates two offences: destroying, defacing, etc. accounts and documents; and using false or misleading accounts or documents in furnishing information.

An offence under s. 17 can be committed by omission as well as by an act. Failing to make an entry in an accounts book, altering a till receipt or supplying an auditor with records that are incomplete may, if accompanied by the other ingredients, amount to an offence.

Unlike theft there is no requirement to prove an intention permanently to deprive but there is a need to show dishonesty. The requirement as to gain and loss is the same as for blackmail (see para. 2.5.1).

The misleading, false or deceptive nature of the information furnished under s. 17(1)(b) must be 'material' to the defendant's overall purpose, i.e. the ultimate gaining or causing of loss. Such an interpretation means that the defendant's furnishing of information need not relate directly to an accounting process and could be satisfied by lying about the status of a potential finance customer (see *R* v *Mallett* [1978] 1 WLR 820).

Where the documents falsified are not intrinsically 'accounting' forms, such as insurance claim forms filled out by policyholders, you must show that those forms are treated for accounting purposes by the victim (*R* v *Sundhers* [1998] Crim LR 497). An application for a mortgage or a loan to a commercial institution is a document required for an accounting purpose, the rationale being that applications for a mortgage or a loan to commercial institutions will, if successful, lead to the opening of an account which will show as credits in favour of the borrower, funds received from the borrower and as debits paid out by the lender to, or on behalf of, the borrower (*R* v *O and H* [2010] EWCA Crim 2233).

### 2.6.11.2 Forgery

Offences classed as 'forgery' include virtually every kind of document *except* bank notes. Coins and currency are the subject of a separate group of offences classed as counterfeiting.

Many of the offences dealt with below are divided into two categories:

- Offences where there is an *intention* by the defendant to pass the document, note or coin off as being genuine. These, more serious offences, attract higher penalties.
- Offences where there is no requirement to prove any ulterior intent.

### 2.6.11.3 Police Powers Regarding False Instruments

A warrant to search for and seize false instruments and materials may be issued under s. 7 of the 1981 Act.

### 2.6.11.4 False Instruments

OFFENCE: **Making a False Instrument with Intent—*Forgery and Counterfeiting Act 1981, s. 1***
- Triable either way • Ten years' imprisonment on indictment
- Six months' imprisonment and/or a fine summarily

The Forgery and Counterfeiting Act 1981, s. 1 states:

A person is guilty of forgery if he makes a false instrument, with the intention that he or another shall use it to induce somebody to accept it as genuine, and by reason of so accepting it to do or not to do some act to his own or any other person's prejudice.

OFFENCE: **Using a False Instrument with Intent—*Forgery and Counterfeiting Act 1981, s. 3***
- Triable either way • Ten years' imprisonment on indictment
- Six months' imprisonment and/or a fine summarily

The Forgery and Counterfeiting Act 1981, s. 3 states:

It is an offence for a person to use an instrument which is, and which he knows or believes to be, false, with the intention of inducing somebody to accept it as genuine, and by reason of so accepting it to do or not to do some act to his own or any other person's prejudice.

OFFENCE: **Copying a False Instrument with Intent**—*Forgery and Counterfeiting Act 1981, s. 2*
- Triable either way • Ten years' imprisonment on indictment
- Six months' imprisonment and/or a fine summarily

The Forgery and Counterfeiting Act 1981, s. 2 states:

It is an offence for a person to make a copy of an instrument which is, and which he knows or believes to be, a false instrument, with the intention that he or another shall use it to induce somebody to accept it as a copy of a genuine instrument, and by reason of so accepting it to do or not to do some act to his own or any other person's prejudice.

OFFENCE: **Using a Copy of a False Instrument with Intent**—*Forgery and Counterfeiting Act 1981, s. 4*
- Triable either way • Ten years' imprisonment on indictment
- Six months' imprisonment and/or a fine summarily

The Forgery and Counterfeiting Act 1981, s. 4 states:

It is an offence for a person to use a copy of an instrument which is, and which he knows or believes to be, a false instrument, with the intention of inducing somebody to accept it as a copy of a genuine instrument, and by reason of so accepting it to do or not to do some act to his own or any other person's prejudice.

---

**KEYNOTE**

The essence of these offences is that they concern documents or instruments which purport to be something which they are not; that is, they 'tell a lie about themselves'.

---

In the defining terms used by s. 9 of the 1981 Act:

(1) An instrument is false for the purposes of this Part of this Act—
  (a) if it purports to have been made in the form in which it is made by a person who did not in fact make it in that form; or
  (b) if it purports to have been made in the form in which it is made on the authority of a person who did not in fact authorise its making in that form; or
  (c) if it purports to have been made in the terms in which it is made by a person who did not in fact make it in those terms; or
  (d) if it purports to have been made in the terms in which it is made on the authority of a person who did not in fact authorise its making in those terms; or
  (e) if it purports to have been altered in any respect by a person who did not in fact alter it in that respect; or
  (f) if it purports to have been altered in any respect on the authority of a person who did not in fact authorise the alteration in that respect; or
  (g) if it purports to have been made or altered on a date on which, or at a place at which, or otherwise in circumstances in which, it was not in fact made or altered; or
  (h) if it purports to have been made or altered by an existing person but he did not in fact exist.

Section 9 goes on to say that:

(2) A person is to be treated for the purposes of this part of this Act as making a false instrument if he alters an instrument so as to make it false in any respect (whether or not it is false in some other respect apart from that alteration).

An 'instrument' is defined in s. 8 of the 1981 Act which states:

(1) Subject to subsection (2) below, in this Part of this Act 'instrument' means—
   (a) any document, whether of a formal or informal character;
   (b) any stamp issued or sold by a postal operator;
   (c) any Inland Revenue stamp; and
   (d) any disc, tape, sound track or other device on or in which information is recorded or stored by mechanical, electronic or other means.

(2) A currency note within the meaning of Part II of this Act is not an instrument for the purposes of this Part of this Act.

(3) A mark denoting payment of postage which a postal operator authorises to be used instead of an adhesive stamp is to be treated for the purposes of this Part of this Act as if it were a stamp issued by the postal operator concerned.

(3A) In this section, 'postal operator' has the same meaning as in the Postal Services Act 2000.

(4) In this Part of this Act 'Inland Revenue stamp' means a stamp as defined in section 27 of the Stamp Duties Management Act 1891.

### 2.6.11.5  Specific Instruments

In addition to the above offences which apply to any instrument, there are several specific offences which apply to specific types of 'formal' instrument.

OFFENCE: **Having Custody or Control of Specific Instruments and Materials with Intent—*Forgery and Counterfeiting Act 1981, s. 5(1) and (3)***
   • Triable either way • Ten years' imprisonment on indictment
   • Six months' imprisonment and/or a fine summarily

The Forgery and Counterfeiting Act 1981, s. 5 states:

(1) It is an offence for a person to have in his custody or under his control an instrument to which this section applies which is, and which he knows or believes to be, false, with the intention that he or another shall use it to induce somebody to accept it as genuine, and by reason of so accepting it to do or not to do some act to his own or any other person's prejudice.

(2) ...

(3) It is an offence for a person to make or to have in his custody or under his control a machine or implement, or paper or any other material, which to his knowledge is or has been specially designed or adapted for the making of an instrument to which this section applies, with the intention that he or another shall make an instrument to which this section applies which is false and that he or another shall use the instrument to induce somebody to accept it as genuine, and by reason of so accepting it to do or not to do some act to his own or any other person's prejudice.

## OFFENCE: **Having Custody or Control of Specific Instruments and Materials— *Forgery and Counterfeiting Act 1981, s. 5(2) and (4)***

- Triable either way • Two years' imprisonment on indictment
- Six months' imprisonment and/or a fine summarily

The Forgery and Counterfeiting Act 1981, s. 5 states:

(2) It is an offence for a person to have in his custody or under his control, without lawful authority or excuse, an instrument to which this section applies which is, and which he knows or believes to be, false.

(3) ...

(4) It is an offence for a person to make or to have in his custody or under his control any such machine, implement, paper or material, without lawful authority or excuse.

The instruments to which the above offences under s. 5 apply are:

(5) ...
   (a) money orders;
   (b) postal orders;
   (c) United Kingdom postage stamps;
   (d) Inland Revenue stamps;
   (e) share certificates;
   (f) ...
   (g) cheques and other bills of exchange;
   (h) travellers' cheques;
   (ha) bankers' drafts;
   (hb) promissory notes;
   (j) cheque cards;
   (ja) debit cards;
   (k) credit cards;
   (l) certified copies relating to an entry in a register of births, adoptions, marriages, civil partnerships or deaths and issued by the Registrar General, the Registrar General for Northern Ireland, a registration officer or a person lawfully authorised to issue certified copies relating to such entries; and
   (m) certificates relating to entries in such registers.

(6) In subsection (5)(e) above 'share certificate' means an instrument entitling or evidencing the title of a person to a share or interest—
   (a) in any public stock, annuity, fund or debt of any government or state, including a state which forms part of another state; or
   (b) in any stock, fund or debt of a body (whether corporate or unincorporated) established in the United Kingdom or elsewhere.

(7) An instrument is also an instrument to which this section applies if it is a monetary instrument specified for the purposes of this section by an order made by the Secretary of State.

...

### 2.6.11.6 Prejudice and Induce

The intent of *inducing* somebody to accept an instrument with the result that he/she does something to his/her own *prejudice* must be read in the light of s. 10 of the 1981 Act which states:

(1) Subject to subsections (2) and (4) below, for the purposes of this Part of this Act an act or omission intended to be induced is to a person's prejudice if, and only if, it is one which, if it occurs—
   (a) will result—
      (i) in his temporary or permanent loss of property; or
      (ii) in his being deprived of an opportunity to earn remuneration or greater remuneration; or
      (iii) in his being deprived of an opportunity to gain a financial advantage otherwise than by way of remuneration; or
   (b) will result in somebody being given an opportunity—
      (i) to earn remuneration or greater remuneration from him; or
      (ii) to gain a financial advantage from him otherwise than by way of remuneration; or
   (c) will be the result of his having accepted a false instrument as genuine, or a copy of a false instrument as a copy of a genuine one, in connection with his performance of any duty.

(2) An act which a person has an enforceable duty to do and an omission to do an act which a person is not entitled to do shall be disregarded for the purposes of this Part of this Act.

(3) In this Part of this Act references to inducing somebody to accept a false instrument as genuine, or a copy of a false instrument as a copy of a genuine one, include references to inducing a machine to respond to the instrument or copy as if it were a genuine instrument or, as the case may be, a copy of a genuine one.

**KEYNOTE**

This section extends the meaning of inducing someone to accept something as genuine to *machines*. The extension is limited to offences under part I of the 1981 Act and therefore does not apply to offences contained elsewhere such as counterfeiting.

# 2.7 Handling Stolen Goods

## 2.7.1 Handling Stolen Goods

OFFENCE: **Handling Stolen Goods—*Theft Act 1968, s. 22***
- Triable either way • 14 years' imprisonment on indictment • Six months' imprisonment and/or a fine summarily

The Theft Act 1968, s. 22 states:

(1) A person handles stolen goods if (otherwise than in the course of the stealing) knowing or believing them to be stolen goods he dishonestly receives the goods, or dishonestly undertakes or assists in their retention, removal, disposal or realisation by or for the benefit of another person, or if he arranges to do so.

---

**KEYNOTE**

Handling can only be committed *otherwise than in the course of stealing*. Given the extent of theft and the fact that it can be a continuing act, it is critical to identify at what point the theft of the relevant property ended. It is also useful, in cases of doubt, to include alternative charges.

You must show that the defendant *knew* or *believed* the goods to be stolen. Mere suspicion, however strong, will not be enough (*R* v *Griffiths* (1974) 60 Cr App R 14). Deliberate 'blindness' to the true identity of the goods would suffice. Because there are practical difficulties in proving the required *mens rea*, s. 27(3) of the 1968 Act makes special provision to allow evidence of the defendant's previous convictions, or previous recent involvement with stolen goods, to be admitted.

'Goods' will include money and every other description of property except land, and includes things severed from the land by stealing (s. 34(2)(b) of the Act).

---

## 2.7.2 Stolen Goods

The Theft Act 1968, s. 24 states:

(1) The provisions of this Act relating to goods which have been stolen shall apply whether the stealing occurred in England or Wales or elsewhere, and whether it occurred before or after the commencement of this Act, provided that the stealing (if not an offence under this Act) amounted to an offence where and at the time when the goods were stolen; and references to stolen goods shall be construed accordingly.

(2) For purposes of those provisions references to stolen goods shall include, in addition to the goods originally stolen and parts of them (whether in their original state or not),—

(a) any other goods which directly or indirectly represent or have at any time represented the stolen goods in the hands of the thief as being the proceeds of any disposal or realisation of the whole or part of the goods stolen or of goods representing the stolen goods; and

(b) any other goods which directly or indirectly represent or have at any time represented the stolen goods in the hands of a handler of the stolen goods or any part of them as being the proceeds of any disposal or realisation of the whole or part of the stolen goods handled by him or of goods so representing them.

(3) But no goods shall be regarded as having continued to be stolen goods after they have been restored to the person from whom they were stolen or to other lawful possession or custody, or after that person and any other person claiming through him have otherwise ceased as regards those goods to have any right to restitution in respect of the theft.

(4) For purposes of the provisions of this Act relating to goods which have been stolen (including subsections (1) to (3) above) goods obtained in England or Wales or elsewhere either by blackmail or subject to subsection (5) below, by fraud (within the meaning of the Fraud Act 2006) shall be regarded as stolen; and 'steal', 'theft' and 'thief' shall be construed accordingly.

(5) Subsection (1) above applies in relation to goods obtained by fraud as if—

(a) the reference to the commencement of this Act were a reference to the commencement of the Fraud Act 2006, and

(b) the reference to an offence under this Act were a reference to an offence under section 1 of that Act.

The Theft Act 1968, s. 24A states:

(7) Subsection (8) below applies for purposes of provisions of this Act relating to stolen goods (including subsection (4) above).

(8) References to stolen goods include money which is dishonestly withdrawn from an account to which a wrongful credit has been made, but only to the extent that the money derives from the credit.

---

**KEYNOTE**

If goods are not stolen there is no handling. Whether they are so stolen is a question of fact for a jury or magistrate(s). There is no need to prove that the thief, blackmailer, etc. has been convicted of the primary offence before prosecuting the alleged handler, neither is it always necessary to *identify* who that person was.

However, care needs to be taken if a defendant is to be accused of handling goods stolen *from a specific person or place*. If that is the case then ownership of the goods will become an integral part of the prosecution case and it will be necessary to provide evidence proving that aspect of the offence (*Iqbal* v *DPP* [2004] EWHC 2567 (Admin)).

Goods obtained by fraud and blackmail are included in the definition of 'stolen goods' under s. 24(4) and s. 24(5). The references to fraud are to the general offence of fraud under s. 1 of the Fraud Act 2006. Clearly goods gained through robbery or burglary will, by definition, be 'stolen' as theft is an intrinsic element of both offences.

'Wrongful credits' are included within the meaning of stolen goods under certain circumstances.

---

## 2.7.3 Section 24 Explained

Under s. 24(1) a person can still be convicted of handling if the goods were stolen outside England and Wales but only if the goods were taken under circumstances which amounted to an offence in the other country.

Under s. 24(2), goods will be classed as stolen only if they are the property which was originally stolen or if they have at some time represented the *proceeds* of that property in the hands of the thief or a 'handler'.

Therefore if a DVD recorder is stolen, sold to an unsuspecting party who then part-exchanges it for a new one at a high street retailer, the first DVD recorder will be 'stolen' goods, the new one will not. If the first person buying the original DVD recorder *knew* or *believed* that it was stolen, the new DVD recorder will be treated as stolen goods.

Under s. 24(3), once goods have been restored to lawful possession they cease to be stolen. This situation does not cause problems when police officers recover stolen property and then wait for it to be collected by a handler (see *Houghton* v *Smith* [1975] AC 476) as the Criminal Attempts Act 1981 and the common-law rulings on 'impossibility' mean that a defendant could be dealt with in a variety of ways:

- Theft—collecting the property will be an 'appropriation'.
- Handling—an *arrangement* to come and collect stolen goods will probably have been made while they were still 'stolen'.
- Criminal attempt—the person collecting the goods has gone beyond merely preparing to handle them.

### 2.7.4 Proof that Goods were Stolen

The Theft Act 1968, s. 27 states:

(4) In any proceedings for the theft of anything in the course of transmission (whether by post or otherwise), or for handling stolen goods from such a theft, a statutory declaration made by any person that he dispatched or received or failed to receive any goods or postal packet, or that any goods or postal packet when dispatched or received by him were in a particular state or condition, shall be admissible as evidence of the facts stated in the declaration, subject to the following conditions:—

(a) a statutory declaration shall only be admissible where and to the extent to which oral evidence to the like effect would have been admissible in the proceedings; and

(b) a statutory declaration shall only be admissible if at least seven days before the hearing or trial a copy of it has been given to the person charged, and he has not, at least three days before the hearing or trial or within such further time as the court may in special circumstances allow, given the prosecutor written notice requiring the attendance at the hearing or trial of the person making the declaration.

---

**KEYNOTE**

The above provisions allow for specific evidence to be admitted in proving that goods 'in the course of transmission' have been stolen. These provisions allow for a statutory declaration by the person dispatching or receiving goods or postal packets as to when and where they were dispatched and when or if they arrived and, in each case, their state or condition (e.g. if they had been opened or interfered with). Such a statutory declaration will only be admissible in circumstances where an oral statement would have been admissible *and* if a copy has been served on the defendant at least seven days before the hearing and he/she has not—within three days of the hearing—served written notice on the prosecutor requiring the attendance of the person making the declaration.

This section is to be construed in accordance with s. 24 generally (s. 27(5)).

---

### 2.7.5 Handling

The offence of handling stolen goods is made up of many facets. Therefore to charge a defendant without specifying a particular form of handling is not bad for duplicity (*R v Nicklin* [1977] 1 WLR 403). However, the offence can be divided for practical purposes into two parts:

- *receiving/arranging to receive* stolen goods, in which case the defendant acts for his/her own benefit, and
- *assisting/acting for the benefit of another* person, in which case that assistance to another or benefit of another must be proved.

### 2.7.6 Receiving

Receiving does not require the physical reception of goods and can extend to exercising control over them. Things in action—such as bank credits from a stolen cheque—can be 'received'.

'Arranging to receive' would cover circumstances which do not go far enough to constitute an attempt—that is, actions which *are* merely preparatory to the receiving of stolen goods may satisfy the elements under s. 22 even though they would not meet the criteria under the Criminal Attempts Act 1981.

If the goods have yet to be stolen, s. 22 *would not apply* and the offence of conspiracy should be considered (see *R v Park* (1988) 87 Cr App R 164).

## 2.7.7 Assisting/Acting for Another's Benefit

Assisting or acting for the benefit of another can be committed by misleading police officers during a search (see *R* v *Kanwar* [1982] 1 WLR 845).

Disposing of the stolen goods or assisting in their disposal or realisation usually involves physically moving them or converting them into a different form (see *R* v *Forsyth* [1997] 2 Cr App R 299).

If the only person 'benefiting' from the defendant's actions is the defendant, this element of the offence will not be made out (*R* v *Bloxham* [1983] 1 AC 109).

Similarly, if the only 'other' person to benefit is a co-accused on the same charge, the offence will not be made out (*R* v *Gingell* [2000] 1 Cr App R 88).

## 2.7.8 Guilty Knowledge in Cases of Handling and Theft

Section 27 of the Theft Act 1968 allows for the admissibility of previous misconduct and states:

(3) Where a person is being proceeded against for handling stolen goods (but not for any offence other than handling stolen goods), then at any stage of the proceedings, if evidence has been given of his having or arranging to have in his possession the goods the subject of the charge, or of his undertaking or assisting in, or arranging to undertake or assist in, their retention, removal, disposal or realisation, the following evidence shall be admissible for the purpose of proving that he knew or believed the goods to be stolen goods—

   (a) evidence that he has had in his possession, or has undertaken or assisted in the retention, removal, disposal or realisation of, stolen goods from any theft taking place not earlier than 12 months before the offence charged; and

   (b) (provided that seven days' notice in writing has been given to him of the intention to prove the conviction) evidence that he has within the five years preceding the date of the offence charged been convicted of theft or of handling stolen goods.

---

**KEYNOTE**

This provision applies to all forms of handling (*R* v *Ball* [1983] 1 WLR 801) but its use is limited as it can only be used in cases where handling is the *only offence* involved in the proceedings.

The question as to what constitutes recent possession is a matter of fact and degree dependent on the circumstances of each case. This presumption can be rebutted by the person offering a true explanation for the possession (*R* v *Schama* (1914) 84 LJ KB 396, *R* v *Garth* [1949] 1 All ER 773, *R* v *Aves* [1950] 2 All ER 330 and *R* v *Williams* [1962] Crim LR 54).

The term 'recent possession' is not defined and so is a question of fact in each case. In *R* v *Smythe* (1981) 72 Cr App R 8, the Court of Appeal held that property found in the possession of an accused, stolen two or three months earlier during some robberies and burglaries, did not amount to recent possession for the offence of handling stolen goods generally.

---

# Proceeds of Crime

## 2.8.1 Proceeds of Crime Act 2002

The offences and powers under the Proceeds of Crime Act 2002 are not just within the purview of specialist financial investigation departments. While 'serious crime' is likely to play a significant part in the use of the powers the Act provides, police officers must remember that the Act is also connected with day to day criminality and therefore involves all police officers whatever rank and role they fulfil. This section provides an overview of the three principal offences relating to 'Money Laundering' created by s. 327 (concealing criminal property), s. 328 (arrangements in relation to criminal property) and s. 329 (acquisition, use and possession of criminal property) of the Act. To begin with, there must be a brief examination of the concepts relating to 'criminal conduct' and 'criminal property'.

## 2.8.2 Criminal Conduct

The Proceeds of Crime Act 2002, s. 340 states:

> (2) Criminal conduct is conduct which—
>   (a) constitutes an offence in any part of the United Kingdom, or
>   (b) would constitute an offence in any part of the United Kingdom if it occurred there.

Section 340(4) states that it is immaterial:

- who carried out the criminal conduct
- who benefited from it
- whether the conduct occurred before or after the passing of the Act.

So criminal conduct not only includes the behaviour of the defendant but also of any other person. Effectively this states that *any offence*, committed by *any person, anywhere* at all and at *any time* is 'criminal conduct'. This represents a significant departure from earlier law which required the prosecution to show that the criminal property existed as a consequence of a specific offence or class of offences. As a consequence of s. 340, a conviction can be obtained under the Proceeds of Crime Act even if the prosecution cannot specify the offence or offences that gave rise to the proceeds or identify the person(s) responsible for the offence(s).

## 2.8.3 Criminal Property

The Proceeds of Crime Act 2002, s. 340 states:

> (3) Property is criminal property if—
>   (a) it constitutes a person's benefit from criminal conduct or it represents such a benefit (in whole or in part and whether directly or indirectly) and,
>   (b) the alleged offender knows or suspects that it constitutes or represents such a benefit.

**KEYNOTE**

Although the offences under ss. 327, 328 and 329 are often referred to as 'money laundering', it should be noted that the definition of 'property' is exceptionally wide and *does not just relate to money*. Section 340(9) of the Act defines property as *all* property *wherever* situated and includes:

- money
- all forms of property, real or personal, heritable or movable, and
- things in action and other intangible or incorporeal property.

(Incorporeal property relates to property or an asset that does not have value in material form, such as a right or a patent.)

The *mens rea* relating to criminal property and therefore to all three offences is knowing or *suspecting*. Dishonesty is not required. In *R* v *Da Silva* [2006] EWCA Crim 1654, it was said that:

> to suspect something, you have to have a state of mind well short of knowing that the matter you suspect is true. It is an ordinary English word ... the dictionary definition of 'suspicion' [is] an act of suspecting, the imagining of something without evidence or on slender evidence, inkling, mistrust.

The Court of Appeal upheld the conviction, concluding that the word 'suspect' meant that the defendant had to think that there was a possibility, which was more than fanciful, that the relevant facts existed. A vague feeling of unease would not suffice. The fact the suspicion alone will suffice means that proving such offences is remarkably less burdensome for the prosecution than the potential alternative to such offences, a charge of handling stolen goods where the defendant must be proved to know or believe that goods are stolen goods.

## 2.8.4 Concealing Criminal Property

OFFENCE: **Concealing Criminal Property—*Proceeds of Crime Act 2002, s. 327***
- Triable either way  •  14 years' imprisonment on indictment and/or a fine
- Six months' imprisonment and/or a fine summarily

The Proceeds of Crime Act 2002, s. 327 states:

(1) A person commits an offence if he—
    (a) conceals criminal property;
    (b) disguises criminal property;
    (c) converts criminal property;
    (d) transfers criminal property;
    (e) removes criminal property from England and Wales and Scotland or from Northern Ireland.
(2) But a person does not commit such an offence if—
    (a) he makes an authorised disclosure under section 338 and (if the disclosure is made before he does the act mentioned in subsection (1)) he has the appropriate consent;
    (b) he intended to make such a disclosure but had a reasonable excuse for not doing so;
    (c) the act he does is done in carrying out a function he has relating to the enforcement of any provision of this Act or of any other enactment relating to criminal conduct or benefit from criminal conduct.
(3) Concealing or disguising criminal property includes concealing or disguising its nature, source, location, disposition, movement or ownership or any rights with respect to it.

**KEYNOTE**

There is a noticeable overlap between the activities relating to concealing criminal property and the offence of handling stolen goods, particularly when considering the list of activities that a defendant may undertake in the commission of both offences. However, whereas handling only occurs 'otherwise than in the course of stealing' and 'by or for the benefit of another', the offence under s. 327 can potentially be committed *during the commission of an offence* and *for the benefit of the thief*. On a literal reading of s. 327, a thief who conceals, disguises or sells property that he has just stolen may thereby commit offences under that section because the definition of criminal property applies to the laundering of an offender's own proceeds of crime as well as those of someone else.

Section 327(2) creates several defences to charges under s. 327.

## 2.8.5 Arrangements in relation to Criminal Property

OFFENCE: **Arrangements in relation to Criminal Property—*Proceeds of Crime Act 2002, s. 328***
- Triable either way • 14 years' imprisonment on indictment and/or a fine
- Six months' imprisonment and/or a fine summarily

The Proceeds of Crime Act 2002, s. 328 states:

(1) A person commits an offence if he enters into or becomes concerned in an arrangement which he knows or suspects facilitates (by whatever means) the acquisition, retention, use or control of criminal property by or on behalf of another person.

### KEYNOTE

To establish an offence under this section, the prosecutor would need to prove that a person entered into or became concerned in an arrangement which he/she knew or suspected would make it easier for another person to acquire, retain, use or control criminal property and that the person concerned also knew or suspected that the property constituted or represented benefit from criminal conduct. This offence will often be apt for the prosecution of those who launder on behalf of others. Not only could this catch persons who work in financial or credit institutions, accountants etc., who in the course of their work facilitate money laundering by or on behalf of other persons, but also family members (husband/wife, partner etc.). The natural and ordinary meaning of s. 328(1) was that the arrangement to which it referred must be one which related to property which was criminal property at the time when the arrangement began to operate on it. To say that it extended to property which was originally legitimate but became criminal only as a result of carrying out the arrangement was to stretch the language of the section beyond its proper limits (*R* v *Geary* (*Michael*) [2010] EWCA Crim 1925).

Section 328 includes the same defences against committing the offence, as are included in s. 327(2).

## 2.8.6 Acquisition, Use and Possession of Criminal Property

OFFENCE: **Acquisition, Use and Possession of Criminal Property—*Proceeds of Crime Act 2002, s. 329***
- Triable either way • 14 years' imprisonment on indictment and/or a fine
- Six months' imprisonment and/or a fine summarily

The Proceeds of Crime Act 2002, s. 329 states:

(1) A person commits an offence if he—
    (a) acquires criminal property;
    (b) uses criminal property;
    (c) has possession of criminal property.

The coincidence between an offence of handling stolen goods and those described from the Proceeds of Crime Act 2002 might provide a dilemma as to which offence to charge. In such a situation, CPS guidance states that if it is possible to charge money laundering or handling stolen goods then money laundering may be more appropriate if 'either a defendant has possessed criminal proceeds in large amounts or in lesser amounts, but repeatedly and where assets are laundered for profit'. However, a money laundering charge should only be considered where proceeds are more than *de minimis* (about minimal things) in any circumstances where the defendant who is charged with the underlying offence has done more than simply consume the proceeds of crime.

# 2.9 | Criminal Damage

## 2.9.1 Introduction

The chances of any police officers going through their career without dealing in some way with an offence of criminal damage are minuscule. The prevalence of offences of criminal damage is well documented and damage in all forms has a harmful effect on the environment, the community and the economy.

## 2.9.2 Simple Damage

OFFENCE: **Simple Damage—*Criminal Damage Act 1971, s. 1(1)***
- Triable either way • Ten years' imprisonment on indictment
- Six months' imprisonment and/or a fine summarily

OFFENCE: **Racially or Religiously Aggravated—*Crime and Disorder Act 1998, s. 30(1)***
- Triable either way • 14 years' imprisonment and/or a fine on indictment
- Six months' imprisonment and/or a fine summarily

The Criminal Damage Act 1971, s. 1 states:

(1) A person who without lawful excuse destroys or damages any property belonging to another intending to destroy or damage any such property or being reckless as to whether any such property would be destroyed or damaged shall be guilty of an offence.

---

**KEYNOTE**

Although triable either way, if the value of the property destroyed or the damage done is less than £5,000, the offence is to be tried summarily (Magistrates' Courts Act 1980, s. 22). If the damage in such a case was caused by fire (arson), this rule will not apply.

The fact that the substantive offence is, by virtue of the value of the damage caused, triable only summarily does not make simple damage a 'summary offence' for all other purposes. If it did, you could only be found guilty of *attempting* to commit criminal damage if the value of the intended damage was more than £5,000 (because the Criminal Attempts Act 1981 does not extend to summary offences). Therefore, where a defendant tried to damage a bus shelter in a way that would have cost far less than £5,000 to repair, his argument that he had only attempted what was in fact a 'summary offence' was dismissed by the Divisional Court (*R* v *Bristol Magistrates' Court, ex parte E* [1999] 1 WLR 390). Note that where the damage caused is less than £300, the offence can be dealt with by way of fixed penalty notice.

If the offence involves only the painting or writing on, or the soiling, marking or other defacing of, any property by whatever means, the power to issue a graffiti notice may apply.

The racially or religiously aggravated form of this offence is triable either way irrespective of the cost of the damage. For details on how offences can become racially or religiously aggravated, see chapter 3.7.

The provisions of s. 30 of the Crime and Disorder Act 1998 only apply to the offence of 'simple' damage under s. 1(1) of the 1971 Act; they do not apply to any of the other offences in this chapter.

---

### 2.9.2.1 Destroy or Damage

Although a key feature of the 1971 Act, the terms 'destroy' or 'damage' are not defined. The courts have taken a wide view when interpreting these terms. 'Destroying' property would suggest that it has been rendered useless but there is no need to prove that 'damage' to property is in any way permanent or irreparable.

Whether an article has been damaged will be a question of fact for each court to determine on the evidence before it. Situations where courts have accepted that property has been damaged include the defacing of a pavement by an artist using only water-soluble paint (*Hardman* v *Chief Constable of Avon and Somerset* [1986] Crim LR 330). It has also been held by the Divisional Court that graffiti smeared in mud can amount to damage, even though it is easily washed off (*Roe* v *Kingerlee* [1986] Crim LR 735).

A good example of the courts' approach can be seen in *R* v *Fiak* [2005] EWCA Crim 2381. In that case the defendant had been arrested and placed in a police cell which he flooded by stuffing a blanket down the cell lavatory and repeatedly flushing. The defendant argued that there was no evidence that the blanket or the cell had been 'damaged'; the water had been clean and both the blanket and the cell could be used again when dry. The Court of Appeal disagreed and held that, while the effect of the defendant's actions in relation to the blanket and the cell was remediable, the reality was that the blanket could not be used until it had been dried and the flooded cell was out of action until the water had been cleared. Therefore both had sustained damage for the purposes of the Act.

It can be seen therefore that putting property temporarily out of use—even for a short time and in circumstances where it will revert to its former state of its own accord—may fall within the definition of 'damage'.

### 2.9.2.2 Property

Property is defined in the 1971 Act by s. 10 which states:

(1) In this Act 'property' means property of a tangible nature, whether real or personal, including money and—
  (a) including wild creatures which have been tamed or are ordinarily kept in captivity and any other wild creatures or their carcasses if, but only if, they have been reduced into possession...or are in the course of being reduced into possession; but
  (b) not including mushrooms growing wild on any land or flowers, fruit or foliage of a plant growing wild on any land.
  ...

---

**KEYNOTE**

This definition has similarities with the definition of 'property' for the purposes of theft but 'real' property (i.e. land and things attached to it) can be damaged even though it cannot be stolen. Trampling flower beds, digging up cricket pitches, chopping down trees in a private garden and even pulling up genetically-modified crops may all amount to criminal damage if accompanied by the required circumstances.

Pets or farm animals are property for the purposes of this Act. Cases of horses being mutilated would, in addition to the offence of 'cruelty' itself, amount to criminal damage. There may also be occasions—such as domestic or neighbour disputes—involving harm or cruelty to such animals where it will be more appropriate and effective to consider offences under the 1971 Act.

---

### 2.9.2.3 Belonging to Another

Section 10 states:

(2) Property shall be treated for the purposes of this Act as belonging to any person—
  (a) having the custody or control of it;

(b) having in it any proprietary right or interest (not being an equitable interest arising only from an agreement to transfer or grant an interest); or

(c) having a charge on it.

---

**KEYNOTE**

This extended meaning of 'belonging to another' is similar to that used in the Theft Act 1968. One result is that if a person damages his/her own property, he/she may still commit the offence of simple criminal damage if that property also 'belongs to' someone else.

---

### 2.9.2.4 Lawful Excuse

Section 5 of the Criminal Damage Act 1971 provides for two occasions where a defendant may have a 'lawful excuse'. These can be remembered as 'permission' (s. 5(2)(a)) and 'protection' (s. 5(2)(b)). Both involve the belief of the defendant.

### 2.9.2.5 Permission

A person shall be treated as having lawful excuse under s. 5(2):

(a) if at the time of the act or acts alleged to constitute the offence he believed that the person or persons whom he believed to be entitled to consent to the destruction of or damage to the property in question had so consented, or would have so consented to it if he or they had known of the destruction or damage and its circumstances...

---

**KEYNOTE**

An example of 'lawful excuse' under s. 5(2)(a) would be if you, as a police officer, were asked by a motorist to help him get into his partner's car after locking the keys inside. If, during that attempt you damaged the rubber window surround, s. 5(2)(a) would provide you with a statutory defence to any later charge of criminal damage by the owner. The key elements here would be:

- the consent of someone whom you believed to be entitled to consent to that damage, and
- the circumstances under which it was caused.

If the driver was not available and your reason for opening the door was to get a better look at some personal documents for intelligence purposes, it is unlikely that the driver or the owner would have consented, either to the damage or the circumstances in which it was caused. Therefore you could not use this particular defence.

---

### 2.9.2.6 Protection

A person shall be treated as having lawful excuse under s. 5(2):

(b) if he destroyed or damaged or threatened to destroy or damage the property in question or, in the case of a charge of an offence under section 3 above, intended to use or cause or permit the use of something to destroy or damage it, in order to protect property belonging to himself or another or a right or interest in property which was or which he believed to be vested in himself or another, and at the time of the act or acts alleged to constitute the offence he believed—

(i) that the property, right or interest was in immediate need of protection; and

(ii) that the means of protection adopted or proposed to be adopted were or would be reasonable having regard to all the circumstances.

### Belief

The 1971 Act goes on to say that it is immaterial whether a 'belief' above was justified as long as it was honestly held (s. 5(3)). This test is problematic because, although it is supposed to be an *objective* one, the evidence will be based largely on what was going through a defendant's mind at the time—or sometimes what was *not* going through his/her mind! In *Jaggard* v *Dickinson* [1981] QB 527 the defendant had broken a window to get into a house. Being drunk at the time, she had got the wrong house but the court accepted that her belief (that it was the right house and that the owner would have consented) had been honestly held, and that it did not matter whether that belief was brought about by intoxication, stupidity, forgetfulness or inattention. That is not to say, however, that *any* honestly held belief will suffice. An example of someone claiming—though unsuccessfully—a defence under both s. 5(2)(a) and (b) can be seen in *Blake* v *DPP* [1993] Crim LR 586. There the defendant was a vicar who wished to protest against Great Britain's involvement in the Gulf War. In order to mark his disapproval, the defendant wrote a quotation from the Bible in ink on a pillar in front of the Houses of Parliament. He claimed:

• that he was carrying out God's instructions and therefore had a lawful excuse based on his belief that God was the person entitled to consent to such damage and that he had in fact consented or would have done so (s. 5(2)(a)); and
• that he had damaged the property as a reasonable means of protecting other property located in the Gulf from being damaged by warfare (s. 5(2)(b)).

Perhaps unsurprisingly the Divisional Court did not accept either proposition holding that, in the first case a belief in the Almighty's consent was not a 'lawful excuse' and, in the second, that the defendant's conduct was too remote from any immediate need to protect property in the Gulf States. The test in relation to the defendant's belief appears then to be largely subjective (i.e. what was/was not going on in the defendant's head at the time) but with an objective element in that the judge/magistrate(s) must decide whether, on the facts as believed by the defendant, his/her acts were capable of protecting property.

Taking a different tack, peace campaigners in *R* v *Jones (Margaret)* [2004] EWCA Crim 1981 argued that their fear of the consequences of war in Iraq—which they claimed to be illegal—prompted them to conspire to cause damage at an airbase and that such fear amounted both to duress and lawful excuse under s. 5(2)(b) above. The Court of Appeal held that a jury would be entitled to consider some of the subjective beliefs of the defendants in determining the reasonableness of their actions.

Finally, a demonstrator at the Guildhall Gallery knocked the head off a statue of Baroness Thatcher and claimed that he acted in fear for his son's future which had been placed in jeopardy by the joint actions of the US and UK governments, and for which Baroness Thatcher was partly responsible. His appeal against conviction brought under s. 5(2)(b)—with a few technicalities added on—failed (*R* v *Kelleher* [2003] EWCA Crim 2846).

The Act also states, at s. 5(4), that a right or interest in property includes any right or privilege in or over land, whether created by grant, licence or otherwise.

Section 5(5) allows for other general defences at criminal law to apply in addition to those listed under s. 5.

It is not an offence to damage your own property unless there are aggravating circumstances. Even if the intention in doing so is to carry out some further offence—such as a fraudulent insurance claim—this fact still does not make it an offence under s. 1(1) of the Criminal Damage Act 1971 (*R* v *Denton* [1981] 1 WLR 1446).

### 2.9.2.7 Recklessness

An offence of criminal damage under s. 1(1) can be proved by showing that the defendant was 'reckless'. In *R* v *G and R* [2003] UKHL 50, the House of Lords held that a person acts recklessly for the purposes of s. 1(1) of the Act:

- with respect to a circumstance when he/she is aware of a risk that existed or would exist;
- with respect to a result or consequence when he/she is aware of a risk that it would occur and it is, in the circumstances known to him/her, unreasonable to take the risk.

In *R* v *G and R*, two children (aged 11 and 12) set fire to some newspapers in the rear yard of a shop premises while camping out. The children put the burning papers under a wheelie bin and left them, expecting the small fire to burn itself out on the concrete floor of the yard. In fact the fire spread causing around £1,000,000 of damage. Under the former law ('objective' recklessness), the children were convicted on the basis that the risk of the fire would have been obvious to any reasonable bystander. However, their convictions were quashed by the House of Lords who reinstated the general subjective element described above.

### 2.9.3 Aggravated Damage

OFFENCE: **Aggravated Damage—*Criminal Damage Act 1971, s. 1(2)***
- Triable on indictment • Life imprisonment

The Criminal Damage Act 1971, s. 1 states:

(2) A person who without lawful excuse destroys or damages any property, whether belonging to himself or another—
   (a) intending to destroy or damage any property or being reckless as to whether any property would be destroyed or damaged; and
   (b) intending by the destruction or damage to endanger the life of another or being reckless as to whether the life of another would be thereby endangered;
shall be guilty of an offence.

---

**KEYNOTE**

The aggravating factor in this offence, and the reason why it attracts such a heavy maximum sentence, is the intention of endangering life or recklessness as to whether life is endangered.

The reference to 'without lawful excuse' does not refer to the statutory excuses under s. 5 which are not applicable here, but to general excuses such as self-defence or the prevention of crime.

For the relevant test of recklessness see para. 2.9.2.7.

You must show that the defendant either intended or was reckless as to either of the following consequences:

- the damage being caused, and
- the risk of endangering the life of another.

The defendant must intend that or be reckless as to whether life would be endangered as a result of the damage. Where a defendant fired a gun through a window pane he was clearly reckless as to the damage his actions would cause. However, the court felt that, even though two people were standing behind the window and they were obviously put in some danger, it was the *missile* which endangered their lives and not the *result of the damage*. Therefore the court held that the defendant was not guilty of this particular offence (*R* v *Steer* [1988] AC 111). In *R* v *Webster and Warwick* [1995] 2 All ER 168, damaging the windscreen of a car or ramming a car was held to be capable of endangering life as a result of the damage. Furthermore, it is the damage which the defendant intended or was reckless about which is relevant, rather than the actual damage that happens to be caused—this could turn out to be minor damage. In *R* v *Dudley* [1989] Crim LR 57, trivial damage was caused but the conviction was upheld since the defendant created a risk of much more serious damage which was capable of endangering life.

## 2.9.4 Arson

OFFENCE: **Arson—*Criminal Damage Act 1971, s. 1(3)***
- Triable either way • Life imprisonment on indictment
- Where life is not endangered six months' imprisonment and/or a fine summarily

The Criminal Damage Act 1971, s. 1 states:

(3) An offence committed under this section by destroying or damaging property by fire shall be charged as arson.

**KEYNOTE**

In any of the above cases of criminal damage, if the destruction or damage is caused by fire, the offence will be charged as 'arson'. Given the potential for extensive damage and danger to life that fire-raising has, the restrictions on the mode of trial for simple damage under s. 1(1) do not apply to cases of arson.

Again, in light of the potential for serious injury and death, the link between this offence and the various homicide offences often arises. An example of where criminal liability for either gross negligence or unlawful act manslaughter arose from an offence of arson can be seen in *R* v *Willoughby* [2004] EWCA Crim 3365. In that case the defendant enlisted the help of another man in burning down a public house on which the defendant owed money. Having poured petrol around the inside of the building, the defendant set fire to it, killing the other person and injuring himself in the process. The defendant was convicted of both arson and manslaughter. The Court of Appeal held that by convicting the defendant of arson, the jury had showed that they were sure that he (on his own or jointly) had deliberately spread petrol by being reckless or with the intention that the premises would be destroyed. Provided that such conduct had been the cause of the death, the jury were therefore also bound to convict the defendant of manslaughter.

Aggravated damage caused by arson is triable only on indictment and carries a maximum penalty of life imprisonment.

## 2.9.5 Threats to Destroy or Damage Property

OFFENCE: **Threats to Destroy or Damage Property—*Criminal Damage Act 1971, s. 2***
- Triable either way • Ten years' imprisonment on indictment
- Six months' imprisonment and/or a fine summarily

The Criminal Damage Act 1971, s. 2 states:

A person who without lawful excuse makes to another a threat, intending that that other would fear it would be carried out,—

(a) to destroy or damage any property belonging to that other or a third person; or

(b) to destroy or damage his own property in a way which he knows is likely to endanger the life of that other or a third person;

shall be guilty of an offence.

---

**KEYNOTE**

This is an offence of *intention*, that is, the key element is the defendant's intention that the person receiving the threat fears it would be carried out.

The s. 2 offence is very straightforward: there is no need to show that the other person actually feared or even believed that the threat would be carried out. There is no need to show that the defendant intended to carry it out; nor does it matter whether the threat was even capable of being carried out.

........................................................................................................

EXAMPLE

If a person, enraged by a neighbour's inconsiderate parking, shouts over the garden wall, '*When you've gone to bed I'm going to pour paint stripper over your car!*', the offence will be complete, provided you can show that the person making the threat intended the neighbour to fear it would be carried out.

........................................................................................................

Where a group of protestors staged a protest in the pods of the London Eye and threatened to set fire to themselves, their conduct was held by the Court of Appeal to be capable of amounting to a threat to damage the property of another contrary to s. 2(a) (*R v Cakmak* [2002] EWCA Crim 500).

In *Cakmak* the court held that the gist of the offence under s. 2(a) was the making of a threat and that any such threat had to be considered objectively.

Whether:

- there has been such a threat to another
- the threat amounted to 'a threat to damage or destroy property'
- the defendant had the necessary state of mind at the time

are all questions of fact for the jury to decide (per *Cakmak*).

While not usually enough to amount to the substantive offence under s. 2 above, a person's *conduct* which represents a threat to damage property may be relevant in triggering police action. This can be seen in yet another case involving a political protest against war. In *Clements v DPP* [2005] EWHC 1279 (Admin) several protestors left a public highway, crossed a ditch and approached the perimeter fence of an RAF base. The defendant ignored a police warning to return to the road and the police attempted to restrain the protestors in order to prevent criminal damage to the fence. After a scuffle the defendant was subsequently convicted of assaulting a police constable in the execution of his duty (as to which **see para. 3.2.14.2**). The key issues at trial were whether the police officer had acted in the course of his duty and the extent to which the officer had reasonable grounds to believe that the defendant would cause criminal damage. The Divisional Court held that the officer had to consider the whole event in context and at the relevant time a political protest was ensuing; the defendant had deliberately left the public highway and refused to return to it; he had no legitimate reason to approach the fence; and it was plainly reasonable for the police officer to believe that he could cause criminal damage to the fence.

---

## 2.9.6 Having Articles with Intent to Destroy or Damage Property

OFFENCE: **Having Articles with Intent to Destroy or Damage Property—*Criminal Damage Act 1971, s. 3***

- Triable either way • Ten years' imprisonment on indictment
- Six months' imprisonment and/or a fine summarily

The Criminal Damage Act 1971, s. 3 states:

A person who has anything in his custody or under his control intending without lawful excuse to use it or cause or permit another to use it—

(a) to destroy or damage any property belonging to some other person; or

(b) to destroy or damage his own or the user's property in a way which he knows is likely to endanger the life of some other person;

shall be guilty of an offence.

---

**KEYNOTE**

This offence covers *anything* which a defendant has '*in his custody or under his control*', a deliberately broader term than 'possession'.

As a result, this offence applies to graffiti 'artists' carrying aerosols and advertisers with adhesives for sticking illicit posters. The key element, once again, is an *intention*. This time the required intention is that the 'thing' be used to cause criminal damage to another's property or to the defendant's own property in a way which the defendant knows is likely to endanger the life of another. Such articles are 'prohibited' articles for the purposes of the power of stop and search under s. 1 of the Police and Criminal Evidence Act 1984.

A conditional intent—that is, an intent to use something to cause criminal damage if the need arises—will be enough (*R* v *Buckingham* (1976) 63 Cr App R 159).

Just as it is not an offence to damage your own property in a way which endangers no one else, neither is it an offence to have something which you intend to use to cause damage under those circumstances.

.............................................................................................................

EXAMPLE

If the owner of a 10 metre high conifer decides to trim the top with a chainsaw and a ladder, putting himself— but no one else—at considerable risk, he commits no offence, either by causing the damage or by having the chainsaw. If he intends to fell the tree in a way which he realises will endanger the life of his neighbours or passers by, then he may commit the offence under s. 3(b).

---

**Police Powers**

There is a statutory power to apply to a magistrate for a search warrant under s. 6 of the Criminal Damage Act 1971 for anything that could be used or is intended to be used to destroy or damage property.

# PART THREE

# Assaults, Drugs, Firearms and Gun Crime

# 3.1 Homicide

## 3.1.1 Introduction

Homicide covers not only the offences of murder and manslaughter, but also other occasions where a person causes, or is involved in, the death of another. The common law which has grown up around the subject of homicide is important, not only because of the gravity of the offences themselves, but also because the cases have defined a number of key issues in criminal law which are applicable to many other offences.

In all cases of homicide the general criminal conduct (*actus reus*) is the same—the killing of another person.

Many assaults can turn into homicides simply by the consequent and causally-connected death of the victim. For this reason, it is necessary that police officers have at least a general understanding of the key concepts.

## 3.1.2 Murder

OFFENCE: **Murder—*Common Law***
  • Life imprisonment (mandatory)

Murder is committed when a person unlawfully kills another human being under the Queen's Peace, with malice aforethought.

---

**KEYNOTE**

A conviction for murder carries a mandatory sentence of life imprisonment (in the case of a defendant who is under 18, 'detention at Her Majesty's pleasure': Powers of Criminal Courts (Sentencing) Act 2000, s. 90).

'Unlawful killing' means actively causing the death of another without justification and includes occasions where someone fails to act after creating a situation of danger (**see chapter 1.2**).

'Another human being' includes a baby who has been born alive and has an existence independent of its mother. 'Existence independent of mother' means that the child is fully expelled from the womb—it is not necessary that the umbilical cord has been cut. If a person injures a baby while it is in its mother's womb and it subsequently dies from those injuries *after being born*, it may be appropriate to bring a charge of murder. If the defendant intended only to cause serious injury to the mother, that intention cannot support a charge of *murder* in respect of the baby if it goes on to die after being born alive. It may, however, support a charge of *manslaughter*. This liability is clear from the House of Lords' ruling in *Attorney-General's Reference (No. 3 of 1994)* [1998] AC 245. The House of Lords ruled that the doctrine of 'transferred malice' does not fully apply in cases of unborn children (*in utero*) and therefore any liability of the defendant for the subsequent death of a child that he/she injured before it was born alive will depend on the defendant's intentions at the time of causing the injury.

'Under the Queen's Peace' appears to exclude deaths caused during the legitimate prosecution of warfare (see the War Crimes Act 1991).

Under the provisions of the Offences Against the Person Act 1861 (s. 9) any British citizen who commits a murder anywhere in the world may be tried in England or Wales. It does not matter what nationality the victim was or where in the world the act took place—all that matters is that at the time the offence was committed, the defendant was a British citizen.

---

It should be noted that the only state of mind or *mens rea* that will support a charge of attempted murder is an *intention to kill*. Nothing less will suffice.

Where a charge of murder is brought there may be specific restrictions on the applicability of a defence that might otherwise be available. For example, a claim of self-defence based on a mistake arising out of voluntary drunkenness will not be allowed in a prosecution for murder (or manslaughter).

### 3.1.2.1 Malice Aforethought

After the cases of *R* v *Moloney* [1985] AC 905 and *R* v *Hancock* [1986] AC 455, the *mens rea* required for murder is an intention:

- to kill, or
- to cause grievous bodily harm.

Murder is therefore a crime of 'specific intent'.

The term 'malice aforethought' is often associated with some form of premeditation; this is not required.

### 3.1.2.2 Year and a Day

Since the Law Reform (Year and a Day Rule) Act 1996 there is no longer a need to show that a victim died within a year and a day of the defendant's actions (s. 1).

If a victim of an alleged murder dies *more than three years after receiving their injury* then the consent of the Attorney-General (or Solicitor-General) is needed before bringing a prosecution (s. 2(2)(a)). That consent is also needed if the defendant has already been convicted of an offence committed under the circumstances connected with the death (s. 2(2)(b)).

## 3.1.3 Voluntary Manslaughter and 'Special Defences'

As a conviction for murder leaves a judge no discretion in sentencing a defendant, a number of 'special defences' have developed around the offence (diminished responsibility, loss of control and suicide pact). Rather than securing an acquittal, they allow for a conviction of 'voluntary manslaughter' instead of murder (hence the term 'partial' defence to murder). Consequently, voluntary manslaughter is more a finding by a court than an offence with which a person can be charged. It should be noted that these 'special defences' are only available to a defendant who is charged with an offence of murder—they cannot be used in answer to any other charge, e.g. attempted murder or s. 18 wounding/GBH.

### 3.1.3.1 Diminished Responsibility

The Homicide Act 1957, s. 2 states:

(1) A person ('D') who kills or is a party to a killing of another is not to be convicted of murder if D was suffering from an abnormality of mental functioning which—
  (a) arose from a recognised medical condition,
  (b) substantially impaired D's ability to do one or more of the things mentioned in subsection (1A), and
  (c) provides an explanation for D's acts and omissions in doing or being party to the killing.
(1A) Those things are—
  (a) to understand the nature of D's conduct;
  (b) to form a rational judgement;
  (c) to exercise self-control.
(1B) For the purposes of subsection (1)(c), an abnormality of mental functioning provides an explanation for D's conduct if it causes, or is a significant contributory factor in causing, D to carry out that conduct.

(2) On a charge of murder, it shall be for the defence to prove that the person charged is by virtue of this section not liable to be convicted of murder.

(3) A person who but for this section would be liable, whether as principal or as accessory, to be convicted of murder shall be liable instead to be convicted of manslaughter.

(4) The fact that one party to a killing is by virtue of this section not liable to be convicted of murder shall not affect the question whether the killing amounted to murder in the case of any other party to it.

---

**KEYNOTE**

The definition requires that the abnormality *substantially* impaired the defendant's ability to do one (or more) of three things and also provides that the defendant's abnormality of mental functioning should be of at least a significant contributory factor in causing the defendant's acts or omissions. The abnormality must arise from a *recognised medical condition*. 'Abnormality of mind' has been held to be 'a state of mind so different from that of ordinary human beings that the reasonable man would term it abnormal' (*R v Byrne* [1960] 2 QB 396). This includes the mental inability to exert control over one's behaviour and to form rational judgement.

'Impairment of mental responsibility'—this impairment must be 'substantial'. Whether or not that is the case will be a question of fact for the jury to decide. Minor lapses of lucidity will not be enough. There may be any number of causes of the 'abnormality' of the mind. Examples accepted by the courts to date have included post-natal depression and pre-menstrual symptoms (*R v Reynolds* [1988] Crim LR 679) and 'battered wives' syndrome' (*R v Hobson* [1998] 1 Cr App R 31). A further example arose in the case of *R v Dietschmann* [2003] UKHL 10 where the House of Lords accepted that a mental abnormality caused by a grief reaction to the recent death of an aunt with whom the defendant had had a physical relationship could suffice. In that case their lordships went on to hold that there is no requirement to show that the 'abnormality of mind' was the *sole* cause of the defendant's acts in committing the killing.

The burden of proving these features lies with the defence and the standard required is one of a balance of probabilities.

---

### 3.1.3.2   Loss of Control

The Coroners and Justice Act 2009, s. 54 states:

(1) Where a person ('D') kills or is a party to the killing of another ('V'), D is not to be convicted of murder if—
   (a) D's acts and omissions in doing or being a party to the killing resulted from D's loss of self-control,
   (b) the loss of self-control had a qualifying trigger, and
   (c) a person of D's sex and age, with a normal degree of tolerance and self-restraint and in the circumstances of D, might have reacted in the same or in a similar way to D.

(2) For the purposes of subsection (1)(a), it does not matter whether or not the loss of control was sudden.

(3) In subsection (1)(c) the reference to 'the circumstances of D' is a reference to all of D's circumstances other than those whose only relevance to D's conduct is that they bear on D's general capacity for tolerance or self-restraint.

(4) Subsection (1) does not apply if, in doing or being a party to the killing, D acted in a considered desire for revenge.

(5) On a charge of murder, if sufficient evidence is adduced to raise an issue with respect to the defence under subsection (1), the jury must assume that the defence is satisfied unless the prosecution proves beyond reasonable doubt that it is not.

(6) For the purposes of subsection (5), sufficient evidence is adduced to raise an issue with respect to the defence if evidence is adduced on which, in the opinion of the trial judge, a jury, properly directed, could reasonably conclude that the defence might apply.

(7) A person who, but for this section, would be liable to be convicted of murder is liable instead to be convicted of manslaughter.

(8) The fact that one party to a killing is by virtue of this section not liable to be convicted of murder does not affect the question whether the killing amounted to murder in the case of any other party to it.

**KEYNOTE**

Section 54 sets out the criteria which need to be met in order for the partial defence of loss of self-control to be successful, those being:

- the defendant's conduct resulted from a loss of self-control,
- the loss of self-control had a qualifying trigger (which is defined in s. 55—see below), and
- a person of the defendant's sex and age with an ordinary level of tolerance and self-restraint and in the circumstances of the defendant might have acted in the same or similar way to the defendant.

Section 54(2) clarifies that the loss of control *need not be sudden*. Although subs. (2) in the partial defence makes clear that *it is not a requirement* for the partial defence that the loss of self-control be sudden, it will remain open for the judge (in deciding whether to leave the defence to the jury) and the jury (in determining whether the killing did in fact result from a loss of self-control and whether the other aspects of the partial defence are satisfied) to take into account any delay between a relevant incident and the killing.

Section 54(3) supplements 54(1)(c) by clarifying that the reference to the defendant's circumstances in that subsection means all of those circumstances except those whose only relevance to the defendant's conduct is that they impact upon the defendant's general level of tolerance and self-restraint. Thus, a defendant's history of abuse at the hands of the victim could be taken into account in deciding whether an ordinary person might have acted as the defendant did, whereas the defendant's generally short temper could not. Consequently, when applying the test in s. 54(1)(c) the jury will consider whether a person of the defendant's sex and age with an ordinary level of tolerance and self-restraint and in the defendant's specific circumstances (in the sense described earlier in this paragraph) might have acted as the defendant did.

Those acting in a considered desire for revenge cannot rely on the partial defence, even if they lose self-control as a result of a qualifying trigger.

**Qualifying Trigger**

Section 55 of the Coroners and Justice Act 2009, explains the phrase 'qualifying trigger' mentioned in s. 54(1)(b). The defendant's loss of self-control must be attributable to:

- *The defendant's fear of serious violence from the victim against the defendant or another identified person*. This will be a subjective test and the defendant will need to show that he/she lost self-control because of a genuine fear of serious violence, whether or not the fear was in fact reasonable. The fear of serious violence needs to be in respect of violence against the defendant or against another identified person. For example, the fear of serious violence could be in respect of a child or other relative of the defendant, but it could not be a fear that the victim would in the future use serious violence against people generally.
- *To a thing or things done or said (or both) which constituted circumstances of an extremely grave character and caused the defendant to have a justifiable sense of being seriously wronged*. Whether a defendant's sense of being seriously wronged is justifiable will be an objective question for a jury to determine. This sets a very high threshold for the circumstances in which a partial defence is available where a person loses self-control in response to words or actions. The effect is to restrict the potential availability of a partial defence in cases where a loss of control is attributable to things done or said.
- *A combination of the above two factors*.

Section 55(6) states that in determining whether a loss of self-control had a qualifying trigger:

- the defendant's fear of serious violence is to be disregarded to the extent that it was caused by a thing which the defendant incited to be done or said for the purpose of providing an excuse to use violence;
- a sense of being seriously wronged by a thing done or said is not justifiable if the defendant incited the thing to be done or said for the purpose of providing an excuse to use violence;
- the fact that a thing done or said constituted sexual infidelity is to be disregarded.

### 3.1.3.3 Suicide Pact

The Homicide Act 1957, s. 4 states:

> (1) It shall be manslaughter, and shall not be murder, for a person acting in pursuance of a suicide pact between him and another to kill the other or be a party to the other being killed by a third person.

**KEYNOTE**

The *defendant* must show that:

- a suicide pact had been made, and
- he/she had the intention of dying at the time the killing took place.

'Suicide pact' is defined by the Homicide Act 1957, s. 4(3) as:

> a common agreement between two or more persons having for its object the death of all of them, whether or not each is to take his own life, but nothing done by a person who enters into a suicide pact shall be treated as done by him in pursuance of the pact unless it is done while he has the settled intention of dying in pursuance of the pact.

## 3.1.4 Involuntary Manslaughter

Involuntary manslaughter occurs where the defendant causes the death of another but is not shown to have had the required *mens* rea for murder. As with murder, defendants on a charge of manslaughter cannot rely on a mistake induced by their own voluntary intoxication in claiming self-defence.

OFFENCE: **Manslaughter—*Common Law***
- Triable on indictment • Life imprisonment

**KEYNOTE**

Manslaughter, like murder, is the unlawful killing of another human being. What it does not require is the intention to kill or to cause grievous bodily harm.

Involuntary manslaughter, that is, those cases which do not involve the 'special defences' under the Homicide Act 1957 or Coroners and Justice Act 2009, can be separated into occasions where a defendant:

- kills another by an *unlawful act* which was *likely to cause bodily harm*, or
- kills another by *gross negligence*.

### 3.1.4.1 Manslaughter by Unlawful Act

In order to prove manslaughter by an unlawful act (also called constructive manslaughter), you must prove:

- An unlawful act by the defendant, that is, an act which is *unlawful in itself*, irrespective of the fact that it ultimately results in someone's death. The act must be *inherently* unlawful. An act that only becomes unlawful by virtue of the way in which it is carried out will not be enough. A good example is 'driving'. Driving is clearly not an inherently unlawful act but becomes so if done dangerously or carelessly on a road or public place. Therefore if someone drives dangerously and thereby causes the death of another, the act of driving—albeit carried out in a way that attracts criminal liability—is *not* an 'unlawful act' for the purposes of constructive manslaughter (see *Andrews* v *DPP* [1937] AC 576). This is one reason why there are statutory offences addressing most instances of death that are caused by poor standards of driving. The act need not be directed or aimed at anyone and can include acts committed against or towards property (*R* v *Goodfellow* (1986) 83 Cr App R 23).

Generally, if the actions of the victim break the chain of causation between the defendant's unlawful act and the cause of death, the defendant will not be responsible for the death of that victim (**see chapter 1.2**).

This is why drug dealers who supply controlled drugs cannot generally be held liable for the ultimate deaths of their 'victims' (see *R* v *Dalby* [1982] 1 WLR 425 and *R* v *Armstrong* [1989] Crim LR 149). This view was affirmed in the case of *R* v *Kennedy* [2007] UKHL 38. The circumstances of the case were that the defendant had prepared a dose of heroin for the deceased and had given the syringe to the deceased before leaving the room they were both in. The deceased injected the drug and as a result died. The House of Lords ruled that a supplier of a drug is not guilty of manslaughter where the deceased freely and voluntarily self-administered the drug. Therefore suppliers of drugs are unlikely to be convicted of an offence of manslaughter unless they have done far more than just supply the drug.

An *omission* to do something will not suffice—manslaughter by unlawful act requires *an act*.

- That *the act* involved a risk of bodily harm. That risk will be judged *objectively*, that is: would the risk be apparent to a reasonable and sober person watching the act? (See *R* v *Church* [1966] 1 QB 59.) Such acts might include dropping a paving stone off a bridge into the path of a train (*DPP* v *Newbury* [1977] AC 500), setting fire to your house (*Goodfellow* above) or firing a gun at police officers and then holding someone else in front of you when the officers return fire (*R* v *Pagett* (1983) 76 Cr App R 279). 'Harm' must be physical; the risk of emotional or psychological harm does not appear to be enough (see *R* v *Dawson* (1985) 81 Cr App R 150). In *R* v *C* [2006] EWCA Crim 17 the deceased—aged 15—had been out walking with friends and had met the defendants who had been drinking alcohol all afternoon. The defendants were verbally abusive and threatening to the deceased and her group. One defendant punched one of the deceased's group and another attacked the deceased herself, pulling her hair back and punching her in the face. Two boys intervened and stopped the attack, at which point the deceased ran off but collapsed and died later that night. The medical evidence showed that, unknown to her doctors or her family, the deceased had a severely diseased heart, and that she might not have died had she not been running.

On appeal it was held that the manslaughter charge (of which the first defendant was convicted) should have been withdrawn from the jury. Although the attack was unpleasant and accompanied by bullying, any injuries caused had been slight. None of the defendants had intended to cause really serious harm to any of the victims and they did not intend that the deceased should die. The Court of Appeal reiterated the general principle that a person who inflicts a slight injury that unforeseeably leads to the death of the victim nevertheless commits manslaughter (per *R* v *Church* [1966] 1 QB 59). However, to hold the defendants liable for the deceased's death in the circumstances of this case would have involved an 'unwarranted extension of the law'. The court observed that the law of unlawful act manslaughter required the commission of an unlawful act which was recognised, by a sober and reasonable person, as being *dangerous* and likely to subject the victim to the risk of *some physical harm which in turn caused the victim's death*. In the instant case the only act committed against the deceased that was 'dangerous' was the assault and the physical harm resulting from it did not cause her death.

- That the defendant had the required *mens rea* for the relevant 'unlawful act' (e.g. for an assault or criminal damage) which led to the death of a victim. If he/she did not have that *mens rea*, the offence of manslaughter will not be made out. See, for example, *R* v *Lamb* [1967] 2 QB 981 where the defendant pretended to fire a revolver at his friend.

Although the defendant believed that the weapon would not fire, the chamber containing a bullet moved round to the firing pin and the defendant's friend was killed. Lamb was charged with manslaughter by unlawful act (the unlawful act being assault) but it could not be proved that Lamb had the *mens rea* required (an intent or recklessness to cause a person to apprehend immediate unlawful violence) for an assault and his conviction for manslaughter was quashed.

If a defendant uses a motor vehicle as a means to commit an 'unlawful act' (e.g. an assault), he/she can be charged with manslaughter as long as the 'act' goes beyond poor driving. The CPS has published a policy document which sets out the way in which it will deal with cases of bad driving. Unlawful act manslaughter will be considered the most appropriate charge when there is evidence to prove that the vehicle was used as an instrument of attack (but where the necessary intent for murder was absent), or to cause fright, and death resulted. There are, however, reasons of policy (see *R v Lawrence* [1982] AC 510) why, in all but the most deliberate of cases, the offences under the Road Traffic Act 1988 should be used.

### 3.1.4.2 Manslaughter by Gross Negligence

Manslaughter is the only criminal offence at common law capable of being committed by negligence. The degree of that negligence has been the source of considerable debate over the years and particular problems have arisen in trying to distinguish the level of negligence required for manslaughter and that required to prove 'recklessness'.

A charge of manslaughter may be brought where a person, by an instance of *gross negligence*, has brought about the death of another. The ingredients of this offence were reviewed and re-stated by the Court of Appeal and essentially consist of death resulting from a negligent breach of a duty of care owed by the defendant to the victim in circumstances so reprehensible as to amount to gross negligence (*R v Misra and Srivastava* [2004] EWCA Crim 2375). The most difficult task in defining the degree of negligence that will qualify as 'gross' falls to the trial judge when addressing the jury. Whether a defendant's conduct will amount to gross negligence is a question of fact for the jury to decide in the light of all the evidence (*R v Bateman* (1925) 19 Cr App R8).

Although the lack of clarity around this offence has resulted in its being challenged under the European Convention on Human Rights, the Court of Appeal has held that its ingredients are sufficiently certain for those purposes (*R v Misra and Srivastava*). What is clear from the decided cases is that civil liability, although a starting point for establishing the breach of a duty of care, is not enough to amount to 'gross negligence', neither is objective 'recklessness' (*R v Adomako* [1995] 1 AC 171).

The test in *Adomako* as summarised by Lord Mackay seems to provide the leading authority on the area. Lord Mackay put the test for the jury as being: '. . . whether, having regard to the risk of death involved, the conduct of the defendant was so bad in all the circumstances as to amount in their judgment to a criminal act or omission'.

It is not possible to bring proceedings for gross negligence manslaughter against a company or other organisation to which the offence under the Corporate Manslaughter and Corporate Homicide Act 2007 applies (s. 20 of the Corporate Manslaughter and Corporate Homicide Act 2007).

### 3.1.5 Corporate Manslaughter and Corporate Homicide Act 2007

An organisation (including a government department) can be convicted of a corporate manslaughter offence if the way in which its activities were managed or organised caused a person's death and amounted to a gross breach of the duty of care owed to the deceased by virtue of that person being held in custody. This is exceptionally important to police officers as a duty that is owed because a person is being held *in police detention or custody* will be regarded as a 'relevant duty of care' for the purposes of the Act (**see para. 3.1.5.1**).

OFFENCE: **Corporate Manslaughter—*Corporate Manslaughter and Corporate Homicide Act 2007, s. 1***

• Triable on indictment • Unlimited fine

The Corporate Manslaughter and Corporate Homicide Act 2007, s. 1 states:

(1) An organisation to which this section applies is guilty of an offence if the way in which its activities are managed or organised—
   (a) causes a person's death, and
   (b) amounts to a gross breach of a relevant duty of care owed by the organisation to the deceased.

---

**KEYNOTE**

The offence is concerned with the way in which an organisation's activities were managed or organised. Under this test, the courts will examine management systems and practices across the organisation, and whether the adequate standard of care was applied to the fatal activity.

The threshold for the offence is gross negligence. The way in which the activities were managed or organised must have fallen far below what could reasonably have been expected.

The failure to manage or organise activities properly must have caused the victim's death.

A duty of care is an obligation that an organisation has to take reasonable steps to protect a person's safety. These duties exist, for example, in respect of the systems of work and equipment used by employees, the condition of worksites and other premises occupied by an organisation and in relation to products or services supplied to customers. The duty must be a *relevant* one. Relevant duties are set out in s. 2 of the Act and include:

• Employer and occupier duties
• Duties connected to:
  ✦ Supplying goods and services
  ✦ Commercial activities
  ✦ Construction and maintenance work
  ✦ Using or keeping plant, vehicles or other things
• Duties relating to holding a person in custody.

In relation to policing and law enforcement in the Act, there are some exceptions to the relevant duty of care obligation (s. 5 of the Act), these are in:

• Operations for dealing with terrorism, civil unrest or serious disorder, that involve the carrying on of policing or law-enforcement activities where officers or employees of the public authority in question come under attack, or face the threat of attack or violent resistance, in the course of the operations
• Activities carried out in preparation for, or directly in support of, such operations as above
• Training of a hazardous nature or training carried out in a hazardous way in order to improve or maintain the effectiveness of officers or employees of the public authority with respect to such operations as above.

Police services and authorities are subject to the Act and could be prosecuted in matters where death relates to the organisation's responsibility *as an employer* (or to others working for the organisation) or as *an occupier of premises*.

---

The Corporate Manslaughter and Corporate Homicide Act 2007, s. 1 states:

(2) The organisations to which this section applies are—
   (a) a corporation;
   (b) a department or other body listed in Schedule 1;

(c) a police force;

(d) a partnership or trade union or employers' association, that is an employer.

The Corporate Manslaughter and Corporate Homicide Act 2007, s. 1 states:

(3) An organisation is guilty of an offence under this section only if the way in which its activities are managed or organised by its senior management is a substantial element in the breach referred to in subsection (1).

### 3.1.5.1 Meaning of 'Relevant Duty of Care'

The Corporate Manslaughter and Corporate Homicide Act 2007, s. 2 states:

(1) A 'relevant duty of care', in relation to an organisation, means any of the following duties owed by it under the law of negligence—

(a) a duty owed to its employees or other persons working for the organisation or performing services for it;

(b) a duty owed as occupier of premises;

(c) a duty owed in connection with—

     (i) the supply by the organisation of goods or services (whether for consideration or not),

     (ii) the carrying on by the organisation of any construction or maintenance operations,

     (iii) the carrying on by the organisation of any other activity on a commercial basis, or

     (iv) the use or keeping by the organisation of any plant, vehicle or other thing;

    (d) a duty owed to a person who, by reason of being a person within subsection (2), is someone for whose safety the organisation is responsible.

(2) A person is within this subsection if—

    (a) he is detained at a custodial institution or in a custody area at a court, a police station or customs premises;

    (aa) he is detained in service custody premises;

    (b) he is detained at a removal centre or a short-term holding facility;

    (c) he is being transported in a vehicle, or being held in any premises, in pursuance of prison escort arrangements or immigration escort arrangements;

    (d) he is living in secure accommodation in which he has been placed;

    (e) he is a detained patient.

---

**KEYNOTE**

The Act applies to deaths of persons owed a duty of care by virtue of:

- being detained at a custodial institution, or *in a custody area at a court or police station*, or a removal centre or short-term holding facility;
- being transported in a vehicle;
- being held in any premises in pursuance of prison escort arrangements or immigration escort arrangements;
- living in secure accommodation in which the person has been placed; or
- being a detained patient (see s. 2(2)).

This means that it ought to be easier to prosecute organisations who hold people in custody, including government departments, for grossly negligent management failings which cause a death, without the need to identify a 'directing mind' of the organisation. Where the death is not attributable to a breach of such a duty of care the organisation might still be liable under other duties contained in the Act (e.g. a duty owed to employees or as occupier of premises etc.—see s. 2(1)(a) to (c)). In addition, individuals might still be liable for gross negligence manslaughter if they were personally at fault (the Act does not affect individual liability).

The Act will apply to all custody providers, whether public or private (i.e. contracted service providers). Liability will ultimately be determined by the courts, depending on the circumstances of the case and e.g. the terms of the contractual arrangements in place.

The commencement of the custody provisions will not apply retrospectively so any offence committed wholly or partly before 1 September 2011 will be considered under the previous law. This will be the case if any of the conduct or events alleged to constitute the offence occurred before the commencement of the provisions.

It is worth noting that the custody provisions do not create additional duties of care. All custody providers already owe duties of care to detainees, to the same extent that they do to e.g. their staff or the public, by virtue of one of the other duties contained in the Act. The specific duty of care owed to detained persons is relevant for the purposes of the offence in the Act.

---

### 3.1.6   Causing or Allowing a Child or Vulnerable Adult to Die or Suffer Serious Physical Harm

This offence came about as a result of the practical difficulties that arise where a child or other vulnerable person dies or suffers serious physical harm as a result of an unlawful act (or omission) of one of several people but it cannot be shown which of them actually caused the death or allowed it to occur.

OFFENCE: **Causing or Allowing a Child or Vulnerable Adult to Die or Suffer Serious Harm—*Domestic Violence, Crime and Victims Act 2004, s. 5***

- Triable on indictment • Where the child or vulnerable adult dies, 14 years' imprisonment or a fine or both • Where the child or vulnerable adult suffers serious physical harm, 10 years' imprisonment or a fine or both

The Domestic Violence, Crime and Victims Act 2004, s. 5 states:

(1) A person ('D') is guilty of an offence if—

    (a) a child or vulnerable adult ('V') dies or suffers serious physical harm as a result of the unlawful act of a person who—

       (i) was a member of the same household as V, and

       (ii) had frequent contact with him,

    (b) D was such a person at the time of that act,

    (c) at that time there was a significant risk of serious physical harm being caused to V by the unlawful act of such a person, and

    (d) either D was the person whose act caused the death or serious physical harm—

       (i) D was, or ought to have been, aware of the risk mentioned in paragraph (c),

       (ii) D failed to take such steps as he could reasonably have been expected to take to protect V from the risk, and

       (iii) the act occurred in circumstances of the kind that D foresaw or ought to have foreseen.

---

**KEYNOTE**

'Child' means a person under the age of 16 and 'vulnerable adult' means a person aged 16 or over whose ability to protect him/herself from violence, abuse or neglect is significantly impaired through physical or mental disability or illness, through old age or otherwise (s. 5(6)).

It is necessary to prove that the victim died or suffered serious physical harm *as a result of the unlawful act* of a person who fits a number of criteria. For these purposes 'act' includes 'omissions' and an act or omission will generally only be 'unlawful' if it would have amounted to an offence (see s. 5(5) and (6)). It must be shown that the defendant was, *at the time of the act*, a member of the same household as the victim *and* had frequent contact with the victim. For these purposes people will be a member of a particular household if they visit it so often and for such periods of time that it is reasonable to regard them as a member of it—even if they do not actually live there (s. 5(4)(a)). Where, as often happens, the victim lived in different households at different times, the 'same household' criterion will mean the household in which the victim was living at the time of the act that caused the death or serious physical harm (s. 5(4)(b)).

Finally it must be shown that, at the time, there was a significant risk of serious physical harm being caused to the victim by the unlawful act of a person meeting these criteria. 'Serious harm' means grievous bodily harm for the purposes of the Offences against the Person Act 1861 (see para. 3.2.12).

Once these elements have been established, the offence is completed in one of two ways: directly (i.e. by the defendant's act causing the victim's death or serious physical harm) or indirectly and the prosecution does not have to prove which alternative applies (see s. 5(2)). However, in cases where indirect causation is suspected, three further things must be shown, namely that:

(1) the defendant was (or ought to have been) aware of the risk of serious physical harm;

(2) the defendant failed to take such steps he/she could reasonably have been expected to take to protect the victim from the risk; *and*

(3) the act occurred in the kind of circumstances that the defendant foresaw (or ought to have foreseen).

Unless the defendant is the mother or father of the victim (a) he/she cannot be charged with an offence under this section if aged under 16 at the time of the act, and (b) restrictions will be made on what steps would have been reasonable for a defendant to have taken while under that age (see s. 5(3)).

---

# 3.2 Non-Fatal Offences Against the Person

## 3.2.1 Introduction

Non-fatal offences against the person covers a wide range of behaviour from a raised fist to a calculated wounding. As these offences are so very common, it is important for police officers to be able to consider what type of assault activity they are dealing with. To enable that choice to be made, this chapter begins by explaining some of the basic areas of assault law before moving on to deal with more serious categories of assault.

## 3.2.2 Assault

An assault is any act which intentionally or recklessly causes another to apprehend immediate unlawful violence (*Fagan* v *Metropolitan Police Commissioner* [1969] 1 QB 439). The mental elements involved, i.e. the intention or recklessness on the part of the defendant and the 'apprehension' on the part of the victim, means that *no physical contact* between the offender and victim is required. For example, if X shouts at Y 'I'm going to kick your head in!', intending Y to believe the threat and Y does believe it, an assault has been committed by X against Y. Assault can only be committed by carrying out an act—it cannot be committed by an omission.

### 3.2.2.1 Mental Elements of Assault

On the part of the defendant, the *mens rea* needed to prove assault is either:

• the intention to cause apprehension of immediate unlawful violence; or
• subjective recklessness ('*Cunningham*' recklessness, **see para. 1.1.4.2**) as to that consequence.

On the part of the victim, the state of mind is an 'apprehension' of immediate unlawful violence.

It is important to remember that the state of mind of the *victim* in an assault is relevant. The victim must apprehend the immediate use of unlawful force—in other words the victim must believe that he/she is going to be subject to that immediate unlawful violence. For this reason, if X threatened Y with an imitation pistol then X could be charged with assault provided Y believed that the pistol was real—the fact that the pistol was an imitation and could never actually physically harm Y is not important as X has caused Y to apprehend immediate force being used (*Logdon* v *DPP* [1976] Crim LR 121). If Y knew that the pistol was an imitation and that it could not be fired to hurt him, then Y would not believe the threat and would not 'apprehend' immediate unlawful violence and there would be no assault committed by X. Likewise, if X threw a stone at Y, who has his back to X when the stone is thrown, and the stone sails past Y's head without Y noticing it, there would be no assault as Y did not 'apprehend' unlawful violence.

'Apprehension' does not mean 'fear' so there is no need to show that the victim was actually in fear. The force or violence apprehended by the victim does not have to be a 'certainty'. Causing a fear of some possible violence can be enough (see *R* v *Ireland* [1998] AC 147) provided that the violence feared is about to happen in the immediate future (see *R* v *Constanza* [1997] 2 Cr App R 492).

### 3.2.2.2 What is 'Immediate'?

Although the force threatened must be immediate, that immediacy is—like most legal interpretation—somewhat elastic. Courts have accepted that, where a person makes a threat from outside a victim's house to the victim who is inside, an assault is still committed even though there will be some time lapse before the defendant can carry out the threat.

In *Ireland* the House of Lords suggested that a threat to cause violence 'in a minute or two' might be enough to qualify as an assault; a threat to provoke some apprehension of violence in the more distant future would not suffice.

The victim must be shown to have feared the use of *force*; it will not be enough to show that a person threatened by words—or silence—feared more calls or letters. The fear of force is the key to assault.

### 3.2.2.3 Words

Words can amount to an assault provided they are accompanied by the required *mens rea*. This was made clear by the decision in *Ireland* where it was held that telephone calls to a victim, followed by silences, could amount to an assault. In *Ireland*, the House of Lords accepted that 'a thing said is also a thing done' and rejected the view that words can never amount to an assault. *Ireland* involved the making of threatening telephone calls which led the victims to fear that unlawful force would be used against them. The House of Lords accepted that, in such cases, even *silence* could fulfil the requirements for the *actus reus* of assault if it brought about the desired consequences (e.g. fear of the immediate use of unlawful force).

Where the words threatening immediate unlawful force come in the form of letters, the Court of Appeal has held that an assault may have been committed (see *Constanza* at **para. 3.2.2.1**). It is therefore only natural to assume that *any form of communication* can be used as the vehicle for an assault. Thus it would be possible to assault someone via an email or a text message.

### 3.2.2.4 Conditional Threats

As well as constituting an assault, words can also *negate* an assault if they make a conditional threat, e.g., where you attend an incident and one person says to another 'If these officers weren't here I'd chin you!' (*Tuberville* v *Savage* (1669) 1 Mod Rep 3). In this type of case the defendant is making a *hypothetical* threat and is really saying 'if it weren't for the existence of certain circumstances, I would assault you'. This should be contrasted with occasions where the defendant makes an immediate threat conditional upon some real circumstance, e.g. 'If you don't cross the road, I'll break your neck'. Such threats have been held, in a civil case, to amount to an assault (*Read* v *Coker* (1853) 138 ER 1437).

### 3.2.3 Battery

A battery is committed when a person intentionally or recklessly (subjectively) inflicts unlawful force on another (*Fagan* v *Metropolitan Police Commissioner* [1969] 1 QB 439). Battery, then, requires physical contact with the victim so the offence could not be carried out via the phone, causing psychiatric injury (*Ireland*), although it is sufficient to constitute battery that the defendant attacks the clothing which another is wearing (*R* v *Day* (1845) 1 Cox CC 207).

The term battery, or the application of 'force', creates a misleading impression as a very small degree of physical contact will be enough, not, as many think, an act involving serious violence.

That force can be applied directly or indirectly. For example, where a defendant punched a woman causing her to drop and injure a child she was holding, he was convicted of the offence against that child (*Haystead v Chief Constable of Derbyshire* [2000] 3 All ER 890). In *DPP v Santa-Bermudez* [2003] EWHC 2908 (Admin), the defendant was held to have committed a battery against a police officer when he falsely assured her that he had no 'sharps' in his possession, and thus caused her to stab herself on a hypodermic needle as she searched him.

### 3.2.4 Assault or Battery?

Although these terms—assault and battery—have distinct legal meanings they are often referred to as simply 'assaults' or 'common assault'. It is, however, important to separate the two expressions when charging or laying an information against a defendant as to include both may be bad for duplicity (*DPP v Taylor* [1992] QB 645). In *Taylor*, the Divisional Court held that all common assaults and batteries are now offences contrary to s. 39 of the Criminal Justice Act 1988 (**see para. 3.2.10**), and that the information must include a reference to that section.

### 3.2.5 Consent

A key element in proving an assault is the *unlawfulness* of the force used or threatened. Although the courts have accepted consent as a feature which negatives any offence, they have been reluctant to accept this feature in a number of notable cases. The two principal questions that may arise in this context are:

- did the alleged victim in fact consent (expressly or by implication) to what was done; and
- if so, do public policy considerations invalidate that consent?

### 3.2.6 Legitimate Consent to Risk of Injury

One of the more straightforward policy considerations would include the implied consent to make contact with others during the course of everyday activities. We are all 'deemed' to consent to various harmless and unavoidable contact such as brushing against another on a crowded train or contact with someone when moving around at a packed concert venue. In these cases it will be a matter of fact to decide whether the behaviour complained of went beyond what was acceptable in those particular circumstances.

Clearly there are times when a person may consent to even serious harm such as during properly conducted sporting events (see *Attorney-General's Reference (No. 6 of 1980)* [1981] QB 715), tattooing and medical operations. Where the activity falls outside those parameters, such as an off-the-ball incident in a football match (*R v Lloyd* (1989) 11 Cr App R (S) 36) or an unauthorised prize fight, the plea of consent will not apply. However, the Court of Appeal has stated that the criminal prosecution of those who inflict injury on another in the course of a sporting event is reserved for those situations where the conduct was sufficiently grave to be properly categorised as criminal (*R v Barnes* [2004] EWCA Crim 3246). In that case the defendant appealed against his conviction for inflicting grievous bodily harm after he caused a serious leg injury by way of a tackle during a football match. The tackle took place after the victim had kicked the ball into the goal but, while accepting that the tackle was hard, the defendant maintained that it had been a fair challenge and that the injury caused was accidental. The court held that where injuries were sustained in the course of contact sports, public policy limited the availability of the defence of consent to situations where there had been implicit consent to what had occurred. Whether conduct reached the required threshold to be treated as 'criminal' would depend on all the circumstances. The fact that the actions of the defendant had been within the rules and practice of the game would be a firm indication that what had occurred was not criminal, although in highly competitive sports even conduct *outside the rules* could be expected to occur in the heat of the moment, and such conduct still might not reach the threshold level required for it to be criminal. The court held that the threshold level was an objective one to be determined by the type of sport, the level at which it was played, the nature of the 'act', the degree of force used, the extent of the risk of injury and the state of mind of the defendant.

Teachers who are employed at schools for children with special needs, including behavioural problems, do not impliedly consent to the use of violence against them by pupils (*H* v *CPS* [2010] EWHC 1374 (Admin)).

What of the situation where the consent of the victim has been obtained by fraud? In *R* v *Richardson* [1999] QB 444 a dentist (Diane Richardson), who had been suspended by the General Dental Council, continued practising dentistry. The suspension came to light and charges of assault were brought. Although initially convicted, the Court of Appeal quashed the conviction on the basis that fraud will only negate consent if it relates to the identity of the person or to the nature and quality of the act. Richardson did not lie about her identity (identity here does not relate to qualifications—your name is your identity) nor about the nature and quality of the act (the dentistry carried out). While her behaviour was reprehensible, it did not amount to an offence. This does not mean that persons without appropriate qualifications sneaking into a surgery and putting on a white coat and calling themselves 'Doctor' followed by their true name could avoid liability if they then made physical contact with another in the guise of providing treatment. While there is plainly no fraud as to identity, any treatment carried out would certainly be caught by a fraud in respect of the nature and quality of the act. Consent would also be negated if a genuine doctor indecently touched his patients on the basis that this was part of a routine medical examination when its true purpose was for sexual gratification (see *R* v *Tabassum* [2000] 2 Cr App R 328).

### 3.2.7  Consent to Sado-masochistic Injuries

Where actual bodily harm (or worse) is deliberately inflicted, consent to it will ordinarily be deemed invalid on the grounds of public policy even if 'victims' know exactly what they are consenting to.

A good example of this approach can be seen in the case of *R* v *Brown* [1994] 1 AC 212. That case involved members of a sado-masochist group who inflicted varying degrees of injuries on one another (under ss. 47 and 20 of the Offences Against the Person Act 1861) for their own gratification. The group claimed that they had consented to the injuries and therefore no assault or battery had taken place. Their lordships followed an earlier policy that *all assaults which result in more than transient harm will be unlawful unless there is good reason for allowing the plea of 'consent'*. Good reason will be determined in the light of a number of considerations:

• the practical consequences of the behaviour
• the dangerousness of the behaviour
• the vulnerability of the 'consenting' person.

Sado-masochistic injury may justifiably be made the subject of criminal law on grounds of the 'protection of health'. It was for this reason that the European Court of Human Rights held that there had been no violation of the defendants' right to respect for private and family life (under Article 8) in *Brown*.

Further difficulties in clarifying what will amount to 'true' or effective consent were added by the decision of the Court of Appeal in *R v Wilson* [1997] QB 47. In that case the court accepted that a husband might lawfully brand his initials on his wife's buttocks with a hot knife provided she consented (as she appeared to have done). The reasoning behind the judgment seems to be based on the fact that the branding was similar to a form of tattooing, but also on the policy grounds that consensual activity between husband and wife is not a matter for criminal investigation. This causes several problems, not least of which is the fact that sado-masochistic 'branding' was denounced by the House of Lords in *Brown*, above. Therefore, if a situation arose where a husband and wife took part in mutual branding in the privacy of their home, their criminal liability would arguably depend on whether they caused the harm for purposes of sado-masochistic pleasure or out of some affectionate wish to be permanently adorned with the mark of their loved one.

### 3.2.8 Lawful Chastisement

For many years the common and statute law allowed for those acting in *loco parentis* (meaning in place of the parent) of a child to be able to use reasonable force in controlling the behaviour of that child. What was 'reasonable' varied widely and became increasingly difficult to define let alone justify given the breadth and depth of social attitudes and conventions within England and Wales. Legislation has assisted to define the boundaries of lawful chastisement as a defence to assault offences.

The School Standards and Framework Act 1998 outlaws corporal punishment in *all* British schools, although staff may use reasonable force in restraining violent or disruptive pupils. The Divisional Court has held that this legislation removes entirely the defence of lawful chastisement from any teacher when they are acting as such (*Williamson* v *Secretary of State for Education and Employment* [2001] EWHC Admin 960, later affirmed by the House of Lords [2005] UKHL 15). The legislation gave effect to a clear parliamentary intention to abolish corporal punishment in *all* schools, including independent schools, and did not infringe the human rights of any of the claimants.

Section 58 of the Children Act 2004 removes the defence of lawful chastisement for parents or adults acting *in loco parentis* where the accused person is charged with assault occasioning actual bodily harm (Offences Against the Person Act 1861, s. 47), wounding or causing grievous bodily harm (Offences Against the Person Act 1861, s. 18 or 20) or child cruelty (Children and Young Persons Act 1933, s.1) to persons less than 16 years of age. However, the lawful chastisement defence remains available for parents and adults acting *in loco parentis* charged with common assault under the Criminal Justice Act 1988, s. 39. CPS charging standards state that if an injury to a child amounts to no more than reddening of the skin, and the injury is transient and trifling, a charge of common assault may be laid against the defendant for whom the lawful chastisement defence remains available. Whether the actions of the defendant are 'reasonable' will be important; physical punishment where a child is hit (causing injury of reddening to the skin) with an implement such as a cane or a belt may well be considered 'unreasonable'. It is important to note that the law does not rule out physical chastisement by a parent etc. but that chastisement should only constitute 'mild smacking' rather than cause injuries subject to assault charges. At the present time the government has ruled out a complete ban on smacking.

### 3.2.9 Assault Offences

Having considered the key common elements in this area, the specific offences are set out below.

## 3.2.10    Common Assault and Battery

OFFENCE:    **Common Assault/Battery—*Criminal Justice Act 1988, s. 39***
  - Triable summarily   • Six months' imprisonment

OFFENCE:    **Racially or Religiously Aggravated—*Crime and Disorder Act 1998, s. 29(1)(c)***
  - Triable either way   • Two years' imprisonment and/or a fine on indictment
  - Six months' imprisonment and/or a fine summarily

---

**KEYNOTE**

The racially or religiously aggravated offence can be tried on indictment without having to be included along-side another indictable offence as is the case with common assaults generally (see Criminal Justice Act 1988, s. 40).

CPS Charging Standards state that a charge under s. 39 of the Act will be appropriate where *no injury or injuries which are not serious* occur. In determining the seriousness of injury, relevant factors may include, for example, the fact that there has been significant medical intervention and/or permanent effects have resulted (whereby a charge of s. 47 assault may be more appropriate).

The injury sustained by the victim should always be considered first, and in most cases the degree of injury will determine whether the appropriate charge is an assault under s. 39 of the Act or a more serious assault under s. 47 of the Offences Against the Person Act 1861.

---

## 3.2.11    Assault Occasioning Actual Bodily Harm

OFFENCE:    **Assault Occasioning Actual Bodily Harm—*Offences Against the Person Act 1861, s. 47***
  - Triable either way   • Five years' imprisonment on indictment
  - Six months' imprisonment and/or a fine summarily

OFFENCE:    **Racially or Religiously Aggravated—*Crime and Disorder Act 1998, s. 29(1)(b)***
  - Triable either way   • Seven years' imprisonment and/or a fine on indictment
  - Six months' imprisonment and/or a fine summarily

The Offences Against the Person Act 1861, s. 47 states:

> Whosoever shall be convicted . . . of any assault occasioning actual bodily harm shall be liable . . . to be kept in penal servitude . . .

---

**KEYNOTE**

The state of mind required is the same as that for an assault or battery.

It must be shown that 'actual bodily harm' was a consequence, directly or indirectly, of the defendant's actions. Such harm can include shock (*R v Miller* [1954] 2 QB 282) and mental 'injury' (*R v Chan-Fook* [1994] 1 WLR 689).

So what is 'actual bodily harm'? In *DPP v Smith* [1961] AC 290, it was noted that the expression needed 'no explanation' and, in *Chan-Fook*, the court advised that the phrase consisted of 'three words of the English language which require no elaboration and in the ordinary course should not receive any. While the phrase 'bodily harm' has its ordinary meaning, it has been said to include any hurt calculated to interfere with the health or comfort of the victim: such hurt need not be permanent, but must be more than transient and trifling (*R v Miller*, above).

---

The Administrative Court has accepted that a momentary loss of consciousness caused by a kick but without any physical injury can be 'actual harm' because it involved an injurious impairment of the victim's sensory abilities which did not fall within the 'trifling' category described in *Donovan* above (see *T* v *DPP* [2003] EWHC 266 (Admin)).

In *DPP* v *Smith* (*Ross Michael*) [2006] EWHC 94 (Admin), the Divisional Court accepted that the cutting of a person's hair against his/her will could amount to actual bodily harm. In *Smith* the defendant cut off his ex-partner's ponytail, deliberately and without her permission. The court held that, even though medically and scientifically speaking, the hair above the surface of the scalp is no more than dead tissue, it remains part of the body and is attached to it. While it is so attached, it falls within the meaning of 'bodily' in the phrase 'actual bodily harm' as it is concerned with the body of the individual victim. Therefore the same would be true of fingernails.

CPS charging standards state that ABH should generally be charged where injuries and overall circumstances indicate that the offence merits clearly more than six months' imprisonment and where the prosecution intend to represent that the case is not suitable for summary trial. Examples may include cases where there is a need for a number of stiches (but not superficial application of steri-strips) or a hospital procedure under anaesthetic.

Where psychiatric injury is relied upon as the basis for an allegation of assault occasioning actual bodily harm, and the matter is not admitted by the defence, then expert evidence must be called by the prosecution (*R* v *Chan-Fook* [1994] 1 WLR 689).

## 3.2.12 Wounding or Inflicting Grievous Bodily Harm

OFFENCE: **Wounding or Inflicting Grievous Bodily Harm—*Offences Against the Person Act 1861, s. 20***
- Triable either way • Five years' imprisonment on indictment • Six months' imprisonment and/or a fine summarily

OFFENCE: **Racially or Religiously Aggravated—*Crime and Disorder Act 1998, s. 29(1)(a)***
- Triable either way • Seven years' imprisonment and/or a fine on indictment
- Six months' imprisonment and/or a fine summarily

The Offences Against the Person Act 1861, s. 20 states:

Whosoever shall unlawfully and maliciously wound or inflict any grievous bodily harm upon any other person, either with or without any weapon or instrument, shall be guilty of a misdemeanour...

**KEYNOTE**

'Maliciously'—although the word maliciously suggests some form of evil premeditation, 'malice' here amounts to subjective recklessness. It means that the defendant must realise that there is a risk of some harm being caused to the victim. The defendant does not need to foresee the degree of harm which is eventually caused, only that his/her behaviour may bring about some harm to the victim.

Wounding means the breaking of the continuity of the whole of the outer skin, or the inner skin within the cheek or lip. A cut which goes right through all the layers of a person's skin, whether caused externally (e.g. a knife wound) or internally (e.g. a punch causing a tooth to puncture the cheek), will amount to a wound. It does not include the rupturing of internal blood vessels.

The definition of wounding may encompass injuries that are relatively minor in nature, e.g. a small cut or laceration. An assault resulting in such minor injuries should more appropriately be charged contrary to s. 47 of the Act. An assault contrary to s. 20 should be reserved for the type of wounds considered to be serious (thus equating the offence with the infliction of grievous, or serious, bodily harm).

The House of Lords in *R* v *Ireland* [1998] AC 147 has made it clear that no 'assault' is needed for this offence and that harm could be 'inflicted' indirectly (in this case by menacing telephone calls inflicting psychiatric harm). Therefore there is now little if any difference between inflicting harm and 'causing' harm. It should be enough to show that the defendant's behaviour brought about the resulting harm to the victim.

There have also been many judicial attempts at defining grievous bodily harm. In *R* v *Saunders* [1985] Crim LR 230 it was held that the expression meant 'serious or really serious harm'. This harm will now include psychiatric harm (*Ireland*). Examples of what will amount to 'grievous bodily harm' can be found in the CPS Charging Standards and include:

- injury resulting in some permanent disability or visible disfigurement
- broken or displaced limbs or bones
- injuries requiring blood transfusion or lengthy treatment.

There is no definitive list of the kind of injuries that may be considered to be serious, but it is clear that a number of individually minor injuries may collectively become grievous. In *R* v *Birmingham* [2002] EWCA Crim 2608, it was held that a large number of minor wounds were capable of amounting to grievous bodily harm on a charge of aggravated burglary.

Following *R* v *Dica* [2004] EWCA Crim 1103, there was an acceptance that the deliberate infection of another with the HIV virus could amount to grievous bodily harm—although there were still significant difficulties with regard to 'consent' if the infection had taken place as a result of consensual sexual activity. This issue was explored further by the Court of Appeal in *R* v *Konzani* [2005] EWCA Crim 706. In that case the defendant appealed against convictions for inflicting grievous bodily harm on three women contrary to s. 20 above. The defendant had unprotected consensual sexual intercourse with the women, but without having disclosed that he was HIV positive. The women subsequently contracted the HIV virus. In hearing the appeals, the court held that there was a critical distinction between taking a risk as to the various potentially adverse (and possibly problematic) consequences of unprotected consensual intercourse, and the giving of informed consent *to the risk of infection with a fatal disease*. Before consent to the risk of contracting HIV could provide a defence, that consent had to be an *informed* consent in this latter sense (see *Dica* above). Therefore, simply having an honestly held belief that the other person was consenting would only help if that consent would itself have provided a defence to the passing of the infection.

This approach was confirmed in *R* v *B* [2006] EWCA Crim 2945, where the Court of Appeal stated that, while a defendant's condition (being HIV positive) was immaterial in relation to the consent issue in an offence of rape, the defendant would have no defence to the harm created by the sexual activity merely by virtue of that consent, as the consent related to the sexual activity and not to the disease.

## 3.2.13    Wounding or Causing Grievous Bodily Harm with Intent

OFFENCE: **Wounding or Causing Grievous Bodily Harm with Intent—*Offences Against the Person Act 1861, s. 18***

- Triable on indictment only  • Life imprisonment

The Offences Against the Person Act 1861, s. 18 states:

Whosoever shall unlawfully and maliciously by any means whatsoever wound or cause any grievous bodily harm to any person with intent to do some grievous bodily harm to any person, or with intent to resist or prevent the lawful apprehension or detainer of any person, shall be guilty of felony...

**KEYNOTE**

Although there are similarities with the offence under s. 20 (see para. 3.2.12), you must show the appropriate *intent* (e.g. to do grievous bodily harm to *anyone* or to resist/prevent the lawful apprehension/detention of *anyone*). Factors that may indicate such a specific intent include:

- a repeated or planned attack
- deliberate selection of a weapon or adaptation of an article to cause injury, such as breaking a glass before an attack
- making prior threats
- using an offensive weapon against, or kicking a victim's head.

Where the intent was to cause grievous bodily harm, the issue of 'malice' will not arise. However, where the intent was to resist or prevent the lawful arrest of someone, the element of maliciousness as set out above (see para. 3.2.12) will need to be proved. The word 'cause', together with the expression 'by any means whatsoever', seems to give this offence a wider meaning than s. 20. However, the increasingly broad interpretation of the s. 20 offence means that there is little difference in the *actus reus* needed for either offence.

In relation to injuries brought about by driving motor vehicles, the Court of Appeal has held that there is nothing wrong in principle in charging a driver with causing grievous bodily harm as well as dangerous driving in appropriate circumstances (*R* v *Bain* [2005] EWCA Crim 7). It follows that bringing about other forms of significant or lasting injury with a motor vehicle could be dealt with under the offences in this part of the chapter. However, in *Bain* it was held that where a driver was charged with both offences (causing grievous bodily harm and dangerous driving), a court could not impose consecutive terms of imprisonment for both offences arising out of the same incident. The Legal Aid, Sentencing and Punishment of Offenders Act 2012 has created a specific offence of causing serious injury by dangerous driving (under s. 143) which may be a far more appropriate charge when the offence has been brought about by driving a mechanically propelled vehicle.

The provisions of ss. 28 and 29 of the Crime and Disorder Act 1998 in relation to racially or religiously aggravated assaults do not apply to this offence. However, the courts must still take notice of any element of racial or religious aggravation when determining sentence (Criminal Justice Act 2003, s. 145—increase in sentences for racial or religious aggravation).

## 3.2.14 Assaults on Police

### 3.2.14.1 Assault with Intent to Resist Arrest

OFFENCE: **Assault with Intent to Resist Arrest—*Offences Against the Person Act 1861, s. 38***
- Triable either way • Two years' imprisonment

The Offences Against the Person Act 1861, s. 38 states:

> Whosoever...shall assault any person with intent to resist or prevent the lawful apprehension or detainer of himself or of any other person for any offence, shall be guilty of a misdemeanour...

**KEYNOTE**

It must be shown that the defendant intended to resist or prevent a lawful arrest. It must also be shown that the arrest was lawful (*R* v *Self* [1992] 1 WLR 657). Provided they were acting within their powers, this offence can apply to arrests made, not only by police officers, but also by any person who has a power of arrest, i.e. the public.

Once the lawfulness of the arrest is established, the state of mind necessary for the above offence is that required for a common assault coupled with an intention to resist/prevent that arrest. It is irrelevant whether or not the person being arrested had actually committed an offence. These principles were set out by the Court of Appeal in a case where the defendant mistakenly believed that the arresting officers had no lawful power to do so. The court held that such a mistaken belief does not provide a defendant with the defence of 'mistake'. Similarly, a belief in one's own innocence, however genuine or honestly held, cannot afford a defence to a charge under s. 38 (above).

### 3.2.14.2 Assaults on Police

There is an offence which deals specifically with assaults on police officers and those assisting them.

OFFENCE: **Assault Police—*Police Act 1996, s. 89***

   • Triable summarily   • Six months' imprisonment and/or a fine

The Police Act 1996, s. 89 states:

(1) Any person who assaults a constable in the execution of his duty, or a person assisting a constable in the execution of his duty, shall be guilty of an offence...

---

**KEYNOTE**

This offence requires that the officer was acting in the execution of his/her duty when assaulted. If this is not proved, then part of the *actus reus* will be missing. Even a minor, technical and inadvertent act of unlawfulness on the part of the officer will mean that he/she cannot have been acting in the lawful execution of his/her duty. While the precise limits of a constable's duty remain undefined, it is clear that a police officer may be acting in the course of his/her duty even when doing more than the minimum the law requires (*R* v *Waterfield* [1964] 1 QB 164). It is also clear that any action amounting to assault, battery, unlawful arrest or trespass to property takes the officer outside the course of his/her duty (*Davis* v *Lisle* [1936] 2 KB 434).

A court may infer from all the circumstances that an officer was in fact acting in the execution of his/her duty (*Plowden* v *DPP* [1991] Crim LR 850).

Where the assault is made in reaction to some form of physical act by the officer, it must be shown that the officer's act was not in itself unlawful.

Other than the powers of arrest and detention, police officers have no general power to take hold of people in order to question them or keep them at a particular place while background inquiries are made about them. Therefore, if an officer does hold someone by the arm for questioning without arrest, there may well be a 'battery' by that officer (*Collins* v *Wilcock* [1984] 1 WLR 1172). The courts have accepted, however, that there may be occasions where a police officer is justified in taking hold of a person to attract his/her attention or to calm him/her down (*Mepstead* v *DPP* [1996] COD 13).

Where a prisoner is arrested and brought before a custody officer, that officer is entitled to assume that the arrest has been lawful. Therefore, if the prisoner goes on to assault the custody officer, that assault will nevertheless be an offence under s. 89(1) even if the original arrest turns out to have been unlawful (*DPP* v *L* [1999] Crim LR 752).

There is no need to show that the defendant knew—or suspected—that the person was in fact a police officer or that the police officer was acting in the lawful execution of his/her duty (*Blackburn* v *Bowering* [1994] 1 WLR 1324). However, if the defendant claims to have been acting in self-defence under the mistaken and honestly held belief that he/she was being attacked, there may not be sufficient *mens rea* for a charge of assault.

These offences are simply a form of common assault upon someone carrying out a lawful function. A similar offence exists in respect of assaulting designated or accredited persons (s. 46(1) of the Police Reform Act 2002).

---

### 3.2.14.3 Obstructing a Police Officer

OFFENCE: **Obstruct Police—*Police Act 1996, s. 89***

   • Triable summarily   • One month's imprisonment and/or a fine

The Police Act 1996, s. 89 states:

(2) Any person who resists or wilfully obstructs a constable in the execution of his duty, or a person assisting a constable in the execution of his duty, shall be guilty of an offence...

As with the offence of assaulting a constable, no offence under s. 89(2) can be committed unless the officer was acting in the lawful execution of his/her duty.

Resistance suggests some form of physical opposition; obstruction does not and may take many forms, e.g. warning other drivers of a speed check operation (*R (DPP)* v *Glendinning* (2005) EWHC 2333 (Admin)—note that the persons warned about the speed check must be actually committing or about to commit the speeding offence), providing misleading information (*Ledger* v *DPP* [1991] Crim LR 439), deliberately drinking alcohol before providing a breath specimen (*Ingleton* v *Dibble* [1972] 1 QB 480), or 'tipping off' people who were about to commit an offence (*Green* v *Moore* [1982] QB 1044). Obstruction has been interpreted as making it more difficult for a constable to carry out his/her duty (*Hinchcliffe* v *Sheldon* [1955] 1 WLR 1207). Refusing to answer an officer's questions is not obstruction (*Rice* v *Connolly* [1966] 2 QB 414), neither is advising a person not to answer questions (*Green* v *DPP* (1991) 155 JP 816)—unless perhaps the defendant was under some duty to provide information. Any obstruction must be *wilful*, that is the defendant must intend to do it. The obstruction will not be 'wilful' if the defendant was simply trying to help the police, even if that help turned out to be more of a hindrance (*Willmot* v *Atack* [1977] QB 498).

Obstruction can be caused by omission but only where the defendant was already under some duty towards the police or the officer. There is also a common law offence of refusing to go to the aid of a constable when asked to do so in order to prevent or diminish a breach of the peace (*R* v *Waugh* (1986) *The Times*, 1 October).

A similar offence exists in respect of obstructing designated or accredited persons (Police Reform Act 2002, s. 46(2)).

## 3.2.15 Threats to Kill

OFFENCE: **Making a Threat to Kill—*Offences Against the Person Act 1861, s. 16***
  • Triable either way • Ten years' imprisonment on indictment • Six months' imprisonment and/or a fine summarily

The Offences Against the Person Act 1861, s. 16 (amended by the Criminal Law Act 1977, s. 65, sch. 12) states:

A person who without lawful excuse makes to another a threat, intending that that other would fear it would be carried out, to kill that other or a third person shall be guilty of an offence...

The proviso that the threat must be made 'without lawful excuse' means that a person acting in self-defence or in the course of his/her duty in protecting life (e.g. an armed police officer) would not commit this offence (provided that his/her behaviour was 'lawful').

You must show that the threat was made (or implied (*R* v *Solanke* [1970] 1 WLR 1)) with the intention that the person receiving it would fear that it would be carried out. It is the *intention* of the person who makes the threat which is important in this offence. It does not matter whether the person to whom the threat is made *does* fear that the threat would be carried out. The threat may be to kill another person at some time in the future or it may be an immediate threat, but the threatened action must be directly linked with the defendant. Simply passing on a threat on behalf of a third person without the necessary intent would be insufficient for this offence.

# 3.3 Child Abduction

There are two offences of abducting children, one which applies to people 'connected with the child' and the second which applies to abduction by others 'not connected to the child'.

## 3.3.1 Person Connected with Child

OFFENCE: **Child Abduction—Person Connected with Child—*Child Abduction Act 1984, s. 1***
  - • Triable either way  • Seven years' imprisonment on indictment  • Six months' imprisonment and/or a fine summarily

The Child Abduction Act 1984, s. 1 states:

(1) Subject to subsections (5) and (8) below, a person connected with a child under the age of 16 commits an offence if he takes or sends the child out of the United Kingdom without the appropriate consent.

### 'Connected with a Child'

The Child Abduction Act 1984, s. 1 states:

(2) A person is connected with the child for the purposes of this section if—
    (a) he is a parent of the child; or
    (b) in the case of a child whose parents were not married to each other at the time of his birth, there are reasonable grounds for believing that he is the father of the child; or
    (c) he is a guardian of the child; or
    (ca) he is a special guardian of the child; or
    (d) he is a person in whose favour a residence order is in force with respect to the child; or
    (e) he has custody of the child.

### 'Appropriate Consent'

The Child Abduction Act 1984, s. 1 states:

(3) In this section 'the appropriate consent' in relation to a child, means—
    (a) the consent of each of the following—
        (i) the child's mother;
        (ii) the child's father, if he has parental responsibility for him;
        (iii) any guardian of the child;
        (iiia) any special guardian of the child;
        (iv) any person in whose favour a residence order is in force with respect to the child;
        (v) any person who has custody of the child; or
    (b) the leave of the court granted under or by virtue of any provision of Part II of the Children Act 1989; or
    (c) if any person has custody of the child, the leave of the court which awarded custody to him.

## 3.3.2 Defence for Person Connected with a Child

The Child Abduction Act 1984, s. 1 states:

(4) A person does not commit an offence under this section by taking or sending a child out of the United Kingdom without obtaining the appropriate consent if—

    (a) he is a person in whose favour there is a residence order in force with respect to the child, and he takes or sends the child out of the United Kingdom for a period of less than one month; or

    (b) he is a special guardian of the child and he takes or sends the child out of the United Kingdom for a period of less than three months.

(4A) Subsection (4) above does not apply if the person taking or sending the child out of the United Kingdom does so in breach of an order under Part II of the Children Act 1989.

(5) A person does not commit an offence under this section by doing anything without the consent of another person whose consent is required under the foregoing provisions if—

    (a) he does it in the belief that the other person—

        (i) has consented; or

        (ii) would consent if he was aware of all the relevant circumstances; or

    (b) he has taken all reasonable steps to communicate with the other person but has been unable to communicate with him; or

    (c) the other person has unreasonably refused to consent.

## 3.3.3 Person Not Connected with Child

OFFENCE: **Child Abduction—Person Not Connected with Child—*Child Abduction Act 1984, s. 2***

        • Triable either way • Seven years' imprisonment on indictment • Six months' imprisonment and/or a fine summarily

The Child Abduction Act 1984, s. 2 states:

(1) Subject to subsection (3) below, a person other than one mentioned in subsection (2) below, commits an offence if, without lawful authority or reasonable excuse, he takes or detains a child under the age of 16—
 (a) so as to remove him from the lawful control of any person having lawful control of the child: or
 (b) so as to keep him out of the lawful control of any person entitled to lawful control of the child.
(2) The persons are—
 (a) where the father and mother of the child in question were married to each other at the time of his birth, the child's father and mother;
 (b) where the father and mother of the child in question were not married to each other at the time of his birth, the child's mother; and
 (c) any other person mentioned in section 1(2)(c) to (e) above.

---

**KEYNOTE**

This offence requires the taking or detaining of a child under 16 years. This will include keeping a child in the place where he/she is found and inducing the child to remain with the defendant or another person. The distinction between subss. (a) and (b) is important. You must show that the defendant acted without lawful authority or reasonable excuse. The consent of the victim is irrelevant. The word 'remove' for the purpose of s. 2(1)(a) means effectively a substitution of authority by a defendant for that of the person lawfully having it and physical removal from a particular place is not required (see *Foster* v *DPP* [2004] EWHC 2955 (Admin)).

Section 2(1)(a) requires the child *there and then* to be in the lawful control of someone entitled to it when he/she is taken or detained, whereas s. 2(1)(b) requires only that the child be kept out of the lawful control of someone entitled to it when taken or detained. Whether or not a person is under the lawful control of another is a question of fact (*R* v *Leather* [1993] Crim LR 516). Proving the absence of reasonable excuse could be difficult. Clearly defendants could argue, particularly in the case of a very young child, that they were acting in the child's best interests, a claim which might be difficult to refute.

---

### 3.3.4 Defence for Person Not Connected with a Child

The Child Abduction Act 1984, s. 2 states:

(3) ... it shall be a defence for [the defendant] to prove—
 (a) where the father and mother of the child in question were not married to each other at the time of his birth—
  (i) that he is the child's father; or
  (ii) that, at the time of the alleged offence, he believed, on reasonable grounds, that he was the child's father; or
 (b) that, at the time of the alleged offence, he believed that the child had attained the age of 16.

# 3.4 | False Imprisonment

## 3.4.1 False Imprisonment

OFFENCE: **False Imprisonment—*Common Law***
  • Triable on indictment  • Unlimited maximum penalty

It is an offence at common law falsely to imprison another person.

---

**KEYNOTE**

This offence is the first in an ascending order of aggravated offences against the person and is more usually dealt with under civil law or as kidnapping/abduction (see para. 3.5).

These offences are particularly relevant to the offence of committing a criminal offence with intent to commit a relevant sexual offence.

The elements required for this offence are the unlawful and intentional/reckless restraint of a person's freedom of movement (*R* v *Rahman* (1985) 81 Cr App R 349). Locking someone in a vehicle or keeping him/her in a particular place for however short a time may amount to false imprisonment if done unlawfully. An unlawful arrest may amount to such an offence and it is not uncommon for such an allegation to be levelled at police officers against whom a public complaint has been made. On the other hand, a *lawful* arrest will provide a defence to the offence as will reasonable defence of property. In respect of the latter, there would be a defence to a charge of false imprisonment if someone detained a person in the genuine belief that the person was a burglar—even if this genuine belief were unreasonable (*R* v *Shwan Faraj* [2007] EWCA Crim 1033). In *Shwan Faraj*, the court stated that there was no reason why a householder should not be entitled to detain someone in his house whom he genuinely believed to be a burglar; he would be acting in defence of his property in doing so. However, a householder would have to honestly believe he needed to detain the suspect and would have to do so in a way that was reasonable.

---

# 3.5 | Kidnapping

### 3.5.1 Kidnapping

OFFENCE: **Kidnapping—*Common Law***

- Triable on indictment • Unlimited maximum penalty

It is an offence at common law to take or carry away another person without the consent of that person and without lawful excuse.

---

**KEYNOTE**

The required elements of this offence are the unlawful taking or carrying away of one person by another by force or fraud (*R* v *D* [1984] AC 778). Force includes the threat of force (*R* v *Archer* [2011] EWCA Crim 2252). These requirements go beyond those of mere restraint needed for false imprisonment. Parents may be acting without lawful excuse, for instance, if they are acting in breach of a court order in respect of their children. The 'taking or carrying away' need not involve great distances—a short distance (just a few yards/metres) will suffice (*R* v *Wellard* [1978] 1 WLR 921).

The taking or carrying away of the victim must be without the consent of the victim. If the victim consents to an initial taking but later withdraws that consent, the offence would be complete. If the consent is obtained by fraud, the defendant cannot rely on that consent and the offence—or attempted offence—will be made out (see *R* v *Cort* [2003] EWCA Crim 2149). In *R* v *Hendy-Freegard* [2007] EWCA Crim 1236 the defendant was a confidence trickster who pretended to be an undercover agent working for MI5 or Scotland Yard. He would tell his victims that he was investigating the activities of the IRA and that his investigations had revealed that they were in danger. This allowed him to take control of their lives for a number of years and in doing so to direct them to move about the country from location to location. The defendant was eventually arrested and convicted of kidnapping on the basis of the Crown's case that the offence of kidnapping had occurred as his victims had made journeys around the country which they had been induced to make as a result of the defendant's false story. The defendant successfully appealed against the kidnapping conviction, with the court stating that causing a person to move from place to place *when unaccompanied by the defendant* could not itself constitute either taking or carrying away or deprivation of liberty, which were necessary elements of the offence.

If the victim is a child, the consent will probably be that of the parents but the more appropriate charge in such a case may be one under the Child Abduction Act 1984.

The state of mind required for this offence is the same as that for false imprisonment, indeed the only thing separating the two offences seems to be *actus reus* (*R* v *Hutchins* [1988] Crim LR 379).

---

# 3.6 Public Order Act 1986 Offences

Many of the most common offences regulating public disorder and threats to public order were formerly contained in the Public Order Act 1936. This left several key offences, such as riot and affray, to the common law. These provisions were felt to be inadequate and the Public Order Act 1986 was passed in an attempt to codify the law in this area.

## 3.6.1 Violence

The Public Order Act 1986, s. 8 provides guidance on when conduct will amount to 'violence':

'violence' means any violent conduct, so that—
(a) except in the context of affray, it includes violent conduct towards property as well as violent conduct towards persons, and
(b) it is not restricted to conduct causing or intended to cause injury or damage but includes any other violent conduct (for example, throwing at or towards a person a missile of a kind capable of causing injury which does not hit or falls short).

**KEYNOTE**

It has been held that the use of the term 'unlawful' in the 1986 Act has been included to allow for the general defences—such as self-defence—to be applicable (see *R* v *Rothwell* [1993] Crim LR 626).

## 3.6.2 Drunkenness

Parliament has specifically catered for self-induced intoxication, not just for the offence of riot, but in relation to other offences under the 1986 Act, by s. 6 which states:

(5) For the purposes of this section a person whose awareness is impaired by intoxication shall be taken to be aware of that of which he would be aware if not intoxicated, unless he shows either that his intoxication was not self-induced or that it was caused solely by the taking or administration of a substance in the course of medical treatment.
(6) In subsection (5) 'intoxication' means any intoxication, whether caused by drink, drugs or other means, or by a combination of means.

## 3.6.3 Violent Disorder

OFFENCE: **Violent Disorder—*Public Order Act 1986, s. 2***
  • Triable either way • Five years' imprisonment and/or a fine on indictment
  • Six months' imprisonment and/or a fine summarily

The Public Order Act 1986, s. 2 states:

(1) Where 3 or more persons who are present together use or threaten unlawful violence and the conduct of them (taken together) is such as would cause a person of reasonable firmness present at the scene to fear for his personal safety, each of the persons using or threatening unlawful violence is guilty of violent disorder.

(2) It is immaterial whether or not the 3 or more use or threaten unlawful violence simultaneously.

(3) No person of reasonable firmness need actually be, or be likely to be, present at the scene.

(4) Violent disorder may be committed in private as well as in public places.

---

**KEYNOTE**

In order to convict a defendant of this offence, you must show that there were three or more people using or threatening unlawful violence. However, while three or more persons must have been present and used or threatened unlawful violence, it is not necessary that three or more persons should actually be charged or prosecuted with the offence. Further, where there are three defendants and two are acquitted of the charge, the remaining defendant can still be convicted of violent disorder (*R* v *Mahroof* (1989) 88 Cr App R 317) as long as *it can be proved that there were three or more people using or threatening violence* (perhaps from CCTV evidence of the incident). If it *cannot be proved* that there were three or more people using or threatening unlawful violence the court should acquit each defendant (*R* v *McGuigan* [1991] Crim LR 719).

In *R* v *NW* [2010] EWCA Crim 404, the circumstances of the case were that a person was violently resisting arrest by a police officer, during which time a crowd gathered and various members of the crowd used or threatened violence. The Court of Appeal held that for the purposes of this section it was not necessary for a person to act deliberately in combination with at least two other people present at the scene, but that it is sufficient that at least three people be present, each separately using or threatening unlawful violence. The court's view was that the phrase, 'where 3 or more persons who are present together use or threaten violence . . .' consists of ordinary words which must be given their ordinary meaning.

The requirements as to the hypothetical effects on an equally hypothetical person of reasonable firmness are the same as for the offence of riot. However, there is no requirement to prove a common purpose.

Again, a defendant must be shown to have *intended* to use/threaten violence or to have *been aware* that his/her conduct may have been violent (s. 6(2)) and the offence may be committed in private as well as in a public place. 'Violence' for these purposes can include violent conduct towards property (s. 8).

---

### 3.6.4 Affray

OFFENCE: **Affray—*Public Order Act 1986, s. 3***

- Triable either way • Three years' imprisonment and/or a fine on indictment
- Six months' imprisonment and/or a fine summarily

The Public Order Act 1986, s. 3 states:

(1) A person is guilty of affray if he uses or threatens unlawful violence towards another and his conduct is such as would cause a person of reasonable firmness present at the scene to fear for his personal safety.

(2) Where 2 or more persons use or threaten the unlawful violence, it is the conduct of them taken together that must be considered for the purposes of subsection (1).

(3) For the purposes of this section a threat cannot be made by the use of words alone.

(4) No person of reasonable firmness need actually be, or be likely to be, present at the scene.

(5) Affray may be committed in private as well as in public places.

---

**KEYNOTE**

This offence can be committed by a single defendant although, if he/she acts with another, the conduct of them taken together will be the relevant factor in determining their criminal conduct (s. 3(2)).

The House of Lords has held that, in order to prove the offence of affray, the threat of unlawful violence has to be towards a person(s) present at the scene (*I* v *DPP* [2001] UKHL 10). Once this element has been proved, it will be necessary to prove the second element, namely, whether the defendant's conduct would have caused a hypothetical person present at the scene to fear for his/her personal safety (*R* v *Sanchez* (1996) 160 JP 321 and *R* v *Carey* [2006] EWCA Crim 17). However, where the likelihood of a hypothetical person of reasonable firmness being present was low this element of the offence was not satisfied. In *R (On the Application of Leeson) v DPP* [2010] EWHC 994 (Admin) a woman had issued a drunken threat to kill her long-term partner whilst holding a knife, in a bathroom, in an otherwise unoccupied house. In these circumstances the court held that there was no possibility of hypothetical bystanders fearing for their safety.

The threat cannot be made by words alone (s. 3(3)), therefore there must be some action by the defendant—even if that 'action' consists of utilising something else such as a dog to threaten the violence (*R* v *Dixon* [1993] Crim LR 579).

The effect of s. 3(4) is that it is not necessary to show that the defendant's behaviour either was or could have been seen by someone at the time. Contrast this with the lesser offence under s. 5.

Although violence is 'not restricted to conduct causing or intended to cause injury or damage but includes any other violent conduct' (s. 8), the expression does not include conduct towards property as it does with the offences under ss. 1 and 2.

Once more, a defendant must be shown to have *intended* to use/threaten violence or to have *been aware* that his/her conduct may have been violent (s. 6(2)).

# 3.7 | Racially, Religiously Aggravated and Homophobic Offences

## 3.7.1 The Offences

The offences that can become racially or religiously aggravated can be grouped in four categories:

- Assaults
  - ◆ wounding or grievous bodily harm—Offences Against the Person Act 1861, s. 20
  - ◆ causing actual bodily harm—Offences Against the Person Act 1861, s. 47
  - ◆ common assault—Criminal Justice Act 1988, s. 39
- Criminal Damage
  - ◆ 'simple' criminal damage—Criminal Damage Act 1971, s. 1(1)
- Public Order
  - ◆ causing fear or provocation of violence—Public Order Act 1986, s. 4
  - ◆ intentional harassment, alarm or distress—Public Order Act 1986, s. 4A
  - ◆ causing harassment, alarm or distress—Public Order Act 1986, s. 5
- Harassment
  - ◆ harassment—Protection from Harassment Act 1997, s. 2
  - ◆ stalking—Protection from Harassment Act 1997, s. 2A
  - ◆ putting people in fear of violence—Protection from Harassment Act 1997, s. 4
  - ◆ stalking involving fear of violence or serious alarm or distress—Protection from Harassment Act 1997, s. 4A.

---

**KEYNOTE**

The first thing that must be established in order to prove that an offence is racially or religiously aggravated is that the *basic offence* has been committed. Only when that is accomplished should consideration then be given as to whether the offence is aggravated *within the meaning of s. 28 of the Act* (**see para. 3.7.2**). While the definition of a 'racist' incident is of critical importance to all police officers, that definition ('a racist incident is any incident which is perceived to be racist by the victim or any other person') must not be confused with the definition of a 'racially or religiously aggravated' offence under s. 28 of the Act.

---

## 3.7.2 'Racially or Religiously Aggravated'

The test for racial or religious aggravation is set out at s. 28 of the Crime and Disorder Act 1998, which states:

(1) An offence is racially or religiously aggravated for the purposes of sections 29 to 32…if—
    (a) at the time of committing the offence, or immediately before or after doing so, the offender demonstrates towards the victim of the offence hostility based on the victim's membership (or presumed membership) of a racial or religious group; or
    (b) the offence is motivated (wholly or partly) by hostility towards members of a racial or religious group based on their membership of that group.

(2) In subsection (1)(a) above—
'membership', in relation to a racial or religious group, includes association with members of that group;
'presumed' means presumed by the offender.
(3) It is immaterial for the purposes of paragraph (a) or (b) of subsection (1) above whether or not the offender's hostility is also based, to any extent, on any other factor not mentioned in that paragraph.
(4) In this section 'racial group' means a group of persons defined by reference to race, colour, nationality (including citizenship) or ethnic or national origins.
(5) In this section 'religious group' means a group of persons defined by reference to religious belief or lack of religious belief.

### 3.7.3    Timing of the Hostility

In a case involving the abuse and assault of a doorman, the Administrative Court held that a racial insult uttered a few moments before an assault was enough to make the offence racially aggravated for the purposes of s. 29 of the Crime and Disorder Act 1998 (*DPP* v *Woods* [2002] EWHC 85 (Admin)). The Divisional Court in *DPP* v *McFarlane* [2002] EWHC 485 (Admin) decided that, where the expressions 'jungle bunny', 'black bastard' and 'wog' were used, the offence was properly made out as the words were used immediately before and at the time of the commission of the offence (contrary to s. 4 of the Public Order Act 1986).

The word 'immediately' in s. 28(1) not only means immediately before but also *immediately after* the commission of the offence.

However, the need for any such hostility to be demonstrated *immediately* means that it must be shown to have taken place in the immediate context of the basic offence. In *DPP* v *Parry* [2004] EWHC 3112 (Admin) the defendant had caused damage to a neighbour's door by throwing nail polish over it. The police attended the scene some 20 minutes after the damage had occurred and spoke to the defendant who was, by that time, sitting in his own house. At this stage the defendant made comments demonstrating hostility based on the victim's membership of a racial group. The defendant was convicted of racially aggravated criminal damage but appealed against this decision—the appeal was upheld and the conviction was quashed. The court held that the wording of the statute meant that any hostility had to be demonstrated *immediately* before or *immediately* after the substantive offence and that the courts below (magistrates') had not been entitled to consider the retrospective effect of the comments made later by the defendant.

### 3.7.4    Demonstration of Hostility

Section 28(1)(a) requires that the defendant demonstrate hostility at the time of committing the offence or immediately before or after doing so. This is not to establish the accused's state of mind, but what he *did* or *said* so as to demonstrate hostility towards the victim. The demonstration will often be by way of words, shouting, holding up a banner etc. or by adherence to a group that is demonstrating racial hostility.

In the context of criminal damage, the Divisional Court has confirmed that the relevant hostility can be demonstrated even if the victim is no longer present or is not present (*Parry*). However, the need for any such hostility to be demonstrated *immediately* means that it must be shown to have taken place in the immediate context of the offence.

### 3.7.5 Hostility

Common to both factors under s. 28(1)(a) and (b) is the notion of hostility.

Hostility is not defined by the Act. The *Oxford English Dictionary* defines 'hostile' as 'of the nature or disposition of an enemy; unfriendly, antagonistic'. It would seem relatively straightforward to show that someone's behaviour in committing the relevant offences was 'unfriendly or antagonistic'.

### 3.7.6 Victim

The demonstration of hostility will be towards the *victim* based on the *victim's* membership or presumed membership of a racial or religious group. This causes no difficulty where the offence is one of assault, public order or harassment where the victim is a person or where the offence is a criminal damage matter and the property is owned by a person (s. 30(3) of the Act provides that the person to whom the property belongs or is treated as belonging, will be treated as the victim). However, there are problems where the victim of criminal damage is a corporate body, e.g. where a bus shelter belonging to a transport company is damaged by racist graffiti. Of course the transport company may have a legal personality but it is impossible for it to have a race or a religion. Therefore it cannot be possible to prove the offence under s. 28(1)(a)—that the hostility was based on the victim's membership or presumed membership of a racial or religious group. In these circumstances the most suitable charge will be under s. 28(1)(b) of the Act (motivation).

Police officers can be victims of these offences and are entitled to the same protection under the legislation as anyone else (see *R v Jacobs* [2001] 2 Cr App R (S) 38).

---

**KEYNOTE**

The victim's perception of the incident (whatever it is) is totally irrelevant.

---

### 3.7.7 Motivation by Hostility

Section 28(1)(b) is concerned with the accused's motivation, which does concern his subjective state of mind. This is harder to prove although it will often be the case that the kind of demonstration referred to in the above paragraph would be evidence of such motivation. In *Taylor* v *DPP* [2006] EWHC 1202 (Admin), it was decided that use of phrases such as 'fucking nigger' and 'fucking coon bitch', patently not used in a jesting manner, must, in the circumstance of the case, have led any judge to find that the offence (in this case, the Public Order Act 1986, s. 5(1)(a)) was motivated, at least in part, by racial hostility as described in s. 28(1)(b). The fact that the offence is motivated only in part by such hostility would not alter the fact that the offence has been committed (motivated wholly or *partly* by such hostility).

### 3.7.8 Racial Groups

Section 28(4) of the Crime and Disorder Act 1998 states that a 'racial group' means a group of persons defined by reference to race, colour, nationality (including citizenship) or ethnic or national origins.

In determining whether or not a group is defined by *ethnic origins*, the courts will have regard to the judgment in the House of Lords in *Mandla* v *Dowell Lee* [1983] 2 AC 548. In that case their lordships decided that Sikhs were such a group after considering whether they as a group had:

- a long shared *history*;
- a *cultural tradition* of their own, including family and social customs and manners, often, but not necessarily, associated with religious observance;
- either a *common geographical origin* or descent from a small number of *common ancestors*;
- a *common language*, not necessarily peculiar to that group;
- a *common literature* peculiar to that group;
- a *common religion* different from that of neighbouring groups or the general community surrounding the group; and
- the characteristic of being a *minority* or an *oppressed* or a *dominant* group within a larger community.

Lord Fraser's dictum in *Mandla* suggests that the first two characteristics above are essential in defining an 'ethnic group', while the others are at least relevant. His lordship also approved a decision from New Zealand to the effect that Jews are a group with common ethnic origins (*King-Ansell* v *Police* [1979] 2 NZLR 531).

---

**KEYNOTE**

When considering whether an offence was racially motivated under s. 28, hostility demonstrated to people who were foreign nationals simply because they were 'foreign' can be just as objectionable as hostility based on some more limited racial characteristic. In *DPP* v *M* [2004] EWHC 1453 (Admin) a juvenile used the words 'bloody foreigners' immediately before smashing the window of a kebab shop. The Divisional Court held that this was capable of amounting to an expression of hostility based on a person's membership or presumed membership of a racial group for the purposes of s. 28(1)(a) of the Crime and Disorder Act 1998. Although the statutory wording used the expression 'a racial group', the court held that a specific and inclusive definition of such a group had to be used by the defendant (e.g. the defendant did not have to single out a specific nationality) and the size of group referred to by a defendant (such as all 'foreigners') was irrelevant. However, in the case of *M* the youth court had inadvertently mixed the two tests of hostility and motivation under s. 28(1)(b) and his appeal was allowed for that reason. This approach was also taken by the Court of Appeal in *R* v *Rogers* [2005] EWCA Crim 2863 where the defendant had called three Spanish women 'bloody foreigners' and told them to 'go back to your own country'. The prosecution case was that the defendant had demonstrated hostility based on the women's membership of a racial group. The court's decision clarifies the position that, for an offence to be aggravated under s. 28, the defendant has first to form a view that the victim is a member of a racial group (within the definition in s. 28(4)) and then has to say (or do) something that demonstrates hostility towards the victim based on membership of that group. However, the Court of Appeal noted that the very wide meaning of racial group under s. 28(4) gives rise to a danger of aggravated offences being charged where mere 'vulgar abuse' had included racial descriptions that did not truly indicate hostility to the race in question. Consequently, s. 28 should not be used unless the prosecuting authority is satisfied that the facts truly suggest that the offence was aggravated (rather than simply accompanied) by racism.

The Divisional Court has held that the words 'white man's arse licker' and 'brown Englishman' when used to accompany an assault on an Asian victim did not necessarily make the assault 'racially aggravated' and that the prosecution had not done enough to show that the assailants' behaviour fell under the definition set out in s. 28 of the 1998 Act (*DPP* v *Pal* [2000] Crim LR 756), a case that is hard to reconcile with s. 28(2).

Traditional Romany gypsies are capable of being a racial group on the basis of ethnic origin (*Commission for Racial Equality* v *Dutton* [1989] QB 783) but travellers are not. English and Scottish people have been held to constitute groups defined by reference to national origins and thus as members of 'racial groups' in the broad sense as defined and protected from discrimination under the Race Relations Act 1976 (now the Equality Act 2010) (*Northern Joint Police Board* v *Power* [1997] IRLR 610). This decision ought logically to extend to Irish and Welsh people. In *Attorney-General's Reference (No. 4 of 2004), sub nom Attorney-General* v *D* [2005] EWCA Crim 889 the use of the word 'immigrant', in its simple implication that a person was 'non-British', was specific enough to denote membership of a 'racial group' within its meaning in s. 28(4) of the Crime and Disorder Act 1998.

### 3.7.9 Religious Groups

Although in other contexts 'religion' has been interpreted as involving a belief in some kind of god or supernatural being (*R* v *Registrar General, ex parte Segerdal* [1970] 2 QB 697), a much broader approach is clearly required in the context of s. 28. It is clear from s. 28(5) that a 'religious group' may, for the purposes of the Act, include a group defined by its lack of religious beliefs. If, for example, D assaults V because V is an atheist or humanist who rejects religious beliefs, D must be guilty of a religiously aggravated offence. The same could be said of an assault on an agnostic.

A purely religious group such as Rastafarians (who have been held not to be members of an ethnic group *per se* (*Dawkins* v *Crown Suppliers (Property Services Agency)* [1993] ICR 517) are covered by the aggravated forms of offences as they are a religious group. In reality, a number of racial groups will overlap with religious groups in any event—Rastafarians would be a good example. An attack on a Rastafarian might be a racially aggravated offence under s. 28 because it was based on the defendant's hostility towards a *racial group* (e.g. African-Caribbeans) into which many Rastafarians fall. Alternatively, an attack might be made on a white Rastafarian based on the victim's religious beliefs (or lack of religious beliefs), i.e. his 'membership of a religious group'. Muslims have also been held not to be a racial group (*JH Walker* v *Hussain* [1996] ICR 291) but Muslims are clearly members of a religious group and, as such, are covered by the Act.

---

**KEYNOTE**

To be guilty of an offence that is racially or religiously aggravated, it is not necessary that the accused be of a different racial, national or ethnic (or religious) group from the victim (*R* v *White* [2001] EWCA Crim 216).

---

### 3.7.10 Membership

An important extension of 'racial or religious groups' is the inclusion of people who associate with members of that group. 'Membership' *for the purposes of s. 28(1)(a)* will include *association* with members of that group (s. 28(2)). This means that a white man who has a black female partner would potentially fall within the category of a 'member' of her racial group—and vice versa. Moreover, people who work within certain racial or religious groups within the community could also be regarded as members of those groups for these purposes.

For the purposes of s. 28(1)(a), 'membership' will also include anyone *presumed by the defendant* to be a member of a racial or religious group. Therefore, if a defendant wrongly presumed that a person was a member of a racial or religious group, say a Pakistani Muslim, and assaulted that person as a result, the defendant's *presumption* would be enough to make his/her behaviour 'racially or religiously aggravated', even though the victim was in fact an Indian Hindu.

Such a presumption would not extend to the aggravating factors under s. 28(1)(b). The only apparent reason for this would seem to be that the s. 28(1)(a) offence requires hostility to be demonstrated towards a particular person ('the victim') while the offence under s. 28(1)(b) envisages hostility towards members of a racial or religious group generally and does not require a specific victim.

Section 28(3) goes on to provide that it is immaterial whether the defendant's hostility (in either case under s. 28(1)) is also based to any extent on *any other factor*. This concession in s. 28(3) only prevents the defendant pointing to another *factor* in order to explain his/her behaviour in committing the relevant offence (assault, criminal damage, etc.). Although it removes the opportunity for a defendant to argue that his/her behaviour was as a result of other factors (e.g. arising out of a domestic dispute), the subsection does not remove the burden on the prosecution to show that the defendant either demonstrated racial or religious hostility or was motivated by it.

### 3.7.11 Offences Involving Racial and Religious Hatred

The Racial and Religious Hatred Act 2006 inserts part 3A into the Public Order Act 1986 created offences of stirring up hatred against persons on religious grounds. This section provides a summary of the offences introduced by the 1986 Act aimed at addressing incidents specifically motivated by racial hatred, and the new offences, created by the Racial and Religious Hatred Act 2006, motivated by religious hatred.

For the purposes of the offences contrary to ss. 18 to 23 of the 1986 Act, 'racial hatred' means hatred against a group of persons defined by reference to colour, race, nationality (including citizenship) or ethnic or national origins (s. 17).

For the purposes of offences contrary to ss. 29B to 29G of the 1986 Act, 'religious hatred' means hatred against a group of persons defined by reference to religious belief or lack of religious belief (s. 29A).

### 3.7.12 Use of Words, Behaviour or Display of Written Material, s. 18

OFFENCE: **Use of Words or Behaviour or Display of Written Material—*Public Order Act 1986, s. 18***

• Triable either way • Seven years' imprisonment and/or a fine on indictment • Six months' imprisonment and/or a fine summarily

The Public Order Act 1986, s. 18 states:

(1) A person who uses threatening, abusive or insulting words or behaviour, or displays any written material which is threatening, abusive or insulting, is guilty of an offence if—
    (a) he intends thereby to stir up racial hatred, or
    (b) having regard to all the circumstances racial hatred is likely to be stirred up thereby.
(2) An offence under this section may be committed in a public or a private place, except that no offence is committed where the words or behaviour are used, or the written material is displayed, by a person inside a dwelling and are not heard or seen except by other persons in that or another dwelling.

---

**KEYNOTE**

This, and the other offences under this part of the Act, may not be prosecuted without the consent of the Attorney-General (or Solicitor-General).

Generally, in order to prove these offences, you must show that a defendant:

• *intended* to stir up racial hatred; or
• that he/she *intended* the relevant words, behaviour or material to be threatening, abusive or insulting; or
• that he/she *was aware* that the relevant words/behaviour/material might be threatening, abusive or insulting.

This offence does not apply to broadcasts in a programme (but **see para. 3.7.16**) and there are exemptions in the case of fair and accurate reports of parliamentary or court proceedings.

---

#### 3.7.12.1 Defence

The Public Order Act 1986, s. 18 states:

(4) In proceedings for an offence under this section it is a defence for the accused to prove that he was inside a dwelling and had no reason to believe that the words or behaviour used, or the written material displayed, would be heard or seen by a person outside that or any other dwelling.

### 3.7.13 Publishing or Distributing Written Material, s. 19

OFFENCE: **Publishing or Distributing Written Material—*Public Order Act 1986, s. 19***
- Triable either way • Seven years' imprisonment and/or a fine on indictment
- Six months' imprisonment and/or a fine summarily

The Public Order Act 1986, s. 19 states:

(1) A person who publishes or distributes written material which is threatening, abusive or insulting is guilty of an offence if—
   (a) he intends thereby to stir up racial hatred, or
   (b) having regard to all the circumstances racial hatred is likely to be stirred up thereby.

(2) ...

(3) References in this Part to the publication or distribution of written material are to its publication or distribution to the public or a section of the public.

---

**KEYNOTE**

Prosecution of this offence needs the consent of the Attorney-General (or Solicitor-General).

---

#### 3.7.13.1 Defence

The Public Order Act 1986, s. 19 states:

(2) In proceedings for an offence under this section it is a defence for an accused who is not shown to have intended to stir up racial hatred to prove that he was not aware of the content of the material and did not suspect, and had no reason to suspect, that it was threatening, abusive or insulting.

### 3.7.14 Use of Words, Behaviour or Display of Written Material, s. 29B

OFFENCE: **Use of Words or Behaviour or Display of Written Material—*Public Order Act 1986, s. 29B***
- Triable either way • Not exceeding seven years' imprisonment and/or a fine on indictment • Not exceeding six months' imprisonment and/or a fine summarily

The Public Order Act 1986, s. 29B states:

(1) A person who uses threatening words or behaviour, or displays any written material which is threatening, is guilty of an offence if he intends thereby to stir up religious hatred or hatred on the grounds of sexual orientation.

(2) An offence under this section is committed in a public or private place, except that no offence is committed where the words or behaviour are used, or the written material is displayed, by a person inside a dwelling and are not heard or seen except by other persons in that or another dwelling.

---

**KEYNOTE**

This differs from the other sections under the 1986 Act which have no specific power of arrest since the provisions of the Serious Organised Crime and Police Act 2005 were introduced.

All of the new offences are similar to that under s. 18 in that they require the consent of the Attorney-General before proceedings can be taken (s. 29L), and the same defences apply to this particular section—no reason to believe the words or behaviour, etc., would be heard or seen outside the dwelling (s. 29B(4)), or where used solely for the purpose of being included in a programming service (s. 29B(5)).

---

Section 29J of the Act provides that the offences of stirring up religious hatred are not intended to limit or restrict discussion, criticism or expressions of antipathy, dislike, ridicule or insult or abuse of particular religions or belief systems or lack of religion or of the beliefs and practices of those who hold such beliefs or to apply to persons newly converted to a religious faith, evangelism or the seeking to convert people to a particular belief or to cease holding a belief.

### 3.7.15 Publishing or Distributing Material, s. 29C

OFFENCE: **Publishing or Distributing Written Material—*Public Order Act 1986, s. 29C***
• Triable either way • Not exceeding seven years' imprisonment and/or a fine on indictment • Not exceeding six months' imprisonment and/or a fine summarily

The Public Order Act 1986, s. 29C states:

(1) A person who publishes or distributes written material which is threatening is guilty of an offence if he intends thereby to stir up religious hatred or hatred on the grounds of sexual orientation.

(2) References in this Part to the publication or distribution of written material are to its publication or distribution to the public or a section of the public.

### 3.7.16 Hatred on the Grounds of Sexual Orientation

Section 74 of and sch. 16 to the Criminal Justice and Immigration Act 2008 extends the offences of inciting hatred against people on religious grounds to cover hatred against people on grounds of sexual orientation, amending part 3A of the Public Order Act 1986 (hatred against persons on religious grounds) to create offences involving stirring up hatred on the grounds of sexual orientation.

Section 29AB of the 1986 Act defines 'hatred on the grounds of sexual orientation'. The definition covers hatred against a group of persons defined by reference to their sexual orientation, be they heterosexual, homosexual or bi-sexual. The amendments to ss. 29B to 29G of the 1986 Act extend the various religious hatred offences in those sections to cover hatred on the grounds of sexual orientation. These offences involve the use of words or behaviour or display of written material (s. 29B), publishing or distributing written material (s. 29C), the public performance of a play (s. 29D), distributing, showing or playing a recording (s. 29E), broadcasting or including a programme in a programme service (s. 29F), and possession of inflammatory material (s. 29G).

In relation to each extended offence the relevant act (namely, words, behaviour, written material or recordings or programme) must be threatening, and the offender must intend thereby to stir up hatred on the grounds of sexual orientation. In the case of the offence under s. 29B, there is a specific defence where the words or behaviour are used or displayed inside a private dwelling and the accused had no reason to believe that they can be heard or seen by a person outside that or any other private dwelling.

The offences differ from the offences of stirring up racial hatred in, part 3 of the 1986 Act, in two respects. First, the offences apply only to 'threatening' words or behaviour, rather than 'threatening, abusive or insulting' words or behaviour. Secondly, the offences apply only to words or behaviour if the accused 'intends' to stir up hatred on grounds of sexual orientation, rather than if hatred is either intentional or 'likely' to be stirred up.

# 3.8 Misuse of Drugs

## 3.8.1 Introduction

This chapter deals, in the main, with offences created by the Misuse of Drugs Act 1971. As some of the concepts associated with drug offences, e.g. 'possession' and 'supply', are so important to assist in understanding the legislation, these concepts are dealt with prior to any offences associated with them. A methodical approach is then taken by dealing with drug offences in the order of possession, supply and production and finishes with an examination of other offences and police powers.

## 3.8.2 Classification

Drugs that are subject to the provisions of the Misuse of Drugs Act 1971 are listed in parts I, II and III of sch. 2 to the Act. The main practical effect of the classification of controlled drugs relates to the mode of trial, available powers and sentencing provisions.

The divisions are made largely on the basis of each substance's potential effects on both the person taking it and society in general.

- **Class A**—This class includes heroin, cocaine, LSD, 'Ecstasy' (MDMA) and methylamphetamine ('crystal meth'). It also includes fungus (of any kind) which contains psilocin (such as 'magic mushrooms').
- **Class B**—This class includes cannabis, codeine and ritalin (methylphenidate).
- **Class C**—This class includes ketamine, diazepam (valium) and gamma hydroxybutyrate (GHB).

If the charge alleges possession of one particular drug then that drug must be identified.

While crystal meth is a Class A drug, the leaves produced by the khat plant (sometimes chewed for a mild stimulant effect) are not controlled drugs for the purposes of the 1971 Act.

Note that, although a substance may appear in sch. 2 to the Act, there may be restrictions on the occasions where possession is treated as an offence (**see para. 3.8.3.7**).

It is not necessary, when prosecuting an offence, to distinguish between the various chemical forms in which a drug exists (i.e. as a salt, ester or other form) (*R* v *Greensmith* [1983] 1 WLR 1124).

A defendant's admission may, in some cases, be relied upon to prove his/her knowledge as to what a particular substance is (see *R* v *Chatwood* [1980] 1 WLR 874).

### 3.8.2.1 Cannabis

The Misuse of Drugs Act 1971, s. 37 states:

> 'cannabis' (except in the expression 'cannabis resin') means any plant of the genus *Cannabis* or any part of any such plant (by whatever name designated) except that it does not include cannabis resin or any of the following products after separation from the rest of the plant, namely—
> (a) mature stalk of any such plant,
> (b) fibre produced from mature stalk of any such plant, and
> (c) seed of any such plant,

'cannabis resin' means the separated resin, whether crude or purified, obtained from any plant of the genus *Cannabis*.

---

**KEYNOTE**

Cannabis is a Class B drug. This means that cannabis, cannabis resin, cannabinol and its derivatives, any preparations or other product containing these substances and any substance which is an ester or ether either of cannabinol or of a cannabinol derivative are also Class B drugs. It should be noted that cannabis oil is also subject to control as a Class B drug. As cannabis and cannabis resin are both in the same class for the purposes of the 1971 Act there would be no duplicity if a person is charged with possessing either one or the other in the same charge (*R v Best* (1979) 70 Cr App R 21).

---

### 3.8.3 Possession

A good starting point in understanding the concept of 'possession' is to realise that it is a neutral concept, not implying any kind of fault, blame or guilt. This is the key feature to recognise before going on to consider specific offences under *any* legislation. There are two elements to possession; the physical element and the mental element (*R v Lambert* [2002] 2 AC 545).

#### 3.8.3.1 Custody or Control

The physical element involves proof that the thing is in the custody of the defendant or subject to his control. For example, if X has a wrap of cocaine in his jacket pocket, X therefore has control of the wrap of cocaine (although *mere custody* does not mean that X is in 'possession' at this stage).

This approach is enlarged by s. 37(3) of the Misuse of Drugs Act 1971 which states that 'For the purposes of this Act the things which a person has in his possession shall be taken to include anything subject to his control which is in the custody of another'.

..................................................................................................................

EXAMPLE

X buys a controlled drug via the Internet, directing that it be sent by post to his home address. X is in possession of that drug from the time it arrives through his letterbox. (*R v Peaston* (1978) 69 Cr App R 203)

..................................................................................................................

#### 3.8.3.2 Knowledge of Possession

The second element involves that the defendant knows that the thing in question is under his/her control. He/she need not know what its nature is, but as long as he/she knows that the thing, whatever it is, is under his/her control, it is in his/her possession.

..................................................................................................................

EXAMPLE

X and Y are walking along a street. X is going through his pockets looking for his wallet and as he is searching for the wallet he hands Y several tablets of Ecstasy and asks him to hold onto them while he continues searching. Y has no idea that the tablets he takes hold of are a controlled drug.

- Y has control of the Ecstasy tablets (they are in his hand)
- Y has knowledge of the presence of the Ecstasy tablets in his hand
- *Therefore Y has possession of the Ecstasy tablets.*

..................................................................................................................

In the above example nobody is suggesting, at this stage, that Y is guilty of an offence. Of course Y could, quite rightly, be arrested on *suspicion* of possessing a controlled drug but arresting on suspicion that a person has committed an offence and *proving* guilt in relation to that offence are two very different things. Indeed, Y's lack of knowledge about what the tablets are may afford him a defence (**see para. 3.8.9**) But the fact remains that ignorance of, or mistake as to the quality of the thing in question does not prevent the accused being in possession of it. *Remember, 'possession' is a neutral concept.*

What if the thing is inside a container, e.g. a box, a bag or a cigarette packet, and the person claims not to have known the thing was inside the container? In such cases, the common law makes the same requirements; you need to show that the person had custody of the container together with a knowledge that it (the container) contained *something*.

....................................................................................................

EXAMPLE

X is given a packet of cigarettes by Y. X believes the packet contains cigarettes only. The packet does contain several cigarettes but also contains a wrap of cocaine. X does not know about the wrap of cocaine and puts the pack of cigarettes into his pocket.

- X has custody of the pack of cigarettes (they are in his pocket)
- X has knowledge of the presence of the pack of cigarettes (X put them there)
- X knows that the pack of cigarettes contains *something*
- *Therefore X has possession of the wrap of cocaine.*

....................................................................................................

Once again, nobody is suggesting X is guilty of an offence—just that he is in 'possession' of the wrap of cocaine.

In *R v Forsyth* [2001] EWCA Crim 2926, the defendant argued that there was a distinction between a person carrying something *in* a container and a person carrying *something inside something else* in a container. In that particular case, the defendant was found in possession of a box which contained a safe; inside the safe was a significant quantity of a controlled drug. The defendant argued that this type of possession should be differentiated from the situation where someone simply had possession of a box with drugs in it. The Court of Appeal ruled that there was no difference and the issues of proof were the same.

A person does not possess something of which he/she is completely unaware—there would be no knowledge of possession. If a drug is put into someone's pocket without his/her knowledge, he/she is not in possession of it (*Warner v Metropolitan Police Commissioner* [1969] 2 AC 256).

### 3.8.3.3 Joint Possession

To show that two or more persons are in possession of a controlled drug requires more than a mere ability to control it (*R v Kousar* [2009] EWCA Crim 139). Mere knowledge of the presence of a drug in the hands of a confederate is not enough; joint possession must be established (*R v Searle* [1971] Crim LR 592). In *Searle* it was stated that this could be established by asking the question 'do the drugs form part of a common pool from which all had the right to draw?' (Lord Widgery CJ). In *R v Strong* (1989) *The Times*, 26 January 1990, the prosecution put the case on the basis that there was joint possession, that is, each of the co-accused had control of one or more of the packages of cannabis. The Court of Appeal followed *Searle*, and said that what was being looked for was whether each person had the right to say what should be done with the cannabis. Mere presence in the same vehicle as the drugs, and knowing they were there, was not sufficient.

Some of the further practical difficulties that can arise from this view of 'possession' were highlighted in *Adams v DPP* [2002] EWHC 438 (Admin). In that case a small quantity of controlled drugs was found in the defendant's home during the execution of a search warrant.

There was no proof that the drugs were owned by the defendant, nor that she was specifically aware of their presence but the defendant *did* know that her home was used by various people who were highly likely to bring controlled drugs into it. She was convicted of possession. In hearing her appeal against conviction by way of case stated, the Administrative Court held that, where knowledge of possession of drugs was limited to the fact that a visitor had brought drugs into the defendant's home intending to take them, that was not sufficient evidence from which it was appropriate to infer that she had control over the drugs.

The court also held that giving consent (explicitly or impliedly) for the use of a controlled drug did not of itself constitute possession. Similarly, an inference that the defendant knew whose drugs had been found in her home did not amount to evidence of control over the drug itself—even though she may well have been able to exercise control over what actually took place in her home.

### 3.8.3.4 Points to Prove

Once 'possession' has been proved it is then necessary to prove that what the defendant possesses is, in fact, a controlled drug. If this is established then the defendant has a case to answer in relation to the offence of possession of a controlled drug.

........................................................................................................

EXAMPLE

X is subject to a stop and search procedure under s. 23 of the Misuse of Drugs Act 1971 (see para. 3.8.17.1). During the search several packets containing cannabis resin are found in X's coat pocket.

In order to prove 'possession' of the cannabis for the purpose of the possession of a controlled drug offence, you must show:

* that X possessed the cannabis (X has custody/control of it and he knows it is in his possession) and
* that the contents of the packets contain a controlled drug.

........................................................................................................

### 3.8.3.5 Quality

In the above example, *you would not have to show that X knew what the resin was*. That is, you do not need to show that X knew the *quality* of what he possessed to prove that X 'possessed' it.

If the defendant admits to knowing that the cannabis resin was there but thought it was chocolate, he is in possession of it (see *R v Marriott* [1971] 1 WLR 187).

Therefore if a defendant had a packet of cigarettes with him and admitted to knowing that he had them, he would be in possession of a controlled drug if one cigarette was shown to have contained cannabis. The fact that the defendant thought they contained tobacco would be irrelevant to the 'possession' concept (*Searle*) (although clearly he may be able to raise the defence under s. 28: see para. 3.8.9).

### 3.8.3.6 Quantity

The *quantity* of a controlled drug, however, may be so small that the defendant could not possibly have known about it; therefore it could not be 'possessed'.

Each case will have to be decided on its merits but the House of Lords has suggested that if something is 'visible, tangible and measurable', that may be sufficient (*R v Boyesen* [1982] AC 768). If the amount recovered is too small to support a charge of possession, it might be used to prove earlier possession of the drug (see *R v Graham* [1970] 1 WLR 113 and *Hambleton v Callinan* [1968] 2 QB 427—traces of a controlled drug in a urine sample held to be possible evidence of earlier possession of that drug).

Quantity is not only relevant to the fact of possession; it is also relevant to the intention of the person in whose possession the drug is found. Larger quantities (particularly if they are also divided into smaller amounts) may be indicative of an intention to supply and may be assumed to be proof of that intention in some circumstances.

Now that the issues surrounding 'possession' have been examined it is appropriate to consider the offence of possession of a controlled drug and the defence to that offence under s. 5 of the Misuse of Drugs Act 1971.

### 3.8.3.7 Possession of a Controlled Drug

OFFENCE: **Possession of Controlled Drug—*Misuse of Drugs Act 1971, s. 5***

    • Triable either way • Class A (seven years' imprisonment and/or a fine on indictment; six months' imprisonment and/or prescribed sum summarily) • Class B (five years' imprisonment and/or a fine on indictment; three months' imprisonment and/or a fine summarily) • Class C (two years' imprisonment and/or a fine on indictment; three months' imprisonment and/or a fine summarily) • See Keynote for possession of cannabis or cannabis resin

The Misuse of Drugs Act 1971, s. 5 states:

(2) Subject to section 28 of this Act and to subsection (4) below, it is an offence for a person to have a controlled drug in his possession in contravention of subsection (1)...

---

**KEYNOTE**

Section 28 provides a general defence to certain drugs offences and is examined at **para. 3.8.9**.

Where the controlled drug involved is a fungus containing psilocin (a class A drug) or an ester of psilocin (commonly known as magic mushrooms) possession will not be unlawful in certain circumstances. In summary, those circumstances are generally where the fungus is growing *uncultivated* and it:

- is picked by a person already in *lawful possession* of it (e.g. the landowner on whose land the mushrooms are growing) for the purpose of delivering it (as soon as is reasonably practicable) into the custody of a person lawfully entitled to take custody of it and it remains in that person's possession for (and in accordance with) that purpose; or
- it is picked by anyone either for the purpose of delivering it (as soon as reasonably practicable) into the custody of a person lawfully entitled to take custody of it or destroying it (as soon as is reasonably practicable) and it is held for that purpose.

Possession of cannabis can be dealt with under the Penalty Notice for Disorder (PND) Scheme. PNDs cannot be issued for any other drug related offences other than possession of cannabis or cannabis derivatives. PNDs may be issued to any adult found in possession of cannabis for personal use; they are not appropriate for offenders under the age of 18.

---

### 3.8.3.8 Section 5—The Defence to Unlawful Possession

Section 5 provides a defence to an offence of unlawful possession:

(4) In any proceedings for an offence under subsection (2) above in which it is proved that the accused had a controlled drug in his possession, it shall be a defence for him to prove—
    (a) that, knowing or suspecting it to be a controlled drug, he took possession of it for the purpose of preventing another from committing or continuing to commit an offence in connection with that drug and that as soon as possible after taking possession of it he took all such steps as were reasonably open to him to destroy the drug or to deliver it into the custody of a person lawfully entitled to take custody of it; or
    (b) that, knowing or suspecting it to be a controlled drug, he took possession of it for the purpose of delivering it into the custody of a person lawfully entitled to take custody of it and that as soon as possible after taking possession of it he took all such steps as were reasonably open to him to deliver it into the custody of such a person.

**KEYNOTE**

This defence envisages two distinct situations. The purpose in taking possession of the controlled drug under s. 5(4)(a) must be to:

- prevent *another*
- from committing (in the future) or
- continuing to commit

an offence in connection with *that* drug.

The first situation might arise where a parent, guardian or carer finds a child in possession of something which appears to be a controlled drug. Provided that that person takes all reasonable steps to destroy the drug or to take it to someone lawfully entitled to possess it (like a general practitioner or police officer), *as soon as possible after taking possession of it*, he/she commits no offence of unlawful possession.

When the accused buried drugs (cannabis) it was not sufficient to satisfy the defence under s. 5(4)(a) that the forces of nature might or would destroy the drug eventually: rather it was for the accused to show that he took all such reasonable steps as were reasonably open to him to destroy them and the acts of destruction must be his (*R* v *Murphy* [2002] EWCA Crim 1587). Relying on the forces of nature did not provide this defence on that occasion.

The second situation (under s. 5(4)(b)) may arise where a person finds what he/she believes to be a controlled drug and he/she takes possession of it *solely for the purpose of delivering it to a person lawfully entitled to take custody of it*. The defendant must prove that this was his/her intention at the time of taking possession (*R* v *Dempsey and Dempsey* (1986) 82 Cr App R 291).

Section 5(4) will not provide a defence to any other offence connected with the controlled drug (e.g. supplying or offering to supply).

Duress of circumstances is not a defence to this, or any other, offence under the Misuse of Drugs Act 1971.

### 3.8.4 Supplying

In *R* v *Maginnis* [1987] AC 303, the House of Lords held that 'supply' involves more than a mere transfer of physical control of the item from one person to another but includes a further concept, namely that of 'enabling the recipient to apply the thing handed over to purposes for which he desires or has a duty to apply it'—in other words *the person to whom the drug is given must derive some benefit from it*.

**KEYNOTE**

In *R* v *Dempsey and Dempsey* (1985) 82 Cr App R 291, a registered drug addict (A) was in lawful possession of a drug. A asked his partner (B) to hold on to some of that drug while he went to administer the remainder of it to himself in a gents' toilet. Both A and B were arrested, A being subsequently charged with 'supplying' B with the drug. The Court of Appeal held that, if B had simply been given the drug for safekeeping until A's return, there would be no 'supplying' by A to B. If, however, she had been given the drug for her own use, then there would clearly be a 'supplying' of that drug (from A to B) and the offence would be complete.

#### Supplying Explained

The key to working out if there has been a 'supply' is to ask 'Does being given the drug benefit the person to whom the drug has been given?'. If the answer is 'Yes' then the person giving the drug is 'supplying' it.

The issue has been further explored in a case involving a person who claimed that he had been coerced into holding controlled drugs for unnamed dealers. When found in possession of the drugs, the defendant claimed the defence of duress and said that he had only been an 'involuntary custodian' of them, intending to return them at a later date. The Court of Appeal decided that it was irrelevant whether a person was a voluntary or involuntary custodian of the drugs and that an intention to return them to their depositor amounted to an 'intention to supply' (*R v Panton* [2001] EWCA Crim 611).

If a police informer provides a controlled drug to another in order that the other be arrested, there will still be a 'supplying' of the drug (*R v X* [1994] Crim LR 827).

### Injecting Others

Injecting another with that person's own controlled drug has been held not to amount to 'supplying' in a case where the defendant assisted in pushing down the plunger of a syringe that the other person was already using (*R v Harris* [1968] 1 WLR 769). It may, however, amount to an offence of 'poisoning' under s. 23 of the Offences Against the Person Act 1861. The problem with charging the supplier of drugs for self-injection by someone who then dies as a result lies in the issues of causation. While there are some authorities which say that supply of a drug for self-injection which leads to the death of the recipient *can potentially* amount to unlawful act manslaughter, great difficulties have arisen and the general view is that the supplier is unlikely to be held liable for *causing* death in such a case (see *R v Dias* [2001] EWCA Crim 2986). Where the defendant actually carries out the injection as opposed to merely the supply of the drug, liability for causing the death of another in this way can be made out however—even if the drug injected is not a controlled drug (see *R v Andrews* [2002] EWCA Crim 3021—injection of insulin with consent).

Dividing up controlled drugs which have been jointly purchased and then handing them out so that persons may use the drug will amount to 'supplying' (*R v Buckley* (1979) 69 Cr App R 371).

The offence of offering to supply a controlled drug is complete when the offer is made. It is irrelevant whether or not the defendant actually has the means to meet the offer or even intends to carry it out (see *R v Goodard* [1992] Crim LR 588). If the offer is made by conduct alone (i.e. without any words), it may be difficult to prove this offence. If words are used, the defence under s. 28 (**see para. 3.8.9**) does not appear to apply (see *R v Mitchell* [1992] Crim LR 723). If the offer is made to an undercover police officer, the offence is still committed and the defendant cannot claim that such an offer was not a 'real' offer (*R v Kray* [1998] EWCA Crim 3211).

### 3.8.4.1    Supplying a Controlled Drug

OFFENCE:    **Supplying Controlled Drug—*Misuse of Drugs Act 1971, s. 4(3)***
  • Triable either way  • Class A (life imprisonment and/or a fine on indictment;
  six months' imprisonment and/or prescribed sum summarily)  • Class B (14 years'
  imprisonment and/or a fine on indictment; six months' imprisonment and/or
  prescribed sum summarily)  • Class C (14 years' imprisonment and/or a fine on
  indictment; three months' imprisonment and/or a fine summarily)

The Misuse of Drugs Act 1971, s. 4 states:

(3)  Subject to section 28 of this Act, it is an offence for a person—
  (a)  to supply or offer to supply a controlled drug to another in contravention of subsection (1)
  above; or
  (b)  to be concerned in the supplying of such a drug to another in contravention of that subsection; or
  (c)  to be concerned in the making to another in contravention of that subsection of an offer to
  supply such a drug.

---

**KEYNOTE**

In order to prove the offence of being concerned in the supply/offer to supply a controlled drug, you must
show:

• the actual supply of, or making of an offer to supply, a controlled drug;
• the participation of the defendant in that enterprise; and
• knowledge by the defendant that the enterprise involved the supply of, or making of an offer to supply,
  a controlled drug (*R* v *Hughes* (1985) 81 Cr App R 344).

---

### Offering to Supply

An offer may be by words or conduct. If it is by words, it must be ascertained whether an
offer to supply a controlled drug was made. Whether the accused had a controlled drug in
his/her possession or had access to controlled drugs or whether the substance in his/her
possession was a controlled drug at all is immaterial. Whether the accused intends to carry
the offer into effect is irrelevant; the offence is complete upon the making of an offer to supply. The offence is committed whether or not the offer is genuine and once an offer is made
it cannot be withdrawn.

### Being Concerned in Supply to Another

The three ingredients of this offence were set out by the Court of Appeal in *R* v *Hughes* (1985)
Cr App R 344:

(a)  The supply of a drug to another, or as the case may be, the making of an offer to supply the drug
  to another in contravention of s. 4(1) of the Misuse of Drugs Act 1971;
(b)  Participation by the accused in an enterprise involving such supply or, as the case may be, such
  an offer to supply; and
(c)  Knowledge by the accused of the nature of the enterprise. i.e. that it involved supply of a drug or,
  as the case may be, offering to supply a drug.

If the object of a conspiracy is to supply a controlled drug to a co-conspirator, any subsequent
charge must make that clear; stating that the defendants conspired to supply the drug to
'another' implies that the supply was to be made to someone *other than any of the conspirators*
(*R* v *Jackson* [2000] 1 Cr App R 97n).

'Supplying' includes distributing (s. 37(1)).

### 3.8.4.2 Specific Situations

The different prevailing circumstances of the 'supply' must be taken into account. Section 4A of the Misuse of Drugs Act 1971 recognises this and requires courts to treat certain conditions as 'aggravating' factors when considering the seriousness of the offence under s. 4(3) if committed by a person aged 18 or over.

The conditions are either:

(1) that the offence was committed on or in the vicinity of school premises at a relevant time. 'Vicinity' is not defined and will be left to each court relying on its local knowledge. Other buildings and premises (e.g. cafes and shopping centres) can fall within this description and courts may decide that a route used to get to or from a school or a place where schoolchildren gather (even if trespassing) may be in the 'vicinity'. School premises are land used for the purposes of a school but *excluding* any land occupied solely as a dwelling *by a person employed at the school* (s. 4A(8)). A 'relevant time' is any time when the school premises are in use by people under the age of 18 (and one hour before the start/after the end of any such time) (s. 4A(5)); or

(2) that in connection with the commission of the offence the offender used a 'courier' who, at the time the offence was committed, was under the age of 18. A person uses a courier if he/she causes or permits another person (the courier):
    (a) to deliver a controlled drug to a third person, or
    (b) to deliver a 'drug related consideration' (basically any money, goods etc. obtained or intended to be used in connection with the supply of a controlled drug) to him/herself or a third person (s. 4A(6) and (7)).

## 3.8.5 Possession with Intent to Supply

This is an offence that brings the concepts of 'possession' and 'supply' together.

OFFENCE: **Possession with Intent to Supply—*Misuse of Drugs Act 1971, s. 5(3)***
• Triable either way • Class A (life imprisonment and/or a fine on indictment; six months' imprisonment and/or a prescribed sum summarily) • Class B (14 years' imprisonment and/or a fine on indictment; six months' imprisonment and/or prescribed sum summarily) • Class C (14 years' imprisonment and/or a fine on indictment; three months' imprisonment and/or a fine summarily)

The Misuse of Drugs Act 1971, s. 5 states:

(3) Subject to section 28 of this Act, it is an offence for a person to have a controlled drug in his possession, whether lawfully or not, with intent to supply it to another in contravention of section 4(1) of this Act.

---

**KEYNOTE**

It is important to note that the lawfulness or otherwise of the *possession* is irrelevant; what matters here is the lawfulness of the intended supply. If a vet or a police officer or some other person is in lawful possession of a controlled drug but he/she intends to supply it unlawfully to another, this offence will be made out.

You must show that the intention was that *the person in possession of the controlled drug* (rather than some third party) would supply it at some point in the future (*R v Greenfield* [1983] 78 Cr App R 179).

If more than one person has possession of the relevant controlled drug, you must show an individual intention to supply it by each person charged; it is not enough to show a joint venture whereby one or more parties simply knew of another's intent (*R v Downes* [1984] Crim LR 552). Given the decision of the Court of Appeal in *Kray* (see para. 3.8.4), possession with intent to supply a controlled drug to a person who is in fact an undercover police officer would appear to amount to an offence under this section.

All that is necessary in proving the offence under s. 5(3) is to show that the defendant had a controlled drug in his possession and intended to supply that substance to another. If the substance in the defendant's possession is a Class A drug and he intended to supply it to another person, the fact that he thought the drug was some other type of drug does not matter (*R* v *Leeson* [2000] 1 Cr App R 233).

While the possession by a defendant of drugs paraphernalia (e.g. clingfilm, paper, scales, contact details, etc.) will be relevant evidence to show that he was an active dealer in drugs generally, it does not prove the intention to supply and the trial judge will give a jury very careful directions as to the probative value of such items found in the defendant's possession (see *R* v *Haye* [2002] EWCA Crim 2476).

Where a Rastafarian was prosecuted for possessing cannabis with intent to supply others as part of their religious worship, he claimed that his rights under Articles 8 and 9 of the European Convention had been unnecessarily and disproportionately interfered with. The Court of Appeal, while reducing the sentence, held that such a prosecution had been properly brought (*R* v *Taylor* [2001] EWCA Crim 2263).

In proving an intention to supply you may be able to adduce evidence of the defendant's unexplained wealth (*R* v *Smith (Ivor)* [1995] Crim LR 940) or the presence of large sums of money with the drugs seized (see *R* v *Wright* [1994] Crim LR 55).

For the purposes of the offence under s. 4 (supplying a controlled drug) and this offence, the 'another' cannot be someone charged in the same count, but can be someone charged in other counts in the same indictment.

## 3.8.6 Supply of Articles

OFFENCE: **Supplying Articles for Administering or Preparing Controlled Drugs—**
*Misuse of Drugs Act 1971, s. 9A*
- Triable summarily • Six months' imprisonment and/or a fine

The Misuse of Drugs Act 1971, s. 9A states:

(1) A person who supplies or offers to supply any article which may be used or adapted to be used (whether by itself or in combination with another article or other articles) in the administration by any person of a controlled drug to himself or another, believing that the article (or the article as adapted) is to be so used in circumstances where the administration is unlawful, is guilty of an offence.

(2) …

(3) A person who supplies or offers to supply any article which may be used to prepare a controlled drug for administration by any person to himself or another believing that the article is to be so used in circumstances where the administration is unlawful is guilty of an offence.

---

**KEYNOTE**

This offence is designed to address the provision of drug 'kits'.

Hypodermic syringes, or parts of them, are not covered by this offence (s. 9A(2)).

The administration for which the articles are intended must be 'unlawful'. Section 9A states:

(4) For the purposes of this section, any administration of a controlled drug is unlawful except—
  (a) the administration by any person of a controlled drug to another in circumstances where the administration of the drug is not unlawful under section 4(1) of this Act, or
  (b) the administration by any person of a controlled drug, other than a temporary class drug, to himself in circumstances where having the controlled drug in his possession is not unlawful under section 5(1) of this Act, or.
  (c) the administration by any person of a temporary class drug to himself in circumstances where having the drug in his possession is to be treated as excepted possession for the purposes of this Act (see s. 7A(2)(c)).

(5) In this section, references to administration by any person of a controlled drug to himself include a reference to his administering it to himself with the assistance of another.

For the law relating to temporary class drugs, see para. 3.8.18.

### 3.8.7 Production of a Controlled Drug

OFFENCE: **Producing Controlled Drug—*Misuse of Drugs Act 1971, s. 4(2)***
- Triable either way • Class A (life imprisonment and/or a fine on indictment; six months' imprisonment and/or prescribed sum summarily) • Class B (14 years' imprisonment and/or a fine on indictment; six months' imprisonment and/or prescribed sum summarily) • Class C (five years' imprisonment and/or a fine on indictment; three months' imprisonment and/or a fine summarily)

The Misuse of Drugs Act 1971, s. 4 states:

(2) Subject to section 28 of this Act, it is an offence for a person—
   (a) to produce a controlled drug in contravention of subsection (1)…; or
   (b) to be concerned in the production of such a drug in contravention of that subsection by another.

---

**KEYNOTE**

'Produce' means producing by manufacture, cultivation or any other method and 'production' has a corresponding meaning (Misuse of Drugs Act 1971, s. 37).

Converting one form of a Class A drug into another has been held to be 'producing' (*R v Russell* (1991) 94 Cr App R 351), as has harvesting, cutting and stripping a cannabis plant (*R v Harris* [1996] 1 Cr App R 369).

Being 'concerned in the production' requires evidence that the accused played an identifiable role in the production of the drug in question. This was not satisfied where the accused simply permitted two others who were producing drugs to use his kitchen (*R v Farr* [1982] Crim LR 745).

---

### 3.8.8 Cultivation of Cannabis

OFFENCE: **Cultivation of Cannabis—*Misuse of Drugs Act 1971, s. 6***
- Triable either way • 14 years' imprisonment and/or a fine on indictment
- Six months' imprisonment and/or prescribed sum summarily

The Misuse of Drugs Act 1971, s. 6 states:

(1) Subject to any regulations under section 7 of this Act for the time being in force, it shall not be lawful for a person to cultivate any plant of the genus *Cannabis*.
(2) Subject to section 28 of this Act, it is an offence to cultivate any such plant in contravention of subsection (1) above.

---

**KEYNOTE**

The definition of 'cannabis' provided by s. 37(1) of the Misuse of Drugs Act 1971 (**see para. 3.8.2.1**) does not apply to the use of the word 'cannabis' in s. 6 of the Act, since the context of the instant offence clearly requires that the plant itself be cultivated.

'Cultivate' is not defined but it appears that you would have to show some element of attention (such as watering or feeding) to the plant by the defendant in order to prove this offence. This offence does not permit police officers to tend plants which have been seized as evidence in order to preserve them as exhibits for court.

In proving the offence, you need only show that the plant is of the genus *Cannabis* and that the defendant cultivated it; you need not show that the defendant knew it to be a cannabis plant (*R v Champ* [1981] 73 Cr App R 367).

A person may be licensed to cultivate cannabis plants by the Secretary of State (under reg. 12 of the Misuse of Drugs Regulations 2001 (SI 2001/3998)).

---

### 3.8.9 General Defence under Section 28

In addition to the generic defences available in criminal law, there is a general defence (available under s. 28 of the Misuse of Drugs Act 1971), to a defendant charged with certain drugs offences. Section 28 applies to offences of:

- unlawful production (s. 4(2))
- unlawful supply (s. 4(3))
- unlawful possession (s. 5(2))
- possession with intent to supply (s. 5(3))
- unlawful cultivation of cannabis (s. 6(2))
- offences connected with opium (s. 9) (not covered in the police promotion examination syllabus).

The defences under s. 28 are *not* available in cases of conspiracy as conspiracy is not an offence under the 1971 Act (*R v McGowan* [1990] Crim LR 399). The defence under s. 28 is compatible with the European Convention on Human Rights and the Human Rights Act 1998 (*R v Lambert* [2001] UKHL 37).

The Misuse of Drugs Act 1971, s. 28 states:

(2) Subject to subsection (3) below, in any proceedings for an offence to which this section applies it shall be a defence for the accused to prove that he neither knew of nor suspected nor had reason to suspect the existence of some fact alleged by the prosecution which it is necessary for the prosecution to prove if he is to be convicted of the offence charged.

(3) Where in any proceedings for an offence to which this section applies it is necessary, if the accused is to be convicted of the offence charged, for the prosecution to prove that some substance or product involved in the alleged offence was the controlled drug which the prosecution alleges it to have been, and it is proved that the substance or product in question was that controlled drug, the accused—

   (a) shall not be acquitted of the offence charged by reason only of proving that he neither knew nor suspected nor had reason to suspect that the substance or product in question was the particular controlled drug alleged; but

   (b) shall be acquitted thereof—

     (i) if he proves that he neither believed nor suspected nor had reason to suspect that the substance or product in question was a controlled drug; or

     (ii) if he proves that he believed the substance or product in question to be a controlled drug, or a controlled drug of a description, such that, if it had in fact been that controlled drug, or a controlled drug of that description, he would not at the material time have been committing any offence to which this section applies.

---

**KEYNOTE**

This defence envisages three distinct situations:

- a lack of knowledge by the defendant of some fact which is alleged by the prosecution;
- a general lack of knowledge by the defendant about the drug in question;
- a conditional belief held by the defendant about the drug in question.

These situations are discussed below.

---

### 3.8.9.1 Lack of Knowledge of Some Alleged Fact

Section 28(2) allows a defence where the defendant did not *know, suspect* or *have reason to suspect* the existence of some fact which is essential to proving the case.

### 3.8.9.2 General Lack of Knowledge about Drug in Question

The wording of s. 28(3)(a) prevents defendants from claiming a 'defence' when what they thought was one type of controlled drug was in fact another, different controlled drug.

Section 28(3)(b) however, has two strands, one concerned with the defendant's general lack of knowledge about the drug in question and the other (see **para 1.6.9.3**) concerning the defendant's conditional belief.

Section 28(3)(b)(i) will allow defendants to prove that they did not believe or suspect the substance in question to be a controlled drug and that they had no reason so to suspect.

This clearly overlaps with s. 28(2) and X in the above example would also be able to claim this lack of knowledge. If he believed the envelope to contain amphetamine when it turned out to contain heroin, however, this lack of knowledge would not be permitted as a defence under s. 28(3).

### 3.8.9.3 Conditional Belief about Drug in Question

In contrast to s. 28(3)(a), the second strand of s. 28(3)(b)(ii) allows defendants to discharge the evidential burden by showing that they *did* believe the drug in question to be a particular controlled drug. It is then open to defendants to claim that, had the drug in question actually been the drug which they believed it to be, then they would not have committed any offences in relation to that drug.

### 3.8.10 Regulated Possession and Supply of Controlled Drugs

The statutory framework governing controlled drugs does not simply ban substances and their possession outright. People working at various levels within the system need to be able to access, analyse and prescribe substances that are controlled by the 1971 Act. To that end, the framework takes account of the differing legitimate activities that may be relevant to individual people or particular circumstances. The majority of the exceptions and conditions imposed on this lawful possession and use can be found in the Misuse of Drugs Regulations 2001 and also in the Misuse of Drugs and Misuse of Drugs (Safe Custody) (Amendment) Regulations (SI 2007/2154).

The importance of the 2001 Regulations lies in the fact that they exempt certain drugs and certain people (pharmacists, medical staff, laboratory workers and police officers etc.) from the main offences of possession, supply and importation *as long as they are reacting lawfully within the parameters set out by those regulations.* So a person in such an occupation who possesses, supplies or imports a controlled drug outside the terms of the exemptions in the regulations will commit an offence.

Among the key regulations (SI 2001/3998) are:

- Regulation 4—which sets out those controlled drugs which will be exempted from the main offences of importation/exportation when they are contained in medicinal products.
- Regulation 5—allowing people holding a licence issued by the Secretary of State to produce, supply, offer to supply or have in their possession a controlled drug.
- Regulation 6—this allows anyone who is *lawfully* in possession of a controlled drug to give the drug back to the person from whom he/she obtained it and would cover registered heroin addicts properly returning methadone to a chemist. Regulation 6 also allows others to possess and supply certain controlled drugs under strict conditions. Regulation 6 allows police constables to have any controlled drug in their possession, or to supply such a drug to anyone who is lawfully allowed to have it (reg. 6(5)–(7)). These exemptions only apply where constables are *acting in the course of their duty as such.*

Other people who are given the same protection are customs and excise officers, postal workers and people engaged in conveying the drug to someone who may lawfully possess it. This last category would include civilian support staff, exhibits officers and others who, although not police constables, are nevertheless properly engaged in conveying controlled drugs to others.

The remainder of the regulations are generally concerned with exemptions for doctors, dentists, vets and others who may need to store or supply controlled drugs; the 2001 Regulations also impose requirements on some such people in relation to record keeping and the provision of information when requested.

### 3.8.11 Occupiers, etc.

OFFENCE: **Occupier or Manager of Premises Permitting Drug Misuse—*Misuse of Drugs Act 1971, s. 8***
 • Triable either way • Class A or B (14 years' imprisonment and/or a fine on indictment; six months' imprisonment and/or prescribed sum summarily) • Class C (14 years' imprisonment and/or a fine on indictment; three months' imprisonment and/or a fine summarily)

The Misuse of Drugs Act 1971, s. 8 states:

A person commits an offence if, being the occupier or concerned in the management of any premises, he knowingly permits or suffers any of the following activities to take place on those premises, that is to say—
 (a) producing or attempting to produce a controlled drug in contravention of section 4(1) of this Act;
 (b) supplying or attempting to supply a controlled drug to another in contravention of section 4(1) of this Act, or offering to supply a controlled drug to another in contravention of section 4(1);

(c) preparing opium for smoking;

(d) smoking cannabis, cannabis resin or prepared opium.

---

**KEYNOTE**

**Occupier**

A person does not have to be a tenant, or to have estate in land, in order to be an 'occupier'. The term 'occupier' should be given a 'common sense' interpretation (see *R* v *Tao* [1977] QB 141). For the purposes of s. 8, a person is in occupation of premises, whatever his/her legal status, if the prosecution can show that the accused exercised control, or had the authority of another, to exclude persons from the premises or to prohibit any of the activities referred to in s. 8 (see *R* v *Coid* [1998] Crim LR 199).

**Concerned in the Management**

To be a manager, the accused must run, organise and plan the use of the premises (see *R* v *Josephs* (1977) 65 Cr App R 253) and so must be involved in more than menial or routine duties.

'Premises' is not defined and has not been clarified at common law but the meaning has been given a wide definition in other legislation.

The permitting or suffering of these activities requires a degree of *mens rea*—*Sweet* v *Parsley* [1970] AC 132—even if that degree is little more than wilful blindness (see *R* v *Thomas* (1976) 63 Cr App R 65). For the purposes of s. 8(b)—and therefore presumably s. 8(a)—it is not necessary to show that the defendant knew exactly which drugs were being produced, supplied etc.; only that they were 'controlled drugs' (*R* v *Bett* [1999] WLR 2109).

However, the precise activities that are described under s. 8 will need to be proved. So, for instance, if the offence charged is one of knowingly permitting the smoking of cannabis (under subs. (d)), it must be shown that this actually took place; it is not enough that the owner/occupier had given permission for this to happen (see *R* v *Auguste* [2003] EWCA Crim 3929). This is also the case when the offence charged is one of supplying or attempting to supply a controlled drug to another (under s. 8(b)), i.e. it must be shown that the supply or attempted supply actually took place (see *R* v *McGee* [2012] EWCA Crim 613).

An occupier who permits the growing of cannabis plants also commits this offence (*Taylor* v *Chief Constable of Kent* [1981] 1 WLR 606).

An occupier will not commit the above offence *in relation to the smoking of cannabis or cannabis resin* if the premises are covered by a research licence from the Secretary of State (see reg. 13 of the Misuse of Drugs Regulations 2001).

---

## 3.8.12 Closure Notices

The Anti-social Behaviour Act 2003 provides a power which allows the police to close premises where drugs offences take place and this unlawful drug activity is accompanied by disorder or nuisance. It might be that such premises are where offences under s. 8 are taking place but that is not necessarily the case as any premises could be subject to a closure order.

The Anti-social Behaviour Act 2003, s. 1 states:

(1) This section applies to premises if a police officer not below the rank of superintendent (the authorising officer) has reasonable grounds for believing—

   (a) that at any time during the relevant period the premises have been used in connection with the unlawful use, production or supply of a Class A controlled drug, and

   (b) that the use of the premises is associated with the occurrence of disorder or serious nuisance to members of the public.

### 3.8.12.1   The Notice

The notice, which must be served by a police officer, must also:

- give notice that an application will be made under s. 2 for the closure of the premises
- state that access to the premises by any person (other than a person who habitually resides in the premises or the owner of the premises) is prohibited
- specify the date and time when and the place at which the application will be heard
- explain the effects of a closure order
- state that failure to comply with the notice amounts to an offence
- give information about the names of and means of contacting people and organisations in the area that provide advice about housing and legal matters.

Service of the notice will be effected by fixing a copy of the notice to:

- at least one prominent place on the premises
- each normal means of access to the premises
- any outbuildings which appear to the constable to be used with or as part of the premises; and

by giving a copy of the notice to at least one person who appears to the constable to have control of or responsibility for the premises and also to any person who lives on the premises or who has control of or responsibility for or an interest in the premises (see s. 1(6)).

For the purpose of effecting service of the notice a constable may enter any premises to which the section applies, using reasonable force if necessary (s. 1(7A)).

### 3.8.12.2   The Closure Order

If a closure notice has been issued under s. 1 a police officer must apply to a magistrates' court for the making of a closure order and that application must be heard by the court not later than 48 hours after the notice has been served (s. 2).

However, the court may adjourn the hearing of the application for a period of not more than 14 days to enable the occupier or another person with control of, responsibility for or an interest in the premises to show why an order should not be made (s. 2(6)).

The magistrates' court cannot use a power under other enactments relating to adjournments to adjourn any hearing of that application for more than 14 days (see *Commissioner of Police for the Metropolis* v *Hooper* [2005] EWHC 340 (Admin)).

The magistrates' court may make a closure order only if it is satisfied that:

- the premises in respect of which the closure notice was issued have been used in connection with the unlawful use, production or supply of a Class A controlled drug
- the use of the premises is associated with the occurrence of disorder or serious nuisance to members of the public, and
- the making of the order is necessary to prevent the occurrence of such disorder or serious nuisance for the period specified in the order.

(s. 2(3))

A closure order is an order that all or any part of the premises are closed to all people for such period (not exceeding three months) as the court decides (s. 2(4)). The police can apply for an order to be extended at any time before it expires but that application must be authorised by an officer not below the rank of superintendent after consultation with the local authority (see s. 5). An order cannot be extended beyond a total of six months (s. 5(5)). Further specific provisions are made by the Act in relation to the discharge of closure notices and the bringing of appeals.

### 3.8.12.3 Enforcement

A police officer or an authorised person may enter the premises in respect of which the order is made and/or do anything reasonably necessary to secure the premises against entry by any person and may use reasonable force to do so (see s. 3).

A police officer or authorised person may also enter the premises at any time while the order is in force for the purpose of carrying out essential maintenance of or repairs to the premises (s. 3(5)).

A police officer or authorised person seeking to enter the premises for these purposes must, if required to do so by or on behalf of the owner, occupier or other person in charge of the premises, produce evidence of his/her identity and authority before entering the premises (s. 3(4)).

### 3.8.12.4 Obstructing or Breaching Closure Order

OFFENCE: **Obstruction and Breaching Closure Order—*Anti-social Behaviour Act 2003, s. 4***
- Triable summarily • Six months' imprisonment and/or a fine

The Anti-social Behaviour Act 2003, s. 4 states:

(1) A person commits an offence if he remains on or enters premises in contravention of a closure notice.
(2) A person commits an offence if—
    (a) he obstructs a constable or an authorised person acting under section 1(6) or 3(2),
    (b) he remains on premises in respect of which a closure order has been made, or
    (c) he enters the premises.

---

**KEYNOTE**

A person does not commit an offence under subs. (1) or subs. (2)(b) or (c) if he/she has a reasonable excuse for entering or being on the premises (as the case may be) (s. 4(4)).

Any person who occupies or owns any part of a building or structure in which closed premises are situated and in respect of which the closure order does not have effect may apply to the court for an order allowing access to any part of the premises.

---

### 3.8.13 Assisting or Inducing Offence Outside United Kingdom

OFFENCE: **Assisting or Inducing Misuse of Drugs Offence Outside UK—*Misuse of Drugs Act 1971, s. 20***

- Triable either way • 14 years' imprisonment and/or a fine on indictment
- Six months' imprisonment and/or a fine summarily

The Misuse of Drugs Act 1971, s. 20 states:

A person commits an offence if in the United Kingdom he assists in or induces the commission in any place outside the United Kingdom of an offence punishable under the provisions of a corresponding law in force in that place.

**KEYNOTE**

In order to prove this offence, you must show that the offence outside the United Kingdom actually took place. The circumstances where this offence is likely to be committed will clearly overlap with the offences of importation/exportation.

'Assisting' has been held to include taking containers to another country in the knowledge that they would later be filled with a controlled drug and sent on to a third country (*R* v *Evans* (1977) 64 Cr App R 237). For an offence to amount to one under 'corresponding law' for these purposes, a certificate relating to the domestic law concerned with the misuse of drugs must be obtained from the government of the relevant country (s. 36).

### 3.8.14 Incitement

OFFENCE: **Incitement—*Misuse of Drugs Act 1971, s. 19***

- Triable and punishable as for substantive offence incited

The Misuse of Drugs Act 1971, s. 19 states:

It is an offence for a person to incite another to commit an offence under any other provision of this Act.

**KEYNOTE**

The Act makes a specific offence of inciting another to commit an offence under its provisions. On the arguments in *DPP* v *Armstrong* [2000] Crim LR 379, it would seem that a person inciting an undercover police officer may commit an offence under s. 19 even though there was no possibility of the officer actually being induced to commit the offence.

### 3.8.15 Importation of Controlled Drugs

Section 3 of the Misuse of Drugs Act 1971 does not create an offence but a prohibition on the import or export of a controlled drug unless authorised by the regulations made under the Act. The relevant offences and their respective penalties are contained in the Customs and Excise Management Act 1979. Schedule 1 to the 1979 Act provides for the following penalties for the improper importation or exportation of controlled drugs:

- Class A—life imprisonment
- Class B—14 years' imprisonment
- Class C—14 years' imprisonment.

## 3.8.16 Travel Restriction Orders

The Criminal Justice and Police Act 2001 makes provision for courts to impose travel restrictions on offenders convicted of drug trafficking offences. Travel restriction orders prohibit offenders from leaving the United Kingdom at any time during the period beginning from their release from custody (other than on bail or temporary release for a fixed period) and up to the end of the order. The minimum period for such an order is two years (s. 33(3)).

Where a court

- has convicted a person of a drug trafficking offence
- and it has determined that a sentence of four years or more is appropriate

it is under a *duty* to consider whether or not a travel restriction order would be appropriate (s. 33). If the court decides not to impose an order, it must give its reasons for not doing so.

Offenders may also be required to surrender their UK passport as part of the order.

The offences which are covered by travel restriction orders include the production and supply of controlled drugs, the importation/exportation offences under s. 3 (**see para. 3.8.15**) along with inciting under the Misuse of Drugs Act 1971, s. 19.

The Secretary of State may add to this list (see s. 34(2)).

An offender may apply to the court that made a restriction order to have it revoked or suspended (s. 35) and the court must consider the strict criteria set out in s. 35 when considering any such suspension or revocation. If an order is suspended, the offender has a legal obligation to be back in the United Kingdom when the period of suspension ends (s. 35(5)(a)).

OFFENCE: **Contravening a Travel Restriction Order—*Criminal Justice and Police Act 2001, s. 36***
- Triable either way
- Five years' imprisonment and/or a fine on indictment
- Six months' imprisonment and/or a fine summarily

The Criminal Justice and Police Act 2001, s. 36 states:

(1) A person who leaves the United Kingdom at a time when he is prohibited from leaving it by a travel restriction order is guilty of an offence...
(2) A person who is not in the United Kingdom at the end of a period during which a prohibition imposed on him by a travel restriction order has been suspended shall be guilty of an offence...

---

**KEYNOTE**

These offences make no specific requirement for a particular state of mind. The first offence simply requires proof of two things—that there was an order in existence in respect of the offender and that he/she left the United Kingdom during the time it was in force. There is no requirement that the person leave the United Kingdom *voluntarily* in order to be guilty (although he/she would have a pretty good argument if he/she were taken out of the jurisdiction against his/her will or without his/her knowledge).

However, travel restriction orders do not prevent the proper exercise of any prescribed power to remove a person from the United Kingdom (see s. 37—the relevant powers are set out in the Travel Restriction Order (Prescribed Removal Powers) Order 2002 (SI 2002/313)). For instance, if the Secretary of State deports someone who is under a travel restriction order, that person would not commit the above offence.

The second offence requires proof that there was a suspended order in existence in respect of the offender and that, at the end of the suspension period, the offender was not in the United Kingdom.

Failing to deliver up a passport when required by an order will be a summary offence carrying six months' imprisonment and/or a fine (s. 36(3)).

### 3.8.17 Police Powers

In addition to the general policing powers available for offences, the 1971 Act provides a number of specific enforcement powers.

#### 3.8.17.1 Powers of Entry, Search and Seizure

The Misuse of Drugs Act 1971, s. 23 states:

(1) A constable or other person authorised in that behalf by a general or special order of the Secretary of State (or in Northern Ireland either of the Secretary of State or the Ministry of Home Affairs for Northern Ireland) shall, for the purposes of the execution of this Act, have power to enter the premises of a person carrying on business as a producer or supplier of any controlled drugs and to demand the production of, and to inspect, any books or documents relating to dealings in any such drugs and to inspect any stocks of any such drugs.

(2) If a constable has reasonable grounds to suspect that any person is in possession of a controlled drug in contravention of this Act or of any regulations or orders made thereunder, the constable may—
   (a) search that person, and detain him for the purpose of searching him;
   (b) search any vehicle or vessel in which the constable suspects that the drug may be found, and for that purpose require the person in control of the vehicle or vessel to stop it;
   (c) seize and detain, for the purposes of proceedings under this Act, anything found in the course of the search which appears to the constable to be evidence of an offence under this Act.

In this subsection 'vessel' includes a hovercraft within the meaning of the Hovercraft Act 1968; and nothing in this subsection shall prejudice any power of search or any power to seize or detain property which is exercisable by a constable apart from this subsection.

(3) If a justice of the peace (or in Scotland a justice of the peace, a magistrate or a sheriff) is satisfied by information on oath that there is reasonable ground for suspecting—
   (a) that any controlled drugs are, in contravention of this Act or of any regulations or orders made thereunder, in the possession of a person on any premises; or
   (b) that a document directly or indirectly relating to, or connected with, a transaction or dealing which was, or an intended transaction or dealing which would if carried out be, an offence under this Act, or in the case of a transaction or dealing carried out or intended to be carried out in a place outside the United Kingdom, an offence against the provisions of a corresponding law in force in that place, is in the possession of a person on any premises,

he may grant a warrant authorising any constable at any time or times within one month from the date of the warrant, to enter, if need be by force, the premises named in the warrant, and to search the premises and any persons found therein and, if there is reasonable ground for suspecting that an offence under this Act has been committed in relation to any controlled drugs found on the premises or in the possession of any such persons, or that a document so found is such a document as is mentioned in paragraph (b) above, to seize and detain those drugs or that document, as the case may be.

> **KEYNOTE**
>
> This is a very wide statutory provision granting authority for a broad range of enforcement measures in connection with controlled drugs.
>
> Particular care will need to be taken when drafting the application for a warrant under s. 23. Where police officers are on premises under the authority of such a warrant it will be important to have established the precise *extent* of the warrant. If such a warrant authorises the search of *premises only*, that in itself will not give the officers authority to search *people* found on those premises unless the officer can point to some other power authorising the search (see e.g. *Hepburn* v *Chief Constable of Thames Valley* [2002] EWCA Civ 1841).
>
> However, where the warrant authorises the search of premises *and* people, the Divisional Court has held that it is reasonable to restrict the movement of people within the premises to allow the search to be conducted properly (see *DPP* v *Meaden* [2003] EWHC 3005 (Admin)).
>
> For the procedure involved in applying for, and executing warrants, **see chapter 1.5** .

PACE Code A applies to the exercise of any power to search people for controlled drugs specifically included in a warrant issued under s. 23.

The Serious Organised Crime and Police Act 2005 has not changed the duration of a warrant issued under s. 23 of the Misuse of Drugs Act 1971. A warrant issued under s. 23 of the Act lasts for a period of *one month* from the date of issue.

### 3.8.17.2 Obstruction

OFFENCE:  **Obstruction—*Misuse of Drugs Act 1971, s. 23(4)***
- Triable either way  • Two years' imprisonment and/or a fine on indictment
- Six months' imprisonment and/or a fine summarily

The Misuse of Drugs Act 1971, s. 23 states:

(4)  A person commits an offence if he—
  (a)  intentionally obstructs a person in the exercise of his powers under this section; or
  (b)  conceals from a person acting in the exercise of his powers under subsection (1) above any such books, documents, stocks or drugs as are mentioned in that subsection; or
  (c)  without reasonable excuse (proof of which shall lie on him) fails to produce any such books or documents as are so mentioned where their production is demanded by a person in the exercise of his powers under that subsection.

### KEYNOTE

The offence of obstructing a person in the exercise of his/her powers is only committed if the obstruction was intentional (*R* v *Forde* (1985) 81 Cr App R 19).

## 3.8.18 Temporary Class Drug Orders

The Home Secretary has the power, under the Misuse of Drugs Act 1971, to make any drug subject to temporary control.

Temporary class drug orders can be made if the following two conditions are met:

(1)  the drug is not already controlled under the Act as a Class A, B or C drug;
(2)  the ACMD [Advisory Council on the Misuse of Drugs] has been consulted and determined that the order should be made, or the Home Secretary has received a recommendation from the Advisory Council that the order should be made, on the basis that it appears to the Home Secretary that:
  (a)  the drug is being, or is likely to be, misused; and
  (b)  the misuse is having, or is capable of having, harmful effects.

A temporary class drug order will come into immediate effect and will last for up to 12 months, subject to Parliament agreeing to it within 40 sitting days of the Order being made. They will enable the government to act faster to protect the public against emerging harmful new psychoactive substances, while full expert advice is being prepared.

A drug placed under a temporary class drug order will be referred to as a 'temporary class drug' and will be a 'controlled drug' for the purposes of the Misuse of Drugs Act 1971, and other legislation such as the Proceeds of Crime Act 2002, unless otherwise stated. With the *exception of the possession* offence, all the offences under the Misuse of Drugs Act will apply. This includes possession in connection with an offence or prohibition, under ss. 3, 4 and 5(3) of the Act, i.e. possession with intent to supply. Offences committed under the Act in relation to a temporary class drug are subject to the following maximum penalties:

- 14 years' imprisonment and an unlimited fine on indictment, and
- six months' imprisonment and a £5,000 fine on summary conviction.

Simple possession of a temporary class drug is not an offence under the 1971 Act; however, law enforcement officers have been given the following powers to enable them to take appropriate action to prevent possible harm to the individual:

- Search and detain a person (or vehicle etc.) where there are reasonable grounds to suspect that the person is in possession of a temporary class drug.
- Seize, detain and dispose of a suspected temporary class drug.
- Arrest or charge a person who commits the offence of intentionally obstructing an enforcement officer in the exercise of their powers.

# 3.9 | Firearms and Gun Crime

## 3.9.1 Introduction

The key piece of legislation governing the possession and use of firearms is the Firearms Act 1968. The Act covers numerous activities involving firearms (such as possession) and also deals with serious offences involving the criminal use of firearms. These activities and other supplementary firearms legislation will be examined in this chapter.

## 3.9.2 Definitions—Firearm, Ammunition and Imitation Firearm

Before examining any offences relating to firearms, it is useful to begin with some basic definitions—particularly those of firearm, ammunition and imitation firearm.

### 3.9.2.1 Firearms

The Firearms Act 1968, s. 57 states:

(1) In this Act, the expression 'firearm' means a lethal barrelled weapon of any description from which any shot, bullet or other missile can be discharged, and includes—
  (a) any prohibited weapon, whether it is such a lethal weapon as aforesaid or not; and
  (b) any component part of such a lethal or prohibited weapon; and
  (c) any accessory to any such weapon designed or adapted to diminish the noise or flash caused by firing the weapon.

---

**KEYNOTE**

'Lethal barrelled weapon' is not defined under the 1968 Act.

The way in which the courts have determined whether or not something amounts to such a weapon is by asking:

- Can any shot, bullet or other missile be discharged from the weapon, or
- Could the weapon be adapted so that any shot, bullet or other missile can be discharged?
- If so, is the weapon a 'lethal barrelled' weapon?

(See *Grace* v *DPP* [1989] Crim LR 365.)

A weapon is a lethal barrelled weapon if it is capable of causing injury, irrespective of the intentions of its maker (*Read* v *Donovan* [1947] KB 326). In determining whether a firearm is in fact a lethal barrelled weapon from which missiles can be discharged a court need not consider any specific evidence of someone who has seen the effects of it being fired. Therefore, where magistrates had heard evidence from a gun shop assistant that an air rifle was in working order, they were entitled to conclude that it fell within the definition even though no evidence was given as to the actual effects of the gun being fired (*Castle* v *DPP* (1998) *The Times*, 3 April).

Air pistols (*R* v *Thorpe* [1987] 1 WLR 383) and imitation revolvers (*Cafferata* v *Wilson* [1936] 3 All ER 149) have all been held to be lethal barrelled weapons. A signalling pistol which fired explosive magnesium and phosphorous flares which was capable of killing at short range has been held to be lethal (*Read* v *Donovan*, above). That is not to say, however, that they will always be so and each case must be determined in the light of the evidence available.

Component parts are not defined in the Act but in *R* v *Rogers* [2011] EWCA Crim 1549, the Court of Appeal ruled that in the absence of a cylinder appropriate for a firearm, an unblocked barrel, frame and trigger could not be regarded as components of a firearm.

---

While silencers and flash eliminators are clearly accessories, a silencer or a flash eliminator *on its own* is not a firearm. However, if a defendant is found in possession of a silencer which has been manufactured for a weapon *that is also in the defendant's possession*, that will be enough to bring the silencer or flash eliminator under s. 57(1). If the silencer is made for a different weapon, it may still come under the s. 57 definition but the prosecution will have to show that it could be used with the defendant's weapon and that he/she had it for that purpose (*R* v *Buckfield* [1998] Crim LR 673). Section 57(1) does not include telescopic sights.

### 3.9.2.2 Deactivation of Firearms

A weapon ceases to be a firearm if it is deactivated in line with the provisions of the Firearms (Amendment) Act 1988, s. 8 which states:

For the purposes of the principal Act and this Act it shall be presumed, unless the contrary is shown, that a firearm has been rendered incapable of discharging any shot, bullet or other missile, and has consequently ceased to be a firearm within the meaning of those Acts, if—

(a) it bears a mark which has been approved by the Secretary of State for denoting that fact and which has been made either by one of the two companies mentioned in section 58(1) of the principal Act or by such other person as may be approved by the Secretary of State for the purposes of this section; and

(b) that company or person has certified in writing that work has been carried out on the firearm in a manner approved by the Secretary of State for rendering it incapable of discharging any shot, bullet or other missile.

#### KEYNOTE

A deactivated weapon must remain in its complete state. Where it is disassembled the parts that are then made available are capable of being reassembled into a working weapon and are therefore component parts of a firearm (*R* v *Ashton* [2007] EWCA Crim 234).

The 'two companies' referred to in s. 8(a) above are the Society of the Mystery of Gunmakers of the City of London and the Birmingham Proof House.

### 3.9.2.3 Ammunition

Ammunition is defined by s. 57 of the Firearms Act 1968 which states:

(2) In this Act, the expression 'ammunition' means any ammunition for any firearm and includes grenades, bombs and other like missiles, whether capable of use with a firearm or not, and also includes prohibited ammunition.

#### KEYNOTE

The definition of ammunition does not include ingredients and components of ammunition; it is only assembled ammunition that is controlled under the Act and not component parts. Empty cartridge cases, for example, are not 'ammunition'. The only exception to this is missiles for ammunition prohibited under s. 5 of the Act, for example expanding or armour-piercing bullets. Such missiles are themselves regarded as 'ammunition' and are subject to control accordingly (s. 5(1A)(g)).

### 3.9.2.4 Imitation Firearm

Some, though not all, offences which regulate the use of firearms will also apply to *imitation* firearms. Whether they do so can be found either in the specific wording of the offence, or by virtue of the Firearms Act 1982.

There are two types of imitation firearms:

- general imitations—those which have the appearance of firearms (which are covered by s. 57 of the Firearms Act 1968); and
- imitations of section 1 firearms—those which both have the appearance of a section 1 firearm and which can be readily converted into such a firearm (which are covered by ss. 1 and 2 of the Firearms Act 1982).

---

**KEYNOTE**

The 'general imitation' firearm definition is by far and away the most commonly used in firearms legislation. That definition is 'anything which has the appearance of being a firearm...whether or not it is capable of discharging any shot, bullet or other missile'.

For that reason, the definition of an imitation of a section 1 firearm will be considered separately and will be dealt with later in this chapter. Therefore, when imitation firearms are referred to in legislation or future Keynotes, think of it as a 'general imitation' unless otherwise stated.

---

The House of Lords has held that the definition in s. 57 requires the defendant to be carrying a 'thing' which is separate and distinct from the person and therefore capable of being possessed (*R v Bentham* [2005] UKHL 18). Holding your fingers under your coat and pretending that this is a firearm—as happened in *Bentham*—will not therefore amount to an imitation firearm for the relevant offences. Their lordships held that an unsevered hand or finger was part of oneself and therefore could not be 'possessed' in the way envisaged by the Act. The 'imitation' must have the appearance of a firearm and it is not necessary for any object to have been constructed, adapted or altered so as to resemble a firearm (*R v Williams* [2006] EWCA Crim 1650). In *K v DPP* [2006] EWHC 2183 (Admin) it was held that in some circumstances a realistic toy gun, in this case a plastic ball bearing gun, could become an imitation firearm. Note that this category does not include anything which resembles a prohibited weapon that is designed or adapted to discharge noxious liquid etc.

Whether or not something has the appearance of being a firearm will be a question of fact for the jury/magistrate(s) to decide in each case.

### 3.9.3 Categories of Firearms and Related Offences

The law regulating firearms classifies weapons into several categories, each of which is specifically defined. These definitions have closely associated offences dealing with activities such as their possession, acquisition and sale. Alongside these offences are exemptions which allow those activities to be lawful.

### 3.9.4 Prohibited Weapon

A prohibited weapon is defined under the Firearms Act 1968, s. 5. The definition not only covers the more powerful or potentially destructive firearms—and their ammunition—(such as automatic weapons and specialist ammunition) but also, since the Firearms (Amendment) Act 1997, covers small firearms which were formerly covered by other parts of the 1968 Act.

The test as to whether a weapon is a 'prohibited' weapon is a purely objective one and is not affected by the intentions of the defendant. Therefore, where a firearm was capable of successively discharging two or more missiles without repeated pressure on the trigger, that weapon was 'prohibited' irrespective of the intentions of the firearms dealer who was in possession of it (*R v Law* [1999] Crim LR 837).

Whereas a firearms certificate is usually needed in order to possess, buy or acquire firearms and ammunition, the authority of the Secretary of State is needed if the firearm or ammunition is a 'prohibited weapon'.

### 3.9.4.1 List of Prohibited Weapons and Ammunition

The full list of prohibited weapons and ammunition is contained in s. 5(1) and (1A) of the Firearms Act 1968 (see *Blackstone's Criminal Practice 2013*, para. B12.52). This list often (but not always) relates to weapons used in a military context and includes:

* automatic weapons
* most self-loading or pump-action weapons
* any firearm which either has a barrel less than 30 cm in length or is less than 60 cm in length overall, other than an air weapon, a muzzle-loading gun or a firearm designed as signalling apparatus
* most smooth bore revolvers
* any weapon, of whatever description, designed or adapted for the discharge of any noxious liquid, gas or other thing
* any air rifle, air gun or air pistol which uses, or is designed or adapted for use with, a self-contained gas cartridge system
* any cartridge with a bullet designed to explode on or immediately before impact
* if capable of being used with a firearm of any description, any grenade or bomb (or other like missile) or rocket or shell designed to explode on or immediately before impact.

---

**KEYNOTE**

In relation to weapons designed or adapted for the discharge of any noxious liquid, gas or other thing, taking an empty Fairy Liquid washing-up bottle and filling it with hydrochloric acid does not amount to adapting it, neither is such a thing a 'weapon' for the purposes of s. 5 (*R v Formosa*, *R v Upton* [1991] 2 QB 1). This is because to do so does not change the nature of the washing-up bottle itself—the bottle has not been adapted or altered and is therefore not a weapon 'designed or adapted' for the discharge of any noxious liquid etc. The same logic applies to a water pistol filled with ammonia (*R v Titus* [1971] Crim LR 279).

An electric 'stun gun' has been held to be a prohibited weapon as it discharges an electric current (*Flack* v *Baldry* [1988] 1 WLR 393) and it continues to be such even if it is not working (*Brown* v *DPP* (1992) *The Times*, 27 March).

---

### 3.9.4.2 Possessing or Distributing Prohibited Weapons or Ammunition

OFFENCE: **Possessing or Distributing Prohibited Weapons or Ammunition—**
**Firearms Act 1968, s. 5**
* Triable either way • Ten years' imprisonment and/or a fine on indictment
* Six months' imprisonment and/or a fine summarily

The Firearms Act 1968, s. 5 states:

(1) A person commits an offence if, without the authority of the Secretary of State or the Scottish Ministers, he has in his possession, or purchases, or acquires, or manufactures, sells or transfers [a prohibited weapon or ammunition]...

This offence is one of strict liability, a position that was confirmed in *R v Zahid* [2010] EWCA Crim 2158 where the defendant had been found guilty of possessing expanding ammunition and sought to appeal on the grounds that he believed the container in which the ammunition was contained actually contained bolts or screws. In rejecting any defence based on such an assertion, the Court of Appeal placed particular emphasis on the public policy considerations of strict and rigorous control of the possession of firearms.

A person may still be in possession of a prohibited weapon even when it is in parts and the accused is in possession of those parts (*R v Pannell* (1982) 76 Cr App R 53), or where the weapon is missing an essential part such as the trigger (*R v Clarke* [1986] 1 WLR 209).

### 3.9.4.3 Possession

As an offence contrary to s. 5 of the 1968 Act is a strict liability offence, it is irrelevant whether or not a person knew he/she was in possession of a firearm or ammunition (*R v Deyemi* [2007] EWCA Crim 2060). In *Sullivan* v *Earl of Caithness* [1976] QB 966, it was held that a person can remain in possession of a firearm even if someone else has custody of it.

There is no need to prove that the accused knew the nature of the thing he/she possessed in order to prove the offence. If an accused is carrying a rucksack and the rucksack contains ammunition for a section 1 firearm, the accused is in 'possession' of the ammunition irrespective of his/her knowledge or ignorance of its presence in the rucksack (see *R v Waller* [1991] Crim LR 381 and *R v Cremin* [2007] EWCA Crim 666).

### 3.9.4.4 Exemptions

There are two sets of exemptions in respect of s. 5 prohibited weapons. They are:

- European exemptions—exemptions to conform with the European Weapons Directive.
- Special exemptions.

#### European Weapons Directive

The effect of the European Weapons Directive (91/477/EEC) is to create exemptions in relation to the possession of, or some transactions in, specified firearms and ammunition by people who have the relevant certificates or who are recognised as collectors under the law of another country.

To this end, s. 5A of the Firearms Act 1968 provides for a number of occasions where the authority of the Secretary of State will not be required to possess or deal with certain weapons under certain conditions.

The main areas covered by s. 5A are:

- authorised collectors and firearms dealers possessing or being involved in transactions of weapons and ammunition;
- authorised people being involved in transactions of particular ammunition used for lawful shooting and slaughtering of animals, the management of an estate or the protection of other animals and humans.

Section 57(4A) of the Firearms Act 1968 makes other provisions in relation to the European directive as an authority for certain uses of firearms.

#### Special exemptions

The list of special exemptions to the offences involving firearms under s. 5(1)(aba) focuses largely on people in jobs where they will need to come into contact with firearms mainly in connection with animals or leisure activities.

The exemptions include:

- **Slaughterers**—A slaughterer, if entitled under s. 10 of the 1968 Act, may possess a slaughtering instrument. In addition, persons authorised by certificate to possess, buy, acquire, sell or transfer slaughtering instruments are exempt from the provisions of s. 5 (s. 2 of the Firearms (Amendment) Act 1997). This is the most common exemption.
- **Humane killing of animals**—This exemption allows a person authorised by certificate to possess, buy, acquire or transfer a firearm solely for use in connection with the humane killing of animals (s. 3 of the Firearms (Amendment) Act 1997). When determining whether a firearm falls within the meaning of a 'humane killer', the definition of a 'slaughtering instrument' under s. 57(4) may be referred to (*R* v *Paul (Benjamin)* [1999] Crim LR 79).
- **Shot pistols for vermin**—This exemption allows a person authorised by certificate to possess, buy, acquire or transfer a 'shot pistol' solely for the shooting of vermin (s. 4(1) of the Firearms (Amendment) Act 1997). A 'shot pistol' is a smooth-bored gun chambered for .410 cartridges or 9mm rim-fire cartridges (s. 4(2)).
- **Treatment of animals**—This exemption allows a person authorised by certificate to possess, buy, acquire or transfer a firearm for use in connection with the treatment of animals or for the purpose of tranquillising or otherwise treating any animal (s. 8 of the Firearms (Amendment) Act 1997). This exemption also applies to offences involving firearms under s. 5(1)(b) and (c).
- **Races at athletic meetings**—A person may possess a firearm at an athletic meeting for the purpose of starting races at that meeting (s. 5(a) of the Firearms (Amendment) Act 1997). Similarly, a person authorised by certificate to possess, buy or acquire a firearm solely for the purposes of starting such races may possess, buy, acquire, sell or transfer a firearm for such a purpose (s. 5(b)).
- **Trophies of war**—A person authorised by certificate to do so may possess a firearm which was acquired as a trophy before 1 January 1946 (s. 6 of the Firearms (Amendment) Act 1997).
- **Firearms of historic interest**—Some firearms are felt to be of particular historical, aesthetic or technical interest. Section 7(4) of the Firearms (Amendment) Act 1997 makes detailed provision for the exemption of such firearms, exemptions which exist in addition to the general exemptions under s. 58 of the Firearms Act 1968 (**see para. 3.9.8**). These provisions are set out in the Firearms (Amendment) Act 1997 (Firearms of Historic Interest) Order 1997 (SI 1997/1537) and the Firearms (Amendment) Act 1997 (Transitional Provisions and Savings) Regulations 1997 (SI 1997/1538).
- **Air weapons**—In relation to air weapons with self-contained gas cartridges, owned before 20 January 2004, owners, if they applied for a firearms certificate before 1 April 2004, may retain their weapons.

### 3.9.5 Section 1 Firearm

There is a group of firearms which, although not a category defined in the 1968 Act, is subject to a number of offences including s. 1 (see below). Firearms which fall into this group are often referred to as 'section 1 firearms' and include all firearms except shotguns (**see para. 3.9.6**) and conventional air weapons. However, shotguns which have been 'sawn off' (i.e. had their barrels shortened) are section 1 firearms, as are air weapons declared to be 'specially dangerous'.

Section 1 ammunition includes any ammunition for a firearm except:

- cartridges containing five or more shot, none of which is bigger than 0.36 inches in diameter;
- ammunition for an airgun, air rifle or air pistol; and
- blank cartridges not more than one inch in diameter (s. 1(4)).

### 3.9.5.1 Conversion

Some weapons which began their life as section 1 firearms or prohibited weapons will remain so even after their conversion to a shotgun, air weapon or other type of firearm (see s. 7 of the Firearms (Amendment) Act 1988).

### 3.9.5.2 Possessing etc. Firearm or Ammunition without Certificate

OFFENCE: **Possessing etc. Firearm or Ammunition without Certificate—*Firearms Act 1968, s. 1***
- Triable either way • Five years' imprisonment and/or a fine on indictment
- Six months' imprisonment and/or a fine summarily

The Firearms Act 1968, s. 1 states:

(1) Subject to any exemption under this Act, it is an offence for a person—
  (a) to have in his possession, or to purchase or acquire, a firearm to which this section applies without holding a firearm certificate in force at the time, or otherwise than as authorised by such a certificate;
  (b) to have in his possession, or to purchase or acquire, any ammunition to which this section applies without holding a firearm certificate in force at the time, or otherwise than as authorised by such a certificate, or in quantities in excess of those so authorised.

---

**KEYNOTE**

This offence relates to those firearms described above as section 1 firearms.

If the firearm involved is a sawn-off shotgun, the offence becomes 'aggravated' (under s. 4(4)) and attracts a maximum penalty of seven years' imprisonment.

The Firearms Act 1982 applies to this section and so the 'general definition' of an imitation firearm *does not* apply. For this offence the definition of an imitation firearm is one 'that has the appearance of a section 1 firearm and which can be readily converted into such a firearm' (which is covered by ss. 1 and 2 of the Firearms Act 1982).

The certificate referred to is issued by the chief officer of police under s. 26A. Such certificates may carry significant restrictions on the types of firearms which the holder is allowed, together with the circumstances under which he/she may have them (see s. 44(1) of the Firearms (Amendment) Act 1997).

The purpose of the legislation regulating the licensing of firearms is to provide certainty and consistency in the effective control of such weapons. Therefore the issue of whether a certificate covers a particular category of weapon is a matter of law for the judge to decide and cannot be affected by the intentions or misunderstanding of the defendant (*R v Paul (Benjamin)* [1998] Crim LR 79).

A person may hold a European firearms pass or similar document, in which case he/she will be governed by the provision of ss. 32A to 32C of the Firearms Act 1968.

If a person has such a certificate which allows the possession etc. of the firearm in question and under the particular circumstances encountered, no offence is committed.

Acquire will include hiring, accepting as a gift and borrowing, and 'acquisition' is to be construed accordingly (s. 57(4) of the Firearms Act 1968).

The Violent Crime Reduction Act 2006 has created a summary offence that restricts the purchase and sale of cap-type primers (primers are components of ammunition designed for use in metallic ammunition for a firearm which contain a chemical compound that detonates on impact) to persons who hold a relevant firearms certificate or who otherwise have lawful authority for having them (s. 35).

---

### 3.9.5.3 Shortening Section 1 Firearm

OFFENCE: **Shortening Barrel of Smooth-bore Section 1 Firearm to Less than 24 Inches—*Firearms (Amendment) Act 1988, s. 6(1)***

- Triable either way • Five years' imprisonment and/or a fine on indictment
- Six months' imprisonment and/or a fine summarily

The Firearms (Amendment) Act 1988, s. 6 states:

(1) Subject to subsection (2) below, it is an offence to shorten to a length less than 24 inches the barrel of any smooth-bore gun to which section 1 of the principal Act applies other than one which has a barrel with a bore exceeding 2 inches in diameter; . . .

---

**KEYNOTE**

The 'principal Act' is the Firearms Act 1968.

Section 6(2) of the Firearms (Amendment) Act 1988 exempts registered firearms dealers from the offence involving shortening a barrel provided the shortening is done *for the sole purpose* of replacing a defective part of the barrel *so as to produce a new barrel having an overall length of at least 24 inches*.

The length of the barrel of a weapon will be measured from its muzzle to the point at which the charge is exploded (s. 57(6)(a) of the 1968 Act).

Once the shortening has taken place, the nature of the firearm will have changed in which case the person will also commit the relevant possession offence unless he/she has the appropriate authorisation.

---

## 3.9.6 Shotguns

A shotgun is defined under s. 1(3)(a) of the Firearms Act 1968. Section 1 (amended by the Firearms (Amendment) Act 1988, s. 2) states:

(3) . . .
- (a) a shotgun within the meaning of this Act, that is to say a smooth-bore gun (not being an airgun) which—
  - (i) has a barrel not less than 24 inches in length and does not have any barrel with a bore exceeding 2 inches in diameter;
  - (ii) either has no magazine or has a non-detachable magazine incapable of holding more than two cartridges; and
  - (iii) is not a revolver gun . . .
- (3A) A gun which has been adapted to have such a magazine as is mentioned in subsection (3)(a)(ii) above shall not be regarded as falling within that provision unless the magazine bears a mark approved by the Secretary of State for denoting that fact and that mark has been made, and the adaptation has been certified in writing as having been carried out in a manner approved by him, either by one of the two companies mentioned in section 58(1) of this Act or by such other person as may be approved by him for that purpose.

---

**KEYNOTE**

When considering the above definition it helps to remember the 'Rule of 2'—a shotgun barrel must be at least 2 feet long, the bore must not exceed 2 inches in diameter and the non-detachable magazine must hold no more than 2 cartridges. A barrel's length is measured from the muzzle to the point at which the charge is exploded on firing the weapon (s. 57(6)(a) of the 1968 Act).

For the 'two companies' referred to in s. 1(3A) above **see para. 3.9.2.2**.

---

### 3.9.6.1 Shotgun Offences

OFFENCE: **Possessing Shotgun without Certificate**—*Firearms Act 1968, s. 2(1)*
- Triable either way • Five years' imprisonment and/or a fine on indictment
- Six months' imprisonment and/or a fine summarily

The Firearms Act 1968, s. 2 states:

(1) Subject to any exemption under this Act, it is an offence for a person to have in his possession, or to purchase or acquire, a shotgun without holding a certificate under this Act authorising him to possess shot guns.

> **KEYNOTE**
>
> A shotgun certificate is granted by a chief officer of police under s. 26B of the 1968 Act and will have certain conditions attached to it. A person failing to comply with those conditions commits the offence below.

OFFENCE: **Failing to Comply with Conditions of Shot gun Certificate**—*Firearms Act 1968, s. 2(2)*
- Triable summarily • Six months' imprisonment and/or a fine

The Firearms Act 1968, s. 2 states:

(2) It is an offence for a person to fail to comply with a condition subject to which a shot gun certificate is held by him.

The conditions and forms used in relation to the grant of shotgun certificates are contained in the Firearms Rules 1998 (SI 1998/1941) and the Firearms (Amendment) Rules 2005 (SI 2005/3344).

### 3.9.6.2 Shortening a Shotgun Barrel

OFFENCE: **Shortening Barrel Of Shotgun to Less than 24 Inches**—*Firearms Act 1968, s. 4(1)*
- Triable either way • Five years' imprisonment and/or a fine on indictment
- Six months' imprisonment and/or a fine summarily

The Firearms Act 1968, s. 4 states:

(1) Subject to this section, it is an offence to shorten the barrel of a shot gun to a length less than 24 inches.

> **KEYNOTE**
>
> The same exclusions as per the offence of shortening a smooth bore section 1 firearm apply to this offence, i.e. registered firearms dealers are excluded from the wording of the conversion offence (s. 6(2) of the Firearms (Amendment) Act 1988) provided the shortening is done *for the sole purpose* of replacing a defective part of the barrel *so as to produce a new barrel having an overall length of at least 24 inches*.
>
> The length of the barrel of a weapon will be measured from its muzzle to the point at which the charge is exploded (s. 57(6)(a) of the 1968 Act).
>
> Once the shortening or conversion has taken place, the nature of the firearm will have changed (e.g. from a shotgun into a section 1 firearm), in which case the person will also commit the relevant possession offence unless he/she has the appropriate authorisation.

### 3.9.7  Air Weapons

Air weapons are defined under s. 1(3)(b) of the Firearms Act 1968. In summary these are air rifles, air guns or air pistols which do not fall within s. 5(1) and which are not of a type declared to be specially dangerous. Any air rifle, air gun or air pistol that uses or is designed or adapted for use with a self-contained gas cartridge system *does* fall within the definition of a prohibited weapon at s. 5(1).

Some air weapons are deemed to be specially dangerous and therefore subject to stricter control than conventional air weapons. Those which are subject to this stricter control are those declared to be so by the Secretary of State. Listed in r. 2 of the Firearms (Dangerous Air Weapons) Rules 1969, as amended, they include:

(1) [any] air rifle, air gun or air pistol—
  (a) which is capable of discharging a missile so that the missile has, on being discharged from the muzzle of the weapon, kinetic energy in excess, in the case of an air pistol, of 6ft lb or, in the case of an air weapon other than an air pistol, of 12ft lb, or
  (b) which is disguised as another object.

Note that this does not include a weapon falling within para. (1)(a) above and which is designed for use only when submerged in water (r. 2(2)).

### 3.9.7.1  Air Weapon Offences

Section 32 of the Violent Crime Reduction Act 2006 imposed a 'face to face' requirement on trade transactions by persons selling air weapons.

OFFENCE: **Sales of Air Weapons by Way of Trade or Business to be Face to Face—*Violent Crime Reduction Act 2006, s. 32***
  • Triable summarily • 51 weeks' imprisonment and/or a fine

The Violent Crime Reduction Act 2006, s. 32 states:

(1) This section applies where a person sells an air weapon by way of trade or business to an individual in Great Britain who is not registered as a firearms dealer.
(2) A person is guilty of an offence if, for the purposes of the sale, he transfers possession of the air weapon to the buyer otherwise than at a time when both—
  (a) the buyer, and
  (b) either the seller or a representative of his,
  are present in person.

---

**KEYNOTE**

A representative of the seller is a reference to a person who is:

• employed by the seller in his/her business as a registered firearms dealer;
• a registered firearms dealer who has been authorised by the seller to act on his/her behalf in relation to the sale; or
• a person who is employed by a person falling within s. 32(3)(b) in his/her business as a registered firearms dealer.

This allows an air weapon to be sent from one registered firearms dealer to another to make the final transfer in person to the buyer. It also enables someone to buy an air weapon from a dealer in a distant part of the country without one or other party to the transaction having to make a long journey, while still preserving the safeguards of a face-to-face handover.

---

OFFENCE: **Firing an Air Weapon Beyond Premises—*Firearms Act 1968, s. 21A***
  • Triable summarily • Fine

The Firearms Act 1968, s. 21A states:

(1) A person commits an offence if—
   (a) he has with him an air weapon on any premises; and
   (b) he uses it for firing a missile beyond those premises.

(2) In proceedings against a person for an offence under this section it shall be a defence for him to show that the only premises into or across which the missile was fired were premises the occupier of which had consented to the firing of the missile (whether specifically or by way of a general consent).

---

**KEYNOTE**

This offence makes it an offence for a person of *any* age to fire an air weapon beyond the boundary of premises. Note that a defence is provided to cover the situation where the person shooting has the consent of the occupier of the land over or into which he/she shoots.

---

OFFENCE: **Failing to Prevent Minors from Having Air Weapons—*Firearms Act 1968, s. 24ZA***

- Triable summarily • Fine

The Firearms Act 1968, s. 24ZA states:

(1) It is an offence for a person in possession of an air weapon to fail to take reasonable precautions to prevent any person under the age of eighteen from having the weapon with him.

(2) Subsection (1) does not apply where by virtue of section 23 of this Act, the person under the age of eighteen is not prohibited from having the weapon with him.

(3) In proceedings for an offence under subsection (1) it is a defence that the person charged with the offence—
   (a) believed the other person to be aged eighteen or over; and
   (b) had reasonable ground for that belief.

The offence does not apply to an antique air weapon held as a curiosity or ornament (s. 58(2) of the 1968 Act), nor, under s. 24ZA(2), does it apply in circumstances where young persons are permitted to have an air weapon with them under one of the exceptions set out in s. 23 of the Act (**see para. 3.9.12**).

### 3.9.8 General Exemptions

The general exemptions, which apply to the provisions of ss. 1 to 5 of the Firearms Act 1968 are mainly concerned with the various occupations of people whom you might expect to be in contact with firearms in one form or another. They include:

#### Police permit holders

Under s. 7(1) of the 1968 Act, the chief officer of police may grant a permit authorising the possession of firearms or ammunition under the conditions specified in the permit.

#### Clubs, athletics and sporting purposes

Section 11 of the 1968 Act provides exemptions for a person:

- borrowing the firearm/ammunition from a certificate holder *for sporting purposes only* but where the person carrying the firearm/ammunition is under 18, this applies only if the other person is aged 18 or over (s. 11(1));
- possessing a firearm at an athletic meeting for the purposes of starting races (s. 11(2));
- in charge of a miniature rifle range buying, acquiring or possessing miniature rifles and ammunition, and using them at such a rifle range (s. 11(4));

- who is a member of an approved rifle club, miniature rifle club or pistol club to possess a firearm or ammunition *when engaged as a club member in target practice* (s. 15(1) of the Firearms (Amendment) Act 1988);
- borrowing a shotgun from the occupier of private premises and using it on those premises *in the occupier's presence* but where the person borrowing the shotgun is under 18, this only applies if the occupier is aged 18 or over (s. 11(5) of the 1968 Act);
- using a shotgun at a time and place approved by the chief officer of police for shooting at artificial targets (s. 11(6)).

### Borrowed rifle on private premises

Section 16 of the Firearms (Amendment) Act 1988 allows a person to borrow a rifle from the occupier of private premises, provided:

- the person is on those premises and in the presence of the occupier (or the occupier's servant); and
- the occupier holds a certificate and the borrowing of the rifle complies with that certificate; and
- where the borrower is aged 17, the occupier in whose presence the rifle is used is 18 or over.

The person borrowing the rifle may buy or acquire ammunition for it in accordance with the certificate's conditions.

### Visitors' permits

Section 17 of the Firearms (Amendment) Act 1988 provides for the issuing of a visitors' permit by a chief officer of police and for the possession of firearms and ammunition by the holder of such a permit.

Visitors' permits will not be issued to anyone without a European firearms pass. It is a summary offence (punishable with six months' imprisonment) to make a false statement in order to get a visitors' permit, and it is a similar offence to fail to comply with any conditions within such a permit (see s. 17(10)).

### Antiques as ornaments or curiosities

Section 58(2) of the 1968 Act allows for the sale, buying, transfer, acquisition or possession of antique firearms *as curiosities or ornaments*. Whether a firearm is such an antique will be a question of fact to be determined by the court in each case. Mere belief in the fact that a firearm is an antique will not be enough (*R v Howells* [1977] QB 614).

### Authorised firearms dealers

Section 8(1) of the 1968 Act provides for registered firearms dealers (or their employees) to possess, acquire or buy firearms or ammunition in the ordinary course of their business without a certificate. If the possession etc. is not in the ordinary course of their business, the exemption will not apply.

---

**KEYNOTE**

In addition to the above, other occupations of people exempt include: auctioneers, carriers and warehouse staff; licensed slaughterers; theatrical performers; ships, aircraft or aerodrome equipment; Crown servants; proof houses; and holders of a museums licence.

---

### 3.9.9 Criminal Use of Firearms

Further to the offences relating to possession etc. of firearms there is a series of offences intrinsically linked to criminal behaviour. The aggravating factor of the presence of a firearm in the commission of such offences is evidenced by the fact that the majority carry a life imprisonment sentence—those that do not still carry ten years' imprisonment.

#### 3.9.9.1 Possession with Intent to Endanger Life

OFFENCE: **Possession with intent to Endanger Life—*Firearms Act 1968, s. 16***
  • Triable on indictment • Life imprisonment and/or a fine

The Firearms Act 1968, s. 16 states:

> It is an offence for a person to have in his possession any firearm or ammunition with intent by means thereof to endanger life or to enable another person by means thereof to endanger life, whether any injury has been caused or not.

---

**KEYNOTE**

This offence *cannot be committed by possessing an imitation firearm.*

The offence involves 'possession' so there is no need for the firearm to be produced or shown to another.

To prove this offence you will have to show an intention by the defendant to behave in a way that he/she knows will in fact endanger the life of another (*R* v *Brown and Ciarla* [1995] Crim LR 328). The life endangered must be the life of 'another', not the defendant's (*R* v *Norton* [1977] Crim LR 478) so that possession with intent to commit suicide would not be covered by the offence. The person whose life is endangered may be outside the United Kingdom (*R* v *El-Hakkaoui* [1975] 1 WLR 396). Note that the intention *is not* to enable the defendant or another to kill.

That intent does not have to be an immediate one and it may be conditional (e.g. an intent to shoot someone if they do not do as they are asked) (*R* v *Bentham* [1973] QB 357).

The firearm must provide the means by which life is endangered; it is not enough to have a firearm at the time when life is endangered by some other means (e.g. by dangerous driving).

There may be occasions when self-defence can be raised in answer to a charge under s. 16 of the 1968 Act but these circumstances will be very unusual (see *R* v *Georgiades* [1989] 1 WLR 759). This defence could apply where the defendant is carrying a weapon for his own defence anticipating an imminent attack (*R* v *Salih* [2007] EWCA Crim 2750).

---

#### 3.9.9.2 Possession with Intent to Cause Fear of Violence

OFFENCE: **Possession with Intent to Cause Fear of Violence—*Firearms Act 1968, s. 16A***
  • Triable on indictment • Ten years' imprisonment and/or a fine

The Firearms Act 1968, s. 16A (added by Firearms (Amendment) Act 1994, s. 1) states:

> It is an offence for a person to have in his possession any firearm or imitation firearm with intent—
>   (a) by means thereof to cause, or
>   (b) to enable another person by means thereof to cause,
> any person to believe that unlawful violence will be used against him or another person.

### 3.9.9.3 Using Firearm to Resist Arrest

OFFENCE: **Using Firearm to Resist Arrest—*Firearms Act 1968, s. 17(1)***
  • Triable on indictment  • Life imprisonment and/or a fine

The Firearms Act 1968, s. 17 states:

(1) It is an offence for a person to make or attempt to make any use whatsoever of a firearm or imitation firearm with intent to resist or prevent the lawful arrest or detention of himself or another person.

### 3.9.9.4 Having Firearm with Intent to Commit Indictable Offence or Resist Arrest

OFFENCE: **Having Firearm with Intent to Commit an Indictable Offence or Resist Arrest—*Firearms Act 1968, s. 18(1)***
  • Triable on indictment  • Life imprisonment and/or a fine

The Firearms Act 1968, s. 18 states:

(1) It is an offence for a person to have with him a firearm or imitation firearm with intent to commit an indictable offence, or to resist arrest or prevent the arrest of another, in either case while he has the firearm or imitation firearm with him.

1340. Despite this narrower meaning, the defendant does not have to be shown to have been 'carrying' the firearm (*R* v *Kelt* [1977] 1 WLR 1365).

**Intention**

In proving the intent for this offence, s. 18 states:

(2) In proceedings for an offence under this section proof that the accused had a firearm or imitation firearm with him and intended to commit an offence, or to resist or prevent arrest, is evidence that he intended to have it with him while doing so.

It is not necessary to show that the defendant intended to *use* the firearm to commit the indictable offence or to prevent/resist the arrest (*R* v *Stoddart* [1998] 2 Cr App R 25).

The mental element is, however, an essential part of this offence. Therefore, if the defendant only formed the intent as a result of duress, this ingredient will not have been established—*R* v *Fisher* [2004] EWCA Crim 1190.

Section 18 does not appear to require that any arrest be 'lawful' and it may be that Parliament intended for this offence to be broader in that respect than the offence under s. 17.

This offence includes imitation firearms in the general sense (see para. 3.9.2.4).

The power of entry and search under s. 47 of the 1968 Act applies to this offence (see para. 3.9.13).

### 3.9.9.5 Possessing Firearm while Committing a Schedule 1 Offence

OFFENCE: **Possessing Firearm while Committing or Being Arrested for sch. 1 Offence—*Firearms Act 1968, s. 17(2)***

- Triable on indictment • Life imprisonment and/or a fine

The Firearms Act 1968, s. 17 states:

(2) If a person, at the time of his committing or being arrested for an offence specified in schedule 1 to this Act, has in his possession a firearm or imitation firearm, he shall be guilty of an offence under this subsection unless he shows that he had it in his possession for a lawful object.

**KEYNOTE**

This offence may be committed in two ways; either by being in possession of the weapon *at the time of committing* the sch. 1 offence or by being in possession of it *at the time of being arrested* for such an offence. Clearly in the second case, there may be some time between actually committing the sch. 1 offence and being arrested for it. Nevertheless, if the defendant is in possession of the firearm at the time of his/her arrest, the offence is committed (unless he/she can show that it was for a lawful purpose).

There is no need for the defendant to be subsequently *convicted* of the sch. 1 offence, nor even to prove the elements of it; all that is needed is to show that the defendant, at the time of his/her arrest for a sch. 1 offence, had a firearm/imitation firearm in his/her possession (*R* v *Nelson* [2000] QB55).

It is for the defendant to prove that the firearm was in his/her possession for a lawful purpose.

This offence includes imitation firearms in the general sense (see para. 3.9.2.4).

### Schedule 1 Offences

The *main* offences listed in sch. 1 are:

- Damage—s. 1 of the Criminal Damage Act 1971.
- Assaults and woundings—ss. 20 and 47 of the Offences Against the Person Act 1861, assault on police (s. 89 of the Police Act 1996) and civilian custody officers (s. 90(1) of the Criminal Justice Act 1991 and s. 13(1) of the Criminal Justice and Public Order Act 1994).

- Rape and other sexual/abduction offences—the following offences under the Sexual Offences Act 2003: s. 1 (rape), s. 2 (assault by penetration), s. 4 (causing a person to engage in sexual activity without consent), where the activity caused involved penetration within subs. (4)(a) to (d) of that section, s. 5 and s. 6 (rape and assault of a child under 13), s. 8 (causing or inciting a child under 13 to engage in sexual activity), where an activity involving penetration within subs. (2)(a) to (d) of that section was caused, s. 30 and s. 31 (sexual activity with/causing or inciting a person with a mental disorder impeding choice), where the touching involved or activity caused penetration within subs. (3)(a) to (d) of that section. Also offences under part I of the Child Abduction Act 1984.
- Theft, robbery, burglary, blackmail and taking a conveyance—Theft Act 1968. (D.A.R.T.)

Although covering several types of assault, sch. 1 does not extend to wounding/causing grievous bodily harm with intent (s. 18 of the Offences Against the Person Act 1861). Schedule 1 also covers the aiding, abetting or attempting to commit such offences.

### 3.9.9.6 Using Someone to Mind a Weapon

OFFENCE: **Using Someone to Mind a Weapon—*Violent Crime Reduction Act 2006, s. 28(1)***

- Triable on indictment • Ten years' imprisonment and/or a fine (firearms, etc.)
- Four years' imprisonment and/or a fine (offensive weapons, etc.)

The Violent Crime Reduction Act 2006, s. 28 states:

(1) A person is guilty of an offence if—
   (a) he uses another to look after, hide or transport a dangerous weapon for him; and
   (b) he does so under arrangements or in circumstances that facilitate, or are intended to facilitate, the weapon's being available to him for an unlawful purpose.
(2) For the purposes of this section the cases in which a dangerous weapon is to be regarded as available to a person for an unlawful purpose include any case where—
   (a) the weapon is available for him to take possession of it at a time and place; and
   (b) his possession of the weapon at that time and place would constitute, or be likely to involve or to lead to, the commission by him of an offence.

---

**KEYNOTE**

The offence was introduced by the 2006 Act to close a perceived loophole in the law where people have escaped prosecution by entrusting their weapon to another person, in particular to a child. Using children in this way may risk injury to them and in the longer term draw them into gun and knife crime as a result of their early association with weapons. Using a minor to mind a firearm is an aggravating factor attracting harsher sentences (s. 29(3)(a)).

A 'dangerous weapon' means a firearm *other than* an air weapon or a component part of, or accessory to, an air weapon; or a weapon to which s. 141 or 141A of the Criminal Justice Act 1988 applies (specified offensive weapons, knives and bladed weapons) (s. 28(3)).

---

## 3.9.10 Further Firearms Offences

Alongside offences associated with the criminal use of firearms are several offences dealing with an offender 'having with him' a firearm in a public place and whilst trespassing.

### 3.9.10.1 Having Firearm or Imitation Firearm in Public Place

OFFENCE: **Having Firearm/Imitation Firearm in Public Place—*Firearms Act 1968, s. 19***
- Triable either way • Seven years' imprisonment and/or a fine on indictment
- 12 months' imprisonment and/or a fine summarily

The Firearms Act 1968, s. 19 states:

A person commits an offence if, without lawful authority or reasonable excuse (the proof whereof lies on him), he has with him in a public place—

(a) a loaded shot gun,

(b) an air weapon (whether loaded or not),

(c) any other firearm (whether loaded or not) together with ammunition suitable for use in that firearm, or

(d) an imitation firearm.

---

**KEYNOTE**

A 'public place' includes any highway and any other premises or place to which, at the material time, the public have or are permitted to have access whether on payment or otherwise (s. 57(4) of the Act).

If the weapon is a shotgun it must be loaded. 'Loaded' here means if there is ammunition in the chamber or barrel (or in any magazine or other device) whereby the ammunition can be fed into the chamber or barrel by the manual or automatic operation of some part of the weapon (see s. 57(6)(b)). If the weapon is an imitation firearm (see para. 3.9.2.4) or an air weapon the offence is committed by the defendant having it with him/her. In the case of other firearms the offence is committed by the defendant having the firearm with him/her together with ammunition suitable for use in it.

For the meaning of 'has with him', see para. 3.9.9.4.

This offence is one of strict liability. Therefore, if you can show that the defendant (X) knew he had something with him and that the 'something' was a loaded shotgun, an air weapon, an imitation firearm, or another firearm with ammunition, the offence is complete (*R* v *Vann* [1996] Crim LR 52). It is for the defendant to show lawful authority or reasonable excuse; possession of a valid certificate does not of itself provide lawful authority for having the firearm/ammunition in a public place (*Ross* v *Collins* [1982] Crim LR 368).

---

### 3.9.10.2 Trespassing with Firearms

OFFENCE: **Trespassing with Firearm in Building—*Firearms Act 1968, s. 20(1)***
- Triable either way (unless imitation firearm or air weapon)
- Seven years' imprisonment and/or a fine on indictment
- Six months' imprisonment and/or a fine summarily

The Firearms Act 1968, s. 20 states:

(1) A person commits an offence if, while he has a firearm or imitation firearm with him, he enters or is in any building or part of a building as a trespasser and without reasonable excuse (the proof whereof lies on him).

---

**KEYNOTE**

This offence can be committed either by entering a building/part of a building or simply by *being* in such a place, in each case as a trespasser while having the firearm. As there is no need for the defendant to have 'entered' the building as a trespasser in every case, the offence might be committed after the occupier has withdrawn any permission for the defendant to be there.

For the interpretation of 'has with him', see para. 3.9.9.4.

---

It will be for defendants to prove that they had reasonable excuse and the standard of that proof will be judged against the balance of probabilities.

If the relevant firearm is an imitation or an air weapon, the offence is triable summarily.

This offence includes imitation firearms in the general sense (see para. 3.9.2.4). If the relevant firearm is an imitation or an air weapon, the offence is triable summarily.

The power of entry and search under s. 47 of the 1968 Act applies to this offence (see para. 3.9.13).

OFFENCE: **Trespassing with Firearm on Land—*Firearms Act 1968, s. 20(2)***
- Triable summarily • Three months' imprisonment and/or a fine

The Firearms Act 1968, s. 20 states:

(2) A person commits an offence if, while he has a firearm or imitation firearm with him, he enters or is on any land as a trespasser and without reasonable excuse (the proof whereof lies on him).

**KEYNOTE**

The elements of this offence are generally the same as those for the s. 20(1) offence above.

As with the s. 20(1) offence, there is no requirement that the defendant had the firearm/imitation firearm with him/her when entering onto the land.

'Land' for these purposes will include land covered by water (s. 20(3)).

This offence includes imitation firearms in the general sense (see para. 3.9.2.4).

The power of entry and search under s. 47 of the 1968 Act applies to this offence (see para. 3.9.13).

### 3.9.11 Possession or Acquisition of Firearms by Convicted Persons

Section 21 of the Firearms Act 1968 places restrictions on convicted persons in respect of their possession of firearms and/or ammunition.

Section 21 generally provides that any person who has been sentenced to:

- custody for *life*, or
- to preventive detention, imprisonment, corrective training, youth custody or detention in a young offender institution for *three years or more*

must not, *at any time*, have a firearm or ammunition in his/her possession, i.e. a life-time ban.

Section 21 goes on to provide that any person who has been sentenced to imprisonment, youth custody, detention in a young offender institution or a secure training order for *three months or more, but less than three years*, must not have a firearm or ammunition in his/her possession at any time before the end of a five-year period beginning on the date of his/her release.

Date of release means, for a sentence partly served and partly suspended, the date on which the offender completes the part to be served and, in the case of a person subject to a secure training order, the date on which he/she is released from detention (under the various relevant statutes) or the date halfway through the total specified by the court making the order, whichever is the latest (s. 21(2A)).

A person holding a licence under the Children and Young Persons Act 1933 or a person subject to a recognisance to keep the peace or be of good behaviour with a condition relating to the possession of firearms, must not, *at any time during the licence or the recognisance*, have a firearm or ammunition in his/her possession (s. 21(3)).

Where sentences or court orders are mentioned, their Scottish equivalents will also apply and a person prohibited in Northern Ireland from possessing a firearm/ammunition will also be prohibited in Great Britain (s. 21(3A)).

Section 21 *does not apply to imitation firearms* as there is no express reference to them in the section and because the reference in the Firearms Act 1982 does not apply.

### 3.9.11.1 Supplying Firearm to Person Prohibited by Section 21

OFFENCE: **Selling or Transferring Firearm to Person Prohibited by s. 21—*Firearms Act 1968, s. 21(5)***

- Triable either way • Five years' imprisonment and/or a fine on indictment
- Six months' imprisonment and/or a fine summarily

The Firearms Act 1968, s. 21 states:

(5) It is an offence for a person to sell or transfer a firearm or ammunition to, or to repair, test or prove a firearm or ammunition for, a person whom he knows or has reasonable ground for believing to be prohibited by this section from having a firearm or ammunition in his possession.

---

**KEYNOTE**

Given that all people are presumed to know the law once it is published, it would seem that the knowledge or belief by the defendant would apply to the *convictions* of the other person, not the fact that possession by that person was an offence.

What you must show is knowledge by the defendant or at least *reasonable ground for believing*; this latter requirement is stronger than mere cause to *suspect*.

---

## 3.9.12 Other Restrictions on Possession or Acquisition

Sections 22 to 24 of the Firearms Act 1968 creates a number of summary offences restricting the involvement of people of various ages in their dealings with certain types of firearm and ammunition.

In summary the age restrictions are as follows:

- a person under 18:
  + must not purchase or hire any firearm or ammunition (s. 22(1)(a));
  + must not have with him/her an air weapon or ammunition for an air weapon (s. 22(4)). An exception to this is where the person is under the supervision of another who is at least 21 years old. However, if the person under 18 fires the weapon beyond the relevant premises, he/she will commit an offence under s. 21A (**see para. 3.9.7.1**) and the person supervising him/her will be guilty of an offence under s. 23(1). It is not an offence under this section for a person aged 14 or over to have with him/her an air weapon or ammunition on private premises with the consent of the occupier (s. 23(3));
  + it is an offence to sell or let on hire an air weapon or ammunition for an air weapon to a person under the age of 18 (s. 24(1)(a)), or to make a gift/part with possession of an air weapon or ammunition for an air weapon to such a person (unless under the permitted circumstances above) (s. 24(4));
  + it is an offence to sell an imitation firearm to a person under the age of 18 (s. 24A(2)), or for a person under 18 to purchase one (s. 24A(1)). It is a defence to show that the vendor believed that the purchaser was 18 or over and had reasonable grounds for that belief (s. 24A(3));
- a person under 15:

- must not have with him/her an assembled shotgun unless supervised by a person aged at least 21 or while the shotgun is securely covered so it cannot be fired (s. 22(3)); and
  - it is an offence to make a gift of a shotgun/ammunition to such a person (s. 24(3));
- a person under 14:
  - must not have in his/her possession a section 1 firearm or ammunition (s. 22(2));
  - must not part with possession of any firearm or ammunition to which s. 15 of the Firearms (Amendment) Act 1988 applies, except in circumstances where under s. 11(1), (3) or (4) of this Act, he/she is entitled to have possession of it without holding a firearm certificate; and
  - it is an offence to make a gift or lend or part with possession of such a firearm/ammunition to such a person (s. 24(2)) (subject to some exceptions relating to sports and shooting clubs—see s. 11 of the Firearms Act 1968 and s. 15 of the Firearms (Amendment) Act 1988).

There is a further provision creating an offence for a person under 18 who is the holder of a certificate using a firearm for a purpose not authorised by the European Weapons Directive (s. 22(1A)).

---

**KEYNOTE**

For the full extent of these restrictions and their exemptions, reference should be made to the 1968 and 1988 Acts. Note that s. 24(5) of the Firearms Act 1968 provides that it is a defence to prove that the person charged with an offence believed that other person to be of or over the age mentioned and had reasonable grounds for the belief.

It is a summary offence (punishable by one month's imprisonment and/or a fine) to be in possession of *any* loaded firearm when drunk (s. 12 of the Licensing Act 1872). There is no requirement that the person be in a public place.

---

## 3.9.13 Police Powers

The Firearms Act 1968, s. 47 states:

(1) A constable may require any person whom he has reasonable cause to suspect—
  (a) of having a firearm, with or without ammunition, with him in a public place; or
  (b) to be committing or about to commit, elsewhere than in a public place, an offence relevant for the purposes of this section,
to hand over the firearm or any ammunition for examination by the constable.

---

**KEYNOTE**

An 'offence relevant to this section' appears to be:

- an offence of having a firearm with intent to commit an indictable offence or resist arrest (contrary to s. 18(1) and (2) of the 1968 Act); or
- an offence of trespassing with a firearm (contrary to s. 20).

It is a summary offence to fail to hand over a firearm or ammunition when required under this section (s. 47(2)).

In order to exercise this power, a police officer may search the person and may detain him/her for that purpose (s. 47(3)). The officer may also enter *any place* (s. 47(5)).

If the officer has reasonable cause to suspect that:

- there is a firearm in a vehicle in a public place, or
- a vehicle is being/about to be used in connection with the commission of an 'offence relevant to this section' (see above)

he/she may search the vehicle and, for that purpose, may require the person driving or in control of the vehicle to stop it (s. 47(4)).

The provisions of the PACE Codes of Practice, Code A, will apply to the exercise of these powers of stop and search.

### 3.9.13.1 Power to Demand Documentation

The Firearms Act 1968, s. 48 states:

(1) A constable may demand, from any person whom he believes to be in possession of a firearm or ammunition to which section 1 of this Act applies, or of a shot gun, the production of his firearm certificate or, as the case may be, his shot gun certificate.

---

**KEYNOTE**

The demand for the relevant documentation may be made where the police officer 'believes' that a person is in possession of a section 1 firearm or ammunition or a shotgun. There is no requirement that the officer's belief be reasonable.

Where the person fails to:

- produce the relevant certificate or
- show that he/she is not entitled to be issued with such a certificate or
- show that he/she is in possession of the firearm exclusively in connection with recognised purposes (collecting/historical/cultural) under the law of another EU Member State

the officer may demand the production of the relevant valid documentation issued in another Member State under any corresponding provisions (s. 48(1A)).

Failing to produce any of the required documents *or* to let the officer read it, or failing to show an entitlement to possess the firearm or ammunition initiates the power of seizure under s. 48(2). It also gives the officer the power to demand the person's name and address.

If the person refuses to give his/her name or address or gives a false name and address, he/she commits a summary offence (s. 48(3)).

A person from another Member State who is in possession of a firearm and who fails to comply with a demand under s. 48(1A) also commits a separate summary offence (s. 48(4)).

---

## 3.9.14 Imitation Firearm Offences

OFFENCE: **Converting Imitation Firearm—*Firearms Act 1968, s. 4(3)***
- Triable either way • Five years' imprisonment and/or a fine on indictment
- Six months' imprisonment and/or a fine summarily

The Firearms Act 1968, s. 4 states:

(3) It is an offence for a person other than a registered firearms dealer to convert into a firearm anything which, though having the appearance of being a firearm, is so constructed as to be incapable of discharging any missile through its barrel.

---

**KEYNOTE**

This offence involves the conversion of anything which has the appearance of a firearm so that it can be fired. Registered firearms dealers are excluded from the offence. Once the conversion has taken place, the nature of the imitation firearm will have changed, in which case the person will also commit the relevant possession offences unless he/she has the appropriate authorisation.

---

Sections 36 to 41 of the Violent Crime Reduction Act 2006 introduced measures to deal with the misuse of firearms. These sections created the three specific summary offences detailed below.

Section 36 makes it an offence to manufacture, import, modify or sell *realistic imitation firearms* as defined in s. 38.

Section 39 makes it an offence to manufacture, modify or import an imitation firearm that does not conform to specifications set out in regulations to be made by the Secretary of State.

Section 40 inserted a new s. 24A into the 1968 Act and makes it an offence to sell an imitation firearm to a person under 18. It also makes it an offence for a person under 18 to purchase an imitation firearm.

---

**KEYNOTE**

For the purposes of the 2006 Act, an 'imitation firearm' is defined as that used in the Firearms Act 1968, i.e. in the 'general sense' (see para. 3.9.2.4). A 'realistic imitation firearm' is effectively a 'sub-category' of an imitation firearm in the general sense. A 'realistic imitation firearm' is defined as an imitation firearm which has an appearance that is so realistic as to make it indistinguishable, for all practical purposes, from a real firearm and is neither a deactivated firearm nor itself an antique (s. 38(1)).

An imitation firearm will be regarded as distinguishable if its size, shape or principal colour is unrealistic for a real firearm (s. 38(3)). The Violent Crime Reduction Act 2006 (Realistic Imitation Firearms) Regulations 2007 (SI 2007/2606) provide defences for an offence under s. 36, and make provision in connection with the definition of 'realistic imitation firearm' in s. 38, specifying the sizes and colours which are to be regarded as unrealistic for a real firearm.

---

# 3.10 | Terrorism and Associated Offences

## 3.10.1 Introduction

The law on terrorism contained in this chapter relates to the Terrorism Act 2000, Terrorism Act 2006, Counter-Terrorism Act 2008 and the Terrorism Prevention and Investigation Measures Act 2011. Another piece of legislation dealing with terrorism is the Anti-terrorism, Crime and Security Act 2001. The 2001 Act, which is not the subject of this chapter, deals with offences designed to combat the potential use by terrorists of poisons and chemical, biological and nuclear weapons, as well as the forfeiture of assets and the disclosure of information by public bodies.

## 3.10.2 Terrorism Defined

Terrorism is defined in the Terrorism Act 2000, s. 1 as:

(1) ...the use or threat of action where—
   (a) the action falls within subsection (2),
   (b) the use or threat is designed to influence the government or an international governmental organisation, or to intimidate the public or a section of the public, and
   (c) the use or threat is made for the purpose of advancing a political, religious, ideological or racial cause.
(2) Action falls within this subsection if it—
   (a) involves serious violence against a person,
   (b) involves serious damage to property,
   (c) endangers a person's life, other than that of the person committing the action,
   (d) creates a serious risk to the health or safety of the public or a section of the public, or
   (e) is designed seriously to interfere with or seriously to disrupt an electronic system.
(3) The use or threat of action falling within subsection (2) which involves the use of firearms or explosives is terrorism whether or not subsection (1)(b) is satisfied.

### KEYNOTE

This definition includes domestic terrorism, and is so broad that it should be considered when dealing with other, more familiar offences such as blackmail, contamination of goods and threats to kill.

The above definition recognises that terrorist activity may be motivated by religious, racial or fundamental reasons rather than simply political ones. The purpose of advancing a 'racial' cause was inserted by s. 75 of the Counter-Terrorism Act 2008. Although a racial cause will in most cases be subsumed within a political or ideological cause, this amendment is designed to put the matter beyond doubt that such a cause is included. The definition also encompasses broad activities (including threats) which, though potentially devastating in their impact on society, may not be overtly violent. Examples of such activity might be interference with domestic water and power supplies or serious disruption of computer networks.

The provision at s. 1(3) means that, where the relevant criminal activity involves the use of firearms or explosives, there is no further need to show that the behaviour was designed to influence the government or to intimidate the public or a section of the public. An example of such activity might be the shooting of a senior military or political figure. A 'firearm' for this purpose includes air weapons (s. 121); it is not clear whether the definition includes imitation firearms.

The reference to 'action' here includes action outside the United Kingdom. Similarly, references to people, property, the public and governments apply to all those features whether in the United Kingdom or elsewhere (s. 1(4)).

### 3.10.2.1  Membership of a Proscribed Organisation

OFFENCE:  **Membership of a Proscribed Organisation—*Terrorism Act 2000, s. 11***
- Triable either way  •  Ten years' imprisonment and/or a fine on indictment
- Six months' imprisonment and/or a fine summarily

The Terrorism Act 2000, s. 11 states:

(1) A person commits an offence if he belongs or professes to belong to a proscribed organisation.

(2) It is a defence for a person charged with an offence under subsection (1) to prove—

  (a) that the organisation was not proscribed on the last (or only) occasion on which he became a member or began to profess to be a member, and

  (b) that he has not taken part in the activities of the organisation at any time while it was proscribed.

---

**KEYNOTE**

Specific organisations are proscribed by the Secretary of State and include some of the most active and widely known terrorist groups across the world, including al-Qaeda (sch. 2 to the Act). What amounts to membership is likely to depend on the nature of an organisation, e.g. membership of a loose and unstructured organisation may not need any formal steps or express process by which a person becomes a member (*R* v *Ahmed* [2011] EWCA Crim 184).

The reverse burden of proof contained in s. 11(2) has been held as imposing an evidential, as opposed to a persuasive, burden of proof (*Attorney-General's Reference (No. 4 of 2002), Sheldrake* v *DPP* [2004] UKHL 43).

Other offences relating to proscribed organisations are provided by s. 12 and include: inviting support; arranging or managing (or assisting in doing so) a meeting of three or more people in public or private, to support, further the activities or be addressed by a person belonging to a proscribed organisation; or addressing a meeting to encourage support or further the activities of the organisation.

The Act also created a summary offence of wearing an item of clothing, or wearing, carrying or displaying an article in such a way or in such circumstances as to arouse reasonable suspicion that the defendant is a member or supporter of a proscribed organisation (s. 13).

---

## 3.10.3  Terrorism Act 2000: Financial Measures

The main financial measures under the Terrorism Act 2000 relate to terrorist fundraising, possession of property and funding arrangements, and include:

- *inviting* another to provide money or other property (s. 15(1));
- *providing* money or other property (s. 15(3));
- *receiving* money or other property (s. 15(2));
- *possessing* money or other property (s. 16(2));
- *arranging* for money or other property to be made available (s. 17);

in each case intending that, or having reasonable cause to suspect that, it may be used for the purposes of terrorism (ss. 15, 16(2) and 17);

- *using* money or other property for the purposes of terrorism (s. 16(1));
- *concealing, moving or transferring* any terrorist property (s. 18).

Each of these offences is punishable by a maximum of 14 years' imprisonment on indictment (s. 22).

## 3.10.4 Terrorism Act 2000: Duty of Disclosure and Tipping Off

The 2000 Act creates a number of offences in relation to the unlawful disclosure of information and provides where disclosure is permissible.

### 3.10.4.1 Disclosure of Information

OFFENCE: **Disclosure of Information—*Terrorism Act 2000, s. 19***
- Triable either way • Five years' imprisonment and/or a fine on indictment
- Six months' imprisonment and/or a fine summarily

The Terrorism Act 2000, s. 19 states:

(1)    This section applies where a person—
   (a)  believes or suspects that another person has committed an offence under any of sections 15 to 18, and
   (b)  bases his belief or suspicion on information which comes to his attention—
       (i) in the course of a trade, profession or business, or
       (ii) in the course of his employment (whether or not in the course of a trade, profession or business).

(1A) But this section does not apply if the information came to the person in the course of a business in the regulated sector.

(2)    The person commits an offence if he does not disclose to a constable as soon as is reasonably practicable—
   (a)  his belief or suspicion, and
   (b)  the information on which it is based.

---

**KEYNOTE**

This section requires banks and other businesses to report any suspicions they may have that someone is laundering terrorist money or committing any of the other terrorist property offences in ss. 15–18. Section 19(1)(b) ensures the offence is focused on suspicions which arise at work.

'Employment' means any employment (paid or unpaid) including work under a contract for services or as an office holder, work experience provided pursuant to a training course or programme or in the course of training for employment, and voluntary work (s. 22A).

It is a defence for a person to prove that he/she had a reasonable excuse for not making the disclosure (s. 19(3)), or that the matters specified were disclosed in accordance with an established procedure for the making of disclosures (s. 19(4)). Disclosure by a professional legal adviser is not required if the information was obtained in privileged circumstances (s. 19(5)).

Section 21A of the Act also provides for an offence of failure to disclose information in the 'regulated sector', i.e. accountancy firms, investment companies, etc., the definition of which is contained in Sch. 3A to the Act.

---

### 3.10.4.2 Disclosure of Information: Permission

The Terrorism Act 2000, s. 20 states:

(1) A person may disclose to a constable—
   (a) a suspicion or belief that any money or other property is terrorist property or is derived from terrorist property;
   (b) any matter on which the suspicion or belief is based.

(2) A person may make a disclosure to a constable in the circumstances mentioned in section 19(1) and (2).

(3) Subsections (1) and (2) shall have effect notwithstanding any restriction on the disclosure of information imposed by statute or otherwise.

(4) Where—
   (a) a person is in employment, and
   (b) his employer has established a procedure for the making of disclosures of the kinds mentioned in subsection (1) and section 19(2),

subsections (1) and (2) shall have effect in relation to that person as if any reference to disclosure to a constable included a reference to disclosure in accordance with the procedure.

---

**KEYNOTE**

Section 20 ensures that businesses can disclose information to the police without fear of breaching legal restrictions.

---

### 3.10.4.3    Information about Acts of Terrorism

OFFENCE:  **Information about Acts of Terrorism—*Terrorism Act 2000, s. 38B***

- Triable either way • Five years' imprisonment and/or a fine on indictment
- Six months' imprisonment and/or a fine summarily

The Terrorism Act 2000, s. 38B states:

(1) This section applies where a person has information which he knows or believes might be of material assistance—
    (a) in preventing the commission by another person of an act of terrorism, or
    (b) in securing the apprehension, prosecution or conviction of another person, in the United Kingdom, for an offence involving the commission, preparation or instigation of an act of terrorism.
(2) The person commits an offence if he does not disclose the information as soon as reasonably practicable in accordance with subsection (3).
(3) Disclosure is in accordance with this subsection if it is made—
    (a) in England and Wales, to a constable . . .

---

**KEYNOTE**

This offence, unlike some of the Act's other provisions, relates to any person who has information that he/she knows or believes might help prevent an act of terrorism or help bring terrorists to justice.

A person resident in the United Kingdom could be charged with this offence notwithstanding that he/she was outside the country when he/she became aware of the information (s. 38B(6)).

It is a defence for a person charged to prove that he/she had a reasonable excuse for not making the disclosure (s. 38B(4)).

---

### 3.10.4.4    Disclosure of and Interference with Information Offences

OFFENCE:  **Disclosure of Information etc.—*Terrorism Act 2000, s. 39***

- Triable either way • Five years' imprisonment and/or a fine on indictment
- Six months' imprisonment and/or a fine summarily

The Terrorism Act 2000, s, 39 states:

(1) Subsection (2) applies where a person knows or has reasonable cause to suspect that a constable is conducting or proposes to conduct a terrorist investigation.
(2) The person commits an offence if he—
    (a) discloses to another anything which is likely to prejudice the investigation, or
    (b) interferes with material which is likely to be relevant to the investigation.
(3) Subsection (4) applies where a person knows or has reasonable cause to suspect that a disclosure has been or will be made under any of sections 19 to 21B or 38B.
(4) The person commits an offence if he—
    (a) discloses to another anything which is likely to prejudice an investigation resulting from the disclosure under that section, or
    (b) interferes with material which is likely to be relevant to an investigation resulting from the disclosure under that section.

### 3.10.5 Terrorism Act 2000: Other Offences

The Terrorism Act 2000 also creates a number of other offences in relation to terrorism. In summary, the key offences are:

- *Directing* the activities of an organisation which is concerned in the commission of acts of terrorism (s. 56). This offence (which is often easier to prove than some of the better known offences) carries a maximum sentence of life imprisonment.
- *Providing or receiving instruction or training* in the making or use of firearms or explosives or radioactive material or weapons designed or adapted for the discharge of any radioactive material, or chemical, biological or nuclear weapons (s. 54).
- *Possessing articles* in circumstances which give rise to a reasonable suspicion that the possession is for a purpose connected with the commission, preparation or instigation of an act of terrorism (s. 57). It must be shown that the defendant(s) possessed extremist material for use in the future to incite the commission of terrorist acts (*R* v *Zafar* [2008] EWCA Crim 184). See also *R* v *G*; *R* v *J* [2009] UKHL 13.
- *Collecting or making a record* of information (including photographs and electronic records) of a kind likely to be useful to a person committing or preparing an act of terrorism, or possessing a document or record containing information of that kind (s. 58). The document, etc. concerned must be of a kind that is likely to provide practical assistance to a person, rather than simply encouraging the commission of terrorist acts (*R* v *K* [2008] EWCA Crim 185). See also *R* v *Muhammed* [2010] EWCA Crim 227. In *R* v *Brown* [2011] EWCA Crim 2751, it was held that s. 58 did not infringe the appellant's right to free speech under ECHR, Article 10, insofar as it penalised the collection and distribution of materials and advice (*The Anarchist Cookbook*) on bomb-making, poisoning and other such activities. This ruling also applies to s. 2 of the Terrorism Act 2006 (**see para. 3.10.6**).
- *Eliciting or attempting to elicit* information about a member of the armed forces or the intelligence services or a constable, which is likely to be useful to a person committing or preparing an act of terrorism, or publishing or communicating information of that kind (s. 58A—inserted by the Counter-Terrorism Act 2008).
- *Inciting* another person to commit an act of terrorism wholly or partly outside the United Kingdom (s. 59).

### 3.10.6 Terrorism Act 2006: Offences

For the purposes of the 2006 Act the offences are grouped into three specific areas; encouragement etc. of terrorism; preparation of terrorist acts and terrorist training; offences involving radioactive devices and materials and nuclear facilities and sites.

### 3.10.6.1 Encouragement etc. of Terrorism

The offences within this group are:

- publishes a statement to encourage the commission, preparation or instigation of acts of terrorism or Convention offences (s. 1(2));
- engages in the dissemination of terrorist publications (s. 2(1)).

For the purposes of both these sections it is necessary to prove that they glorify the act of terrorism and that members of the public could reasonably be expected to infer that what is being glorified is being glorified as conduct that should be emulated by them in existing circumstances. 'Glorification' includes any form of praise or celebration, and cognate expressions are to be construed accordingly (s. 20(2)). The 'Convention offences' mentioned in s. 1(2) are those offences listed in sch. 1 to the Act and include offences in relation to explosives, biological weapons, chemical weapons, nuclear weapons, hostage-taking, hijacking, terrorist funds, etc.

In relation to an offence under s. 2 of the Act it was held that videos uploaded onto the internet of scenes showing attacks on soldiers of the Coalition forces in Iraq and Afghanistan by insurgents were depicting scenes of terrorism within the definition of s. 1 of the 2000 Act (*R v Gul* [2012] EWCA Crim 280). Under this section, although the accused is free to argue that the prosecution constituted an unacceptable interference with the applicant's right to freedom of speech at common law, this defence is always a matter to be determined by the jury (see *R v Brown* [2011] EWCA Crim 2751 and *Faraz v R* [2012] EWCA Crim 2820).

Section 3(1) provides that the offences under ss. 1 and 2 can be committed by publishing a statement electronically, i.e. via the Internet. 'Statement' includes a communication of any description, including a communication without words consisting of sounds or images or both (s. 20(6)). The section provides for a notice to be served by a constable on the person electronically publishing the statement declaring that it is, in the constable's opinion, unlawfully terrorism-related and requiring its removal or modification (s. 3(3)). The methods for giving such a notice are provided in s. 4 of the Act. The offences under ss. 1 and 2 are punishable on indictment by a term of imprisonment not exceeding seven years or a fine or both, and summarily by a term of imprisonment not exceeding six months or a fine or both.

### 3.10.6.2 Preparation of Terrorist Acts and Terrorist Training

The offences within this group are:

- preparation for terrorist acts (s. 5(1));
- providing instruction or training in any of the skills mentioned for the commission or preparation of acts of terrorism or Convention offences (s. 6(1));
- receiving instruction or training in any of the skills mentioned for the commission or preparation of acts of terrorism or Convention offences (s. 6(2));
- attendance at a place used for terrorist training s. 8(1).

For an offence under s. 5(1) it is irrelevant whether the intention and preparations relate to one or more particular acts of terrorism, acts of terrorism of a particular description or acts of terrorism generally (s. 5(2) and see *R v Roddis* [2009] EWCA Crim 585). The punishment for an offence under this section is imprisonment for life.

In relation to the offences of providing or receiving instruction or training under s. 6, the skills mentioned include: the making, handling or use of a noxious substance, the use of any method or technique for doing anything capable of being done for the purposes of terrorism, and the design or adaptation for the purposes of terrorism of any method or technique for doing anything. In *R v Da Costa* [2009] EWCA Crim 482, it was held that the person delivering the training had to know that one or more of those receiving it intended to use it for a terrorist purpose. The punishment on indictment for an offence under s. 6(1) and (2) is a term of imprisonment not exceeding ten years or a fine or both, or on summary conviction imprisonment for a term not exceeding six months or a fine, or both.

The offence under s. 8(1) may be committed either in the United Kingdom or elsewhere. It must be shown that the person either knew or believed that the instruction or training was wholly or partly for purposes connected with the commission or preparation of acts of terrorism, or that the person could not reasonably have failed to understand the purpose of such instruction or training (s. 8(2)). The punishment on indictment for an offence under this section is a term of imprisonment not exceeding ten years or a fine or both, or on summary conviction imprisonment for a term not exceeding six months or a fine, or both.

### 3.10.6.3 Radioactive Devices and Materials and Nuclear Facilities and Sites

The offences within this group are:

- making and possession of devices or materials (s. 9(1));
- misuse of devices or material and misuse and damage of facilities (s. 10(1) and (2));
- terrorist threats relating to devices, materials or facilities (s. 11(1) and (2));
- trespassing etc. on nuclear sites (s. 12 which amends s. 128 of the Serious Organised Crime and Police Act 2005).

The offence under s. 9(1) is committed where a person intends using the device or material in the course of or in connection with the commission or preparation of an act of terrorism or for the purposes of terrorism, or making it available to be so used. The punishment for an offence under this section is imprisonment for life.

A person commits an offence under s. 10(1) if he/she uses a radioactive device or radioactive material in connection with an act of terrorism. For the offence under s. 10(2) the person must use or damage a nuclear facility in a manner which causes a release of radioactive material or creates or increases a risk that such material will be released. The punishment for both these offences is imprisonment for life.

In relation to s. 11(1), this offence deals with a demand for the supply of a radioactive device, radioactive material, a nuclear facility, or for access to such a facility, for him/herself or another, and supports such a demand with a threat that a reasonable person would assume that there is a real risk of the threat being carried out if the demand is not met. Section 11(2) deals with a threat to use radioactive material, a radioactive device, or use or damage a nuclear facility in a manner that releases radioactive material or creates or increases a risk of its release. The punishment for both these offences is imprisonment for life.

Where a person does anything outside the United Kingdom that would constitute an offence falling within ss. 1, 6 or 8 to 11 of the Act, he/she is deemed to be guilty of that offence. This includes conspiracy, incitement, attempt, aiding, abetting, counselling or procuring the commission of such offences. Proceedings for any such offence may be taken at any place in the United Kingdom irrespective of whether the person is a British citizen or, in the case of a company, a company incorporated in a part of the United Kingdom (s. 17). Proceedings for any of the offences may only be instituted in England and Wales with the consent of the DPP. However, where an offence has been committed outside the United Kingdom or for a purpose wholly or partly connected with the affairs of another country the DPP's consent may only be given with the permission of the Attorney-General (s. 19).

### 3.10.7 Terrorism Act 2000: Police Powers

The Terrorism Act 2000 provides the police with many wide-ranging powers which exist *in addition* to any more general powers that the police may have. They include powers of arrest, search of persons and vehicles, authorisations of stop and search in specified locations, and the power to set up cordons.

### 3.10.7.1 Arrest without Warrant

The Terrorism Act 2000, s. 41 states:

(1) A constable may arrest without a warrant a person whom he reasonably suspects to be a terrorist.

---

**KEYNOTE**

The definition of a terrorist is broadly a person who has committed one of the main terrorism offences under the Act (including ss. 11, 12, 15–18, 54 and 56–63), or is or has been concerned in the commission, preparation or instigation of acts of terrorism (s. 40).

A magistrate's warrant may be obtained authorising any constable to enter and search the specified premises for the purpose of arresting the person to whom s. 41 applies (s. 42).

---

### 3.10.7.2 Search of Persons

The Terrorism Act 2000, s. 43 states:

(1) A constable may stop and search a person whom he reasonably suspects to be a terrorist to discover whether he has in his possession anything which may constitute evidence that he is a terrorist.

(2) A constable may search a person arrested under section 41 to discover whether he has in his possession anything which may constitute evidence that he is a terrorist.

(3) ...

(4) A constable may seize and retain anything which he discovers in the course of a search of a person under subsection (1) or (2) and which he reasonably suspects may constitute evidence that the person is a terrorist.

(4A) Subsection (4B) applies if a constable, in exercising the power under subsection (1) to stop a person whom the constable reasonably suspects to be a terrorist, stops a vehicle (see section 116(2)).

---

**KEYNOTE**

Where a vehicle is stopped the constable may search the vehicle, and anything in or on it, to discover whether there is anything which may constitute evidence that the person concerned is a terrorist, and may seize and retain anything which the constable discovers in the course of such a search, and reasonably suspects may constitute evidence that the person is a terrorist (s. 43(4B)). Nothing in s. 43(4B) confers a power to search any person but the power to search in that subsection is in addition to the power in subsection (1) to search a person whom the constable reasonably suspects to be a terrorist (s. 43(4C)).

In relation to s. 43(4A), s. 116(2) provides that the power to stop a person includes the power to stop a vehicle (other than an aircraft which is airborne).

---

### 3.10.7.3 Search of Vehicles

The Terrorism Act 2000, s. 43A states:

(1) Subsection (2) applies if a constable reasonably suspects that a vehicle is being used for the purposes of terrorism.

(2) The constable may stop and search—

(a) the vehicle;

(b) the driver of the vehicle;

(c) a passenger in the vehicle;

(d) anything in or on the vehicle or carried by the driver or a passenger;

to discover whether there is anything which may constitute evidence that the vehicle is being used for the purposes of terrorism.

### 3.10.7.4    Stop and Search in Specified Locations

The Terrorism Act 2000, s. 47A states:

(1) A senior police officer may give an authorisation under subsection (2) or (3) in relation to a specified area or place if the officer—
   (a) reasonably suspects that an act of terrorism will take place; and
   (b) reasonably considers that—
      (i) the authorisation is necessary to prevent such an act;
      (ii) the specified area or place is no greater than is necessary to prevent such an act; and
      (iii) the duration of the authorisation is no longer than is necessary to prevent such an act.
(2) An authorisation under this subsection authorises any constable in uniform to stop a vehicle in the specified area or place and to search—
   (a) the vehicle;
   (b) the driver of the vehicle;
   (c) a passenger in the vehicle;
   (d) anything in or on the vehicle or carried by the driver or a passenger.
(3) An authorisation under this subsection authorises any constable in uniform to stop a pedestrian in the specified area or place and to search—
   (a) the pedestrian;
   (b) anything carried by the pedestrian.

### 3.10.7.5    Cordoned Areas

The Terrorism Act 2000, s. 33 states:

(1) An area is a cordoned area for the purposes of this Act if it is designated under this section.
(2) A designation may be made only if the person making it considers it expedient for the purposes of a terrorist investigation.
(3) If a designation is made orally, the person making it shall confirm it in writing as soon as is reasonably practicable.

### 3.10.7.6    Power to Designate

The Terrorism Act 2000, s. 34 states:

  (1)  Subject to subsections (1A), (1B) and (2), a designation under section 33 may only be made—
      (a) where the area is outside Northern Ireland and is wholly or partly within a police area, by an officer for the police area who is of at least the rank of superintendent, and
      (b) ...
  (1A) ...
  (1B) ...
  (1C) ...
  (2)  A constable who is not of the rank required by subsection (1) may make a designation if he considers it necessary by reason of urgency.
  (3)  Where a constable makes a designation in reliance on subsection (2) he shall as soon as is reasonably practicable—
      (a) make a written record of the time at which the designation was made, and
      (b) ensure that a police officer of at least the rank of superintendent is informed.
  (4)  An officer who is informed of a designation in accordance with subsection (3)(b)—
      (a) shall confirm the designation or cancel it with effect from such time as he may direct, and
      (b) shall, if he cancels the designation, make a written record of the cancellation and the reason for it.

### 3.10.7.7    Cordons and Police Powers

The Terrorism Act 2000, s. 36 states:

  (1) A constable in uniform may—
      (a) order a person in a cordoned area to leave it immediately,
      (b) order a person immediately to leave premises which are wholly or partly in or adjacent to a cordoned area,

(c) order the driver or person in charge of a vehicle in a cordoned area to move it from the area immediately,

(d) arrange for the removal of a vehicle from a cordoned area,

(e) arrange for the movement of a vehicle within a cordoned area,

(f) prohibit or restrict access to a cordoned area by pedestrians or vehicles.

---

**KEYNOTE**

The officer giving the order or making the arrangements and prohibitions set out here must be in uniform. Therefore detectives or other plain clothes officers involved in the terrorist investigation will not have these powers available to them.

The powers under s. 36 are among those that can be conferred on a Police Community Support Officer designated under sch. 4 to the Police Reform Act 2002.

Failing to comply with an order, prohibition or restriction under this section is a summary offence punishable by three months' imprisonment and/or a fine (s. 36(2) and (4)).

This wording will presumably cover refusal. There is a defence if the person can show that he/she had a reasonable excuse for the failure.

A superintendent or above may request passenger, service and crew information from an owner or agent of a ship or aircraft which is arriving, or expected to arrive, at any place in the United Kingdom or is leaving, or expected to leave, from any place in the United Kingdom (Immigration, Asylum and Nationality Act 2006, s. 32(2)). There is a similar power to request freight information from the owners or agents of a ship or aircraft, and in the case of a vehicle, the owner or hirer (s. 33(2) and (3)).

It is an offence if without reasonable excuse a person fails to comply with a requirement imposed under ss. 32(2) or 33(2). The request must be for a police purpose, i.e. the prevention, detection, investigation or prosecution of criminal offences; safeguarding national security; and such other purposes as may be specified (s. 33(5)).

---

## 3.10.8 Terrorism Prevention and Investigation Measures

Terrorism Prevention and Investigation Measures (TPIM), created by the Terrorism Prevention and Investigation Measures Act 2011, are a civil preventative measure intended to protect the public from the risk posed by suspected terrorists who can be neither prosecuted nor, in the case of foreign nationals, deported, by imposing restrictions intended to prevent or disrupt their engagement in terrorism-related activity.

The Secretary of State may impose requirements, restrictions and other provision which may be made in relation to an individual by serving a Terrorism Prevention and Investigation Measures notice on him/her if certain conditions are met (s. 2(1)).

The five conditions required to be met are provided by s. 3 of the Act which states:

(1) Condition A is that the Secretary of State reasonably believes that the individual is, or has been, involved in terrorism-related activity (the 'relevant activity').

(2) Condition B is that some or all of the relevant activity is new terrorism-related activity.

(3) Condition C is that the Secretary of State reasonably considers that it is necessary, for purposes connected with protecting members of the public from a risk of terrorism, for terrorism prevention and investigation measures to be imposed on the individual.

(4) Condition D is that the Secretary of State reasonably considers that it is necessary, for purposes connected with preventing or restricting the individual's involvement in terrorism-related activity, for the specified terrorism prevention and investigation measures to be imposed on the individual.

(5) Condition E is that—

(a) the court gives the Secretary of State permission under section 6, or

(b) the Secretary of State reasonably considers that the urgency of the case requires terrorism prevention and investigation measures to be imposed without obtaining such permission.

For the purposes of Condition A, involvement in 'terrorism-related activity' is any one or more of the following:

(a) the commission, preparation or instigation of acts of terrorism;

(b) conduct which facilitates the commission, preparation or instigation of such acts, or which is intended to do so;

(c) conduct which gives encouragement to the commission, preparation or instigation of such acts, or which is intended to do so;

(d) conduct which gives support or assistance to individuals who are known or believed by the individual concerned to be involved in conduct falling within paragraphs (a) to (c).

It is immaterial whether the acts of terrorism in question are specific acts of terrorism or acts of terrorism in general (s. 4(1)).

In relation to Condition B, s. 3(6) provides that a 'new terrorism-related activity' means:

• if no TPIM notice relating to the individual has ever been in force, terrorism-related activity occurring at any time (whether before or after the coming into force of this Act);

• if only one TPIM notice relating to the individual has ever been in force, terrorism-related activity occurring after that notice came into force; or

• if two or more TPIM notices relating to the individual have been in force, terrorism-related activity occurring after such a notice came into force most recently.

The measures that may be imposed are set out in Sch. 1 to the Act and have a time limit of two years. They may include a requirement for an individual to stay overnight at a specified address, to report daily to a police station, exclusion from specific places or areas, prevention of contact with particular individuals, and prohibition of travelling overseas.

### 3.10.8.1 Contravening a Terrorism Prevention and Investigation Measure

OFFENCE: **Contravening a Terrorism Prevention and Investigation Measure—**
***Terrorism Prevention and Investigation Measures Act 2011, s. 23***
   • Triable either way • Five years
   • Six months' imprisonment and/or a fine summarily

The Terrorism Prevention and Investigation Measures Act 2011, s. 23 states:

(1) An individual is guilty of an offence if—
   (a) a TPIM notice is in force in relation to the individual, and
   (b) the individual contravenes, without reasonable excuse, any measure specified in the TPIM notice.

If the individual has the permission of the Secretary of State by virtue of Sch. 1 for an act which would, without that permission, contravene such a measure, the individual contravenes that measure by virtue of that act if the act is not in accordance with the terms of the permission (s. 23(2)).

### 3.10.8.2 Terrorism Prevention and Investigation Measures: Police Powers

The Terrorism Prevention and Investigation Measures Act 2011, Sch. 5 states:

1 This Schedule confers powers of entry, search, seizure and retention on constables in connection with the imposition of measures on individuals.

2 A power conferred on a constable by virtue of this Schedule—

(a) is additional to powers which the constable has at common law or by virtue of any other enactment, and

(b) is not to be taken as affecting those powers.

3 A constable may detain an individual for the purpose of carrying out a search of that individual under a power conferred by virtue of this Schedule.

4 A constable may use reasonable force, if necessary, for the purpose of exercising a power conferred on the constable by virtue of this Schedule.

---

**KEYNOTE**

Broadly, the powers of entry, search, seizure and retention include:

Without a warrant

- entry and search of premises to locate an individual to serve a TPIM notice (or other specified notices) on that individual;
- search of an individual or premises at the time of serving a TPIM notice for the purpose of discovering anything that might breach any measure specified in the TPIM notice;
- search of premises on suspicion that an individual subject to a TPIM notice has absconded;
- search of an individual subject to a TPIM notice for public safety purposes.

With a warrant

- search of an individual or premises for purposes of determining whether the individual is complying with the measure specified in the TPIM notice.

Anything that is seized under a power conferred by virtue of this Schedule may be subjected to tests and retained for as long as is necessary in all the circumstances. In particular if a constable has reasonable grounds for believing that the thing is or contains evidence in relation to an offence, it may be retained for use as evidence at a trial for an offence, or for forensic examination or for investigation in connection with an offence; and if a constable has reasonable grounds for believing that the thing has been obtained in consequence of the commission of an offence, it may be retained in order to establish its lawful owner (Sch. 5, para. 11).

---

### 3.10.9 Offences Involving Explosive Substance

OFFENCE: **Causing Explosion Likely to Endanger Life or Property—*Explosive Substances Act 1883, s. 2***

  • Triable on indictment  • Life imprisonment

The Explosive Substances Act 1883, s. 2 states:

(1) A person who in the United Kingdom or (being a citizen of the United Kingdom and Colonies) in the Republic of Ireland unlawfully and maliciously causes by any explosive substance an explosion of a nature likely to endanger life or to cause serious injury to property shall, whether any injury to person or property has been actually caused or not, be guilty of an offence.

---

**KEYNOTE**

The consent of the Attorney-General (or Solicitor-General) is required before prosecuting this offence (s. 7(1) of the 1883 Act).

'Explosive substance' includes any materials for making any explosive substance; any implement or apparatus used, or intended or adapted to be used for causing or aiding any explosion (s. 9(1)).

The definition of 'explosive' under the Explosives Act 1875 also applies to this offence (see *R v Wheatley* [1979] 1 WLR 144). Therefore fireworks and petrol bombs will be covered (*R v Bouch* [1983] QB 246).

Articles which have been held to amount to 'explosive substances' include:

- shotguns (*R* v *Downey* [1971] NI 224);
- electronic timers (*R* v *Berry (No. 3)* [1995] 1 WLR 7 and *R* v *G* [2009] UKHL 13);
- gelignite with a fuse and detonator (*R* v *McCarthy* [1964] 1 WLR 196).

You must prove that the act was carried out 'maliciously'.

Sections 73 to 75 of the Explosives Act 1875 provide powers to search for explosives in connection with the above offence and offences under ss. 3 and 4 below.

OFFENCE: **Attempting to Cause Explosion or Keeping Explosive with Intent—** *Explosive Substances Act 1883, s. 3*

- Triable on indictment  - Life imprisonment

The Explosive Substances Act 1883, s. 3 states:

(1) A person who in the United Kingdom or a dependency or (being a citizen of the United Kingdom and Colonies) elsewhere unlawfully and maliciously—

    (a) does any act with intent to cause, or conspires to cause, by an explosive substance an explosion of a nature likely to endanger life, or cause serious injury to property, whether in the United Kingdom or elsewhere, or

    (b) makes or has in his possession or under his control an explosive substance with intent by means thereof to endanger life, or cause serious injury to property, whether in the United Kingdom or elsewhere, or to enable any other person so to do

shall, whether any explosion does or does not take place, and whether any injury to person or property is actually caused or not, be guilty of an offence...

OFFENCE: **Making or Possessing Explosive under Suspicious Circumstances—** *Explosive Substances Act 1883, s. 4*

- Triable on indictment  - 14 years' imprisonment

The Explosive Substances Act 1883, s. 4 states:

(1) Any person who makes or knowingly has in his possession or under his control any explosive substance under such circumstances as to give rise to a reasonable suspicion that he is not making it or does not have it in his possession or under his control for a lawful object, shall, unless he can show that he made it or had it in his possession or under his control for a lawful object, be guilty of felony...

**KEYNOTE**

The offence under s. 3 is one of specific intent.

Both of the above offences require the consent of the Attorney-General (or Solicitor-General) before a prosecution can be brought.

It would seem that the wording of these offences requires the prosecution—in cases of 'possession'—to prove that a defendant *had* the relevant article in his/her possession and that he/she *knew* the nature of it (see *R* v *Hallam* [1957] 1 QB 569). This should be contrasted with the usual approach to offences involving 'possession' where the second part (knowledge of the 'quality' of an item) does not need to be shown. However, the concept of 'in your possession' or 'under your control' is a wide one, as illustrated in a case where the defendant had moved out of his property and left homemade bombs and other articles in some boxes with a friend. New tenants in the property had discovered the boxes which later turned up on a rubbish tip. The defendant went to the police station after learning that he was a suspect and he claimed that he had collected the articles many years previously when he was too young to appreciate how dangerous they were. Although he had left the boxes with his friend he was nevertheless convicted of the above offence as he still had the explosives under his control when he left the property (*R* v *Campbell* [2004] EWCA Crim 2309).

'Reasonable suspicion' in this case will be assessed *objectively*, that is, you must prove that the circumstances of the possession or making of the explosive substance would give rise to suspicion in a reasonable and objective bystander (*R* v *Fegan* (1971) 78 Cr App R 189 and *R* v *G* [2009] UKHL 13).

Whether a person's purpose in having the items prohibited by these offences is a 'lawful object' will need to be determined in each case (*Fegan*). In *R* v *Riding* [2009] EWCA Crim 892, the defendant alleged he had made a pipe bomb out of mere curiosity, using explosives drained from a number of fireworks. The defence contended that 'lawful object' meant the absence of a criminal purpose rather than a positive object that was lawful. However, the court was satisfied it meant the latter and mere curiosity could not be a 'lawful object' in making a lethal pipe bomb.

There is no need to show any criminal intent or an unlawful purpose on the part of the defendant (see *Campbell*, above).

## 3.10.10 Offences Relating to Gunpowder

The Offences Against the Person Act 1981 creates further offences in relation to gunpowder:

- causing bodily injury by gunpowder or other explosive substance (s. 28);
- causing gunpowder or other explosive substance to explode, sending an explosive substance or throwing corrosive fluid with intent (s. 29);
- placing gunpowder or other explosive substance near a building etc. with intent to do bodily injury to any person (s. 30);
- making or having gunpowder, explosive substance, or any dangerous or noxious thing etc. with intent to enable any person to commit a felony (s. 64).

All offences are triable on indictment only. Section 28 and 29 offences have a maximum penalty of imprisonment for life; s. 30 offences imprisonment for up to 14 years; and s. 64 offences imprisonment for up to two years.

## 3.10.11 Animal Experiments and Vivisection

The activities of anti-vivisection campaigners and others opposed to the 'commercial exploitation' of animals can be significant and serious in policing terms. These activities have led to specific changes in legislation and also significant policing operations to protect individuals who work with animals in certain circumstances. Some activities that are seen as necessary within our society—such as formal animal experiments—rely on secrecy in order to avoid disruption and the intimidation of staff. For this reason the Animals (Scientific Procedures) Act 1986—under which animal experiments are licensed—creates an offence of improperly disclosing information to others (s. 24).

The Serious Organised Crime and Police Act 2005 provides two offences in relation to animal research organisations as outlined below.

### 3.10.11.1 Interference with Contractual Relationship so as to Harm Animal Research Organisation

OFFENCE: **Interference with Contractual Relationships so as to Harm Animal Research Organisation—*Serious Organised Crime and Police Act 2005, s. 145(1)***
- Triable either way • Five years' imprisonment and/or a fine on indictment
- 12 months' imprisonment and/or a fine summarily

The Serious Organised Crime and Police Act 2005, s. 145 states:

(1) A person (A) commits an offence if, with the intention of harming an animal research organisation, he—
  (a) does a relevant act, or
  (b) threatens that he or somebody else will do a relevant act, in circumstances in which that act or threat is intended or likely to cause a second person (B) to take any of the steps in subsection (2).

(2) The steps are—
  (a) not to perform any contractual obligation owed by B to a third person (C) (whether or not such non-performance amounts to a breach of contract);
  (b) to terminate any contract B has with C;
  (c) not to enter into a contract with C.

(3) For the purposes of this section, a 'relevant act' is—
  (a) an act amounting to a criminal offence, or
  (b) a tortious act causing B to suffer loss or damage of any description;
  but paragraph (b) does not include an act which is actionable on the ground only that it induces another person to break a contract with B.

---

**KEYNOTE**

To commit this offence the defendant needs to do a relevant act—this means a criminal offence or a tortious act causing loss or damage—or to threaten that he/she or another will commit a crime or such a tortious act. A tortious act is an act that is a civil wrong but is not a criminal offence. It then needs to be shown that the conduct of the defendant was likely or intended to cause the person against whom the crime/tortious act is committed (or threatened) to fail to perform a contractual obligation, to terminate a contract or to decide not to enter into a contract.

The intent to harm an animal research organisation needs to be proved. 'Animal research organisation' has two specific meanings for the purposes of ss. 145 and 146:

- A person or organisation who is the owner, lessee or licensee of premises constituting or including:
  ◆ a place specified in a licence granted under ss. 4 or 5 of the Animals (Scientific Procedures) Act 1986,
  ◆ a scientific procedure establishment designated under s. 6 of that Act, or
  ◆ a breeding or supplying establishment designated under s. 7 of that Act (s. 148(2)).
- A person or organisation employed or engaged under a contract for services, as:
  ◆ the holder of a personal or project licence granted under the 1986 Act,
  ◆ a person specified under ss. 6(5) or 7(5) of that Act

(s. 148(3)).

'Harming' an animal research organisation means to cause such an organisation loss or damage of any description, or to prevent or hinder such an organisation from carrying on any of its activities (s. 145(5)).

By virtue of s. 145(3)(b), no offence is committed if the only relevant tortious act is an inducement to break a contract. This means that no offence is committed by people peacefully arguing, or representing, that one person should cease doing business with another on the basis of the other's involvement with an animal research organisation.

Generally this section does not apply to any act done wholly or mainly in contemplation or furtherance of a trade dispute (s. 145(6)). However, there are some changes to the definition of such a dispute that need to be taken into account (see s. 145(7)).

No proceedings for an offence under either of those sections may be instituted except by or with the consent of the DPP.

Further guidance on the implementation of this section can be found in Home Office Circular 34/2005.

### 3.10.11.2  Intimidation of Persons Connected with Animal Research Organisation

OFFENCE:  **Intimidation of Persons Connected with Animal Research Organisation—*Serious Organised Crime and Police Act 2005, s. 146(1)***
- Triable either way • Five years' imprisonment and/or a fine on indictment
- 12 months' imprisonment and/or a fine summarily

The Serious Organised Crime and Police Act 2005, s. 146 states:

(1) A person (A) commits an offence if, with the intention of causing a second person (B) to abstain from doing something which B is entitled to do (or to do something which B is entitled to abstain from doing)—

    (a) A threatens B that A or somebody else will do a relevant act, and

    (b) A does so wholly or mainly because B is a person falling within subsection (2).

---

**KEYNOTE**

Subsection (2) is a lengthy and very comprehensive list. In summary, a person falls within this subsection if he/she is:

- an employee or officer of an animal research organisation;
- a student at an educational establishment that is an animal research organisation;
- a lessor or licensor of any premises occupied by an animal research organisation;
- a person with a financial interest in, or who provides financial assistance to, an animal research organisation;
- a customer or supplier of an animal research organisation. (s. 146(2)).

A person who is contemplating becoming someone within the categories covered by the third, fourth and fifth bullet points is covered, as is a person who is (or is contemplating becoming) a customer or supplier of such people/organisations.

Employees and employers of someone within the above descriptions are covered, as are people with a financial interest in, or providing financial assistance to the above.

Subsection (2) also extends to spouses, civil partners, friends or relatives, or people known personally to someone within any of the above descriptions.

As with the offence under s. 145, this section does not generally apply to any act done wholly or mainly in contemplation or furtherance of a trade dispute and no proceedings for an offence under either of those sections may be instituted except by or with the consent of the DPP.

Further guidance on the implementation of this section can be found in Home Office Circular 34/2005.

---

# 3.11 Cybercrime

## 3.11.1 Introduction

Cybercrime is defined as the use of any computer network for criminal activity. Given the extent to which computers are a part of everyday life for millions of people in the workplace and/or in the home, it becomes clear that the impact of criminal activity via a computer network has huge implications for the government, businesses and for the individual and therefore it is essential that police officers have an understanding of the law that relates to this area of criminality.

There is no single piece of legislation that deals with cybercrime; rather there is the legislation dealing with the end result of the use of a computer network for criminal activity e.g. the Fraud Act 2006 and then a variety of legislation dealing with computer misuse (particularly 'hacking'), data protection and malicious communications (activities dealt with by the Computer Misuse Act 1990, the Data Protection Act 1998 and the Malicious Communications Act 1998).

It is worthwhile noting that s. 20 of the Police and Criminal Evidence Act 1984 specifically deals with powers of seizure in respect of information stored in electronic form.

## 3.11.2 Offences under the Computer Misuse Act 1990

The Computer Misuse Act 1990 was enacted to address the growth in the use of computers and the inadequacy of the existing legislation in dealing with offences involving computers, such as 'hacking'.

The Police and Justice Act 2006 amended the 1990 Act to ensure the United Kingdom's compliance with the European Union Framework Decision on Attacks Against Information Systems. This compliance requires that penalties relating to 'hacking' into computer systems, unauthorised access to computer material, and the intentional serious hindering of a computer system, reflect the seriousness of the criminal activities that can be involved in committing these offences.

### 3.11.2.1 Unauthorised Access to Computer Materials

OFFENCE: **Unauthorised Access to Computer Material ('Hacking')—*Computer Misuse Act 1990, s. 1***
  • Triable either way  • Two years' imprisonment and/or a fine on indictment
  • Six months' imprisonment and/or a fine summarily

The Computer Misuse Act 1990, s. 1 states:

(1) A person is guilty of an offence if—
  (a) he causes a computer to perform any function with intent to secure access to any program or data held in any computer;
  (b) the access he intends to secure is unauthorised; and
  (c) he knows at the time when he causes the computer to perform the function that that is the case.

(2) The intent a person has to have to commit an offence under this section need not be directed at—

    (a) any particular program or data;

    (b) a program or data of any particular kind; or

    (c) a program or data held in any particular computer.

---

**KEYNOTE**

This offence involves 'causing a computer to perform any function', which means more than simply looking at material on a screen or having any physical contact with computer hardware. In the latter case an offence of criminal damage may be appropriate. Any attempt to log on would involve getting the computer to perform a function (even if the function is to deny you access!). 'Computer' is not defined and therefore must be given its ordinary meaning. Given the multiple functions of many electronic devices such as mobile phones, this could arguably bring them within the ambit of the Act.

Any access must be 'unauthorised'. If the defendant is authorised to *access* a computer, albeit for restricted purposes, then it was originally held that he/she did not commit this offence if he/she then *used* any information for some other unauthorised purpose (e.g. police officers using data from the Police National Computer (PNC) for private gain (*DPP* v *Bignell* [1998] 1 Cr App R 1)). However, this case was overruled by the House of Lords where an employee of American Express accessed accounts that fell outside her normal scope of work and passed on the information to credit card forgers. Their lordships held that, although she was authorised to access certain data generally, she was not authorised to access the specific data involved—*R* v *Bow Street Metropolitan Stipendiary Magistrate, ex parte Government of the USA* [2000] 2 AC 216. This case still illustrates that the purpose of the Act is to address unauthorised access as opposed to unauthorised use of data and behaviour such as looking over a computer operator's shoulder to read what is on the screen would not be covered.

In order to prove the offence under s. 1 you must show that the defendant intended to secure access to the program or data. This is therefore an offence of 'specific intent' and lesser forms of *mens rea* such as recklessness will not do.

You must also show that the defendant knew the access was unauthorised.

The Privacy and Electronic Communications (EC Directive) Regulations 2003 (SI 2003/2426) regulate the use of cookies and internet tracking devices, along with the use of unsolicited email and text messages. Guidance in their extent and practical effect is prepared by the Office of the Information Commissioner.

The powers of entry, search and seizure under the Police and Criminal Evidence Act 1984 apply to this offence.

---

## 3.11.2.2    Definition of Terms

The 1990 Act defines a number of its terms at s. 17 which states:

(2) A person secures access to any program or data held in a computer if by causing a computer to perform any function he—

    (a) alters or erases the program or data;

    (b) copies or moves it to any storage medium other than that in which it is held or to a different location in the storage medium in which it is held;

    (c) uses it; or

    (d) has it output from the computer in which it is held (whether by having it displayed or in any other manner);

    and references to access to a program or data (and to an intent to secure such access or to enable such access to be secured) shall be read accordingly.

(3) For the purposes of subsection (2)(c) above a person uses a program if the function he causes the computer to perform—

    (a) causes the program to be executed; or

    (b) is itself a function of the program.

(4) For the purposes of subsection (2)(d) above—

    (a) a program is output if the instructions of which it consists are output; and

    (b) the form in which any such instructions or any other data is output (and in particular whether or not it represents a form in which, in the case of instructions, they are capable of being executed or, in the case of data, it is capable of being processed by a computer) is immaterial.

(5) Access of any kind by any person to any program or data held in a computer is unauthorised if—

(a) he is not himself entitled to control access of the kind in question to the program or data; and

(b) he does not have consent to access by him of the kind in question to the program or data from any person who is so entitled,

but this subsection is subject to section 10.

(6) References to any program or data held in a computer include references to any program or data held in any removable storage medium which is for the time being in the computer; and a computer is to be regarded as containing any program or data held in any such medium.

...

(8) An act done in relation to a computer is unauthorised if the person doing the act (or causing it to be done)—

(a) is not himself a person who has responsibility for the computer and is entitled to determine whether the act may be done; and

(b) does not have consent to the act from any such person.

In this subsection 'act' includes a series of acts.

---

**KEYNOTE**

Securing access will therefore include:

- altering or erasing a program or data;
- copying or moving a program or data to a new storage medium;
- using data or having it displayed or 'output' in any form from the computer in which it is held.

Under s. 17(5) access is 'unauthorised' if the person is neither entitled to control that type of access to a program or data, nor does he/she have the consent of any person who is so entitled. The provision under s. 17(5)(a) was the basis for the decision in *Bow Street* above. This definition does not affect the powers available to any 'enforcement officers', i.e. police officers or other people charged with a duty of investigating offences (s. 10).

---

### 3.11.2.3 Unauthorised Access to Computers with Intent

OFFENCE: **Unauthorised Access with Intent to Commit Further Offences— *Computer Misuse Act 1990, s. 2***

- Triable either way • Five years' imprisonment and/or a fine on indictment
- Six months' imprisonment and/or a fine summarily

The Computer Misuse Act 1990, s. 2 states:

(1) A person is guilty of an offence under this section if he commits an offence under section 1 above ('the unauthorised access offence') with intent—

(a) to commit an offence to which this section applies; or

(b) to facilitate the commission of such an offence (whether by himself or by any other person); and the offence he intends to commit or facilitate is referred to below in this section as the further offence.

(2) This section applies to offences—

(a) for which the sentence is fixed by law; or

(b) for which a person of twenty-one years of age or over (not previously convicted) may be sentenced to imprisonment for a term of five years (or, in England and Wales, might be so sentenced but for the restrictions imposed by section 33 of the Magistrates' Courts Act 1980).

(3) It is immaterial for the purposes of this section whether the further offence is to be committed on the same occasion as the unauthorised access offence or on any future occasion.

(4) A person may be guilty of an offence under this section even though the facts are such that the commission of the further offence is impossible.

### 3.11.2.4 Unauthorised Acts with Intent to Impair Operation of Computer, etc.

OFFENCE: **Unauthorised Acts with Intent to Impair, or with Recklessness as to Impairing, Operation of Computer, etc.—*Computer Misuse Act 1990, s. 3***

- Triable either way • Ten years' imprisonment and/or a fine on indictment
- 12 months' imprisonment and/or a fine summarily

The Computer Misuse Act 1990, s. 3 states:

(1) A person is guilty of an offence if—
  (a) he does any unauthorised act in relation to a computer;
  (b) at the time when he does the act he knows that it is unauthorised; and
  (c) either subsection (2) or subsection (3) below applies.
(2) This subsection applies if the person intends by doing the act—
  (a) to impair the operation of any computer;
  (b) to prevent or hinder access to any program or data held in any computer; or
  (c) to impair the operation of any such program or the reliability of any such data.
(3) This subsection applies if the person is reckless as to whether the act will do any of the things mentioned in paragraphs (a) to (c) of subsection (2) above.

### 3.11.2.5 Making, Supplying or Obtaining Articles for Use in Offences under sections 1 or 3

OFFENCE: **Making, Supplying or Obtaining Articles for Use in Offences under sections 1 or 3—*Computer Misuse Act 1990, s. 3A***

- Triable either way • Two years' imprisonment and/or a fine on indictment
- 12 months' imprisonment and/or a fine summarily

The Computer Misuse Act 1990, s. 3A states:

(1) A person is guilty of an offence if he makes, adapts, supplies or offers to supply any article intending it to be used to commit, or to assist in the commission of, an offence under section 1 or 3.
(2) A person is guilty of an offence if he supplies or offers to supply any article believing that it is likely to be used to commit, or to assist in the commission of, an offence under section 1 or 3.
(3) A person is guilty of an offence if he obtains any article with a view to its being supplied for use to commit, or to assist in the commission of, an offence under section 1 or 3.
(4) In this section 'article' includes any program or data held in electronic form.

---

**KEYNOTE**

This section creates three offences designed to combat the growing market in electronic tools, such as 'hacker tools' which can be used for hacking into computer systems, and the increase in the use of such tools in connection with organised crime. These offences comply with Article 6(1)(a) of the 2001 Council of Europe Cybercrime Convention requiring the criminalisation of the distribution or making available of a device, program or computer password or similar data by which a computer system is capable of being accessed with the intention to commit an offence.

---

## 3.11.3  The Data Protection Act 1998

The Data Protection Act 1998 brought UK law into line with the European Union Data Protection Directive 95/46/EC that requires Member States to protect people's fundamental rights and freedoms and in particular their right to privacy with respect to the processing of personal data.

The 1998 Act is intended to strike a balance between the rights of individuals to privacy and the ability of organisations to use data for the purposes of their business. It introduced basic rules of registration for users of data and rights of access to that data for the individuals to which it related.

Data protection law applies whenever a data controller processes personal data. A data controller is the person who determines the purposes for which, and the manner in which, any personal data is, or is likely to be, processed (s. 1(1)). A typical example of a data controller is an employer. The data controller must register with the Information Commissioner who has overall responsibility to ensure that personal data is protected in observance with the Act.

The Information Commissioner provides guidance and information, resolves complaints, and prosecutes those who commit offences under the Act. The DPP may also prosecute offences or give consent to such prosecutions.

### 3.11.3.1  Personal Data

The Data Protection Act 1998, s. 1 states:

(1) In this Act, unless the context otherwise requires— 'data' means information which—
(a) is being processed by means of equipment operating automatically in response to instructions given for that purpose,
(b) is recorded with the intention that it should be processed by means of such equipment,
(c) is recorded as part of a relevant filing system or with the intention that it should form part of a relevant filing system, or
(d) does not fall within paragraph (a), (b) or (c) but forms part of an accessible record as defined by section 68, or
(e) is recorded information held by a public authority and does not fall within any of paragraphs (a) to (d).

The 1998 Act seeks to protect 'personal data', that is,

> data which relate to a living individual who can be identified, (a) from those data, or (b) from those data and other information which is in the possession of, or is likely to come into the possession of, the data controller, and includes any expression of opinion about the individual and any indication of the intentions of the data controller or any other person in respect of the individual (s. 1(1)).

---

**KEYNOTE**

In *Johnson* v *Medical Defence Union Ltd (No. 2)* [2007] EWCA Civ 262 it was held that the compilation of information from various manual and electronic files in a computer-related document is not necessarily the creation of data capable of being processed under s. 1(1).

The individual must be capable of being identified from the data that the data controller has or is likely to get. This does not mean that the person's name and/or address must be known. If it is possible to distinguish the individual from other people (e.g. by email addresses which contain the person's name or from CCTV film of that person) then it may be that the above test is satisfied.

Data controllers must give data subjects the right of access to their personal data. An individual may request access to all personal data of which he/she is the subject and which is being processed by the data controller. There are exemptions from these access rules in certain limited circumstances.

'Personal data' means data which relates to a living individual who can be identified from those data, or from those data and other information which are in the possession of, or are likely to come into the possession of, the data controller. It includes any expression of opinion about the individual and any indication of the intentions of the data controller or any other person in respect of the individual.

The definition of personal data would apply to data held on police computers about suspected and convicted offenders and may well apply to other similar paper records. Personal data held on the PNC clearly falls within this category (see *R* v *Rees* [2000] LTL 20 October).

---

### 3.11.3.2  Sensitive Personal Data

The 1998 Act makes special provision in relation to 'sensitive personal data' which it defines (at s. 2) as:

> personal data consisting of information as to—
> (a) the racial or ethnic origin of the data subject,
> (b) his political opinions,
> (c) his religious beliefs or other beliefs of a similar nature,
> (d) whether he is a member of a trade union (within the meaning of the Trade Union and Labour Relations (Consolidation) Act 1992),
> (e) his physical or mental health or condition,
> (f) his sexual life,
> (g) the commission or alleged commission by him of any offence, or
> (h) any proceedings for any offence committed or alleged to have been committed by him, the disposal of such proceedings or the sentence of any court in such proceedings.

---

**KEYNOTE**

Data controllers are not permitted to process sensitive data about an individual unless: the processing is in connection with current or prospective legal proceedings or consultations; or is in the substantial public interest; or the explicit, informed and freely given consent of the individual has been obtained. This consent of the individual must be in writing, he/she must be informed of what information is to be processed, and no detriment must be suffered by an individual refusing to give consent.

---

### 3.11.3.3　Data Protection Principles

A crucial element in the 1998 Act is the data protection principles set out at sch. 1. As well as introducing the principles, s. 4(4) makes it clear that it is the duty of the relevant 'data controller' to comply with those principles wherever they apply. Part I of sch. 1 sets out the principles as being:

1. Personal data shall be processed fairly and lawfully and, in particular, shall not be processed unless—
   (a) at least one of the conditions in Schedule 2 is met, and
   (b) in the case of sensitive personal data, at least one of the conditions in Schedule 3 is also met.
2. Personal data shall be obtained only for one or more specified and lawful purposes, and shall not be further processed in any manner incompatible with that purpose or those purposes.
3. Personal data shall be adequate, relevant and not excessive in relation to the purpose or purposes for which they are processed.
4. Personal data shall be accurate and, where necessary, kept up to date.
5. Personal data processed for any purpose or purposes shall not be kept for longer than is necessary for that purpose or those purposes.
6. Personal data shall be processed in accordance with the rights of data subjects under this Act.
7. Appropriate technical and organisational measures shall be taken against unauthorised or unlawful processing of personal data and against accidental loss or destruction of, or damage to, personal data.
8. Personal data shall not be transferred to a country or territory outside the European Economic Area unless that country or territory ensures an adequate level of protection for the rights and freedoms of data subjects in relation to the processing of personal data.

---

**KEYNOTE**

Under the first data protection principle, a data controller must justify its processing of personal data under one of the following conditions:

- the data subject has given his/her consent to the processing;
- the processing is necessary for the performance of a contract or the entering into of a contract to which the data subject is a party;
- the processing is necessary for compliance with any legal obligation to which the data controller is subject;
- the processing is necessary in order to protect the vital interests of the data subject;
- the processing is necessary for the administration of justice; or
- the processing is necessary for the purposes of legitimate interests pursued by the data controller provided such processing does not harm the rights and freedoms or legitimate interests of data subjects.

The 1998 Act creates certain offences from the first data protection principle. Section 55 of the Act provides that a person must not knowingly or recklessly, without the consent of the data controller, obtain or disclose data or the information contained in personal data, or procure its disclosure to another person (s. 55(1)). However, this subsection does not apply where the obtaining, disclosing or procuring was necessary for the purpose of preventing or detecting crime (s. 55(2)(a)). In *R (On the Application of Catt) v ACPO* [2013] EWCA Civ 192, it was held that the personal information relating to the appellant held on the National Domestic Extremism Database was in breach of Article 8 of the European Convention on Human Rights (Right to respect for privacy and family life). For many years the appellant had been an ardent and frequent protestor against what he saw as a variety of forms of injustice. The appellant's entry on the database arose from his attendance at protests where he associated with those who have a propensity to violence and crime. However, he personally had never been the specific target of any observations and it was not suggested that he indulged in criminal activity or actively encouraged those that do.

Other exemptions from subs. (1) are contained within s. 55.

---

## 3.11.4 Malicious Communications

OFFENCE: **Malicious Communications—*Malicious Communications Act 1988, s. 1(1)***
  • Triable summarily • Six months' imprisonment and/or a fine

The Malicious Communications Act 1988, s. 1 states:

(1) Any person who sends to another person—
    (a) a letter, electronic communication or article of any description which conveys—
        (i) a message which is indecent or grossly offensive;
        (ii) a threat; or
        (iii) information which is false and known or believed to be false by the sender; or
    (b) any article or electronic communication which is, in whole or part, of an indecent or grossly offensive nature,
is guilty of an offence if his purpose, or one of his purposes, in sending it is that it should, so far as falling within paragraph (a) or (b) above, cause distress or anxiety to the recipient or to any other person to whom he intends that it or its contents or nature should be communicated.

---

**KEYNOTE**

The offence is not restricted to threatening or indecent communications and can include giving false information provided that *one* of the sender's purposes in so doing is to cause distress or anxiety. 'Purposes' is simply another way of saying 'intention'.

In addition to letters, the above offence also covers *any* article; it also covers electronic communications which include any oral or other communication by means of an electronic communications network. This will extend to communications in electronic form such as emails, text messages, pager messages etc. (see s. 1(2A)).

'Sending' will include transmitting.

The relevant distress or anxiety may be intended towards the recipient *or* any other person.

It is clear from s. 1(3) that the offence can be committed by using someone else to send, deliver or transmit a message. This would include occasions where a person falsely reports that someone has been a victim of a crime in order to cause anxiety or distress by the arrival of the police.

Section 1(1)(b) covers occasions where the article itself is indecent or grossly offensive (such as putting dog faeces through someone's letter box).

---

### 3.11.4.1 Defence Regarding Malicious Communications

Section 1 of the 1988 Act goes on to state:

(2) A person is not guilty of an offence by virtue of subsection (1)(a)(ii) above if he shows—
    (a) that the threat was used to reinforce a demand made by him on reasonable grounds; and
    (b) that he believed, and had reasonable grounds for believing, that the use of the threat was a proper means of reinforcing the demand.

---

**KEYNOTE**

The wording of the statutory defence has been changed (by the Criminal Justice and Police Act 2001) to make the relevant test objective. It will no longer be enough that the person claiming the defence under s. 1(2) believed that he/she had reasonable grounds; the defendant will have to show:

• that there were in fact reasonable grounds for making the demand;
• that he/she believed that the accompanying threat was a proper means of enforcing the demand; and
• that reasonable grounds existed for that belief.

---

Given the decisions of the courts in similarly worded defences under the Theft Act 1968 (e.g. blackmail; **see chapter 2.5**), it is unlikely that any demand could be reasonable where agreement to it would amount to a crime.

The defence is intended to cover financial institutions and other commercial concerns who often need to send forceful letters to customers. However, for the offence of unlawfully harassing debtors, see s. 40 of the Administration of Justice Act 1970.

### 3.11.5 Mutual Legal Assistance Treaties (MLATs)

Cybercrime, like the internet itself, is not limited by national boundaries. An investigation that begins in one country may quickly lead elsewhere, but without the co-operation of other nations, it may be impossible to track down the offender(s) and secure convictions.

To assist countries to enforce the law, bilateral and multilateral mutual legal assistance treaties (MLATs) exist to aid the exchange and gathering of information on an international basis. The agreements as a whole are intended to facilitate both the extradition of individuals charged with transnational crimes along with the gathering and sharing of information needed to investigate and prosecute those crimes. Procedurally it should be noted that:

- any request for information from countries other than the United Kingdom will be dealt with by Interpol Liaison;
- requests for data from the United States of America may be dealt with initially via the Regulation of Investigatory Powers Act 2000 (special agreement);
- the request may be for intelligence purposes only;
- any request for evidential material will be facilitated via an MLAT;
- evidential preservation orders can be requested via an MLAT.

### 3.11.5.1 International Letter of Request (ILOR)

An international letter of request (which may also be referred to a 'letter rogatory') is a customary method of obtaining judicial assistance from abroad in the absence of a treaty (such as an MLAT) or executive agreement. Such a letter is a request from the courts in one country to the judiciary of a foreign country requesting the performance of an act which, if done without the sanction of the foreign court, could constitute a violation of that country's sovereignty. A recent example of such a request was where the Scottish authorities sent an ILOR to the Libyan authorities to assist in the ongoing investigation into the Lockerbie bombing which took place in 1988. Procedurally it should be noted that:

- an ILOR is issued by a judge or justice of the peace on the request of a prosecuting authority;
- it is used for gathering evidence likely to be of evidential value in proceedings;
- requests for intelligence should not be made via an ILOR;
- the process of obtaining an ILOR will be dealt with by the CPS who will give written notice to the appropriate court.

# PART FOUR

# Sexual Offences

# 4.1 Sexual Offences

### 4.1.1 Introduction

Sexual offences represent a particularly important area of criminal law for two main reasons: the sensitivity required in their investigation and prosecution and their potential effect on the victim. It is important to note that there is overlap between many of the offences, for example a mentally disordered person could be raped under s. 1 (because of his/her lack of ability to give true consent) or subjected to sexual activity contrary to s. 30 (due to an inability to refuse). In all circumstances it is essential that the most appropriate option is chosen.

### 4.1.2 Human Rights Considerations

Sexual activities are aspects of a person's 'private life' as protected by Article 8 of the Convention (see *Dudgeon* v *United Kingdom* (1981) 3 EHRR 40 and *ADT* v *United Kingdom* [2000] 31 EHRR 33). This concept applies to homosexual and heterosexual relationships (*X* v *United Kingdom* (1997) 24 EHRR 143).

The Sexual Offences Act 2003 and its compatibility with the European Convention on Human Rights were considered in *R* v *G & Secretary of State for the Home Department* [2006] EWCA Crim 821. The Court of Appeal held that the imposition of strict liability in relation to the offence under s. 5 of the Act (rape of a child under 13) did not infringe Article 6.2 of the Convention (presumption of innocence).

### 4.1.3 Anonymity

Under the Sexual Offences (Amendment) Act 1992, victims of most sexual offences (including rape, incest, and indecency with children) are entitled to anonymity throughout their lifetime. This means that there are restrictions on the way in which trials and cases may be reported and the courts have powers to enforce these provisions. Further protection preventing victims from cross-examination by their alleged attackers is provided by the Youth Justice and Criminal Evidence Act 1999. The 1999 Act also imposes restrictions on the introduction of evidence in most of the sexual offences covered in this chapter.

# 4.2 The Sexual Offences Act 2003

## 4.2.1 Introduction

The large majority of offences in this chapter are dealt with under the Sexual Offences Act 2003. The Act provides practical measures such as the presumptions about consent that will be made by a court under certain circumstances. In many of the mainstream offences it creates, the Act uses the approach of describing actions of a hypothetical offender 'A' towards the victim 'B'.

The Act has some recurring themes and terms; in order to understand—and prove—many of the offences set out in the Act, it is necessary to understand some of the themes and terms first.

## 4.2.2 The Definition of 'Sexual'

Section 78 of the Act defines the term 'sexual' and provides that penetration, touching or any other activity will be sexual if a reasonable person would consider that:

(a) whatever its circumstances or any person's purpose in relation to it, it is sexual by its very nature or,
(b) because of its nature it *may* be sexual and because of its circumstances or the purpose of any person in relation to it, it is sexual.

Therefore, activity under (a) covers things that a reasonable person would always consider to be sexual (for example, masturbation), while activity under (b) covers things that may or may not be considered sexual by a reasonable person depending on the circumstances or the intentions of the person carrying it out (or both). For instance, a doctor inserting a finger into a vagina might be sexual under certain circumstances, but if done for a purely medical purpose in a hospital, it would not be.

If the activity would not appear to a reasonable person to be sexual, then it will not meet either criterion and, irrespective of any sexual gratification the person might derive from it, the activity will not be 'sexual'. Therefore weird or exotic fetishes that no ordinary person would regard as being sexual or potentially sexual will not be covered. This pretty well follows the common law developments in this area (see e.g. *R v Court* [1989] AC 28 and *R v Tabassum* [2000] 2 Cr App R 328).

## 4.2.3 The Definition of 'Touching'

This activity is relevant to a number of specific offences. Section 79(8) states that touching includes touching:

• with any part of the body
• with anything else
• through anything

and in particular, touching amounting to penetration.

'Touching' for the purposes of an offence under s. 3 (**see para. 4.4.2**) includes the touching of a victim's clothing. This is clear from the Court of Appeal's decision in *R v H* [2005] EWCA Crim 732. There it was held that it was not Parliament's intention to preclude the touching of a victim's clothing from amounting to a sexual 'assault'. Where touching was not automatically by its nature 'sexual' the test under s. 78(b) applies (**see para. 4.2.2**). In a case where that section applies it will be appropriate for a trial judge to ask the jury to determine whether touching was 'sexual' by answering two questions. First, would the jury, as 12 reasonable people, consider that the touching could be sexual and, if so, whether in all the circumstances of the case, they would consider that the purpose of the touching *had in fact been* sexual.

# 4.3 Rape

## 4.3.1 Rape

OFFENCE: **Rape—*Sexual Offences Act 2003, s.1***
- Triable on indictment • Life imprisonment

The Sexual Offences Act 2003, s. 1 states:

(1) A person (A) commits an offence if—
    (a) he intentionally penetrates the vagina, anus or mouth of another person (B) with his penis,
    (b) B does not consent to the penetration, and
    (c) A does not reasonably believe that B consents

---

**KEYNOTE**

Rape is an offence that can *only* be committed via the use of the penis. It can be committed if the defendant penetrates the vagina, anus or mouth of the victim with the penis.

Consent is a key aspect of rape. In proving rape you must show that the victim did not in fact consent at the time and that the defendant did not reasonably believe that he/she consented. The wording is supported by the further provision that whether or not the defendant's belief is reasonable will be determined having regard to all the circumstances (s. 1(2)). Both this, and the aspects of the criminal conduct required to prove rape are considered in greater detail below.

Sections 75 and 76 apply to this offence (**see paras 4.3.4** and **4.3.5**).

If the victim is a child under 13, you simply have to prove intentional penetration and the child's age. No issue of 'consent' arises and a specific offence under s. 5 is committed.

Section 103(2)(b) of the Criminal Justice Act 2003 provides that a defendant's propensity to commit offences of the kind with which he is charged may (without prejudice to any other way of doing so) be established by evidence that he has been convicted of an offence of 'the same category'. An offence under s. 1, if committed in relation to a person under the age of 16, or under s. 5 (including aiding, abetting, counselling, procuring, inciting or attempting the commission of such an offence) falls within the relevant sexual offences category. A number of other sexual offences that follow in this chapter are also covered and will fall within the relevant sexual offences category (see the Criminal Justice Act 2003 (Categories of Offences) Order 2004 (SI 2004/3346)).

---

## 4.3.2 Criminal Conduct

To prove rape you must show that the defendant penetrated the vagina, mouth or anus of the victim. It should be noted that penetration is a continuing act from entry to withdrawal (s. 79(2)). The 'continuing' nature of this act is of practical importance when considering the issue of consent and the statutory presumptions (**see para. 4.3.3**). While it is not necessary to prove ejaculation, clearly the presence of semen or sperm is important in proving the elements of a sexual offence, as is other scientific evidence recovered from the victim, the offender and the scene etc. References to a part of the body (for example, penis, vagina) will include references to a body part which has been surgically constructed, particularly if it is through gender reassignment (s. 79(3)).

### 4.3.3 Consent

The issue of consent is a question of fact and is critical to proving the offence of rape. It is also potentially the most difficult aspect of the offence to prove and that is why the legislation has included some specific sections raising presumptions and conclusions in certain circumstances. Whereas an act of intercourse or physical intimacy may be proved or corroborated by forensic evidence, the true wishes of the victim at the time of the offence are much more difficult to prove beyond a reasonable doubt. Any consent given must be 'true' consent, not simply a *submission* induced by fear or fraud. Some people however are not capable of giving the required consent—these are generally addressed in further sections of this chapter.

The starting point in examining consent is s. 74 which states that a person consents if he/she agrees by choice and has the freedom and capacity to make that choice. Therefore, if the person does not have any real choice in the matter, or the choice is not a genuine exercise of free will, then he/she has not 'consented'.

A graphic example of how 'true' consent operates is the case involving PC Stephen Mitchell who committed a number of sexual offences against vulnerable women over a period of eight years. On one occasion Mitchell drove one of his victims to a dirt track and told her that if she did not do as he said he would ensure her children were taken away from her for good, and then raped her. Any 'consent' given by the victim could not be 'true' because her choice to participate in the act of sexual intercourse would not be by the genuine exercise of free will (a 'gun to the head'-type scenario).

In *Assange* v *Sweden* [2011] EWHC 2489 (Admin) the Divisional Court held that it would be open to a jury to hold that, if a complainant had made it clear that she would consent to sexual intercourse only if the appellant used a condom, there would be no consent if, without her consent, he did not use a condom, or removed or tore the condom without her consent.

In *R* v *B* [2006] EWCA Crim 2945, the Court of Appeal stated that whether an individual had a sexual disease or condition, such as being HIV positive, was not an issue as far as consent was concerned. The case related to a man who was alleged to have raped a woman after they had met outside a nightclub in the early hours of the morning. When arrested, the man informed the custody officer that he was HIV positive, a fact he had not disclosed to the victim prior to sexual intercourse. At the original trial, the judge directed that this non-disclosure was relevant to the issue of consent. On appeal the court stated that this was not the case and that the consent issue for a jury to consider was whether or not the victim consented to sexual intercourse, not whether she consented to sexual intercourse with a person suffering from a sexually transmitted disease.

The next key considerations in relation to consent are the important provisions set out at ss. 75 and 76. These are presumptions about consent and can be divided into *evidential* presumptions and *conclusive* presumptions.

### 4.3.4 Section 75—Evidential Presumptions and Consent

The Sexual Offences Act 2003, s. 75 states:

(1) If in proceedings for an offence to which this section applies it is proved—
    (a) that the defendant did the relevant act,
    (b) that any of the circumstances specified in subsection (2) existed, and
    (c) that the defendant knew that those circumstances existed,
the complainant is to be taken not to have consented to the relevant act unless sufficient evidence is adduced to raise an issue as to whether he consented, and the defendant is to be taken not to have reasonably believed that the complainant consented unless sufficient evidence is adduced to raise an issue as to whether he reasonably believed it.

This means that, if the prosecution can show that the defendant carried out the relevant act in relation to certain specified sexual offences (for example, penetration in rape) and that any of the circumstances below existed and the defendant knew they existed, it will be presumed that the victim did not consent. Then the defendant will have to satisfy the court, by reference to evidence, that this presumption should not be made.

The circumstances are that:

(a) *any person* was, at the time of the relevant act (or immediately before it began), using violence against *the complainant* or causing *the complainant* to fear that immediate violence would be used against him/ her;

(b) *any person* was, at the time of the relevant act or immediately before it began, causing *the complainant* to fear that violence was being used, or that immediate violence would be used, against *another person*;

(c) *the complainant* was, and the defendant was not, unlawfully detained at the time of the relevant act;

(d) *the complainant* was asleep or otherwise unconscious at the time of the relevant act;

(e) because of *the complainant's* physical disability, *the complainant* would not have been able at the time of the relevant act to communicate to the defendant whether the complainant consented;

(f) *any person* had administered to or caused to be taken by the complainant, without the complainant's consent, a substance which, having regard to when it was administered or taken, was capable of causing or enabling the complainant to be stupefied or overpowered at the time of the relevant act.

It can be seen that these conditions cover a range of circumstances, including the use or threat of violence by any person (not just the defendant) against the victim of the sexual offence and circumstances where the victim was asleep or had been drugged.

The 'relevant act' for each offence covered by s. 75 will generally be obvious but is set out specifically at s. 77.

### 4.3.5 Conclusive Presumptions about Consent

Section 76 of the Sexual Offences Act 2003 states that, if it is proved in some sexual offences (listed in s. 77) that the defendant did the relevant act and that he/she:

(a) intentionally deceived the complainant as to the nature or purpose of the relevant act or

(b) intentionally induced the complainant to consent to the relevant act by impersonating a person known personally to the complainant,

there will be a *conclusive* presumption both that the victim did not consent and also that the defendant did not believe he/she consented.

These provisions deal with the problems where the defendant either misrepresents the nature or purpose of what he/she is doing (for example, pretending that inserting a finger into the victim's vagina is for medical reasons) or impersonates the victim's partner. Section 76 requires that a misunderstanding was created by the defendant and that it was done deliberately. Once it is proved, beyond a reasonable doubt, that these circumstances existed then it is conclusive and the defendant cannot argue against them. An example of a deception as to the purpose of the act comes from the case *R* v *Devonald* [2008] EWCA Crim 527. In this case, the defendant (a male) posed as a young woman and induced the complainant to masturbate in front of a web cam. The complainant only did so because he thought that he was masturbating for the sexual gratification of a young woman. The court held that the complainant had been deceived as to the purpose of the masturbation.

It is important to emphasise the fact that s. 76 deals with situations where the defendant either:

- deceives the victim regarding the nature and purpose of the act or
- induces the victim to consent to the relevant act by impersonating a person known personally to the complainant.

If the deception/inducement does not relate to either of these aims then s. 76 has no application. For example, in *R v Jheeta* [2007] EWCA Crim 1699, the defendant deceived the complainant into having sex more frequently than she would have done otherwise. In these circumstances the conclusive presumptions under the Sexual Offences Act 2003 had no relevance as the complainant had not been deceived as to the nature or purpose of the sexual intercourse.

As with s. 75, the 'relevant act' for each offence covered by s. 76 will generally be obvious but is set out specifically at s. 77.

Even if freely given, consent may still be withdrawn at any time. Once the 'passive' party to sexual penetration withdraws consent, any continued activity (for example, penetration in rape—*R v Cooper* [1994] Crim LR 531) can amount to a sexual offence provided all the other ingredients are present.

# 4.4

# Sexual Assualt

There are several specific offences dealing with types of sexual assault: these are discussed below.

## 4.4.1 Assault by Penetration

> OFFENCE: **Assault by Penetration—*Sexual Offences Act 2003, s. 2***
> • Triable on indictment • Life imprisonment

The Sexual Offences Act 2003, s. 2 states:

(1) A person (A) commits an offence if—
   (a) he intentionally penetrates the vagina or anus of another person (B) with a part of his body or anything else,
   (b) the penetration is sexual,
   (c) B does not consent to the penetration, and
   (d) A does not reasonably believe that B consents.

---

**KEYNOTE**

As with all the offences in the Sexual Offences Act 2003 except rape, this offence can be committed by a male or a female against a male or female.

This offence involves penetration by any part of the body or anything else whatsoever. It is therefore a very broad offence covering insertion into the vagina or anus (though not the mouth) of *anything*, provided that the penetration is 'sexual'. Penetration must be intentional, made without the consent of the victim and you must show that the defendant did not reasonably believe that the victim did consent. Whether a belief is reasonable is to be determined having regard to all the circumstances, including any steps the defendant has taken to ascertain whether the victim consents (s. 2(2)).

Sections 75 and 76 apply to this offence.

If the victim is a child under 13, you simply have to prove intentional, sexual penetration and the child's age. No issue of 'consent' arises and a specific offence under s. 6 is committed.

---

## 4.4.2 Sexual Assault by Touching

> OFFENCE: **Sexual Assault by Touching—*Sexual Offences Act 2003, s. 3***
> • Triable either way • If victim is child under 13—14 years' imprisonment; otherwise ten years' imprisonment on indictment • Six months' imprisonment summarily

The Sexual Offences Act 2003, s. 3 states:

(1) A person (A) commits an offence if—
   (a) he intentionally touches another person (B),
   (b) the touching is sexual,
   (c) B does not consent to the touching, and
   (d) A does not reasonably believe that B consents.

There is no requirement for force or violence: the lightest touching will suffice. The part of the body touched does not have to be a sexual organ or orifice. Touching for the purposes of the above offence includes touching a person's clothing. Therefore, where a man approached a woman and asked '*Do you fancy a shag?*', grabbing at a pocket on her tracksuit bottoms as she tried to walk away, he was properly convicted of the s. 3 offence even though he did not touch her person (*R* v *H* [2005] EWCA Crim 732). The victim need not be aware of being touched, so the offence was committed where the accused secretly took his penis out of his trousers and ejaculated onto a woman's clothing when pressed up against her dancing at a nightclub (*R* v *Bounekhla* [2006] EWCA Crim 1217). It is unclear whether ejaculation onto a victim without contact with any part of the accused's body would constitute an offence of sexual touching.

You need to prove that the conduct was intentional (rather than reckless or accidental), that it was sexual, that the victim did not consent and that the defendant did not reasonably believe that the victim consented.

Whether a belief is reasonable is to be determined having regard to all the circumstances, including any steps the defendant has taken to ascertain whether the victim consents (s. 3(2)).

Sections 75 and 76 apply to this offence.

If the victim is a child under 13, you simply have to prove intentional, sexual touching and the child's age. No issue of 'consent' arises and a specific offence under s. 7 is committed.

### 4.4.3 Causing Sexual Activity without Consent

OFFENCE: **Causing a Person to Engage in Sexual Activity without Consent—**
**_Sexual Offences Act 2003, s. 4_**

 • If involves penetration: of the victim's anus or vagina, of victim's mouth with penis, of any other person's anus or vagina with a part of victim's body or by victim, or of any person's mouth by victim's penis—triable on indictment; life imprisonment  • Otherwise triable either way; ten years' imprisonment on indictment; six months' imprisonment summarily

The Sexual Offences Act 2003, s. 4 states:

(1)  A person (A) commits an offence if—
   (a)  he intentionally causes another person (B) to engage in an activity,
   (b)  the activity is sexual,
   (c)  B does not consent to engaging in the activity, and
   (d)  A does not reasonably believe that B consents.

The offence can involve a number of permutations—for example a woman making a man penetrate her, a man forcing someone else to masturbate him, a woman making another woman masturbate a third person or even an animal. It would include causing a person to act as a prostitute. Apart from the defendant and the victim, there may be others involved who also consent. Clearly they may be liable for aiding and abetting under the right circumstances.

The term 'activity' is not defined and is capable of being given a wide interpretation, although it must have actually taken place. The activity engaged in must be 'sexual' in accordance with s. 78. It can include engaging someone in a conversation of a sexual nature (*R* v *Grout* [2011] EWCA Crim 299).

This offence overlaps partly with rape in that it deals with vaginal, anal and oral penetration. The offence is wider than rape, in that rape can only be committed by a man, as a principal, and does not involve penetration with an object. The offence can be committed by and against persons of either sex and includes cases of 'female rape', i.e. where A causes B to penetrate her vagina with his penis. Furthermore, the offence makes

A criminally liable for causing B to engage in sexual activity where B cannot himself be convicted of any offence because he has a defence such as duress or is under the age of criminal responsibility.

Whether a belief is reasonable is to be determined having regard to all the circumstances, including any steps the defendant has taken to ascertain whether the victim consents (s. 4(2)).

Sections 75 and 76 apply to this offence.

There is a specific offence of causing or *inciting* a child under 13 to engage in sexual activity (s. 8). It is important to remember that an individual can commit an offence of incitement even if the activity he/she is encouraging, etc. does not take place. In *R v Walker* [2006] EWCA Crim 1907, the Court of Appeal held that s. 8 of the Act created two offences: (i) intentionally causing, and (ii) intentionally inciting a child under 13 to engage in sexual activity. The offence was centred on the concept of incitement and the acts had to be intentional or deliberate, but it was not a necessary ingredient for incitement of sexual activity that the defendant had intended the sexual activity to take place.

# 4.5 | Child Sex Offences

## 4.5.1 Introduction

The Sexual Offences Act 2003 creates several specific offences relating to sexual activity involving or directed towards children. These are set out below. In considering each offence it is important to remember the relevant ages, both of offenders and victims. In addition, the Act makes special exceptions to some offences of aiding, abetting or counselling some offences involving children (**see para. 4.5.5** for such an example).

The full list of offences is set out in s. 73(2); basically it covers specific offences against children under 13 and offences involving sexual activity with a child under 16.

## 4.5.2 Sexual Activity with a Child

OFFENCE: **Sexual Activity with a Child—*Sexual Offences Act 2003, s. 9***
- If involves penetration: of victim's anus or vagina by a part of defendant's body or anything else, of victim's mouth with defendant's penis, of defendant's anus or vagina by a part of victim's body or of defendant's mouth by victim's penis—triable on indictment; 14 years' imprisonment • Otherwise triable either way; 14 years' imprisonment on indictment; six months' imprisonment summarily

The Sexual Offences Act 2003, s. 9 states:

(1) A person aged 18 or over (A) commits an offence if—
    (a) he intentionally touches another person (B),
    (b) the touching is sexual, and
    (c) either—
       (i) B is under 16 and A does not reasonably believe that B is 16 or over, or
      (ii) B is under 13.

---

**KEYNOTE**

The person committing this offence must be at least 18. If the defendant is under 18, he/she commits a specific offence, punishable by five years' imprisonment (if tried on indictment) under s. 13. Similarly, if the person committing the offence is in a position of trust in relation to the victim, he/she commits a specific offence under s. 16.

You must show that the defendant intentionally touched the victim sexually and either that the victim was under 13 (in which case the offence is complete) or that the victim was under 16 and that the defendant did not reasonably believe he/she was 16 or over. In either case consent is irrelevant.

There is a further specific offence (s. 10) of a person aged 18 or over intentionally causing or inciting another to engage in the type of sexual activity set out above. The sexual activity caused or envisaged may be with the defendant or with a third person. In the case of incitement there is no need for the sexual activity itself to take place. If the person committing the offence is in a position of trust in relation to the victim, he/she commits a specific offence under s. 17.

---

### 4.5.3 Sexual Activity in Presence of a Child

OFFENCE: **Engaging in Sexual Activity in the Presence of a Child—***Sexual Offences Act 2003, s. 11*

> • Triable either way • Ten years' imprisonment on indictment • Six months' imprisonment summarily

The Sexual Offences Act 2003, s. 11 states:

(1) A person aged 18 or over (A) commits an offence if—
   (a) he intentionally engages in an activity,
   (b) the activity is sexual,
   (c) for the purpose of obtaining sexual gratification, he engages in it—
      (i) when another person (B) is present or is in a place from which A can be observed, and
      (ii) knowing or believing that B is aware, or intending that B should be aware, that he is engaging in it, and
   (d) either—
      (i) B is under 16 and A does not reasonably believe that B is 16 or over, or
      (ii) B is under 13.

---

**KEYNOTE**

The person committing this offence must be at least 18. If the defendant is under 18, he/she commits a specific offence, punishable by five years' imprisonment (if tried on indictment) under s. 13. Similarly, if the person committing the offence is in a position of trust in relation to the victim, he/she commits a specific offence under s. 18.

The activity in which the offender is engaged must be 'sexual' and intentional and must be in order to obtain sexual gratification (for the defendant). The display of sexual images or sexual activity might, in certain circumstances, be appropriate, for example, for medical or educational reasons, hence the requirement that the offence depended on the corrupt purpose of 'sexual gratification'. However, the offence under s. 12 of the Act does not require that such gratification has to be taken immediately; i.e. the section does not require that the offence can only be committed if the purposed sexual gratification and the viewed sexual act, or display of images, were simultaneous, contemporaneous or synchronised. For example, the defendant may cause a child to watch a sexual act to put the child in a frame of mind for future sexual abuse, as well as where the defendant does so to obtain enjoyment from seeing the child watch the sexual act (*R* v *Abdullahi* [2006] EWCA Crim 2060). The approach to 'sexual gratification' taken in *Abdullahi* appears equally applicable to other offences where this phrase appears (the offence under s. 11 of the Act, for example).

You must show that a person under 16 is present or is in a place from which the defendant can be observed *and* that the defendant knew, believed or intended that the child was aware that he/she was engaging in that activity. Therefore, it is not necessary to show that the child was in fact aware of the activity in every case (although that would clearly help in terms of proving the defendant's state of mind). Because of the wording in s. 79(7), 'observation' includes direct observation or by looking at any image.

In relation to the child you must show also that either the child was under 13 (in which case the offence is complete) or that he/she was under 16 and that the defendant did not reasonably believe him/her to be 16 or over.

This offence is aimed at, for example, people masturbating in front of children or performing sexual acts with others where they know they can be seen (or they want to be seen) by children directly or via a camera/video phone etc.

---

### 4.5.4 Causing a Child to Watch a Sex Act

OFFENCE: **Causing a Child to Watch a Sexual Act—***Sexual Offences Act 2003, s. 12*

> • Triable either way • Ten years' imprisonment on indictment • Six months' imprisonment summarily

The Sexual Offences Act 2003, s. 12 states:

(1) A person aged 18 or over (A) commits an offence if—
   (a) for the purpose of obtaining sexual gratification, he intentionally causes another person (B) to watch a third person engaging in an activity, or to look at an image of any person engaging in an activity,
   (b) the activity is sexual, and
   (c) either—
      (i) B is under 16 and A does not reasonably believe that B is 16 or over, or
      (ii) B is under 13.

---

**KEYNOTE**

The person committing this offence must be at least 18. If the defendant is under 18, he/she commits a specific offence, punishable by five years' imprisonment (if tried on indictment) under s. 13. Similarly, if the person committing the offence is in a position of trust in relation to the victim, he/she commits a specific offence under s. 19.

While the related offence under s. 11 is concerned with the engaging in sexual activity which the person knows, believes or intends to be observed by a child, the above offence is concerned with intentionally causing a child to watch a third person engaging in such activity *or* to look at an image of a person *engaging in such activity*. 'Image' includes a moving or still image and includes an image produced by any means and, where the context permits, a three-dimensional image (s. 79(4)); it also includes images of an imaginary person (s. 79(5)).

As with the s. 11 offence, you must show that the defendant acted for the purposes of obtaining sexual gratification. For issues in relation to the term 'sexual gratification' see the explanation given in **para. 4.5.3**. Similarly, you must also show that either the child was under 13 (in which case the offence is complete) or that he/she was under 16 and that the defendant did not reasonably believe him/her to be 16 or over.

---

## 4.5.5 Arranging Intended Child Sex Offences

OFFENCE: **Arranging or Facilitating Commission of Child Sex Offences—*Sexual Offences Act 2003, s. 14***
   • Triable either way • 14 years' imprisonment on indictment • Six months' imprisonment summarily

The Sexual Offences Act 2003, s. 14 states:

(1) A person commits an offence if—
   (a) he intentionally arranges or facilitates something that he intends to do, intends another person to do, or believes that another person will do, in any part of the world, and
   (b) doing it will involve the commission of an offence under any of sections 9 to 13.

---

**KEYNOTE**

This offence addresses the activities of those who arrange or facilitate child sex offences. The relevant offences are those set out in ss. 9–13 of the Act set out in the earlier paragraphs of this chapter.

The offence applies to activities by which the defendant intends to commit one of those relevant child sex offences him/herself, or by which the defendant intends or believes another person will do so, in either case in any part of the world. The offence is complete whether or not the sexual activity actually takes place. Examples of the offence would include a defendant approaching a third person to procure a child to take part in sexual activity with him or where the defendant makes travel arrangements for another in the belief that the other person will commit a relevant child sex offence.

This part of the Act specifically excludes the actions of those who are protecting the child in question. The exception will apply to those acting for the child's protection who arrange or facilitate something that they believe another person will do, but that they do not intend to do or intend another person to do. Acting for the child's protection must fall within one of the following:

- protecting the child from sexually transmitted infection,
- protecting the physical safety of the child,
- preventing the child from becoming pregnant, or
- promoting the child's emotional well-being by the giving of advice,

and not for obtaining sexual gratification or for causing or encouraging the activity constituting the relevant child sex offence or the child's participation in it. This statutory exception (contained in s. 14(2) and (3)) covers activities such as health workers supplying condoms to people under 16 who are intent on having sex in any event and need protection from infection; it also potentially extends to covert investigative operations.

OFFENCE: **Meeting a Child Following Sexual Grooming—*Sexual Offences Act 2003, s. 15***

> • Triable either way • Ten years' imprisonment on indictment • Six months' imprisonment summarily

The Sexual Offences Act 2003, s. 15 states:

(1) A person aged 18 or over (A) commits an offence if—
    (a) A has met or communicated with another person (B) on at least two occasions and subsequently—
        (i) A intentionally meets B,
        (ii) A travels with the intention of meeting B in any part of the world or arranges to meet B in any part of the world, or
        (iii) B travels with the intention of meeting A in any part of the world,
    (b) A intends to do anything to or in respect of B, during or after the meeting mentioned in paragraph (a)(i) to (iii) and in any part of the world, which if done will involve the commission by A of a relevant offence,
    (c) B is under 16, and
    (d) A does not reasonably believe that B is 16 or over.

**KEYNOTE**

This offence was created to deal with child grooming, often as a result of contact being made via the Internet. The initial action of the defendant involves either a meeting or a communication with the victim (who must be under 16) on at least two previous occasions. Such meetings or communications can be innocuous, such as family occasions or during the course of youth activities, sports fixtures and so on. The only requirement prior to an intentional meeting during which an offender intends to do anything to a complainant which, if carried out, would involve the commission by the offender of a relevant offence is a meeting or communication 'on at least two occasions'. There is no requirement that either communication be sexual in nature (*R* v *G* [2010] EWCA Crim 1693).

The communications can include text messaging or interactions in Internet 'chat rooms'. Such contact can have taken place in any part of the world.

Once these earlier meetings or communications have taken place, the offence is triggered by:

- an intentional meeting with the victim;
- a defendant travelling with the intention of meeting the victim;
- the victim travelling to meet the defendant in any part of the world.

The activity at s. 15(1)(a)(iii) means that an offence will be committed by an adult where a child under 16 travels to meet the adult or the adult arranges to meet the child.

At the time of any of the above activities, the defendant must intend to do anything to or in respect of the victim, during or even after the meeting, that would amount to a relevant offence. A relevant offence here is generally any offence under part I of the Act (all the offences covered in this chapter). Note that the intended offence does not have to take place.

You must show that the victim was under 16 and that the defendant did not reasonably believe that he/she was 16 or over.

## 4.5.6    Sex Offences with Family Members

OFFENCE:    **Sexual Activity with Child Family Member—*Sexual Offences Act 2003,* *ss. 25 and 26***

- Where defendant is 18 or over at the time of the offence and if involves penetration: of victim's anus or vagina by a part of defendant's body or anything else, of victim's mouth with defendant's penis, of defendant's anus or vagina by a part of victim's body or of defendant's mouth by victim's penis—triable on indictment: 14 years' imprisonment • Otherwise triable either way; 14 years' imprisonment on indictment; six months' imprisonment and/or a fine summarily • Or, where defendant is under 18 at the time of the offence; five years' imprisonment on indictment; six months' imprisonment and/or a fine summarily

The Sexual Offences Act 2003, s. 25 states:

(1) A person (A) commits an offence if—
   (a) he intentionally touches another person (B),
   (b) the touching is sexual,
   (c) the relation of A to B is within section 27,
   (d) A knows or could reasonably be expected to know that his relation to B is of a description falling within that section, and
   (e) either—
      (i) B is under 18 and A does not reasonably believe that B is 18 or over, or
      (ii) B is under 13.

### KEYNOTE

Where the defendant intentionally incites another person (the victim) to touch him/her or to allow him/herself to be touched by the defendant, there is a specific—and to all practical purposes identically worded—offence under s. 26.

For the relevant definitions of touching and sexual see the earlier paragraphs in this chapter.

There are two further elements that must be proved in relation to these offences. The first is the existence of the relevant family relationship between the defendant and the victim, the second is the age of the victim.

Note that, where the relevant family relationship is proved, it will be presumed that the defendant knew or could reasonably have been expected to know that he/she was related to the victim in that way. Similarly where it is proved that the victim was under 18, there will be a presumption that the defendant did not reasonably believe that the victim was 18 or over. In respect of both the relationship and the age of the defendant under these circumstances, the defendant will have an evidential burden to discharge in that regard (see s. 25(2) and (3)).

The relevant family relationships are set out in s. 27. These cover all the close family relationships that you would expect, along with adoptive relationships. In summary the relationships are where:

- the defendant or the victim is the other's parent, grandparent, brother, sister, half-brother, half-sister, aunt or uncle or
- the defendant is or has been the victim's foster parent.

Additional categories are where the defendant and victim live or have lived in the same household, or the defendant is or has been regularly involved in caring for, training, supervising or being in sole charge of the victim and:

- one of them is or has been the other's step-parent,
- they are cousins,
- one of them is or has been the other's stepbrother or stepsister, or
- they have the same parent or foster parent.

For a full definition of the various familial relationships and their application to the specific offences, reference should be made to the statutory text.

There are exceptions for situations where the defendant and the victim are lawfully married at the time or where (under certain circumstances) the sexual relationship pre-dates the family one—for example, where two divorcees each have a child of 17 who are engaged in a sexual relationship before their respective parents marry and move all four of them into the same household.

### 4.5.7    Other Offences with Family Members

The Sexual Offences Act goes on to clarify and extend a number of other sexual offences involving adult family members (see ss. 64–65). These create either way offences punishable by up to two years' imprisonment. They can be committed by both parties where one relative (who is 16 or over) intentionally penetrates the vagina or anus of another relative (aged 18 or over) with anything, or penetrates his/her mouth with his penis and in each case the relative knows (or could reasonably be expected to know) that he/she is related to the other in the way described. The relatives are parent, grandparent, child, grandchild, brother, sister, half-brother, half-sister, aunt, uncle, nephew or niece. The Criminal Justice and Immigration Act 2008 amended ss. 64 and 65 of the Sexual Offences Act 2003 so that the offences of sex with an adult relative are committed where an adoptive parent has consensual sex with his/her adopted child when the child is aged 18 or over. The adopted person does not commit this offence unless he/she is aged 18 or over.

### 4.5.8    Indecent Photographs

OFFENCE:  **Indecent Photographs—*Protection of Children Act 1978, ss. 1, 1A and 1B***
• Triable either way • Ten years' imprisonment on indictment • Six months' imprisonment and/or a fine summarily

The Protection of Children Act 1978, s. 1 states:

**1 Indecent photographs of children**
(1) Subject to sections 1A and 1B, it is an offence for a person—
(a) to take, or permit to be taken or to make, any indecent photograph or pseudo-photograph of a child . . . ; or
(b) to distribute or show such indecent photographs or pseudo-photographs; or
(c) to have in his possession such indecent photographs or pseudo-photographs, with a view to their being distributed or shown by himself or others; or
(d) to publish or cause to be published any advertisement likely to be understood as conveying that the advertiser distributes or shows such indecent photographs or pseudo-photographs, or intends to do so.
(2) For purposes of this Act, a person is to be regarded as distributing an indecent photograph or pseudo-photograph if he parts with possession of it to, or exposes or offers it for acquisition by, another person.
(3) . . .
(4) Where a person is charged with an offence under subsection (1)(b) or (c), it shall be a defence for him to prove—
(a) that he had a legitimate reason for distributing or showing the photographs or pseudo-photographs or (as the case may be) having them in his possession; or
(b) that he had not himself seen the photographs or pseudo-photographs and did not know, nor had any cause to suspect, them to be indecent.
(5) References in the Children and Young Persons Act 1933 (except in sections 15 and 99) to the offences mentioned in Schedule 1 to that Act shall include an offence under subsection (1)(a) above.

For the definition of a 'photograph' or 'pseudo-photograph' see below.

The consent of the DPP is needed before prosecuting an offence under the Protection of Children Act 1978.

A person will be a 'child' for the purposes of the Act if it appears from the evidence as a whole that he/she was, at the material time, under the age of 18 (Protection of Children Act 1978, s. 2(3)).

Once the defendant realises, or should realise, that material is indecent, any distribution, showing or retention of the material with a view to its being distributed will result in a prima facie offence being made out under the 1978 Act if the person depicted turns out to be a child (*R* v *Land* [1999] QB 65).

However, if the impression conveyed by a pseudo-photograph is that the person shown is a child or where the predominant impression is that the person is a child, that pseudo-photograph will be treated for these purposes as a photograph of a child, notwithstanding that some of the physical characteristics shown are those of an adult (s. 7(8) of the 1978 Act).

'Distributing' will include lending or offering to another. Clearly cases falling within the above legislation will vary significantly and there needs to be some distinction between the seriousness of different types of material. The Court of Appeal has set out five broad levels of seriousness and these are of use, not only in helping police officers and investigators understand how the offences will be dealt with by the criminal courts, but also in explaining this to victims and witnesses. The levels are:

(1) images depicting erotic posing with no sexual activity;

(2) sexual activity between children, or solo masturbation by a child;

(3) non-penetrative sexual activity between adults and children;

(4) penetrative sexual activity between children and adults; and

(5) sadism or bestiality.

(*R* v *Oliver* [2002] EWCA Crim 2766)

The Court of Appeal also recognised that much of this material involves abuse of the child featuring in it and held that, so far as an offender's involvement was concerned, the seriousness of an offence increased with the offender's proximity to, and responsibility for, the original abuse. In considering all these factors, courts will distinguish between pseudo-photographs which had involved no abuse or exploitation of children, and photographic images that involved real children. The Court of Appeal indicated that imprisonment would normally follow where the material had been shown or distributed to others or where the offender had been in possession of a large amount of level 2 material or a small amount of material of level 3 or above.

Note that although the offences include video recordings, possession of exposed but undeveloped film (i.e. film in the form in which it is taken out of a camera) does not appear to be covered. The offence at s. 1(1)(b) and (c) of the 1978 Act can only be proved if the defendant showed/distributed the photograph etc. or intended to show or distribute the photograph etc. to someone else. This is clear from the decisions in *R* v *Fellows* [1997] 1 Cr App R 244 and *R* v *T* [1999] 163 JP 349. If no such intention can be proved, or if the defendant only had the photographs etc. for his/her own use, the appropriate charge would be under s. 160 of the Criminal Justice Act 1988.

Sections 1 and 2 of the Criminal Evidence (Amendment) Act 1997 apply to an offence under s. 1 of the Protection of Children Act 1978 (and to conspiracies, attempts or incitements in the circumstances set out in the 1997 Act).

A legitimate purpose for possessing such material might be where someone has the material as an exhibits officer or as a training aid for police officers or social workers.

The Protection of Children Act 1978, s. 1A states:

**1A Marriage and other relationships**

(1) This section applies where, in proceedings for an offence under section 1(1)(a) of taking or making an indecent photograph or pseudo-photograph of a child, or for an offence under section 1(1)(b) or (c) relating to an indecent photograph or pseudo-photograph of a child, the defendant proves that the photograph was of the child aged 16 or over, and that at the time of the offence charged the child and he—

(a) were married, or civil partners of each other or

(b) lived together as partners in an enduring family relationship.

(2) Subsections (5) and (6) also apply where, in proceedings for an offence under section 1(1)(b) or (c) relating to an indecent photograph or pseudo-photograph of a child, the defendant proves that the photograph was of the child aged 16 or over, and that at the time when he obtained it the child and he—

(a) were married, or civil partners of each other or

(b) lived together as partners in an enduring family relationship.

(3) This section applies whether the photograph or pseudo-photograph showed the child alone or with the defendant, but not if it showed any other person.

(4) In the case of an offence under section 1(1)(a), if sufficient evidence is adduced to raise an issue as to whether the child consented to the photograph or pseudo-photograph being taken or made, or as to whether the defendant reasonably believed that the child so consented, the defendant is not guilty of the offence unless it is proved that the child did not so consent and that the defendant did not reasonably believe that the child so consented.

(5) In the case of an offence under section 1(1)(b), the defendant is not guilty of the offence unless it is proved that the showing or distributing was to a person other than the child.

---

**KEYNOTE**

**Defences to Indecent Photographs—Marriage and Other Relationships**

There is a specific defence to offences under s. 1(1)(a), (b) and (c) of the Protection of Children Act 1978 (making, distributing or possessing with a view to distributing). This defence arises where the defendant can prove that the photograph was of a child aged 16 or over, the photograph only showed the defendant and the child, and that, at the time of the offence, they were married, in a civil partnership or lived together as partners in an enduring family relationship (s. 1A). If the defendant cannot show these elements, the defence will not apply. If the defendant can show these elements, then the following further conditions of the defence will apply:

• In the case of an offence under s. 1(1)(a) (taking or permitting to be taken etc.), the defendant will have an evidential burden of showing that the child consented or that the defendant reasonably believed that the child consented to the making of the photograph (s. 1A(4)).

• In the case of an offence under s. 1(1)(b) (distributing or showing), you must prove that the distributing or showing was to a person other than the child in the photograph (s. 1A(5)).

• In the case of an offence under s. 1(1)(c) (possession with a view to distribution or showing etc.), the defendant will have an evidential burden of demonstrating that the image was to be shown/distributed to no person other than the child and that the child consented to the defendant's possession of the photograph (s. 1A(6)).

Similar provisions are made in relation to the offence under s. 160 of the Criminal Justice Act 1988 (possession)—see s. 160A below.

---

The Protection of Children Act 1978, s. 1B states:

**1B Exception for criminal proceedings, investigations etc.**

(1) In proceedings for an offence under section 1(1)(a) of making an indecent photograph or pseudo-photograph of a child, the defendant is not guilty of the offence if he proves that—

(a) it was necessary for him to make the photograph or pseudo-photograph for the purposes of the prevention, detection or investigation of crime, or for the purposes of criminal proceedings, in any part of the world,

(b) at the time of the offence charged he was a member of the Security Service or the Secret Intelligence Service, and it was necessary for him to make the photograph or pseudo-photograph for the exercise of any of the functions of that Service, or

(c) at the time of the offence charged he was a member of GCHQ, and it was necessary for him to make the photograph or pseudo-photograph for the exercise of any of the functions of GCHQ.

**Exception of Indecent Photographs—Criminal Proceedings and Investigations**

There is a limited defence in relation to the making of an indecent photograph or pseudo-photograph contrary to s. 1(1)(a) of the Protection of Children Act 1978 where the defendant proves that:

- it was necessary for the defendant to make the photograph or pseudo-photograph for the purposes of the prevention, detection or investigation of crime or for criminal proceedings in any part of the world, or
- at the time the defendant was a member of the Security Service, Secret Intelligence Service or GCHQ (Government Communications Headquarters) and it was necessary for the exercise of any of the functions of that Service/GCHQ (s. 1B).

In order to assist police officers and prosecutors the Association of Chief Police officers (ACPO) and the Crown Prosecution Service (CPS) have published a Memorandum of Understanding. This Memorandum sets out the factors that will be taken into account in deciding whether the intention of someone accused of an offence under s. 1(1)(a) attracted criminal liability when 'making' a photograph etc. As the Memorandum points out:

This reverse burden is intended to allow those people who need to be able to identify and act to deal with such images to do so. It also presents a significant obstacle to would-be abusers and those who exploit the potential of technology to gain access to paedophilic material for unprofessional (or personal) reasons.

The purpose of the Memorandum is therefore twofold: to reassure those whose duties properly involve the prevention, detection or investigation of this type of crime and also as a warning to others who might claim this defence having taken it upon themselves to investigate such offences. In summary the following criteria will be considered:

- How soon after its discovery the image was reported and to whom.
- The circumstances in which it was discovered.
- The way in which the image was stored and dealt with, and whether it was copied.
- Whether the person's actions were reasonable, proportionate and necessary.

**What is a Photograph?**

Section 7 of the Protection of Children Act 1978 provides a definition of a photograph for the purposes of the Act and states:

(1)   The following subsections apply for the interpretation of this Act.

(2)   References to an indecent photograph include an indecent film, a copy of an indecent film, and an indecent photograph comprised in a film.

(3)   Photographs (including those comprised in a film) shall, if they show children and are indecent, be treated for all purposes of this Act as indecent photographs of children and so as respects of pseudo-photographs.

(4)   References to a photograph include—

(a)  the negative as well as the positive version; and

(b)  data stored on a computer disc or by other electronic means which is capable of conversion into a photograph.

(4A)  References to a photograph also include—

(a)  a tracing or other image, whether made by electronic or other means (of whatever nature)—

(i)  which is not itself a photograph or pseudo-photograph, but

(ii)  which is derived from the whole or part of a photograph or pseudo-photograph (or a combination of either or both); and

(b)  data stored on a computer disc or by other electronic means which is capable of conversion into an image within paragraph (a);

and subsection (8) applies in relation to such an image as it applies in relation to a pseudo-photograph.

(5)   'Film' includes any form of video-recording.

(6)   'Child', subject to subsection (8), means a person under the age of 18.

(7)   'Pseudo-photograph' means an image, whether made by computer graphics or otherwise howsoever, which appears to be a photograph.

(8)  If the impression conveyed by a pseudo-photograph is that the person shown is a child, the pseudo-photograph shall be treated for all purposes of this Act as showing a child and so shall a pseudo-photograph where the predominant impression conveyed is that the person shown is a child notwithstanding that some of the physical characteristics shown are those of an adult.

(9)  References to an indecent pseudo-photograph include—

(a)  a copy of an indecent pseudo-photograph; and

(b)  data stored on a computer disc or by other electronic means which is capable of conversion into an indecent pseudo-photograph.

---

**KEYNOTE**

'Pseudo-photographs' include computer images and the above offences will cover the situation where part of the photograph is made up of an adult form. The widespread use of the Internet to facilitate offences relating to indecent photographs has led to a great deal of case law on the subject, much of which involves technical issues surrounding the way such images are downloaded, stored and viewed. What follows is a summary of several key decisions by the courts on these issues:

- Downloading images from the Internet will amount to 'making' a photograph for the purposes of s. 1(1)(a) of the 1978 Act (*R* v *Bowden* [2001] QB 88).

- 'Making' pseudo-photographs includes voluntary browsing through indecent images of children on and from the Internet. Once an image is downloaded, the length of time it remains on the screen is irrelevant (*R* v *Smith and Jayson* [2002] EWCA Crim 683).

- In the same case the Court of Appeal held that a person receiving an unsolicited e-mail attachment containing an indecent image of a child would not commit the offence under s. 1(1)(a) by opening it if he/she was unaware that it contained or was likely to contain an indecent image. This was because s. 1(1)(a) does not create an absolute offence.

- Copying onto a hard drive and storing 'pop-ups' containing indecent images of children amounts to possessing those images (*R* v *Harrison* [2007] EWCA Crim 2976).

- If images have been deleted from a computer so that their retrieval is impossible and, at the material time, a person cannot gain access to them and the images are beyond a person's control, that person cannot be in possession of them (*R* v *Porter* [2006] EWCA Crim 560).

- Evidence indicating an interest in paedophile material generally along with evidence to show how a computer had been used to access paedophile news groups, chat lines and websites can be relevant to show that it was more likely than not that a file containing an indecent image of a child had been created deliberately (*R* v *Mould* [2001] 2 Cr App R(S) 8).

- An image consisting of two parts of two different photographs taped together (the naked body of a woman taped to the head of a child) is not a 'pseudo-photograph'. If such an image were to be photocopied it could be (*Goodland* v *DPP* [2000] 1 WLR 1427).

- Where a defendant had knowledge that images were likely to be accessed by others, any images would be downloaded 'with a view to distribute' (*R* v *Dooley* [2005] EWCA Crim 3093).

---

OFFENCE:  **Indecent Photographs—*Criminal Justice Act 1988, s. 160***

- Triable either way • Five years' imprisonment on indictment • Six months' imprisonment and/or a fine

The Criminal Justice Act 1988, ss. 160 and 160A state:

**160 Possession of indecent photograph of child**

(1)  Subject to section 160A, it is an offence for a person to have any indecent photograph or pseudo-photograph of a child in his possession.

(2)  Where a person is charged with an offence under subsection (1) above, it shall be a defence for him to prove—

(a)  that he had a legitimate reason for having the photograph or pseudo-photograph in his possession; or

(b)  that he had not himself seen the photograph or pseudo-photograph and did not know, nor had any cause to suspect, it to be indecent; or

(c) that the photograph or pseudo-photograph was sent to him without any prior request made by him or on his behalf and that he did not keep it for an unreasonable time.

**160A  Marriage and other relationships**

(1) This section applies where, in proceedings for an offence under section 160 relating to an indecent photograph or pseudo-photograph of a child, the defendant proves that the photograph or pseudo-photograph was of the child aged 16 or over, and that at the time of the offence charged the child and he—

    (a) were married, or civil partners of each other or

    (b) lived together as partners in an enduring family relationship.

(2) This section also applies where, in proceedings for an offence under section 160 relating to an indecent photograph or pseudo-photograph of a child, the defendant proves that the photograph or pseudo-photograph was of the child aged 16 or over, and that at the time when he obtained it the child and he—

    (a) were married, or civil partners of each other or

    (b) lived together as partners in an enduring family relationship.

(3) This section applies whether the photograph or pseudo-photograph showed the child alone or with the defendant, but not if it showed any other person.

(4) If sufficient evidence is adduced to raise an issue as to whether the child consented to the photograph or pseudo-photograph being in the defendant's possession, or as to whether the defendant reasonably believed that the child so consented, the defendant is not guilty of the offence unless it is proved that the child did not so consent and that the defendant did not reasonably believe that the child so consented.

---

**KEYNOTE**

For the meaning of 'photograph' and 'pseudo-photograph' see the previous Keynote.

A person will be a 'child' for the purposes of the Act if it appears from the evidence as a whole that he/she was, at the material time, under the age of 18 (Criminal Justice Act 1988, s. 160(4)).

The statutory defence under s. 160(2)(b) of the 1988 Act above is broader than it seems at first. Although the wording requires that the defendant (1) has not seen the material and (2) did not know or have any cause to suspect it was indecent, the defendant will be acquitted of the offence under s. 160 if he/she proves that (1) he/she had not seen the material and (2) did not know (and had no cause to suspect) that it was an indecent photograph of a child. This was confirmed by the Court of Appeal in *R* v *Collier* [2004] EWCA Crim 1411 and arose from an argument where the material relating to children had been among other adult material that the defendant did know was indecent—he just did not know that it was an indecent photograph of a child.

---

## 4.5.9    Harmful Publications

OFFENCE:  **Harmful Publications—*Children and Young Persons (Harmful Publications) Act 1955, s. 2***

    • Triable summarily  • Four months' imprisonment and/or a fine

The Children and Young Persons (Harmful Publications) Act 1955, s. 2 states:

(1) A person who prints, publishes, sells or lets on hire a work to which this Act applies, or has any such work in his possession for the purpose of selling it or letting it on hire, shall be guilty of an offence...

---

**KEYNOTE**

A prosecution for this offence can only be brought with the consent of the Attorney-General (or Solicitor-General). The sort of 'works' to which the Act applies are set out in s. 1 and include books, magazines or other like works of a kind likely to fall into the hands of children or young persons which consist wholly or mainly of stories told in pictures which portray:

- the commission of crimes, or
- acts of violence or cruelty, or
- incidents of a repulsive or horrible nature,

in such a way that the work as a whole would tend to corrupt a child or young person.

### Power of Search

A search warrant may be issued under s. 3 of the 1955 Act.

### Defence

The Children and Young Persons (Harmful Publications) Act 1955, s. 2 states:

(1) ...in any proceedings taken under this subsection against a person in respect of selling or letting on hire a work or of having it in his possession for the purpose of selling it or letting it on hire, it shall be a defence for him to prove that he had not examined the contents of the work and had no reasonable cause to suspect that it was one to which this Act applies.

## 4.5.10 Possession of Prohibited Images of Children

OFFENCE: **Possession of Prohibited Images of Children—*Coroners and Justice Act 2009, s. 62***

- Triable either way • Three years' imprisonment on indictment and/or a fine
- Six months' imprisonment and/or a fine

The Coroners and Justice Act 2009, s. 62 states:

(1) It is an offence for a person to be in possession of a prohibited image of a child.
(2) A prohibited image is an image which—
  (a) is pornographic,
  (b) falls within subsection (6), and
  (c) is grossly offensive, disgusting or otherwise of an obscene character.

---

**KEYNOTE**

An image is 'pornographic' if it is of such a nature that it must reasonably be assumed to have been produced solely or principally for the purpose of sexual arousal.

An image falls within subsection (6) if it is an image which focuses solely or principally on a child's genitals or anal region, or portrays any of the acts mentioned below. Those acts are:

- the performance by a person of an act of intercourse or oral sex with or in the presence of a child;
- an act of masturbation by, of, involving or in the presence of a child;
- an act which involves penetration of the vagina or anus of a child with a part of a person's body or with anything else;
- an act of penetration, in the presence of a child, of the vagina or anus of a person with a part of a person's body or with anything else;
- the performance by a child of an act of intercourse or oral sex with an animal (whether dead or alive or imaginary);
- the performance by a person of an act of intercourse or oral sex with an animal (whether dead or alive or imaginary) in the presence of a child.

Penetration is a continuing act from entry to withdrawal.

Section 62(4) of the offence states that where (as found in a person's possession) an individual image forms part of a series of images, the question of whether it is pornographic must be determined by reference both to the image itself and the context in which it appears in the series of images. Where an image is integral to a

---

narrative (for example a mainstream or documentary film) which when it is taken as a whole could not reasonably be assumed to be pornographic, the image itself may not be pornographic, even though if considered in isolation the contrary conclusion might have been reached (s. 62(5)). This is related to the exclusion from the scope of the offence of certain excluded images under s. 63 of the Act.

Proceedings for an offence under subs. (1) may not be instituted in England and Wales, except by or with the consent of the DPP.

### Meaning of 'Image' and 'Child'

Section 65 states that an 'image' includes a moving or still image (produced by any means) such as a photograph or film, or data (stored by any means) which is capable of conversion into a movable or still image such as data stored electronically (as on a computer disk), which is capable of conversion into an image. This covers material available on computers, mobile phones or any other electronic device. It should be noted that the term 'image' *does not* include an indecent photograph, or indecent pseudo-photograph, of a child as these are subject to other controls (see s. 160 of the Criminal Justice Act 1988 above).

A 'child' means a person under the age of 18 (s. 65(5)). Where an image shows a person the image is to be treated as an image of a child if the impression conveyed by the image is that the person shown is a child, or the predominant impression conveyed is that the person shown is a child despite the fact that some of the physical characteristics shown are not those of a child (s. 65(6)).

References to an image of a person include references to an image of an imaginary person. References to an image of a child include references to an image of an imaginary child.

### 4.5.10.1 Defence

The Coroners and Justice Act 2009, s. 64 states:

(1) Where a person is charged with an offence under section 62(1), it is a defence for the person to prove any of the following matters—
   (a) that the person had a legitimate reason for being in possession of the image concerned;
   (b) that the person had not seen the image concerned and did not know, nor had any cause to suspect, it to be a prohibited image of a child;
   (c) that the person—
      (i) was sent the image concerned without any prior request having been made by or on behalf of the person, and
      (ii) did not keep it for an unreasonable time.

This section sets out a series of defences to the s. 62 offence of possession of prohibited images of children. These defences are the same as those for the offence of possession of indecent images of children under s. 160(2) of the Criminal Justice Act 1988.

### 4.5.11 Possession of Extreme Pornographic Images

This offence is set out under ss. 63–67 of the Criminal Justice and Immigration Act 2008. The offence is not intended to extend the law to cover additional material beyond what is illegal to publish under the Obscene Publications Act 1959. Indeed this offence covers a more limited range of material than the Obscene Publications Act. It creates a possession offence in respect of a sub-text of extreme pornographic material which is defined in s. 63 of the Act.

OFFENCE: **Possession of Extreme Pornographic Images—*Criminal Justice and Immigration Act 2008, s. 63***

> • Triable either way • Three years' imprisonment on indictment and/or a fine (where the images contain life-threatening acts or serious injury) • Two years' imprisonment on indictment and/or a fine (where the images contain acts of necrophilia or bestiality) • Six months' imprisonment and/or a fine summarily

The Criminal Justice and Immigration Act 2008, s. 63 states:

> (1) It is an offence for a person to be in possession of an extreme pornographic image.

---

**KEYNOTE**

Proceedings cannot be instituted without the consent of the DPP.

There are three elements to the offence. An image must come within the terms of all three elements before it will fall foul of the offence. Those elements are:

- that the image is pornographic;
- that the image is grossly offensive, disgusting, or otherwise of an obscene character, and
- that the image portrays in an explicit and realistic way, one of the following extreme acts:
  - ✦ an act which threatens a person's life (this could include depictions of hanging, suffocation or sexual assault involving a threat with a weapon);
  - ✦ an act which results in or is likely to result in serious injury to a person's anus, breasts or genitals (this could include the insertion of sharp objects or the mutilation of the breasts or genitals);
  - ✦ an act involving sexual interference with a human corpse (necrophilia);
  - ✦ a person performing an act of intercourse or oral sex with an animal (whether dead or alive) (bestiality);
- and a reasonable person looking at the image would think that the people and animals portrayed were real.

The key to assessing s. 63 accurately is to apply all three elements to an example under consideration. To focus on just one element in isolation inevitably leads to false conclusions about what is caught. The three elements, when taken together, should ensure that the offence only covers material which it is an offence to publish under the Obscene Publications Act 1959.

An 'extreme pornographic image' is an image which is both pornographic and an extreme image. An image is 'pornographic' if it is of such a nature that it must reasonably be assumed to have been produced solely or principally for the purpose of sexual arousal. Section 63(4) and (5) provides that where an image is integral to a narrative (for example a mainstream or documentary film) which taken as a whole could not reasonably be assumed to be pornographic, the image itself may be taken not to be pornographic even though if considered in isolation the contrary conclusion would have been reached.

An 'image' means either still images (such as photographs) or moving images (such as those in a film). The term also incorporates any type of data, including that stored electronically (as on a computer disk), which is capable of conversion into an image. This covers material available on computers, mobile phones or any other electronic device. The scope of the definition of image is also affected by the requirement that the persons or animals portrayed in an image must appear to be real. This requirement has the effect of excluding animated characters, sketches, paintings and the like (s. 63(8)). References to parts of the body include body parts that have been surgically constructed (s. 63(9)).

Section 64 of the Act provides an exclusion from the scope of the offence under s. 63 for classified films (films that have been classified by the British Board of Film Classification).

---

### 4.5.11.1 General Defences

Several general defences to the offence of possession of extreme pornographic images are set out in s. 65 of the Act. They are:

- that the person had a legitimate reason for being in possession of the image; this will cover those who can demonstrate that their legitimate business means that they have a reason for possessing the image;
- that the person had not seen the image and therefore neither knew, nor had cause to suspect, that the images held were extreme pornographic images; this will cover those who are in possession of offending images but are unaware of the nature of the images; and
- that the person had not asked for the image—it having been sent without request—and that he/she had not kept it for an unreasonable period of time; this will cover those who are sent unsolicited material and who act quickly to delete it or otherwise get rid of it.

### 4.5.11.2 Defence: Participation in Consensual Acts

Section 66 of the Act provides an additional defence for those who participate in the creation of extreme pornographic images. The defence is limited and will not cover images relating to bestiality and necrophilia images that depict a real corpse.

To use the defence, a defendant must prove (on the balance of probabilities) that he/she directly participated in the act or acts portrayed in the image and that the act(s) did not involve the infliction of non-consensual harm on any person. Where the image depicts necrophilia the defendant must also prove that the human corpse portrayed was not in fact a corpse. Non-consensual harm is harm which is of such a nature that, in law, a person cannot consent to it being inflicted on him/herself, or harm to which a person can consent but did not in fact consent.

### 4.5.12 Offences Outside the United Kingdom

Section 72(1) of the Sexual Offences Act 2003 (as amended by the Criminal Justice and Immigration Act 2008) makes it an offence for a UK national to commit an act outside the United Kingdom which would constitute a relevant sexual offence if done in England and Wales. The amended section removes the previous requirement that the act committed must have been illegal in the country where it took place, in respect of the prosecution of UK nationals.

| 4.6 | Protection of Children |

### 4.6.1  Introduction

The application of the law and the use of measures to protect children, particularly those relating to 'police protection', are amongst some of the most contentious issues that any police officer may be involved in.

### 4.6.2  Children Act 1989

When first enacted the Children Act 1989 was the most comprehensive piece of legislation affecting children ever seen in England and Wales. The Act has been supplemented by a further substantial and far-reaching statute, the Children Act 2004. Throughout the 1989 Act, which makes provision for the care and treatment of children in virtually every aspect of their development, there is a common theme of the child's rights. Among those rights are the right to protection from harm and the Act imposes many duties on local authorities. It also provides powers for the protection of children and, in particular, for situations where emergency protection is needed.

### 4.6.3  Police Protection

The police have specific statutory powers to deal with the threat of significant harm posed to children and these are set out below.

Section 46 of the Children Act 1989 states:

(1) Where a constable has reasonable cause to believe that a child would otherwise be likely to suffer significant harm, he may—
  (a) remove the child to suitable accommodation and keep him there; or
  (b) take such steps as are reasonable to ensure the child's removal from any hospital, or other place, in which he is then being accommodated is prevented.
(2) For the purposes of this Act, a child with respect to whom a constable has exercised his powers under this section is referred to as having been taken into police protection.

---

**KEYNOTE**

For most purposes of the 1989 Act, someone who is under 18 years old is a 'child' (s. 105).

The wording of s. 46(1) means that an officer may use the powers at s. 46(1)(a) and (b) if he/she has reasonable cause to believe that, if the powers are not used, a child is likely to suffer significant harm. The issues arising from similar wording in relation to powers of arrest have been considered by the courts on a number of occasions. Generally, tests of reasonableness impose an element of objectivity and the courts will consider whether, in the circumstances, a reasonable and sober person might have formed a similar view to that of the officer.

'Harm' is a very broad term and is defined under s. 31(9). It covers all forms of ill treatment including sexual abuse and forms of ill treatment that are not physical. It also covers the impairment of health (physical or mental) and also physical, intellectual, emotional, social or behavioural development. The definition also extends to impairment suffered from seeing or hearing the ill-treatment *of any other person*.

---

When determining whether harm to a child's health or development is '*significant*', the child's development will be compared with that which could reasonably be expected of a similar child (s. 31(10)).

The power under s. 46 is split into two parts:

- a power to *remove* a child to suitable accommodation and keep him/her there, and
- a power to take reasonable steps to *prevent* the child's removal from a hospital or other place.

The longest a child can spend in police protection is 72 hours (s. 46(6)). It should be remembered that this is the *maximum* time that a child can be kept in police protection, not the norm.

As soon as is reasonably practicable after using the powers under the Act, the 'Initiating Officer' (the officer who takes the child into police protection and undertakes the initial inquiries) must do a number of things as set out above. These things include:

- telling the local authority within whose area the child was found what steps have been, and are proposed to be, taken and why. This aspect of communicating with the local authority is a critical part of the protective powers;
- giving details to the local authority within whose area the child is ordinarily resident of the place at which the child is being kept;
- telling the child (if he/she appears capable of understanding) of what steps have been taken and why, and what further steps may be taken;
- taking such steps as are reasonably practicable to discover the wishes and feelings of the child;
- making sure that the case is inquired into by a 'designated officer' (**see para. 4.6.4**);
- taking such steps as are reasonably practicable to inform:
  - ✦ the child's parents
  - ✦ every person who is not the child's parent but who has parental responsibility for the child and
  - ✦ any other person with whom the child was living immediately before being taken into police protection,
- of the steps that the officer has taken under this section, the reasons for taking them and the further steps that may be taken with respect to the child. This element of informing the child, parent and/or relevant carers of what is happening and why is also a vital part of the protective process.

Where the child was taken into police protection by being removed to accommodation which is not provided by or on behalf of a local authority or as a refuge (under s. 51), the officer must, as soon as is reasonably practicable after taking a child into police protection, make sure that the child is moved to accommodation provided by the local authority. Every local authority must receive and provide accommodation for children in police protection where such a request is made (s. 21).

The requirement under s. 46(3)(c) to give the child information, reflects the 1989 Act's theme that children should have some influence over their own destiny.

The 'Initiating Officer' and the 'Designated Officer' must not carry out these two separate roles (Home Office Circular 17/2008). The Circular also states that a police station is not 'suitable accommodation' and children should not be brought to a police station except in exceptional circumstances, such as a lack of immediately available local authority accommodation, and then only for a short period. *On no account* should a child who has been taken into police protection be taken to the cellblock area of a police station.

Note that, when considering action under s. 46, it is possible that the child may already be the subject of an Emergency Protection Order (EPO) applied for by a local authority or authorised body under s. 44.

In considering the proper approach under these circumstances the Court of Appeal has held that:

- There is no express provision in the Act prohibiting the police from invoking s. 46 where an EPO is in place and it is not desirable to imply a restriction which prohibits a constable from removing a child under s. 46 where the constable has reasonable cause to believe that the child would otherwise be likely to suffer significant harm.

- The s. 46 power to remove a child can therefore be exercised even where an EPO is in force in respect of the child.
- Where a police officer knows that an EPO is in force, he/she should not exercise the power of removing a child under s. 46, unless there are compelling reasons to do so.
- The statutory scheme accords primacy to the EPO procedure under s. 44 because removal under that section is sanctioned by the court and involves a more elaborate, sophisticated and complete process of removal than under s. 46.
- Consequently, the removal of children should usually be effected pursuant to an EPO, and s. 46 should only be invoked where it is not reasonably practicable to execute an EPO.
- In deciding whether it is practicable to execute an EPO, the police should always have regard to the paramount need to protect children from significant harm.
- Failure to follow the statutory procedure may amount to the police officer's removal of the child under s. 46 being declared unlawful.

(*Langley* v *Liverpool City Council and Chief Constable of Merseyside* [2005] EWCA Civ 1173.)


## 4.6.4 Designated Officer

The reference at s. 46(3)(e) of the Act to a 'designated officer' is a reference to the appropriate officer designated for that police station for the purposes of this legislation by the relevant chief officer of police. This is a key role in ensuring the effective use of the statutory framework set up for the protection of children in these circumstances. The responsibility for ensuring that the case is inquired into by the designated officer, together with the other responsibilities under s. 46(3) and the responsibility for taking steps to inform people under s. 46(4), clearly rest with the police officer exercising the power under s. 46.

Practically, the designated officer must inquire fully and thoroughly into the case; he/she must also do what is reasonable in all the circumstances for the purpose of safeguarding or promoting the child's welfare (having regard in particular to the length of the period during which the child will be so protected) (s. 46(9)(b)).

Where a child has been taken into police protection, the designated officer shall allow:

- the child's parents
- any person who is not a parent of the child but who has parental responsibility for the child
- any person with whom the child was living immediately before being taken into police protection
- any person in whose favour a contact order is in force with respect to the child
- any person who is allowed to have contact with the child by virtue of an order under s. 34 and
- any person acting on behalf of any of those persons,

to have such contact (if any) with the child as, in the opinion of the designated officer, is both reasonable and in the child's best interests (s. 46(10)).

The designated officer may apply for an 'emergency protection order' under s. 44 (s. 46(7)). Such an order allows the court to order the removal of the child to certain types of accommodation and to prevent the child's removal from any other place (including a hospital) where he/she was being accommodated immediately before the making of the order (s. 44(4)). An emergency protection order gives the applicant 'parental responsibility' for the child while it is in force. It also allows the court to make certain directions in relation to contact with the child and a medical or psychiatric assessment. Section 44A allows the court to make an order excluding certain people from a dwellinghouse where the child lives and to attach a power of arrest accordingly.

While the designated officer can apply for an emergency protection order without the local authority's knowledge or agreement (see s. 46(8)), there should be no reason why, given proper multi-agency co-operation and a well-planned child protection strategy, this situation would come about. On completing the inquiry into the case, the designated officer must release the child from police protection *unless he/she considers that there is still reasonable cause for believing that the child would be likely to suffer significant harm if released* (s. 46(5)).

While a child is in police protection, neither the officer concerned nor the designated officer will have parental responsibility for the child (s. 46(9)(a)).

When a local authority is informed that a child is in police protection, they have a duty to make 'such enquiries as they consider necessary to enable them to decide whether they should take any action to safeguard' the child (s. 47(1)(b)). A court may issue a warrant for a constable to assist a relevant person to enter premises in order to enforce an emergency protection order.

### 4.6.5 Contravention of Protection Order or Police Protection

OFFENCE: **Acting in Contravention of Protection Order or Power Exercised under s. 46—*Children Act 1989, s. 49***

- Triable summarily • Six months' imprisonment

The Children Act 1989, s. 49 states:

(1) A person shall be guilty of an offence if, knowingly and without lawful authority or reasonable excuse, he—
  (a) takes a child to whom this section applies away from the responsible person;
  (b) keeps such a child away from the responsible person; or
  (c) induces, assists or incites such a child to run away or stay away from the responsible person.
(2) This section applies in relation to a child who is—
  (a) in care;
  (b) the subject of an emergency protection order; or
  (c) in police protection,
and in this section 'the responsible person' means any person who for the time being has care of him by virtue of the care order, the emergency protection order, or section 46, as the case may be.

---

**KEYNOTE**

Where a child is taken in contravention of s. 49 above, the court may issue a 'recovery order' under s. 50. Such an order, which is also available where a child is missing or has run away, requires certain people to produce the child to an authorised person (which includes a constable (s. 50(7)(b)) or to give certain information about the child's whereabouts to a constable or officer of the court (s. 50(3)). It can also authorise a constable to enter any premises and search for the child.

Under s. 102 of the 1989 Act a court may issue a warrant to enter premises in connection with certain provisions of the Act which regulate children's homes, foster homes, child-minding premises and nursing homes for children. Section 102 allows for constables to assist any person in the exercise of their powers under those provisions. It also makes allowances for a constable to be accompanied by a medical practitioner, nurse or health visitor (s. 102(3)).

---

### 4.6.6 Disclosure of Information Regarding Child

Where a child is reported missing problems can arise once the child is discovered to be safe and well but one of the parents wants the police to disclose the whereabouts of the child. This situation arose in *S v S (Chief Constable of West Yorkshire Police Intervening)* [1998] 1 WLR

1716 and the Court of Appeal provided some clarification of the issues. In that case the mother left home with her three-year-old child after a marriage breakdown. The father reported the child's absence to the police who found the child and her mother in a refuge. At the request of the mother, the police advised the father that both she and the child were safe but refused to disclose their whereabouts. The father applied 'without notice' (i.e. without telling the police) to the county court which then made an order under s. 33 of the Family Law Act 1986, requiring the police to disclose the information. The chief constable was granted leave to intervene and, following another order from the court to disclose the child's whereabouts, the chief constable appealed. The Court of Appeal held that it was only in exceptional circumstances that the police should be asked to divulge the whereabouts of a child under a s. 33 order. Their primary role in such cases should continue to be finding missing children and ensuring their safety.

However, the court went on to say that, in such cases:

- The police are *not* in a position to give 'categoric assurances' of confidentiality to those who provide information as to the whereabouts of a child. The most they could say is that, other than by removing the child, it would be *most unlikely* that they would have to disclose the information concerning the child's whereabouts.
- An order under s. 33 provides for the information to be disclosed to the court, not to the other party or his/her solicitor.
- An order under s. 33 should not normally be made in respect of the police without their being present (ex parte).

Note that the provision of information by police officers in relation to civil proceedings involving children is governed by regulations; specific advice should therefore be sought before disclosing any such information.

# 4.7 Sexual Offences Against People with a Mental Disorder

## 4.7.1 Introduction

The Sexual Offences Act 2003 is centred largely upon the fact that certain mental disorders deprive the sufferer of the ability to refuse involvement in sexual activity. This is different from, and wider than, a lack of consent at the time and focuses on the victim's inability to refuse.

## 4.7.2 Definition of 'Mental Disorder'

The relevant definition of a 'mental disorder' is that of s. 1(2) of the Mental Health Act 1983 which defines mental disorder as meaning any disorder or disability of the mind.

## 4.7.3 Sexual Activity with Mentally Disordered Person

OFFENCE: **Sexual Activity with a Person with a Mental Disorder—*Sexual Offences Act 2003, s. 30***
> • If involves penetration of victim's anus or vagina, of victim's mouth with defendant's penis, or of defendant's mouth by victim's penis—triable on indictment; life imprisonment • Otherwise triable either way; 14 years' imprisonment on indictment; six months' imprisonment and/or a fine summarily

The Sexual Offences Act 2003, s. 30 states:

(1) A person (A) commits an offence if—
  (a) he intentionally touches another person (B),
  (b) the touching is sexual,
  (c) B is unable to refuse because of or for a reason related to a mental disorder, and
  (d) A knows or could reasonably be expected to know that B has a mental disorder and that because of it or for a reason related to it B is likely to be unable to refuse.

---

### KEYNOTE

In order to prove the above offence you must show, not only that the sexual touching was intentional, but also that the victim was *unable to refuse* and that this inability was because of, or for a reason related to a mental disorder. The Act goes on to provide that a person is unable to refuse if:

• he/she lacks the capacity to choose whether to agree to the touching (whether because of a lack of sufficient understanding of the nature or reasonably foreseeable consequences of what is being done, or for any other reason), or
• he/she is unable to communicate such a choice to the defendant.

s. 30(2).

Once you have established these elements, you must also show that the defendant knew or could reasonably have been expected to know both that the victim had a mental disorder *and* that because of it (or for a reason related to it) he/she was likely to be unable to refuse. In *Hulme* v *DPP* [2006] EWHC 1347 (Admin), the Divisional Court examined a decision reached by a magistrates' court in relation to a complainant who was a cerebral palsy sufferer with a low IQ (aged 27). The magistrates' court had decided that the complainant was unable to refuse to be touched sexually; the Divisional Court agreed and the conviction against the defendant (who was 73) was upheld.

If the defendant obtains the victim's agreement to sexual touching by means of any inducement (offered or given), or a threat or deception for that purpose, the defendant commits a specific (and similarly punishable) offence under s. 34. An example of such an offence would be where the defendant promises to give the victim some reward in exchange for allowing sexual touching or where the defendant deceives the victim into believing that the touching is necessary for some other purpose. If the defendant uses an inducement, threat or deception to *cause* the victim to engage in or agree to engage in sexual activity, there is a further specific offence (similarly punishable) under s. 35.

In these specific cases of inducements, threats or deception there is still the need to prove that the defendant knew (or could reasonably have been expected to know) of the victim's mental disorder but *no need to prove that the victim was unable to refuse*.

Causing or inciting a person with a mental disorder impeding choice to engage in sexual activity with another person generally (i.e. without threats, inducements or deception) is a separate offence, punishable in the same way, under s. 31. As that is an 'incomplete' or unfinished offence it is not necessary to prove that the sexual activity took place.

## 4.7.4 Sexual Activity in Presence of Mentally Disordered Person

OFFENCE: **Sexual Activity in Presence of a Person with a Mental Disorder—** *Sexual Offences Act 2003, s. 32*

• Triable either way • Ten years' imprisonment on indictment • Six months' imprisonment and/or a fine summarily

The Sexual Offences Act 2003, s. 32 states:

(1) A person (A) commits an offence if—
  (a) he intentionally engages in an activity,
  (b) the activity is sexual,
  (c) for the purpose of obtaining sexual gratification, he engages in it—
    (i) when another person (B) is present or is in a place from which A can be observed, and
    (ii) knowing or believing that B is aware, or intending that B should be aware, that he is engaging in it,
  (d) B is unable to refuse because of or for a reason related to a mental disorder, and
  (e) A knows or could reasonably be expected to know that B has a mental disorder and that because of it or for a reason related to it B is likely to be unable to refuse.

### KEYNOTE

As with the previous offence, you will need to show that the defendant intentionally engaged in sexual activity; you will also have to show that he/she did so:

• when a person (who was unable to refuse because of, or for a reason related to, a mental disorder) was present or in a place from which the defendant could be observed, and

• that the defendant knew/believed/intended that the mentally disordered person was aware that the defendant was engaging in that activity for the purposes of sexual gratification.

For the requirements in proving the victim's inability to refuse see the previous offence under s. 30.

Because of the wording of s. 79(7), 'observation' includes direct observation or by looking at any image. For the specific offence of causing a person with a mental disorder impeding choice to watch a sexual act or an image of such an act see para. 4.7.5.

If the victim agrees to be present or in the place referred to in s. 32(1)(c)(i) above because of any inducement (offered or given), or a threat or deception practised by the defendant for that purpose, the defendant commits a specific (and similarly punishable) offence under s. 36. An example of such an offence would be where the defendant pays the mentally disordered person to stay in a particular place while the activity occurs. In these specific cases of inducements, threats or deception there is still the need to prove that the defendant knew (or could reasonably have been expected to know) of the victim's mental disorder but *no need to prove that the victim was unable to refuse*.

## 4.7.5 Causing Person with Mental Disorder to Watch Sexual Act

OFFENCE: **Causing a Person with a Mental Disorder to Watch a Sexual Act—** *Sexual Offences Act 2003, s. 33*

> • Triable either way • Ten years' imprisonment on indictment • Six months' imprisonment summarily

The Sexual Offences Act 2003, s. 33 states:

(1) A person (A) commits an offence if—
   (a) for the purpose of obtaining sexual gratification, he intentionally causes another person (B) to watch a third person engaging in an activity, or to look at an image of any person engaging in an activity,
   (b) the activity is sexual, and
   (c) B is unable to refuse because of or for a reason related to a mental disorder, and
   (d) A knows or could reasonably be expected to know that B has a mental disorder and that because of it or for a reason related to it B is likely to be unable to refuse.

---

**KEYNOTE**

For the key elements to prove in relation to this offence see the earlier offences above.

While the related offence under s. 32 is concerned with engaging in sexual activity which the person knows, believes or intends to be observed by a person with a mental disorder impeding their choice, the above offence is concerned with intentionally causing such a person to watch a third person engaging in such activity *or* to look at an image of a person engaging in such activity. 'Image' includes a moving or still image and includes an image produced by any means and, where the context permits, a three-dimensional image (s. 79(4); it also includes images of an imaginary person (s. 79(5)).

If the victim agrees to watch or look because of any inducement (offered or given), or a threat or deception practised by the defendant for that purpose, the defendant commits a specific (and similarly punishable) offence under s. 37. An example of such an offence would be where the defendant (with the appropriate motive) deceives the mentally disordered person into watching a film which is actually a live video feed of sexual activity. In these specific cases of inducements, threats or deception there is still the need to prove that the defendant knew (or could reasonably have been expected to know) of the victim's mental disorder but *no need to prove that the victim was unable to refuse*.

---

## 4.7.6 Care Workers

There are specific sexual offences that apply to people who are involved in the care of the mentally disordered victim. These offences follow similar wording to those general offences set out above (namely engaging in, causing or inciting sexual activity, sexual activity in the presence of a mentally disordered person etc.). In proving these offences (which appear in ss. 38–41 of the Act) you must show that the person was in a relationship of care as defined at s. 42. These are generally people whose employment has brought them into regular face-to-face contact with the victim in care homes, voluntary homes or hospitals. The offences are similar to those involving a position of trust. In these offences there is no need to prove that the victim was unable to refuse to take part in the activity but you must show that the defendant knew or could reasonably have been expected to know that the victim has a mental disorder. Given that the defendant will be a care worker with direct personal knowledge of the victim's circumstances, there is a presumption against the defendant that he/she had (or could reasonably have been expected to have) such knowledge and defendants will have to discharge an evidential burden in that regard if they are using this issue as part of their defence.

# 4.8  Offences Relating to Prostitution

## 4.8.1  Introduction

There are many offences connected with prostitution. Some of these offences specifically involve children and these are addressed elsewhere in this chapter.

While some European Union Member States have 'zones of toleration' where some forms of prostitution are permitted within controlled limits, the laws regulating prostitution and soliciting in England and Wales are quite clear and do not allow for such zones as presently drafted.

## 4.8.2  Definition of a Prostitute

The Sexual Offences Act 2003 defines prostitution and provides that a prostitute is a person (A) who:

- on at least one occasion and
- whether or not compelled to do so,
- offers or provides sexual services to another person
- in return for payment or a promise of payment to A or a third person.

(s. 51(2)).

This definition applies to both men and women.

## 4.8.3  Offence of Causing, Inciting or Controlling Prostitution

OFFENCE: **Causing, Inciting or Controlling Prostitution—*Sexual Offences Act 2003, s. 52***
- Triable either way • Seven years' imprisonment on indictment • Six months' imprisonment and/or a fine summarily

The Sexual Offences Act 2003, s. 52 states:

(1)  A person commits an offence if—
  (a)  he intentionally causes or incites another person to become a prostitute in any part of the world, and
  (b)  he does so for or in the expectation of gain for himself or a third person.

The Sexual Offences Act 2003, s. 53 states:

(1)  A person commits an offence if—
  (a)  he intentionally controls any of the activities of another person relating to that person's prostitution in any part of the world, and
  (b)  he does so for or in the expectation of gain for himself or a third person.

---

**KEYNOTE**

Where the victim of these offences is under 18, the specific offence under s. 48 should be considered.

The first offence above is concerned with intentional causing or inciting—in the case of the latter, this is an incomplete offence.

The second offence above addresses those who intentionally control the activities of prostitutes (pimps).

In each case, unlike the offence involving persons under 18, you must show that the defendant acted for, or in the expectation of, gain—either for him/herself or another. Gain means any financial advantage, including the discharge of an obligation to pay or the provision of goods or services (including sexual services) gratuitously or at a discount or the goodwill of any person which is or appears likely, in time, to bring financial advantage (s. 54). This is a wide definition covering the actions of someone who hopes to build up a relationship with, say, a drug dealer who will eventually give the defendant cheaper drugs as a result of his/her activities. Although you do not need to show that money, goods or financial advantage actually passed to the defendant, you must show that he/she wanted or at least expected that someone would benefit from the conduct.

## 4.8.4 Paying for Sexual Services of a Prostitute Subjected to Force

OFFENCE: **Paying for Sexual Services of a Prostitute Subjected to Force—*Sexual Offences Act 2003, s. 53A***
  • Triable summarily • Fine

The Sexual Offences Act 2003, s. 53A states:

(1) A person (A) commits an offence if—
  (a) A makes or promises payment for the sexual services of a prostitute (B),
  (b) a third person (C) has engaged in exploitative conduct of a kind likely to induce or encourage B to provide the sexual services for which A has made or promised payment, and
  (c) C engaged in that conduct for or in the expectation of gain for C or another person (apart from A or B).
(2) The following are irrelevant—
  (a) where in the world the sexual services are to be provided and whether those services are provided,
  (b) whether A is, or ought to be, aware that C has engaged in exploitative conduct.
(3) C engages in exploitative conduct if—
  (a) C uses force, threats (whether or not relating to violence) or any other form of coercion, or
  (b) C practises any form of deception.

### KEYNOTE

This section creates an offence which is committed if someone pays or promises payment for the sexual services of a prostitute who has been subject to exploitative conduct of a kind likely to induce or encourage the provision of sexual services for which the payer has made or promised payment. The person responsible for the exploitative conduct must have been acting for or in the expectation of gain for him/herself or another person, other than the payer or the prostitute.

It does not matter where in the world the sexual services are to be provided. An offence is committed regardless of whether the person paying or promising payment for sexual services knows or ought to know or be aware that the prostitute has been subject to exploitative conduct. In other words the offence is one of *strict liability* and *no mental element* is required in respect of the offender's knowledge that the prostitute was forced, threatened, coerced or deceived.

## 4.8.5 Brothels

There are several summary offences aimed at landlords, tenants and occupiers of premises used as brothels (see ss. 34–36 of the Sexual Offences Act 1956). The Sexual Offences Act 2003 extended the relevant offences so that they covered brothels used by male prostitutes and created the following offence:

OFFENCE: **Keeping a Brothel Used for Prostitution—*Sexual Offences Act 1956, s. 33A***

 • Triable either way • Seven years' imprisonment on indictment • Six months' imprisonment and/or a fine summarily

The Sexual Offences Act 1956, s. 33A states:

(1) It is an offence for a person to keep, or to manage, or act or assist in the management of, a brothel to which people resort for practices involving prostitution (whether or not also for other practices).

---

**KEYNOTE**

A brothel is a place to which people resort for the purposes of unlawful sexual intercourse with more than one prostitute. However, it is not necessary that full sexual intercourse takes place or is even offered. A massage parlour where other acts of lewdness or indecency for sexual gratification are offered may be a brothel. While the old summary offence of keeping, managing or assisting with the management of a brothel (under s. 33) still remains, it is unlikely to be used very often in light of the above offence.

Prostitution means offering or providing sexual services, whether under compulsion or not, to another in return for payment or a promise of payment to the prostitute or a third person (see s. 51(2)).

---

OFFENCE: **Keeping a Disorderly House—*Common Law***

 • Triable on indictment • Unlimited sentence

It is an offence at common law to keep a disorderly house.

---

**KEYNOTE**

To prove the offence of keeping a disorderly house you must show that the house is 'open' (i.e. to customers); that it is unregulated by the restraints of morality; and that it is run in a way that violates law and good order (*R* v *Tan* [1983] QB 1053).

There must be 'knowledge' on the part of the defendant that a house is being so used (*Moores* v *DPP* [1992] QB 125).

The offence also requires some persistence and will not cover a single instance, e.g. of an indecent performance.

---

4.8.6 **Soliciting**

OFFENCE: **Soliciting by Persons—*Street Offences Act 1959, s. 1***

 • Triable summarily • Fine

The Street Offences Act 1959, s. 1 states:

(1) It shall be an offence for a person whether male or female persistently to loiter or solicit in a street or public place for the purpose of prostitution.

(2) ...

(3) Repealed

(4) For the purposes of this section:

(a) conduct is persistent if it takes place on two or more occasions in any period of three months;

(b) any reference to a person loitering or soliciting for the purposes of prostitution is a reference to a person loitering or soliciting for the purposes of offering services as a prostitute.

OFFENCE: **Soliciting by 'Kerb-crawling'—*Sexual Offences Act 2003, s. 51A***

   • Triable summarily • Fine

The Sexual Offences Act 2003, s. 51A, (as amended) states:

(1) It is an offence for a person in a street or public place to solicit another (B) for the purpose of obtaining B's sexual services as a prostitute.

(2) The reference to a person in a street or public place includes a person in a vehicle in a street or public place.

## 4.8.7 Placing Adverts for Prostitutes Near Public Phones

OFFENCE: **Placing an Advertisement—*Criminal Justice and Police Act 2001, s. 46***

   • Triable summarily • Six months' imprisonment and/or a fine

The Criminal Justice and Police Act 2001, s. 46 states:

(1) A person commits an offence if—
   (a) he places on, or in the immediate vicinity of a public telephone, an advertisement relating to prostitution, and
   (b) he does so with the intention that the advertisement should come to the attention of any other person or persons.

to prostitution' there is a presumption that it meets the requirements of this section (s. 46(3)). This presumption is, however, rebuttable.

'Public telephone' here means any telephone which is

- located in a public place *and*
- made available for use by the public or a section of the public

and includes any kiosk, booth, acoustic hood, shelter or other structure housing or attached to the telephone (s. 46(5)).

Given this wide definition, the offence will cover the placing of advertisements on or within the immediate vicinity of, not just the telephone itself, but also the kiosk, booth, etc. Therefore, although the magistrate(s) will decide whether an act fell within the immediate vicinity as a question of fact, the offence is capable of being committed by placing advertisements on pavements or shop windows immediately adjacent to a public telephone kiosk.

Section 46(5) gives a very specific definition of 'public place' for the purposes of this offence, namely:

- any place to which the public have or are permitted to have access (on payment or otherwise), *other than*
- a place to which children under 16 years of age are not permitted to have access (by law or otherwise), or
- premises used wholly or mainly as residential premises.

This means that public areas where children under 16 are not allowed, either because they are prevented by law (e.g. licensing laws) or for some other reason (e.g. where a landowner is holding a public event and has barred children from attending), will not be caught by this legislation.

## 4.8.8 Trafficking for Sexual Offences

OFFENCE: **Trafficking Into, Within or Out of the UK for Sexual Exploitation—**
*Sexual Offences Act 2003, ss. 57–59*
- Triable either way • 14 years' imprisonment on indictment • Six months' imprisonment and/or a fine summarily

The Sexual Offences Act 2003, s. 57 states:

(1) A person commits an offence if he intentionally arranges or facilitates the arrival, or the entry into, the United Kingdom of another person (B) and either—
  (a) he intends to do anything to or in respect of B, after B's arrival but in any part of the world, which if done will involve the commission of a relevant offence, or
  (b) he believes that another person is likely to do something to or in respect of B, after B's arrival but in any part of the world, which if done will involve the commission of a relevant offence.

The Sexual Offences Act 2003, s. 58 states:

(1) A person commits an offence if he intentionally arranges or facilitates travel within the United Kingdom by another person (B) and either—
  (a) he intends to do anything to or in respect of B, during or after the journey and in any part of the world, which if done will involve the commission of a relevant offence, or
  (b) he believes that another person is likely to do something to or in respect of B, during or after the journey and in any part of the world, which if done will involve the commission of a relevant offence.

The Sexual Offences Act 2003, s. 59 states:

(1) A person commits an offence if he intentionally arranges or facilitates the departure from the United Kingdom of another person (B) and either—
  (a) he intends to do anything to or in respect of B, after B's departure but in any part of the world, which if done will involve the commission of a relevant offence, or

(b) he believes that another person is likely to do something to or in respect of B, after B's departure but in any part of the world, which if done will involve the commission of a relevant offence.

---

**KEYNOTE**

These three offences address the trafficking of people for sexual exploitation. Worded almost identically, the three sections deal with the intentional arranging or facilitation of the person's arrival in, travel within, or departure from the United Kingdom. In each case you must show the defendant's intention to do something to or in respect of the victim which would involve the commission of a relevant offence *or* the defendant's belief that someone else is likely to do so. The relevant offence, intended or believed likely by the defendant, can take place in any part of the world provided it is after the victim's arrival, during or after his/her journey, or after his/her departure respectively.

A relevant offence is any offence under part I of the Sexual Offences Act 2003 (virtually all regularly occurring sexual offences) and an offence under s. 1(1)(a) of the Protection of Children Act 1978 (taking, permitting to be taken or making indecent photographs of a child—**see para. 4.5.8**); it also includes anything done outside England and Wales which is not an offence in that country but would be if done in England and Wales where the offender is a British citizen, a British overseas territories citizen, a British National (Overseas), a British Overseas citizen, a person who is a British subject under the British Nationality Act 1981 or a British protected person within the meaning given by s. 50(1) of that Act (s. 60).

The wording of the offences means that bringing victims into the United Kingdom temporarily on their way to another destination will be caught.

Note that it is the intention or belief of the defendant that is the central feature—the fact that the relevant sexual offence never actually took place will not prevent this offence being committed. Similarly, if the intention or belief is not present, there is no offence under these provisions. This protects transport companies and their staff who are often unwittingly used in these offences. Nevertheless, the wording of the offences is wide enough to deal with any intentional involvement in planning, organising or carrying out arrangements in furtherance of trafficking where the relevant state of mind or knowledge is present.

---

# 4.9 Preparatory Offences

In addition to the many substantive offences covered by this chapter, there are specific provisions to prevent the consequences set out in those offences from happening.

## 4.9.1 Any Offence with Intent to Commit Sexual Offence

OFFENCE: **Committing Criminal Offence with Intent to Commit a Sexual Offence—*Sexual Offences Act 2003, s. 62***
- Where the offence committed is kidnapping or false imprisonment—triable on indictment only; life imprisonment • Otherwise triable either way; ten years' imprisonment on indictment; six months' imprisonment and/or a fine summarily

The Sexual Offences Act 2003, s. 62 states:

(1) A person commits an offence under this section if he commits any offence with the intention of committing a relevant sexual offence.

---

**KEYNOTE**

Relevant sexual offence means an offence under part I of the Act (virtually all regularly occurring sexual offences) including aiding, abetting, counselling or procuring such an offence (s. 62(2)). It *does not extend* to other sexual offences such as those under the Protection of Children Act 1978.

This offence is designed to deal with the commission of any criminal offence where the defendant's intention is to commit a relevant sexual offence. In addition to the more obvious offences of kidnapping and false imprisonment, this would appear to cover a vast array of possible circumstances where the defendant's ulterior motive in committing the first offence is to carry out the relevant sexual offence. As there is no express requirement for there to be any immediate link in time between the two offences, the wording appears to cover any situation from the theft of drugs or equipment to be used in the course of the sexual offence and going equipped for burglary, to the taking of a vehicle or even dangerous driving with the intention in each case of committing the further relevant sexual offence.

---

## 4.9.2 Trespass with Intent to Commit Sexual Offence

OFFENCE: **Trespass with Intent to Commit a Relevant Sexual Offence—*Sexual Offences Act 2003, s. 63***
- Triable either way • Ten years' imprisonment on indictment • Six months' imprisonment and/or a fine summarily

The Sexual Offences Act 2003, s. 63 states:

(1) A person commits an offence if—
   (a) he is a trespasser on any premises,
   (b) he intends to commit a relevant sexual offence on the premises, and
   (c) he knows that, or is reckless as to whether, he is a trespasser.

### 4.9.3    Administering Substance with Intent

OFFENCE:   **Administering Substance with Intent—*Sexual Offences Act 2003, s. 61***
  • Triable either way  • Ten years' imprisonment on indictment  • Six months' imprisonment and/or a fine summarily

The Sexual Offences Act 2003, s. 61 states:

(1)  A person commits an offence if he intentionally administers a substance to, or causes a substance to be taken by, another person (B)—

(a)  knowing that B does not consent, and

(b)  with the intention of stupefying or overpowering B, so as to enable any person to engage in a sexual activity that involves B.

# Offences in Immigration Enforcement and Asylum (This section is for Immigration Enforcement and National Crime Agency Candidates **only**)

This Part covers offences under the Immigration Act 1971, the Immigration and Asylum Act 1999, the Asylum and Immigration (Treatment of Claimants, etc.) Act 2004, the Immigration, Asylum and Nationality Act 2006, the UK Borders Act 2007, the Identity Documents Act 2010, as well as the associated powers. It also covers the Police and Criminal Evidence Act 1984 (Application to Immigration Officers and Designated Customs Officials) Order 2013 and offences in relation to marriage.

The information in this Part is fully testable for candidates from Immigration Enforcement and the National Crime Agency *only*. Please see **How to use Blackstone's Police Investigators' Manual 2014** on page xvii for further information.

PART FIVE

Offences in Immigration
Enforcement and Asylum
(This section is for Immigration
Enforcement and National Crime
Agency Candidates only)

# 5.1 The Immigration Act 1971

This chapter is only for examination candidates from Immigration Enforcement and the National Crime Agency.

### 5.1.1 Introduction

The Immigration Act 1971 is the main Act of Parliament dealing with immigration issues in the United Kingdom. The Act regulates the entry and stay of individuals in the United Kingdom, creates several offences relating to such behaviour and provides a variety of powers to immigration officers and the police.

When considering *all* immigration related offences, it should be noted that the United Kingdom is bound by the Council of Europe Treaty ratified by the government on 17 December 2008 (in force 1 April 2009) which places specific and positive obligations upon EU States to prevent and combat trafficking and protect the rights of victims. It provides for the possibility of not imposing penalties on victims for their involvement in unlawful activities to the extent that they have been compelled to do so.

Adults and children arrested by the police and charged with committing criminal offences might be the victims of trafficking. This most frequently arises when they have been trafficked here to commit criminal offences. But trafficked victims may also be apprehended by law enforcement where they are escaping from their trafficking situation. Therefore, officers must be alert to the fact that the suspect may be a victim of trafficking and consider referring the suspect through the national referral mechanism (NRM) to the competent authority for victim identification and referral to appropriate support.

### 5.1.2 The Immigration Act 1971—Offences

The Immigration Act 1971 provides a number of offences relating to unlawful entry to the United Kingdom.

#### 5.1.2.1 Illegal Entry

OFFENCE: **Illegal Entry—*Immigration Act 1971, s. 24***
- Triable summarily • Six months' imprisonment and/or a fine

The Immigration Act 1971, s. 24 states:

(1) A person who is not a British citizen shall be guilty of an offence . . . in any of the following cases—
    (a) if contrary to this Act he knowingly enters the United Kingdom in breach of a deportation order or without leave;
    (aa) . . .
    (b) if, having only a limited leave to enter or remain in the United Kingdom, he knowingly either—
      (i) remains beyond the time limited by the leave; or
      (ii) fails to observe a condition of the leave;

(c) if, having lawfully entered the United Kingdom without leave by virtue of section 8(1) above, he remains without leave beyond the time allowed by section 8(1);

(d) if, without reasonable excuse, he fails to comply with any requirement imposed on him under Schedule 2 to this Act to report to a medical officer of health or to attend, or submit to a test or examination, as required by such an officer;

(e) if, without reasonable excuse, he fails to observe any restriction imposed on him under Schedule 2 or 3 to this Act as to residence, as to his employment or occupation or as to reporting to the police or to an immigration officer or to the Secretary of State;

(f) if he disembarks in the United Kingdom from a ship or aircraft after being placed on board under Schedule 2 or 3 to this Act with a view to his removal from the United Kingdom;

(g) if he embarks in contravention of a restriction imposed by or under an Order in Council under section 3(7) of this Act.

---

**KEYNOTE**

All of the offences in s. 24 can only be committed by a person who is *not* a British citizen.

Section 24 is concerned generally with non-British citizens who enter the United Kingdom illegally or who 'overstay' having been granted limited leave to be here; it also addresses occasions where such people disregard some other lawful requirements placed upon them. The offence requires actual entry and *will not* have been committed if entry has not occurred.

For the offence to be committed, a person must *knowingly* enter in breach of a deportation order or without leave. By contrast, a person is an illegal entrant (for removal purposes) simply if he/she unlawfully enters or seeks to enter in breach of a deportation order or of the immigration laws.

A person commits an offence under s. 24(1)(b)(i) on the day when he/she first knows that the time limited by his/her leave has expired and continues to commit it throughout any period which he/she is in the United Kingdom thereafter, but that person shall not be prosecuted under the provision more than once in respect of the same limited leave.

The reference in s. 24(1)(c) to 'section 8(1)' refers to the special provisions made for seamen, aircrew, etc. landing lawfully in the United Kingdom.

Although the burden of proof is normally on the prosecution, an exception is made in relation to the offence under s. 24 if the case is brought within six months of the date of entry. In these cases the burden is on the accused to show on the balance of probabilities that he/she entered the United Kingdom legally (Immigration Act 1971, s. 24(4)(b)).

Section 28 of the Immigration Act 1971 provides that an extended time limit will apply to the prosecution of the offence under s. 24. An information relating to an offence under s. 24 may, in England and Wales, be tried by a magistrates' court if it is laid within six months of the commission of the offence *or* it is laid within three years of the commission of the offence and not more than two months after the date certified by a police officer *above* the rank of chief superintendent to be the date on which evidence sufficient to justify proceedings came to the notice of an officer of the police force to which he/she belongs. A person charged with such an offence may be tried where the offence was committed or at any place he/she may be.

---

### 5.1.2.2 Use of Deception to Enter or Remain

OFFENCE: **Use of Deception—*Immigration Act 1971, s. 24A***

- Triable either way • Two years' imprisonment on indictment
- Six months' imprisonment and/or a fine summarily

The Immigration Act 1971, s. 24A states:

(1) A person who is not a British citizen is guilty of an offence if, by means which include deception by him—

(a) he obtains or seeks to obtain leave to enter or remain in the United Kingdom; or

(b) he secures or seeks to secure the avoidance, postponement or revocation of enforcement action against him.

This offence is aimed at the more calculated actions by non-British citizens to get (or try to get) leave to enter or stay in the United Kingdom, or to evade deportation.

'Deception' here has its ordinary meaning and is not specifically defined within the 1971 Act.

This offence can be committed in a control zone in France or Belgium and powers of arrest (see para. 5.1.3.1) are exercisable there.

The offence can be committed by *seeking to enter* as well as *actually by entering*, and also embraces action taken to remain in the United Kingdom and to prevent and defer removal. It has been used against failed asylum-seekers who have sought asylum again under a false identity (*R v Nagmadeen* [2003] EWCA Crim 2004). The deception must be material (but it does not have to be the sole means of obtaining entry etc.) and must be by the immigrant personally.

It is worth noting that the relevant criminal conduct by the defendant here can be *any means which includes deception by him*. Therefore, although the entire course of conduct by the defendant need not amount to a deception, it will be necessary to show that the defendant him/herself carried out some act of deception (e.g. giving false details, providing misleading information, etc.). It will not be enough for this offence to show that someone else practised a deception in order to bring about the consequences at s. 24A(1)(a) and (b) for another person (but see later for further offence of assisting and harbouring).

'Enforcement action' means:

- the giving of removal directions;
- the making of a deportation order; or
- removal.

Section 31 of the Immigration and Asylum Act 1999 sets out defences, based on Article 31 of the Convention Relating to the Status of Refugees ('the Refugee Convention'), to the offence under s. 24A. Section 31 of the Immigration and Asylum Act 1999 states that it is a defence to the deception offence (s. 24A) and certain other offences, including offences under s. 4 or 6 of the Identity Documents Act 2010 (see para. 5.6.4), for a refugee who has come to the United Kingdom directly from another country to show that he/she:

(a) presented him/herself to the UK authorities without delay;

(b) showed good cause for his/her illegal entry or presence in the United Kingdom; and

(c) made a claim for asylum as soon as was reasonably practicable after his/her arrival in the United Kingdom.

The statutory defence applies only to those persons ultimately recognised as refugees—it *does not* apply to the offence of illegal entry under s. 24 (*Sternaj* v *DPP* [2011] EWHC 1094 (Admin)).

The extended time limit discussed in **para. 5.1.2.2** *does not* apply to this offence.

### 5.1.2.3    Assisting Unlawful Immigration and Asylum-Seekers

OFFENCE: **Assisting Unlawful Immigration to Member State—*Immigration Act 1971, s. 25***

- Triable either way • 14 years' imprisonment on indictment
- Six months' imprisonment and/or a fine summarily

The Immigration Act 1971, s. 25 states:

(1)  A person commits an offence if he—

(a)  does an act which facilitates the commission of a breach of immigration law by an individual who is not a citizen of the European Union,

(b)  knows or has reasonable cause for believing that the act facilitates the commission of a breach of immigration law by the individual, and

(c)  knows or has reasonable cause for believing that the individual is not a citizen of the European Union.

**KEYNOTE**

This offence requires that the defendant facilitated the commission of any breach of immigration law by someone who is not an EU citizen.

The offence refers to an act which 'facilitates' a breach of 'immigration law'. Thus, the first element in the offence is complicit dishonesty on the part of the person whose entry or stay is facilitated (e.g. that the visa applicant knew that the documents with which he had been provided by the accused and on which he relied in making his visa application were false); proof of dishonesty on the part of the accused is not sufficient (*R* v *Kaile* [2009] EWCA Crim 2868).

'Immigration law' means a law in a Member State (which includes Norway and Iceland) and which controls, in respect of some or all people who are not nationals of the State, entitlement to enter, travel across or be in the State (s. 25(2)). This means that the offence covers acts of facilitating entry or stay in *other Member States*. In *R* v *Kapoor* [2012] EWCA Crim 435, the Court of Appeal held that for the purposes of s. 25(2) an immigration law is a law which determines whether a person is lawfully or unlawfully either entering the UK, or in transit or being in the UK. Thus, if a person, with the necessary knowledge or reasonable cause to believe, facilitates the unlawful entry or unlawful presence in the United Kingdom of a person who is not a citizen of the EU, he commits the offence. The court held that s. 2 of the Asylum and Immigration (Treatment of Claimants) Act 2004 (**see para. 5.3.1**) was not an 'immigration law' for the purposes of s. 25(2).

The Secretary of State may make an order prescribing additional States which are to be regarded as 'Member States' for the purposes of the section if he considers it necessary for the purpose of complying with the United Kingdom's EU obligations (see s. 25(7)).

A document issued by the relevant government of a Member State will be conclusive in certifying any matter of law in this regard (s. 25(3)).

You must show that, in doing so, the defendant *knew* or had *reasonable cause for believing* both that their act facilitated the commission of the breach of immigration law and also that the person was not an EU citizen.

It also includes acts assisting non-EU citizens who entered the United Kingdom lawfully to remain unlawfully. In *R* v *Javaherifard* [2005] EWCA Crim 3231, the Court of Appeal held that it is possible to facilitate entry by acts close to but following actual entry (e.g. by making arrangements to get illegal entrants away quickly from the port of disembarkation).

This offence can be committed outside the United Kingdom by British citizens and others with relevant forms of British citizenship (see s. 25(4)).

The accused cannot rely on the protection of Article 31 of the Refugee Convention (**see para. 5.1.3**) in relation to facilitating the entry into the United Kingdom of another (*Sternaj*).

It is worth noting the Court of Appeal's observations that drivers and others involved in these types of offences are often of previous good character—in fact that is one of the criteria by which they are selected by the main organisers so as not to arouse suspicion of the authorities (*R* v *Salem* (2003) LTL 5 February).

### 5.1.2.4 Helping Asylum-Seekers to Enter the United Kingdom

OFFENCE: **Helping Asylum-Seeker to Enter United Kingdom—*Immigration Act 1971, s. 25A***

- Triable either way • Fourteen years' imprisonment on indictment
- Six months' imprisonment and/or a fine summarily

The Immigration Act 1971, s. 25A states:

(1) A person commits an offence if—
  (a) he knowingly and for gain facilitates the arrival in, or the entry into, the United Kingdom of an individual, and
  (b) he knows or has reasonable cause to believe that the individual is an asylum-seeker.

In order to prove this particular offence you must show that the defendant acted in the *knowledge* that they facilitated the arrival in the United Kingdom of a person whom they *knew* was (or had *reasonable cause to believe* to be) an asylum-seeker and that, in so doing, that they acted 'for gain'—the whole essence of this offence is profiteering thus financial gain is an essential element of the offence.

'Asylum-seeker' means a person who *intends* to claim that to remove them from, or require them to leave, the United Kingdom would be contrary to the United Kingdom's obligations under the Refugee Convention or the Human Rights Convention (in each case as defined under s. 167(1) of the Immigration and Asylum Act 1999) (s. 25A(2)). This presumably means that a person could be guilty of this offence even though the immigrant did not make a claim under the Refugee Convention or the ECHR, provided it can be established that the immigrant intended to make such a claim.

Section 25A applies in the case of an asylum-seeker who arrives in or enters the United Kingdom without any breach of immigration law being committed by the person gaining entry (*Sternaj*).

The right to claim asylum is protected by the Universal Declaration of Human Rights so the act of assisting asylum-seekers to arrive in the United Kingdom and claim asylum cannot therefore be unlawful per se, hence this offence does not apply to anything done by a person acting on behalf of an organisation which aims to assist asylum-seekers and *does not charge for its services* (s. 25A(3)).

A conspiracy to 'assist persons claiming asylum in the UK' is not an offence known to law (*R v Hadi* [2001] EWCA Crim 2534).

## 5.1.2.5 Assisting Entry to United Kingdom in Breach of Deportation Order

OFFENCE: **Assisting Entry to United Kingdom in Breach of Deportation Order—** *Immigration Act 1971, s. 25B*

- Triable either way • Fourteen years' imprisonment on indictment
- Six months' imprisonment and/or a fine summarily

The Immigration Act 1971, s. 25B states:

(1) A person commits an offence if he—
   (a) does an act which facilitates a breach of a deportation order in force against an individual who is a citizen of the European Union, and
   (b) knows or has reasonable cause for believing that the act facilitates a breach of the deportation order.
(2) ...
(3) A person commits an offence if he—
   (a) does an act which assists the individual to arrive in, enter or remain in the United Kingdom,
   (b) knows or has reasonable cause for believing that the act assists the individual to arrive in, enter or remain in the United Kingdom, and
   (c) knows or has reasonable cause for believing that the Secretary of State has personally directed that the individual's exclusion from the United Kingdom is conducive to the public good.

This offence applies *only* where the person being assisted is a citizen of the European Union.

For the first offence, there must be a deportation order in force and this will need to be proved before someone can be convicted. Additionally, the defendant must have *known* or *had reasonable cause for believing* that their act facilitated a breach of that order (therefore they must have *known/had reasonable cause to believe* that there was such an order in existence). This offence also applies where the Secretary of State personally directs that the exclusion from the United Kingdom of an individual who is a citizen of the European Union is conducive to the public good (an exclusion order) (s. 25B(2)).

The second offence is broader in scope than the offence under s. 25A (**see para. 5.1.2.4**) and applies to acts that assist the person to arrive in, enter or remain in the United Kingdom. Again, however, the relevant knowledge or cause for belief are crucial.

It is a defence that the accused did not know or have reason to believe that the person being assisted was the subject of a deportation or exclusion order.

### 5.1.2.6 Obstructing an Immigration Officer

OFFENCE: **Obstructing an Immigration Officer—*Immigration Act 1971, s. 26(1)(G)***
  • Triable summarily  • Six months' imprisonment and/or a fine

The Immigration Act 1971, s. 26 states that a person shall be guilty of an offence:

> (1)(g) if, without reasonable excuse, he obstructs an immigration officer or other person lawfully acting in the execution of this Act.

## 5.1.3 The Immigration Act 1971—Powers

Immigration officers are provided with essential powers of arrest and search in order to deal with offences outlined in **para. 5.1.2** and related offences—these powers can be found in s. 28 of the Immigration Act 1971.

### 5.1.3.1 Arrest Without Warrant

There are a number of powers of arrest set out in the Immigration Act 1971.

The Immigration Act 1971, s. 28A states:

> (1) An immigration officer may arrest without warrant a person—
>   (a) who has committed or attempted to commit an offence under section 24 or 24A; or
>   (b) whom he has reasonable grounds for suspecting has committed or attempted to commit such an offence.
> (2) But subsection (1) does not apply in relation to an offence under section 24(1)(d).
> (3) An immigration officer may arrest without warrant a person—
>   (a) who has committed an offence under section 25, 25A or 25B; or
>   (b) whom he has reasonable grounds for suspecting has committed that offence.

---

**KEYNOTE**

The power of arrest under s. 28(1) relates to the offences under s. 24 (illegal entry) and s. 24A (use of deception). Note that this power does not relate to the offence under s. 24(1)(d) (failing to comply with a requirement to report to a medical officer etc.) but **see para. 5.1.3.2** for a power of arrest to deal with this offence.

In relation to the power conferred at s. 28(3)(b), it is immaterial that no offence has been committed (s. 28(1)).

---

> (5) An immigration officer may arrest without warrant a person ('the suspect') who, or whom he has reasonable grounds for suspecting—
>   (a) has committed or attempted to commit an offence under section 26(1)(g); or
>   (b) is committing or attempting to commit that offence.
> (6) The power conferred by subsection (5) is exercisable only if either the first or the second condition is satisfied.
> (7) The first condition is that it appears to the officer that service of a summons (or, in Scotland, a copy complaint) is impracticable or inappropriate because—

(a) he does not know, and cannot readily discover, the suspect's name;

(b) he has reasonable grounds for doubting whether a name given by the suspect as his name is his real name;

(c) the suspect has failed to give him a satisfactory address for service; or

(d) he has reasonable grounds for doubting whether an address given by the suspect is a satisfactory address for service.

(8) The second condition is that the officer has reasonable grounds for believing that arrest is necessary to prevent the suspect—

(a) causing physical injury to himself or another person;

(b) suffering physical injury; or

(c) causing loss of or damage to property.

(9) For the purposes of subsection (7), an address is a satisfactory address for service if it appears to the officer—

(a) that the suspect will be at that address for a sufficiently long period for it to be possible to serve him with a summons (or copy complaint); or

(b) that some other person specified by the suspect will accept service of a summons (or copy complaint) for the suspect at that address.

---

**KEYNOTE**

The power of arrest under s. 28(5) relates to the offence under s. 26(1)(g) (obstructing an immigration officer).

In relation to the exercise of the power conferred by subs. (5), it is immaterial that no offence has been committed (s. 28(10)).

In Scotland the powers conferred by s. 28(3) and (5) may also be exercised by a constable (s. 28(11)).

---

### 5.1.3.2 Arrest with Warrant

The Immigration Act 1971, s. 28AA states:

(1) This section applies if on an application by an immigration officer a justice of the peace is satisfied that there are reasonable grounds for suspecting that a person has committed an offence under—

(a) section 24(1)(d), or

(b) section 21(1) of the Immigration, Asylum and Nationality Act 2006.

(2) The justice of the peace may grant a warrant authorising any immigration officer to arrest the person.

(3) In the application of this section to Scotland a reference to a justice of the peace shall be treated as a reference to the sheriff or a justice of the peace.

---

**KEYNOTE**

The offence under the Immigration, Asylum and Nationality Act 2006 relates to employing a person knowing that they are subject to immigration control when they have not been granted leave to enter or remain in the United Kingdom.

---

### 5.1.3.3 Search and Arrest by Warrant

The Immigration Act 1971, s. 28B states:

(1) Subsection (2) applies if a justice of the peace is, by written information on oath, satisfied that there are reasonable grounds for suspecting that a person ('the suspect') who is liable to be arrested for a relevant offence is to be found on any premises.

(2) The justice may grant a warrant authorising any immigration officer or constable to enter, if need be by force, the premises named in the warrant for the purpose of searching for and arresting the suspect.

(3) Subsection (4) applies if in Scotland the sheriff or a justice of the peace is by evidence on oath satisfied as mentioned in subsection (1).

(4) The sheriff or justice may grant a warrant authorising any immigration officer or constable to enter, if need be by force, the premises named in the warrant for the purpose of searching for and arresting the suspect.

---

**KEYNOTE**

A 'relevant offence' means an offence under s. 24(1)(a) to (f) (illegal entry) and s. 24A (use of deception). It also applies to the offences under ss. 2 and 35(3) of the Asylum and Immigration (Treatment of Claimants) Act 1999 (see chapter 5.3) and to the offence under s. 21 of the Immigration, Asylum and Nationality Act 2006 (see chapter 5.4).

'Premises' includes any vehicle, vessel, aircraft or hovercraft, any offshore installation, any renewable energy installation and any tent or moveable structure.

---

### 5.1.3.4 Search and Arrest Without Warrant

The Immigration Act 1971, s. 28C states:

(1) An immigration officer may enter and search any premises for the purpose of arresting a person for an offence under section 25, 25A or 25B.

---

**KEYNOTE**

The power may be exercised only to the extent that it is reasonably required for that purpose and only if the officer has reasonable grounds for believing that the person whom he is seeking is on the premises (s. 28(C)(2)).

In relation to premises consisting of two or more separate dwellings, the power is limited to entering and searching any parts of the premises which the occupiers of any dwelling comprised in the premises use in common with the occupiers of any such other dwelling and any such dwelling in which the officer has reasonable grounds for believing that the person whom he is seeking may be (s. 28(C)(3)).

The power may be exercised only if the officer produces identification showing that he is an immigration officer (whether or not he is asked to do so) (s. 28C(4)).

---

### 5.1.3.5 Business Premises: Entry to Arrest

The Immigration Act 1971, s. 28CA states:

(1) A constable or immigration officer may enter and search any business premises for the purpose of arresting a person—
   (a) for an offence under s. 24,
   (b) for an offence under s. 24A, or
   (c) under paragraph 17 of Schedule 2.

---

**KEYNOTE**

The power may be exercised only to the extent that it is reasonably required for the purpose of arresting a person (s. 28CA(2)(a)).

The constable or immigration officer has to have reasonable grounds for believing that the person whom he/she is seeking is on the premises (s. 28CA(2)(b)).

In the case of an immigration officer, the power may only be exercised with the authority of the Secretary of State (this will be given on behalf of the Secretary of State by a civil servant of at least the rank of Assistant Director) and if the immigration officer produces identification showing his/her status (s. 28CA(2)(c) and (d)). The authority will expire at the end of a period of seven days beginning with the day on which it was given (s. 28CA(3)).

In the case of a police officer, the power may only be exercised with the authority of an officer of the rank of chief superintendent or above (s. 28CA(2)(c)).

---

Where a constable or immigration officer enters premises in reliance on this section, and detains a person on the premises, a detainee custody officer may enter the premises for the purpose of carrying out a search (s. 28CA(5) and (6)). A 'detainee custody officer' means a person in respect of whom a certificate of authorisation is in force under s. 154 of the Immigration and Asylum Act 1999 and 'search' means a search under para. 2(1)(a) of sch. 13 to that Act (escort arrangements; power to search detained person).

### 5.1.3.6 Entry and Search of Premises

The Immigration Act 1971, s. 28D states:

(1) If, on the application made by an immigration officer, a justice of the peace is satisfied that there are reasonable grounds for believing that—
  (a) a relevant offence has been committed,
  (b) there is material on the premises specified in the application which is likely to be of substantial value (whether by itself or together with other material) to the investigation of the offence,
  (c) the material is likely to be relevant evidence,
  (d) the material does not consist of or include items subject to legal privilege, excluded material or special procedure material, and
  (e) any of the conditions specified in subsection (2) applies,
he may issue a warrant authorising an immigration officer to enter and search the premises.
(2) The conditions are that—
  (a) it is not practicable to communicate with any person entitled to grant entry to the premises;
  (b) it is practicable to communicate with a person entitled to grant entry to the premises but it is not practicable to communicate with any person entitled to grant access to the evidence;
  (c) entry to the premises will not be granted unless a warrant is produced;
  (d) the purpose of a search may be frustrated or seriously prejudiced unless an immigration officer arriving at the premises can secure immediate entry to them.

### KEYNOTE

An immigration officer may seize and retain anything for which the search has been authorised (s. 28D(3)).

'Relevant offence' covers a whole series of offences including offences under s. 24(1)(a) to (f) (illegal entry), s. 24A (use of deception), s. 25 (assisting unlawful immigration to a member state), s. 25A (helping an asylum-seeker) and s. 25B (assisting entry in breach of a deportation/exclusion order). It also applies to offences under ss. 2 and 35(3) of the Asylum and Immigration (Treatment of Claimants) Act 1999 (see chapter 5.3) and to the offence under s. 21 of the Immigration, Asylum and Nationality Act 2006 (see chapter 5.4).

For the meaning of items 'subject to legal privilege', 'excluded material' and 'special procedure material', see paras 1.5.3.8 to 1.5.3.10.

### 5.1.3.7 Entry and Search of Premises following Arrest

The Immigration Act 1971, s. 28E states:

(1) This section applies if a person is arrested for an offence under this Part at a place other than a police station.
(2) An immigration officer may enter and search any premises—
  (a) in which the person was when arrested, or
  (b) in which he was immediately before he was arrested,
for evidence relating to the offence for which the arrest was made ('relevant offence').
(3) The power may be exercised—
  (a) only if the officer has reasonable grounds for believing that there is evidence on the premises; and
  (b) only to the extent that it is reasonably required for the purpose of discovering relevant evidence.

### 5.1.3.8    Entry and Search of Premises following Arrest under Section 25, 25A or 25B

The Immigration Act 1971, s. 28F states:

(1) An immigration officer may enter and search any premises occupied or controlled by a person arrested for an offence under section 25, 25A, 25B.

(2) The power may be exercised—
  (a) only if the officer has reasonable grounds for suspecting that there is relevant evidence on the premises;
  (b) only to the extent that it is reasonably required for the purpose of discovering relevant evidence; and
  (c) subject to subsection (3), only if a senior officer has authorised it in writing.

(3) The power may be exercised—
  (a) before taking the arrested person to a place where he is to be detained; and
  (b) without obtaining an authorisation under subsection (2)(c),

if the presence of that person at a place other than one where he is to be detained is necessary for the effective investigation of the offence.

### 5.1.3.9    Search for Personal Records: Warrant Unnecessary

The Immigration Act 1971, s. 28FA states:

(1) This section applies where—
  (a) a person has been arrested for an offence under section 24(1) or 24A(1),
  (b) a person has been arrested under paragraph 17 of Schedule 2,
  (c) a constable or immigration officer reasonably believes that a person is liable to arrest for an offence under section 24(1) or 24A(1), or
  (d) a constable or immigration officer reasonably believes that a person is liable to arrest under paragraph 17 of Schedule 2.

(2) A constable or immigration officer may search business premises where the arrest was made or where the person liable to arrest is if the constable or immigration officer reasonably believes—

(a) that a person has committed an immigration employment offence in relation to the person arrested or liable to arrest, and

(b) that employee records, other than items subject to legal privilege, will be found on the premises and will be of substantial value (whether on their own or together with other material) in the investigation of the immigration employment offence.

(3) A constable or officer searching premises under subsection (2) may seize and retain employee records, other than items subject to legal privilege, which he reasonably suspects will be of substantial value (whether on their own or together with other material) in the investigation of—

(a) an immigration employment offence, or

(b) an offence under section 105 or 106 of the Immigration and Asylum Act 1999 (c. 33) (support for asylum-seeker: fraud).

---

**KEYNOTE**

Section 28FA(4) states that the power under subs. (2) may be exercised only to the extent that it is reasonably required for the purpose of discovering employee records other than items subject to legal privilege. The constable or immigration officer must produce identification showing his/her status (only when the premises are occupied) and the constable or immigration officer must reasonably believe that at least one of the following conditions applies.

Those conditions are—

- that it is not practicable to communicate with a person entitled to grant access to the records;
- that permission to search has been refused;
- that permission to search would be refused if requested; and
- that the purpose of a search may be frustrated or seriously prejudiced if it is not carried out in reliance on subs. (2) (s. 28FA(5)).

In this section 'immigration employment offence' means an offence under s. 21 of the Immigration, Asylum and Nationality Act 2006 (employment) (s. 28FA(7)).

'Business premises' means premises (or any part of premises) not used as a dwelling (Immigration Act 1971, s. 28L(2)).

'Employee records' means records which show an employee's name, date of birth, address, length of service, rate of pay, nationality or citizenship (Immigration Act 1971, s. 28L(3)).

For 'items subject to legal privilege', see para. 1.5.3.8.

---

### 5.1.3.10 Search for Personnel Records: With Warrant

The Immigration Act 1971, s. 28FB states:

(1) This section applies where on an application made by an immigration officer in respect of business premises a justice of the peace is satisfied that there are reasonable grounds for believing—

(a) that an employer has provided inaccurate or incomplete information under section 134 of the Nationality, Immigration and Asylum Act 2002 (compulsory disclosure by employer),

(b) that employee records, other than items subject to legal privilege, will be found on the premises and will enable deduction of some or all of the information which the employer was required to provide, and

(c) that at least one of the conditions in subsection (2) is satisfied.

(2) Those conditions are—

(a) that it is not practicable to communicate with a person entitled to grant access to the premises,

(b) that it is not practicable to communicate with a person entitled to grant access to the records,

(c) that entry to the premises or access to the records will not be granted unless a warrant is produced, and

(d) that the purpose of a search may be frustrated or seriously prejudiced unless an immigration officer arriving at the premises can secure immediate entry.

(3) The justice of the peace may issue a warrant authorising an immigration officer to enter and search the premises.

### 5.1.3.11 Searching Arrested Persons

The Immigration Act 1971, s. 28G states:

(1) This section applies if a person is arrested for an offence under this Part at a place other than a police station.

(2) An immigration officer may search the arrested person if he has reasonable grounds for believing that the arrested person may present a danger to himself or others.

(3) The officer may search the arrested person for—

    (a) anything which he might use to assist his escape from lawful custody; or

    (b) anything which might be evidence relating to the offence for which he has been arrested.

### 5.1.3.12 Searching Persons in Police Custody

The Immigration Act 1971, s. 28H states:

(1) This section applies if a person—

    (a) has been arrested for an offence under this Part; and

    (b) is in custody at a police station or in police detention at a place other than a police station.

(2) An immigration officer may, at any time, search the arrested person in order to see whether he has anything—

    (a) which he might use to—

        (i) cause physical injury to himself or others;

        (ii) damage property;

        (iii) interfere with evidence; or

        (iv) assist his escape; or

    (b) which the officer has reasonable grounds for believing is evidence relating to the offence in question.

For the meaning of 'an offence under this Part', **see para. 5.1.3.6.**

For the meaning of 'police detention', **see para. 1.6.5.2.**

For the meaning of 'custody officer', **see para. 1.6.2.**

The power may be exercised only to the extent that the custody officer concerned considers it to be necessary for the purpose of discovering anything of a kind mentioned in subs. (2) (s. 28H(3)).

The officer searching a person under this section may seize and retain anything he/she finds, if he/she has reasonable grounds for believing that that person might use it for one or more of the purposes mentioned in subs. (2)(a), in which case it may be retained by the police, or if it is evidence relating to the offence in question, in which case it may be retained by an immigration officer (s. 28H(4) to (6)).

The person from whom something is seized must be told the reason for the seizure unless he/she is:

- violent or appears likely to become violent; or
- is incapable of understanding what is said to him/her (s. 28H(7)).

An intimate search *may not* be conducted under this section (s. 28H(8)). For the meaning of an 'intimate search, **see para. 1.6.19.**

The person carrying out the search under this section *must* be the same sex as the person searched (s. 28H(9)).

# 5.2 The Immigration and Asylum Act 1999

> This chapter is only for examination candidates from Immigration Enforcement and the National Crime Agency.

## 5.2.1 Introduction

The Immigration and Asylum Act 1999 provides a significant power enabling the removal of a person who is not a British citizen from the United Kingdom. In addition to legislation available to deal with individuals who possess and/or use false documents in relation to immigration matters, the Act provides several offences to deal with false and dishonest representations made in respect of part VI of the Act. Part VI of the Act acknowledges that an asylum-seeker and his/her dependants may need support from the State in the form of accommodation or provision for essential living needs (including meals and personal care items) or both.

## 5.2.2 Removal of Certain Persons Unlawfully in the United Kingdom

The Immigration and Asylum Act 1999, s. 10 states:

(1) A person who is not a British citizen may be removed from the United Kingdom, in accordance with directions given by an immigration officer, if—
  (a) having only a limited leave to enter or remain, he does not observe a condition attached to the leave or remains beyond the time limited by the leave;
  (b) he has obtained leave to remain by deception; or
  (c) directions ('the first directions') have been given for the removal, under this section, of a person ('the other person') to whose family he belongs.
(2) Directions may not be given under subsection (1)(a) if the person concerned has made an application for leave to remain in accordance with regulations made under section 9.
(3) Directions may not be given under subsection (1)(c) unless the Secretary of State has given the person concerned written notice, not more than eight weeks after the other person left the United Kingdom in accordance with the first directions, that he intends to remove the person concerned from the United Kingdom.
(4) If such a notice is sent by the Secretary of State by first class post, addressed to the person concerned's last known address, it is to be taken to have been received by that person on the second day after the day on which it was posted.
(5) Directions for the removal of a person under subsection (1)(c) cease to have effect if he ceases to belong to the family of the other person.
(6) Directions under this section—
  (a) may be given only to persons falling within a prescribed class;
  (b) may impose any requirements of a prescribed kind.
(7) In relation to any such directions, paragraphs 10, 11, 16 to 18, 21 and 22 to 24 of Schedule 2 to the 1971 Act (administrative provisions as to control of entry), apply as they apply in relation to directions given under paragraph 8 of that Schedule.

(8) Directions for the removal of a person given under this section invalidate any leave to enter or remain in the United Kingdom given to him before the directions are given or while they are in force.

(9) The costs of complying with a direction given under this section (so far as reasonably incurred) must be met by the Secretary of State.

---

**KEYNOTE**

Anyone who had been lawfully in the United Kingdom but who no longer had any entitlement to remain would normally be subject to administrative removal rather than deportation. This section provides that those who have failed to observe the conditions attached to their leave, overstayers and those who have obtained leave to remain by deception, i.e. those currently liable to deportation action under s. 3(5)(a) and (aa) of the 1971 Act, and the family members of such people, will be subject to administrative removal procedures. These procedures mirror those which apply in respect of illegal entrants. Deportation action applies to cases where the Secretary of State deems the person's removal to be conducive to the public good and to court-recommended cases (s. 3(5)(b) and (6) of the 1971 Act) and to the family members of someone deported on those grounds.

Section 10(2) makes it clear that an overstayer who has applied for leave to remain under the special arrangements set out in s. 9 *cannot* be removed under the removal procedures (if an application is subsequently *refused*, the person concerned *will be* subject to deportation proceedings and will have a right of appeal to the Immigration Appellate Authority).

Section 10(3) places a time limit on taking removal action against the family member of someone who is being, or has been, removed.

---

## 5.2.3 Offences under the Immigration and Asylum Act 1999

False or dishonest representations in support of an asylum-seeker are dealt with by the Immigration and Asylum Act 1999.

### 5.2.3.1 False Representations in Respect of Support for an Asylum-Seeker

OFFENCE: **False Representations—*Immigration and Asylum Act 1999, s. 105***
- Triable summarily • Three months' imprisonment and/or a fine

The Immigration and Asylum Act 1999, s. 105 states:

(1) A person is guilty of an offence if, with a view to obtaining support for himself or any other person under any provision made by or under this Part, he—
   (a) makes a statement or representation which he knows is false in a material particular;
   (b) produces or gives to a person exercising functions under this Part, or knowingly causes or allows to be produced or given to such a person, any document or information which he knows is false in a material particular;
   (c) fails, without reasonable excuse, to notify a change of circumstances when required to do so in accordance with any provision made by or under this Part; or
   (d) without reasonable excuse, knowingly causes another person to fail to notify a change of circumstances which that other person was required to notify in accordance with any provision made by or under this Part.

### 5.2.3.2 Dishonest Representations in Respect of Support for an Asylum-Seeker

OFFENCE: **Dishonest Representations—*Immigration and Asylum Act 1999, s. 106***
- Triable either way • Seven years' imprisonment and/or a fine on indictment
- Six months' imprisonment and/or a fine summarily

The Immigration and Asylum Act 1999, s. 106 states:

(1) A person is guilty of an offence if, with a view to obtaining any benefit or other payment or advantage under this Part for himself or any other person, he dishonestly—
  (a) makes a statement or representation which is false in a material particular;
  (b) produces or gives to a person exercising functions under this Part, or causes or allows to be produced or given to such a person, any document or information which is false in a material particular;
  (c) fails to notify a change of circumstances when required to do so in accordance with any provision made by or under this Part; or
  (d) causes another person to fail to notify a change of circumstances which that other person was required to notify in accordance with any provision made by or under this Part.

(2) ...

(3) In the application of this section to Scotland, in subsection (1) for 'dishonestly' substitute 'knowingly'.

---

**KEYNOTE**

The power to enter and search (under s. 28E of the Immigration Act 1971) applies to these offences (see para. 5.1.3.7).

The power to search a person (under s. 28G of the Immigration Act 1971) applies to a person arrested for these offences (see para. 5.1.3.11).

# The Asylum and Immigration (Treatment of Claimants, etc.) Act 2004

> This chapter is only for examination candidates from Immigration Enforcement and the National Crime Agency.

## 5.3.1 Introduction

In addition to the more general immigration offences and provisions discussed in **chapter 5.1**, there are specific statutory measures designed to deal with other immigration offences. These are dealt with by the Asylum and Immigration (Treatment of Claimants, etc.) Act 2004.

## 5.3.2 Offences

There has been a steady flow of offences covered by s. 2 of the Act (failing to produce an immigration document) and the offence under s. 35 (fail to comply with a requirement) is high on the agenda across Immigration Enforcement. In addition, the offence relating to trafficking people into, within or out of the United Kingdom for the purpose of exploitation is constantly in the media spotlight due to its increasing occurrence.

### 5.3.2.1 Entering the United Kingdom without a Passport, etc.

OFFENCE: **Entering the United Kingdom without a Passport etc.—*Asylum and Immigration (Treatment of Claimants, etc.) Act 2004, s. 2***
- Triable either way • Two years' imprisonment and/or a fine on indictment
- Six months' imprisonment and/or a fine summarily

The Asylum and Immigration (Treatment of Claimants) Act 2004, s. 2 states:

(1) A person commits an offence if at a leave or asylum interview he does not have with him an immigration document which—
   (a) is in force, and
   (b) satisfactorily establishes his identity and nationality or citizenship.
(2) A person commits an offence if at a leave or asylum interview he does not have with him, in respect of any dependent child with whom he claims to be travelling or living, an immigration document which—
   (a) is in force, and
   (b) satisfactorily establishes the child's identity and nationality or citizenship.
(3) But a person does not commit an offence under subsection (1) or (2) if—
   (a) the interview referred to in that subsection takes place after the person has entered the United Kingdom, and

(b) within the period of three days beginning with the date of the interview the person provides to an immigration officer or to the Secretary of State a document of the kind referred to in that subsection.

(4) It is a defence for a person charged with an offence under subsection (1)—

(a) to prove that he is an EEA national,

(b) to prove that he is a member of the family of an EEA national and that he is exercising a right under the Community Treaties in respect of entry to or residence in the United Kingdom,

(c) to prove that he has a reasonable excuse for not being in possession of a document of the kind specified in subsection (1),

(d) to produce a false immigration document and to prove that he used that document as an immigration document for all purposes in connection with his journey to the United Kingdom, or

(e) to prove that he travelled to the United Kingdom without, at any stage since he set out on the journey, having possession of an immigration document.

(5) It is a defence for a person charged with an offence under subsection (2) in respect of a child—

(a) to prove that the child is an EEA national,

(b) to prove that the child is a member of the family of an EEA national and that the child is exercising a right under the Community Treaties in respect of entry to or residence in the United Kingdom,

(c) to prove that the person has a reasonable excuse for not being in possession of a document of the kind specified in subsection (2),

(d) to produce a false immigration document and to prove that it was used as an immigration document for all purposes in connection with the child's journey to the United Kingdom, or

(e) to prove that he travelled to the United Kingdom with the child without, at any stage since he set out on the journey, having possession of an immigration document in respect of the child.

(6) Where the charge for an offence under subsection (1) or (2) relates to an interview which takes place after the defendant has entered the United Kingdom—

(a) subsections (4)(c) and (5)(c) shall not apply, but

(b) it is a defence for the defendant to prove that he has a reasonable excuse for not providing a document in accordance with subsection (3).

(7) For the purposes of subsections (4) to (6)—

(a) the fact that a document was deliberately destroyed or disposed of is not a reasonable excuse for not being in possession of it or for not providing it in accordance with subsection (3), unless it is shown that the destruction or disposal was—

(i) for a reasonable cause, or

(ii) beyond the control of the person charged with the offence, and

(b) in paragraph (a)(i) 'reasonable cause' does not include the purpose of—

(i) delaying the handling or resolution of a claim or application or the taking of a decision,

(ii) increasing the chances of success of a claim or application, or

(iii) complying with instructions or advice given by a person who offers advice about, or facilitates, immigration into the United Kingdom, unless in the circumstances of the case it is unreasonable to expect non-compliance with the instructions or advice.

(8) A person shall be presumed for the purposes of this section not to have a document with him if he fails to produce it to an immigration officer or official of the Secretary of State on request.

---

**KEYNOTE**

If a person is unable to produce an immigration document at a leave or asylum interview in respect of either himself or a child with whom he claims to be living or travelling then he will commit an offence. A person does not commit the offence if the interview takes place after the person has entered the United Kingdom and within the period of three days beginning with the date of that interview the person provides an immigration document to an immigration officer or to the Secretary of State.

There are various defences to the charges. In respect of a person's failure to produce his own document it will be a defence for the him to prove that:

(a) he is an EEA national,

(b) he is a member of the family of an EEA national and he is exercising a right under the Community Treaties in respect of entry to or residence in the United Kingdom,

(c)  he has a reasonable excuse for not being in possession of an immigration document, or

(d)  he travelled to the United Kingdom without, at any stage since he set out on that journey, having possession of an immigration document.

It is also a defence for a person to produce a false immigration document and to prove that he used that document as an immigration document for all purposes in connection with his journey to the United Kingdom.

In respect of a person's failure to produce a document for a child with whom he claims to be living or travelling it will be a defence for him to prove that:

(a)  the child is an EEA national,

(b)  the child is a member of the family of an EEA national and that he is exercising a right under Community Treaties in respect of entry to or residence in the United Kingdom,

(c)  the person has a reasonable excuse for not being in possession of an immigration document in respect of the child, or

(d)  that he travelled to the United Kingdom with the child without, at any stage since he set out on the journey, having possession of an immigration document in respect of the child.

It is also a defence for a person to produce a false immigration document and to prove that it was used as an immigration document for all purposes in connection with the child's journey to the United Kingdom.

A person *will not* be able to rely on the deliberate destruction or disposal of a document as their excuse for not being in possession of it unless it was done for a reasonable cause or was beyond his control. It will not be a reasonable cause, however, if the document was destroyed or disposed of with a view to delaying a claim or increasing its chances of success or on the instructions or advice of a facilitator—unless it would have been unreasonable to expect non-compliance.

An immigration officer or a police constable who has a reasonable suspicion that an offence under the section has been committed may arrest the person without a warrant (s. 2(10)).

'EEA national' means a national of a State which is a contracting party to the Agreement on the European Economic Area signed at Oporto on 2 May 1992 (as it has effect from time to time).

An 'immigration document' means:

(a)  a passport, and

(b)  a document which relates to a national of a State other than the United Kingdom and which is designed to serve the same purpose as a passport.

The phrase 'leave or asylum interview' means an interview with an immigration officer or an official of the Secretary of State at which a person—

(a)  seeks leave to enter or remain in the United Kingdom, or

(b)  claims that to remove him from or require him to leave the United Kingdom would breach the United Kingdom's obligations under the Refugee Convention or would be unlawful under s. 6 of the Human Rights Act 1998 as being incompatible with his Convention rights.

For the purposes of this section a document which purports to be, or is designed to look like, an immigration document, is a false immigration document, and an immigration document is a false immigration document if and in so far as it is used—

(i)  outside the period for which it is expressed to be valid,

(ii)  contrary to provision for its use made by the person issuing it, or

(iii)  by or in respect of a person other than the person to or for whom it was issued.

## 5.3.2.2    Trafficking People for Exploitation

OFFENCE:  **Trafficking People for Exploitation—*Asylum and Immigration (Treatment of Claimants, etc.) Act 2004, s. 4***
  - • Triable either way  • Fourteen years' imprisonment and/or a fine on indictment
  - • Six months' imprisonment and/or a fine summarily

The Asylum and Immigration (Treatment of Claimants etc.) Act 2004, s. 4 states:

(1) A person commits an offence if he arranges or facilitates the arrival in, or the entry into the United Kingdom of an individual (the 'passenger') and—
  (a) he intends to exploit the passenger in the United Kingdom or elsewhere, or
  (b) he believes that another person is likely to exploit the passenger in the United Kingdom or elsewhere.

(2) A person commits an offence if he arranges or facilitates travel within the United Kingdom by an individual (the 'passenger') in respect of whom he believes that an offence under sub-section (1) may have been committed and—
  (a) he intends to exploit the passenger in the United Kingdom or elsewhere, or
  (b) he believes that another person is likely to exploit the passenger in the United Kingdom or elsewhere.

(3) A person commits an offence if he arranges or facilitates the departure from the United Kingdom of an individual (the 'passenger') and—
  (a) he intends to exploit the passenger outside the United Kingdom, or
  (b) he believes that another person is likely to exploit the passenger outside the United Kingdom.

**KEYNOTE**

This offence covers arranging or facilitating the arrival in, departure from or travel within the United Kingdom of a whole series of different vulnerable categories of person, in each case with the relevant intention or belief with regard to that person's exploitation.

For the purposes of this section a person is exploited if:

- they are the victim of behaviour that contravenes Article 4 of the European Convention on Human Rights (slavery and forced labour);
- they are encouraged, required or expected to do anything as a result of which they (or another person) would commit an offence under the Human Organ Transplants Act 1989;
- they are subjected to force, threats or deception designed to induce them to provide services, to provide another person with benefits or to enable another person to acquire benefits of any kind;
- they are requested or induced to undertake *any activity*, having been chosen on the grounds that they are mentally or physically ill or disabled, young or have a family relationship with a person and a person without the illness, disability, youth or family relationship would be likely to refuse the request or resist the inducement (s. 4(4)).

Where the offence is committed within the context of employment there are further considerations and offences and the advice of the Home Office Immigration and Nationality Directorate should be sought.

### 5.3.2.3 Deportation or Removal: Cooperation

The Asylum and Immigration (Treatment of Claimants, etc.) Act 2004, s. 35 states:

(1) The Secretary of State may require a person to take specified action if the Secretary of State thinks that—
  (a) the action will or may enable a travel document to be obtained by or for the person, and
  (b) possession of the travel document will facilitate the person's deportation or removal from the United Kingdom.

(2) In particular, the Secretary of State may require a person to—
  (a) provide information or documents to the Secretary of State or to any other person;
  (b) obtain information or documents;
  (c) provide fingerprints, submit to the taking of a photograph or provide information, or submit to a process for the recording of information, about external physical characteristics (including, in particular, features of the iris or any other part of the eye);
  (d) make, or consent to or cooperate with the making of, an application to a person acting for the government of a State other than the United Kingdom;
  (e) cooperate with a process designed to enable determination of an application;
  (f) complete a form accurately and completely;
  (g) attend an interview and answer questions accurately and completely;
  (h) make an appointment.

**KEYNOTE**

Under s. 35(3), a person commits an offence if he fails without *reasonable excuse* to comply with a requirement of the Secretary of State under s. 35(1). Fear of persecution in the home country was held *not* to constitute a reasonable excuse for non-compliance with a requirement to attend for interview by officials of that country's Embassy in *R* v *Tabnak* [2007] EWCA Crim 380. Reasonable excuse should relate to *ability*, not willingness, to comply. Home Office guidance on the Act indicates that travel difficulties and health emergencies might constitute reasonable excuses.

The offence is triable either way and punishable with two years' imprisonment and/or a fine on indictment or, on summary conviction, to imprisonment for six months' and/or a fine.

If a constable or immigration officer reasonably suspects that a person has committed an offence under s. 35(3) then he/she may arrest the person without warrant (s. 35(5)).

A 'travel document' means a passport or other document which is issued by or for Her Majesty's Government or the government of another State and which enables or facilitates travel from the United Kingdom to another State.

The term 'removal from the United Kingdom' means removal under—

(a) sch. 2 to the Immigration Act 1971 (control on entry) (including a provision of that schedule as applied by another provision of the Immigration Acts);
(b) s. 10 of the Immigration and Asylum Act 1999 (removal of person unlawfully in United Kingdom), or
(c) sch. 3 to this Act.

# The Immigration, Asylum and Nationality Act 2006

This chapter is only for examination candidates from Immigration Enforcement and the National Crime Agency.

## 5.4.1 Introduction

In the same way that a 'handler' of stolen property may be seen to encourage offences of theft, those who employ persons who are subject to immigration control may be seen to encourage immigration offences.

## 5.4.2 Offences

Sections 21 and 22 of the Immigration, Asylum and Nationality Act 2006 create offences dealing with individuals and bodies corporate who employ persons subject to immigration control.

### 5.4.2.1 Employing Persons Known to be Not Entitled to Work in the United Kingdom

OFFENCE: **Employing Persons—*Immigration, Asylum and Nationality Act 2006, s. 21***
- Triable either way • Two years' imprisonment and/or a fine on indictment
- Six months' imprisonment and/or a fine summarily

The Immigration, Asylum and Nationality Act 2006, s. 21 states:

(1) A person commits an offence if he employs another ('the employee') knowing that the employee is an adult subject to immigration control and that—
 (a) he has not been granted leave to enter or remain in the United Kingdom, or
 (b) his leave to enter or remain in the United Kingdom—
  (i) is invalid,
  (ii) has ceased to have effect (whether by reason of curtailment, revocation, cancellation, passage of time or otherwise), or
  (iii) is subject to a condition preventing him from accepting the employment.

**KEYNOTE**

Section 21 creates an offence of employing a person knowing that they are an adult subject to immigration control who has not been granted leave to enter or remain (unless granted permission to work by the Secretary of State), or whose leave to remain is invalid, has ceased to have effect (whether by reason of curtailment, revocation, cancellation, passage of time or otherwise) or subject to a condition preventing him from accepting the employment.

The Immigration, Asylum and Nationality Act 2006, s. 22 states:

(1) For the purposes of section 21(1) a body (whether corporate or not) shall be treated as knowing a fact about an employee if a person who has responsibility within the body for an aspect of the employment knows the fact.

(2) If an offence under section 21(1) is committed by a body corporate with the consent or connivance of an officer of the body, the officer, as well as the body, shall be treated as having committed the offence.

(3) In subsection (2) a reference to an officer of a body includes a reference to—
    (a) a director, manager or secretary,
    (b) a person purporting to act as a director, manager or secretary, and
    (c) if the affairs of the body are managed by its members, a member.

(4) Where an offence under section 21(1) is committed by a partnership (whether or not a limited partnership) subsection (2) above shall have effect, but as if a reference to an officer of the body were a reference to—
    (a) a partner, and
    (b) a person purporting to act as a partner.

---

**KEYNOTE**

Section 22 defines the liability of bodies corporate, officers of bodies, and members of partnerships in relation to the criminal offence in s. 21.

---

5.5

# The UK Borders Act 2007

> This chapter is only for examination candidates from Immigration Enforcement and the National Crime Agency.

## 5.5.1 Introduction

This is a large piece of legislation but only one offence is dealt with in this chapter—assaulting an immigration officer.

## 5.5.2 Assaulting an Immigration Officer

OFFENCE: **Assaulting an Immigration Officer—*UK Borders Act 2007, s. 22***
- Triable summarily • Six months' imprisonment and/or a fine

The UK Borders Act 2007, s. 22 states:

(1) A person who assaults an immigration officer commits an offence.

> **KEYNOTE**
>
> Whilst this offence specifically caters for an assault committed on an immigration officer, other assault offences (under the Offences Against the Person Act 1861—see chapter 3.2) may be more appropriate should the nature of the injury warrant it.

# 5.6 The Identity Documents Act 2010

> This chapter is only for examination candidates from Immigration Enforcement and the National Crime Agency.

## 5.6.1 Introduction

You may have noticed that in the section dealing with 'Fraud' (**see chapter 2.6**) there was no mention of false passports or immigration documents in the offence dealing with custody or control of specific instruments and materials (Forgery and Counterfeiting Act 1981, s. 5(2) and (4)). This is because the Identity Cards Act 2006 specifically dealt with these documents under s. 25. The Identity Cards Act 2006 was, in turn, repealed on 21 January 2011 by the Identity Documents Act 2010, s. 1(1). Offences and definitions that appeared in the Identity Cards Act 2006 now appear as offences and definitions in the 2010 Act.

## 5.6.2 Offences under the Identity Documents Act 2010

The main offences associated with false identity documents are provided for under ss. 4 to 6 of the Act.

### 5.6.2.1 Possession of False Identity Documents, etc. with Improper Intention

OFFENCE: **Possession of False Identity Documents etc. with Improper Intention—*Identity Documents Act 2010, s. 4***
- Triable on indictment • Ten years' imprisonment and/or a fine

The Identity Documents Act 2010, s. 4 states:

(1) It is an offence for a person ('P') with an improper intention to have in P's possession or under P's control—
  (a) an identity document that is false and that P knows or believes to be false,
  (b) an identity document that was improperly obtained and that P knows or believes to have been improperly obtained, or
  (c) an identity document that relates to someone else.
(2) Each of the following is an improper intention—
  (a) the intention of using the document for establishing personal information about P;
  (b) the intention of allowing or inducing another to use it for establishing, ascertaining or verifying personal information about P or anyone else.
(3) In subsection (2)(b) the reference to P or anyone else does not include, in the case of a document within subsection (1)(c), the individual to whom it relates.

OFFENCE: **Apparatus Designed or Adapted for the Making of False Identity Documents etc.—*Identity Documents Act 2010, s. 5***
- Triable on indictment • Ten years' imprisonment and/or a fine

The Identity Documents Act 2010, s. 5 states:

(1) It is an offence for a person ('P') with the prohibited intention to make or to have in P's possession or under P's control—
   (a) any apparatus which, to P's knowledge, is or has been specially designed or adapted for the making of false identity documents, or
   (b) any article or material which, to P's knowledge, is or has been specially designed or adapted to be used in the making of such documents.
(2) The prohibited intention is the intention—
   (a) that P or another will make a false identity document, and
   (b) that the document will be used by somebody for establishing, ascertaining or verifying personal information about a person.

OFFENCE: **Possession of False Identity Documents etc. without Reasonable Excuse—*Identity Documents Act 2010, s. 6***

- Triable either way • Two years' imprisonment and/or a fine on indictment
- Six months' imprisonment and/or a fine summarily

The Identity Documents Act 2010, s. 6 states:

(1) It is an offence for a person ('P'), without reasonable excuse, to have in P's possession or under P's control—
   (a) an identity document that is false,
   (b) an identity document that was improperly obtained,
   (c) an identity document that relates to someone else,
   (d) any apparatus which, to P's knowledge, is or has been specially designed or adapted for the making of false identity documents, or
   (e) any article or material which, to P's knowledge, is or has been specially designed or adapted to be used in the making of such documents.

### 5.6.2.2 Meaning of 'Identity Document'

The Identity Documents Act 2010, s. 7 states:

(1) For the purposes of sections 4 to 6 'identity document' means any document that is or purports to be—
   (a) an immigration document,
   (b) a United Kingdom passport (within the meaning of the Immigration Act 1971),
   (c) a passport issued by or on behalf of the authorities of a country or territory outside the United Kingdom or by or on behalf of an international organisation,
   (d) a document that can be used (in some or all circumstances) instead of a passport,
   (e) a licence to drive a motor vehicle granted under Part 3 of the Road Traffic Act 1988 or under Part 2 of the Road Traffic (Northern Ireland) Order 1981, or
   (f) a driving licence issued by or on behalf of the authorities of a country or territory outside the United Kingdom.
(2) In subsection (1)(a) 'immigration document' means—
   (a) a document used for confirming the right of a person under the EU Treaties in respect of entry or residence in the United Kingdom,
   (b) a document that is given in exercise of immigration functions and records information about leave granted to a person to enter or to remain in the United Kingdom, or
   (c) a registration card (within the meaning of section 26A of the Immigration Act 1971).
(3) In subsection (2)(b) 'immigration functions' means functions under the Immigration Acts (within the meaning of the Asylum and Immigration (Treatment of Claimants, etc.) Act 2004).
(4) References in subsection (1) to the issue of a document include its renewal, replacement or re-issue (with or without modifications).
(5) In this section 'document' includes a stamp or label.
(6) The Secretary of State may by order amend the definition of 'identity document'.

### 5.6.2.3 Meaning of 'Personal Information'

The Identity Documents Act 2010, s. 8 states:

(1) For the purposes of sections 4 and 5 'personal information', in relation to an individual ('A'), means—
   (a) A's full name,
   (b) other names by which A is or has previously been known,
   (c) A's gender,
   (d) A's date and place of birth,
   (e) external characteristics of A that are capable of being used for identifying A,
   (f) the address of A's principal place of residence in the United Kingdom,
   (g) the address of every other place in the United Kingdom or elsewhere where A has a place of residence,
   (h) where in the United Kingdom and elsewhere A has previously been resident,
   (i) the times at which A was resident at different places in the United Kingdom or elsewhere,
   (j) A's current residential status,
   (k) residential statuses previously held by A, and
   (l) information about numbers allocated to A for identification purposes and about the documents (including stamps or labels) to which they relate.
(2) In subsection (1) 'residential status' means—
   (a) A's nationality,
   (b) A's entitlement to remain in the United Kingdom, and
   (c) if that entitlement derives from a grant of leave to enter or remain in the United Kingdom, the terms and conditions of that leave.

### 5.6.2.4 Other Definitions

The Identity Documents Act 2010, s. 9 states:

(1) 'Apparatus' includes any equipment, machinery or device and any wire or cable, together with any software used with it.
(2) In relation to England and Wales and Northern Ireland, an identity document is 'false' only if it is false within the meaning of Part 1 of the Forgery and Counterfeiting Act 1981 (see section 9(1)).
(3) An identity document was 'improperly obtained' if—
   (a) false information was provided in, or in connection with, the application for its issue to the person who issued it, or
   (b) false information was provided in, or in connection with, an application for its modification to a person entitled to modify it.
(4) In subsection (3)—
   (a) 'false' information includes information containing any inaccuracy or omission that results in a tendency to mislead,
   (b) 'information' includes documents (including stamps and labels) and records, and
   (c) the 'issue' of a document includes its renewal, replacement or re-issue (with or without modifications).
(5) References to the making of a false identity document include the modification of an identity document so that it becomes false.
(6) This section applies for the purposes of sections 4 to 6.

---

**KEYNOTE**

The three offences at ss. 4, 5 and 6 are effectively the same as the older offence under s. 25 of the Identity Cards Act 2006. The s. 25(5) offence was considered in *R* v *Unah* [2011] All ER (D) 97 (Jul), in which it was held that whether the defendant's ignorance of a document's falsity would amount to a 'reasonable excuse' for possessing must be a question of fact. The same must be true for the offence under s. 6.

---

# 5.7 The Police and Criminal Evidence Act 1984—Powers

## The Police and Criminal Evidence Act 1984 (Application to Immigration Officers and Designated Customs Officials) Order 2013

> This chapter is only for examination candidates from Immigration Enforcement and the National Crime Agency.

### 5.7.1 The Order

The purpose of the 2013 Order is to apply certain provisions of the Police and Criminal Evidence Act 1984 (PACE) to criminal investigations conducted by immigration officers and designated customs officials and to persons designated by customs officials. This includes powers of arrest, search of premises and seizure of evidence as well as obligations in respect of persons detained on suspicion of having committed customs offences.

Immigration officers have not previously had access to the PACE powers. Customs officials currently have access to certain PACE powers relating to the criminal investigation and detention of suspects by virtue of the Police and Criminal Evidence Act 1984 (Application to Revenue and Customs Order) 2007 ('the 2007 PACE Order'). These powers were provided via application of s. 22 of the Borders, Citizenship and Immigration Act 2009. This Order extends certain PACE powers (such as arrest, search and seizure) to immigration officers carrying out criminal investigations and effectively replicates the PACE powers already available to customs officials under the 2007 PACE Order with the addition of some extra PACE provisions. It also repeals some of the provisions of the Borders, Citizenship and Immigration Act 2009.

Schedules 1 and 2 detail the provisions of PACE that are now applied to investigations conducted by immigration officers (sch. 1) and to investigations conducted, and to persons detained, by designated customs officials (sch. 2).

In relation to PACE, the following provisions apply to an investigation conducted by an immigration officer:

Section 8(1) to (6) (power of justice of the peace to authorise entry and search of premises) (subject to the modification in art. 8) (**see chapter 1.5**).
Section 9(1) (special provisions as to access) and sch. 1 (special procedure) (**see chapter 1.5**).
Section 15 (search warrants: safeguards) (**see chapter 1.5**).
Section 16 (execution of warrants) (**see chapter 1.5**).
Section 17(1)(a)(i), (1)(b), (1)(cb)(i), (1)(d), (2) and (4) (entry for purpose of arrest etc.) (**see chapter 1.5**).

Section 18 (entry and search after arrest) (subject to the modification in art. 10) (**see chapter 1.5**).

Section 19 (general power of seizure etc.) (subject to the modification in art. 9(1)) (**see chapter 1.5**).

Section 20 (extension of powers of seizure to computerised information) (**see chapter 1.5**).

Section 21 (access and copying) (subject to the modification in art. 9(3)) (**see chapter 1.5**).

Section 22(1) to (4) and (7) (retention) (subject to the modification in art. 11) (**see chapter 1.5**).

Section 24(1) to (5)(c)(iii) and (5)(d) to (5)(f) (arrest without warrant: constables) (subject to the modification in art. 7).

Section 28 (information to be given on arrest).

Section 29 (voluntary attendance at police station etc.).

Section 30(1) to (4)(a) and (5) to (13) (arrest elsewhere than at police station).

Section 31 (arrest for further offence).

Section 32(1) to (9) (search upon arrest).

Section 46A(1) and (1A) to (3) (power of arrest for failure to answer to police bail) (**see chapter 1.9**).

Section 51(b) (savings).

Section 107(2) (police officers performing duties of higher rank).

The Police and Criminal Evidence Act 1984 should be consulted for a full explanation of the above sections.

# 5.8 | Offences in Relation to Marriage

> This chapter is only for examination candidates from Immigration Enforcement and the National Crime Agency.

## 5.8.1 Introduction

'Sham' marriages are becoming a more common occurrence; some as an individual incident and others facilitated on a large scale. Although there may be a variety of immigration-related offences that individuals may be prosecuted for when involved in such behaviour, it is also worth considering certain offences relating to marriage that have been on the statute books for a little longer.

## 5.8.2 Bigamy

OFFENCE: **Bigamy—*Offences Against the Person Act 1861, s. 57***
  - Triable either way • On indictment seven years' imprisonment and/or a fine
  - Six months' imprisonment and/or a fine summarily

The Offences Against the Person Act 1861, s. 57 states:

> Whosoever, being married, shall marry any other person during the life of the former husband or wife, whether the second marriage shall have taken place in England or Ireland or elsewhere, shall be guilty of [an offence], and being convicted thereof shall be liable to [imprisonment] for any term not exceeding seven years....: Provided, that nothing in this section contained shall extend to any second marriage contracted elsewhere than in England and Ireland by any other than a subject of Her Majesty, or to any person marrying a second time whose husband or wife shall have been continually absent from such person for the space of seven years then last past, and shall not have been known by such person to be living within that time, or shall extend to any person who, at the time of such second marriage, shall have been divorced from the bond of the first marriage, or to any person whose former marriage shall have been declared void by the sentence of any court of competent jurisdiction.

### KEYNOTE

The *actus reus* of bigamy is committed where the defendant 'marries' another person whilst still lawfully married to a surviving spouse. No offence is committed, however, where the defendant's original spouse has been missing for seven years or more; nor is any offence committed under English law where a foreigner commits bigamy abroad, even if his original marriage was registered in England. If, however, the defendant is a British (or British overseas etc.) citizen, it is irrelevant where the bigamous marriage takes place, because bigamy is punishable in England and Wales (or in Northern Ireland) if committed by a person anywhere in the world (*R v Earl Russell* [1901] AC 446).

The defendant must go through a ceremony of marriage that purports to be legally binding. The defendant does not commit bigamy where, for example, he contracts an unregistered Islamic marriage in England without disclosing the existence of a subsisting marriage (*Al-Mudaris* v *Al-Mudaris* [2001] All ER (D) 288 (Feb)).

The burden is on the prosecution to prove that the defendant was validly married on an earlier occasion and that this marriage was still subsisting at the time of the second ceremony.

To establish the defence (continually absent for seven years), the defendant must adduce evidence of continual absence for that period. The prosecution must then prove either that there was no such continual absence or that the defendant knew his/her spouse to be alive at some time during that period.

## 5.8.3 False Statements with Reference to Marriage

OFFENCE: **False Statements with Reference to Marriage—*Perjury Act 1911, s. 3***

- Triable either way • On indictment seven years' imprisonment and/or a fine
- Six months' imprisonment and/or a fine summarily

The Perjury Act 1911, s. 3 states:

(1) If any person—
  (a) For the purpose of procuring a marriage, or a certificate or licence for marriage, knowingly and wilfully makes a false oath, or makes or signs a false declaration, notice or certificate required under any Act of Parliament for the time being in force relating to marriage; or
  (b) knowingly and wilfully makes, or knowingly and wilfully causes to be made, for the purpose of being inserted in any register of marriage, a false statement as to any particular required by law to be known and registered relating to any marriage; or
  (c) forbids the issue of any certificate or licence for marriage by falsely representing himself to be a person whose consent to the marriage is required by law knowing such representation to be false, or
  (d) with respect to a declaration made under section 16(1A) or 27B(2) of the Marriage Act 1949—
    (i) enters a caveat under subsection (2) of the said section 16, or
    (ii) makes a statement mentioned in subsection (4) of the said section 27B, which he knows to be false in a material particular.
  he shall be guilty of [an offence].
(2) No prosecution for knowingly and wilfully making a false declaration for the purpose of procuring any marriage out of the district in which the parties or one of them dwell shall take place after the expiration of eighteen months from the solemnization of the marriage to which the declaration refers.

### KEYNOTE

An offence under s. 3 is committed *only* by a person who acts for the purposes of procuring a marriage or licence etc. but whether or not he/she succeeds in this purpose is irrelevant. A false statement cannot, however, give rise to liability under s. 3(1)(a) or (b), unless it concerns something which must be by law stated correctly (*R* v *Frickey* [1956] Crim LR 421).

A similar offence in respect of civil partnerships exists (see Civil Partnership Act 2004, s. 80).

Section 13 of the Perjury Act 1911 (corroboration is required in perjury cases) will apply to this offence (see also para. 1.12.1).

Every person who aids, abets, counsels, procures or suborns another person to commit an offence against this Act [Perjury Act 1911] shall be liable to be proceeded against, indicted, tried and punished as if he/she were a principal offender (Perjury Act 1911, s. 7(1)).

Every person who incites another person to commit an offence against this Act shall be guilty of [an offence], and, on conviction thereof on indictment, shall be liable to imprisonment, or to a fine, or to both such imprisonment and fine (Perjury Act 1911, s. 7(2)).

# PART SIX

# Offences in Customs and Excise Management and Serious Organised Crime
# (This section is for National Crime Agency Candidates **only**)

This Part covers offences under the Customs and Excise Management Act 1979 and the Serious Organised Crime and Police Act 2005, as well as the associated powers. There is also coverage of offenders assisting investigations and prosecutions.

The information in this Part is fully testable for candidates from the National Crime Agency *only*. Please see **How to use** *Blackstone's Police Investigators' Manual 2014* on page xvii for further information.

# 6.1 The Customs and Excise Management Act 1979

| This chapter is only for examination candidates from the National Crime Agency. |
| :--- |

## 6.1.1 Introduction

Until 2005 the Inland Revenue and Customs and Excise were separate government departments. As a consequence of this historical separation, the legislation creating offences against the public revenue and the powers associated with them are contained in different Acts of Parliament, although the major piece of legislation dealing with this area of the law is the Customs and Excise Management Act 1979.

## 6.1.2 Powers under the Customs and Excise Management Act 1979

As you might expect, there are a large number of powers available to an authorised officer under the Act; this section examines powers under parts III, IV, XI and XII of the Act.

### 6.1.2.1 Officers' Powers of Boarding

The Customs and Excise Management Act 1979, s. 27 states:

(1) At any time while a ship is within the limits of a port, or an aircraft is at an aerodrome, or a vehicle is—
  (a) entering, leaving or about to leave the United Kingdom,
  (b) within the prescribed area,
  (c) within the limits of or entering or leaving a port or any land adjacent to a port and occupied wholly or mainly for the purpose of activities carried on at the port,
  (d) at, entering or leaving an aerodrome,
  (e) at, entering or leaving an approved wharf, transit shed, customs warehouse or free zone, or
  (f) at, entering or leaving any such premises as are mentioned in subsection (1) of section 112 below,

  any officer and any other person duly engaged in the prevention of smuggling may board the ship, aircraft or vehicle and remain therein and rummage and search any part thereof.

> **KEYNOTE**
>
> A 'ship' includes any boat or other vessel whatsoever (and, to the extent provided in s. 2, any hovercraft). All other provisions of the customs and excise Acts shall apply as if references (however expressed) to goods or passengers carried in or moved by ships or vessels included references to goods or passengers carried in or moved by hovercraft (Customs and Excise Management Act 1979, s. 1).
>
> A 'port' means a port appointed by the Commissioners under s. 19 of the Customs and Excise Management Act 1979.
>
> An 'aerodrome' means any area of land or water designed, equipped, set apart or commonly used for affording facilities for the landing and departure of aircraft (Customs and Excise Act 1971, s. 1).

For the definitions of the terms 'vehicle', 'approved wharf' and 'transit shed', see para. 6.1.2.1.

For the purposes of subs. (1), 'customs warehouse' means a victualling warehouse or a place approved by the Commissioners under Article 98 of Council Regulation (EEC) No. 2913/92 or Article 505 of Commission Regulation (EEC) No. 2454/93 (s. 27(1A)).

The Treasury may, by order, designate any area in the United Kingdom as a special area for customs purposes. An area so designated shall be known as a 'free zone' (Customs and Excise Management Act 1979, s. 1).

Subsection (1) of s. 112 states, ' An officer may, subject to subsection (2) below, at any time enter upon any premises of which entry is made, or is required by or under the revenue trade provisions of the customs and excise Acts to be made, or any other premises owned or used by a revenue trader for the purposes of his trade and may inspect the premises and search for, examine and take account of any machinery, vehicles, vessels, utensils, goods or materials belonging to or in any way connected with that trade' (Customs and Excise Management Act 1979, s. 112(1)).

A further power and associated offence is provided for at s. 27(2):

The Commissioners may station officers in any ship at any time while it is within the limits of a port, and if the master of any ship neglects or refuses to provide—

(a) reasonable accommodation below decks for any officer stationed therein; or

(b) means of safe access to and egress from the ship in accordance with the requirements of any such officer,

the master shall be liable on summary conviction to a penalty of level 2 on the standard scale.

### 6.1.2.2 Officers' Powers of Access

The Customs and Excise Management Act 1979, s. 28 states:

(1) Without prejudice to section 27 above, the proper officer shall have free access to every part of any ship or aircraft at a port or aerodrome and of any vehicle which falls within paragraphs (a) to (f) of subsection (1) of section 27 above or is brought to a customs and excise station, and may—

(a) cause any goods to be marked before they are unloaded from that ship, aircraft or vehicle;

(b) lock up, seal, mark or otherwise secure any goods carried in the ship, aircraft or vehicle or any place or container in which they are so carried; and

(c) break open any place or container which is locked and of which the keys are withheld.

---

**KEYNOTE**

'Proper' in relation to the person by, with or whom, or the place at which, anything is to be done, means the person or place appointed or authorised in that behalf by the Commissioners (Customs and Excise Management Act 1971, s. 1).

For 'ship', 'port' and 'aerodrome', see para. 6.1.3.1.

For 'goods', 'vehicle' and 'container', see para. 6.1.2.1.

Any goods found concealed on board any such ship, aircraft or vehicle shall be liable to forfeiture (s. 28(2)).

---

### 6.1.2.3 Power to Inspect Aircraft, Aerodromes, Records, etc.

The Customs and Excise Management Act 1979, s. 33 states:

(1) The commander of an aircraft shall permit an officer at any time to board the aircraft and inspect—

(a) the aircraft and any goods loaded therein; and

(b) all documents relating to the aircraft or to goods or persons carried therein;

and an officer shall have the right of access at any time to any place to which access is required for the purpose of any such inspection.

(2) The person in control of any aerodrome shall permit an officer at any time to enter upon and inspect the aerodrome and all buildings and goods thereon.

(3) The person in control of an aerodrome licensed under any enactment relating to air navigation and, if so required by the Commissioners, the person in control of any other aerodrome shall—

(a) keep a record in such form and manner as the Commissioners may approve of all aircraft arriving at or departing from the aerodrome;

(b) keep that record available and produce it on demand to any officer, together with all other documents kept on the aerodrome which relate to the movement of aircraft; and

(c) permit any officer to make copies of and take extracts from any such record or document.

---

**KEYNOTE**

'Commander' in relation to aircraft, includes any person having or taking the charge or command of the aircraft (Customs and Excise Management Act 1979, s. 1).

For 'goods', see para. 6.1.2.1.

For 'aerodrome', see para. 6.1.3.1.

If any person contravenes or fails to comply with any of the provisions of this section he shall be liable on summary conviction to a penalty of level 4 on the standard scale or to imprisonment for a term not exceeding 3 months, or to both (s. 33(4)).

---

### 6.1.2.4 Power to Prevent Flight of Aircraft

The Customs and Excise Management Act 1979, s. 34 states:

(1) If it appears to any officer or constable that an aircraft is intended or likely to depart for a destination outside the United Kingdom and the Isle of Man from—

(a) any place other than a customs and excise airport; or

(b) a customs and excise airport before clearance outwards is given,

he may give such instructions and take such steps by way of detention of the aircraft or otherwise as appear to him necessary in order to prevent the flight.

---

**KEYNOTE**

A 'customs and excise airport' means an aerodrome for the time being designated as a place for the landing or departure of aircraft for the purposes of the customs and excise Acts by an order made by the Secretary of State with the concurrence of the Commissioners which is in force under an Order in Council made in pursuance of s. 60 of the Civil Aviation Act 1982 (Customs and Excise Management Act 1979, s. 1).

Any person who contravenes any instructions given under subs. (1) shall be liable on summary conviction to a penalty of level 4 on the standard scale, or to imprisonment for a term not exceeding 3 months, or to both (s.34(2)).

If an aircraft flies in contravention of any instruction given under subs. (1) or notwithstanding any steps taken to prevent the flight, the owner and the commander thereof shall, without prejudice to the liability of any other person under subs. (2), each be liable on summary conviction to a penalty of level 4 on the standard scale, or to imprisonment for a term not exceeding three months, or to both, unless he proves that the flight took place without his consent or connivance (s. 34(3)).

---

### 6.1.2.5 Forfeiture of Goods Improperly Imported

The Customs and Excise Management Act 1979, s. 49 states:

(1) Where—

(a) except as provided by or under the Customs and Excise Acts 1979, any imported goods, being goods chargeable on their importation with customs or excise duty, are, without payment of that duty—

(i) unshipped in any port,

(ii) unloaded from any aircraft in the United Kingdom,

(iii) unloaded from any vehicle in, or otherwise brought across the boundary into, Northern Ireland, or

(iv) removed from their place of importation or from any approved wharf, examination station or transit shed; or

(b) any goods are imported, landed or unloaded contrary to any prohibition or restriction for the time being in force with respect thereto under or by virtue of any enactment; or

(c) any goods, being goods chargeable with any duty or goods the importation of which is for the time being prohibited or restricted by or under any enactment, are found, whether before or after the unloading thereof, to have been concealed in any manner on board any ship or aircraft or, while in Northern Ireland, in any vehicle; or

(d) any goods are imported concealed in a container holding goods of a different description; or

(e) any imported goods are found, whether before or after delivery, not to correspond with the entry made thereof; or

(f) any imported goods are concealed or packed in any manner appearing to be intended to deceive an officer, those goods shall, subject to subsection (2) below, be liable to forfeiture.

(2) Where any goods, the importation of which is for the time being prohibited or restricted by or under any enactment, are on their importation either—

(a) reported as intended for exportation in the same ship, aircraft or vehicle; or

(b) entered for transit or transhipment; or

(c) entered to be warehoused for exportation or for use as stores,

the Commissioners may, if they see fit, permit the goods to be dealt with accordingly.

---

**KEYNOTE**

For 'goods', 'vehicle', 'approved wharf', 'examination shed' and 'transit shed', see para. 6.1.2.1.

'Lands', in relation to aircraft, includes alighting on water (Customs and Excise Management Act 1979, s. 1).

---

### 6.1.2.6 Provisions as to Detention of Persons

The Customs and Excise Management Act 1979, s. 138 states:

(1) Any person who has committed, or whom there are reasonable grounds to suspect of having committed, any offence for which he is liable to be detained under the customs and excise Acts may be detained by any officer or any member of Her Majesty's armed forces or coastguard at any time within 20 years from the date of the commission of the offence.

---

**KEYNOTE**

'The customs and excise Acts' means the Customs and Excise Management Act 1979 and any other enactment for the time being in force relating to customs or excise (Customs and Excise Management Act 1979, s. 1).

'Officer' means, subject to s. 8(2), a person commissioned by the Commissioners. Subject to s. 8(2) means any person, whether an officer or not, engaged by the orders or with the concurrence of the Commissioners (whether previously or subsequently expressed) in the performance of any act or duty relating to an assigned matter which is by law required or authorised to be performed by or with an officer, shall be deemed to be the proper officer by or with whom that act or duty is to be performed (Customs and Excise Management Act 1979, ss. 1 and 8(2)).

Where it was not practicable to detain any person so liable at the time of the commission of the offence, or where any such person having been then or subsequently detained for that offence has escaped, he may be detained by any officer or any member of Her Majesty's armed forces or coastguard at any time and may be proceeded against in like manner as if the offence had been committed at the date when he was finally detained (s. 138(2)).

Where any person who is a member of the crew of any ship in Her Majesty's employment or service is detained by an officer for an offence under the customs and excise Acts, the commanding officer of the ship shall, if so required by the detaining officer, keep that person secured on board that ship until he can be brought before a court and shall then deliver him up to the proper officer (s. 138(3)).

Where any person has been arrested by a person who is not an officer by virtue of this section or by virtue of s. 24 of the Police and Criminal Evidence Act 1984 in its application to offences under the customs and excise Acts, or by virtue of art. 26 of the Police and Criminal Evidence (Northern Ireland) Order 1989 in its application to such offences, the person arresting him shall give notice of the arrest to an officer at the nearest convenient office of customs and excise (s. 138(4)).

### 6.1.2.7 Provisions as to Detention, Seizure and Condemnation of Goods, etc.

The Customs and Excise Management Act 1979, s. 139 states:

(1) Any thing liable to forfeiture under the customs and excise Acts may be seized or detained by any officer or constable or any member of Her Majesty's armed forces or coastguard.

(2) Where any thing is seized or detained as liable to forfeiture under the customs and excise Acts by a person other than an officer, that person shall, subject to subsection (3) below, either—
  (a) deliver that thing to the nearest convenient office of customs and excise; or
  (b) if such delivery is not practicable, give to the Commissioners at the nearest convenient office of customs and excise notice in writing of the seizure or detention with full particulars of the thing seized or detained.

(3) Where the person seizing or detaining any thing as liable to forfeiture under the customs and excise Acts is a constable and that thing is or may be required for use in connection with any proceedings to be brought otherwise than under those Acts it may, subject to subsection (4) below, be retained in the custody of the police until either those proceedings are completed or it is decided that no such proceedings shall be brought.

(4) The following provisions apply in relation to things retained in the custody of the police by virtue of subsection (3) above, that is to say—
  (a) notice in writing of the seizure or detention and of the intention to retain the thing in question in the custody of the police, together with full particulars as to that thing, shall be given to the Commissioners at the nearest convenient office of customs and excise;
  (b) any officer shall be permitted to examine that thing and take account thereof at any time while it remains in the custody of the police;
  (c) nothing in section 31 of the Police (Northern Ireland) Act 1998 shall apply in relation to that thing.

(5) Subject to subsections (3) and (4) above and to Schedule 3 to this Act, any thing seized or detained under the customs and excise Acts shall, pending the determination as to its forfeiture or disposal, be dealt with, and, if condemned or deemed to have been condemned or forfeited, shall be disposed of in such manner as the Commissioners may direct.

(6) Schedule 3 to this Act shall have effect for the purpose of forfeitures, and of proceedings for the condemnation of any thing as being forfeited, under the customs and excise Acts.

(7) If any person, not being an officer, by whom any thing is seized or detained or who has custody thereof after its seizure or detention, fails to comply with any requirement of this section or with any direction of the Commissioners given thereunder, he shall be liable on summary conviction to a penalty of level 2 on the standard scale.

(8) Subsections (2) to (7) above shall apply in relation to any dutiable goods seized or detained by any person other than an officer notwithstanding that they were not so seized as liable to forfeiture under the customs and excise Acts.

### 6.1.2.8 Forfeiture of Ships, etc. used in Connection with Goods Liable to Forfeiture

The Customs and Excise Management Act 1979, s. 141 states:

(1) Without prejudice to any other provision of the Customs and Excise Acts 1979, where any thing has become liable to forfeiture under the customs and excise Acts—
  (a) any ship, aircraft, vehicle, animal, container (including any article of passengers' baggage) or other thing whatsoever which has been used for the carriage, handling, deposit or concealment of the thing so liable to forfeiture, either at a time when it was so liable or for the purposes of the commission of the offence for which it later became so liable; and
  (b) any other thing mixed, packed or found with the thing so liable,
shall also be liable to forfeiture.

(2) Where any ship, aircraft, vehicle or animal has become liable to forfeiture under the customs and excise Acts, whether by virtue of subsection (1) above or otherwise, all tackle, apparel or furniture thereof shall also be liable to forfeiture.

(3) Where any of the following, that is to say—

   (a) any ship not exceeding 100 tons register;

   (b) any aircraft; or

   (c) any hovercraft,

becomes liable to forfeiture under this section by reason of having been used in the importation, exportation or carriage of goods contrary to or for the purpose of contravening any prohibition or restriction for the time being in force with respect to those goods, or without payment having been made of, or security given for, any duty payable thereon, the owner and the master or commander shall each be liable on summary conviction to a penalty equal to the value of the ship, aircraft or hovercraft or level 5 on the standard scale, whichever is the less.

### 6.1.2.9    Power to Search Premises: Search Warrant

The Customs and Excise Management Act 1979, s. 161A states:

(1) If a justice of the peace is satisfied by information upon oath given by an officer that there are reasonable grounds to suspect that anything liable to forfeiture under the customs and excise Acts is kept or concealed in any building or place, he may by warrant under his hand authorise any officer, and any person accompanying an officer, to enter and search the building or place named in the warrant.

---

**KEYNOTE**

Section 161A(2) states that an officer or other person so authorised has power—

(a) to enter the building or place at any time, whether by day or night, on any day, and search for, seize, and detain or remove any such thing, and

(b) so far as is necessary for the purpose of such entry, search, seizure, detention or removal, to break open any door, window or container and force and remove any other impediment or obstruction.

Where there are reasonable grounds to suspect that any still, vessel, utensil, spirits or materials for the manufacture of spirits is or are unlawfully kept or deposited in any building or place, subss. (1) and (2) apply in relation to any constable as they would apply in relation to an officer (s. 161A(3)).

The powers conferred by a warrant under this section are exercisable until the end of the period of one month beginning with the day on which the warrant is issued (s. 161A(4)).

A person other than a constable shall not exercise the power of entry conferred by this section by night unless accompanied by a constable (s. 161A(5)).

---

### 6.1.2.10    Power to Search Vehicles or Vessels

The Customs and Excise Management Act 1979, s. 163 states:

(1) Without prejudice to any other power conferred by the Customs and Excise Acts 1979, where there are reasonable grounds to suspect that any vehicle or vessel is or may be carrying any goods which are—

   (a) chargeable with any duty which has not been paid or secured; or

   (b) in the course of being unlawfully removed from or to any place; or

   (c) otherwise liable to forfeiture under the customs and excise Acts,

any officer or constable or member of Her Majesty's armed forces or coastguard may stop and search that vehicle or vessel.

(2) If when so required by any such officer, constable or member the person in charge of any such vehicle or vessel refuses to stop or to permit the vehicle or vessel to be searched, he shall be liable on summary conviction to a penalty of level 3 on the standard scale.

### 6.1.2.11 Power to Search Vehicles or Vessels

The Customs and Excise Management Act 1979, s. 163A states:

(1) Without prejudice to any other power conferred by the Customs and Excise Acts 1979, where there are reasonable grounds to suspect that a person in the United Kingdom (referred to in this section as 'the suspect') has with him, or at the place where he is, any goods to which this section applies, an officer may—

(a) require the suspect to permit a search of any article that he has with him or at that place, and

(b) if the suspect is not under arrest, detain him (and any such article) for so long as may be necessary to carry out the search.

### 6.1.2.12 Power to Search Persons

The Customs and Excise Management Act 1979, s. 164 states:

(1) Where there are reasonable grounds to suspect that any person to whom this section applies (referred to in this section as 'the suspect') is carrying any article—

(a) which is chargeable with any duty which has not been paid or secured; or

(b) with respect to the importation or exportation of which any prohibition or restriction is for the time being in force under or by virtue of any enactment,

an officer may exercise the powers conferred by subsection (2) below and, if the suspect is not under arrest, may detain him for so long as may be necessary for the exercise of those powers and (where applicable) the exercise of the rights conferred by subsection (3) below.

(2) The officer may require the suspect—

(a) to permit such a search of any article which he has with him; and

(b) subject to subsection (3) below, to submit to such searches of his person, whether rub-down, strip or intimate,

as the officer may consider necessary or expedient; but no such requirement may be imposed under paragraph (b) above without the officer informing the suspect of the effect of subsection (3) below.

An intimate search means any search which involves a physical examination (i.e. an examination which is more than simply a visual examination) of a person's body orifices (Customs and Excise Management Act 1979, s. 164(5)).

If the suspect is required to submit to a search of his person, he may require to be taken—

(a) except in the case of a rub-down search, before a justice of the peace or a superior of the officer concerned; and

(b) in the excepted case, before such a superior;

and the justice or superior shall consider the grounds for suspicion and direct accordingly whether the suspect is to submit to the search (s. 164(3)).

This section applies to the following persons, namely—

- any person who is on board or has landed from any ship or aircraft;
- any person entering or about to leave the United Kingdom;
- any person within the dock area of a port;
- any person at a customs and excise airport;
- any person in, entering or leaving any approved wharf or transit shed which is not in a port;
- any person in, entering or leaving a free zone;
- in Northern Ireland, any person travelling from or to any place which is on or beyond the boundary.

# 6.2 Serious Organised Crime and Police Act 2005

> This chapter is only for examination candidates from the National Crime Agency.

## 6.2.1 Introduction

Part 2 of the Serious Organised Crime and Police Act is divided into six chapters. This chapter of the Manual examines elements of chapters 1 and 2 of part 2.

## 6.2.2 Chapter 1: Investigatory Powers of the DPP

Chapter 1 enables designated members of staff of SOCA, police constables or officers of Revenue and Customs, acting under the supervision of the Director of Public Prosecutions (DPP), the Director of Revenue and Customs Prosecutions or the Lord Advocate, to compel people to cooperate with an investigation by producing documents and answering questions.

### 6.2.2.1 Disclosure Notices

The Serious Organised Crime and Police Act 2005, s. 62 states:

(1) If it appears to the Investigating Authority—
  (a) that there are reasonable grounds for suspecting that an offence to which this Chapter applies has been committed,
  (b) that any person has information (whether or not contained in a document) which relates to a matter relevant to the investigation of that offence, and
  (c) that there are reasonable grounds for believing that information which may be provided by that person in compliance with a disclosure notice is likely to be of substantial value (whether or not by itself) to that investigation,
he may give, or authorise an appropriate person to give, a disclosure notice to that person.
(2) In this Chapter 'appropriate person' means—
  (a) a constable,
  (b) a member of the staff of SOCA who is for the time being designated under section 43, or
  (c) an officer of Revenue and Customs.
(3) In this Chapter 'disclosure notice' means a notice in writing requiring the person to whom it is given to do all or any of the following things in accordance with the specified requirements, namely—
  (a) answer questions with respect to any matter relevant to the investigation;
  (b) provide information with respect to any such matter as is specified in the notice;
  (c) produce such documents, or documents of such descriptions, relevant to the investigation as are specified in the notice.
(4) In subsection (3) 'the specified requirements' means such requirements specified in the disclosure notice as relate to—
  (a) the time at or by which,
  (b) the place at which, or
  (c) the manner in which,

the person to whom the notice is given is to do any of the things mentioned in paragraphs (a) to (c) of that subsection; and those requirements may include a requirement to do any of those things at once.

(5) A disclosure notice must be signed or counter-signed by the Investigating Authority.

(6) This section has effect subject to section 64 (restrictions on requiring information etc.) [**see para. 6.2.2.3**].

**Production of Documents**

The Serious Organised Crime and Police Act 2005, s. 63 states:

(1) This section applies where a disclosure notice has been given under section 62.

(2) An authorised person may—
   (a) take copies of or extracts from any documents produced in compliance with the notice, and
   (b) require the person producing them to provide an explanation of any of them.

(3) Documents so produced may be retained for so long as the Investigating Authority considers that it is necessary to retain them (rather than copies of them) in connection with the investigation for the purposes of which the disclosure notice was given.

(4) If the Investigating Authority has reasonable grounds for believing—
   (a) that any such documents may have to be produced for the purposes of any legal proceedings, and
   (b) that they might otherwise be unavailable for those purposes,
they may be retained until the proceedings are concluded.

(5) If a person who is required by a disclosure notice to produce any documents does not produce the documents in compliance with the notice, an authorised person may require that person to state, to the best of his knowledge and belief, where they are.

(6) In this section 'authorised person' means any appropriate person who either—
   (a) is the person by whom the notice was given, or
   (b) is authorised by the Investigating Authority for the purposes of this section.

(7) This section has effect subject to section 64 (restrictions on requiring information etc.) [**see para. 6.2.2.3**].

### 6.2.2.3 Restrictions on Requiring Information

The Serious Organised Crime and Police Act 2005, s. 64 states:

(1) A person may not be required under section 62 or 63—
   (a) to answer any privileged question,
   (b) to provide any privileged information, or
   (c) to produce any privileged document,
except that a lawyer may be required to provide the name and address of a client of his.

**KEYNOTE**

A 'privileged question' is a question which the person would be entitled to refuse to answer on grounds of legal professional privilege in proceedings in the High Court (s. 64(2)).

'Privileged information' is information which the person would be entitled to refuse to provide on grounds of legal professional privilege in such proceedings (s. 64(3)).

A 'privileged document' is a document which the person would be entitled to refuse to produce on grounds of legal professional privilege in such proceedings (s. 64(4)).

Section 64(5) states that a person may not be required under s. 62 to produce any excluded material (as defined by s. 11 of the Police and Criminal Evidence Act 1984).

In the application of this section to Scotland, subss. (1) to (5) do not have effect, but a person may not be required under s. 62 or 63 to answer any question, provide any information or produce any document which he would be entitled, on grounds of legal privilege, to refuse to answer or (as the case may be) provide or produce.

In subs. (6)(b), 'legal privilege' has the meaning given by s. 412 of the Proceeds of Crime Act 2002. That means 'protection in legal proceedings from disclosure, by virtue of any rule of law relating to the confidentiality of communications'; and 'items subject to legal privilege' are communications between a professional legal adviser and his/her client or communications made in connection with or in contemplation of legal proceedings and for the purpose of those proceedings.

Section 64(8) states that a person may not be required under s. 62 or 63 to disclose any information or produce any document in respect of which he owes an obligation of confidence by virtue of carrying on any banking business, unless—

(a) the person to whom the obligation of confidence is owed consents to the disclosure or production, or

(b) the requirement is made by, or in accordance with a specific authorisation given by, the Investigating Authority.

Subject to the preceding provisions, any requirement under s. 62 or 63 has effect despite any restriction on disclosure (however imposed) (s. 64(9)).

### 6.2.2.4 Restrictions on Use of Statements

The Serious Organised Crime and Police Act 2005, s. 65 states:

(1) A statement made by a person in response to a requirement imposed under section 62 or 63 ('the relevant statement') may not be used in evidence against him in any criminal proceedings unless subsection (2) or (3) applies.

(2) This subsection applies where the person is being prosecuted—
    (a) for an offence under section 67 of this Act, or
    (b) for an offence under section 5 of the Perjury Act 1911 (c. 6) (false statements made on oath otherwise than in judicial proceedings or made otherwise than on oath), or
    (c) for an offence under section 2 of the False Oaths (Scotland) Act 1933 (c. 20) (false statutory declarations and other false statements without oath) or at common law for an offence of attempting to pervert the course, or defeat the ends, of justice.

(3) This subsection applies where the person is being prosecuted for some other offence and—
    (a) the person, when giving evidence in the proceedings, makes a statement inconsistent with the relevant statement, and
    (b) in the proceedings evidence relating to the relevant statement is adduced, or a question about it is asked, by or on behalf of the person.

---

**KEYNOTE**

This section provides that a statement made by a person in response to a requirement imposed under this chapter cannot be used in evidence in criminal proceedings against them, other than proceedings for an offence under s. 67 or for an offence of giving a false statutory declaration or statement. The only exception is where the person seeks in other criminal proceedings to use another statement which is inconsistent with the statement made in response to the requirement under this chapter.

---

### 6.2.2.5 Power to Enter and Seize Documents

The Serious Organised Crime and Police Act 2005, s. 66 states:

(1) A justice of the peace may issue a warrant under this section if, on an information on oath laid by the Investigating Authority, he is satisfied—
    (a) that any of the conditions mentioned in subsection (2) is met in relation to any documents of a description specified in the information, and
    (b) that the documents are on premises so specified.

(2) The conditions are—
    (a) that a person has been required by a disclosure notice to produce the documents but has not done so;
    (b) that it is not practicable to give a disclosure notice requiring their production;
    (c) that giving such a notice might seriously prejudice the investigation of an offence to which this Chapter applies.

(3) A warrant under this section is a warrant authorising an appropriate person named in it—

    (a) to enter and search the premises, using such force as is reasonably necessary;

    (b) to take possession of any documents appearing to be documents of a description specified in the information, or to take any other steps which appear to be necessary for preserving, or preventing interference with, any such documents;

    (c) in the case of any such documents consisting of information recorded otherwise than in legible form, to take possession of any computer disk or other electronic storage device which appears to contain the information in question, or to take any other steps which appear to be necessary for preserving, or preventing interference with, that information;

    (d) to take copies of or extracts from any documents or information falling within paragraph (b) or (c);

    (e) to require any person on the premises to provide an explanation of any such documents or information or to state where any such documents or information may be found;

    (f) to require any such person to give the appropriate person such assistance as he may reasonably require for the taking of copies or extracts as mentioned in paragraph (d).

(4) A person executing a warrant under this section may take other persons with him, if it appears to him to be necessary to do so.

(5) A warrant under this section must, if so required, be produced for inspection by the owner or occupier of the premises or anyone acting on his behalf.

(6) If the premises are unoccupied or the occupier is temporarily absent, a person entering the premises under the authority of a warrant under this section must leave the premises as effectively secured against trespassers as he found them.

(7) Where possession of any document or device is taken under this section—

    (a) the document may be retained for so long as the Investigating Authority considers that it is necessary to retain it (rather than a copy of it) in connection with the investigation for the purposes of which the warrant was sought, or

    (b) the device may be retained for so long as he considers that it is necessary to retain it in connection with that investigation,

as the case may be.

(8) If the Investigating Authority has reasonable grounds for believing—

    (a) that any such document or device may have to be produced for the purposes of any legal proceedings, and

    (b) that it might otherwise be unavailable for those purposes,

it may be retained until the proceedings are concluded.

(9) Nothing in this section authorises a person to take possession of, or make copies of or take extracts from, any document or information which, by virtue of section 64, could not be required to be produced or disclosed under section 62 or 63.

---

**KEYNOTE**

This section provides for a magistrate, or sheriff in Scotland, to issue a warrant to enter and seize documents where someone has failed to provide documents specified in a disclosure notice or it is not practicable to give a disclosure notice or doing so might seriously prejudice an investigation. The warrant would authorise a constable, a member of SOCA's staff or an officer of HMRC to enter, using force if necessary, and search the premises and seize and retain any specified documents. The constable or other person authorised by the warrant may take other people with him on the search, but must show the warrant to the occupier of the premises on request.

---

### 6.2.2.6    Offences in Connection with Disclosure Notices or Search Warrants

OFFENCE: **Fail to Comply/Make False Statement/Wilful Obstruction—Serious Organised Crime and Police Act 2005, s. 67**

- Triable either way • Two years' imprisonment and/or a fine
- Six months' imprisonment and/or a fine

The Serious Organised Crime and Police Act 2005, s. 67 states:

(1) A person commits an offence if, without reasonable excuse, he fails to comply with any requirement imposed on him under section 62 or 63.
(2) A person commits an offence if, in purported compliance with any requirement imposed on him under section 62 or 63—
   (a) he makes a statement which is false or misleading, and
   (b) he either knows that it is false or misleading or is reckless as to whether it is false or misleading.
'False or misleading' means false or misleading in a material particular.
(3) A person commits an offence if he wilfully obstructs any person in the exercise of any rights conferred by a warrant under section 66.

### 6.2.2.7 Manner in Which Disclosure Notice May Be Given

The Serious Organised Crime and Police Act 2005, s. 69 states:

(1) This section provides for the manner in which a disclosure notice may be given under section 62.
(2) The notice may be given to a person by—
   (a) delivering it to him,
   (b) leaving it at his proper address,
   (c) sending it by post to him at that address.
(3) The notice may be given—
   (a) in the case of a body corporate, to the secretary or clerk of that body;
   (b) in the case of a partnership, to a partner or a person having the control or management of the partnership business;
   (c) in the case of an unincorporated association (other than a partnership), to an officer of the association.
(4) For the purposes of this section and section 7 of the Interpretation Act 1978 (c. 30) (service of documents by post) in its application to this section, the proper address of a person is his usual or last-known address (whether residential or otherwise), except that—
   (a) in the case of a body corporate or its secretary or clerk, it is the address of the registered office of that body or its principal office in the United Kingdom,
   (b) in the case of a partnership, a partner or a person having the control or management of the partnership business, it is that of the principal office of the partnership in the United Kingdom, and
   (c) in the case of an unincorporated association (other than a partnership) or an officer of the association, it is that of the principal office of the association in the United Kingdom.
(5) This section does not apply to Scotland.

---

**KEYNOTE**

This section provides that a disclosure notice may be given to a person by delivering it to him, leaving it at his proper address or sending it by post to him at that address. The definition of a person's 'proper address' is his usual or last-known address.

---

### 6.2.3 Chapter 2: Offenders Assisting Investigations and Prosecutions

Chapter 2 places the mechanism by which a defendant can plead guilty and offer Queen's Evidence in return for a discounted sentence on a statutory footing.

### 6.2.3.1 Assistance by Offender: Immunity from Prosecution

The Serious Organised Crime and Police Act 2005, s. 71 states:

(1) If a specified prosecutor thinks that for the purposes of the investigation or prosecution of any offence it is appropriate to offer any person immunity from prosecution he may give the person a written notice under this subsection (an 'immunity notice').

(2) If a person is given an immunity notice, no proceedings for an offence of a description specified in the notice may be brought against that person in England and Wales or Northern Ireland except in circumstances specified in the notice.

(3) An immunity notice ceases to have effect in relation to the person to whom it is given if the person fails to comply with any conditions specified in the notice.

(4) Each of the following is a specified prosecutor—
  (a) the Director of Public Prosecutions;
  (b) the Director of Revenue and Customs Prosecutions;
  (c) the Director of the Serious Fraud Office;
  (d) the Director of Public Prosecutions for Northern Ireland;
  (e) a prosecutor designated for the purposes of this section by a prosecutor mentioned in paragraphs (a) to (d).

(5) The Director of Public Prosecutions or a person designated by him under subsection (4)(e) may not give an immunity notice in relation to proceedings in Northern Ireland.

(6) The Director of Public Prosecutions for Northern Ireland or a person designated by him under subsection (4)(e) may not give an immunity notice in relation to proceedings in England and Wales.

(7) An immunity notice must not be given in relation to an offence under section 188 of the Enterprise Act 2002 (c. 40) (cartel offences).

---

**KEYNOTE**

This section provides for a designated prosecutor from the Crown Prosecution Service, the Revenue and Customs Prosecutions Office, the Serious Fraud Office or the Northern Ireland Director of Public Prosecutions office to grant a person a conditional immunity from prosecution. The immunity notice itself must be written and specify the offences for which the person will be immune from prosecution in England and Wales or Northern Ireland. The notice will normally include conditions, breach of which would lead to the immunity being revoked.

---

### 6.2.3.2 Assistance by Offender: Undertakings as to Use of Evidence

The Serious Organised Crime and Police Act 2005, s. 72 states:

(1) If a specified prosecutor thinks that for the purposes of the investigation or prosecution of any offence it is appropriate to offer any person an undertaking that information of any description will not be used against the person in any proceedings to which this section applies he may give the person a written notice under this subsection (a 'restricted use undertaking').

(2) This section applies to—
  (a) criminal proceedings;
  (b) proceedings under Part 5 of the Proceeds of Crime Act 2002 (c. 29).

(3) If a person is given a restricted use undertaking the information described in the undertaking must not be used against that person in any proceedings to which this section applies brought in England and Wales or Northern Ireland except in the circumstances specified in the undertaking.

(4) A restricted use undertaking ceases to have effect in relation to the person to whom it is given if the person fails to comply with any conditions specified in the undertaking.

(5) The Director of Public Prosecutions for Northern Ireland or a person designated by him under section 71(4)(e) may not give a restricted use undertaking in relation to proceedings in England and Wales.

(6) The Director of Public Prosecutions or a person designated by him under section 71(4)(e) may not give a restricted use undertaking in relation to proceedings in Northern Ireland.

(7) Specified prosecutor must be construed in accordance with section 71(4).

---

**KEYNOTE**

This section provides for a designated prosecutor (as specified in *subs. (4)* of s. 71) to grant a person a conditional undertaking that any information that individual provides will not be used in any criminal proceedings, or proceedings under part 5 of the Proceeds of Crime Act 2002, against that person in England and Wales or Northern Ireland. The notice containing the undertaking must be in writing and specify the circumstances in which the information provided will not be used against that person. The notice will normally include conditions, breach of which would lead to the undertaking being revoked.

---

### 6.2.3.3    Assistance by Defendant: Reduction in Sentence

The Serious Organised Crime and Police Act 2005, s. 73 states:

(1) This section applies if a defendant—

    (a) following a plea of guilty is either convicted of an offence in proceedings in the Crown Court or is committed to the Crown Court for sentence, and

    (b) has, pursuant to a written agreement made with a specified prosecutor, assisted or offered to assist the investigator or prosecutor in relation to that or any other offence.

(2) In determining what sentence to pass on the defendant the court may take into account the extent and nature of the assistance given or offered.

(3) If the court passes a sentence which is less than it would have passed but for the assistance given or offered, it must state in open court—

    (a) that it has passed a lesser sentence than it would otherwise have passed, and

    (b) what the greater sentence would have been.

(4) Subsection (3) does not apply if the court thinks that it would not be in the public interest to disclose that the sentence has been discounted; but in such a case the court must give written notice of the matters specified in paragraphs (a) and (b) of subsection (3) to both the prosecutor and the defendant.

(5) Nothing in any enactment which—

    (a) requires that a minimum sentence is passed in respect of any offence or an offence of any description or by reference to the circumstances of any offender (whether or not the enactment also permits the court to pass a lesser sentence in particular circumstances), or

    (b) in the case of a sentence which is fixed by law, requires the court to take into account certain matters for the purposes of making an order which determines or has the effect of determining the minimum period of imprisonment which the offender must serve (whether or not the enactment also permits the court to fix a lesser period in particular circumstances),

affects the power of a court to act under subsection (2).

(6) If, in determining what sentence to pass on the defendant, the court takes into account the extent and nature of the assistance given or offered as mentioned in subsection (2), that does not prevent the court from also taking account of any other matter which it is entitled by virtue of any other enactment to take account of for the purposes of determining—

    (a) the sentence, or

    (b) in the case of a sentence which is fixed by law, any minimum period of imprisonment which an offender must serve.

(7) If subsection (3) above does not apply by virtue of subsection (4) above, sections 174(1)(a) and 270 of the Criminal Justice Act 2003 (c. 44) (requirement to explain reasons for sentence or other order) do not apply to the extent that the explanation will disclose that a sentence has been discounted in pursuance of this section.

(8) In this section—

    (a) a reference to a sentence includes, in the case of a sentence which is fixed by law, a reference to the minimum period an offender is required to serve, and a reference to a lesser sentence must be construed accordingly;

    (b) a reference to imprisonment includes a reference to any other custodial sentence within the meaning of section 76 of the Powers of Criminal Courts (Sentencing) Act 2000 (c. 6) or Article 2 of the Criminal Justice (Northern Ireland) Order 1996 (S.I. 1996/ 3160).

(9) An agreement with a specified prosecutor may provide for assistance to be given to that prosecutor or to any other prosecutor.

(10) References to a specified prosecutor must be construed in accordance with section 71.

---

**KEYNOTE**

This section provides that the Crown Court, when sentencing defendants who plead guilty in proceedings before that court and who have entered into a written agreement to provide assistance in any investigation or prosecution, can take account of the nature and extent of that assistance. Section 73(3) requires the court in passing a lower sentence to set out what the sentence would otherwise have been, unless it is in the public interest not to do so (in which case the court must provide a written notice of what the sentence would have been to the prosecutor and the defendant). This section applies to offences for which there is a minimum sentence and also to sentences fixed by law in determining the minimum period of imprisonment that a person must serve.

The intention is that the court can in exceptional circumstances exercise its power under s. 73(2) to reduce a person's sentence or minimum period of imprisonment, as the case maybe, to reflect the assistance provided or offered.

Section 73(6) provides that the court's decision (or not) to take into account the assistance provided or offered by a person does not affect any other power it may have when determining that person's sentence or minimum term for imprisonment.

Section 73(7) disapplies the specified provisions, which would otherwise require the court to explain the reasons for passing its sentence on a person, where the court has decided (under s. 73(4)) that it is not in the public interest to make such an explanation.

### 6.2.3.4    Assistance by Defendant: Review of Sentence

The Serious Organised Crime and Police Act 2005, s. 74 states:

(1)  This section applies if—
    (a)  the Crown Court has passed a sentence on a person in respect of an offence, and
    (b)  the person falls within subsection (2).
(2)  A person falls within this subsection if—
    (a)  he receives a discounted sentence in consequence of his having offered in pursuance of a written agreement to give assistance to the prosecutor or investigator of an offence but he knowingly fails to any extent to give assistance in accordance with the agreement;
    (b)  he receives a discounted sentence in consequence of his having offered in pursuance of a written agreement to give assistance to the prosecutor or investigator of an offence and, having given the assistance in accordance with the agreement, in pursuance of another written agreement gives or offers to give further assistance;
    (c)  he receives a sentence which is not discounted but in pursuance of a written agreement he subsequently gives or offers to give assistance to the prosecutor or investigator of an offence.
(3)  A specified prosecutor may at any time refer the case back to the court by which the sentence was passed if—
    (a)  the person is still serving his sentence, and
    (b)  the specified prosecutor thinks it is in the interests of justice to do so.
(4)  A case so referred must, if possible, be heard by the judge who passed the sentence to which the referral relates.
(5)  If the court is satisfied that a person who falls within subsection (2)(a) knowingly failed to give the assistance it may substitute for the sentence to which the referral relates such greater sentence (not exceeding that which it would have passed but for the agreement to give assistance) as it thinks appropriate.
(6)  In a case of a person who falls within subsection (2)(b) or (c) the court may—
    (a)  take into account the extent and nature of the assistance given or offered;
    (b)  substitute for the sentence to which the referral relates such lesser sentence as it thinks appropriate.
(7)  Any part of the sentence to which the referral relates which the person has already served must be taken into account in determining when a greater or lesser sentence imposed by subsection (5) or (6) has been served.
(8)  A person in respect of whom a reference is made under this section and the specified prosecutor may with the leave of the Court of Appeal appeal to the Court of Appeal against the decision of the Crown Court.
(9)  Section 33(3) of the Criminal Appeal Act 1968 (c. 19) (limitation on appeal from the criminal division of the Court of Appeal) does not prevent an appeal to the Supreme Court under this section.
(10)  A discounted sentence is a sentence passed in pursuance of section 73 or subsection (6) above.
(11)  References—
    (a)  to a written agreement are to an agreement made in writing with a specified prosecutor;
    (b)  to a specified prosecutor must be construed in accordance with section 71.
(12)  In relation to any proceedings under this section, the Secretary of State may make an order containing provision corresponding to any provision in—
    (a)  the Criminal Appeal Act 1968 (subject to any specified modifications), or

(b) the Criminal Appeal (Northern Ireland) Act 1980 (c. 47) (subject to any specified modifications).

(13) A person does not fall within subsection (2) if—

(a) he was convicted of an offence for which the sentence is fixed by law, and

(b) he did not plead guilty to the offence for which he was sentenced.

(14) Section 174(1)(a) or 270 of the Criminal Justice Act 2003 (c. 44) (as the case may be) applies to a sentence substituted under subsection (5) above unless the court thinks that it is not in the public interest to disclose that the person falls within subsection (2)(a) above.

(15) Subsections (3) to (9) of section 73 apply for the purposes of this section as they apply for the purposes of that section and any reference in those subsections to subsection (2) of that section must be construed as a reference to subsection (6) of this section.

---

**KEYNOTE**

This section provides that where a person is still serving a sentence imposed by the Crown Court and one of the conditions in s. 74(2) applies, a specified prosecutor may refer the person's sentence back to the court for review (where possible to the original sentencing judge), where he considers it is in the interests of justice to do so. The conditions are that the defendant received a reduced sentence on the basis of an agreement to assist, but then knowingly failed to give that assistance; or the defendant gives or agrees to give assistance after they have been sentenced.

Section 74(5) gives the court a power to substitute a greater sentence where it considers the person has failed to assist (not exceeding the sentence it could have passed but for the agreement). However, where a person has provided assistance or offered to assist, s. 74(6) gives the court a power to take that into account and to reduce the individual's sentence accordingly.

Section 78(8) and (9) provide that normal avenues of appeal against sentence apply.

---

### 6.2.3.5 Proceedings under s. 74: Exclusion of the Public

The Serious Organised Crime and Police Act 2005, s. 75 states:

(1) This section applies to—

(a) any proceedings relating to a reference made under section 74(3), and

(b) any other proceedings arising in consequence of such proceedings.

(2) The court in which the proceedings will be or are being heard may make such order as it thinks appropriate—

(a) to exclude from the proceedings any person who does not fall within subsection (4);

(b) to give such directions as it thinks appropriate prohibiting the publication of any matter relating to the proceedings (including the fact that the reference has been made).

(3) An order under subsection (2) may be made only to the extent that the court thinks—

(a) that it is necessary to do so to protect the safety of any person, and

(b) that it is in the interests of justice.

(4) The following persons fall within this subsection—

(a) a member or officer of the court;

(b) a party to the proceedings;

(c) counsel or a solicitor for a party to the proceedings;

(d) a person otherwise directly concerned with the proceedings.

(5) This section does not affect any other power which the court has by virtue of any rule of law or other enactment—

(a) to exclude any person from proceedings, or

(b) to restrict the publication of any matter relating to proceedings.

---

**KEYNOTE**

This section provides that a court in dealing with a defendant under s. 74 can exclude people from the court or impose reporting restrictions, but only to the extent that it is necessary to protect the safety of any person and it is in the interests of justice. The court cannot exclude court staff, parties to the proceedings (or their legal representatives) or others directly concerned with the proceedings.

# Index

## A

**Abandoned property** 2.1.5
**Abduction**
  child abduction
    persons connected with child 3.3.1–3.3.2
    persons not connected with
      child 3.3.3–3.3.4
  kidnapping 3.5.1
  possessing firearms with intent 3.9.9.5
**Abroad** *see* **Foreign suspects**
**Absconding**
  escaping from legal custody 1.12.7
  ground for refusal of bail 1.9.6
  statutory offence 1.9.11
**Abuse of position** 2.6.5
**Accessories**
  arranging intended child sex
    offences 4.5.5
  assisting escape 1.12.7
  assisting or inducing drug offences
    abroad 3.8.13
  defined 1.2.6
  handling stolen goods 2.7.7
  immigration and asylum offences
    assisting entry in breach of deportation
      order 5.1.2.5
    assisting unlawful immigration to
      EU 5.1.2.3
    assisting unlawful immigration to
      UK 5.1.2.4
  perjury 1.12.1.1
  state of mind 1.2.6.1
  using someone to mind weapon 3.9.9.6
**Actual bodily harm** 3.2.11
*Actus reus*
  *see also* **Specific offences**
  causal link with crime 1.2.4
  coincidence with *mens rea* 1.2.2.2
  essential requirements 1.2.2
  facts in issue 1.11.3
  importance 1.2.1
  voluntary acts 1.2.2.1
**Administering substances with
  intent** 4.9.3
**Administration of justice**
  concealing relevant offences 1.12.6
  contempt of court 1.12.8
  ground for refusal of bail 1.9.6
  harming witnesses 1.12.4
  offences relating to offenders
    assisting offenders 1.12.5
    escaping from legal custody and
      harbouring 1.12.7
  perverting the course of justice
    principal offence 1.12.2
    protection of witnesses and
      others 1.12.3
**Admissibility of evidence**
  decision by judge 1.11.2
  fingerprints 1.8.5.1
  interviews 1.7.3.1
  reasons for exclusion 1.11.2.2
  unlawfully seized material 1.5.3.6

**Adverse inferences**
  audio recorded interviews 1.7.10
  delay of rights 1.6.20
  restrictions on 1.7.5
  silence at trial 1.7.2.5
  silence when arrested
    failure to account for presence 1.7.2.4
    failure to account for things 1.7.2.3
  silence when questioned or
    charged 1.7.2.2
  statutory provisions 1.7.2
  visual recorded interviews 1.7.17
**Advice** *see* **Legal advice**
**Affray** 3.6.4
**Aggravated offences**
  assault
    actual bodily harm 3.2.11
    common assault and battery 3.2.10
    grievous bodily harm 3.2.12
  burglary
    statutory provisions 2.3.1
    weapons and explosives 2.3.2
  criminal damage
    aggravated damage 2.9.3
    simple damage 2.9.2
  hatred for sexual orientation 3.7.16
  overview 3.7.1
  racial or religious offences generally
    associates of members of group 3.7.10
    motivation 3.7.7
    need for hostility 3.7.5
    publishing or distributing written
      material 3.7.13, 3.7.15
    racial groups 3.7.8
    religious groups 3.7.9
    statutory test 3.7.2
    stirring up hatred 3.7.11
    things said or done 3.7.4
    timing of hostility 3.7.3
    use of words, behaviour or written
      displays 3.7.12, 3.7.14
    victim's membership or presumed
      membership of group 3.7.6
  supplying drugs 3.8.4.2
**Aiding and abetting** *see* **Accessories**
**Air weapons**
  children 3.9.7.1
  defined 3.9.7
  face to face sales 3.9.7.1
  firing beyond premises 3.9.7.1
  special exemption 3.9.4.4
**Aircraft**
  access for customs officers 6.1.2.2
  inspection of aircraft and
    aerodromes 6.1.2.3
  prevention of aeroplane flying
    6.1.2.4
**Alibi witnesses** 1.10.10.7
**Ammunition**
  defined 3.9.2.3
  possession or distribution 3.9.4.2
  restrictions on possession or
    acquisition 3.9.12
  section 1 firearms 3.9.5

**Animals**
  exemption for prohibited weapons 3.9.4.4
  extreme pornographic images 4.5.11
  research organisations
    interference with contractual
      relationships 3.10.11.1
    intimidation of connected
      persons 3.10.11.2
    source of serious crime 3.10.11
**Anonymity**
  custody records 1.6.6.1
  informants
    leading to search warrants 1.5.4.1
  sexual offences 4.1.3
**Antique firearms** 3.9.4.4, 3.9.8
**Appropriate adults**
  charging procedure 1.6.17
  disclosure of evidence to
    interviewees 1.10.10.7
  general requirements 1.6.5
  identification procedures
    consent 1.8.3.1
    general requirements 1.8.3
    parades 1.8.9
    video identification 1.8.8
  initial action 1.6.7
  intimate searches 1.6.19
  relevant persons 1.6.5.4
  summary of provisions 1.6.21
**Appropriation** 2.1.4
**Arrests**
  assault on police 3.2.14.1
  detention of persons under arrest 1.6.7.1
  firearms
    having with intent 3.9.9.4
    using 3.9.9.3
  grounds for suspicion 1.7.2.1
  illegal immigrants
    with warrant 5.1.3.2
    without warrant 5.1.3.1
  requirements for caution 1.7.2
  search powers
    after arrest 1.5.5.2
    indictable offences 1.5.5.3
    when making an arrest 1.5.5.1
  street bail
    arrest for non-compliance 1.9.2.7
    attendance at police station and
      re-arrest 1.9.2.4
    failure to comply 1.9.9
    no requirement to attend police
      station 1.9.2.1
    procedure for release 1.9.2.2
  terrorism 3.10.7.1
**Arson** 2.9.4
**Assault**
  conditional threats 3.2.2.4
  consent
    'deemed' consent 3.2.6
    overview 3.2.5
    sado-masochism 3.2.7
  defined 3.2.2
  immediate threats 3.2.2.2
  immigration officers 5.5.2